Revolt of the Saints

Revolt of the Saints

Memory and Redemption in the Twilight
of Brazilian Racial Democracy

JOHN F. COLLINS

Duke University Press   Durham and London   2015

Printed in the United States of America on acid-free paper

Designed and typeset by Julie Allred, BW&A Books, Inc.

Library of Congress Cataloging-in-Publication Data

Collins, John F., 1965 April 19–

Revolt of the saints : memory and redemption in the twilight

of Brazilian racial democracy / John F. Collins.

pages cm

Includes bibliographical references and index.

ISBN 978-0-8223-5306-5 (hardcover : alk. paper)

ISBN 978-0-8223-9570-6 (e-book)

ISBN 978-0-8223-5320-1 (pbk. : alk. paper)

1. Pelourinho (Salvador, Brazil)—Social conditions.

2. Pelourinho (Salvador, Brazil)

—Race relations. 3. Blacks—Brazil—Salvador. I. Title.

F2651.S136P4535 2015

981'.42—dc23

2015008870

Cover photo by John Collins

Duke University Press gratefully acknowledges the support
of Queens College, City University of New York, and the
Queens College Foundation, which provided funds toward
the publication of this book.

To F. W. Manasek

Contents

Preface and Acknowledgments

Long before I thought much about anthropology, or about writing a book such as this one, I would spend lazy afternoons on the Praça Municipal (Municipal Plaza) in front of Salvador, Brazil's Lacerda Elevator. There, on the bluff that separates the neighborhoods known respectively as the "Upper" and "Lower" Cities, I used to savor sunsets set off by the Bay of All Saints and listen as the "Ave Maria" took over the evening radio waves. Fresh out of college and excitedly abroad, I would also watch with interest as an elderly man displayed his electric eel from the exotic Amazon. He would promise to make his fish light an incandescent bulb if the gathering crowd would purchase the bars of homemade soap whose sale allowed him to feed his family. And I would dream of traveling up the Atlantic coast from Salvador so as to follow the Amazon to its source in the Andes. And, later, when I returned to Salvador after having fulfilled this fantasy, I would watch the eel, still in its Styrofoam cooler in front of the elevator. This almost always led me to fight off an urge to reach out and touch the fish, just to see what such an experience would be like.

The eel man's main competitor for space and attention was a magician, known simply as "O Mago," who would perform remarkable escapes and risky tricks. The Mago was, even from my backpacker perspective, relatively unconcerned with personal hygiene. Usually grimy from wriggling out of chains, drinking gasoline, or dragging himself around on the cobblestones as passersby cheered, he loved to spit—on his hands, when he swished water in his mouth before a difficult routine, on the ground so as to build suspense or indicate disgust, and, without a moment's hesitation, on hecklers or those who would threaten his pot of audience donations. The Mago also liked to curse and had a runny, almost-closed eye from which he could not see. Nonetheless, he typically aimed it at interlocutors so that they would not perceive the voracity with which he observed them with his other, functioning eye.

My friend "Fat Carlos" and the Mago were neighbors who encouraged me to transform my own defects, as they did theirs, into sources of power or greater understanding. Thus around 1990 the magician and I began a friendship. Like the clarity of his analysis of social relations, the Mago's ostensible purposefulness always struck me. He never seemed to be without a plan, or a scheme, or a problem that cried out for analysis and resolution. Yet one day, as we reviewed neighborhood gossip or a particularly thorny philosophical question—I do not recall which, since the two so often overlapped in Salvador's Pelourinho of the early 1990s—the Mago commented, "Rapaz, neste mundo existem muitos filhos de Deus que tomam muitas posições. Mas a melhor posição a tomar é não tomar nenhuma posição" (Man, in this world there are many children of God who take many positions in life. But the best position to take is to take none at all!). Later, after reading the work of the anthropologist Roberto da Matta and the poet and novelist Mário de Andrade, I would come to recognize this slippery positionality as an important part of now-canonical definitions of a Brazilian people. But at the moment I believed that the Mago had explained quite well some of the ways Pelourinho residents related to their neighbors and the government institutions already pressuring them to leave their soon-to-be valuable residences.

Some years later, already involved in anthropological research, I bumped into the Mago during carnival. Freshly scrubbed, his fingernails polished with a clear lacquer, and sporting a silk shirt, he told me he had disappeared from the "area" because he had gone to live in Edinburgh, Scotland. He then introduced me to his charming wife, a Scottish university student. She was well mannered in the high-cultured sense of *educação* as used in Bahia. This led me to tease the magician about his change of fortunes, his ability to make wishes become true, and his chic new look. He agreed quickly that the wildest of his dreams, and machinations, had become real, especially in terms of material benefits. He had married out of Bahia's red light district into a world of privilege, far beyond the Praça Municipal.

The Mago now flew across the Atlantic in British Airways jets and found himself making a decent living and consuming as he had always desired. Thus, despite his earlier claim that the best position to take is none at all, this man seemed to have taken on a specific position in the so-called First World. In a manner similar to his escapes from the padlocked chains in which he wrapped his body alongside the elevator, the magician had moved from one position to another in an attempt to survive and to prosper.

As these opening paragraphs about a young North American and a Bahian magician are designed to underscore, *Revolt of the Saints* is often about, and formulated from within, fantasies, the possibility of their realization, and their relationship to global imaginaries and geopolitical difference. It is a story of the making of a UNESCO World Heritage site out of the Maciel/Pelourinho, one of Salvador's most stigmatized neighborhoods until the 1990s, one of Brazil's richest fonts of African-tinged identities, and today a largely empty shopping area for tourists that Bahia's new, more progressive government elected in 2006 struggles to manage as more than a cash cow for elites and a jewel for visitors. For all of these reasons, this book is also about transformation, redemption, loss, and new possibilities in the face of adversity. And it is written from a very particular perspective, as are, I suppose, all texts.

I did not arrive in the Pelourinho as an anthropologist. I did not face the task of choosing a site, or a "people," or even a "problem" that I seized upon because it related to my academic interests. Rather, the Pelourinho chose me without my full understanding or consent. And this occurred as part of what I must admit was a very high modernist, privileged, metropolitan search for difference that I began in 1987, soon after graduating from, of all places, Yale College. My years in New Haven, that beacon of *lux et veritas*, were marked by a Comparative Literature Department that had just witnessed the apogee of poststructuralism. Paul De Mann had died the year before I arrived on campus, Jacques Derrida gave frequent guest lectures, and Geoffrey Hartman, Harold Bloom, and J. Hillis Miller directed undergraduates who were able to deconstruct any text, often without really concentrating on much beyond the contingency of meaning as enacted in plays of signifiers.

Upon graduation, awash in theory, I fled into experience in the so-called developing world as have so many other seemingly well-educated, kind, and liberal children of First-World privilege, and hence so many anthropologists. I ended up spending years in Latin America, interspersed with short returns to the United States. At one point, as my money ran out during Brazil's hyperinflation of the early 1990s, I happened upon a Spaniard who had dropped out of a PhD program in chemistry in England. He was making and selling tourist jewelry along the coasts of the states of Pernambuco and Alagoas. We fell in together, enjoying the nearly middle-class incomes, mobility, and freedom to talk to whomever we desired that our artisan status afforded us. We eventually split up in Salvador, where I remained in a cheap rented room of plywood partitions that failed to separate the Pelourinho's floating population of hustlers, artisans, guides, prostitutes, laborers, street vendors, and washwomen. One day two artisan friends, Rai and Márcio, let me in on a sweet deal: The manager of the Olodum social movement/music group's weekly Sunday night concerts, Seu Léo, had given them permission to set up their jewelry stands. They had been allowed to sell their crafts along the bleachers mobbed by fans of Olodum, which had just returned from cutting an album with Paul Simon. At the top of the Bahian cultural hierarchy, and thus one of Brazil's principal social movements and artistic forces, Olodum attracted enormous attention to the Pelourinho and to its message of Afro-Brazilian empowerment. Rai and Márcio spoke to Léo on my behalf, pointing out that despite being a *parmalat* (milky-white guy), I was also *gente boa* (good people). And Léo agreed to allow the three of us to serve as exclusive artisans for Olodum's Tuesday night rehearsals.

I soon fell into a pleasant rhythm, living in the Pelourinho, surviving, and treating neighbors with respect. Making fine use of my elite language training, I sold trinkets to the visitors from throughout the world who flooded Olodum's rehearsals so as to experience Afro-Bahian culture as mobilized by a grassroots social movement. Working away, humbly, I saw literary and social scientific luminaries whose books I had read, and continue to read, pass me by as they conducted "research." Meanwhile, I twisted wire into beguiling designs and molded the plumbing resin called "Durepoxi" into exotic representations of ostensibly traditional objects. The researchers, like most of my clients, frequently mistook me for an Argentine due to my height, color, and, at the time, Spanish-inflected Portuguese. They usually failed to imagine that a North American would work as an artisan, or what Brazilians call a *maluco* (crazy). Unless visitors asked, I was usually silent on who I was and where I came from. I let my work and bearing speak for themselves, as if doing so could resolve the thorny issues of authorship, authenticity, and exoticism that are so much a part of what the Pelourinho, and I, have become in the ensuing decades.

The experience I sought as part of a grand tour available to the privileged nonetheless turned me into a resident of the *mangue* (mangrove), or the Maciel/Pelourinho red light district. There, on multiple occasions, I faced police beatings, threats of assassination as an unprotected individual, and active discrimination by middle-class Bahians who came to believe I was but a troublesome artisan from a neighboring republic. But at the same time, it granted me a bit of popular credibility not usually afforded to *gringos* in Bahia. This powerful yet troubling authenticity of the type so often celebrated by anthropologists and refugees from the metropole haunts and yet encourages me today, when, as a *doutor*, I return to perform social science in the Pelourinho or sit down to write about the people who shared, and at times hid, so much from and with me.

Like colonial expatriates or, in Bahia, the bohemian men of letters I discuss below, I have come over the course of my career and the writing of this book to mix an exploratory and orientalist fascination with the mangrove with a professionalizing gaze and sentimentalized engagement with its residents intended, but never quite able, to overcome the inequalities that structure this meeting point. Yet those contradictions have brought a certain knowledge and perspective that might mitigate against orientalism and professionalism even as some readers may conclude that they only reinforce the two, albeit in a more obscure or theoretically developed manner. Such knowledge helps bring home the fundamental contradictions, and even ridiculousness, of this "adventure."

What to do, then? Should I be silent and ignore the inequalities, immature searches, and redemptive fantasies that led me to an intellectual position, and career, via the Pelourinho? Shall I deny what I understand to have been the ragged and initial steps in the genesis of the book you are to read? Or might I drown out such truths within a rhetoric of engaged, professional, investigation and political commitment? Shall I then end this preface by taking many positions, or none at all?

In response, I report that I have struggled to take a position and to reveal it in all its ugliness and beauty in relation to a North American in Bahia as well as a new citizen of Europe who employed his ability to wriggle out of restraints so as to make a life in a new location. I have indicated that a similar desire, albeit generated under remarkably different circumstances, took me to the Pelourinho. These affinities, or mirrorings, between self and Other suggest the importance not only of introspection and communication, but also of interrogating how and why such reflections and engagements become possible.

I am not suggesting that I will somehow transcend a subject-object distinction, or, even more concretely, the many separations of the wealthy and the impoverished at play in the pages that follow. Nor will I manage to escape such dichotomizations that get to the heart of inequalities even as they help gloss over similarities and the work performed by claims to shared experience. But I do imagine that at some level, in some way, the account that follows may provide insights that may help generate openings for accomplishing such goals someday. And this is why I emphasize the importance of examining the ways that unequal, yet in some sense, shared, experience is put together at different historical junctures and in distinct yet connected places. In doing so I am foreshadowing my interest in the UNESCO World Heritage Site, a technology directed at portraying qualitatively different, yet similarly human, practices as shared or comparable possessions of that humanity. How, then, might one take a position that does justice to such identities and differences?

In carving out my position(s) in the chapters that follow I have relied on the advice and help of many. In Brazil a number of colleagues have been enormously accommodating and hospitable. I thank especially Ordep Serra, Carlos Caroso, Jocélio Teles dos Santos, João Reis, Naomar Almeida Filho, Vagner Gonçalves da Silva, José Reginaldo Gonçalves, Olívia Maria Gomes da Cunha, Livio Sansone, finado Ubiratan Reis, Fábio Lima, Alain Kaly, Jorge Mattar Villela, and Roca Alencar for their companionship and intellectual fervor. I am also indebted to a number of people within IPAC, the staffs of IPAC's library, the Arquivo Público do Estado da Bahia, the Santa Casa da Misericórdia, and the Secretaria Municipal do Planejamento, Urbanismo e Meio Ambiente. Professor Vivaldo da Costa Lima, who passed away in 2011, was an inspiring interlocutor, a rough but kind teacher, and he remains a boisterous presence in this book and in memories of a bohemian red light district that is now a memorial to the culture around which Costa Lima's life revolved.

In mentioning eminent social scientists, I cannot forget the people in Salvador's Pelourinho, and elsewhere in the city, who were so important to our joint project of analyzing state power and the production of the past. Among the many who helped me, I thank especially Nilson, Carlos, Nivaldo, Dona Patrícia, Bira, Dona Aidil, Seu Joel, and all of the família Gomes de Jesus, Jubiacy, Lula, finada Topa, Aurelino Filho, Garimpeiro, Zefa, Eduardo, Gil, Caximbada, Dona Isa and children, Irênio, finada Veveu, Rita, finado Claudio, Jailson, Zé, Indio, Joseval, Jaca, Gaginho, Olodum, finada Dona Ne, Dinha, finado Cachorrão, Carlete, Mano Lel, It, finada Quésia, finado Moisés, Conceição, Seu Ademar, Dona Zulmira, Manuel, Rogério, Michel, Preta, Mestre Caboclo, Evandro, Dona Célia, Dona Cecília, Lia Hollywood, finada Cintia, Bira Boi, Fátima, finado Osnir and Paula and children, Capixaba, William, finado Mestre Decente, finado Mestre Dois de Olho, finado Mestre Boi Manso, finado Sabão de Mula, Cebolinha, Dona Tió, Baraúna, finado Cabeção, Neném, Fábio, Lasca, Zilton, Luiz Alberto, Paulo Anunciação, Edinho Cheiro Mole, Bigode, Neinha and family, Seu Régis, Macaco, finada Luisa, Clarindo Silva, finado Tremendão, Surrindo, Tõ, Nivio, Toinho Malvadeza, and all my other friends, associates and interlocutors in Salvador. Even if you are not named here, you are not forgotten, just underappreciated for the moment.

Fieldwork would have been impossible without financial support from the Brazilian Fulbright Commission, PSC-CUNY, the U.S. National Science Foundation, and the Wenner-Gren Foundation for Anthropological Research. The completion of this book benefited from a Mellon Fellowship at the City University of New York's (CUNY) Center for the Humanities. While at Queens College and the CUNY Graduate Center's Department of Anthropology I have appreciated especially the encouragement and insightful comments provided by Alessandro Angelini, Akissi Britton, Christopher Parisano, Jorge Alves, Kevin Birth, Amy Chazkel, Vincent Crapanzano, Warren Deboer, Mauricio

Font, Murphy Halliburton, Mandana Limbert, Louise Lennihan, Marc Edelman, Shirley Lindenbaum, and Leith Mullings.

Audiences at many universities and various professional meetings and associations have also done much to improve the account that follows. Sueann Caulfield, E. Valentine Daniel, Conrad Kottak, and, especially, Ann Stoler have been kind and inspiring interlocutors for decades. In related ways, I have benefited from years of advice and readings from James Herron, Carole McGranahan, Paul Kobrak, Peter Kalliney, Rachel Meyer, Aaron Ansell, Roger Sansi, Rebecca Scott, Andrew Shryock, Fernando Coronil, Richard and Sally Price, Joanne Rappaport, Thomas Abercrombie, Andrew Canessa, Joseph Masco, Jean Jackson, John Burdick, Sid Greenfield, and Daryle Williams.

It is important to recognize the generosity of the Society for Cultural Anthropology and the American Ethnological Society for permitting me to employ in chapters 5 and 6 certain of the descriptions that appeared in articles published previously in the two societies' journals. The first, "'But What if I Should Need to Defecate in *Your* Neighborhood, Madame?': Empire, Redemption and the 'Tradition of the Oppressed' in a Brazilian Historical Center," appeared in *Cultural Anthropology* 23(2). The second, "Melted Gold and National Bodies: The Hermeneutics of Depth and the Value of History in Brazilian Racial Politics," was published in *American Ethnologist* 38(4). Within the world of publishing, I owe an enormous debt at Duke University Press, especially to Valerie Milholland who first engaged me about this manuscript, and Gisela Fosado who helped bring it to life.

As is normal at moments such as this one, I save my greatest thanks for my family. I would be unable to refer to "privilege" in the paragraphs above were it not for the sacrifices of my parents, John and Marlene. Nor would I have come to love investigating the social world were it not for their encouragement. And as I look into the future, I thank Gabriel for accompanying me across much of the initial fieldwork while wrapped in his baby carrier, and then for easing the occasional pains of writing with our discussions of dinosaurs, australopithecines, and Salvador's mass transit system that permitted me to explain why it is not "cavemen," but culture and history, that interest me as an anthropologist. This litany brings me to Ana, who I thank not simply because of all you have done for me, but because of all of my love for you. Nonetheless, in the end, and rather than looking into the future, I must look into the past, once more. Here I thank a Bohemian quite different from the bohemians discussed in this book: I have always been inspired by the brilliance, the creativity, and the drive of my grandfather, Francis W. Manasek. In a feat of endurance that appears quite magical from my current perspective, he fled the implosion of the Austro-Hungarian Empire and made a life in the United States. Here he began, but never finished, his studies at the City University of New York. Inspired by those efforts I am honored to have honed my writings with input from more recent students, including some from Brazil, who continue to add to the intellectual life of North America's largest public urban university system.

As the reader who has reached this point may notice, then, I understand this as both a very personal and a very Bahian book that wraps around to tell a variety of stories—often in the excruciating detail and parabolic style favored in the Maciel/Pelourinho—so as to speak to multiple processes around the world. Perhaps, then, this text moves toward fulfilling the utopian promises of UNESCO. I hope it does. But I hope also that it does so while helping us to cast a critical eye on what happened in Bahia at the turn of the millennium, and in ways that might help upstage or alleviate the impossible contradictions I so frequently see reflected in that carefully wrapped, precious, and nonetheless troubling bundle celebrated today as "cultural heritage."

Introduction

Being, through the Archive

Why does it disquiet us to know that Don Quixote is a reader of the *Quixote*, and Hamlet is a spectator of *Hamlet*? I believe I have found the answer: those inversions suggest that if the characters in a story can be readers or spectators, then we, their readers or spectators, can be fictitious. In 1833 Carlyle observed that universal history is an infinite sacred book that all men write and read and try to understand, and in which they too are written.

—Jorge Luis Borges, "Partial Enchantments of the *Quixote*"

According to officials in Salvador, capital of the northeastern state of Bahia, Brazil's history and the world's cultural heritage faced grave threats at the turn of the millennium. Each year, during the May through August rainy season, colonial mansions in the city's imposing Pelourinho Historical Center would collapse, sometimes with losses of life. People's deaths, like the disintegration of architectural treasures, lent direction to accounts of national belonging and urgency to the efforts of the Institute of Artistic and Cultural Patrimony (IPAC) and the Bahian Regional Development Company (CONDER), the state institutions responsible for the neighborhood's development as a UNESCO World Heritage Site.[1] Meanwhile, the buildings' working-class and mostly Afro-Brazilian occupants listened for snapping beams, gauged tremors that might indicate a need to flee, and perfected techniques for propping up the often crumbling, Baroque and Neoclassical structures that they had come to occupy across the twentieth century. In spite of such attention to objects and phenomena construed by the Bahian state as icons of a shared attachment to the nation, but which their inhabitants cared for as a matter of

Figure I.1. Collapsed, but inhabited, building at number 18 Saldanha da Gama Street.

survival, IPAC and the Bahian press linked the loss of Brazil's patrimony to a populace it painted as exacerbating a threatening nature and the passage of time. From the Bahian state's perspective, then, managing the relationship between supposedly disorderly populations and a vulnerable cultural patrimony would help ground the claims to shared destiny, common or complementary origins, and attentiveness to cultural difference so basic to development projects and liberal democratic politics today.

In late 1997 I stood in the rubble of a collapsed building pressed into service as both a parking lot and a soccer field. I watched, shocked, as dozens of drug misusers swayed to the music of a Pelourinho-based, born-again Christian, reggae band called the Bem Aventurados (The Blessed). Known to locals as the 28th of September (the 28), this Pelourinho subregion had been dubbed "*cracolândia*" by police and the press due to its status as the main open-air market for the crack cocaine that first appeared in the colonial center's streets in 1996. And in a nod to the pipe-smoking, not-quite-human, black trickster figure known in Brazilian folklore as the *saci pererê*, residents had come to refer to the crack users who flocked to their neighborhood as *sacis*.[2] Thus, on that dull gray afternoon, I joined a circle of opposition politicians and Black Movement activists who sought to organize the residents of the 28 against a dispossession intended to permit the Bahian state to reconstruct their homes as part of the neighborhood's $100-million "restoration." But rather than organizing local people, we found ourselves listening in uncomfortable silence as the Bem

Aventurados sang, "Saci, saci, saci, é uma paranoia," or "The saci, saci, saci, it's really a state of paranoia."

The lyrics linked ongoing violence against Afro-Brazilians to the folkloric imagery seemingly brought to life in the Pelourinho's transformation into a historical center, or one of those special zones found around the world in which states and private institutions seek to bring history to life as a tool of capital accumulation and the education of consent.[3] The song also spurred the dancers to shout and hoist the aluminum foil–covered mineral-water cups used as crack pipes in Salvador. Thus drug misusers drawn by money coursing through the still incompletely restored UNESCO site celebrated a song intended by its authors as a denunciation of the urban reform and cocaine scourge ravaging their neighborhood.[4] Today, near the end of its transformation into a historical center dependent on the aura and lifeways of the thousands of inhabitants removed since 1992, this colonial-era downtown, long configured as both a source of infection and an enduring piece of the nation's past, glistens as a depopulated monument to what has been presented repeatedly in official discourse as the valuable, and yet uncomfortable, vitality of an Afro-Brazilian people.

Since 1992, IPAC culture managers have focused on the reconstruction of Pelourinho buildings and the removal or re-education of what the state institution presents as those structures' morally suspect occupants. The staff of IPAC paints this exercise in accumulation by dispossession as a renewal of Brazil's first capital city and a celebration of its Afro-Brazilian character.[5] But the restorative project, one based on the allegedly faithful preservation of collective memories and popular culture, works in practice as an alienating and future-oriented attempt to redeem a black population presented as needing civilizational improvement. Here redemption is not simply some attempt at moral uplift. Nor is it a critique of capitalism or an attempt to move beyond trauma like that examined by Jason James in relation to heritage programs in former East Germany.[6] The Pelourinho project is instead an approach to development and capital accumulation that rests on a UNESCO-supported canonization of selected residents of the neighborhood as producers of practices that function as both commodities and a civilizing, supposedly shared milieu called "culture." The resulting attempts to purify the Pelourinho and its populace, a project officials often referred to until quite recently as a "moralization of the soil," gave rise to the expulsion of nearly all residents in the period between 1992 and 2006. Only people with close relationships to politicians, able to "shake down" IPAC bureaucrats, or who produce especially valuable expressive culture and whom IPAC thus deems ready to represent Afro-Brazilian culture to the world, have managed to remain.

The painstakingly orchestrated but ultimately confusing process of counting, knowing, and culling a populace portrayed as in need of salvation has permitted state officials to lay claim to formerly abandoned mansions (*sobrados*) and large colonial buildings with courtyards (*solares*) that impoverished citizens reoccupied across the second half of the twentieth century. In so doing, IPAC has focused on and evaluated occupants' quotidian practices with techniques it celebrates as holistic care of people and landscapes associated with the essences of the Brazilian nation. Such efforts to treat minority subjects' everyday lives as sources of value and belonging for all, and accumulation by a few, are critical grounds for figuring identity, personhood, and politics in historical centers around the world today. But in Salvador's Pelourinho, many of those subject to IPAC's violent "care" interpret their state's moralizing evaluation of their human qualities as both an attack upon, and a reification of, their very being.[7] And such management of people and things, and people as things, is key to understanding shifts in Brazilian racial politics today.

Yet on that dispiriting afternoon on the 28th of September, as the Bem Aventurados' audience twisted warnings about illegal substances and the seizure of homes into commemorations of drug use in a neighborhood being transformed into a symbol of tradition dependent on the lifeways of expelled residents, I thought little about the overlaps between buildings and people in IPAC's cynical language of faithful restoration and disempowering care. I also failed to recognize the importance of misreading to communication, the links between residents' vocabularies and state-directed pathologizations of Afro-Brazilian culture, or the ways ethnographic documentation of Pelourinho social ills props up accounts of the state's protection of cultural treasures and redemption of ostensibly problematic citizens. Nor did I imagine that contests over space and history as forms of property woven around the celebration and denigration of Afro-Brazilian practices would lead me to argue that state-directed attempts to produce heritage and history were more about a moralizing surveillance of the Pelourinho's population than the landmarking of buildings or the celebration of heroes and remarkable events. Most of all, I did not even begin to consider how a future decision to describe collapsing buildings and illegal drug users in opening a book about history and racial politics might tie into a tradition of "streetcorner ethnography," or anthropological fascinations with supposedly marginal, impoverished, and usually nonwhite populations construed as an underclass.[8] But how it ties into this tradition is a critical part of understanding the ways that in Salvador's Pelourinho the bureaucratic securing of a hybrid category of property and humanity moves in tandem with, and thus both supports and emerges from, overlapping shifts in Brazilian racial politics, historical imaginaries, and citizenship categories.

Instead, and in what would turn out to be a first step in understanding the extent to which the everyday habits of Pelourinho residents have long reverberated in government archives and development organizations' boardrooms, on that day in 1997 I managed only to scribble field notes and listen to Senator Luiz Alberto dos Santos. Luiz Alberto, as he likes to be called, is an organizer in Salvador's petrochemical workers union and a leader in Brazil's Unified Black Movement (MNU). He explained,

> For a long time the Movement forgot about people like this. We were concentrating on consciousness, on workers and more middle class Bahians excluded from the political process and economic empowerment because of their race. But the Pelourinho was . . . important . . . in our struggle. It was even the spot where we met in the 1980s to plan our moves. . . . But I have to say, we ignored this population, we turned our backs on these people here . . . who are, quite frankly, very difficult to organize politically. Now we have to return and make an effort at reaching them, to include them in our vision of a more just Brazil.

Following the election of leftist President Luiz Inácio "Lula" da Silva in 2002, leaders in Brazil's Workers Party (PT) and its allies would draw on their experiences in the Pelourinho to foment more equitable cultural policies at both the state and federal levels. This attempt to draw on cultural policy in fomenting social justice has continued during the administrations of Lula's successor, president Dilma Rousseff, and the Bahian officials from the Workers Party swept into office on the heels of the PT victories. For this new group of politicians, culture is more a medium for empowering, rather than exploiting, the former inhabitants of the red light district.[9] But in 1997, Luiz Alberto and his allies frequently found themselves checked, and even physically assaulted, by those aligned with Antonio Carlos Magalhães (ACM). Magalhães, whose grandson is now mayor of Salvador and a leader in a conservative coalition still invested in monetizing the citizenry's everyday habits, was, until his death in 2006, Brazil's most powerful late-twentieth-century populist politician, the patron of the Pelourinho reconstruction, and Bahia's authoritarian "governor," infamous for his attempts to appropriate Afro-Brazilian culture. Perhaps it was the violent, paternalistic power of this man that caused Luiz Alberto, as he spoke in the parking lot, to turn morosely toward a soon-to-be displaced Pelourinho resident wearing a T-shirt that bore the portrait of a politician aligned with ACM. With a nod, the senator continued softly, "See what we're facing. How can that woman support Marcos Medrado? How can we counter this sort of embedded patron-clientelism that fosters an ongoing marginalization of Afro-Brazilians? How can the PT compete when the people think of politics as an exchange, a road to material compensation, rather than a means of changing the system?"

This is a book about race, historical destinies, and the uncertain boundaries between human beings and objects in a once-denigrated neighborhood born in the Atlantic Triangle Trade, subsequently abandoned by elites and occupied by Afro-Brazilians, and restored today as a shimmering and often disorienting space for the enactment of Brazilian and diasporic histories. In it I argue that in the Pelourinho, a neighborhood whose name means "Pillory" and that serves today as Brazil's most resonant symbol of blackness and tradition, people have come to be configured as a form of national patrimony. This so-called development is both a symptom and a motor of shifts in racial politics in that it has helped configure race as a historical, and historicized, property in a nation where the relative weakness of a genealogical version of racial belonging has long set off racial politics as somehow different from those in places like the United States or South Africa. Yet my account of the historicization of race and its reification as a property is not a lament about the loss of some original humanity to the commodification of culture, a claim that race now exists where it was once absent or mutable, or even an argument about the true nature of a history obscured by IPAC's whitewashing of Bahia's violent pasts as the shared and proud legacy of Brazil's history of interracial communion. On the contrary, it is a detailed ethnographic journey into some of the ways race twists and turns as it latches onto, and is infiltrated by, areas of social life that may at first glance appear rather different, or unrelated, to ethno-racial politics.[10]

Revolt of the Saints is thus an intentionally bewildering and oftentimes frustrating and painful story of social action and historical engagement. It offers no neat outside, as it focuses in on how the IPAC-directed attempt to purify a population and bundle culture and history as valuable goods ties into racial politics. This involves an account of the configuration of history and culture as tangible and alienable properties, and of the truths such attempts to reify social relations make possible and draw on at a moment when the "care" of minority cultures has become part and parcel of democratic governance inflected by neoliberal, multicultural initiatives.[11] The result is something of a community study that congeals around iconoclastic, but influential, forms of agency catalyzed as conflicts between a state and its Afro-Bahian citizenry help transform the meanings of blackness and everydayness in relation to a space called history and a place called the Pillory. But this examination of the destruction of a neighborhood called the Maciel and the construction of a UNESCO World Heritage Site is one that looks critically at how this heritage machine has been put together as a historicized entity and an ideological project that is influential in

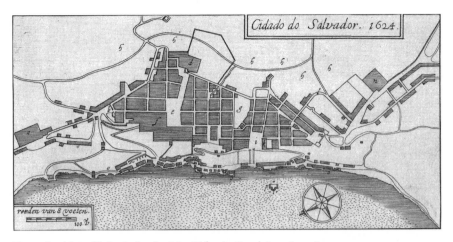

Figure I.2. Map of Salvador's colonial grid for the Dutch invasion, 1624.

transformations of the nature of collective belonging. And I perform this analysis as part of a larger argument about how the attempts by Afro-Bahians both excluded from and included in the restored Pelourinho to situate themselves in the often pathologizing, and at times triumphant, histories being written upon their backs come to play a fundamental role in how race is constructed, and deployed, in contemporary Brazil.

To clarify the genesis and implications of what my reader may come to judge to be a disturbing, or even misplaced, take on race, space, and history, it is worth considering Luiz Alberto's representation of Pelourinho politics in relation to a longer history of Salvador's role in a nationalism that depends on Afro-Brazilian lives and landscapes. In so doing, I hope to begin to do justice to the struggles of people who face state-sponsored redemption, to examine their ambiguous canonization as symbolic ancestors to the national community, and thus to come to understand more clearly how all citizens of modern liberal democracies may engage the ways of knowing and being in the world that substantiate ethno-racial politics' enduring and yet potentially capricious truth-effects. How such forms of belonging converge with long-standing means of redeeming a national people, and thus of negotiating what across the nineteenth and twentieth centuries Brazilian intellectuals so often described as a peripheral position in the capitalist world order, is a story that begins long before my arrival in the Pelourinho. And the ways these relations unfolded at earlier moments provide a powerful introduction to the Brazilian conundrums, and attempted resolutions, in which today's still-unfinished Pelourinho reforms participate in novel as well as time-worn manners.

Modernist Origins

On a hot summer morning in January 1927, three years before the authoritarian Getúlio Vargas would gain the presidency and begin to solidify the modern, twentieth-century Brazilian nation out of whose millennial redirection the present account emerges, a twenty-three-year-old Bahian writer named Godofredo Filho guided a visiting poet, Manuel Bandeira, through the Pelourinho's twisting alleys. This already-decaying center of the northeastern city of Salvador, Brazil's first capital and the administrative center of the Portuguese South Atlantic Empire from the early sixteenth through the late eighteenth centuries, would become critical to the nationalizing project that Bandeira, Filho, their avant-garde associates in southern Brazil, and their regionalist associates in northeastern states, helped make a reality in the 1920s and 1930s.[12]

Given Bandeira's importance to the São Paulo–based modernist movement that in the 1920s sought to create an autonomous national identity by cannibalizing and subverting European cultural forms that denied Brazil's modernity, the visitor wished to experience the most authentic of tropical Bahia's traditions and charms. This led to cobblestone alleyways, grand plazas dominated by monuments to Catholic religious orders, and the colonial mansions, abandoned by Salvador's upper classes at the end of the nineteenth century, which working families and women of ostensible ill-repute had begun to occupy and subdivide in the late 1920s. At lunchtime Godofredo Filho, who would go on to head the Bahian office of Brazil's national heritage bureaucracy (IPHAN), and his guest, who would help establish IPHAN and spend a significant portion of his life singling out Brazilian wonders for inclusion in the register of national historic places, stopped by "Black Eva's" home-style cooking stand. There, on simple benches and among Bahia's already storied African population, Bandeira tested Bahia's signature African-influenced *moqueca*, a stewed delicacy he later described as "the most stupendous mixtures of palm oil and hot peppers."[13]

The visitor, born in the neighboring state of Pernambuco but a resident of cosmopolitan Rio de Janeiro at the time of his Bahian sojourn, adored his tour of Brazil's blackest region.[14] He spent a total of four days with Godofredo Filho and waxed to his São Paulo–based mentor, the influential novelist, poet, folklorist, and founding force in Brazil's modernist movement, Mário de Andrade, "The Pelourinho Square is the urban space that a Brazilian can show to a Frenchman without worrying about being cuckolded by the Champs Élysées or the Avenue of the Opera."

After staking this vociferously masculine and deliberately Brazilian claim to an autochthonous modernity based on the Pelourinho's architecture, but not necessarily its people, Bandeira continued,

Figure I.3. The "urban space that a Brazilian can show to a Frenchman without worrying about being cuckolded by the Champs-Élysées," filled with decorations portraying Bahian and national archetypes following carnival in 1999.

I'm in love with Bahia! It's a stupendous place! THE BRAZILAN CITY. Hundreds, hundreds, hundreds of huge colonial mansions with four floors and a cellar. If I could I'd take one back for you and one for me. Mansions with strong and serious seigniorial lines, with polished rock doorways and family crests, doors of deep hardwoods and baroque peacock's tails—all inhabited by little black ladies, prostitutes and people so poor, so poor, the poorest of them all! You look down through the cracks into a cellar where you would imagine that only rats could live and you see a little altar, lit by a flickering oil lamp.[15]

The poet's description foreshadows Bahia's twentieth-century consecration as the mythic site of Brazil's African soul, or the proper place for establishing the traditional and locating the black component of the nation's foundational national myth of "racial democracy." This racial democracy, for which Brazil has for so long been well known, is a supposedly seductive account of a peaceful "brown" nation born of a cultural and racial fusion of Portuguese, African, and Native peoples in northeastern Brazil. As such, it is both a historical misrepresentation that obscures five centuries of violence and a durable ideology to which millions of Brazilians still ascribe even as racism and intolerance are increasingly recognized as negatively affecting the lives of so many citizens.[16]

Figure I.4. Early morning in the Pelourinho's cobblestone streets.

Figure I.5. Proud
Pelourinho father, a
resident of a ruined
building like those
that surprised
Bandeira.

Dependent for its power on a story of relations between the male members of a colonial planter class and their female domestics, and thus between the colonial planter's mansion and its kitchens and servants quarters, Brazil's racial democracy (which is not really democratic), turns on spatial relationships expressed in a variety of spheres and moments in Brazilian life. Over the next seven chapters I track agreements and disagreements between Pelourinho residents and a state cultural-heritage bureaucracy in order to examine how this relationship between people, landscapes, and the Brazilian nation is both essential to, and modified by, the Pelourinho's restoration today. Nonetheless, as the Brazilian anthropologist Roberto Da Matta suggested as early as 1981, the equation of national history to a fable of three great races and their mixture turns racial democracy into an ahistorical master trope for understanding Brazil, lending direction to a multitude of important political battles and research plans but simplifying much more complex issues.[17] Thus I do not set up racial democracy as some sort of legacy or enduring construction that makes sense in itself and against which people fight in the present.[18] The term is seductively descriptive for the uninitiated, but it is not all-encompassing in spite of its role as a master symbol for so many political movements and so much of Brazilianist scholarship. In fact, one of my most basic points across this book is that race and racisms are historical formations. Thus race and racisms function, and signify, differently across time and space.

In the decades surrounding Bandeira's visit in 1927, Brazilian intellectuals had begun to agree more and more vociferously that race mixture, instead of explaining a backwardness attributed to Latin America by Victorian science and the eugenics that followed, could be an engine of development. Gilberto Freyre, the scion of a planter family in the state of Pernambuco who studied for a short time at Columbia University under Franz Boas and rose to prominence as perhaps Brazil's best-known twentieth-century intellectual, is widely credited with coining the term "racial democracy" even though the expression seems to have been used for the first time by the social psychologist and medical doctor Arthur Ramos in 1941. So although Freyre apparently avoided this wording, his 1926 poem "Bahia of all Sins" celebrates the sort of interracial sexual relations and the making public of culinary and domestic habits associated today with the concept of racial democracy:

Bahia of all saints (and almost all sins)
Houses climbing[19] licentiously, one on top of the other
Houses, colonial mansions, churches . . .

All of Bahia is one fat maternal city
As if out of her taut wombs . . .

Old Black women of Bahia
Selling gruel, manioc paste and bean fritters . . .
Mothers of the most beautiful *mulattas* . . .

Mulattas with angelic hands
Making little boy children grow bigger
Creating great Sirs almost equal
To those of the Empire

One day, with time to spare, I will return to your
Brown Brazilian breast . . .
Your market women's tables where X is laid out
(And that X is the future of Brazil)[20]

Written after a visit to Bahia, a state whose planter families' stories he would muster as evidence for his discussion of interracial relations in the colonial household that grounded his 1933 magnum opus *Casa grande e senzala* (The Masters and the Slaves), Freyre's prognosis for a "whitening" or mixed-race Brazil rests on successive generations' move away from blackness into a nationalist brownness dependent on domestic servants and the tables of its market women.[21] Brazil's most famous twentieth-century intellectual thus outlines a view of race mixture as an engine for "improving" a postcolonial nation whose "great Sirs" nursed by nonwhite women might challenge their Lusitanian colonialist ancestors' civilization. As a result, and as miscegenation came to be consecrated as a reason for and a symbol of citizens' allegedly creative ability to move between identities that were elsewhere fixed in law and social practice, Brazil's mixed-race character became a source of pride for nationalists rather than the site of infection and explanation for the underdevelopment foreign observers described.[22]

In his examination of changes in Bahia's political economy and the types of networks among black Bahians to which those shifts contributed at the end of the twentieth century, Michel Agier identifies two main currents to the ideologies of mixture that are so formative in Brazilian nationalism. He highlights the emphasis on undercutting fixed categories of race through relationships between women of color and socially empowered white men, relationships that across much of the twentieth century are girded by a powerful state-supported emphasis on miscegenation. To this "intimacy in inter-racial relations . . . [that] would generate a reciprocal habit of living with racial differences," Agier adds an emphasis on codes of conduct, or cordiality and "manners [that] . . . usually succeed, in eliminating the effects of . . . social differentiation and domination within the public domain."[23] What should be clear from Agier's historical gloss on claims about miscegenation and his analysis of social conventions is that what passes for racial democracy is a moral narrative, or a national history, that draws on the making public of intimate habits alongside the formalization of codes of conduct related to race so as to redeem what nationalist intellectuals portrayed as a Brazil that, negatively tinged by contact with Africa, was unable to join the club of modern nations.[24] Racial democracy is, then, most basically a historical narrative. But here history looks to the future rather than just at the past.

I add two observations to Agier's understanding of what he presents as a double veiling of socio-racial differences in Brazil. In his letter to Andrade, Bandeira reveals an interest in national origins, here in the form of imposing manor houses inhabited by black women whom he characterizes as prostitutes and who it would thus appear should not occupy such architecture.

The wrong, or the not-quite-right, sort of people are present in these origins and something must be done about them. Yet as is evident in the delight Bandeira takes in Black Eva's lunch tables, it is not clear that he wishes to do away with those residents of Pelourinho basements, something Bahia's cultural heritage and political establishment would seek to accomplish in the 1990s. On the contrary, Bandeira seems interested in people he never admits to seeing, but recognizes as present on the basis of their flickering altar lights. Thus an Afro-Brazilian populace, a symbolic "peoplehood," becomes visible in the poet's account by means of the material signs of their piety.[25] It would seem that the people who are not quite fit to inhabit buildings that rival the Champs-Élysées nonetheless offer the visitor a promise of redemption. And this is the second issue that both introduces and grounds this book's approach to race, history, and urban space.

Brazil is usually presented as rather exceptional, at least when compared to the United States or South Africa, in its emphasis on racial mutability. Heavily influenced by Lamarckian conceptions of evolution, whereby alterations in one's physical form generated by environmental influences across one's lifetime can be passed on to one's offspring, it is, or was for much of the twentieth century, a nation in which one biological sibling might be classified as "white" or "brown" and another as "black." And in this "new world in the tropics" the claim that there is no racism even as there are hierarchies of color has long served, at least according to many commentators, to veil racism.[26] Such a separation of color and race may seem strange to North American sensibilities, and this distinction is precisely what so many Brazilians are challenging today as part of a process that at least some observers have suggested is overly influenced by foreign ideas about race.[27] But if color, or one's classification, is something that, like sullied origins, might be changed or improved in relation to contexts or a community's interpretation of what that color means and is, then race in Brazil, where "racial belonging . . . has traditionally been based more on an individual's appearance than on descent," is not quite like race in the United States. An important political corollary to this understanding of Brazilian approaches to color and corporate belonging is the "assumption that there are no absolute borders between different races."[28]

In an analysis first published in 1954, the Brazilian sociologist Oracy Nogueira crystallized something of the perplexing nature of race, color, and the qualities or traits thought to establish the boundaries, or lack thereof, of social groups in Brazil. He argued, "When racial prejudice takes form in relation to appearance . . . one might say that it functions in relation to marks; but when the claim that a person is a descendant of a particular ethnic group is enough to unleash prejudice, then we might say that this is an issue of origins."[29] For

Nogueira, as for myriad commentators in ensuing decades, there seems to exist in Brazil what Livio Sansone dubs "blackness without ethnicity," or a conjuncture in which powerful forms of discrimination are not necessarily accompanied by concomitantly powerful forms of corporate, racial solidarity. And as noted by none other than Marvin Harris, whose post–World War II studies in rural Bahia uncovered evidence of racial prejudice, this "calculus" of racial identity seems to be an issue of "referential ambiguity."[30] I take reference seriously—and rather differently from Harris for whom it was largely an issue of relatively unexplored "cognition" rather than the resolutely public, semiotic approach developed for Brazilian racial politics across this book—by exploring how what goes on in a UNESCO historical center speaks to, and seemingly even influences, Bahian conceptualizations of the relationships between "marks" and "origins" that have informed such a large swathe of social scientific approaches to Brazilian race over the last fifty years. In doing so I concentrate not on contesting what the UNESCO historical center's technologies for resuscitating the past do to representations of what has happened, but on the ways that an ongoing yet shifting chain of symbolizations changes the very nature of representation. This ground or "nature" from which future representations spring is fundamental to the shape taken by those future representations, and race is, in the end, a representation or issue of reference. Thus I approach alterations in racial ideologies not by investigating identities and related histories per se, but by examining the presuppositions and interpretive lenses, or, in Webb Keane's descriptive framework, "semiotic ideologies," through which state and citizen have come to understand the production of value and the molding of consent in Brazil around the reified forms of culture and history that seem to point incessantly at stories of racial mixture.[31]

The term "semiotic ideology" is a welcome shorthand for describing, and thus for raising to consciousness so as to trace, the implications for politics and social life of the myriad manners through which signs refer to the world, and thus to one another. As should be clear in relation to the distinction by Nogueira between physical marks that transmit some social hierarchy in the present and physical marks that point to origins in order to instantiate social hierarchies in the present—and thus to issues of inheritance and continuity ostensibly carried within the body of their bearer rather than to the contextual array of ostensibly given or preexisting forms of difference within racial systems—I employ "reference" to talk about a semiotic relationship whereby certain meaning-producing vehicles stand in and take the place of the things or processes at which they gesture. Yet in concentrating on referentiality and its significance to racial politics I am emphasizing that semiosis is not simply about the ways that a sign points to or depicts that which is already present.

Rather, my approach turns on the careful consideration of "participation frameworks," or the rules and assumptions by which previous interpretations become the objects of, and come to influence, successive representations.[32]

My concern with the details of the ongoing reinterpretation of representations of the world may appear fairly basic, especially given the extent to which theorists of Latin American social movements have argued that a key aspect of political change involves the "resignification" of politics and identities.[33] Conversely, it may also seem so abstract a concern as to mean little to an analysis of the attempt to restore the origins of the Brazilian nation around a cultural heritage management that involves the replacement of a living population with commodified and archived signs of that vitality. Nonetheless, even for readers uninterested in semiotic mediation and its effect on, for example, IPAC's or my own ability to group disparate processes like sexual reproduction, religiosity, and the management of a historical center's everyday life as issues or nodes within some linked, historical, and yet contradictory thread like "vitality," an investigation of the details of the ways that particular stances toward the world may become habitual ways of interpreting and acting within it may resonate more forcefully in relation the ways that skin of an indeterminate hue is commonly deemed "white" in the world today.

This objectifying claim, or a simplification about blurry qualities perceived and then identified as objects in relation to a usually occluded array of prompts and assumptions, is ordinarily taken up in the analysis of racial politics as an issue of "categorization." But in breaking down and moving ethnographically beyond "categorization," I seek to understand the crossfertilizations that unite ostensibly disparate areas of social life in a longer and more entwined chain of implication and interpretation. Such a braiding of previously unconnected or differentially wrapped strands for making sense of the world—as in, for example, the lashing of concerns with descent to worries over the potential for future degeneration of a national population as made manifest in perceptions of color—assigns broader as well as more specific meanings to existing simplifications about pigmentation or cultural identities. As a result, I am not interested in the fact of categorization or even all that concerned with announcing that categories loop back to produce their objects.[34] Rather, I seek to understand a much fuller array of semiotic operations whose workings challenge the very assumptions through which social scientists and citizens work through categorization to sort the world.

Among the recursive implications that complicate what I have referred to as a "simplification" about perceivable skin color, and that most interest me in their naturalization, and application in Brazil today, is the assumption (or conclusion) that the bearer of white skin is somehow descended from northern

Europeans. In this particular and yet broad "racial situation" well known in a contemporary United States in which racial belonging is typically understood as a function of descent or cultural affiliation, some material sense or trace of northern Europeanness is imagined as passed down as part of a thread that unites peoples, times, and places.[35] Critical to such transmission of ideas about affiliation and difference that come to make sense as "legacies" with a powerful influence on the present are the modes by which forms of reference are taken up in successive communicative interactions so that a representation comes to participate in broader contests over its meaning and effects. In other words, any attempt to describe or represent both begins as, and relies across its trajectory on, specific propositions about the nature of what is being discussed and how its significance may be communicated, or understood. These propositions may snowball, or even become stripped away and altered fundamentally, in engagements that change the meaning and political effects of what was once a sign of something else, but which may eventually become an object of further signification.[36] Perhaps this is but a way of saying that signs take on new meanings, and thus little more than a case of a well-known social constructivism parading about in fancy clothes. But how one wears one's clothes, how one struts, and how one conceives of, for example, the space or overlap between clothes and bodies, state institutions and the sources of their power, and history or tradition and racial inequality come together in this book to reveal much more than the fact that traditions invented in the UNESCO cultural heritage center play a key role in the construction of categories of identity.

Lived Archives, or Being in History

Race, so often approached as a problem of classification, turns on signification and reference. And as I have begun to foreshadow, signs, like people, participate in the world in different ways that alter fundamentally how these vehicles for communicating meaning, force, and value are perceived and structure social relations. In one, relatively well-known example of this process, signs may butt up against or meld into that which they transmit or to which they refer; point at or direct attention to those referents; or hew to convention and call up arbitrarily what they stand for, pulling referents together on the basis of interpretive or communicative conventions. In perhaps his best-known trichotomy, the philosopher of language and science Charles Sanders Peirce recognizes the variability of forms of reference in the world and accordingly separates semiotic vehicles into icons, indexes, and symbols, or three classes of sign that generate significance differentially (along the lines of the three examples I have just introduced).

Put more prosaically, a sign that takes form as a relative icon like the "White House"—which may stand in for the U.S. presidency—signifies through likeness, shared substance, or metonymy. An index, which includes those entities that linguistic anthropologists dub "shifters," exerts its force upon the world by pointing to that usually proximate thing to which it refers, as does smoke to fire or a weather vane to the wind. Meanwhile, what Peirce referred to pointedly as "the symbol" represents by means of a conventional, learned, relationship to its object or objects. This third example involves the sort of significance emphasized by the linguist Ferdinand de Saussure and usually referred to as "arbitrary" because there is no relationship of contiguity or likeness between the sign vehicle and the object to which it refers. Instead, a given speech community learns, on the basis of habit, to match the signifier ("representamen" in Peirce's vocabulary) to its referent (the "object," for Peirce) in relation to an interpretation or interpreter (or "interpretant" in the Victorian thinker's lexicon). Across this book I suggest that a detailed recognition of this triadic relation and highly variable terrain of social communication, and thus of significance etched in relation to a real object in the world, a sign vehicle whose very materiality adds to its significance, and an interpretant that is attached to and influences each of the other two terms as they do in relation to the interpretant and to one another, is key to understanding why shifts in the production of history are so much a part of alterations in racial ideologies in Brazil today.[37] And the potential for everyday habits to come into new semiotic relationships as part of their objectification and storage as something called "heritage" gives rise to a situation in which archival conventions, social scientific methods, and market relations that transform quotidian actions into commodified culture become a real part of conceptions of personhood and belonging in the Pelourinho today.

In recent analyses of histories as actively produced in the present, rather than gleaned from the excavation of facts and figures from a putatively stable entity called the past, social scientists have come to examine archives not simply as primary sources that contain information about what has taken place, but as historical and historicized sites of inquiry whose contents come to justify multiple presents by means of semiotic entanglements. These entanglements may arise due to some intentional manipulation of evidence and interpretation, but more commonly they take form below the level of notability. An important companion to this insight, developed most complexly in recent decades by Ann Stoler, involves Peirce's recognition that, if signification involves not simply an arbitrary or conventional relationship, but also an iconic or indexical one, then the meaning transmitted will change along with the materiality or shape of the vehicle that conveys it. Thus whether a sign refers by convention (a symbol), points at (an index), or shares matter with or resembles its object (an icon), is remarkably important to the meanings generated. From such a perspective, documentary sources do not simply present the intrepid investigator with an opportunity to learn what really happened by gathering evidence that reflects, however poorly or perfectly, some reality that stands outside and beyond the interpreter and the text. Instead, archives and their architecture become more recognizable as key sites for the production of knowledge, and thus the semiotic mediation of evidence and stances taken toward that evidence.

Rather than repositories of facts to be interpreted, archives might be approached as unstable borders between a society's shifting truths and the techniques that produce and substantiate those facts.[38] Much more than sources or symbolic registers, then, archives stand as "filing systems" that produce "assemblages of control and specific methods of domination."[39] Again, these assemblages are stances, not categories. And their contents, more than scraps of paper that indicate what happened, are in themselves contested remainders whose ongoing inscription and reordering changes what those objects mean, and do. Matthew Hull describes this approach to the production of history as an "attempt to look *at*, rather than *through* documents."[40] And I take this means of facing the archive as basic to understanding how Pelourinho residents' iconoclastic approaches to evidence configure people, their institutions, and their politics in specific ways that both arise from and contribute to the ongoing, and yet variable, deployment of race in Brazilian politics.

Again, to really look at race by considering IPAC's documentation of Pelourinho residents' habits as capable of establishing a horizon of intelligibility obligates the ethnographer to recognize that historical records are not simply arbitrary or habitual signs whose meaning can be decoded via some sort of detached interpretation or valorization of history as "what really happened." This suggests in turn that the attempt to make up for centuries of violence by rescuing those excluded from official histories through a celebration of their attempt to craft new, competing versions of what those documents describe as having taken place may also fall short in the effort to comprehend what history really does in Bahia today. In response, and thus in an attempt to analyze what has happened in the Pelourinho over the last decades, I follow the production and treatment of social scientific and heritage documents as material entities in the world, rather than as objectified reflections of some other reality detached from their formal qualities and concrete presence or arrayal in the archive. This leads me to suggest that what has taken place across the Bahian state's attempt to transform living Afro-Brazilians and their archived habits into signs of Brazilian pasts is a consequence of radically different forms of "reading" and authentication of evidence developed as Pelourinho residents have become habituated to the IPAC social scientists who have produced reams of sociological and ethnographic data about their lifeways.

In the eyes of the people who are concerned with dispossession, the possession of information has been less a question of interpretations related to identities or claims to the past and more an issue of what interested parties *do* with materials. And what people do with IPAC documents often seems to be informed by the manipulation of these material objects in relation to residents' desire to profit from the indemnification process or remain in their homes, IPAC's ritualized or repetitive gathering of evidence, and existing "dispositions" toward written records. In this context, looking *at* documents also affords a new perspective on what it means to look *through* them.

Salient among the uses made of documents by a number of Pelourinho residents in the early 1990s was a rummaging through trash outside businesses and government offices so as to find clean pieces of paper in which they might package the peanuts, cheese, and marijuana sold across the historical center. And yet, since the late 1960s, state-directed social scientific interventions into people's domestic spaces and intimate relations have filled IPAC's patrimonializing archives with a standing reserve of written data. This sociological and ethnographic material is now available as a resource for still-unwritten histories of the Pelourinho, of the Black Atlantic, and of government efficacy and responsibility in cleansing an Afro-Brazilian peoplehood while safeguarding the nation's patrimony. Thus in a process critical to understanding the shifts in racial politics that accompany this development, the very act of generating data and storing it in particular forms has given rise to a specific stance toward history. This is most pronounced in relation to residents whose long-term concern with documents as the raw material for wrapping everyday objects has been transformed into a concern with the ways their everyday habits quite literally compose, or fill, the sheaves of paper that enclose and permit the circulation, for example, of peanuts, marijuana, and information. Thus residents' specific disposition toward archives and the histories they are typically thought to index revolves not so much around the past, as on relationships between the form in which ethnographic data is wielded and the political economic impact, or potential impact, of historical discourse as a vehicle for surviving, prospering, and getting things done. Here engaging history becomes less an issue of somehow understanding "better" what really happened and with what effects, than of manipulating as resources in and of the present the data that become, in the process, signs of what supposedly really happened. As such, history—which I struggle to delineate here as not simply a "commodity" but also as an idiom that veers between and serves multiple functions and social domains—serves the Pelourinho's inhabitants as a way of positioning their contemporary selves rather than of commenting on the past, a horizon of little concern to the majority of those displaced in the recent urban reform. As a result, a careful, ethnographic, look at the composition and use of documents suggests the importance of attending to the materiality of the ways that residents look through documents, and in the process come to see themselves.

Revolt of the Saints is in great measure the fruit of a bifocal ethnographic perspective that Pelourinho residents taught me: Across my period of fieldwork my friends and interlocutors, and at times even my enemies, insisted on the importance of blackmailing IPAC employees with whom they might enter into a sexual relationship that could be documented or alluded to in conversation, trailing architects and sociologists in city streets in order to listen in on plans for the removal of buildings' occupants, pretending not to understand foreign languages so as to react during their interactions to researchers' metacommentaries and in the process alter those ethnographers' results, and lying to, or composing domestic scenes for, field researchers seeking to conduct neighborhood censuses that would soon be filed in IPAC archives. The goal was to inflect how IPAC would represent those people in its patrimonializing ledgers, or those "'rituals of possession'" that cultural bureaucrats would manipulate so as to determine who could remain downtown and who, at what price, would be forced to leave through a combination of police pressure and indemnification.[41] And the basic supposition was not that historical sources might reveal what had taken place so that people could rescue their pasts, but that by attending to the research and documentation process in their iconoclastic manners Pelourinho residents might inflect what takes place in the present.

Residents have found themselves riveted by the ways that information is produced and then placed into and extracted from IPAC's archives in a process with important consequences for their survival. But people are not interested in contesting state officials' interpretations of data, except in cases in which they or a family member have been left out of a survey that might play a role in the size of their indemnification or their ability to claim a living space. Therefore, possession of archival information is not a sign of one's attachment to a particular history that has been silenced. Rather, people approach history as a practical medium that revolves around the manipulation, rather than simply the interpretation, of data. In short, the state-directed archiving of their habits has alerted residents to the fact that rather than the resuscitation or definition of what really happened, the production of history is indeed a production of new knowledge that nonetheless always carries with it traces of other processes and associations that inflect how it is used and interpreted.

To understand how different actors produce, and array, information about daily life in the Pelourinho and then wield it like a sledgehammer or fine-toothed comb in attempts to protect property or extract indemnifications, I would typically don leather shoes and what friends in the neighborhood referred to with admiration as my khakhi "sucker pants" (*calça de otário*) to visit culture managers' offices. "Be a fool," they would counsel, "Drink the hot coffee and the water they'll bring you. When they give you the papers [*as folhas*] put them in your binder and we'll see what we can do with them." Later—or often earlier, since so many Pelourinho residents arose so early to work in demanding jobs across Salvador—I would exchange my fancy pants and leather shoes for rubber flip-flops and shorts and visit the homes of precisely those people facing down and cutting deals with the representatives of IPAC who sought their removal. The perspective facilitated by the alterations in my social skin was especially important when observing, or taking part in, meetings between IPAC officials and the community, between police and those they sought to dislodge, and between leaders of social movements from across Salvador and the infamous residents of the "Mangrove," whom they found so frustratingly difficult to organize and yet so symbolically important to the wider cause.

Changing clothes was important not because it offered some context for interpreting what I saw and experienced, but because by shape-shifting in this manner I began to participate in the transductions of evidence going on around me. And I did so not simply by manipulating the content of representations, but by inflecting their trajectories on the basis of what I looked like, and thus by means of who people took me—rightly or wrongly—to be. As part of this experience I came to experience data not only as authorizing bits of knowledge and concrete mediators of the relationships between different actors, but also as somehow active in the composition of experience as a marked substance that loops around to permeate and contour the outlines and densities of human bodies, the habits it supposedly describes, and the tastes and sounds of the Pelourinho.

One of the most important results of fieldwork involved my firsthand involvement with the construction and transfer of data back and forth, and thus through, bureaucratic structures, residents' homes and hands, formal interviews, and instruments such as ethnographic field notes, sociological questionnaires, and the archives and filing systems in which they became lodged. I was present and sat, often silently, as state officials engaged residents to gather information. Then, later, I would don my valuable pants and follow up with the heritage authorities who tabulated and recoded that information only to emerge from their offices and demand that people turn over their homes or content themselves with the size of an indemnification justified through the results of IPAC research.[42] As a result, over the course of my more than fifteen-year-long professional engagement with the Pelourinho and its residents I have witnessed many transformations as information coproduced by residents and professional social scientists passes out of everyday life, into the archive, and into history and the monumentalization of the quotidian so basic to the Pelourinho's workings: Facts and data about multiple presents, then, take on the status of historical evidence about still-unrealized futures as time wears on or as culture managers force information in the present to stand in for their imagined versions of the origins of Brazil. Central to this dynamic is a social science–based indemnification, expulsion, and configuration of Pelourinho residents as living ancestors to the national community, and thus as central actors and producers of the content of histories of that collectivity.

My approach adds to a burgeoning anthropological and historical interest in the materiality of written records and the influence of that materiality on interpretation. And yet it differs from most analyses of what documents do because I do not locate this materiality in either the archive or the document itself—or the "object," if you will—but in a distributed sense of materiality arising from residents' proleptic approaches to history: People would alter their habits and stories with the goal of inflecting how they were represented in written records of the encounter that they knew would pass into IPAC's archives.[43] And they knew that such information—which they seemed to fetishize not simply as paper documents but also as "data" that had form and shape—might come to shift the conditions for negotiating their claims to personhood and belonging in the Pelourinho, and thus IPAC's evaluation of their suitability for residence in the restored historical center or compensation in return for their departure. Given the importance of money and housing, people's inflections of the shape, contents, and circulation of the records produced about their everyday lives thus became both the raw material of history and an issue of survival, in the barest of senses.[44]

Put too simply, then, this is a book about the writing of Brazilian and Atlantic history through the state-directed sanitization of urban space and the social science–based sanctification of the Afro-Bahians who once occupied, and continue to claim, the ruins of the sumptuous first capital of Brazil. The argument that the Pelourinho restoration involves the sanctification, or what I refer to also as the canonization, of its residents may confuse readers who know something about the expulsion of approximately four thousand Pelourinho residents between 1992 and the present so as to make room for tourist boutiques, hotels, NGO offices, and apartments for the middle class.[45] Yet it is a perspective I stand by: the Pelourinho reconstruction that began in 1992 and continues today has turned the transformation of the vast majority of the neighborhood's former populace into a species of folkloric, quasi-human "data." As information distilled and stored by state institutions, these people's life histories and everyday practices signal the presence of Afro-Brazilians in the Brazilian nation. But

Figure I.6. A resident of the Ladeira da Misericórdia stands in the façade of his home, 1997.

they do so without permitting residents' and former residents' presence within, and thus potential disruption of, the UNESCO-sanctioned representation of that nation via the Pelourinho Historical Center as an urban neighborhood. Nonetheless, this data stands as an archive for future histories of the Brazilian nation and it is, in a number of ways I will seek to make clear through an analysis influenced by Charles Peirce's approaches to signification, a means of representing and/or touching up against an everyday life whose management is critical to the historicity of race, nation, and citizenry in Brazil. And this means that residents' concerns with the production of information about their quotidian lifeways may open a certain room for maneuver. But before outlining further my approach to the rather iconoclastic substantiation of racial politics in the Pelourinho, it is worth presenting a bit of Salvador's more standard history so that the dynamics contemplated here may become more palpable to the reader unfamiliar with the space of difference that is the origin of Brazil.

"The Cradle of Brazil"

The restoration of Brazil's Pelourinho, or Pillory, provides a window onto the ways that the Brazilian state and its citizens negotiate the shifting meanings of race and history in a nation whose pasts as well as futures have long been presented as thinkable only through racial mixture. This mythic origin of the "extreme west" that is Bahia, transformed at the end of the twentieth century from northeastern Brazil's most infamous red light district to an incompletely antiseptic stage, commands the high bluffs that look across the Bay of All Saints, a body of water whose surrounding Recôncavo region was one of the Americas' earliest and richest plantation belts.[46] The Pelourinho's Baroque architecture, so important to twenty-first-century Brazilian identity as presented by nationalist culture managers, is thus one manifestation of the massive wealth and labor of slaves in an Atlantic complex that would come to tie London and Luanda, Baltimore and the Bight of Benin, and Havana and Salvador.[47]

The colonial administrative center for the Portuguese South Atlantic, the first capital of Brazil, and the seat of the High Court of Appeals in Brazil (*Relação*), the Pelourinho began a long decline as the eighteenth-century Caribbean eclipsed northeastern Brazil in the sugar trade and Brazil's capital was transferred to Rio de Janeiro in 1763.[48] By the end of the nineteenth century the wealthy owners of the Pelourinho's mansions had moved to seaside neighborhoods after renting, abandoning, or ceding their homes to domestic servants, trusted family associates and, increasingly, new immigrants from Portugal, Spain, and the Middle East. By the middle of the twentieth century, Salvador's

Map I.1. Salvador and Brazil

central Pelourinho appeared regularly in song, published literature, popular gazettes (*literatura de cordel*), and news reports as a "Brown Mother" and the "Cradle of Brazil," even as it gained a reputation as a fantastic cauldron of behaviors felt to be impossible in other areas of Brazil. At times, men from the city's "best" families left their wives to live in the Pelourinho with their Eastern European mistresses who passed as French, or, worse yet in the eyes of a society purportedly enamored of racial democracy, to live with black Bahians who had fled domestic service in upper-class homes in favor of prostitution. Poor and so-called dishonored women from throughout Brazil fled to its brothels and boarding houses, where they could earn a living washing, cooking, and caring for the children of other working women in this "city within a city" of Salvador, which Ruth Landes dubbed the "city of women" in her monograph of the same name published in 1947.

Some of the women who, to use the local idiom for prostitution, "made a life" in the Pelourinho, subsequently rose to positions of political influence as the lovers and advisors of powerful men. At the same time, "respectable" Bahian women usually refused to enter or be associated in any way with the neighborhood. Certain residents of the city center amassed fortunes running clubs, cabarets, restaurants, illicit drug-dealing operations, and general stores that allowed them to move away from the Pelourinho and sometimes blend into the bourgeoisie as Salvador expanded from a city of four hundred thousand in 1950 to nearly three million inhabitants today. The Pelourinho's population constitutes the actual and metaphorical descendents of the black people in the windows of manor houses, the prostitutes, and "the poorest of them all" that Manuel Bandeira spied on in 1927 but did not ever really see.

For most of the postwar period the Pelourinho provided a space for the erotic and economic relations between middle- and upper-class men and mixed-race or black women. Politicians and intellectuals anchored their claims to popular authenticity, and to communion with the people and their culture, by drinking, carousing, fighting, and visiting the neighborhood's famous houses of prostitution, known locally as "castles." Here interracial relations produced an unstable public authenticity for white men and politicians like Bahia's "governor" Antonio Carlos Magalhães, who reveled in Bahianness on the basis of their knowledge of a red light zone often called the "mangrove."[49] This authentication of populist politics and interclass exploitation through a myth of ostensibly salutary and paradigmatically Brazilian sexual interaction between public men and Afro-descendent women is so powerful that in 2000 the owner of Maria da Vovó, the Pelourinho's last remaining castle, insisted to me that Luis Eduardo Magalhães, the deceased leader of Brazil's lower house of representatives and son of Antonio Carlos Magalhães, frequently conducted high-level

Figure I.7. Street scene prior to the historical center's restoration.

political meetings there until the time of his death. Whether or not the story is apocryphal, it gives some idea of the Pelourinho's importance to the interclass and interracial sexual relations that are so much a part of Bahian political life.

Even as the neighborhood's sex trade gave way to the drug trade in the 1980s, the Pelourinho became a hotbed for the black cultural production—especially the neighborhood's famed carnival associations (*blocos afros*)—and political movements that swept Salvador as Brazil emerged from twenty years of military rule.[50] By this time, colonial homes had begun to collapse and residents built multifloored shantytowns alongside the interior walls of gutted mansions, preserving the façades and creating a vibrant but economically marginalized community that would become the object of state attention, especially after the federal government declared the area a part of national patrimony in 1984 and UNESCO included it in its list of World Heritage sites in 1985.

In 1992 the state government of Bahia, under the leadership of Brazil's then-most powerful populist politician, Antonio Carlos Magalhães, began a still-unfinished $100-million-dollar restoration of the Pelourinho managed by IPAC until 2001 and, subsequently, by CONDER. In the process, the state government converted a crumbling red light zone into a pastel-hued mnemonic device that continues to attract foreign investment and serve as a system of governance. This plan emphasizes regeneration, a reconstruction of Brazil around its first major settlement, the Pelourinho, and the celebration of Bahia as the African

Figure I.8. Salvador's Sussuarana neighborhood, a destination for many residents forced out of the Pelourinho.

root of a nation ostensibly built on the fusion of the African, Portuguese, and Native Brazilian.

The vast majority of the people who inhabited the Pelourinho before 1992 have been forced to accept indemnifications ranging from US$200 to US$5,000 and to move to Salvador's outlying neighborhoods, or areas of the city that municipal and state authorities consider more appropriate to their ways of life. A select group of between four hundred and six hundred people, mainly those with ties to powerful politicians or who have convinced heritage officials of their cultural competence in embodying the attributes necessary to enactors of origins, has managed to remain in the Pelourinho and participate in this new popular public sphere and marketplace that draws thousands of people weekly from throughout Salvador and the world.[51]

The Pelourinho's central role in the development of capitalism and the Atlantic world, its importance to Brazilian nationalism, and the extent to which its populace—made intimate with their state government and city's upper classes through almost a century of sexual, affective, bureaucratic, and workplace contacts—is understood as both diseased, degenerate, and dangerous as well as special and quintessentially Brazilian makes the neighborhood a special place for understanding how such worlds are put together today. And cultural heritage management seems to be one of the most convincing methods available today for lashing people to local, national, and diasporic communities.

Is Patrimony Good to Think?

The configuration of relations between states, territories, and populations constitutes one of the most basic of modernity's political operations. Cultural heritage, or what is usually called "cultural patrimony" (*patrimônio cultural*) in Brazil and across Latin America, is made up of the popular manifestations, the slices of everyday life, and the artistic and architectural expressions that legal registry and the state's rituals of possession transform into collective assets. This means of representing the past and entifying people's practices as cultural "goods" is thus a type of property as well as a technology that mediates the relations between landscapes, political units, and peoplehoods by holding aloft the promise of shared—even alternative—futures carved out of what it configures as common experiences and collective properties. These properties range from cuisines and statues to "qualities" like taste, gait, and even sexuality. And in this engagement with simultaneously abstract and particular political forms like "the community" or "humanity," cultural heritage management both particularizes and makes commensurable cultures and peoples around their putatively specific, and knowable, contents.

Such a classically liberal view of culture—and peoples—as national possessions highlights how much cultural heritage relies on an objectifying relation in which delineation and possession specify the supposedly intrinsic nature not simply of the object, but of the "possessor." In Bahia today, this way of holding on to an identity may generate a felt attachment to regional identities; enrich the political class; justify the confiscation of the property of populations construed as irresponsible; encourage people to perform political subjectivities as if they owned them; and, in a relationship central to the Pelourinho, rank different populations in space and time.[52] In short, patrimony promises to materialize culture by making visible as a type of belonging those qualities that supposedly lie behind, within, and anterior to social relations. And here I am using "belonging" as both a noun and a verb in an attempt to underscore how this technology may turn almost anything into a possession of the nation or, in the case of UNESCO, of a potentially commensurable "humankind": Battlefields, slave routes, buildings, people, mountainous or urban landscapes populated by minority peoples, languages, "traditional" knowledges, DNA codes, carnival celebrations, ways of worshipping, and even samba, capoeira, and foods such as Bahian black-eyed-pea fritters (*acarajé*) are included in UNESCO and Brazilian registries of patrimonialized objects today.

Instrumental to the transformations of previously privately held properties—as well as habits and objects understood as public precisely because they have not yet been circumscribed—into collective possessions is attention to some aspect of everyday life by legal and hygienic institutions. Thus battles over what may be patrimonialized are also at base disputes over ethics, or what comes to attract attention in a particular society. Moreover, such debates are also, at least implicitly, ways of specifying the types of experts authorized to attend to that society's everyday, its approaches to the past, and its conceptualizations of property.[53] In making conspicuous what in retrospect come to appear as life's unmarked or hidden qualities, cultural heritage establishes specific vocabularies for communicating perceptions of the world and defining what fills or alters it: To elevate quotidian relations to the level of treasured objects is to make claims about the efficacy of routinized practices and to suggest that what appears to be little more than a collection of unappreciated behaviors is in fact something material or definitive of the nature of belonging. Discussions of patrimony are thus engagements with both the categories available for valorizing objects and understanding social ontologies—"historical" monuments, "popular" practices, or "natural" treasures, for example—and with the arguments about what is special or intrinsic to the practices that are to be recuperated as historical, popular, or natural. In its consecration of the normal as special, this process is both a nominative and a divinatory science. As a result, to tell a story of Brazilian origins around cultural heritage is to weave an account of how things *are* in the world.

A delineation and symbolic elevation of aspects of the quotidian is also basic to anthropological understandings of religion and the sacred. This is one reason that students of patrimony generally follow the sociologist Dean MacCannell in referring to these collective belongings as a "secular sacred."[54] When a society or societies come to valorize, or even fetishize, patrimony, the sacralized object serves as a space for rethinking standard ways of doing things. It becomes also a type of metacommentary, or metaculture, prized as a technique for getting at or identifying something configured in the process as essential or shared.[55] Patrimonialization, even as espoused today by a UNESCO increasingly invested in a processual version of cultural belonging, is thus about the production of essences in the present in the name of protecting that which is presented as deeply historical and tied to shared legacies. But the very concept of legacy—understood as an enduring linkage of pertinent phenomena and people—obscures the heavy labor necessary to establish the coherence of that tradition and its linked entities.

Today, the idea that circumscribing something as heritage protects it from the market seems relatively anachronistic since culture is increasingly presented as a fungible good. I thus direct my inquiry at the ways social relations solidify as objects that are then linked to, and divided from, one another as a part of human struggles that are nonetheless ordinarily presented within capitalism as some identification of properties intrinsic to those objects. An important part of this spiraling commodification basic to capitalism as well as the semiotic processes that gird intersubjective communication involves the ways that, as the patrimonialized object comes into being, its emergence allows that which is left over to be considered as some *thing* in itself: Engaged ethnographically, the making of patrimony thus brings the everyday or the quotidian into being as a substance actively produced, rather than simply a residue or ground that sets off and contextualizes events and monuments.

Preservation, like transvestitism, promises to make visible what is not there, and in the process make it there. Yet Marjorie Garber points out that dominant approaches ordinarily "erase the third term to appropriate the cross-dresser 'as' one of the two sexes . . . not to see crossdressing except as male or female *manqué* . . . and this tendency might be called an underestimation of the object."[56] A similar lack of attention to the reworkings of the object of both analysis and memorialization is typical in critical discussions of cultural heritage management, a technology many social scientists portray as either radically inauthentic or in fact consonant with the practices of—and thus appropriate to—a community.[57] For Garber, however, the third term that escapes the male/female polarities is a space of possibility. And drawing on Garber's insight, I treat the heritage-making process as a set of state-directed, objectifying techniques whose analysis supports the claim that the person "who wishes to know the truth about life in its immediacy must scrutinize its estranged form."[58] Heritage might even become at times what Martin Heidegger called a "techne" that stands alongside a revelatory poiesis so as to bring forth the grounds of everydayness and belonging.[59] As Garber's emphasis on a third term suggests, and even if one is troubled by Heidegger's approach to ontology and politics, scrutiny of patrimony's historical content is not simply an issue of battles over correct and incorrect, exclusionary and more just, or elite versus subaltern perspectives on tradition. It involves much more complex questions about the techniques that link different moments and produce the past as a salient part of, and means of authorizing, the present. And this is why life itself is one of this book's principal areas of investigation.

The Many Lives of Heritage

Richard Handler pointed out nearly thirty years ago that cultural heritage planning "focuses on life itself as the object to be preserved, documented, and displayed."[60] Since then, this insight has been explored relatively timidly and almost entirely in the realm of "commodification of culture" arguments concerned with the effects in neoliberal Latin America of the packaging of

Figure I.9. Everyday life in the ruins of Lusitania.

people's habits and the manufacturing of traditions in attempts to cash in on culture. From such a perspective, the "life" of the heritage machine appears to transpire in a resolutely social or cultural arena of everyday habits and politics. These practices and politics appear relatively separate from the biological functioning of a group or species. And in the few accounts that have begun to integrate into the heritagescape the unravelings of the nature/culture divide so much a part of the social sciences today—symptoms of broader processes that may very well be partially responsible for UNESCO's supplementation of existing "natural" and "cultural" heritage categories with "intangible heritage" in 2003—this patrimony is presented rather like an inert "resource" like oil or corn or social capital. From such a perspective, the basket of relations packaged as heritage emanates logically from the workings of capital even when authors recognize people's creativity in engaging the twisted logic of commodification. As a result, commodification is seen as deployed in quite understandable, and thus rather reasonable, manners by subalterns who seize hold of an alienated culture/humanity/biology that resists anything but the most perspicacious of ethnographic engagements.[61] But as I have begun to signal, this book is a rather unreasonable account, albeit one still tempered by the violence of the reasoning that circulates around me to demand particular and rather habitual forms of accountability.

My claim to "unreason" emanates from a propensity to take seriously arguments by Pelourinho residents that, for example, they are themselves patrimonialized objects who gain a special, sacral status akin to that of buildings set off and reconstructed by heritage officials. In examining this drawing together of people and buildings as monuments, I build on the work of Michel Foucault, especially his concerns with what he dubbed the "biopolitical" management of the life or abstract vitality of a people. Foucault associates this power to cultivate a broadly defined life in relation to death—and thus produce self-governing, "normalized" subjects—with the system of control he called "governmentality."[62] Systems of governmentality, understood as concerns with the "conduct of conduct," arose in relation to what Foucault called "biopower," or a form of diffuse, capillary power "situated and exercised at the level of life, the species, the race, and the large-scale phenomena of population."[63] And sexuality is a key node in the transfer, and thus the productivity, of this power. Hence the Pelourinho, as a former red light zone turned into a UNESCO site, or a source of national and world history produced around the social scientific examination of the intimate habits of a population still tinged by its association with deviant sexuality, might be approached as a critical arena for understanding the details of the biopolitical management of national unity around history, hygiene, and race.

Throughout this book I draw on Foucault's insights, and work to tie them to a concern with political economic relations, in order to make out the extent to which concerns with biology, vitalism, and human essences come face-to-face with a confusion of people and buildings in the Pelourinho of the last fifty years. But here it is worth noting that, at least according to Doris Sommer, Latin America's national romantic novel arose as a "foundational fiction" capable of tying together the nation through the public dissemination of a domestic narrative. Thus the romantic novel helped to establish nascent American republics that were "ostensibly grounded in 'natural' heterosexual love and in the marriages that provided a figure for apparently nonviolent consolidation during internecine conflicts."[64] And, like the national romance in the mid-nineteenth century, the early-twenty-first-century Latin American cultural heritage center is a critical genre for producing foundational fictions that might unite the Brazilian nation in spite of the violence naturalized in those narratives. In this capacity, as in Gilberto Freyre's mid-twentieth-century fictions of Brazilian "non-racialism" located in the "mansions and the shanties" and the "big house and the slave quarters," the Pelourinho permits the establishment of a Brazilian ecumene by revealing what IPAC-authorized observers identify as taking place in ostensibly more intimate or affective locations such as the household, the bed, or at the stove.[65] Within this dynamic, visitors' ability to appreciate a dance step somehow associated with a sexualized Afro-Brazilian essence, or the boiling of peanuts in large vats, or even particular types of kinship relations, motivate the representations of the Pelourinho that attract tourist dollars and Inter-American Development Bank (IDB) lending.

Life in the Pelourinho, especially given the historical center's construction in relation to a Brazilian tradition of Lamarckian blurrings of the biological and the social, comes into being around a conjuring of essences that seems to collapse the sentimental, the biological, and the social. Clearly, the affective aspects of the heterosexual love and marriage that Sommer locates at the core of Latin American nationalism are not the same as the biological life of the species. And yet, in the writings of Gilberto Freyre, reproduction, affect, scent, Lusitanian and African cultural traditions, skin color, architecture, bathing habits, corporeal rhythms, modes of stroking or cuddling, cuisine, Native Brazilian agricultural techniques, and innumerable other qualities and knowledges—only some likely to be recognizable to most North Americans today as somehow biological—stew in a vital milieu to produce a uniquely Brazilian ethos that Freyre claimed would propel the nation into a mixed-race future. Given the extent to which IPAC patrimonializing initiatives activate such by-now habitual ways of recognizing Brazilian selves and communities, the Pelourinho takes form in an environment or through technologies that look rather like those that commentators associate with the recent growth of technoscience in the United States.

According to Nikolas Rose, citizens in the contemporary United States find themselves enmeshed in a transition away from a view of life writ large as an "unalterable fixed endowment."[66] More specifically, and given, for example, the commodification of the human around trade in its body parts and a transformation of biological processes into coded information, a growing reliance on genetic testing as a form of prognostication, the development of "genetic" and "biological" citizenship, and what Rose argues are increasingly somaticized senses of self, it seems that people relate more and more to "biology" as some blurred form of "nature/culture."[67] From this perspective, it would seem that technoscientific advance has generated in the contemporary United States a melding of the social and biological in ways that encourage a variety of effects that are strikingly similar to mid-twentieth-century Brazilian approaches to life, organicism, and the relationship between landscapes and people. Thus reference to "life" involves proliferating series of vital relations open to biosocial improvement, a rather Lamarckian situation that propels Didier Fassin to argue that while Foucault concerned himself with a power over life, today we find ourselves within regimes of "biolegitimacy" that are imprinted by "the power *of* life" on lives, in an ethical sense.[68] Hence a life lived poorly may spur institutions to withdraw care in a move that results in biological death. And for Rose, when such ostensible civilizational inadequacy is translated into a biological condemnation to death, or exclusion from health, the resultant expanded notion of life and its associated technologies of calculability and anticipation help orient societies toward the future. Yet this is a somewhat provincial observation.

In a markedly different analysis, some of the first investigators of the social impact of technoscience and recent reconfigurations of nature/culture in Latin America argue that, in Brazil, interpretations of genetics point back in time "to reassert the important proportions of African and Amerindian ancestry in contemporary white Brazilians."[69] In other words, in spite of the concern with futurity associated with the disaggregation of the human body into alienable parts in North America, it would appear that similar technologies produce an interest in specifying origins in new ways in Brazil, the second most populous democracy in the Americas and a nation long characterized as predicated on future aspirations rather than a strong sense of tradition. Yet technoscience is not the only realm in which such a concentration, and specification, of origins is taking place in Brazil today.

Brazilian claims to modernity are increasingly secured today through a particularization of national pasts thought to produce origins. In a myth of national hybridity like that enunciated by Gilberto Freyre and his colleagues, origins were approached as idealized starting points mobilized in the service of future exchanges. While an interest in such futures has not been extinguished today, by the 1990s Brazilian histories produced by both the state and new social movements tended toward the restoration of origins portrayed as lost or having decayed from an earlier "purer" state.[70] The modification in emphasis from the mid-twentieth-century *construction* of a modernist utopia in Brasilia to the 1992–present *reconstruction* of Salvador's colonial center, Brazil's originary urban space, is emblematic of this shift in the nation's most salient temporalities.[71] Increasingly, dominant actors in the Brazilian state and in civil society posit history as a recuperative act limited to specific groups, rather than a future-oriented narrative directed to the majority of citizens.[72] Such public recognition of exclusionary specificities both draws on and adds to the importance of the heritage zone in producing the nation today.

I do not, in what follows, make any concerted argument about some relationship between technoscience and Brazilian race relations. Nonetheless, I do recognize biotechnologies' potential for altering the relations between pasts, presents, and futures that my research suggests are manipulated in Bahia by patrimony. And I address questions of genetics in chapters 5 and 6, as Bahians seek to assign identities to the skeletons uncovered under the largest plaza in the Pelourinho. More important, however, I note that the Euro-North American fascination with the unraveling of nature/culture distinctions linked by scholars like Nikolas Rose to incitements to futurity points to the importance of considering debates about "vitality" in the heritage center, and thus the ways these discussions help focus attention on issues of origins. This seems especially appropriate in the Pelourinho due to its associations with sexuality, reproduction, death, immoral acts, and bodily fluids. In fact, I concentrate in what follows on how in Salvador a social scientific gaze cast upon what is construed as an undifferentiated, biosocial everyday life linked to long-standing concerns with the health and vitality of an Afro-Brazilian population comes to play a key role in charting shifting webs of associations that make believable specific conceptions of human being and its attachments to politics. And this leads me, finally, to this book's title and the reason I am so concerned with saints in a historical ethnography of cultural heritage, urban reform, and the production of the past.

From People, to Things, to Spirits, and Back Again?

This book bears the title "Revolt of the Saints" for several reasons: First, it examines a state-directed elevation of people as patrimony—that secular form of the sacred—that gives rise to a certain understanding on the part of those citizens as to their own historicization in the context of an attempt to make them serve as both internal Others and exemplars of national development. Such a coming into being congeals as a result of residents' growing realization that the IPAC techniques designed to produce the past *rely* on Pelourinho residents' participation. The revolt that this engenders is a deep, guttural feeling of *revolta* that is akin to the English nausea. Therefore, the saints' revolt is not a counternarrative to some official history of the Pelourinho and Brazil, but involves the sense that the technocratic production of what passes as history is noxious and disturbing in ways that force people to engage space and time in new ways.

Second, canonical Brazilian culture as packaged in Bahia today revolves around the Afro-Brazilian divination-based religion Candomblé. Candomblé turns around possession, or the eruption of forces that are not one's own. Such forces are typically interpreted by academics and activists as giving rise to alternative histories, and thus to future possibilities never imagined in everyday spaces. As Joan (Colin) Dayan observes of Candomblé's cousin, Haitian vodou, the "dispossession accomplished by slavery became the model for possession in vodou: for making a man not into a thing but into a spirit."[73] But such eruptions have become commonplace in Salvador. They are now normal, even canonical, ways of telling histories as put forth by a state government deeply involved in the fomenting of Candomblé as a quintessentially Bahian religion. Seemingly as a result of their association of Candomblé with the patrimonialization process, as well as the rapid growth of Protestant churches across all of Latin America, many of the residents of the Pelourinho demonstrate an affinity for iconoclastic versions of Pentecostal Protestantism. These religious practices challenge Catholicism, Candomblé—the now hegemonic cultural model for Bahian identity and Brazilian history—and the Bahian state's attempt to derive legitimacy through the appropriation of Afro-Brazilian culture. As a result, and even as I continue to appreciate the beauty of Candomblé and the political roles of its leadership in relation to an Afro-Brazilian population and attempts to carve out a space of political possibility in the face of ongoing state-led efforts to appropriate the religion's symbols, I follow the residents of the Pelourinho into a confusing, musealized urban space of Evangelical conversion set amidst the iconography of Roman Catholic cathedrals, grand monuments to Lusitania, and the estranging, apparently secular, rituals of canonization through cultural heritage.

In this environment, "possession" stands not simply as some spiritual or spirit-based medium for escaping the entanglements of a debauched, physical world. Instead, and drawing on the ways that spirituality, material images, and particular shrines or locations have long been confused in Iberian and Latin American popular religiosity, it seems that meaning, selves, and agency may lie closer to objects than usually recognized in modern social science. Here it is worth repeating my assertion that the rather special ways of facing the archive developed by Pelourinho residents, who I will come to refer to as "properly historical subjects" in relation to their concerns with propriety, property, and their self-insertions into history as a pragmatic field, suggest that history in Salvador's colonial downtown is about knowing how to situate oneself in flows that may generate palpable material benefits. In doing so people make a variety of claims about their own status as historical beings *da antiguidade* (from antiquity) who nonetheless exist in the present. Inhabitants of the Pelourinho often come to see themselves as human heritage objects whom IPAC seeks to restore by means of social hygienic techniques akin to those applied to the reconstruction of monuments and statues. In these overlaps, the canonization of people as patrimony converges with long-standing traditions in Iberian and Latin American folk Catholicism, as well as Candomblé, in which saints, people, and material things often appear remarkably indistinct, and thus potentially interchangeable.

Roman Catholic conventions stipulate a rather dogmatic path to sainthood, including the beatification and subsequent canonization of ostensibly exemplary individuals as mediators between God and human beings. Yet in the Catholicism of northeastern Brazil there is significant overlap between consecrated saints, folk saints, religious icons that might be described misleadingly as representing saints, and their devotees.[74] One effect of this overlap is that the relationship between saints themselves, and images of those saints, seems to have developed in ways that challenge dominant social scientific approaches to representation. In what follows I build on this ambivalence, as well as saints' roles as "persons in heaven," or mediators entitled to veneration and authorized to intercede with the gods on behalf of "normal" mortals, in order to illustrate how cultural heritage-based manipulations of the "division of the sensible" alter conceptions of humanity and vitality, and thus of race and political struggle.[75] Basic to this assertion is the observation that Pelourinho residents, like saints and even Candomblé deities across Bahia, are iconic, mediating figures who are often confused with national monuments.

Order of the Chapters

Even in their totality, the chapters leave much, and many people, out of my account of the reconstruction of a neighborhood known as the nation's "heart." This is not my intention. But if I were to include all that I desire, this book would quickly approach the mass and problematic yet fictional unity of IPAC's archives. And thus, before moving on, I would like to make a request: If you have not done so already, please read the preface. Many of your questions— which may soon become worries—about how and why I have come up with certain ideas, or have chosen to represent relationships in particular ways, may be addressed (if not quite answered) by the short account there. That preface is important for understanding who I was when I quite literally bumped into members of the group that would come to be known as "S.O.S. Children of the Historical Center," or simply the Bem Aventurados (The Blessed). And I have noticed in ensuing years that the query, "Who are you, John, and how are you in any way authorized to tell that story in the way you do?" is a common reaction among readers of this account. So, please, read the preface so as to join me in a more complete understanding of this book's goals and genesis so that we might all assess more critically the chapters that follow.

Chapter 1, "The Eighteenth Battalion of Love" shakes up the classic scene of ethnographic arrival by following as both the anthropologist and his Bahian interlocutors step into the histories represented in this book, even as no one seems prepared to do so successfully. This ramble intended to transmit a feel for the Pelourinho is not about "how I arrived." Rather, it is about a panoply of people who begin on the wrong foot and then find bits of themselves within semiotic systems that feel so foreign, but that eventually thicken so as to offer a perch from which to engage, and even alter, the world.[76] And this, in turn, is about some of the ways that accepted techniques for producing truths and making claims about groups come to be highlighted in manners that may lead to their dismantling or alteration. The account opens with memories I put together with one of my closest friends in Salvador, moves through an encounter with a famous music producer and a plate of rice and beans eaten by the wrong man, and then smacks into a false philanthropic extravaganza organized around "street children" but designed to enrich its organizers. Next, it enters a wily game of dominoes before ending up at a reggae concert. There, an audience's misinterpretation of lyrics about violent police officers has important implications for the rise of a Pelourinho-based social movement composed of former street children and the illegitimate sons and daughters of powerful Bahian men and women of the red light district. Chapter 1 thus offers a glimpse into the ruses, setbacks, and feints and contradictions so much a part of Pelourinho life. But in doing so it also puts forth a theory of agency and historicity and sets up a scene that will come to fruition, or perhaps make sense, only as the reader completes this book.

Chapter 2 is rather different: It offers a history of patrimonialization initiatives, bracketed by the "discovery" of Brazil and my "discovery" in 2000 of the quincentennial commemorations of that moment of contact, that suggests that Bahia's cultural heritage initiatives are unthinkable without the presence of marginal women of imperfect morals. I structure this argument around a series of letters, including one that ends up in the middle of *Macunaíma*, a well-known modernist novel authored by the man who would also put together the original plan for SPHAN, Brazil's federal heritage bureaucracy (later IPHAN). The chapter, which situates patrimony in longer histories of colonial and postcolonial Brazil, thus sets up chapter 3. This next chapter offers a detailed analysis of interactions between Pelourinho residents and the IPAC social scientists who, soon after the establishment of the heritage institution in 1967, set forth to map the Maciel red light district and its population. The IPAC initiative would do much to shape how the Pelourinho Historical Center has come into being today. And thus my emphasis is once again on morality and gender as I work across this chapter about the nature and development of Bahian social science and cultural heritage management to suggest that Pelourinho-based patrimonializing initiatives effect a melding of the human and the monumental around sexuality. This surprising concatenation is something that residents will by the 1990s pick up and wield against IPAC and in relation to their own attempts to understand personhood in neoliberal Brazil.

Chapter 4 carries the reader into the turn of the millennium by offering a detailed history of ownership, and dispossession, around the "Gueto," or the building from which the Children of the Historical Center sallied forth in an attempt to seize hold of history and claim their property as recounted in chapter 1. But in chapter 4 the reader is privy to the end of the Gueto as IPAC and police forces succeed in driving out all residents. The chapter follows as this experience gives rise to a series of claims to "properties" that permit residents to assert a patrimonialized status on which they draw, often profitably, in their interactions with state authorities. I tag along as IPAC seeks to sort out legal title to buildings and establishes an indemnification program that residents rapidly overwhelm, creating fictitious families, registering relatives from thousands of miles away, and even attempting to compile their own dossiers and questionnaires so as to blackmail bureaucrats. This discussion of human and cultural properties and state techniques for coming to know a population thus sets up chapter 5, an account of excavations on the Pelourinho's largest plaza where the unexpected discovery of hundreds of human skeletons sets off a frenzied search for treasure and an attempt to identify the bodies uncovered. Citizens' and institutions' struggles to find what lies underneath the fabric of naturalized landscapes and give form to remains that people come to identify as ancestors index important shifts in Bahian racial ideologies, which are explored in this chapter in relation to accounts of lost slaves, semi-free laborers, British interference in mid-nineteenth-century Bahia, and some of the approaches to property introduced in chapter 4.

In chapter 6 the narrative narrows, focusing on a single interaction between a public health team and a group of HIV-positive residents of the Ladeira da Misericórdia, one of Salvador's most stigmatized locales in the 1990s. The account develops my approach to cultural heritage, northeastern Brazilian saintliness, and iconoclasm by examining the "gutsy insurrection" of a woman nicknamed Topa (or "I'm up for anything," in Bahian slang) who seizes hold of a public health performance and, by following its pedagogical implications to the letter, leaves the health professionals speechless in a move that interpellates them as actors within Topa's drama. Here I concentrate, in a discussion that extends the attempts to move across a representational field introduced in chapter 1, on the ways that the patrimonialization process in the Pelourinho has made residents keenly aware of their special roles in the neighborhood's sacralization, their places in shifting definitions of historical truth, and thus their importance to the nation as a political project. I describe this state as "proper historicity" and demonstrate how it is performed through specific approaches to narrative and interpretation.

Chapter 7 builds on Topa's fascination with technique and rejection of the right to interpretation by looking at a surprising form of translation performed by thousands of working-class youths who travel to the Pelourinho on Sunday nights to sing in unison as they transform the English of classic Jamaican reggae songs into Portuguese entirely on the basis of the songs' prosody. I examine how discussions of commodities and consumption in the Pelourinho "translations" interact with the ways that remaining Pelourinho residents—precisely those who were able to make claims to Pelourinho identities by convincing the state of their ability to properly represent Africans in the official national triad of black, Native Brazilian, and Portuguese mixture—vehemently reject this elision of language's referential features. Chapter 7 extends my earlier considerations of residents' negotiations of state power and history. It focuses on the shapes taken by the semiotic pathways that link the seen and the unseen and the voiced and the unvoiced in order to make properties present. In this way, chapter 7 loops back to consider how the production of cultural heritage in the Pelourinho ties into shifting approaches to racial identity in relation to a series of social practices that may at first glance seem unrelated to Brazilian racial formations.

A Coda to an Introduction

This is not a book designed to be chopped into digestible chapters or assigned as discrete arguments about an easily identifiable thing called "Brazil," or "history," or "racial politics," or even that familiar, sentimentalized object that I might describe as "those poor people who were expelled from their homes." Rather, it is an account of love, and pain, and confusion that makes a variety of specific and, I hope, clear points about the ways that shifting approaches to the past and modes of claiming truth factor into Brazil's democratic transitions. It is also a rather specific engagement with propriety and dignity, concepts central to life in the Pelourinho in spite of the level of discrimination residents face from outsiders. Yet the dignity to which I refer is not some ideal, bourgeois,

North American dignity. It is instead a properly historical approach that may at times feel irreverent to those attached to neat definitions of moral actions.

Given what my time in the Pelourinho suggests are social scientists' potential difficulties in questioning their own worldviews and taking seriously what the people with whom they work actually say and do—as opposed to what "we" the enlightened analysts want them to say and do—I suspect that some readers will find rather off-putting my occasional honesty or irony about interactions and phenomena on which I would at times rather not report. But I do not know any other way to convey my perceptions of how my friends and former neighbors engaged a state seeking to define and burrow into the very bases of their humanity. And thus, perhaps as a result of this commitment and its attendant difficulties, as well as the importance of the present account to who I am today, I must admit that this book is an artifact of a story that has gotten, and will continue to get, away from me. Sometimes I believe this occurs because I want too much to make good, and put my version of the patrimonialization of the Pelourinho into the box of the professional social science from which it did not emerge. But that limiting, professionalizing option has proved impossible.

Now, in retrospect, I introduce these pages by concluding only that my inability to circumscribe the story as some neat building block that fits nicely into established theoretical canons that secure professional knowledge and politics as we know them must have something to do with the fact that the images that unfold do more than depict a people, a place, or a set of problems. What lies before you, dear reader, is a story that, more than working as some theoretical or empirical intervention, produces its own author as a fictional character, or a social scientist, with much too much power over the misrepresentations that drive Bahia's political economy of development today. Perhaps, then, this is a theoretical intervention that might prove useful to those interested in the politics of race and history. And thus, in drawing here self-consciously and humbly on an expression with weighty historical associations when wielded by travelers to tropical lands, I can say without modesty that my manipulation of symbols and traditions that play such key roles in Bahia's political economy has proved to be a heavy burden. But it is a burden shared also by the many Bahians who are expected by their state, and often by their society and their neighbors, to serve as living archetypes of a history that is, and can never be entirely, their own.

CHAPTER 1

"The Eighteenth Battalion of Love"

Failure and the Dissemination of Misinterpretation

The very involuntariness of love, even where it has not found itself
a practical accommodation beforehand, contributes to the whole as
soon as it is established as a principle.
—Theodor W. Adorno, *Minima Moralia*

I n June 2009, during a break in the winter rains that sent chunks of
masonry crashing onto homes built along the interior walls of collapsed buildings, I joined a friend at the corner of João de Deus and
Gregório de Mattos Streets. This crossroads served for most of the
twentieth century as the symbolic heart of the Maciel, as the western side of today's Pelourinho Historical Center was called prior to
1992, when IPAC initiated its most recent round of urban reforms. My
companion, whom I will call Malaquias, had been one of the neighborhood's many infamous *malandros*, or old-school hard men who
refused to tolerate affronts to their honor even as, like the Mago introduced in the preface above, he often "took no position at all" while
making do at the edges of the so-called formal economy. By the mid-
1990s Malaquias had parlayed this renown as a bender of rules, and
thus as a fixture in the Maciel/Pelourinho, into a career as a reggae
musician. And as we traversed streets where the smells of wet lime,
garbage, and rotting hardwoods had been replaced by stale beer and
fresh paint, my friend compared his life to the increasingly depopulated Historical Center.

Malaquias' autobiography, which I have heard in many iterations,
usually involves escape from his overbearing cowhand father in Bahia's dry backlands (the *sertão*); childhood struggles to survive alone

in the once lively streets of the Maciel/Pelourinho; confrontations with, and crafty confoundings of, infamous detectives; stints in the penitentiary under aliases that spared him a record and thus permitted him to travel to Europe; reacquaintance with his mother, a domestic servant who had been forced to send him to live with his father so she could care for others' children in Salvador; conversion to Pentecostal Protestantism; and, finally, consecration as a Rastafarian leader, or a holy man celebrated due in part to widely perceived links to the Afro-Brazilian tradition packaged and disseminated in the Pelourinho's reconstruction. Malaquias, then, has become well known, and a person (*gente*) rather than a street child or convict, on the basis of travails and a struggle for truth that he argues has led him to an appreciation of Afro-Brazilian identity and rather Christian notions of restoration and self-examination.

As Malaquias and I left the Maciel, we stopped by the Praça das Artes, Cultura, e Memória (Plaza of Arts, Culture, and Memory), an interior courtyard restored by IPAC in 1999. There a sculpture called "Redemption" gurgled hopefully. Encrusted with semiprecious stones whose safeguarding requires that the artwork be enclosed by an iron fence, the fountain announces that:

water washes away evil as compassionate tears sacralize this contemporary ritual. In the end, then, the place's negative energies are inverted.

The Pelourinho's destructive aspects evaporate, and from this we extract its regenerative power.

Out of condemned material we extract magical power, the mana of the condemned, whose magic is that of knowing how to reinvent life in a ritualized form again and again, again and again.

But Malaquias and I did not even glance at words that suggested that we were crossing a landscape whose regeneration, we had learned through bitter experience, rested on the ritual sacrifice and careful presentation of data—the "mana of the condemned"—about its inhabitants. All too familiar with this state-directed monumentalization of the Pelourinho's populace over the last two decades, we pointed out the corner in which Bira "the Ox" and Fat Carlos used to tether their fighting cocks. And we spat, nearly in unison, below a tiled sign that announced our arrival at the Praça das Artes, Cultura, e Memória. Not by chance, then, its first vertical column was louvered at a thirty degree angle so as to guide the viewer's eye toward "A-C-M," the initials and well-known nickname of Bahia's "Governor" Antonio Carlos Magalhães.

Unnerved by the spectral power of the iron-fisted patron of "Arts, Culture and Memory" whose architects, neighborhood residents agreed, rarely missed a chance at nervous obeisance, we followed Rua João de Deus.[1] We walked

Figure 1.1. "A-C-M" present in the Plaza of Arts, Culture and Memory

silently past the military police post established in 1992 as part of the state's initial attempts to control the Maciel and paused at the handicrafts market that had replaced a brothel formerly known as the Buraco Doce (Sweet Hole). After Malaquias collected a small sum owed to him, we crossed onto the bustling Terreiro de Jesus Square. There, bookended by Salvador's Cathedral and the gold leaf of the Baroque Igreja de São Francisco (São Francisco Church), *baianas do acarajé* slathered black-eyed-pea fritters (*acarajé*) with fish paste and okra while *capoeira* fighters drummed up an audience in the drizzle.[2] At the Square's opposite edge we turned toward the still-stigmatized 28th of September Street. Descending pitted hillsides (*ladeiras*), we sought to recall the names of sealed buildings' former occupants. At times we stuttered and stumbled, disoriented on slippery cobblestones that had once reassured in their uneven familiarity.

Now, nearly two decades after they had shuttered the first of the Maciel's buildings, workers were transforming colonial *sobrados*, built for planter and merchant elites but occupied across the twentieth century by impoverished quasi-citizens, into quarters for the philanthropies and state institutions that would help cement the Pelourinho as a cultural destination. Due to hiccups in IDB funding supported by arguments that planners had neglected the population, they were also converting a number into apartments for the police and the bureaucrats reviled, and envied, by Malaquias and his former neighbors: In response to pressure to enliven a now-depopulated architectural jewel, IPAC and

Figure 1.2.

its institutional sibling, state-level urban planning body CONDER, had joined federal credit institutions to structure mortgages for public servants. But this meant that working-class Afro-Bahians without formal labor documents (*carteira assinada*) or the marks of bourgeois propriety demanded by lending officers had little hope of returning to Brazil's soon-to-be-reconstructed African heart.[3]

As Malaquias and I reached the corner of the 28th of September and Saldanha da Gama Streets, we paused before the doorway of the charred shell of number 18, a building that still bore the coat of arms of the Santa Casa da Misericórdia, the Americas' oldest philanthropic organization. In 1998 one

Figure 1.3. Police at the corner of Rua São Francisco and 28th of September Streets not long after residents' removal.

IPAC official had described to me the edifice—dubbed the "Gueto" (Ghetto) by its vocal group of mainly Pentecostal and Rastafarian occupants so as to emphasize their kinship with residents of poor areas of Kingston, Jamaica—as "a vile nest of dangerous snakes, the absolute worst there is in the Pelourinho!" But in 2009 we approached it as Malaquias' former home, a space he had filled with friends from the Bahian sertão he fled before arriving in Salvador as what observers usually call a "street child."[4]

Military police regarded us warily as we kicked at construction scraps and ran our hands along graffitied walls. Some stared, seeking to understand what the gap-toothed Rastafarian wearing an expensive watch might be passing surreptitiously to the large gringo. Savvier civil police detectives shouted ostensibly welcoming, yet decidedly menacing, greetings.[5] These gatekeepers skilled at torturing supposed miscreants recognized us as one of the neighborhood's many odd pairs: While still subject to the threat of summary abuse, Malaquias

Figure 1.4. In 1995, prior to their dispossession, residents celebrate a birthday near the corner of Rua São Francisco and 28th of September Streets while neighbors play dominoes.

and I had gained a measure of safety due to an association with the heritage landscape and the social science so essential to its reconstruction. This is not to equate our experiences or the risks borne by a white, U.S. citizen and a working-class, Afro-Bahian, but rather to emphasize their interrelatedness in a UNESCO World Heritage site that served as a hub for communication across and between transnational networks and Salvador's working-class neighborhoods.

The felt identification that residents referred to in the wake of their expulsion as *da antiguidade* (again, being or arising from antiquity), authorized Malaquias and me as performers within and interpreters of a Pelourinho-based quotidian. At the time, IPAC had worked assiduously to separate out, and then mobilize, this everyday life as an economic resource and index of supposedly shared beginnings. Indeed, the foreign anthropologist who had become a *doutor* on the basis of his knowledge of an antique land's social relations, and this former convict and self-described *flagelado* (sufferer, beaten one) who had become a reggae phenomenon as a result of his representations of his struggles in those same streets, fit quite nicely into, and even helped animate and give form to, the historical center as a sensuous, at-times enjoyable, and much-discussed reconstruction of Brazil's colonial origins. In part as a result, it is difficult to find a visitor to Salvador who fails to exclaim something like, "Wow, Bahia's really beautiful. The art, the music, the Afro-Brazilian culture. It's really the heart of Brazil!" Or, in a slightly different but related version, one may hear, "I despise the Pelourinho. It's so touristy and false, so filled with hustlers and street children, so commercial, and so brutal!" This book does not evaluate either claim. Instead, it burrows into a novel Bahia that comes into being in direct dialogue with the national and diasporic pasts produced in Salvador's downtown heritage machine. The Pelourinho as a quite literally re-membered formation, so real and so illusory in its reconstruction of what never existed until now, is simultaneously commercial, beautiful, traditional, novel, and, yes, still so brutal.

This first chapter is both an argument and a panorama. Designed to stand in for anthropology's classic "Imagine yourself suddenly set down surrounded by all your gear, alone on a tropical beach close to a native village" introduction to a field site, while still offering the reader a shared path into a panorama rife with description and dislocation, it revolves around a failed event in a neighborhood seemingly anchored in feints, dodges, and unauthorized appropriations.[6] This approach to narrative origins is intended to carve out and describe an inchoate and provisional, yet formative, perch from which the rest of this book flows. And the sentimental space that emerges from the enveloping, bittersweet love out of which I conceptualize and introduce the group of Pelourinho residents who would become the neighborhood social movement "S.O.S. Filhos do Centro Histórico" (also "Children of the Historical Center" or "S.O.S."), and with whom I traversed Bahia's streets and bureaucracies in developing the standpoints I seek to share across the present ethnography of the making of a historical center, is not the neatly encompassing, idealized love of inclusion.

A focus on setbacks, ruses, missed opportunities, petty insults, misinterpretations, potent threats, and, of course, the love that shrouds and shreds us all does more than reflect the many literary traditions that present this love as an involuntary feeling that is strongest or most clearly apparent when denied or unrequited: It also mimics the often conflictual yet powerful forms of association relied on by a group of close friends, most of them former "street children," in their everyday dealings with their state and with one another.[7] Such contradictory, at times even violent, love seems most appropriate for drawing you, my reader, into the intimacy of the encounter between a state and its people in Salvador's Historical Center over the course of its state-directed "improvement." This is true in part because, I venture to argue cross-culturally and relatively ahistorically, the declaration of love, even if made cynically or never fulfilled,

Figure 1.5. An adolescent hit by a police bullet shows his injuries while sitting on the Ladeira da Misericórdia.

alters the reception, and shape, of those phenomena associated with the precarity of the promise, its enunciator, and all those connected by the utopian possibility of pure communion with an Other.

As we walked, and in an example of productive negation and the Pelourinho's place in suturing disparate phenomena, moments, and people, Malaquias and I recalled a misty night five years earlier. Compadre Washington, the producer of Brazil's then-most famous band, the *pagode* music supergroup "É o Tchan," had screeched to a halt to leap from his black Mercedes and join us at an impromptu bar made up of aluminum chairs set on the 28.[8] And thus while Malaquias and I traversed a neighborhood now nearly devoid of inhabitants, we chuckled about how we had pointed out to Compadre Washington that as he was appearing on television and enjoying the good life, his former friends from the Maciel/Pelourinho had remained in crumbling, squatted buildings to face intensifying violence from the feared *Choque* (Shock) military police units sent to root out the last of the neighborhood's long-term residents.

Figure 1.6. The Praça da Sé under "restoration," March 1999.

Due to the Choque's boots, fists, and nightsticks, people nicknamed its patrols the *timbalada* in honor of the powerful beats of another Bahian institution, the Timbalada music group led by the well-known percussionist Carlinhos ("Charlie") Brown.[9] And as Brown and his musicians traveled abroad and gained fame, they built in his home neighborhood, the Candeal de Brotas, a concert space modeled after the Pelourinho's colonial architecture. This venue came to attract large numbers of the city's elite to its Sunday performances even as the state-sanctioned and malignant version of Brown's Timbalada would storm into the Gueto to search for lawbreakers, collect debts from criminals they controlled, and support IPAC attempts to dislodge residents. By 2001 these enforcers had been largely replaced in the Pelourinho by a specially trained force modeled on Mayor Rudolph Giuliani's New York City–based community policing initiative.

While it would be incorrect to suggest that Bahia's military police are now pacific monitors in a Pelourinho their state has sought to assemble as an idealized community of Afro-Brazilians and objectified popular practices, the transition from brutal Choque to white-gloved tourist police is emblematic of an entwined violence and state-directed care basic to millennial Brazil and the production of Bahian heritage as a form of communal property. In Salvador this involves race, history, and hygienic surveillance of public and private spaces by the police, as well as by "softer" institutions like IPAC and putatively beneficent NGOs.

During the more than two decades I have watched them interact with Pelourinho residents, IPAC's social services administrators have often counterposed themselves to the state's more repressive forces even as they rely on them for tasks they usually wish to deny. This often bewildering interplay of repression and concern for a citizenry configured as requiring improvement was evident as Malaquias and I climbed the hill from the Gueto and, leaving the 28, moved toward colonial Salvador's main square, the Praça da Sé.

As we rounded a corner where the words "Isso Não e Verdade" (that's not true), splashed across a wall in the 1990s, had been painted over and that now provided a vantage point for a policewoman watching over camera-toting tourists and researchers like myself, we passed a flock of fresh-faced IPAC interns drawn from Salvador's expanding university system.[10] Clipboards in hand, they were updating censuses intended to detail remaining inhabitants' practices. This data, which IPAC would soon sequester and then redeploy selectively to justify a variety of initiatives and provide the authorizing content of histories of a Brazil supposedly born in the Pelourinho, provoked Malaquias to remark slyly, "Hey, John, remember when I became a human sandwich? You know, the day I became a living notebook?" We chuckled and recalled how Malaquias had left the Gueto to begin the public protest that would launch S.O.S. Children of the Historical Center. But we laughed hardest, and felt most forcefully the bittersweet nostalgia in which we wrapped our past lives and interpreted the present unfolding before us, when we remembered how Malaquias had returned home to the Gueto some ten years earlier.

A Politics of Failure

Frustrated and sweating in the January 1998 sun, Malaquias returned to his home built into a collapsed colonial mansion only to find his friend and housemate, Augusto, helping himself to the plate of liver and onions on brown beans and manioc flour that their neighbor Dona Valmira had sent over for Malaquias, whom she always called "son." But unlike the inhabitants of number 18 Saldanha da Gama Street, or "the Gueto," who had incurred IPAC's wrath by refusing to leave the fire-gutted Baroque structure, Dona Valmira owned her own neatly kept, if structurally unsound, home on the infamous 28. As these blocks stood separate from, yet connected to, the restored Pelourinho, they became known as one of Salvador's most violent districts. Yet Valmira's courtyard, where she kept tortoises (cágados) from her home region in the sertão, and her kitchen, where she cooked and served lunches to many of the residents, the 28 presented a certain security.

Dona Valmira could shout across the wall her house shared with the Gueto

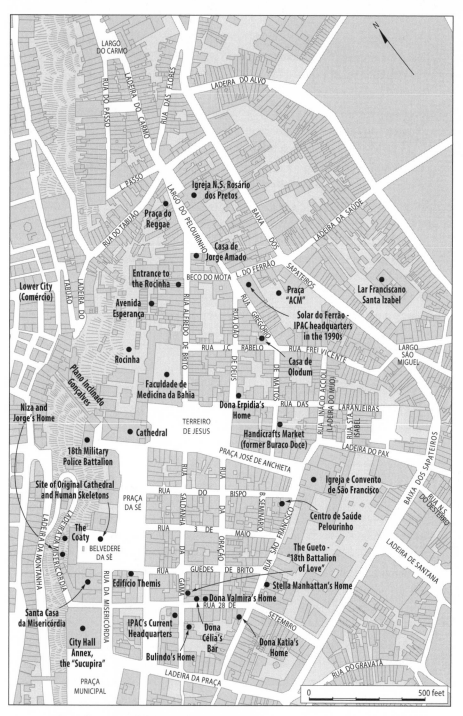

Map 1.1. Pelourinho region of Salvador's historical center

to advise Augusto and his roommates, Pepeta and Diego, that lunch was ready. These young men's section of the Gueto included a tower from which they blasted evangelical radio broadcasts designed to "soften up" (*amolecer*) marauding police patrols. Although unable to see her neighbors, Valmira heard their sacred radio and felt thuds and screams during police raids. Such invasions never took place in her building. There, in addition to serving meals, she rented rooms to boarders, all long-term residents of the Maciel/Pelourinho. Her home combined aspects of what social scientists typically present as dominant Brazilian bourgeois values—an attempted separation of "house and street," the care of family, and a policing of specifically gendered domestic spaces—even as Valmira remained attached to the Pelourinho's infamous nightlife of the 1960s.[11] Like Dona Célia, the septuagenarian proprietor of the bar two doors up the street whose grace, wit, and fluid samba steps are still remembered with admiration throughout Salvador, Valmira had once worked at the Rumba Dance Nightclub. Her success with middle-class male patrons who purchased dances by the song, and later her cooking for the workers at the nearby cable cars that link Salvador's Upper City and Lower City, enabled her to acquire legally a house on the 28. This street was a redoubt of Salvador's post–World War II "bohemians," or upper-class male patrons who socialized in downtown bars, cabarets, houses of prostitution, and bookstores from the first decades of the twentieth century until the end of the 1970s.[12] In spite of this association with prostitution and a red light district increasingly stigmatized by former visitors as a dangerous space of drug abuse and ruined buildings, Valmira had by the early 1990s taken on the status of respected, elderly, and honorable woman who maintained her house, fed neighbors, watched after grandchildren, and refused to tolerate affronts to her reputation and authority.

Dona Valmira arrived in Salvador as a teenager to work as a maid but prospered by dancing and cooking in the red light district. This trajectory is important to an intimate public sphere in which powerful women, as well as state institutions run by the types of men in whose families' kitchens and bedrooms many of these women once toiled, struggled across the second half of the twentieth century to rework definitions of morality and associated economic activities performed by the women for whom the Maciel offered a means of survival and a space for relative independence.[13] As Valmira explained when interviewed in 1997 by reporters from the *Correio da Bahia*, "Here I raised myself. Here I had my children. And here I live."[14] She told me later her statement was a *desabafo*, or an attempt to get something off her chest. The vehicle in which her desabafo appeared is significant, as *Correio da Bahia* is owned by the family of Antonio Carlos Magalhães, described by residents as a frequent visitor to the 28th of September and its bawdy establishments in his youth. This triumvirate of state, press, and Bahia's best-known political dynasty infuriated Valmira, who considered Magalhães a hypocrite who embodied and ran a government seeking to confiscate her property by painting her as a prostitute, or somebody who didn't know how to keep her house.

The claim to life, family, and self by a woman authorities described to me as dissolute, and hence in need of supervision, hygienic education, and "aid" in the form of technical advice and an indemnification that might facilitate her resettlement far from the coveted Historical Center, illustrates a growing recognition on the part of residents of the roles of intimate practices, Pelourinho domestic life, and assertions of moral status in the packaging of their lifeways as public culture. In fact, Valmira's emphasis on propriety, and her claim to home and personhood in a former red light district, came into clear view on the day that her neighbor Malaquias marched like a human sandwich across their neighborhood.

Frustrated Analysis

On the afternoon of January 6, 1998, as Malaquias embarked on a foray into the refurbished Pelourinho Square ringed with establishments designed to cater to middle-class Bahians and tourists eager to experience the neighborhood touted as Brazil's most traditional and authentic African space, all eyes seemed to follow Carla Perez. Perez was a new type of dancer in the Pelourinho, one to whom Valmira denied affiliation: Renowned across Brazil for her suggestive steps, her blond hair and narrow nose, her "African" body, and her starring role in Compadre Washington's "É o Tchan" musical group, Perez performed in large clubs and on the TV Globo network rather than in the neighborhood's defunct cabarets. For the elderly women of the Pelourinho, a place where the word *família* painted on the front doors of certain buildings had once marked sharply the lines between family groups' dwellings and neighboring houses of prostitution and dance halls, the scantily clad Perez's gyrations offered up a public exhibition of moves they felt should remain sequestered in cabarets, and thus separate from "the street."[15] They argued also that Perez's dancing marked the stark immorality of a Bahian public culture distilled from their lives but marketed by people whom Dona Valmira described as the "lost" and corrupted descendents of men who had once frequented the Pelourinho's dance halls where they "knew how to treat a woman."[16] For Valmira, such propriety was a function of long-term, ostensibly affective, and clearly material ties between men from across Salvador and their companions in the Maciel.[17]

On the day she appeared on the Pelourinho Square, Perez had been invited to film a video for what she understood as a philanthropic institution dedicated to helping street children. Thus when the Pelourinho street child aptly nicknamed "Avisa-lá," (Spread the News) interrupted the Gueto's daily domino game to report the presence of television cameras just a few blocks away, Malaquias and his neighbors who would become S.O.S. Children of the Historical Center lay down their plastic rectangles marked with black dots. Electrified by the possibility of publicizing their struggle and of taking a spot in the neighborhood's pantheon of globally disseminated social movements and cultural groups like Olodum or Filhos de Gandhi, they pulled out a piece of cardboard that Gueto resident Diego, crippled as a child street vendor after a vengeful customer threw him down a flight of stairs, had fished from the trash the night before. Between ten and twelve men and women living in the Gueto sat in Malaquias' home and dictated a collective message they wrote down in the working-class register of Portuguese as spoken, and written, in the Pelourinho. They asked me to translate this appeal into "bad" English so that no one would know there was a gringo involved in their "movement." It read, as penned by Augusto:

Front of Sign (Original, Portuguese)
Denucia [sic]
Nosso Governador, Nosso Senador, Vocês
Sabem o que Está Aconte-
Cendo???
IPAC (Instituto Patrimônio Artistico
e cultural) Esta tirando nossas
casas; Passei minha infancia
Inteira Aqui (Saldanha da Gama 18 centro historico)
Agora eles me dao 1,200 Rais na
Minha casa, E Justo??
Cadê nossos direitos?
Não creio que nosso Governador saiba disso; e ao conhecimento do nosso
     senador tudo
Sera resolvido.
Obrigado

Back of Sign (Original, English trans.)
Denucia [sic]
Do You Know what IS
happening here?
IPAC (Instituto Patrimônio Artistico e cultural)
takes our houses, I Passed

my entire childhood here.

Now my house, Is this Justice?

Where are our rights?

I do not believe governor know about this.

And when our Senator knows he

will resolve everything

Front of Sign (This author's subsequent translation of the Portuguese
    original for purposes of this book)

Complaint

Our Governor, Our Senator, Do you

Know what is Happening?

IPAC (the Cultural and Artistic Patrimony Institute [sic])

Is taking our houses

I spent my entire childhood here (Saldanha da Gama Street, number 18,
    Historical Center)

Now they give me 1,200 Reais in exchange

For my house. Is this just?

Where are our rights?

I do not think that our Governor knows about this

And when he learns of it, everything will be

Resolved

Thank you.

When Malaquias returned home, hungry and still bearing the petition upon his torso, his enthusiasm had dissipated. Augusto shouted, spraying bits of Valmira's beans, "What up, Mala!?! How'd it go? Did ya get on TV?!?" as a crowd of friends gathered.[18]

"Eh Eh Eh Eh Eh Eh Eh Eh Eh Eh, I may be a st-t-t-t-tutterer, left-handed, black, illiterate, and need a set of f-f-f-false teeth, but I'll beat anyone in the b-b-b-b-b-ullshit category,"[19] responded Malaquias, trying to evade his housemate's question even as he revealed a penchant for turning supposed disabilities into creatively inflected aspects of his sense of Pelourinho-based selfhood.

"So did you denounce them, did you let everyone know what's happening?" asked Gula, the most earnest of the group and one of only two of the organizers who had not moved to the Pelourinho as an orphan or a child separated from parents in the countryside.

"I denounced, I denounced in the name of our Lord Jesus Christ! God help YOU!!" responded Malaquias, shaking and even more agitated than he had been earlier that morning after losing a soccer game in the city hall parking lot down the hill from the Gueto.

"Out with it, man, what happened? You on TV or what!?!" bellowed Umbuzada, a nattily dressed seventy-five-year-old retired sanitation supervisor who in 1962 left his first family in the working-class neighborhood of Liberdade in order to move downtown to the Pelourinho. He claims that there he could smoke marijuana freely and live with Dona Pió on "Piss Hill" (*Ladeira do Mijo*), a street now crowded with boutiques, galleries, NGO offices, and parking garages designed to facilitate middle-class access to the historical center.

Malaquias avoided his elder's question and attacked his weakest colleague, "G-G-G-G-G-Gula, you t-t-t-talk too much. That's your problem. You talk t-t-t-t-too damn much. Of course I-I-I-I denounced everything."

"Were you on [the] Rede Globo [television network]?" persisted Augusto.[20]

"Television!? You and the devil's messenger![21] Everyone was looking at Carla Perez shake rattle and roll . . . in front of the Jorge Amado Museum. She was dancing . . . just the way that Babylon likes it.[22] But people saw me! I talked to Mundinho on the way out, he called me over, 'Hey, human sandwich, what the hell ya doing?' So I told him about our movement, about 'SOS: Children of the Historical Center.' I'll tell *you*, I'm sick of this human sandwichboard thing. No more." Malaquias slipped from the placards with Rastafarian-colored red, gold, green, and black lettering. "Next time it's Augusto or Raimunda who's going. And Gula, go tell your politician buddies to shove it. I've had it up to here with politricks!"[23]

From "Youthful Action" to "Doubtful Action"

Malaquias and his collaborators, beginning a battle to remain in the Pelourinho in the face of IPAC efforts to replace working class people's physical presence with social scientifically mediated representations of their lifeways, found themselves launching something of a social movement in January 1998. Their grumbling about, interpretations of, and unrealized oppositions to government plans, conducted previously in the plays of shadow and light characteristic of the neighborhood's Baroque architecture, thus moved into the open on the day a previously obscure philanthropic group from São Paulo called Youthful Action united the stars of Bahia's culture industry. In attaching themselves to this moment, the neighbors sought to appeal to the benevolence of, but not embarrass or challenge directly, "Governor" Magalhães.

By carrying complaints onto the Pelourinho Square amid the singing and dancing of Brazil's most famous musicians, the not-quite-residents' association sought to drive a wedge between Magalhães, his handpicked successor in the Governor's mansion, and IPAC. They hoped they might remain in the neighborhood and even take on the positions and authority held by cultural bureaucrats.

Nonetheless, Malaquias' effort appeared to have been drowned out by the hullabaloo surrounding the recording idols. These included the inimitable Perez and Brazil's ambassador to UNICEF, the "Queen of Axé (music)," Daniela Mercury.[24] Seemingly as a result of this array of talent, the protest had elicited a response only from Mundinho, Malaquias' old friend. And Mundinho simply laughed at his neighbor-turned-human-sandwichboard.

No one but Mundinho noticed the public event that launched S.O.S. No one had glanced away from the stone stage in front of the museum dedicated to Jorge Amado, Bahia's renowned novelist whose writings about o povo (the people) fetishize lusty mulattas and immortalize Pelourinho rogues and heroes like Malaquias. Or if they had, they had missed the Rastafarian dressed as a sandwich in Brazil's most important space for black and national identities. To add insult to injury, the next day's newspapers revealed that the benefit was a farce: The spectacle ostensibly intended to raise public awareness of, and funds for, underprivileged children was in fact designed to produce for-profit footage of celebrities.[25] Its organizers had claimed sponsorship from Projeto Axé, the prizewinning Italian philanthropy that works with street children; from UNESCO; from the Brazilian National Bishops' Council (CNBB); from UNICEF; and from the National Ministry of Sports, headed at the time by the soccer star Pelé, who, it was rumored, would be attending. But these organizations soon denounced the fraud and newspapers rechristened the group that called itself "Youthful Action" (Ação Jovem) as "Doubtful Action" (Ação Duvidosa).[26]

Local people had been overshadowed by corporate con artists claiming to speak for street children. Or rather, the effort by former street children to work their way into a soon-to-be discredited spectacle had not resulted in attention. Proud of their negotiation of difficult childhoods, the plasticity of the identities they claimed as their own enraged the Children of the Historical Center. And, together with Dona Valmira and the other former dancers who now served as their self-described mothers and community leaders, the Gueto's inhabitants were offended. In fact, the residents, many who had served prison terms or survived through prostitution, focused on Perez's perceived licentiousness as an example of the immorality of a state that declared itself in charge of a neighborhood's, and their own, "restoration." The complaints were thus more than quibbles over spaces. They were debates about ways of being, of leading and directing lives, of raising families, of conceiving of themselves in a former red light district, and of the moralizing foundations of the histories being put together in their neighborhood. They are also one reason why I concentrate across this book on the relationships between moralization, historicization, and the emergent claims to Afro-Brazilian culture that I refer to as "proper historicity."

The concept of proper historicity turns on manners of situating selves in economies of signs coproduced by Pelourinho residents and a Bahian state that works to turn citizens' every gesture into an icon or an index of an ostensibly shared tradition. This heritage functions in turn as a potentially alienable product of an Afro-Bahian people whose centuries of labor on plantations and in manor houses and factories are thus compounded by an emphasis on the re-presentation of their everyday habits today as fungible culture. Yet proper historicity, and thus also "properly historical subjects," is not simply some analytic category that describes a particular instantiation of today's burgeoning alienation of culture as a commodity. It is not a celebration of cultural objectifications or of the Pelourinho's populace's seizing from social scientists the techniques necessary to realize such entifications. Rather, and as should become clear across this book, it is an attempt to describe how a people comes into their own as a people, with a variety of political effects, at a moment when the alienation of a biocultural substance called everyday life is touted as a tool of democratic governance and capitalist development. As a result, residents begin to link social scientific methods for defining propriety, or precisely that basket of moral attributes put forth by the Bahian state as a prerequisite for remaining in the sanitized Historical Center, to a series of dispossessions that generate in turn critical displacements that permit people to develop iconoclastic ways of belonging to, or making themselves present by "being besides themselves" in, the valuable, sentimental structures fomented in the Pelourinho's reconstruction.[27]

On the day Malaquias returned home to find his best friends devouring his lunch, what most upset the Gueto's former street children who had survived to adulthood was the ease with which a "herd of candy-asses" (*rebanho de bunda mole*) could appropriate their experiences of creative survival. How, they wondered, could businessmen and recording stars, not to mention politicians, carry off those simultaneously marginal and essentially Bahian identities? Who were these interlopers who sought to control the expert knowledge that would allow them to speak for the neighborhood? And, in a question important to this book as a whole, how did the different groups agitating for a right to the Pelourinho acquire the knowledge of everyday life on which they based their claims to authority?

The Logic of the Scam

In 1998 a group of businessmen set up the counterfeit philanthropic event they dubbed "Youthful Action." The scam highlights the value of a Pelourinho understood as the heart of a sensuous and beautiful Bahian culture that is anchored by a special group of Afro-Brazilians, the actual and metaphorical "children of the Historical Center." In the 1990s, street children became a growth area for philanthropic organizations in or near Salvador's city center. The most successful groups shared space, funds, and personnel with government institutions as UNESCO officials, social scientists, and visitors celebrated such apparently novel global assemblages.[28] Some of the best-known existed primarily on paper so as to capture donations or, a variety of officials insisted to me, to launder illicit funds from abroad. Nonetheless, and independently of their efficacy and intent in caring for children or cleansing currency, the presence of so many groups focused on children exposes how the Pelourinho reconstruction relies for its claims to inclusion and authenticity on a contradictory attention to a national family, its everyday practices, and the sentiments and aspirations associated with those practices. As I will detail in subsequent chapters, anthropological investigations of kinship and domestic practices have been basic to this process. And in this light, the fact that former street children from the unrestored 28th of September adopted the name "S.O.S. Children of the Historical Center" raises to consciousness, and thus both instantiates and may help dismantle, a naturalized relationship between ruined buildings and Afro-Bahian Pelourinho residents, on the one hand, and the government-directed restoration and recuperation of Brazilian history, on the other.

The Pelourinho's influence on national and regional politics at a moment of widespread questioning of Brazil's unifying narratives emanates from its centrality to different groups' attempts to establish the proper relationship between landscape, property, people, and state power. From IPAC's perspective, this involves the regeneration of a national populace and reconstruction of iconic buildings. In this way a historical people—like those described here who redirect their patrimonialization by calling themselves "Children of the Historical Center"—may come to appear to emanate naturally from a landscape prepared and cared for by a supposedly beneficent state.

As Manuel Bandeira hinted at the beginning of the twentieth century and Youthful Action's logics demonstrated at its end, morality and proper family structure have long helped secure the ground of national politics.[29] Around the world childhood and family are charged sites for the management of community identities, in no small part because of salient ideas about human development, potentiality, and thus the hopefulness of futures and the hubris of those who would improve the lots of Others. Such inchoate horizons are prefigured in the Pelourinho by a population whose association with history and racialized underdevelopment renders it malleable, or open to manipulations of milieus long central to Brazilian nationalism and analyzed throughout the chapters that follow. Social scientific techniques that focus attention on the neighborhood's populace—precisely those people who, in the wake of Malaquias' march onto the Pelourinho Square, self-consciously dubbed themselves the "Children of the Historical Center"—are in turn critical to understanding IPAC's attempted regeneration of a population, the simultaneous displacement of that population, and the multiple roles of Pelourinho children who move promiscuously from what one IPAC report issued in 1970 called "little artists" on to the "street children" of the early twenty-first century.

Dominant Bahian institutions paint the Pelourinho's inhabitants as vile marginals—recall the "nest of snakes" metaphor invoked by the IPAC technician quoted at the beginning of this chapter—as well as, like children, unformed citizens in need of tutelage, kindness, and education.[30] They are thus resonant signs, or as-yet unfulfilled figures, onto whom a nation's collective aspirations and fears of failure or infection might be projected. Such polyvalent representations cast this symbolic population of Afro-Bahians as objects of a history of progressive state involvement in both caring for and excising Brazil's maladies. They also throw doubt on residents' ability to participate in a modern, democratic Brazil since these images both emerge from and encourage the cataloging and taxonomic exhibition of residents as childlike, African-associated, ancestors to the mixed-race nation.

Convincing Restorations and the Antinomies of Care

The Pelourinho project emerges from and supports claims about anachronism, purification, and national kinship that might be redeployed in furthering development projects predicated on the commodification of everyday life. These political initiatives, which are dependent on government claims about its responsibility for the collective well-being of people and monuments, and people as monuments, rose to the forefront when I first visited IPAC: At the moment I dropped by in July 1994, the head of public relations was circulating an exposé on Pelourinho transvestites suffering from AIDS. It had been published by Antonio Carlos Magalhães' family newspaper, the same *Correio da Bahia* whose reporters interviewed Dona Valmira. The official, who received the researcher from the United States with kindness, ordered an assistant to photocopy the article. Trained as a sociologist, he addressed my ethnographic sensibilities by confiding,

> Look how the press treats these people. For the press, the people of the Pelourinho are a problem. They are marginals; a scourge, diseased. But here at IPAC we understand the social nature of these problems and we work to find them homes, to valorize them, and to get them into treatment centers.

The official did not realize that my preanthropological residence in the Maciel meant that a number of those portrayed as in need of valorization were my former neighbors. I knew that many of the HIV-infected residents of the Rua São Francisco—the Pelourinho's "transvestite street" in the 1980s and 1990s—were among those forced out around the time of my visit.[31] I knew also that they complained about IPAC's recourse to the police and its intransigence in meeting demands for higher indemnifications or the right to remain or return after the "reforms."

Familiarity with neighborhood social relations was not simply a resource that enabled me to see through false claims, but also a Pelourinho-influenced way of being, and facing state power, that led me to keep quiet and listen, agreeably, to the bureaucrat's arguments about pollution and beneficence. It prepared me to appreciate the multiple edges of IPAC's emphasis on the management of the population and to follow them, intently, in the hope that they might provide me with a tool for analysis, a flash of insight, or even a free cup of government coffee. As my friend Gula had once whispered to me, "I'm a spider. And I spin and spin and spin; whatever falls into my web is mine!" This is an approach I seek to replicate and expand on, alongside and in dialogue with the Pelourinho residents with whom I have struggled to analyze their state across the last twenty years.

Careful grooming by IPAC of human subjects through the bureaucratic definition and management of childbearing, sexual morality, household and personal hygiene, economic activities, and racial identity, all of which were understood in the pre-1992 Pelourinho and among residents of Salvador's working-class neighborhoods as ideally outside the purview of the state and even one's neighbors, has helped establish residents as simultaneously marginal to the social body and essential to national progress. In introducing IPAC and its interventions in the Pelourinho through HIV-positive residents, the spokesperson configured that population as infected, or as a problem generated by inappropriate yet social scientifically amenable behaviors. He did so by speaking of viral statuses, or the quality of people's blood.[32] As transvestite prostitutes with AIDS, the article's subjects were made to seem diseased, tinged by sex work and activities like assaults on customers. This made them worthy of an attention focused on sexual proclivities, kinship and residence patterns, seropositive status, and permanence in the Pelourinho. Related topics, as I will detail in chapter 3, had been at the center of IPAC research since the late 1960s. Yet by arguing that IPAC existed in order to guarantee care at a moment of rampant dispossession in tandem with the deployment of information about these people's everyday habits and inner states, the official deflected the conclusion that he sought to exclude them. Instead, given the terms in which the AIDS epidemic was understood in 1990s Bahia, residents stood ostensibly as examples of their own depravity and sexual immorality even as IPAC's spokesman used his attention to their unseen infection as an example of his institution's democratic responsiveness to the needs and deficiencies it defined on the basis of its researchers' claims to social scientific expertise.

The attention IPAC afforded residents immediately preceding their removal generates, like life in an AIDS hospice or living with retrovirals, a special status that empowers in a number of contradictory ways.[33] Here the active management of an impending end, or a symbolic or actual death, helps place members of the Pelourinho community—who were among the first in Salvador to suffer on a large scale from the AIDS epidemic—into a category of personhood, and a form of historicity, that allows them to demand increased consideration from the state. In the mid-1990s, poor Bahians often interpreted HIV positive status as a helpful development, an ontological state that reflected how their everyday habits might also be resituated. Additionally, their status as "carriers" (*portadores*) granted them access to federal disability pensions and aid from philanthropies, while police who might otherwise mistreat them recognized them as a special class of citizen and transmitters of a biological scourge. This status and the marks of impending death, or that liminal status that arises from suspecting one's end is near, turned HIV-positive Bahians into citizens who received more attention than the uninfected precisely at the moment when IPAC sought to musealize the Pelourinho's population as a whole. In fact, many residents told me that they were glad they were infected because this had allowed them to gain attention from those—including people like myself, they sometimes admitted—who would not have entered their lives otherwise.

As I learned when I spent a period of several months accompanying, and advocating for, my friend Indio during his quest to gain a government disability pension on the basis of his HIV status, such valorization of precisely those Afro-Bahians construed as problematic and thus destined for removal from the revalorized city center suggests the extent to which the Pelourinho-based sanitization of Brazil's origins and their human subjects encourages both bureaucrats and residents to consider the relationship between observable habits and the unseen or inner values to which they supposedly point: As we would sit in government offices getting documents stamped, seeing doctors, paying small fees, and demonstrating our good intentions to an array of bureaucrats who often sought an excuse to ask us to return another day, Indio would wonder at length about unseen *micobrios* [*sic*], or "microbes," a word (*microbios*) he pronounced in a markedly working-class Bahian manner due to the placement of the letter *r*. He would then link his infection to his actions across life, wild habits he understood as resulting from his *natureza ruim* (bad nature), which caused him to run away from his family in the neighborhood of Liberdade and begin a life of crime and intravenous drug use in the Pelourinho's streets. And such musings were almost invariably spurred by a visit to a government office or an interview with a public health official.

One Pelourinho resident who was especially concerned with both state power and surface appearances, and the ontological states those appearances are so often thought to index within accepted North American semiotic ideologies, is "Dandinha." Said to be a former marine sergeant, and today a leader of the historical center's street merchants' association, he stands close to two meters and weighs nearly one hundred and fifty kilograms. Dandinha uses silicone to enhance his breasts, cheeks, and buttocks but announces proudly that the two girls he raised are his biological daughters. He also brags that when IPAC refuses to meet his demands, he dons a bikini and stands in the lobby of its headquarters, screaming for the director. But Dandinha claims that his most effective techniques involve loosing obscenities while impugning staffers' virility on the basis of their inability to own up to their own purported homosexuality. Dandinha reports also that when IPAC proves intractable he repeats such scenes in the lobby of the *Correio da Bahia*, the Magalhães family newspaper.[34] Although I have never accompanied Dandinha on those pilgrimages, I have observed many *travesti* residents of the Rua São Francisco setting up IPAC employees for blackmail by gathering information about their private lives or enticing them into a sexual encounter or another type of shared intimacy. And in a public display of force and the making public of what pass as secrets, I have seen Dandinha flatten against a wall an IPAC construction worker who had laughed at him. Dandinha bellowed, "You, you, you're a faggot but you can't admit it! You want me! You know you want me! But you can't be me! Go home to your wife and tell her I had you today at work, you shameless little creep," as he let the terrified man slide to the ground.

Most everyone in the Pelourinho respects, fears, or enjoys Dandinha's strength and humor: He served as an intermediary between residents and Magalhães' government and has been granted restored houses in areas reserved for locals who integrate themselves into IPAC's patron-client relations. In fact, Dandinha came to oversee the daily management of "São João do Pelô," a June (St. John's) harvest festival sponsored by the *Correio da Bahia* in its attempt to unseat a competing newspaper's festival and thus extend the Magalhães family's reach into politics and leisure.

Dandinha's interactions with workers who might mock him, and officials who might dislodge him, rework and, at times, reproduce dominant gender relations. He exhibits his copiously siliconed body so as to frighten or shame officials into giving him what he wants in a striptease that is not so much a revelation of nakedness as a demonstration of the extent to which draping signs across the body promises, and thus makes real, the existence of something underneath that bikini. He intimidates and claims to have penetrated a rough construction worker who had the temerity to laugh at him. And often he relives these exploits with neighbors over a cold beer. Dandinha thus turns against his aggressors a language of morality celebrated by people like the IPAC technicians whose job it is to decide who may remain. And in an example of how "transvestitism is not so much about imitation as it is about revealing how meaning is constructed," his manipulation of his body serves as a weapon in relation to historically and geographically specific definitions of propriety, and thus transgression and responsibility.[35] Nonetheless, Dandinha does not just confound or deconstruct gender binaries. Nor is he simply an authentic vestige of the red light district whose description in an ethnography might help the anthropologist strip away the artifices of the restored UNESCO heritage zone and its cultural bureaucrats.[36] Dandinha supports state attempts to populate the heritage center with interesting and exotic types. Construction workers, who are typically residents of Salvador's periphery or the Bahian interior and thus initially unaccustomed to the specific mores of the city center, often mentioned that some of their fondest Pelourinho memories involved Dandinha. Many told me they respected his macho "style," or way of being, and his prowess in verbal duels and fisticuffs. Likewise, I know surfers in Rio de Janeiro and college students in São Paulo who recall Dandinha as a Pelourinho "figure" (figura) they encountered during vacation-time pilgrimages to Brazil's first capital. Thus, even as institutions interpellate travestis as problems, and Dandinha redirects those discourses, his creativity supports the Pelourinho as a zone of extravagant Bahianness crafted around sexual moralities and liminal yet central figures. Like Malaquias, Dandinha is a colorful subject who has helped make the Pelourinho the Pelourinho, and Bahia Bahia. Both prop up the historical center's fictions, even as the polyvalence of the state's methods for composing those fictions may come to alter how people like Dandinha and Malaquias support, or undercut, the status quo.

I have heard both men and women recount with great mirth the story of the year that Dandinha dressed as a witch and set off to the nearby Praça Castro Alves to "play" (brincar) and "jump" (pular) carnival. At some point another reveler knocked off Dandinha's tall black hat, causing him to react with a flurry of blows. But in the ensuing fight Dandinha's costume was torn and, as people who claim to have been present recount, this breach in his social skin seems to have "set Dandinha off" (ele rodou à baiana). He began to throw barrages of wild, roundhouse punches. Due to his size and the strange ferocity that overcame him, Dandinha thus cleared a large section of the plaza, a singular occurrence on the Castro Alves Square, which is a packed carnival space where even police patrols must fight their way through crowds with great difficulty. The vehemence of Dandinha's reaction to a tear in his costume, a violent reprisal during which observers emphasized that Dandinha seemed to "lose himself" (*se perdeu por completo*), suggests that his clothing was not simply an outfit draped across his body but, like a bikini that hides nakedness, an integral and material part of the very constitution of that body.[37] Dandinha's loss of control reveals the value of a costume as a set of material signs basic to producing its wearer. And it does so in a Pelourinho where IPAC increasingly construes surface signs such as witches' hats, costumes recognized as folklorically Afro-Bahian, or Baroque architectural details considered iconic of a Portuguese colonial fundament to the nation, as pointing neatly to their supposedly secure and objectively available contents or referents.

Figuring Pelourinho Futures

In Bahia today, subjects who rise above events and peers due to a creative ability to arrange the self in a manner that connotes an unexpected, interiorized, and creative power are often dubbed *figuras*.[38] The emphasis is on human form as both malleable and rooted, or on someone special, almost holy, who can nonetheless shape-shift the self across the many barriers of harshly divided Salvador.[39] The observation "ele é um figura" (he is a figure)—something frequently directed at Dandinha who argues that he is not a travesti, but simply himself—is a powerful, disarming compliment when made in a neighborhood bar, during a domino game, or by a circle of men perched on the border between acceptance and violence. Usually directed at men, but in a Pelourinho filled with powerful female entrepreneurs frequently directed at women also, the term refers to a difficult-to-pin-down and yet somehow materially and affectively evident strength indexed by a creative alterity and a sense of depth. This is especially significant given the extent to which working-class Bahians so often reject claims about psychic interiority, and thus psychological models of detached contemplation of inner essences and sublimated experiences.[40]

To be a "figura" is to act in a manner that suggests, but does not necessarily reveal, larger-than-life, exceptional, and thus almost sacral qualities and being: Figuration in Salvador posits an orientation toward the future, often expressed by one of the sentences most critical to the establishment of Bahian masculinity: "I have no fear of dying" (*Eu não tenho medo de morrer não*). Thus a figura may pass, untouched and in a manner that generates laughter, respect, and goodwill, through Salvador's violently segregated spaces. After all, those who look death in the face are even more powerful than those who simply fear no evil.

Figuration is in the Pelourinho an intensely local amalgam of qualities that points to the universal through a baroque embellishment of everyday dispositions. Such mimetic exaggeration lifts the bearer's qualities out of the quotidian without the assurance that they are anything more than a façade, or part of a game, even as this process produces a contradictory rootedness for the person designated a figura. Pelourinho residents often tie this remarkably porous form of subjectivity, which seems to give weight to the body as a result of its bearer's performances rather than any physical density, to the celebration of Bahia as a timeless yet traditional land of enchantment where an explicitly racialized deviation from norms produces a regional iconoclasm. From this perspective, and in influential representations in advertising, fiction, and academic writing, Brazil's nexus of tradition appears as a place where Roman Catholic saints come to be taken over by Candomblé's African spirits; where one may leave for work early in the morning and become swept up, dancing in a carnival celebration for days; or, as in the Pelourinho, where an impoverished Afro-Bahian teenager from the backlands may come to be associated with the very core of what makes Brazil complete. Yet concerns with figuration are not exclusively Bahian, or modern.

Early Roman Catholic theologians drew on the Greek and Latin *figura* to develop a mode of interpretation that would transform the Old Testament from a compilation of everyday practices and laws and a history of the Israelites into a prefiguration of Christ's death and resurrection. Like the social science and rituals IPAC and UNESCO employed to wrest everyday practices from the quotidian and inscribe them in a higher register ostensibly available to and reflective of the future of all humanity, ancient Christian theories of figuration posited that an already-existing content lay concealed, awaiting fulfillment. This completion supposedly emerged naturally from the very materiality of the signs assembled in Christian eschatology and the movement of a sacred universe.[41] Such a connection between redemption, religion, and a universal history, which is not about sublation or the end of history, but phenomena that appear to fulfill antecedents construed retroactively as presaging them, mirrors IPAC's attempt to transform a red light district into a piece of UNESCO world patrimony by isolating cultural traits in the present. The state heritage institution then treats them as representative tokens of the histories and essences IPAC argues it reconstructs on the basis of their physical form and supposedly enduring, historical roots.

The Pelourinho "restoration" suggests how much the process of heritage reconstruction, which strives to rescue and preserve everyday practices understood as pregiven, formerly unnoticed, or uncared for but worthy of protection, approaches its objects from within philosophical traditions that reanimate them as fundamentally new things. This contradicts heritage's claims about authenticity and originality. Yet even when IPAC recognizes its alteration of what it supposedly preserves, it emphasizes an auratic originality, and thus the presence of something ongoing, existent, and seemingly real. From this perspective, enduring qualities take tangible form as a result of the state's care and technical prowess in preserving what is supposedly already there, but unrecognized or uncared for. How this takes place, and with what effects, is a core concern of this book about the burgeoning influence of ideas about race and interiority— or those hidden qualities and legacies that supposedly lie inside a person's DNA or cultural legacies—in a Brazil riddled by cultural heritage projects. It is also one reason why I have opened this ethnography with a description of Malaquias' march onto the Pelourinho Square, an event that has not yet come to fruition but that will take on a special meaning by the end of this account.

Here, perhaps overly influenced by my figura friend Malaquias or by the joy Dandinha took in interpellating state officials by hiding his nakedness with the promise of a striptease in a bikini he never removed, I ask you, my reader, to suspend any expectation of further interpretation, for just a short time: Before developing my introduction to the ways the Brazilian state and Pelourinho residents come to know, and trick, one another on the symbolic ground of the historical center in manners that produce the possibility of agentive intervention for those Afro-Bahians the state seeks to convert into living human actors in its own origins stories, I offer a brief description of downtown Salvador. My goal in doing so is to draw my reader into the neighborhood that is so essential to understanding the performance of Afro-Brazilianness today.

Shifting Geographies

The Pelourinho (O Pelourinho) is known officially today as Salvador's "Centro Histórico," or Historical Center.[42] Its inhabitants appear in the press, fiction, government reports, police blotters, and academic treatises as exotic archetypes, as humble sufferers in need of philanthropic and state aid, and as dangerous "marginals" the state must excise in order to pave the way for Brazil's national motto, "Order and Progress." Such a tension between the regeneration and exclusion of an Afro-Bahian population, made increasingly visible as the state writes history in urban space through the exclusion of people in favor of the social scientific collection of signs of their habits, reveals much about the production, the uses, and the lived experience of the past in Brazil today. And it owes much to the fact that officials typically describe the Pelourinho as the largest Baroque architectural complex in Latin America. This is significant in a nation where, since at least the 1920s, Baroque architecture has served as a core symbol of unity and tradition, and hence fodder for cultural heritage. Nonetheless, Afro-Bahian culture, especially its role in the "cultural development" celebrated by the Ministry of Culture and international lending agencies since the mid-1990s, is even more of an impetus to the neighborhood's reconstruction than are its ornate buildings. Together, these people and buildings in need of "repair," and associated by authorities with mysteries, depths, and ornate or dilapidated façades that need to be protected and restored through techniques of cultural heritage management so as to bear witness to their supposedly deeply held truths, make for one of Brazil's most important pilgrimage sites.

This Pelourinho gained form as a heritage zone rather than a red light district following the federal landmarking in 1984 of ten central neighborhoods that contained approximately seven thousand residents and three thousand buildings and monuments dating mainly from the seventeenth through the nineteenth centuries. In this way the districts of Santo Antônio Além do Carmo, the Passo, the Carmo, the Pelourinho Square, the Maciel, the Taboão, the Misericórdia, the Terreiro de Jesus, the Praça da Sé/Misericórdia, and the 28th of September Street came to be recognized as making up a "Centro Histórico," a unit inscribed in 1985 by UNESCO as number 309 in the World Heritage List maintained by the International Commission on Monuments and Historic Sites (ICOMOS). The borders of the historical center have been enlarged, subsequently, and are in fact almost constantly in flux as authorities seek to put forth new plans intended to capture funds and "re-urbanize" the city of Salvador.

With the exception of Santo Antônio Além do Carmo (Santo Antônio), until recently a home to many ne'er-do-well members of the powerful families who had abandoned the city center by the early twentieth century in favor of Salvador's newer "noble" neighborhoods, by the 1980s all of the subdistricts had fallen into disrepair. This degradation is first mentioned in accounts from the 1920s, a decade that witnessed numerous downtown arrests for prostitution as poorer Bahians began to take over once-proud mansions. These newcomers rented buildings from Catholic Church orders, which had typically received them as donations from wealthy residents who found themselves unable to keep up family estates, and divided them into small rooms separated by plywood panels (*tabiques*).

After President Getúlio Vargas took power in 1930 and consolidated what would become his 1937–1945 Estado Novo (New State) dictatorship, Salvador's police began to force prostitutes to register and, in conjunction with city planners, obligated all sex workers to move to the area surrounding the 28th of September, then called the Street of Bricks (*Rua do Tijolo*).[43] This urban sliver deemed appropriate to prostitution was expanded several times in the 1930s,

1940s, and again in the late 1960s, eventually including most of what is now the historical center. In an example of the linked trajectories of buildings and people, IPAC estimates that by 1992 over 70 percent of the structures in the Maciel, the heart of the area restored that year and the region to which many houses of prostitution moved as buildings on the 28th of September became increasingly unstable, were in "ruins." These were home to many who earned a living in prostitution and the handicrafts, domestic service, tourist, and drug trades. Nonetheless the population consisted of a majority of residents who actively avoided and condemned illegal activities or prostitution, an activity that is not illegal under Brazil's legal codes. It also included those who lived with, loved, and did business with lawbreakers but worked in more legitimate professions: Like any neighborhood, the Pelourinho was, and still is, in a state of ongoing becoming.

When in 1997 I returned as a neophyte social scientist to the neighborhood in which I had once lived as an artisan, IPAC had already restored significant portions of the Maciel, Carmo, Pelourinho, and Terreiro de Jesus. The state government of Bahia had spent almost R$100 million for the restoration of 610 of a total of 900 buildings requiring structural interventions. This restoration hinged on the removal of residents between 1993 and the end of 2010.[44] The majority accepted indemnifications in exchange for homes. Typical payments ranged from US$1,200 to US$3,000 for residential properties and averaged just under US$2,000 per family. IPAC claims to have relocated in restored Pelourinho apartments 176 of the 1,870 families displaced. These people pay rent equal to 20 percent of a minimum monthly salary, which ranged from US$50 to US$300 between 1997 and 2010. Between 2006 and 2011, thirty more families were "provisionally relocated" on what were described as humanitarian grounds, with their fates unclear. Another group has been granted apartments in a housing project near the entrances to the peripheral neighborhoods of São Gonçalo do Retiro and Engomadeira, a low-prestige destination from which it is difficult to return to the city center. It may come as little surprise to my reader that this housing project—"Conjunto ACM"—is named after Antonio Carlos Magalhães!

Between 1997 and 2005 residents displaced in the first stages of the 1992-to-present restoration could find space in adjoining, not-yet-gentrified areas like the Misericórdia and the 28. These people would transfer their residences again and again, often with another indemnification in their pocket, as the reforms caught up to their perambulations. Many moved to other parts of downtown Salvador, including the Pilar, the Gameleira, the Contorno, the São Miguel, the Julião, and the Dois de Julho neighborhoods. People from all of these areas had maintained kin ties, economic relationships, and friendships

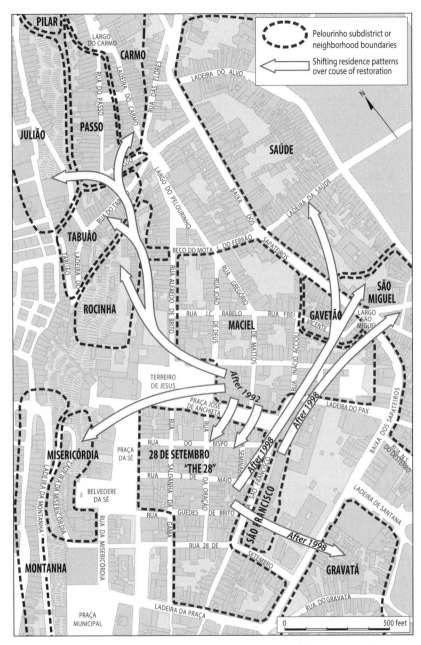

Map 1.2. Pelourinho subdistricts and adjoining neighborhoods (white arrows indicate salient movements of residents following people's dispossession in successive waves of Pelourinho "reforms")

with Pelourinho residents since at least the end of World War II. A larger group of approximately three thousand people employed indemnifications to purchase homes in working-class Salvador, the interior of Bahia, and, in a handful of cases, the peripheries of São Paulo and Rio de Janeiro. A small number of sex workers are reported to have used their indemnifications to travel to Europe.

Government statistics about the movement of former residents correspond roughly to my experience with a much smaller number of people. Yet I find it difficult to quantify IPAC's ethnography or my own: Given my long-term residence that predates an involvement in anthropology, I was in frequent contact during my official fieldwork period with more than the thirty families and approximately fifty individuals not living in kin groups whom I might classify as ethnographic interlocutors. Our encounters ranged from intense friendships to a brief updating, typical of former neighbors, while on a beach, catching a bus, standing in line in a public health office, dancing during carnival, or visiting Salvador's Lemos de Brito Penitentiary. Given the Pelourinho's central role in the life of working-class Bahians, this "methodology" put me in touch with an enormous number of people. These contacts inform my account in ways that I can know only partially, but struggle to recognize in their usefulness for resisting a quantification of people in the name of the social science and state power I present here as inextricably entangled. I do count, and I do quantify, but I also present an ethnographically grounded and theoretically informed portrayal without reproducing the sociological techniques so important to the state's construction of heritage. I believe firmly that this has produced a substantially truthful version of what has taken place during the Pelourinho's reconstruction. Nonetheless, at least for the moment, back to statistics!

The Pelourinho's still-unfinished restoration—between 1997 and 2012, its central square, the Praça da Sé, and approximately 30 percent of its area around the 28th of September remained unrestored or unfinished—created a neighborhood divided by a visible line and formed by the contrast between gleaming architectural gems and crumbling ruins along the eastern edge of the Terreiro de Jesus. To the northwest, heading into the former Maciel, shone the nineteen square blocks into which the government had poured its resources since 1992. To the east of the Terreiro de Jesus lies the 28th of September. Facing southeast, the delineated historical center ends at the escarpment that separates Salvador's "Upper City" from its waterfront commercial center, known as the "Lower City." The Historical Center's Misericórdia and Rocinha subdistricts, important settings for chapters 4 and 6, lie on this steep, tree-lined hillside overlooking one section of Salvador's dockside Lower City, the "Comércio."

Between 1997 and 2002, as IPAC removed almost all residents and sealed buildings in preparation for a yet-to-begin restoration of the 28, hundreds of

Figure 1.7. Resident of the Misericórdia looks out over Salvador's Lower City financial and commercial district known as the "Comércio."

crack addicts, often minors, raced about the streets surrounding Dona Valmira's home. Drawn by the neighborhood's importance to the marketing of the form of cocaine that became readily available for the first time in late 1996 and the availability of funds derived from visitors to the center, the drug users helped IPAC produce graphic evidence of the importance of removing residents and beginning the restoration. By generalizing crack users' behavior and concentrating on the "degenerate" status of residents, IPAC united ideas drawn from architecture, a profession concerned with the form, function,

Figure 1.8. Antonio Carlos Magalhães greeting, and being greeted by, citizens at the inauguration of the fifth stage of the Pelourinho reconstruction, 1999.

and substance of dwellings, and the social scientific quantification and examination of human populations. In this way a give-and-take between popular initiatives instrumentalized by state institutions and practices observed and appropriated by residents brought the "problem" of "seigniorial mansions" and "wizened black women" noted by Manuel Bandeira in 1927 to the forefront of debates about the Pelourinho's restoration in the late twentieth century. This give-and-take suggests that at the turn of the millennium, in Bahia, unlike in other regions of Brazil such as those examined recently by Teresa Caldeira and James Holston, the manipulation of space remains a key means of generating the social.[45]

The Pelourinho reconstruction, in keeping with its social prophylactic nature, has been planned and realized in stages (*etapas*). Up until about 2007, as participatory budgeting initiatives spread across Brazilian municipalities and the Workers Party–allied cultural bureaucrats who replaced IPAC's leaders under Antonio Carlos Magalhães began to reflect the state's concern with economic inequality and social justice, IPAC would select an area for an across-the-board intervention in which all residents were required to abandon all buildings. It would then gut and restore the architectural monuments en masse. According to officials, this approach prevented residents from returning or staying on and confounding still incomplete work. This claim is instructive in highlighting planners' suspicion and fear of a population understood as crafty, plotting, and able to infiltrate and exploit every nook and cranny.

Each step in IPAC's restoration protocols includes substages that revolve around a survey, the removal of residents, the sealing of buildings, designs for

Figure 1.9. Moving truck hired by IPAC *awaits residents moving out of buildings surrounding the Pelourinho Square.*

the restoration of those buildings, plans for their future occupancy, and then physical reconstruction. Researchers begin by dividing inhabitants between those suitable for future resettlement in the Historical Center and those to be pushed elsewhere through indemnifications just large enough to allow for the purchase of a house in a squatter settlement, or *invasão* as they are known locally.

Today there are very few people left in the Pelourinho. In order to effect this displacement, engineers and architects assessed people's homes while interns from Salvador's universities, supervised by IPAC sociologists and anthropologists, counted residents and produced statistics designed to quantify quotidian existence. Following the removal of residents and their possessions in flatbed trucks hired by IPAC, workers boarded up houses in preparation for reconstruction and leasing to new occupants. People often expressed satisfaction with the professional movers. In a dynamic that recalls the government's interest in AIDS patients, residents liked this perk and felt special, almost privileged, as they waved goodbye to former neighbors from atop high trucks and entered a bracketed, and yet still-undefined type of space/time akin to that which Yael Navaro-Yashin has described in post-conflict Cyprus as a "make-believe space."[46]

According to sources within IPAC and among storeowners, up through the fifth stage Antonio Carlos Magalhães handpicked new occupants of restored buildings. Subsequently, as Magalhães moved to Brasilia as president of the national senate, the IPAC manager residents referred to as Seu Leal came to be recognized as responsible for meting out space. Yet the reconstruction of buildings and people, begun in earnest in November 1992, moved forward only fitfully. IPAC had planned to begin restoring the 28's buildings by June 2002, but work began only in mid-2007 under the leadership of the Workers Party coalition that had opposed Magalhães throughout the 1990s. The gap between the sixth and seventh stages was approximately eight years, even as IPAC paid indemnifications to residents in late 2001 and early 2002. Through the end of the first decade of the new millennium, and after spending their indemnifications on daily needs, many of these people still lived precariously in their homes and awaited word from IPAC as to their fates.

As a result, and even as the state government has sought to restore the Pelourinho in the name of democratic rights, shared heritage, and popular culture, it has forced residents to confront what it means to reside in a historical center and thus to focus on how a transformation of their very identities into communal properties and evidence about Brazilian pasts and presents alters their life chances. This process rests on suspending existing social relations and then excluding physical bodies, acting selves, and "real" populations in favor of the exhibition of signs that evoke those removed. While Bahia's new, more progressive administration led by Governor Jacques Wagner now seeks to reverse this process, much of the damage has been done. Thus the Pelourinho reforms, like Brazil, which over the last decade has emerged as more democratic and much more just, must be read not simply as a triumphant democratization of culture, but a contradictory engagement with objectified culture's often troubling roles in the world today.

Of Sandwichmen and Sign Vehicles

The Pelourinho, like heritage zones around the world, enables the colonization and exposition of something known as daily life that is basic to the representations so valuable, and so influential, within advanced capitalism. Cultural heritage management is thus critical to understanding shifts in subjectivities, the management of urban space, and the ways alterations in market systems impact systems of meaning and feeling.[47] Walter Benjamin, in his analysis of an earlier moment in capitalism by means of his Parisian arcades project, followed the "sandwichman," or the worker paid to advertise products and businesses by wearing placards. Such advertisements, common in Brazilian city centers today, seem to be what Mundinho referred to when he called Malaquias a "human sandwich" in the midst of Youthful Action's spectacle.

For Benjamin, the sandwichman exemplified the melding of the human and the commodity necessitated by expanding capitalist relations. And today's packaging and culling of the Pelourinho's population is an example of some salient, contemporary manners by which human figures and human actions have come to be a part of relations of production and consumption.[48] But in donning placards in an attempt to air his grievances, Malaquias was not selling someone else's product, or himself. He was protesting efforts to exchange money for his home. He used the texts in an attempt to influence imminent urban reforms that would displace him, and thus also the interpretations of Brazilian history for which IPAC attempted to muster him as evidence so as to justify those interventions in the name of the hygienic city and the protection of shared heritage. Malaquias' emergence is thus one manifestation of flows of capital and struggles to stay alive in the Pelourinho, issues that prompt him to struggle to understand the forms of Afro-Bahian personhood his state presents as commodities and vectors for governing an unruly population. But the placards are not simply evidence of residents' conversion into a species of human commodity, an argument I will nonetheless make across this book.[49]

On the day in January 1998 that he paraded about in an attempt to exhibit his experience so as to alter events, Malaquias was quite literally a sign vehicle. He offered to an unsuspecting public a version of his life that included his future aspirations, problems, and doubts, as well as a description of growing up in the rough and tumble prerestoration Pelourinho. The narrative that covered and in effect became the flesh of Malaquias' torso was, more than just a protest, a claim to rootedness that described the historical situation of being made into a fundament of, and a foil against, the nation. The Gueto's residents posed this interpretation of the goings-on in the Pelourinho as a problem for themselves and for Bahia's political elite: "Do you know?" queried the placard, challenging the governor's and the senator's knowledge of the workings of their historical center. "Is this Justice?" asked Malaquias as he claimed special status for having spent his childhood in the city center and announced in Portuguese, but not English, that the state was forcing him to accept R$1,200 in exchange for his home.[50] By keeping the language of the sign open and refusing to denounce the senator and governor by arguing that they did not know what was happening in the Pelourinho, residents produced a "denunciation" that demonstrated how they began to make sense of their state's intervention into something called history and memory. Yet this account, as his friend

Mundinho laughingly pointed out, turned Malaquias into a sandwich—or a specifically layered being that took on a form dependent on a definite inside, outside, and content—rather than the author of his own destiny.

At the moment Malaquias marched onto the Square, IPAC was transforming everyday habits into the building blocks of one version of Brazilian and Black Atlantic history that would be justified and disseminated in the future. As I explore in detail in subsequent chapters, the Bahian state would begin this dissemination by constituting, and then drawing on, IPAC's archive of folkloric traits produced through social scientists' attention to Malaquias and his neighbors from the late 1960s to the present. But given the reactions of the Bahians crowding the square, Malaquias seems not to have gone very far in spreading his analysis of state power. Nonetheless, in imagining the placards' English and Portuguese-speaking readership and the most effective manner of capturing that public's attention, the Children of the Historical Center produced a pragmatic, motile reading of their everyday: Malaquias' Afrocentrically decorated placards influenced by the black aesthetic sweeping the neighborhood in the 1990s, were, in their very invisibility, evidence of hegemonic ways of doing business and forging alliances in the Pelourinho.

The Children of the Historical Center sought to hold on to a piece of their neighborhood and, in the process, rub up against the stars of Brazil's recording industry and a formation called "national history." As they counseled me to do on multiple occasions so as not to risk a direct confrontation with the likes of Antonio Carlos Magalhães and his henchman, they struggled to do so not only by challenging their erasure directly but by conforming to, and in the process potentially deforming, salient rules for manipulating patron/client relations, for presenting evidence, and for arguing truth and falsity in a neighborhood being transformed into an anachronistic space that locates Afro-Brazilians in history, but not in the future.

In seeking to overshadow Youthful Action's spectacle and to dislodge IPAC and curry favor with the governor and the senator, the Children of the Historical Center worked not against the grain, but along the grain.[51] Thus the Children of the Historical Center's rise as historical beings, or progeny molded by the process of transforming history and culture into building blocks of capitalist accumulation, is not a case of the resistant deployment of existing, but hidden, "transcripts."[52] Rather, it took form as a specific type of embrace of the social relations and equipment that permit Afro-Brazilian expressive culture and everyday life, or the subject of the representational strategies and documentary evidence cobbled together by unscrupulous businessmen and IPAC social scientists alike, to be cast in a new light. But how, exactly, do the Children of Historical Center grab on to those technologies so as to come into being as the progeny of the Historical Center? How does a group of people painted by their state as "marginals" and "street children" open to assassination come to be known as the Children of the Historical Center? And what does the on-going experience of facing the erasure of one's struggle do to, or for, that effort?

The Birth of the Children of the Historical Center

The man I call Zezinho, chief of staff for the then Workers Party (PT) city councilman Zilton Rocha, who threw his support behind Gueto residents resisting eviction during the late 1990s and who was thus the politician Malaquias accused of "politricks" as he disrobed from his placards, took me aside on more than one occasion to whisper that the Gueto residents' movement did not arise unmediated from the 28. Zezinho insisted that he, and not Malaquias, Caboré, Pretinha, Augusto, Maromba, Diego, Pepeta, Jorginho, or any other member of the group my reader will meet in ensuing chapters, had proposed the name "S.O.S. Children of the Historical Center" and that Zilton's cabinet had tutored the residents carefully before permitting them to act.[53]

A sharp strategist and student leader during Brazil's redemocratization in the late 1980s and early 1990s, Zezinho had been a high school classmate of a founding member of S.O.S., and the two had reinitiated contact after meeting in the Historical Center during protests organized as residents of the Gueto sought to avoid dispossession. Perhaps, then, Zezinho had proposed the name adopted by Malaquias and his housemates. Yet S.O.S., as a heterogeneous collection of neighbors who seek to understand the state and "turn an act of diagnosis into an act of self-description," is neither an imposition by a wily politician intent on attacking the conservative coalition that ran Bahia in the late 1990s, nor the expression of the sincere desires of an oppressed underclass seeking to hold on to their homes.[54] Rather, it is both, and much which falls between those poles: At certain moments S.O.S. is a meal ticket, or a part of the profusion of NGOs that provide steady, relatively comfortable employment at above-market wages to thousands of Bahians today. At other junctures it functions as a shield that allows its members to claim that they are not the drug dealers, tourist touts, prostitutes, vagabonds, and thieves that the police and gentrification authorities accuse them of being. The attempt to inhabit the status of the "Children of the Historical Center" allows them to argue that they are instead professionals acting in the area of culture, or important people able to walk as "natives" into city hall and be served coffee and water by secretaries before meeting with powerful men and women. Meanwhile, at other moments, the Children of the Historical Center stand as an oppositional group that confounds police plans, bureaucracies, and even the politicians who support them.

The Children of the Historical Center's mimetic approach to the signs and rhetorics that exclude them, or their attempt to gain notice by inhabiting semiotic systems that the state seeks to employ to dispossess them, makes visible the extraordinary intimacy between the most powerful members of Bahian society and some of its most marginalized people: The Children of the Historical Center, in name, actions, and symbolic paternity, emerge from a series of attempts to objectify culture, the past, and personhood in the service of state power. Yet they manage to confound, at certain moments and often by lashing themselves to that which threatens them, these processes. S.O.S., as well as its members-as-children-of-history, does not, then, emanate simply and rationally from political discussions between a Workers Party representative and enraged Gueto residents. In fact, it might be more accurate to say the Children of the Historical Center arose most clearly within a domino game held in the Gueto nearly every evening from about 1995 to 1999. And this was precisely the contest in which residents of the Gueto were engrossed when television crews rolled onto the Pelourinho Square to begin filming that infelicitous, and eventually delegitimized, event known as "Youthful Action."

The Gueto game of dominoes is fast-paced, sonorous, and full of pain that stems from the force of smashing pieces on a board supported by the laps of all four players who sit in tactile, visual, and aural communication as limbs, fingers, and words clash and meld into one another. The game makes apparent the violence and solidarity of the surrounding neighborhood. It does so not from an observer's perspective or by direct commentary, but via the iterative performance of embodied relationships among players who smack the shared surface of the board and threaten and cajole one another. They respond with verbal challenges, a visual counting of dots, and an exchange of crashing plastic. Here what is important is not how well one makes mental representations of what is "really going on," but rather how one as a sign among signs finds one's niche or one's angle of repose in the direction of a flow that takes on a status independent of, but nonetheless tethered to, its components. Thus the game, however much it emerges from or enables analysis of Pelourinho life, is not a space for the contemplation of the true significance of the playing of dominos in a colonial ruin coveted by the state. Unlike, for example, Steven Feld's attempt to link people's performance of bird sounds to the myths that hold together Kaluli society, or even Clifford Geertz's approach to the Balinese cockfight as a "native" text that comments on social reality, the Gueto domino game reveals something more contingent, dialogical, and powerfully agonistic even as it no doubt comments on its surroundings.[55]

Dominoes is played with twenty-three heavy white pieces marked with between two and twelve dots, and one blank "ace" without markings. Participants are not interested in the "real" meanings of each piece, or the ways that such a piece might signify its historical construction or relationship to wider social relations such as, for example, the status and etymologies of an "ace" or "snake eyes." Those who join the game strive to position themselves as winners within a game, and they understand that this ludic milieu they constitute collectively reflects in surprising ways their own social situations. But there is little pressure to classify the world through dominoes or to produce a clear conceptual apparatus that might distinguish historical moments and human motivations. People focus instead on semiotic interfaces as part of temporary, if permeable, economies of signs that gain material significance as sources of pleasure, honor, bragging rights, winning bets, and thus also the development of specific personas in the historical center.

The play of surfaces in dominoes highlights the possibility of communication, of solidarity, and of a knowledge produced not through shared symbols that point to deeper realities presented as people's true beliefs, but by means of the slight inflections and deflections somehow brought about in the interfaces of signs both in the game and in the everyday lives of players.[56] To know how to succeed at the game is not to impute some determinate relation between the world and dominoes, between the everyday and the ludic, but to look at, or more precisely, to enter into the flow of, the relations within the circuit of its pieces. A related, but different, skill that inserts a relatively more involved type of objectification into the play is the ability to count the game, and thus estimate the pieces placed next on the board, without breaking up its fluid counterclockwise rotation.[57] To interrupt is to risk a barrage of shouts, garbage, or even fists. The surest way for a player or team to lose is to be left without moves or pairings for the pieces at hand. And this becomes apparent to neighbors because, in the face of such an impasse, the smacking of dominoes ceases. The noises end abruptly in favor of a significant silence often remarked on or filled in by spectators or nearby people who, due to the absence of sound, are interpellated as participants but not necessarily players.

Following the punctive, and hence indexical, silence of the impasse that ends the match, participants and nearby neighbors erupt into a loud analysis of what has happened. One of Gueto residents' favorite descriptions of this inability to move is, "Presinho da Silva!" "Da Silva" is one of the most common working-class names in Brazil, and especially the northeast, as exemplified by Luiz Inácio da Silva ("Lula"), Brazil's working-class former president, born in the neighboring state of Pernambuco. *Preso* means "caught," "trapped," or "jailed." Its diminutive, *presinho*, functions as both an adjective and a noun. As an adjective it describes an immobile or unfree state akin to panopticity or suspension in a system. As a noun, it describes a jailed, not-quite fictive, person named "da Silva." In the Gueto, winning players, and even spectators, would often pretend they were jailors, calling out to immobile colleagues ensnared in their own, and the game's, folds.

In addition to "Presinho da Silva," a common saying at a moment of stasis was "'Tá com o rabo preso," or, literally, "Your ass is imprisoned." To have one's "rabo preso" is to owe another person, to have received an act of kindness, duty, or a gift, and not returned that favor, often because its grantor refuses one's reciprocation in favor of a greater price at a later date. The implication of this highly gendered term on the 28 is that eventually one will have to pay an extraordinarily high price, perhaps even offering one's body as the passive recipient in homosexual sex as is common among real-life Presinhos da Silva. As Richard Parker in Rio de Janeiro and Don Kulick in the Pelourinho have discussed, gender identities often hinge on one's status as sexual penetrator or penetree or the incitement of another's desiring gaze. The rape and sexual abuse of children in the prerestoration Pelourinho was common. And men defined as heterosexual frequently engage in paid sexual relations with other men across Bahia, and especially when foreigners' cash is involved in places like the Pelourinho. Within S.O.S. the mention of homosexual sex with foreigners, while considered masculine if the Brazilian were the penetrator, would result in snickers about friends who, like the travestis on the nearby Rua São Francisco, permitted themselves to be objects of male desire. To have one's "rabo preso" in this way, and to be open to penetration by another man, denoted an enormous disadvantage in power and status even as, at times, certain accepted and respected male residents of the Gueto engaged in sexual commerce with male foreigners.

The language of prison, gendered violence, and commercial sex highlights the domino game as a space for inversions that emphasize certain dynamics from the wider society even as its movement as a game requires specific semiotic responses to the laying of differentially numbered plastic rectangles on the board suspended over players' laps. This suggests the difficulty of drawing boundaries between a game and an "outside" even as I recognize the difficulty and immense problems that are so much a part of generalizing and applying literally to a wider realm that which takes place in the ludic space of dominoes or joking relations. Nonetheless, as suggested by their quick equipping of Malaquias with placards following the news that television cameras were rolling on the Pelourinho Square, the game was also an affective space within which S.O.S.'s members formulated not only their reputations within a group of friends, but also their reactions to their state's appropriations of their habits and homes.

The game attracted visitors like myself and the Workers Party's Zezinho as well as musicians, intellectuals, and political figures. People exchanged ideas and insults as they smashed pieces onto the board. Residents of the Gueto who were not playing, but washing clothes, resting, eating, bathing, and even making love, would shout out across thin walls to comment on the game and its participants. In this way residents became united in a complexly layered, yet shared, soundscape. And they employed this system to analyze and comment on the experiences onto and from which the performance leaked and arose. The sounds of the game, and the feel of the pieces, were thus a critical part of this shared experience whose ebbs and flows, rather than intentional actions, generated an NGO called "S.O.S. Children of the Historical Center."

At the center of the Gueto's homegrown NGO—a group of men and women who ranged from their late teens to their early seventies but most of whom were in their thirties and forties and had become Evangelical Christians while serving time in jail—stood Malaquias. In an account that may or may not be apocryphal, and that is presaged in the first pages of this chapter, Malaquias often recounts his arrival in the Maciel/Pelourinho as a result of the day he waited until his ranch-hand father took off his boots. Seeing his father sockless, and knowing that this would grant him a few extra minutes with which to escape a tedious and abusive life in the parched sertão, he launched himself into a long, bramble-infested irrigation ditch that led to a highway. Upon reaching the road, Malaquias continued as far as Salvador, where he grew up, alone, on the streets of the Maciel. He suffered a long imprisonment for an armed robbery designed to glean enough money to spend a night in a short-stay, but luxurious, motel with a girlfriend. After the intended victim began shooting back, Malaquias fled only to be hunted down by military police. While serving time under an assumed name for this crime that he claims led to his salvation through the discovery of the Bible, Malaquias began to follow the teachings of Rastafarianism. He was introduced to the new religion by fellow prisoners, radio stations, and accounts by now-Minister of Culture Gilberto Gil of his contacts with Jamaican musicians while exiled in London under the military dictatorship, which lasted from 1964 to 1985.

Returning to the Maciel/Pelourinho after his release, Malaquias became a relatively important marijuana trafficker who employed a number of *aviões* (airplanes), or underlings. This led to additional short imprisonments and continuing problems with the well-known narcotics detective Barbosinha, a violent master of disguise who Maciel residents claim would pass confiscated drugs to his brother, a trafficker in Salvador's distant *suburbio ferroviário* region. Nonetheless, due to his reputation for standing up to police, relatively ample cash, amiable character, Christian faith, attempts at repentance for earlier involvement with robberies, elaborate dreadlocks and status as a leader in the nascent reggae movement, and generally respectful behavior toward neighbors, Malaquias came to be admired across the Pelourinho by the end of the 1980s. This was just prior to the moment at which IPAC began to contemplate seriously the restoration of the Pelourinho, something that would become a reality with the re-election of Antonio Carlos Magalhães to the governor's seat in 1991.

Throughout the 1990s, Malaquias remained a community leader even as he became embroiled in serious conflicts with many from the PT, the Children of the Historical Center, and his reggae band, the Bem Aventurados. Such strife was frequently a result of his desire to serve as unquestioned boss in all activities in which he participated. In explaining why he should take this role, Malaquias frequently invoked disparate justifications. These included veiled threats of violence, his own hard work and intelligence, and, most of all, the example set by Bahia's "Governor" Antonio Carlos Magalhães in his management of the Pelourinho and Bahian culture. Here it bears noting that Magalhães, the senior figure to whom Malaquias appealed textually on the day he dressed as a sandwichman, is also the individual identified across Brazil as most directly responsible for the Pelourinho's 1992–present restoration.

Everyone Writes the Colonel

The Pelourinho reconstruction makes manifest multiple forces and influences that exceed the struggles of any individual. Nonetheless, "Governor" Antonio Carlos Magalhães' involvement guaranteed that what went on there from 1992–2007 reverberated at the highest echelons of national politics. Such influence might be understood in light of the Brazilian system of *coronelismo*, or patron-based strongman politics.[58] Yet Magalhães and his allies were not some enduring manifestation of underdevelopment or tradition. They represented instead a modern regional political coalition that did much to set the terms of Brazilian politics through the first years of the new millennium even as this conservative alliance's policies contrasted markedly with the progressive work of the national state and Bahia's opposition politicians who took office during the Lula presidency.

Magalhães secured his power base in the 1960s as Brazil moved to a military regime that reworked regional relations and embarked on an ambitious and authoritarian modernization program. This vengeful and masterful manipulator of patronage and state bureaucracy often called "ACM," "Tony Malignant," "White Head," or the "Strong Arm of Bahia," has thus served twice as mayor of Salvador, as unelected representative to congress during the military dictatorship, and as minister of communications during the return from military rule in the 1980s, a post that earned his family the Bahian franchise

Figure 1.10. Bar in Santo Antonio Além do Carmo subdistrict of the
historical center reads "ACM: The Force of Bahia and Brazil."

for Rede Globo, Brazil's largest television network. From 1994 to 2001 he was
president of the Brazilian Senate. Magalhães has also been governor of Bahia
three times, each time handpicking his successors. As Dona Valmira recognized in her *desabafo* recounted above, he was also the de facto owner of the
state's second-largest newspaper, the *Correio da Bahia*, and much of Salvador's
prime real estate.

Magalhães was the Pelourinho's patron: Residents claimed that, after having personally selected all those granted commercial concessions in the area
between 1992 and 1995, he continued to supervise its reforms in the late 1990s
while serving as "the president of the President [Fernando Henrique Cardoso]."
Even as such assertions may overstate his power, and Magalhães was forced to
give up his presidency of the senate due to a scandal in which he broke into the
upper house's "secret" vote counting system, Bahians re-elected him as senator
in 2002. Nonetheless, soon after his return to Brasilia he found himself again
the center of investigations due to his tapping of the phone lines of over three
hundred allies and enemies. This scandal, as well as his age and the ascen-
dancy of the PT and Lula to the presidency, weakened Magalhães and allowed
Workers Party candidates to win Salvador's mayoral and Bahia's gubernatorial
races by the end of 2006. Yet he remained a potent force in both local and national politics until his death in 2007 and his grandson, ACM Neto, is mayor
of Salvador today.

Bahians often paint Magalhães as the man who oversaw their state's modernization as Salvador grew from a languishing provincial capital to the center

of the Brazilian culture industry and an industrial and agricultural power-house with nearly three million inhabitants today. In the 1990s they pro-claimed, "ACM rouba, mas faz." This saying, "ACM robs, but he gets things done," reflects Magalhães' power and involvement with public works projects such as the Pelourinho reconstruction, often channeled to a series of construc-tion companies associated with the Magalhães family.

Antonio Carlos was the son of Francisco Peixoto de Magalhães Neto, a med-ical doctor, the head of the Bahian Institute for Geography and History, and professor of sanitary engineering. Part of the group of intellectuals who mixed an interest in urbanism, public hygiene, and Afro-Brazilian culture in order to focus on a people and "moralize" Bahian urban life in the mid-twentieth century, Magalhães Neto was a peer of the engineer Mario Leal Ferreira, who studied at Harvard on a Rockefeller Foundation grant in the 1930s. Ferreira created a never-instituted master plan for Salvador, along the lines of Brasília's all-encompassing modernist blueprint for a new type of city that might domi-nate its barbaric roots in American soil. Magalhães Neto's son Antonio Carlos resuscitated and made manifest aspects of Ferreira's unrealized project while mayor and governor, something he mobilized in the 1990s to portray the Pe-lourinho as part of a march forward predicated on stewarding Bahia's past.

Magalhães grew up across the street and up a steep hill from the Pelou-rinho's 28th of September. Elderly residents claim to remember him, a member of the infamous "Campo da Pólvora" gang in the 1950s, as a capoeira fighter, a drinker, and a visitor to the Pelourinho's brothels.[59] They consider him a "lover of Bahian culture and history," as one septuagenarian told me. Later in life Magalhães became virtually synonymous with Bahia by patronizing cultural manifestations like the Afro-Brazilian religion Candomblé, the dance/martial art capoeira, Bahian cuisine, and the city's precarnavalesque street celebra-tions. In 1997 the novelist Jorge Amado, frequently cited by the Nobel Prize Committee in Literature and a committed member of the Brazilian Commu-nist Party (PCB) during the 1930s and 1940s, called ACM "the father of the re-vitalization of the Pelourinho."[60]

Among Amado's fictional treatments of life in the Pelourinho, where he lived while a student, are *Capitães de Areia* (Captains of the Sand), an explo-ration of the lives of street children, and *Suor* (Sweat), an account of life in one of the Pelourinho's boarding houses. But even more relevant to the post-1992 restoration process is his *Tenda dos milagres* (Tent of Miracles), which tells the story of a mixed-race, organic intellectual from the Pelourinho who enters into conflict with, and ends up being misrepresented due to the influence of, a noted North American professor from Columbia University who becomes markedly interested in Bahia. The protagonist, Pedro Archanjo, is himself an

Figure 1.11. Young boy performs "Governor" Antonio Carlos Magalhães along the route of Bahia's independence celebrations.

author of pamphlets about important themes in the present work, including "Daily Life in Bahia," "The African Influence on the Customs of Bahia," "Notes on Miscegenation in the Families of Bahia," and a "Cookbook." Additionally, Amado produced *O Sumiço da Santa* (War of the Saints), a fictionalization of a real dispute over religious icons protagonized by Antonio Carlos Magalhães and the governor of the adjoining state of Pernambuco, the birthplace of Gilberto Freyre and Manuel Bandeira and Bahia's northeastern rival as a seat of black and colonial culture in modern Brazil. *War of the Saints* follows a religious image that, after coming "alive" during its journey to Salvador's art museum, becomes lost in the streets of Salvador.[61]

In addition to Amado, and in an example of the prescience of the novelist's interest in the complex overlaps between human beings and images, many lesser-known Bahians agree publicly that ACM personifies Bahia and that this personification is somehow related to the coming to life of historical figures. The boy pictured in figure 1.11 attempted to incarnate Magalhães in the Santo Antônio neighborhood during the city's celebration of Bahian independence on July 2, 1998. He mimicked the patriarch's gestures, modes of speech, dress, and physical appearance, quite literally anchoring ACM's image in a historical setting, in this case a stage for enacting the story of Bahia's independence from Portugal in the early nineteenth century. The boy performed for appreciative crowds and, as the official government delegation passed by, for Antonio Carlos himself. Magalhães smiled, waved, and began in turn to imitate the signature Magalhães gestures the child used to impersonate him. As the populist politician and the Pelourinho's populace mirrored one another, they highlighted the historical center as a coproduction of an entwined state and people who are nonetheless sometimes at odds over the reconstruction, its meanings, and its uses.

Antonio Carlos Magalhães, as the "father" of the Pelourinho reforms and the figure to whom the Children of the Historical Center addressed their petition in January 1998, was an integral part of the political horizon that makes the Pelourinho intelligible as a source of tradition. In his paternalism and brutal masculinity he served as a symbol of a past that he updated through violent manipulations of space and culture. And information-gathering was key to his machinations. Not only did IPAC provide him with information as to the habits of the people among whom he is thought to carouse: As Malaquias stresses in practice and points out explicitly when criticized by IPAC bureaucrats who find him overly bureaucratic, Antonio Carlos Magalhães relied across his career on dossiers, files, and secret recordings. Today, as memories of Magalhães and his governance circulate among current and former Pelourinho residents who regale new neighbors and visitors with stories of witnessing barroom brawls or knowing secrets about Magalhães' relationship to his security guards, the techniques associated with ACM's attempts to secure power in Bahia and the federal senate serve as guides to the making of selves and the garnering of influence.

Cordial Men and Rectilineal Lines

Magalhães and his coalition typically claimed to be acting to return Brazil's most expressive and foundational architecture to its previous brilliance, or "building the future by preserving the past" in the name of a glorious Bahia located at the heart of Brazil.[62] In an interview in 1998 with *Veja*, Brazil's dominant news magazine, Magalhães defined Bahianness in the following manner:

Reporter: What is Bahianness?

ACM: It's a spiritual state produced in relationship to this land through which one experiences all of Bahia's special characteristics, attributes like religious syncretism and cordiality that no other land possesses.

The Bahian people are the most cordial of any in Brazil. In Bahia there is no racism, no prejudice.

Reporter: How can there not be any?

ACM: No, there isn't any.

Reporter: You are a Catholic and you go to Candomblé?

ACM: I go to Candomblé, but I believe in Dom Eugenio [Bahia's Catholic Bishop at the time]. Anyone who doesn't really know Candomblé cannot govern Bahia. I don't go to Candomblé because of my beliefs, I go on the basis of Bahianness.[63]

A recourse to the possession and divination-based religion Candomblé demonstrates the importance of Bahian popular culture in legitimating Magalhães' political coalition in the post-1984 move away from, but not entirely beyond, a politics associated with Brazil's military regimes.[64] But most important, Bahia is, according to Magalhães, without prejudice and filled with Brazil's most "cordial" citizens. This is an allusion to the noted historian Sérgio Buarque de Holanda's canonical description of the Brazilian as the "cordial man," an idea put forth in his *Raizes do Brasil* (Roots of Brazil), a milestone in the reworking of Brazilian origins and racial ideologies of the 1930s.

In a formulation repeated by many even today, Buarque de Holanda argued that a Portuguese colonial venture that resulted in a timid yet rapacious colonization, limited to coastal areas, failed to establish institutions necessary for national development. First published in 1936, three years after Gilberto Freyre's treatise on Brazil's debt to miscegenation, *The Masters and the Slaves*, Buarque de Holanda's text also tied national character to colonial spatial configurations. While Freyre argued Brazilian particularity around the tensions and intercourse between big houses and slave quarters, Buarque de Holanda read the haphazard engineering and lack of "rectilinear lines" in colonial cities as reflecting a Portuguese colonial incompetence.[65]

Brasilia, built in the form of an airplane in the distant interior and designed to index Brazil's future is, in part, a reaction to perceptions about backwardness related to those enunciated by Buarque de Holanda. The new capital was put together in the 1950s, and idealized for decades beforehand, as a means of effacing and moving beyond Brazil's uncertain and unpalatable origins. In fact, a fascination with the past and with tradition girded Brasilia's designers' experiments in modernist architecture.[66] And Magalhães' invocation of Buarque de Holanda recalls again the governor's motto, "Building the new, without forgetting the old." Thus the Pelourinho project goes one step farther than Brasilia does: Rather than abandoning colonial Brasil for a new city, as did Brasilia's planners who nonetheless sought to ground their modern architecture in

Figure 1.12. Crowds on the Carmo Hill (Ladeira do Carmo) on their way to Bahia's July 2 independence day celebrations pass by banners draped across historic buildings thanking ACM for bringing a Ford Motors plant to Bahia.

Brazil's colonial Baroque, Magalhães oversaw a project that refurbishes the nation's traditional heart. This integrates, redeems, and improves upon the twisting colonial alleyways lamented by Buarque de Holanda, and celebrated by Manuela Bandeira, in the process reconstructing Brazil's history in multiple ways.

Most basically, the restored urban physiognomy that makes national memories real may thus create a spiritual bond between a population and a landscape that indexes a purported Bahian essence that the "governor" ties into so as to ground his political legitimacy. On another level, Magalhães undermines Buarque de Holanda's concerns with national backwardness. He celebrates the Pelourinho, the historical heart of Brazil and thus that originary national space that Buarque de Holanda claimed lacked so much in comparison to Spanish and British cities in the Americas. But to do so, he establishes a modern infrastructure, belowground.

Magalhães' technicians created an unseen firmament that attests to political power and ability to reconfigure that which girds society: Underneath the Pelourinho's cobblestones and within its colonial homes are miles of fiber-optic cables, a new sewage system, and telephone lines hooked into the internet cafes housed in colonial walls originally sealed with sperm-whale oil. Perhaps most important, middle-class Bahians, tourists from throughout the world, and the new group of working-class Bahians with cash to spend, who residents often call the "beautiful blacks" (*negros lindos*), visit the neighborhood to consume and frolic in the signs of the past that ACM took credit across his life for preserving. He performed this feat through the restoration of façades and the implementation of a new, technological base that, according to IPAC, has revolutionized approaches to heritage restoration. Magalhães thus seems to have configured the historical center by picking up specific components of nationalist projects through which Brazilian intellectuals reworked their nation's status in the mid-twentieth century. And yet, as suggested by the rise of a discussion of "negros lindos" among Pelourinho residents, this shifting constellation may be deployed in ways that favor, or attract, people who describe themselves as "Afro-Brazilian" or "black" even as these may be heterogeneous categories.

As I point out in the introduction to this book, a key component of the bundle of tactics and claims called "racial democracy" that were so much a part of Magalhães' administrations' concern with Afro-Brazilian customs, urban space, and Bahianness is not simply an emphasis on religious syncretism, which in the Bahia of the 1990s was often read as a synonym for race mixture since a strong critique of syncretism on the part of the most respected houses of Candomblé was a basic component of their rejection of racial democracy alongside Black Movement allies, but also a politeness or cordiality tied to the rhetorical denial of forms of social differentiation that are nonetheless often glaringly obvious. Such conventions are precisely what lead the anthropologist Robin Sheriff to argue that Afro-Brazilians have long interpreted the experience of racism through opposing black and white groups even as politeness dictates that they not comment explicitly, except in certain unguarded moments, about such situations.[67] One result of this "silencing" is a situation in which intense discrimination may coexist with a failure to identify specifically racial prejudice as a driver of inequality. As William Hanks has argued for the colonial Spanish Americas, spatial relations and rhetoric may overlap to make manifest discursive and corporeal orientations, or an "indexical binding" that renders certain things enunciable or commensurable while muffling others.[68] Social conventions, like grammars and urban planning, help establish the conditions of possibility for making certain types of conceptual linkages—like noting discrimination and tying those practices to the color of one's skin—or for missing such connections entirely or policing oneself into ignoring them.

For Magalhães and his state institutions invested in reconstructing Brazil's colonial spaces, cordiality and "syncretism" are possessions of his land and parts of a modular toolkit whose parts may be recombined over time. To point out that ACM is a "traditional" northeastern political leader who set himself up as master of a restored historical zone animated by talk akin to that associated with racial democracy is thus to reify tradition and interracial relations, or precisely the terrain within which he constructed his political legitimacy. But to note how a shifting constellation of claims may be resituated alongside new technologies, whether fiber-optic cables or the bundling of everyday life as a cultural patrimony that attracts tourists, is to recognize the malleability, and hence the endurance in novel guises, of that which has been glossed as racial democracy. One might, like Senator Luiz Alberto, the leaders of Salvador's houses of Candomblé, or the members of black leisure associations like the Pelourinho-based Olodum that formed as Salvador industrialized across the 1970s and 1980s, take a firm stand against such a racial ideology. In this respect Malaquias and his housemates agree with Luiz Alberto since they are clear that, in valorizing African roots and their own blackness they are taking an explicitly political position against the violence of a racist state and its claims that they are a beautiful, creative, and resolutely hybrid Afro-Lusitanian-Indigenous Brazilian people. But by what process might one come into that consciousness when, like the Children of the Historical Center who seek to hold onto their home rather than counter the abstract, and nonetheless influential, narratives of sensuous Brazilian mixture into which Magalhães and his allies dragoon them, one's survival requires a focus on the quotidian mechanisms of exclusion? How, then, do those Bahians so often denied formal employment, educational opportunities, and even bourgeois propriety come to align experience, evidence, and social convention in ways that permit them to define publicly the nature of their state's attempt to produce Brazilian futures by removing them physically while enshrining their habits as vestiges of a past that cultural heritage management transforms into a communal property?

Failure and the Objectification of the Everyday

In their attempts to do justice to subaltern voices, anthropologists and historians frequently develop new sources, creative ways of reading, and more inclusive modes of writing. Yet a quest for alternative lifeways and creative expressions, for unrepressed popular actions, and for histories beyond Europe is in many ways the story of Brazilian nationalism, a formation that rests on accounts of resistant tricksters like Malaquias, the ostensible inversions of social order provoked by festivals like carnival, the creative deformation of imperial projects, and the presumed redemption of sullied origins by racial mixing. For this reason Malaquias' near-emergence is of such interest.

Rather than contributing immediately and positively to IPAC's, residents', or visitors' interpretations of the past, or to the future directions of such readings, Malaquias' struggle gives rise to a symptomatic, and thus potentially revelatory, frustration.

After his walk around the Pelourinho, Malaquias returned to the Gueto and renounced the neighbors and politicians he believed had put him up to the embarrassing public presentation of his personal history, calling these people's support "politricks" (*politicagem*). Pelourinho residents commonly employ this term to describe patron/client relationships that inhibit social change and contribute to personal enrichment emanating from nefarious backroom accords and maneuverings. Yet through such failure, Malaquias helped lay bare assumptions about the place of Afro-Brazilians, and their experiences in the Pelourinho, in the Brazilian politics of the 1990s.

How Malaquias' actions congealed as an event, a process that includes the descriptions on this page, became clearer in 1999 as IPAC moved to evict the bulk of holdouts on the 28. Recognizing the possibility that his time in the Gueto was coming to an end, one of Malaquias' housemates, and a member of S.O.S. Children of the Historical Center named Antonio Carlos, wrote a song that he imagined would memorialize the rotting ruin for which he felt such affection, his first home in Salvador after arriving from the countryside in 1995. "Décimo Oitavo Batalhão do Amor," or "Eighteenth Battalion of Love," is an ode to the Gueto on Saldanha da Gama Street that expresses what Antonio Carlos, who like many Bahian men born since the late 1960s, shares a name with his state's "governor," described to me as desires for peace, love, and to be left alone so as to benefit from neighborhood friendships, low-cost housing, a central location, and proximity to cultural events. Yet the song's intended message, a celebration of the Gueto as the home Pepeta was able to construct as part of his difficult move to the city of Salvador, was soon overshadowed by another distinct interpretation.

By the end of 1999 IPAC had forced most bars and musical venues in the Pelourinho catering to working-class Bahians to close and relocate to an enormous walled patio, called the "Praça do Reggae." The fortified Praça do Reggae, or Reggae Square, lies across the Pelourinho Square from the site of Youthful Action's scam. At the time of the plaza's construction, government officials transformed a move designed to limit citizens' mobility into a project portrayed as a source of Afro-Bahian pride and an example of state attention to citizens' needs by announcing that they had contributed to the fomenting of popular culture by producing the nation's first Reggae Square. The construction of the Reggae Square thus added to a long history of the absorption of blackness in the name of national consolidation by means of a walling off, or attempted sanitation, of Afro-Brazilian culture and its enactment by working-class Brazilians.[69]

In June 1999, Albino Apolinário, a military policeman during the day, the grandson of a proprietor of a famous, defunct Pelourinho house of leisure, and the Reggae Square's principal concessionaire, invited S.O.S.'s band, the Bem Aventurados, to play on a Saturday night. Made up mainly of members of Children of the Historical Center, including Antonio Carlos, the Bem Aventurados brought along as an opening act a man I will call "Ras Miro Dimas." Miro's final song to the square packed with revelers from working-class neighborhoods was "Brother Policeman." Presented in both English and Portuguese, the lyrics warn that corruption will get police nowhere and, quoting from the Bible, that "the wages of sin are death." The officers on duty in the square that night became upset by Miro's denunciations and they pushed aggressively toward the stage. Fortunately for Miro, the reggae crowd is hostile to the police, rarely allowing them to move freely and actively challenging their authority in close quarters that make it difficult to use firearms. After the singer finished without incident, the Bem Aventurados' lead vocalist, Gula, took the stage to harangue the crowd about Jesus Christ, Jah Rastafari, and the active persecution of Rastafarians in the Pelourinho.[70] Then his bandmate Pepeta stepped up and launched into a set that culminated with the song "Eighteenth Battalion of Love."

Pepeta's ode to survival in the Gueto, or the colonial house at number 18 Saldanha da Gama Street (figure I.1) to which I will return repeatedly across ensuing chapters, began to mean something new in the packed Reggae Square. In the wake of "Brother Policeman," and in the midst of evidence of state efforts to sanitize the Pelourinho, the song broke free of the moorings intended by its author. It took on a strange, disconcerting materiality, almost floating above us: As Pepeta closed his eyes and announced that he would begin "The Eighteenth Battalion of Love," the bassist Augusto plucked out thick "roots reggae" chords, and Malaquias clasped his hands and thanked Jah for blessing the crowd, concertgoers began to hoot, holler, and point at the police. People turned and watched the patrols from the Eighteenth Battalion of the Military Police (*Décimo Oitavo Batalhão da Policia Militar da Bahia*) as they reacted to a message of peace and love. Some began also to laugh, understanding the unintended joke that was just becoming apparent in the space between the (Blessed) Children of the Historical Center, the police, and a culture industry predicated on attempts to bracket Afro-Brazilian habits as Brazilian culture.

Rather than talking as he had intended about the Gueto, whose actual address on the Rua Saldanha da Gama and nickname the majority of revelers did not know, Antonio Carlos seemed to most listeners to be talking about and to the police. "Eighteenth Battalion of Love" had come on the heels of another song about the Gueto. This was "Gueto Chuvoso," or "Rainy Ghetto," an account of residents' awaiting IPAC technicians as stone walls collapsed around them during the rainy season. In the interpretation of "Eighteenth Battalion" that the audience heard soon after "Rainy Ghetto" and "Brother Policeman," a reggae band called "The Blessed" (Bem Aventurados) had thus renamed the Pelourinho's military police battalion: Rather than the terrifying and violent 18th Military Police Battalion, the police became, if just for a few hours on one night and, in the future when they encountered the Bem Aventurados and the Children of the Historical Center, the "18th Battalion of Love." Like rain, the police seemed yet another quasi-natural force that bore down upon the ruins occupied by Pelourinho residents. In large part inadvertently, the Bem Aventurados had thus taken public the function of their sacred radio perched high atop Augusto's tower in the Gueto. This was not just an instance of talking about the police, but of talking to and recodifying the authorities in public through music broadcast across the Pelourinho and through an emphasis on God as a higher force. As a result of this performative misfire young, working-class, and black Bahians began to call the neighborhood's police the "18th Battalion of Love."[71] Over the next years Pelourinho frequenters and residents in the know would shout out ironically, "Hey, Eighteenth Battalion of Love!" as police patrols trundled past.

It would be untrue to claim that the misinterpretation of "Eighteenth Battalion of Love" in the Praça do Reggae caused police to become more responsive to the populace. It did not. Much more significant was the development of the neighborhood as a heritage zone dedicated to the desires of the bourgeoisie. In this space, mostly evacuated of its Afro-Bahian and working-class populations, Bahia's rulers do not usually tolerate flagrant police abuses of the type common during the heyday of the Maciel red light district. Thus the song's misinterpretation is, from most perspectives, a minor development, something that a majority of police, heritage officials, residents, and visitors do not even know or care about. But unlike Malaquias' attempt at protest that generated almost no commentary, in the days following the Praça do Reggae concert, the Bem Aventurados' neighbors began to laugh about "The Eighteenth Battalion of Love." However, this Battalion of Love was not composed of Gueto residents, as the song's author intended, but police patrols. The feared military police battalion, or what residents had previously referred to as the Timbalada, had passed from a repressive force to an ironized structure of feeling.

The misinterpretation passed on by the Reggae Square crowd, even as it did not transform police into soft and friendly guardians, provided an opening in which the violent representatives of a state seeking to sanitize the Pelourinho could be configured in new ways. Or rather, the song permitted a possibility of reconceiving the ties between Afro-Bahian Pelourinho residents and revelers and the government that claimed to rescue their history. In fact, the very existence and title of Antonio Carlos' song, prior to reinterpretation by his public, suggested that this relationship between Bahian memories, state power, and the Pelourinho's population was already in the midst of a difficult-to-evaluate yet enormous change.

Through the first years of the new millennium, Pelourinho residents almost never approached their homes as sentimental spaces, as signs of a cognized history, or even as inviting places. They claimed overwhelmingly that buildings were simply resources that would protect them by providing a place to "lay their heads" (*deitar a cabeça*). Yet the "Eighteenth Battalion of Love" celebrates a filthy, burnt out, and dangerous ruin. Even as tourists and heritage officials understood the building as either a folkloric remainder of an idealized past or a degenerate mark of the Pelourinho's former status, and thus as iconic of what the Pelourinho project is believed both to recuperate and to preserve, most inhabitants refused such mythifications. One told me,

> this is a terrible place to live . . . you come in during the day and I'm with you and you think it's all cool. But at night, when the roof leaks and the pieces of concrete crash down and the crackheads come in looking to steal whatever they can, it's not a very romantic place to be. I'd give anything to be able to afford a safe and clean place near the center of the city and get away from these people. John, you have no idea what it is to wake up at night and find Bonzinho [a neighbor] smoking crack on my doorstep. And if I say anything to him. . . . Well, you know how it is. I'm tired of risking my life standing up to Jurema's nephews and to the death squads that run after them. The Gueto is not a place for people [gente].

In the face of his neighbor's emphasis on subhuman conditions and residents, the fact that Antonio Carlos thought to praise the Gueto indicates an imminent shift in the relationship between residents and their homes. One result of the government's perverse attention to tradition, history, Pelourinho buildings, and the people who inhabited them is that nostalgia seems to have crept into Pelourinho social relations amid the neighborhood's transformation: Prior to Antonio Carlos' song, in my nearly two decades of residence in, and association with, the Pelourinho I had encountered only one person who expressed wistfulness, or even fondness about, a dwelling. This was, tellingly, a former president of the Pelourinho neighborhood association. After a painful and very personal battle against IPAC and Antonio Carlos Magalhães, "Jackson" looked out his window with tears in his eyes on the day he would be indemnified and removed from the home in which he grew up, and blurted,

> Jackson: John, do you ever sit looking at that amazing building over there [Lar Franciscano Santa Izabel] and think it is beautiful?
>
> John Collins: No, I hadn't noticed.
>
> Jackson: I used to draw its lines all the time when I was a kid. I think that's why I'm a cabinetmaker today. I'll miss it when I'm off there in Periperi [a peripheral neighborhood to which he was moving]. But we have to get out of here. I can't take the [government] pressure any more. This is just the way it is.

Jackson went on to lament the day the military police, "sent by ACM," entered the once-abandoned shell of a building he had occupied and in which he had built his cabinetry business. "My tools are still locked up; they took my tools!" he blurted out, flecks of spit showering me. "When they took my tools I realized I was done. I mean, I'm still finding work. I borrow tools. I might even make more than I did before because I'm forced to go out and hustle. But, of course, my expenses are higher. But, in the end, what's a cabinetmaker without his tools?"

National pasts are part of constellations of practices and objects that permit felt identifications, and thus senses of community belonging. For this reason patrimony, in its unification of ideas about the past and the possession or shared ownership of a society's most exalted resources, is such a resonant arena for understanding politics today. But this nationalism, rather than some instrumental ideology, elite project, or purely imaginative formulation, might be imagined as what Martin Heidegger referred to as an "equipmental whole."[72] From this perspective, one might think of Jackson's shop not as a smoothly running place of employment, but as a space of production molded by the relationships between saws, cabinets, hammers, pencils, and even the fighting cocks he raised and often kept tethered in his shop. The functions of such a whole, which like the heritage center is constructed around things valued for their objectness and thus particular ways of standing in for or in relation to other things and ideas, stand below the level of interpretation and cognition until one or more such objects break or become "unavailable." At that moment, a fabric of shop life that had once appeared natural might take on new roles. Quotidian but now useless objects out of order, like a hammer unsuitable for driving nails, shock by their very uselessness, at least as defined in a narrow, mechanistic manner. Understood another way, broken and useless tools might aid in establishing new perspectives by making clear the relative fragility of a world based on their bygone usefulness. Such novel viewpoints might also arise when a Pelourinho malandro, well known for "taking no position at all," stands up and drapes himself with textual slabs that outline a philosophy cobbled together in an attempt to remain in place, rather than slip effortlessly between contradictory positions. Such a state of affairs pushes for an understanding of those moments when histories no longer belong entirely to the state, and new types of battalions of love patrol a historical center built in the name of an Afro-Bahian people. But it does not do so as a careful accretion of intentional acts. Nor is it simply some individual manifestation that becomes explainable, and thus reasonable, in relation to a specific context.

A Landscape in Flux

In this chapter offered up as a taste of the Pelourinho and my approach to its ethnography, I have jumped from as-yet unfulfilled memories shared with Malaquias to Augusto's appropriation of my friend's lunch. This led to an introduction to Valmira, and some of her neighbors, and my rendition of Malaquias' apparently unsuccessful foray into the Pelourinho Square. Augusto's open-mouthed interrogation of Malaquias upon his return thus makes more visible IPAC's alienation of everyday habits as cultural heritage. Here, now-broken ties to neighbors like Valmira, who once extinguished Malaquias' hunger, stoke an indignation, and a breach, through which the formation of objects of inquiry and a positing of causes and effects and origins and endpoints begins to transform a landscape in flux. In this environment, eating lunch is no longer just eating, but rather a habit cognized as Afro-Brazilian culture supervised by the state. One result is a recognition of breakdown, or that which does not work or no longer works properly. This transformation takes place as habitual activities and interpretations become impossible due to specific types of objectifications that alter participants' relationships to everydayness, and thus to their own status as subjects and objects of histories produced in the Pelourinho.

National history and global heritage were not salient issues for most Pelourinho residents until after 1992, a time when IPAC began to manage the past as patrimony by excluding a vast number of residents from the historical zone. Until this moment, the importance and proximity of something called history lay below the level of perception, a naturalized aspect of the Brazilian nation-state not yet brought into being as an entity available for interrogation. Yet in the midst of an odd juncture, a group of people ringed by military police on the Praça do Reggae came together not as enunciators of some fresh, alternative, and subaltern counterhistory to the Pelourinho's restoration, but as people who had come to look in new ways at their state's attention to the Pelourinho's buildings and the pasts associated with those structures and their inhabitants. The subaltern had not necessarily come to speak on the Pelourinho Square. Rather, the extent to and means by which the state was packaging the Historical Center as a fleeting structure of feeling that might produce a unifying sense of identity around national love had become slightly more apparent over the course of a misunderstanding catalyzed by a song that turned denigrated squatters into the offspring of Brazilian history. To understand more clearly how such confusion came to be, it is worth turning away from the Children of the Historical Center for just a moment so as to track in the next chapter the institutional development of Brazilian techniques for harnessing minority subjects and everyday life as guarantors of national development.

CHAPTER 2

Letters to the Amazons

Porto-Seguro of Vera Cruz

May 1, 1500

Sire,
The admiral of this fleet . . . will write to Your Majesty telling you the
news of . . . this new territory of Your Majesty's which has just been
discovered. . . . But I, too, cannot but give my account of this matter . . .
as well as I can, though I know that my powers of telling and relating it
are less than any man's. May it please Your Majesty, however, to let my
good faith serve as an excuse for my ignorance, and to rest assured that
I shall not set down anything beyond what I have seen and reflected
on, either to add beauty or ugliness to the narrative. . . . Therefore, Sire,
I begin what I have to tell.

Pero Vaz de Caminha,
His Majesty's Scribe

Sometimes it makes sense to start at the beginning. And Pero Vaz
de Caminha's letter to King Manuel, written between April 22 and
May 1, 1500, is the text most commonly credited with narrating Brazil into existence.[1] Produced by a Portuguese scribe and bordering on
the fantastic, this testament to the arrival of a flotilla commanded by
Admiral Pedro Álvares Cabral would come to hold great power despite its claims to modesty and imprecise reflection. The document
lies today in Lisbon's Torre do Tombo, the Portuguese national archives whose contents the British navy carried to Brazil in the face of
Napoleon's invasion of Iberia in 1808. As such stewardship of archival
holdings suggests, stories that prop up origins typically require great
care and well-organized factual support.

In 1998, two years before Caminha's letter was exhibited throughout Brazil in celebration of the nation's quincentennial, I received my first copy of this document often referred to as "Brazil's birth certificate." Diego, the Gueto resident and former street child introduced in the previous chapter, handed it to me after discovering a 1963 edition while rummaging through Salvador's trash. Thus Caminha's letter might be approached not simply as a foundational document, but as a found text that highlights how objects help construct traditions in their movements through the hands of those who claim the authority to protect or interpret them. I might argue, then, that my account emanates not from a canonical description whose significance is assured by confinement in a government building, but from a stained remnant extracted from the trash by a resident of a ruined colonial edifice occupied by former street children, coveted by a state government for whom these residents secure a certain contested historical truth, and central to an urban renewal designed to attract capital, tourists, and political legitimacy. As such, the fragment's perambulations in this book and in the hands of a Pelourinho resident branded a "marginal" by the police and heritage authorities becomes helpful for understanding manipulations of origins and pastness in Brazil today.

As I begin to suggest that this chapter emerges not from the most authoritative sources of a Portuguese colonial tradition, but from the hands of an impoverished, disabled, Bahian, my words appear quite silly, almost ridiculous. It is as if an ethnographer's appeal to disabilities and fragmentary status might guarantee impossible authority and perverse truth in the face of questions about origins. Presented self-consciously, however, claims to having captured an alternative, popular reality highlight issues of interpretive authority, knowledge transformation, and the importance of exclusions to traditions' coherence. The movements, and the relationship to conceptions of community and canonicity, of my copy of Caminha's letter are in this sense critical to a history of the development of Brazil's cultural heritage movement, an account I nestle in this chapter within a consideration of how social relations coded as popular knowledge may be recuperated in erudite discourse in ways that render narratives of community solidarity truthful or meaningful to a range of interpreters. To follow this process, then, is to present both a theoretical argument and a detailed history of what heritage does, and how it works. But in the end, these pages are really little more than a series of responses to questions about the reasons, methods, and historical developments around which Pelourinho residents have become accepted as sources of historical truth despite their expulsion from the historical center.

Lost Texts and Rediscovered Origins

Within an Atlantic literary tradition forged in the interactions between Iberian kingdoms and their colonial possessions that extends at least from Miguel de Cervantes Saavedra's *Don Quixote* (1603) to Gabriel García Márquez's *One Hundred Years of Solitude* (1967), the found document stands as a device that supports an illusion of authority in its decentering of its creator. It is thus an important vehicle for considering truth and evidence, especially since the origin stories told about such interloping shreds of evidence tend to emphasize their own materiality and conditions of emergence. Found texts, then, permit authors and characters to deny their creative roles even as they invent subjects and objects to whom they ascribe the power to make and remake a reality construed in the process as outside the text itself.[2] While this sentence may provoke in anthropological readers some discomfort, or even an appreciation of the extent to which ethnography depends on an emplotment of people and institutions in a tense dialogue with truth and reality, my goal is not to lash social scientists or even to celebrate ethnographic writing's facticity. Instead, I am interested in the development of a heritage bureaucracy and the overlapping workings of race and gender in the accounts of national belongings authorized by the circulations of material signs of what these documents help define as shared pasts. And this is why a piece of paper that sets into motion a fictitious, yet convincing, story of origins that masquerades as unmediated reality provides such a promising path for a history of Brazilian statecrafting around sacred, as well as denigrated, objects and populations.

Don Quixote's narrator insists that its author purchased his manuscript, in the form of a torn Arabic text, from a boy in an outdoor market. Glancing about for an Arabic speaker, the buyer had it read by a "Spanish-speaking Morisco."[3] This hybrid translator informs Cervantes, its "discoverer," that the text's creator is "Cid Hamete Benengeli, an Arabian historian."[4] Thus an early-seventeenth-century rescue of a piece of Spanish history, which enables Cervantes to tell the stories of provincial lives within a dusty European interior dependent for its identity on Islam and the farthest corners of the Indies, involves the extraction from the market of a once-overlooked account allegedly written by a historian among the vanquished conquerors of a still inchoate Spanish people. Translated by another internal Other hired in the marketplace, *Don Quixote* describes an errant knight who espouses a chivalric code that is outdated, and thus no longer "alive" as recognizably Iberian culture. It thus parodies, by means of anachronisms worthy of twenty-first-century heritage-based attempts to resuscitate Brazil's colonial landscape and fading folkloric practices in a Pelourinho Historical Center filled with cash machines, police surveillance cameras, and seas of sunburned tourists disgorged by cheap charters, a fictional genre popular, though reviled by intellectuals, in early modern Spain.

Cervantes modeled the faux-chivalric *Don Quixote* on domestic fictions popular at the time. His work emerged in relation to disqualified knowledge whose passage from the domestic to the public, and thus its concern with an everydayness coded as transparently authentic due to the dissemination of apparently private knowledge, would become critical to the identities of its readers as a distinctly Spanish community. And *Don Quixote* comments on the tastes and desires of this incompletely modern public even as its fiction of origins directs attention to its own production, and hence its relationship to tradition: Cervantes makes his foundational narrative about everyday life dependent on an expert gaze that extracts tattered pages from the market so that a hired, interstitial translator may transform them into a Spanish vernacular. In this resituation of a once-overlooked object whose thematic concerns mimic its supposed passage out of the realm of scraps and into literature, the pages recount a species of pilgrimage. Here Cervantes not only recovers parchments, but also celebrates, or discovers, the power of everyday life, its objects, and its translators in constructing a national people around moral dramas and a Spanish landscape pockmarked by windmills, rural inns, and women whose questionable honor the protagonist seeks to defend.

Macunaíma, the early twentieth-century Brazilian novel whose structure and specifically gendered relationship to everydayness I employ in latter sections of this chapter in order to delve into its author's foundational role in establishing Brazil's national heritage bureaucracy, draws complexly on Cervantes. But I do not mention *Don Quixote* to emphasize the connections between early modern Spain and modernist Brazil. Instead, Cervantes, a self-conscious chronicler of traditions whose writings are typically accepted as producing the first modern novel, provides insights into patrimony's role in producing a collectivity.

Like the novel, heritage reconstruction establishes its specific space/time, or what Mikhail Bakhtin referred to as a "chronotope," by engulfing and piggybacking upon competing genres and the details of everyday life.[5] In encountering his text Cervantes quite literally lifts it out of an everyday life that lies at the center of a story Jorge Luis Borges once described as written "as if a novelist of our day were to sketch a satirical caricature of, say, service stations."[6] In other words, a purchase in an antiques market enables a connoisseur of literary texts named Miguel Cervantes to save something that might have gone unnoticed, namely, a piece of a Moorish past that comes into view soon after Spain reconquered itself after four hundred years of occupation by the oriental power that begin to unite and make modern a disparate collection of Iberian fiefdoms.[7]

*Figure 2.1. Crowds celebrate July 2, the Bahian independence holiday, a date com-
memorated by the caboclo, or Native Brazilian figure associated with Candomblé
and thus popularly interpreted as indicative of formative mixtures. Pelourinho
Square, July 2, 2000.*

Not only does Cervantes emphasize the importance of a temporal gap, of the
power of anachronism to permit a reinterpretation of one's perspective or historical situation, but he also makes clear that finding the text relies on a superior, trained eye, and a "natural" curiosity.

In the Pelourinho, the Bahian state does not purchase, but confiscates
through a mix of forced indemnification, police violence, and social scientific
research, the everyday objects and habits of an Afro-Bahian populace as part
of an attempt to reconstruct itself around a stigmatized population. By means
of its generally ethnographic or sociological research, IPAC experts define previously unrecognized nuggets of Bahian material culture, history, and social
relations and make them into apparently inalienable, community possessions
appreciated by a wider audience whom they mold in turn as a citizenry. This
process of making the community's "heritage" palpable, resonant, and permanent helps bring Brazil and Brazilianness into being as objects of felt identification. But in setting off previously overlooked objects, Cervantes' narrator
relies on more than eyes.

The Spaniard who removed Cid Hamete Benengeli's writings from circulation becomes sure of the parchments' historical and literary value when his
Morisco interpreter laughs at a joke in the margins about the maid Dulcinea, a

figure of desire and hence a motor of the plot. Here a marginal woman becomes central to a masculine expertise presented as a challenge to the market. And, as introduced above, the residents of the Pelourinho for the most part removed in the 1990s were typically referred to by outsiders and the state as marginals (*marginais*). This will become important as I examine the experiences in São Paulo's red light district of the protagonist of *Macunaíma*, and, in chapter 3, of Salvador's ethnographers whose research in the Pelourinho across the last four decades of the twentieth century was fundamental to the constitution of modern Bahian social science and its cultural objects.[8] But here I emphasize simply how parchments, everyday life, and value are apprehended in a specifically gendered field, essential to the nation, which takes form in the dim light of anachronism and as an apparently natural outgrowth of a masculine expertise dependent on a marginal, female figure.

Witnessing Encounters/Framing Origins: A Contemporary Recourse to Mixture

In April 2000 Brazilians celebrated their quincentennial. Or rather, they celebrated what people often called "the 500 years of discovery," a commemoration of the April 22, 1500, Portuguese arrival in what is now the state of Bahia. Bahians overwhelmingly understood their history as beginning with Admiral Pedro Álvares Cabral's landfall rather than, for example, from the arrival of the Portuguese Court in Salvador in 1808—an event that made Salvador, and later Rio de Janeiro, the American seat of Lusitania's empire—or from either the nation's independence struggles of the 1820s or the formal declaration of the republic in 1889.[9] This conception of Brazil as emanating from a colonial encounter between Europeans and Native Americans near the present-day Bahian city of Porto Seguro (Safe Harbor) encourages a view of historical continuity arising from a foundational mixture. And such an emphasis was fundamental to the representations of the Pelourinho put forth by IPAC, the Brazilian media, and Governor Antonio Carlos Magalhães' political coalition during the quincentennial and throughout the 1990s and first years of the new millennium.

For example, on January 6, 1999, some sixteen months before the celebrations of the anniversary of Portuguese arrival, Brazil's most important newsmagazine carried an advertisement intended to attract visitors and celebrate Bahia's role in the colonial encounters so influential to commemorations of a Brazilian nation. Sponsored by the Government of Bahia, the two-page spread in *Veja* set an unclothed Native Brazilian woman, her back to the reader, against a green background crisscrossed by light lines that suggested colonial voyagers' routes. This homogeneous, relatively empty space of exploration, seemingly contained and set off by a golden Baroque frame, mimics early modern maps of the Atlantic. The advertisement's "native" protagonist thus reaches out onto a cartographic space already scratched with navigators' guidelines. With her painted body reminiscent of the descriptions of natives elaborated in colonial travelogues, the woman clutches a writing instrument so as to embody as well as trace an invitation to Brazil's upcoming quincentennial. Presented in epistolary form, *Veja*'s Native Brazilian guide's invitation to formative encounters recalls Pero Vaz de Caminha's "Letter of Discovery" to the Portuguese Court, drafted on May 1, 1500. Yet it is dated *a full week earlier* than the Portuguese account of Brazil's birth with which I opened this chapter. The resultant postcolonial Brazilian, rather than Portuguese, account of discovery reads,

> Bahia. April 22, 1500
> On one side, the Lusitanian prow. On the other side, the Tupis' beach. A starry night glided by in silence, full of omens. The next morning, two peoples assess one another, face-to-face. They exchange glances, gestures, signs. And then comes the dance of encounters. The first morning of a new world. Of a world called Brazil. Yes. Brazil was born in Bahia. And soon the blacks arrived—with their smiles, rites, and rhythms. In this way our heart became complete. And that is exactly why Bahia begins, right away, to beat its drums. To celebrate its 500 years of the life of Brazil. And to invite the Brazilian people to place this nation at the center of our attention.[10]

The native author's letter to a Brazilian people is impressive in its mixture of races and temporalities, especially as advertising copy that reads in part, "And that is exactly why Bahia begins, right away, to beat its drums. To celebrate its 500 years of the life of Brazil." This superimposes promotional literature for the tourist trade with the suggestion that Bahia's culture industry extends in a line to a still-immediate moment of contact. The source of such supposedly unbroken creativity appears as a flash of recognition structured by Lusitanian and Amerindian evaluatory glances, a "dance of encounters," catalyzed in the advertising copy and in national ideologies of racial mixture by the presence of a corporeal and ritual fervor traced to Africans. Bahia thus arises as historically adjacent to, as well as a late twentieth-century road into, a moment of discovery made real through a denial of violence around a cultural fusion of the type celebrated in the Pelourinho. And this story of foundational racial mixture, well known and roundly criticized today, turns on the invention of specific types of actors presented as natural to, or at home in, the Pelourinho Historical Center.

Like Cervantes in relation to his Spanish public, the *Veja* text inserts a stereotyped, minority author into the stories of community belonging and belongings rehearsed between 1999 and 2000. Somewhat like the working-class Afro-Bahians who I argue in subsequent chapters are cultivated by their state as of the subjects and objects of versions of history enacted in the Pelourinho, and the fictional character Macunaíma invented by Mário de Andrade and discussed at length in this chapter, this Native Brazilian appears as an authenticating witness to a history not quite her own. "Her" language recalls early and mid-twentieth nationalist tracts that espouse a Brazilian exceptionalism predicated on racial hybridity. Yet its putative author resembles physically the individuals commonly featured today in Brazilian media depictions of Yanomami people from the Amazon, thousands of kilometers from Bahia. And in a denial of the encroachments, the diseases, the sexual exploitation, and the facilitating ethnographic study faced by Native Brazilians, whether twentieth-century Yanomami or sixteenth-century Tupinambá from Bahia's coast, the *Veja* text celebrates a teleological mixing of races that supposedly makes the nation's "heart complete."

To point out today that modern Brazil took form upon an emotional story of racial mixture is to restate the naturalized bases of national life espoused, identified with, and increasingly challenged by millions of citizens and quasi-citizens over the last decades.[11] To critique this formation in an attempt to highlight how it both unites the nation and elides racialized exploitation is thus to support progressive politicians, academics, and the MNU.[12] Yet I do not write explicitly here *against* Brazil's now infamous myth. Instead, I am interested in something more basic: Even as I am convinced of racial democracy's role in masking violence and oppression, I understand it as but one attempted solution to a quandary of origins.[13] This is a problem inherent in the liberal democratic nation-state that is imperfectly resolved in modern Brazil through recourse to race. Bahian patrimony today, then, involves mutations in, as well as recuperations of, relatively ignored technologies for producing the "solution" to a problem of origins in the modern state and its relationship to a national people.

Seeing and Being in Brazilian Origins

In contemporary anthropology, as in cultural heritage restoration, a making comprehensible of seemingly incommensurable practices as a common legacy or contested idiom called "culture" often rests on recourse to a hidden, explicative grammar. This unifying code, or epistemological glue, guides the ways things become enunciable or comparable. Michel De Certeau analyzed such an arrangement around one of the earliest ethnographic treatments of South America's Atlantic coast, the Huguenot Jean de Léry's *History of A Voyage to the Land of Brazil* (1563). In his account of flight from European religious strife and the attempt to write down what he has "experienced, seen, heard, and observed among the American savages," Léry provides an initial description of Brazilian everyday life and ritual:

> I drew near the place where I heard the chanting; the houses of the savages are very long and of a roundish shape. Since they are covered . . . in order to see as well as I might wish, I made with my hands a little opening. . . . I beckoned the two Frenchmen . . . and we all three entered the house. Seeing that our entering did not disturb the savages as the interpreter thought it would, but rather, maintaining admirably their ranks and order, they continued their chants, we quietly withdrew into a corner to drink in the scene.[14]

The explorers imbibe the Tupinambá display of practices akin to those that will, by the time of the Pelourinho reforms of the 1990s, become recognizable as a medium called culture. Léry's description of the dwelling thus provides a primal scene based upon rules of writing that make the Tupinambá fit for cosmopolitan knowledge. And here the act of translating practices into a scriptural register, or a sacred ledger that predates UNESCO heritage registries, may confine the figure of the Tupinambá to a premodern space of orality.

Like the perusal of the living spaces of recently dispossessed Pelourinho residents by IPAC researchers, something I explore in the four chapters that follow, the ritual described by Léry occurs in an interior into which excited explorers peer through a keyhole. This uncovering of a previously hidden intermingling of savage bodies that promises to reveal to Europeans the true nature of the Tupinambá sets up the world and everything in it, whether Tupinambá woman or the European social body, as potentially legible spaces for cosmopolitan knowledge-gathering. For De Certeau, such formative inventions undertaken under the sign of the written may appear to eliminate real difference from objective knowledge as a commensurating system called ethnology overdetermines its own object.[15] And critics of cultural heritage initiatives often argue something similar by counterposing heritage to more trustworthy histories and suggesting that a development technique predicated on the invention of tradition is radically inauthentic in its enclosure of everyday life. Such arguments, exemplified by Timothy Mitchell's claims that the very enframing devices appropriated by Egyptian officials from European displays of "primitive" culture in fact produce their own referent, namely, an original and exotic nineteenth-century Egypt, are important to understanding the convincing power of UNESCO heritage centers.[16] They are also salutary critiques of ethnography and modes of representation that require a distance between observer and observed.

Figure 2.2. State-sponsored carnival decorations, Pelourinho Square, February 1999.

Nonetheless, like De Certau's suggestion that ethnology is but a fantasy of the observer, neat denunciations of heritage's lack of authenticity are both stimulating and overwrought: Nominalist claims about the narrative production of a world, while insightful, overemphasize the power of metropolitan representations and underplay the extent to which actors coproduce shared narratives, with diverse effects. Enactments of difference like those put together by Léry have become widely diffused forms of statecrafting, development expertise, subject production, and thus capital accumulation today. The twenty-first-century Pelourinho demonstrates the extent to which ethnography, and its quotidian concerns, has become salient in development discourse. Given the productive roles of everydayness and difference in the global political economy today, then, I am not simply exhibiting cultural heritage's inventions of its own objects but introducing the *continuing* and, as will become apparent in relation to Pelourinho residents' engagements with their state, often unexpected relevance of ethnography in places like the Pelourinho. One aspect of ethnography's ongoing significance involves its availability as a technique around which people may develop modes of contestation that draw on and at times rework the terms of their own exclusion. Such sites of contention may provide human beings with perches for putting together an ethics of self-preservation, and thus self-invention.[17] But this is not to suggest that it is easy, or even possible, to find some redemptive space of popular agitation against the manipulations of Afro-Brazilian culture going on in the Pelourinho.

Pelourinho-based representations draw heavily on the interplay between European and Native desires, gazes, and intercourse. Figure 2.2 depicts a state-sponsored rendition of Portuguese explorers, spyglass in hand, gazing upon Brazilian shores and peoples. And figure 2.3 shows a pair of working-class Afro-descendent visitors to the Pelourinho posing for a photograph in front of this only partially enframed diorama, a mockup of the arrival of Bahia's first Portuguese governor, Tomé de Souza. What the two photographs may not reveal as immediately is that the representation of indigenous Brazilian women is located midway between the nautical mockup of the Portuguese fleet's arrival and the camera wielded by the North American ethnographer capturing the scene.[18] This encounter of foreign gazes mediated by representations of Tupinambá women, who look forward and backward as they inhabit a carefully constructed stage, suggests some of the challenges that arise in the Pelourinho today. There, the Bahian state has sought to instantiate its own legitimacy around the management of a tradition grounded in a cultural and racial fusion both celebrated and contested by Bahians, as well as invented in dialogues between social scientists and a non-white citizenry.

Salvador's urban spaces, the Pelourinho community's memories, IPAC's projects, and Brazilian collective identities *cannot* be configured seamlessly. Still, they often appear to fit together. How, then, has a historical field been constituted in which such decorations became not simply possible at the end of the twentieth century but, as in the photograph of Afro-descendent citizens snapping portraits in front of the mockup of the Portuguese explorers, somewhat unremarkable or even enjoyable? And what types of circulation, and sorts of resituations, of objects like snapshots and Caminha's letter of Portuguese discovery of a South American landmass and associated exotic practices and attractive bodies has this motivated and drawn upon?

The fact that the people depicted in figure 2.3 seek to have their pictures taken in front of the Portuguese vessel foreshadows how I am using "unremarkable." The photographer within the image I snapped told me that he and his friends find the representation of a Portuguese gaze quite "cool." Yet this noteworthiness intrigues: In the future, their photo albums may include images of a trip to a historical center that I argue has been produced around the exposition of Afro-Bahian intimacies. Thus the Pelourinho, as a public space whose claims to a clear and truthful exposition rest ultimately on the state's presentation of evidence about domestic or hidden relations, becomes in turn a part of the memories of a group of Afro-Brazilians. What remains unremarked in this intermingling of family and public space is the history of exploitation

Figure 2.3.

that is so much a part of the colonizer's gaze that stands as a backdrop to visitors' self-portraits. And how the violence of colonial dispossession, Atlantic slavery, and national consolidation disappears from view has much to do with the ways modern cultural heritage management, whether understood as a means of boxing in everyday life or as a proliferating technology that opens up new possibilities for resistance and the apperception of life's contradictions, has been put together as a field of expert knowledge.

Overcoming "Civilization and Barbarism"

In 1922, the southern Brazilian metropolis of São Paulo, its commercial and agricultural leaders flush with profits from the state's coffee boom, gave rise to a remarkable movement: "Modern Art Week" was an event around which artists and culture managers who sought to reverse the terms of Brazilian dependence on European and North American traditions came to publicize what they dubbed *"antropofagia."* This term might be translated poorly as the creative devouring of cosmopolitan culture by peripheral societies whose very legitimation requires the ingestion of the foreign. Such cannibalism provided a basis for reworking independence by presenting as strengths Latin America's non-white racial "infection" and dependence on foreign finance and cultural capital, technology, and expertise. From this perspective, which meshed with European modernists' concurrent fascination with primitive difference, divergence from metropolitan norms appears to be an asset.

The relationship between cities and their hinterlands was critical to antropofagia and related currents within Brazilian modernism. Since at least the late 1840s, Latin Americans had wrestled with "civilization versus barbarism," or what Fernando Coronil highlights as an internalization of nineteenth-century European and North American evaluations of Latin Americans' mixed-race "degeneracy," and hence the region's supposed unsuitability to civilizational advancement.[19] This explanation posed Latin American nature, and thus the countryside, as a premodern space that threatened the European civilization, and the creole and mestizo elites resident in large cities, with a civilizational backsliding into savagery. An important aspect of such degeneracy theory was an approach to the overlaps of biology and culture, which clashed rather markedly with Darwinian theories of natural selection.

Darwinian approaches to heredity and the physical form taken by organisms emphasize genetic material as a shifting blueprint, dependent on mutations, whose manifestations at the phenotypical level are influenced by their biological contexts. From this perspective, alterations in physical form wrought by environments across living beings' lifetimes will not, with the exception of cases like nuclear contamination that spur some alteration at the chromosomal level, seep back into the body to alter permanently its component parts in ways that might be passed down directly to future generations. Meanwhile, the Lamarckian biology that came to be accepted in influential Latin American intellectual and political circles across the early and mid-twentieth century suggested that changes in an individuals' milieu across his or her lifetime could provoke fundamental alterations in the organism that might be passed on, in some ill-defined but relatively direct manner, to future generations.[20]

While it would be incorrect to classify its polymath author as a strict Lamarckian, a concern with the power of milieu and landscape in the mutability of the human form—or what seems a fundament of planners' attempts to rework the symbolic origins of Brazil through a sanitizing dispossession of Afro-Brazilian cultural producers in the Pelourinho from the late 1960s to the present—is basic to one of Brazil's foundational fictions, the engineer and journalist Euclides da Cunha's *Rebellion in the Backlands* (1902). In this positivist ethnography of Bahian life da Cunha argues that Brazilians,

> do not possess a unity of race, and it is possible we shall never possess it. We are pre-destined to form a historic race in the future, providing the

autonomy of our national life endures long enough to permit it. In this respect we are inverting the natural order of events. Our biological evolution demands the guaranty of social evolution. . . . We are condemned to civilization. Either we shall progress or we shall perish. So much is certain, and our choice is clear.[21]

Da Cunha's prescription for development, a "condemnation to civilization," inverts "the natural order" so that interventions into the nation's landscapes alter the biological makeup of its inhabitants, a people that becomes essentially, and problematically, Brazilian in relation to the contradictions of their environment. As da Cunha makes clear in a text that focuses relentlessly on the dessicated landscapes of Bahia's sertão, and its inhabitants who have adapted to life there so well that they blend into its contours in terms of physical bearing as well as existential status, biology follows social intervention. Approached through the prism of civilization and barbarism then, the renovation of insalubrious environments like the Pelourinho red light district or the accessorizing of cities with the trappings of European commodities might elevate a citizenry's moral and physical status. And cultural heritage in contemporary Bahia seems to draw on this distinctly Latin American postcolonial position within which a rather eugenicist attention to racial development, history, and physical and moral landscapes girds national advancement.

One well-known national-level, and thus perhaps familiar, example of the overlaps between modernism and tradition and civilization and barbarism that have structured Bahian cultural heritage involves the decision in 1956 to locate the new capital of Brasilia on a plateau deep within the nation's interior: From a perspective influenced by explicators of civilization and barbarism like da Cunha, whose *Rebellion in the Backlands* is one Brazil's most canonical works, the transportation of a CIAM-designed city's crisp modernist lines to undeveloped scrub forests would propel the nation and its people into the future.[22] Thus Brazilian landscape, understood as a milieu that bridges post-Enlightenment categories of nature and culture, is not a backdrop that reinvigorates, as in Thoreau's and North America's Walden Pond. Rather, the everyday associated with national landscapes is in the early twentieth century a contradictory medium that requires sanitizing vigilance if Latin American nations are to improve the terms of postcolonial independence. This is one reason the social prophylaxis unleashed on the Pelourinho in the 1990s is so convincing in its promises to redeem a national degeneracy while, in the process, turning blackness, mixed-race status, and the supposedly savage Latin American nature associated with them, into sources of exceptional unity and capitalist development through the commodification of culture.

If high modern Brasilia promised an intervention into a future realized through a transformation of savage backlands, today's Pelourinho restoration rests on a resuscitation and renewal of lost or degraded origins, in this case Brazil's first capital city. The two initiatives separated by almost half a century are thus different, albeit complementary, approaches to redemption. And, as I will support ethnographically in ensuing chapters, they are joined most basically, and powerfully, by Lamarckian logics and ethnographic techniques directed at race, sexuality, and public/private boundaries in a neighborhood supposedly filled with diseased and immoral people. Related concerns permeate the literary production of the man who would be charged with planning Brazil's federal cultural heritage bureaucracy.

Displaced Origins, or a "Letter to the Amazons"

In 1928 Mário de Andrade, a leader in São Paulo's modern art movement, published an astonishing novel. In its valorization of language and topography, lifeways, and ethnic diversity as distinctly Brazilian, *Macunaíma: o heroi sem nenhum caráter* (Macunaíma: The Hero without Any Character) enunciates a remarkable solution to problems associated with degeneration, racial impurities, and unclear origins. On a structural level, the novel confuses origins and endpoints by reversing the standard plot of Latin America's early-twentieth-century telluric "novels of the land." In such texts a protagonist emerges from the city to discover a frightening, promising, and still-barbaric interior distinct from the capital city's civilization. A picaresque travelogue, *Macunaíma* instead inflects this format with Macunaíma, Jiguê, and Maanape, three Native Brazilian brothers who make their way *from* the Amazon hinterlands *to* modern São Paulo. The book thus emerges, in terms of both genesis and narrative, from São Paulo's industrialization while pointing to Brazil's movement toward a centralized national state as the First Republic, founded in 1889, fell deeper into crisis in the late 1920s. It also highlights the growing importance of a nationalist folklore to the definition of modern Brazil, a dynamic that would provide core content for the cultural policy developed following President Getúlio Vargas' rise in 1930 and, especially, after 1937 when he declared martial law and put together the developmentalist dictatorship known as the Estado Novo. This "New State," run by the populist Vargas, who would lead Brazil until 1945 and then again from 1951 to 1954, managed national consolidation around sets of corporatist institutions it concentrated at the federal level. This legacy came be dismantled, or rethought, only during, and in the wake of, late-twentieth-century neoliberalism.

Macunaíma presents movements in folklore and modernist thought that would gird the Estado Novo's emphasis on national culture. The novel suggests that the future is about not only rectifying problematic and barbaric regions, but also carving out an independent path for a Latin American modernity that would valorize aspects of the continent's history and culture in a world dominated by European notions of order and progress. Thus, in an example of the reworking of perceived disabilities so important to Brazilian nationalism, the countryside and its folk become sources of inspiration, rather than of debilitating alterity, within Andrade's celebration of objects and everyday life beholden to a tradition of found texts, epistles, and narrative disavowals associated with *Don Quixote.*

The reader may recall Andrade's receipt of a letter dated January 18, 1927, from the poet and future national heritage bureaucrat Manuel Bandeira, who, while visiting Salvador's Pelourinho, became fascinated by the "little black ladies" and colonial buildings he claimed would impress even a Frenchman. In the months surrounding Bandeira's visit to Bahia, he and Andrade discussed at length drafts of *Macunaíma.* This correspondence, read alongside the novel and Andrade's subsequent work in setting up the federal heritage institution SPHAN (Service for the Protection of the National Historical and Artistic Patrimony), reveals certain of the presuppositions about vernacular culture developed by a group of intellectuals who would define Brazilian patrimony at various points across the twentieth century and, increasingly, today.[23]

One section of *Macunaíma* that fascinated and troubled Andrade as he wrote, and on which Bandeira therefore offered advice around the time of his visit to Salvador, was chapter 9, "A Letter to the Amazons." This epistle, which Andrade later described as his favorite part of *Macunaíma,* appears near the middle of the seventeen-chapter novel. Written to his Amazonian affines by the protagonist Macunaíma, a black Native Brazilian who would become white during the journey that forms the novel's plot, this ethnographic description of modern Brazil highlights a series of concerns and solutions that Andrade's national civilizing narrative was itself intended to work out: "King" Macunaíma, who, in a social ascension reminiscent of impoverished Portuguese immigrants' marriages to planters' creole daughters during Bahia's colonial heyday, became sovereign after marrying the Amazons' queen, wrote to his subjects to report that he had discovered Brazil after arriving in São Paulo. He describes a metropolis of industrious inhabitants, multiple job categories, stone carvings, and the hardwoods found by Portuguese explorers. But Macunaíma encountered São Paulo's Brazilwood, which gave its name to the nation, already carved into pleasing and useful modern articles. This inverts a standard story of discovery: Rather than traveling from Europe to discover a tropical Eden, Macunaíma leaves his home village in Amazonia and discovers an exotic modernity around industrial production.

The letter indicts, in its studied realism, an industrializing Brazil and dependent modernity by portraying a *paulista* everyday of the 1920s that drips with the impish roguishness that is so much a part of early-twentieth-century Brazilian attempts to define national character. And the ostensibly transparent yet self-consciously obfuscatory language of his letter to an Amazonian people who have lost their Queen recalls Pero Vaz de Caminha's promise to Portugal's King on May 1, 1500: "I shall not set down anything beyond what I have seen and reflected." Macunaíma furthers Andrade's rewriting of colonial conquest when he laments the forfeiture to a capitalist monster of the amulet he received as a gift from the Amazons and their deceased queen. Macunaíma's loss of, and attempts to retrieve, the talisman recalls a similar incident of loss with Native Brazilians as recounted in Caminha's letter to the Portuguese king. But Andrade's reconfiguration of Brazil's epistolary foundations becomes most explicit as Macunaíma wanders São Paulo. While Caminha praised Native Brazilian women as "so well made and so rounded, and her private parts (of which she made no privacy) so comely that many women in our country would be ashamed," Macunaíma exclaims in a letter home to the Amazons, and in a reference to Caminha as well as the waves of immigrant women flooding Atlantic port cities in the wake of European pogroms,

Now, we shall speak . . . of that brilliant group of ladies of Polish origin who live here and rule open-handedly. They are unusually animated in their deportment. . . . Like you, dear ladies, these women form a community . . . the men living with them being reduced to slavery and condemned to . . . serving them . . . they do not call themselves men, but respond to the barbarism "Garcon! [Waiter!]" They are very polite and quiet, and always wear the same unobtrusive livery.

These women live cloistered together in the same area, called the . . . red-light district; it is significant that the afterbirth of these expressions is not polite and would not be worthy of inclusion in this report of affairs in São Paulo were it not for our anxiety to use exact and unambiguous terms.[24] However, even if, like you, these darling ladies form a female clan, most of you are very different from them in looks, life style and beliefs. . . . They live by night, they do not devote themselves to the affairs of Mars, nor do they destroy their right breast. . . . And, as for their bosoms, they keep us captivated by them. . . . They speak any number of languages, . . . they are widely traveled and well educated; they are all equally obeisant at all times; further . . . they appear to have originated, jointly and severally, in only one country. Add to this that every one of them is referred to . . . by the same name—"Frenchwoman." Our suspicion is that these dames by no means all come from Poland, but that if the truth be known, they are Spanish, Italian, German, Turkish, Argentinean, Peruvian, in fact from any populated region in one hemisphere or the other.

We shall rejoice if you will . . . Amazon ladies . . . invite some of these women to live in your realms . . . so that you can learn from them a modern and more rewarding way of life which would do much to augment your Emperor's wealth.[25]

At the center of the novelistic rewriting of language, landscape, and nationalist history by the man who would draft Brazil's heritage legislation, the protagonist proposes that São Paulo's immigrant women and Eastern European prostitutes who pass as French might teach the virgin Amazons "modern and more rewarding ways of life." And in the story encompassing the letter, Macunaíma imagines resolving the difficulties occasioned by the loss of his wealth-producing amulet by becoming the Amazons' pimp. Here the migrant from the Amazon takes on the identity of a "dangerous" immigrant archetype that attracted great attention from police and public health authorities at the turn of the century in South Atlantic port cities.[26] In both cases, uncertainly defined foreign women as described by a not-quite-indigenous Native Brazilian help construct the nation contrapuntally. Like Dulcinea at the manuscript's margins or the Moor who became a Spaniard and translated the texts based on domestic fiction that became *Don Quixote*, the liminal women of São Paulo's red light district make public the often embarrassing or unsanitary practices that function as the kernels against which an emergent nationalism takes form.

In Andrade's text, degraded natives who can no longer live as noble savages are recuperated, contradictorily, by their journey across Brazil. This destroys Macunaíma and his brothers as Indians and makes them Brazilians—a new type of irreverent "native"—even as they ironize positivist modernity, voraciously misinterpreting its fashions in a studied naïveté that demonstrates the poor fit of foreign ideas.[27] The most resonant site for this reworking of the relationship between metropole and colony is a letter in which Macunaíma lectures his Amazonian subjects on the morality and economic life he encounters in São Paulo's red light district. This letter, or a supposedly trustworthy, but in fact dissimulatory, genre, holds a certain kinship with the ethnographic reports about unruly women written from Salvador's Pelourinho red light district of the 1960s and 1970s, or the primary sources that gird both my next chapter and the claims about the essences of Brazil formulated by IPAC today.

Both the Native Brazilian discoverer of modern Brazil and the immigrant women whose immorality Macunaíma misrecognizes due to his ignorance of proper mores are examples of a not-quite-white population that Andrade's picaresque narrator redeems as Brazil's greatest asset. This populace, an object of concern in the wake of abolition in 1888, appears in *Macunaíma* as a source of national potential rather than of national embarrassment. The text recuperates immigrants and "black" Native Brazilians, who then become white. But it is not simply the novel's content that ties it to an emergent Brazilian nationalism predicated on the recuperation of a mixed-race citizenry. It is also, as in Caminha's letter of discovery, its object status.

Andrade underscores the importance of the dispatch at the center of *Macunaíma* by having Macunaíma refer explicitly to "an epistolary communication."[28] Epistolary novels, which often include female narrators or men posing as women, function rather well for formulating selves and ideas otherwise silenced by dominant modes of expression. Letter writing also functions as a meditation on misdirection, misconstrual, and misreading, important aspects of Macunaíma's trickster-laden personality and a Brazilian modernity in which an emphasis on slippery mediation would help define the nation's ostensible character. But in terms of the novel *Macunaíma*'s ties to cultural heritage, what is most important is that, as with the found text, part of the epistle's effectiveness stems from the first-person fragment's invocation of authenticity, of being there, that buttresses an illusion of truth for a work or tradition as a whole. Such false yet compelling sincerity, something essential to the impact of its protagonist's letter to the Amazons, is an effect that many post-Enlightenment authors have sought to deploy strategically so as to inhabit or hail a figure of the Other.

Soon after the publication of *Macunaíma*, the Estado Novo would come to mediate and monitor the modernists' production of exemplary national figures. At that moment President Getúlio Vargas' advisors, especially the intellectuals from the state of Minas Gerais who had come to run the Ministry of Education and Culture, began to engage in a broad manipulation of the ties between a people and a nation in a manner that invented both as modern. *Macunaíma* is thus an important text for thinking through a variety of relations.

First, the novel is an artifact of a rethinking of national culture that will contribute significantly, at the level of personnel and ideas, to the legitimation and subsequent influence of a corporatist nation-state during the Vargas era. The 1920s, and *Macunaíma*, foreground the rise of a state-directed involvement in popular culture from 1930 to 1945, and then again during the years preceding Brasilia's construction, two periods generally accepted as constitutive of the modern Brazilian state reformulated by President Fernando Henrique

Cardoso's administration during the 1990s and Luiz Inácio da Silva's and Dilma Rousseff's in the following decades. Second, the miscegenatory terms proposed by people like Andrade, and instantiated by intellectuals incorporated into the Estado Novo, soon became sanctioned mythology for the nation and powerful logics drawn on by IPAC in the Pelourinho's restoration during the 1990s. As in Macunaíma's "Letter to the Amazons," family and sexuality are critical to this overall discourse. Additionally, and building on this second point, ethnography and everyday life would come to justify the archetypes and histories produced by the intellectuals and bureaucracies they founded in the first half of the century. Andrade's own trajectory within the Estado Novo demonstrates this in a way that makes clear the extent to which *Macunaíma* is not just a commentary about a historical juncture or a building block in Brazilian traditions. Rather, it is the most influential text written by a man who would envision the shape of Brazil's heritage bureaucracy. This suggests that the sexual politics discussed in Andrade's/Macunaíma's "Letter to the Amazons" are not supplementary to Brazilian nationalism or the nuances of his concern with the everyday. They are instead crucial to understanding the relationships between a bourgeoisie that began to produce images of Brazil and a peoplehood the modernists struggled to represent and bring into being.

The Rise of the National State: An Interior Colonization

On November 10, 1937, shortly after President Getúlio Vargas addressed the Brazilian people to announce the establishment of his Estado Novo, which was designed to counter the "Universal suffrage . . . [that] has become the instrument of the astute, the mask which thinly disguises the connivings of personal ambition and greed,"[29] Francisco Campos, Vargas' Minister of Education from 1930 to 1934 and the drafter of the Estado Novo's new 1937 constitution, solemnly burned the flags of each of Brazil's twenty states in a public ceremony in Rio de Janeiro.[30] As the symbolic pyrotechnics by one of the regime's principle ideologues suggest, the bloodless coup represented an unprecedented move toward a restructuring of Brazilian society around a centralized state. After disbanding congress, Vargas embarked on what he described as a process of "interior colonization."[31] This consisted of the "expansion within its own territory, conquering itself and the integration of the State, making its dimensions as vast as the country."[32]

As Francisco Martins, a planner in the Geographical and Historical Institute, explained in 1941, the key to state power lay in "a hierarchization of activities, a coordination of means, and a continuity of action."[33] Important figures in the authoritarian Estado Novo moved to establish and to oversee universal health care, maternity leave, a national system of labor unions, free and compulsory public education, federal unemployment insurance, a pervasive system of censorship, and a well-oiled and intrusive police force. Another area of the care of social life to which the Vargas regime directed special attention was that of record keeping and national statistics, a science that Talal Asad reminds us, "imposes not just by creating administrative rulings but by determining classifications within which people must think of themselves and the actions that are open to them."[34]

The Estado Novo represented a marked increase in the quality and the quantity of technocratic impulses around patrimony and statistics, including what are known as *livros de tombo*, or archival registries of heritage objects. National patrimony thus depended on and constituted a particular type of archive as a part of the Estado Novo statecrafting project. And while a discourse of preservation or restoration or origins usually accompanies an emphasis on patrimony, cultural heritage management is ostensibly designed to safeguard community possessions for future generations. Patrimony may thus be, like statistics, forward-looking and capable of helping to temper the contours of the future historical interpretations by means of which the past is supposedly preserved in a recuperative, retrospective movement.

The quotidian objects transformed into national patrimony after being enshrouded in ritual and set off from the everyday may constitute material influences on the range of explanations available to future interpreters of their nation's past. The debates and specific archival and preservation techniques surrounding the transformation of such heirlooms into collective possessions may thus also impact, in turn, the future histories that might be told around them. This is not to say that the objects and the moment in which they are patrimonialized *determine* the future. This is not the case. But nor do future histories written around these objects emanate solely from the future presents from which they will be crafted. Rather, as I will explore subsequently, there is a complex interplay between a future moment of interpretation and the evidence as collected, stored, and codified into existence in the period between that moment of collection and subsequent moments of retrospective significance.

But here, as happens so frequently, I get ahead of myself: Presidential Decree Number 25, issued on November 30, 1937, just twenty days after the closing of the national congress and Francisco Campos' burning of state flags, heralded the midcentury importance of national patrimony to the Estado Novo's project of national consolidation. The decree's thirty articles outlined the responsibilities and organization of SPHAN. Article One defined historical and artistic patrimony as the "set of mobile and immobile goods that exist in the nation whose conservation is of public interest, whether because of their ties to memorable facts of Brazilian history or because of their exceptional archaeological, ethnographic, bibliographic or artistic value." The decree was co-signed by Gustavo Capanema, Vargas' politically moderate yet powerful Minister of Education and Health. Capanema was renowned for his ability to attract and retain artists and intellectuals to the Estado Novo in spite of the Vargas regime's social conservatism and repression of popular dissent.

The newly formed SPHAN fell under the administrative control of the Ministry of Education and Health, whose Minister Capanema wrote to Getúlio Vargas, "The Ministry of Education and Health is destined to prepare, to compose, and to perfect the Brazilian man. This ministry is really the Ministry of Man."[35] Education, hygiene, and cultural preservation were thus allied as part of a rather holistic management of the nation's population and their quotidian practices in a mandate that combined Catholic Church teachings; eugenicist and corporatist thought from Italy, Spain, Germany, and the United States; and a midcentury Brazilian emphasis on popular culture as filtered through the racialized lenses of thinkers such as Gilberto Freyre and Mário de Andrade. However, in spite of its establishment as a subsidiary of the Ministry of Education and Health, whose twin areas of intervention intrigue in their relationship to national culture by suggesting some of the overlap between concerns with health and sexuality and concerns with culture and everyday life that I develop later in this book, SPHAN was little involved with either citizens' health or with popular cultural expressions.[36]

Instead of protecting expressive culture or worrying about people's everyday habits, SPHAN focused almost exclusively during the first decades of its existence on the built environment of the states of Minas Gerais, São Paulo, Rio de Janeiro, and Bahia. This concentration of resources and attention to the architectural heritage of four of the country's largest and most populous states, under the guidance of another Andrade, Director Rodrigo M. F. de Andrade, reflected the distribution of regional political power after World War II. It also typified the activities of a federal institution that would remain somewhat outside the debates over popular culture that characterized Brazilian statecrafting and national identity during the period from Vargas' downfall in 1945 to the establishment of a nationalist military dictatorship in 1964. This later dictatorship would reanimate certain of the Estado Novo's racialized claims to Brazilianness, thus substantially affecting the course of Brazilian politics and the Pelourinho restoration in the 1970s and 1980s. But before examining this history, it is worthwhile to consider the years surrounding the establishment of SPHAN.

A Modernist Intellectual's Proposal for National Patrimony

Together with Manuel Bandeira, the poet, musicologist, ethnologist, folklorist and novelist Mário de Andrade was among the intellectuals drawn into the Estado Novo by Minister Gustavo Capanema. His influence on SPHAN was enormous, and he is still considered a symbolic mentor by many federal heritage bureaucrats within its successor, IPHAN. In his 1936 planning document (*anteprojeto*) for Capanema and Vargas, Andrade defined patrimony "as all pure or applied artworks, popular or erudite, national or foreign, that belong to public powers, social organisms, individual citizens, and foreign citizens resident in Brazil."[37] His outline called for these "pure or applied artworks" to be divided into eight categories and listed in one of four *livros de tombo*, or registries.[38] The eight basic categories were:

1. Archaeological Art
2. Amerindian Art
3. Popular Art
4. Historical Art
5. National Erudite Art
6. Foreign Erudite Art
7. National Applied Arts
8. Foreign Applied Arts[39]

The four registries into which objects in the above categories of artistic production would be inserted and codified were, in Andrade's words, the:

1. Archaeological and Ethnographic Registry, corresponding to the first three categories of arts: archaeology, Amerindian, and popular
2. Historical Registry, corresponding to the fourth category, historical art
3. Fine Arts Registry—National Gallery of Fine Arts, corresponding to the fifth and sixth categories: national and foreign erudite arts
4. Applied Arts Registry and the Museum of Applied Arts and Industrial Technologies, corresponding to the seventh and eighth categories: national and foreign applied arts[40]

Andrade's super-catalogue of Brazil's possessions separates popular, erudite, and applied arts. These divisions revolve around objects' valorization in three areas: an association with a Brazilian people; supposedly transcendent aesthetic or "fine" arts criteria; and industry, an area of intense interest during the Estado Novo. This is significant in terms of understandings of the future of a midcentury, modernizing Brazil in which the nation is composed of its so-called popular, erudite, and applied or industrial sectors.

Two concerns were especially salient in Andrade's attempts to give substance to the nation. The first was an interest in ethnography that led him to a fascination with creative process, or with the techniques, types of knowledge, care, and creativity with which common Brazilians produced the nation's material culture. The second was an event-based theory of history in which culture stood as a mark of development. Both approaches reflect Andrade's historical moment, experiences managing São Paulo's cultural office, and, as histories of patrimony emphasize, his particular genius.

Andrade's involvement with SPHAN had come about in a curious manner. From 1934 until the coup that in 1937 ushered in the Estado Novo, he headed the city of São Paulo's cultural affairs division. There he developed a series of cultural initiatives, museum and educational programs, ethnographic expeditions to Brazil's "wild" Northeast where Salvador is located, and exchanges with notable foreign ethnologists like Dina and Claude Lévi-Strauss. Yet with President Getúlio Vargas' disenfranchisement of elected officials in 1937, Andrade found himself unemployed. He traveled to Rio, then Brazil's capital. There, Gustavo Capanema slowly recruited Andrade for his Ministry of Education and Health, which functioned as a de facto Ministry of Culture. Most important to the present discussion is not, however, Andrade's co-optation by Capanema, but the ways that the author of *Macunaíma* imagined his nation's cultural heritage once he joined the nationalizing effort under way in Rio de Janeiro.

In Andrade's suggestion for the listing of the objects to be protected for the future benefit of all Brazilians, the "popular" arts included the Amerindian and the archaeological, thus revealing the temporal and ethnic bases of a national imaginary that draws heavily on a relatively unexplained, and thus apparently assumed, relationship between the cultural production of Native Brazilians in the present (Amerindians) and Native Brazilians in the past (the producers of "Archaeological Arts"). Here, at a critical moment in the development of ideas about racial mixture in Brazil and roughly contemporaneously with Gilberto Freyre's *The Masters and the Slaves*, the organization of the nation's patrimony locates Amerindian and popular culture in a historical time linked to archaeological investigation. Andrade's move suggests that within an ideology of supposedly egalitarian and exemplarily Brazilian mixture there exist a range of distinctions and evolutionary evaluations that undermine a dominant discourse on the forward movement of a "brown" national race. Thus racial ideologies invoked by Brazil's most talented folklorists under Vargas relied on an evolutionary scheme that anchored certain groups in the past even as the nation supposedly hurtled toward a shared democratic and mixed-race future.

The Ministry of Education and Health's intellectuals and administrators raised a number of objections to Andrade's plan, among them that, "[if] there are objects that belong to more than one category . . . in which book to inscribe them . . . in which Museum to place them?" A peeved Andrade replied that,

> Such doubts will always exist and are typical of lazy minds. We simply need to adopt preliminary criteria. It will be sufficient that these criteria should be appropriate and reasonable; it is not necessary that they resolve unsolvable aesthetic issues. What criteria might we adopt? For example:
>
> An object that is at the same time historical and of true artistic value . . . will be archived in accordance with its historical value. Of course, there are exceptions, like paintings or sculptures that address a historical theme but which are simply evocative and not reproductions of real events.[41]

Andrade excludes from the category of history and classifies as erudite those works of art that depict historical events evocatively, and thus in what he understands as an empirically unfaithful manner. Here he reveals himself, in accordance with Brazilian historiographical conventions of the mid-1930s, as a realist in relation to the historical record. And he establishes "historical value" as more important than aesthetic value when it comes to national artistic possessions. History, in Andrade's version of the state bureaucracy that was designed to establish and preserve those human expressions intended to define Brazil as a nation, is the basis of that nation. Such historical value arises, in Andrade's conceptualization of SPHAN's bureaucracy, from verifiable relations between a representation and real events in that nation's past.

The understandings of history that gird Andrade's version of patrimony revolve around the marking of events through the preservation of artifacts associated with them. This theory of artifactuality, to employ a concept used by Tony Bennett to underscore the power of exhibited objects to conjure up seemingly veridical histories, is a critical part of the attunements between people's everyday habits and their understanding of Brazilian nation that takes place in the Pelourinho in the 1990s.[42] But by the 1980s the nation's collective possessions as registered by SPHAN—later rechristened IPHAN, or the National Institute of Historical and Artistic Patrimony—will revolve less around an association between those objects and historical events and individual people, and more around collective habits, or what is often referred to as national culture. Such national culture will be associated with ideas about everyday life drawn from anthropological theorizations of the culture concept produced by a group of IPHAN intellectuals who consciously resuscitate Andrade's approach to national patrimony at a moment of return from military rule. In the Bahian Pelourinho of the 1990s, however, national patrimony will continue to revolve around a production of historical events grounded in the habits of the neighborhood's residents. This is in fact a philosophy quite congruent with Andrade's original intentions for SPHAN.

Although Andrade stresses in his proposal in 1936 that SPHAN should be established around a monumentalized and event-based approach to national history, in the years surrounding his work for Vargas and the Ministry of Education and Health he produced an extraordinary number of studies of popular habits—especially music and language—or what he generally referred to as folklore or "Brazilianisms." These studies, as well as the prominence given to the "Amerindian" and "popular" arts in his SPHAN proposal, indicate something of Andrade's interest in the processes by which he sought to uncover and showcase what he presented insistently as a remarkable and very Brazilian creative spirit that lay in the nation's people. And Andrade was quite proud of his own use of an everyday, and specifically *Brazilian*, Portuguese in producing both the SPHAN project proposal as well as his literary works, including *Macunaíma*.[43]

For Andrade, folklore was the creative cultural production of Brazil's non-lettered classes, whether northeasterners, the descendents of slaves, European immigrants to São Paulo, Amazonian natives, or any of the residents of the nation's vast interior. Andrade's studies, sometimes conducted in the late 1930s on weekend excursions to show Claude Lévi-Strauss the cowboy culture of the rural São Paulo state, often focused on the importance of Native Brazilians' customs to defining Brazil as exceptional among modern nations.[44] Given his association with the modernist movement, which valorized the figure of the Native Brazilian, this emphasis is not entirely surprising. But it is significant in terms of *Macunaíma*, the literary masterpiece that emerged from Andrade's interests in Amazonia and the social changes and stresses he associated with Brazilian modernity. It is also noteworthy in terms of the reanimation of Andrade's ideas that would take place among heritage bureaucrats during Brazil's redemocratization, out of which the Pelourinho reforms emerge, but do not follow, in the 1990s.

Some Histories of Patrimony

While international involvement in heritage, organized supranationally today by UNESCO and ICOMOS, grew rapidly during the postwar period, Brazilian patrimony has typically evolved in ways that both reflect and condense, as well as contradict, international trends. Following Mário de Andrade's proposal that stressed the processual nature of national culture and sought to valorize and document popular creativity, SPHAN would by the 1950s move away from such ethnological approaches. Under the guidance of Rodrigo M. F. de

Andrade from 1937 to 1967, SPHAN came to register mostly buildings and monuments. This Andrade, a lawyer, seemed to enjoy bureaucratic process as much as Mário de Andrade valorized the ethnographic excavation of creativity.

Under Rodrigo M. F. de Andrade, SPHAN largely ignored the discussions of miscegenation and national popular culture that have come to define images of post–World War II Brazil. In the two decades following the war, SPHAN surveyed monuments in constructing a canon of Brazilianness linked tightly to ideas about Portuguese Baroque contributions to the nation. This European, high cultural, and thus distinctive version of Brazilianness, especially when compared to the nationalizing brownness gaining more widespread currency during the Estado Novo and ensuing decades, did not become hegemonic in representations of Brazil at home or abroad. In this way, SPHAN's activities suggest something of the extent to which representations of the nation were torn between visions of harmonious mixture, on the one hand, and an enduring attachment to Portugal's virtues, on the other. Illustrative of the extent to which "racial democracy" is not a seamless thing or coherent discourse, this seems to be a reaction to an elite and southern-Brazilian-based aversion to discussions of African and northeastern regional influences in the internal development of the nation as a whole. It is also emblematic of a disjuncture between Brazil's federal cultural heritage bureaucracy and the activities, heritage, and interests of the majority of its citizenry and artists in the post–World War II period. During this time Brazil experienced great cultural and intellectual ferment, something dampened only by the military dictatorship. But with the exception of SPHAN's interventions into the built environments of select cities, heritage institutions played a relatively small role in the postwar florescence. In spite of the interest in folklore and everyday, popular practices Mário de Andrade had enunciated over the course of his career and within his *anteprojeto*, for most of the mid- to late twentieth century the federal heritage bureaucracy that today champions minority rights and multicultural initiatives stood as a purveyor of Brazilian ideas about European culture. This began to change only when cultural planning became progressively more politicized with the gathering opposition to military rule in the late 1970s.

Under the leadership of Aloisio Magalhães, appointed director in 1979, SPHAN began to expand beyond the architecture-based orientation of earlier decades. Planners working with the municipality of São Paulo, such as the social historian Silvia Lara, and Bahian intellectuals, including the anthropologist Ordep Serra, were important actors in this shift. And in an environment of United Nations challenges to the industrialized world's stranglehold on patents and intellectual property in the 1970s and 1980s, SPHAN—by then already "IPHAN"—reinstated a more processual understanding of national culture akin to Mário de Andrade's approach to folklore. The late 1970s thus saw a multiplication of municipal, state-level, federal, and quasi-governmental agencies concerned with patrimony. Intellectuals sought to reverse what they considered to be racist and Eurocentric criteria. This rethinking led to the registry in 1982 of Salvador's oldest continually functioning Candomblé temple (*terreiro*) in Salvador, and the town of Palmares, the site of a sixteenth-century maroon community (*quilombo*) in the state of Alagoas.[45]

Efforts to address social struggle by including Afro-Brazilian and working-class heritage as patrimony gained momentum as prodemocracy activists turned increasingly to culture as a force that might be mobilized to open the political system during the dictatorship. Article 216 of the new constitution, drafted in 1988 as Brazil reconstituted its democratic institutions, made this orientation into law, defining "cultural patrimony as goods of a material and immaterial nature, taken individually or as a group, which are significant to the identity, action, or memory of the different groups that make up Brazilian society." The constitutional article, written as indigenous rights were becoming a major issue in Amazonia and internationally, points to what might be read today as an incipient multiculturalism, given its reference to social groups increasingly distinguished and painted as making up Brazilian society. By avoiding a language of monuments or simplistic exceptionality tied to national essence, it also discourages the high-cultural orientation common under Rodrigo M. F. de Andrade's SPHAN. Instead, the new constitution defined patrimony in relation to the significance of cultural manifestations to particular communities, which in turn make up the nation. This helped create room for individual states to move to protect and foment practices that could be defined under the mantle of Brazilian culture.

Article 270 of the state constitution of Bahia, drafted in 1989, specified that cultural policy should "facilitate the population's access to the production, distribution, and consumption of cultural goods" and "guarantee . . . communities' own abilities to direct popular, traditional, and contemporary cultural manifestations." But despite the beauty of the new Bahian constitution's legal language, the state's largest twentieth-century cultural initiative, the restoration of the Pelourinho, took form by the beginning of the 1990s as a top-down packaging of culture for the benefit of elites and outsiders. In fact, and in an example of the often contradictory entanglements of politics and the economy that are so much a part of neoliberalism, the renaissance in heritage planning associated with the return to democracy had by the final years of the 1980s come to an end as President Fernando Collor de Mello, the first democratically elected president to take office following Brazil's return to civilian rule in 1985, sought to balance the budget by abolishing the Ministry of Culture. Following Collor de Mello's impeachment and the two-year administration of his vice-president Itamar Franco, a neoliberal assault began again in earnest with the election of Fernando Henrique Cardoso to the presidency in 1994.

To the chagrin of many who had struggled alongside Cardoso and his minister of culture Francisco Weffort during the 1960s and 1970s, Weffort's ministry came to approach culture as a national property that might be auctioned off to the highest bidder or used to generate cash flow for paying down debt. As Weffort, an expert on Gramsci, stated in a World Bank meeting in New Orleans' restored French Quarter in 2000, "We must turn history around to combine development and heritage preservation."[46] This shift away from culture as a source of national pride and sovereignty and toward culture as an economic resource came at a moment in which supranational definitions of patrimony also underwent significant alteration.

By the mid-1990s UNESCO planners had begun to contemplate another, third, realm of patrimony that would expand upon the existing "cultural patrimony" and "natural patrimony" designations. Its planners understood this "intangible" or "immaterial" patrimony as "embracing all forms of traditional and popular or folk culture, that is, collective works originating in a given community and based on tradition." For UNESCO, intangible patrimony is "an essential source of an identity deeply rooted in the past" that looks much like the processual version of attention to national culture written into the SPHAN proposal by Mário de Andrade. UNESCO warns that "the essentially ephemeral nature of this intangible heritage makes it highly vulnerable" and that "it is not easy to map out the boundaries of what is called the cultural heritage of humanity."[47]

According to UNESCO, intangible heritage adheres to landscapes and individuals, and states should cultivate and preserve this heritage through attention to a class of people, generally those considered experts in oral, performative, and artisanal traditions. Near the turn of the millennium, UNESCO identified these exceptional beings as "Living Human Treasures." This term, which UNESCO largely abandoned after 2004, suggests a transnational valorization and objectification of human being. Thus the new "intangible" program fused life, economics, and the preservation or care of treasured selves and populations. It did so within a system predicated on what Michel Foucault described as "governmentality"—again, the management of the conduct of conduct— under which accepted, modern boundaries between human beings and things would come to be confused following IPAC's massive "reconstruction" of Salvador's colonial core.

While Brazilian statecrafting efforts of the 1930s and 1940s rested prominently on efficient statistical, public relations, and policing tools familiar to citizens today, the rolling back of the Estado Novo's corporatist labor, industrial, and pension systems in the 1990s occurred alongside UNESCO's celebration of a form of patrimony that not only organizes and objectifies national populations and their everyday practices, but renders them enunciable within guidelines that local people also associate with an array of relatively inert monuments. At the same time, the World Bank and Inter-American Development Bank have piggybacked on UNESCO initiatives in the cultural realm and focused on local cultures as motors for development. Reversing earlier stands in which the banks believed that culture, which stands as "traditional" economic activities and beliefs in this context, retarded development, these institutions encourage governments to foster cultural expressions attractive to tourists. Such shifts suggest not only changes in conceptualizing culture but also a greater involvement in the packaging and definition of everyday habits.

If national states and colonial powers have long sought to cultivate moral populations to police the borders between different groups, guarantee healthy bodies for the colonial venture, and aid in workforce reproduction, at a contemporary moment of attention to heritage the assembly of healthy families and "Living Human Treasures" and the UNESCO categorizations that have replaced them has become important in new ways. Previous concerns with everyday lives focused on a population's labor power and the diacritical practices through which, for example, colonials carved out their own identities in the face of "native" designations. Today intangible patrimony helps showcase the everyday as a means of defining nations and spurring investment, rather than producing labor power. The exposition of populations' practices—something apparent in Cervantes' as well as Léry's early modern writings—has become critical to national identity, political legitimacy, and the forms of power that support the two. At the same time, this exhibiting of the everyday involves enormous investments and promises to attract more and more capital.

Despite the global influence of UNESCO's most recent category of heritage, it would be a mistake to imagine that the Bahian heritage management of the last twenty years described in the next chapters is simply some local or national instantiation of a United Nations program. In August 2000 Brazil's Presidential Decree 3.551 in effect anticipated UNESCO's establishment in 2003 of the new category of "immaterial heritage," thus augmenting the cultural ledgers envisioned by Mário de Andrade. This initiative specified that immaterial cultural heritage should be subdivided into four volumes:

1. The Book of Knowledges (*Livro dos Saberes*)
2. The Book of Celebrations (*Livro das Celebrações*)
3. The Book of Expressive Forms (*Registro das Formas de Expressão*)
4. The Book of Places (*Registro dos Lugares*)

Decree 3.551 was designed specifically to address the sections of Brazil's 1988 constitution that treat cultural heritage.[48] As such, it can be read as a response to a growing international interest in immaterial heritage across the 1990s, to the work of Mário de Andrade in the 1930s, and to the excitement and wealth of innovative proposals that surrounded culture during Brazil's return from military rule in the 1980s. In other words, innovations promulgated by IPHAN and institutions like Bahia's IPAC near the end of the twentieth century did not give rise to UNESCO's subsequent initiatives. The same is true of the relations between IPAC and Pelourinho residents, an important nexus that I begin to examine in the next chapter. But both IPHAN and IPAC initiatives are something of a parallel discourse to their transnational cousins, or a bundle of techniques that arose not in the United Nations or even in IPHAN meeting rooms. Rather, as I will detail in the next chapter, they were worked out in a specifically Bahian context in ways that reflected Bahian race and class relations in the period after World War II. As such, they speak to and are no doubt influenced by multiple heritage initiatives developed around the world, including UNESCO's "Living Human Treasures" program. But they carry with them a special character that might be expected to influence how a now-codified immaterial heritage will be reworked in Bahia.

Since the ratification in Brazil in 2006 of UNESCO's 2003 convention for immaterial patrimony, innumerable cultural manifestations have been registered as Bahian and the "world's" intangible heritage. In Bahia a musical genre called samba de roda was listed in 2004. In 2006 the women who prepare black-eyed-pea fritters called *acarajé* joined the immaterial club, only to be followed in 2008 by the dance/martial art capoeira. Since then, the carnival of the Bahian town of Maragojipe, the carnival parades of the Afro-Bahian musical and social organizations known as *afoxés*, the skills employed by Bahian cowboys in the sertão, and the Afro-Brazilian women's religious society known as the *Irmandade da Boa Morte* (Sisterhood, or Catholic lay Association, of the Good End) in the town of Cachoeira have all been declared immaterial patrimony. No doubt the list will grow as the federal, as well as individual state's, cultural bureaucracies become increasingly invested in the purportedly intangible habits of their citizenries.

But I am not really committed here to listing cultural manifestations or commenting in depth on the spiraling influence and institutional development of UNESCO or state and national-level "pastification" initiatives around immaterial heritage.[49] The enormously complex, and often creative, approaches to culture put together in the last ten years by an IPHAN that, long a world leader in heritage management, has been bolstered by Workers Party support following Lula's rise to the presidency, warrant a book in themselves.[50] So I constrain myself, for the moment, to tracing a series of connections between seemingly separate areas of political and cultural life. Their interplay in the formal structures of governance erected around culture across the twentieth century will become important to my arguments about the shifts in personhood and politics that are part of twenty-first-century Brazilian engagements with the everyday practices and creativity of a national people.

The Significance of a Letter to the Amazons

Concerns with gender and intimate spaces provided Mário de Andrade, as they did for thinkers like Gilberto Freyre at about the same time, with a mode of thinking through origins by means of the manipulation of a medium available in their presents. This was culture. The resultant SPHAN bureaucracy largely avoided addressing race in any explicit manner. This is not unexpected in a nation predicated on the denial of racial difference, yet constructed upon the techniques developed to perform this negation. Here it seems important that Andrade's modernist literary production, and his subsequent proposal for organizing patrimony, demonstrate a faith in a people he conceives of as producers of an authentic and valuable culture. For Andrade, the intellectual's duty was to catalogue and encourage such manifestations of creativity in a manner that would allow the people's energies, neither European nor African nor Amerindian, but hybridly Brazilian, to define Brazil against the tired civilizations of Europe and North America.

Macunaíma suggests just how much Andrade's moment, and heritage proposal, revolved around ideas about gender and race. In Andrade's reworking of the terms of Brazilian modernity, the sexual lives of almost-white women and the downtown space of male sociability they animate take center stage. Apparently influenced, like his confidant Manuel Bandeira, by fears of being symbolically "cuckolded by a Frenchman" in the march toward modernity discussed in this book's introduction and fleshed out in this chapter's latter sections, Andrade constructed origins out of a nationalist interracial love. This is not to say that such an ideal became real or that I am commenting on his individual desires, but rather that São Paulo's red light district provided a stage for an influential mid-twentieth-century national fantasy that may reappear in multiple manifestations.

At the end of the twentieth century, as a variety of race-based political movements struggled for equal representation in Bahia, Antonio Carlos Magalhães and his political coalition sought to resuscitate the Pelourinho as a space for purportedly healthy interracial interactions similar to those idealized in Andrade's midcentury fiction. Thus I have not argued here for a continual and even ideology of racial democracy, but rather for a reanimation at a moment of need of a series of possibilities preserved in a variety of erudite and popular idioms. And subsequently, in the first decade of the new millennium, a discourse of racial mixture has faded in the Pelourinho in the face of an intense concern with rooted essences, or a more historical version of racial being. Patrimonialized possessions, as items and people that circulate and take on the appearance of content in their movement out of the everyday and into state registers, thus served in the 1990s as one site for the instantiation of mixture at a moment when many Brazilians argued that long-standing emphases on miscegenation were about to be eclipsed as a convincing discourse or solution to the predicaments of postcolonial Latin America. And, given the rise in ethno-racial identification in Brazil today, it appears they were correct. But does this mean that the imagination of content and the ethnographic organization of Brazil's everydayness through patrimony have come to work in new ways also? Or might one recognize in the Pelourinho today some sort of uneven distribution and ongoing modification of techniques first directed at patrimony under the Estado Novo, and influential in current political realignments?

In the next chapter I move to a consideration of an entwined popular and erudite system of enunciability in the Pelourinho, as developed with the establishment of IPAC during Brazil's military dictatorship in the late 1960s. I thus continue this chapter's historical move away from the images of the Pelourinho of the 1990s introduced in chapter 1, something I will reverse in chapter 4's return to the present. And in doing so, I focus on a red light district, the sort of space that stands as an origin of the Brazilian nation in *Macunaíma*. This is not to say that red light districts in themselves have a special role in Brazilian or Bahian patrimony. Rather, following this chapter's emphasis on the ways that specific types of entities come into being as answers to pressing questions about Bahian origins, in the 1970s and 1980s the Bahian state's reconstruction of the Pelourinho has attenuated certain unresolved ideas about political legitimacy and national fundaments. And, like Andrade of the 1930s, IPAC has located the sources of the nation in a possible redemption that would be unthinkable were it not for the supposedly imperfect morals of the women of the red light zone. For this reason I turn in chapter 3 to the results of state concern with female morality during a period of military dictatorship, and thus to an argument that injects gender and sexuality into that national property so well known as "patrimony." But before doing so, it is worthwhile to recall, if only briefly and in a move that mimics irreverently some of the descriptions and self-fashionings performed by modernist intellectuals and Portuguese explorers, from where I have come in engaging the Pelourinho, its residents, and you, my sovereign reader.

A Journey to the Source

Salvador

May 1, 2000

Dear Reader,

Many others, possessing a greater knowledge of the exact sciences of demography, cartography and philology, will provide you with more extensive accounts of recent attempts to restore the origins of the Brazilian nation. But I, too, cannot but endeavor to represent to you something that I might describe humbly as the beauty, difficulty, and significance of travel in these tropical areas of the Americas.

Just this week, my wife, my toddler son, and I made our way south from Salvador, the capital of the state of Bahia, to Porto Seguro in order to attend Brazil's quincentennial celebrations. Porto Seguro (Safe Harbor) is today a touristic city, located near the site of the Portuguese disembarkation on April 22, 1500, and favored by international and southern Brazilian sun lovers. Although I cannot quite reproduce in its entirety the experience for your perusal here, our automobile journey to the nation's professed birthplace involved traversing the Bay of All Saints by ferryboat, zipping across the lush Island of Itaparica into the Bahian Recôncavo—the seventeenth century's richest source of tropical commodities and the region where Daniel Defoe's fictional character Robinson Crusoe owned a large and productive plantation—and descending to the gleaming sands and historical cities of Bahia's "Coast of Discovery," a region advertised by the state government of Bahia with the slogan "Bahia: Brazil was Born Here."

Excited by this break from anthropological fieldwork concerned with the production of history in Salvador's Pelourinho Historical Center, I watched my son, just shy of three, and recalled my own 1976 voyage to New York's Operation Sail in celebration of the United States' bicentennial. My wife and I talked about national commemorations and Brazilian and North American exceptionalisms as we drove through an area whose economic and political decline began at about the time of the U.S. Declaration of Independence. I wondered what my son would recollect about this journey, undertaken with his Bahian mother and North American father, into the celebration of Brazilian national history. Not surprisingly, given the importance of forgetting to individual and collective identity, it turns out that he remembers only southern Bahia's beaches and the Brazilian Air Force's English Spitfire propeller planes that buzzed overhead. And his scattered memories have spurred me to recall a similar event in my own life, or the way the North American bicentennial celebrations' Operation Sail in New York Harbor had helped introduce me to geopolitics and cultural difference.

Traveling into upper Manhattan from New York's suburban Westchester County in the summer of 1976, I experienced a West Side Highway closed to cars and filled with street vendors in dashikis and Afro-style haircuts—this was the 1970s, after all—from which crowds viewed a flotilla of military vessels. My brothers and I wanted to climb down the embankment and wet our toes in the Hudson River, but our mother did not allow us because there were men down there, drinking beer to the sounds of Fania Records' increasingly popular disseminations of salsa music.

The international visitors parading around Manhattan Isle that day included the Chilean Navy's dark-hulled sailing ship, infamous as a floating torture chamber following Salvador Allende's U.S.-supported overthrow. I remember the *Esmeralda* because of the protesters milling about its berth. And I recall being shocked at the sight of ruddy pink naval officers in safari shorts aboard a South African frigate. Both images still stand out as moments of curious disjuncture: "Why were people protesting the most beautiful three-masted ship in Operation Sail?" I questioned my parents. And "Why aren't the Africans black?" I recall wondering as I learned of Pinochet's bloody coup and apartheid. It seemed that Operation Sail, in addition to images of striking tall ships and military technology, had left me with memories that contradicted the official messages the celebrations were intended to elicit.

I was jolted out of this reverie about 200 kilometers short of the city of Porto Seguro as we happened upon Juan, an artisan and a friend from Salvador, who was also headed for Brazil's festivities. Juan had arrived in Brazil after fleeing his native Argentina and the trauma of serving in the 1982–83 Falkland Islands war that sealed the fate of Argentina's military dictatorship, linked in the 1970s and 1980s to Pinochet's Chilean torturers and the United States' and Brazil's militaries. As I pondered briefly how post–World War II military alliances in the Americas complicated the interconnections between Operation Sail and Porto Seguro's celebration of Brazil's 500 years, we offered our Argentine compatriot a ride and helped him transfer to our trunk his jerry-rigged airport luggage cart, fished from the garbage in one of Salvador's middle-class neighborhoods.

Upon arriving in Eunápolis, a county seat, the entrance to the coastline that harbors Porto Seguro, and a stronghold of the political party in charge of Bahia at the time—the PFL—we found ourselves in a massive traffic jam. As we sat, stalled in the advancing darkness, members of the Movimento dos Trabalhadores Sem Terra, or the Landless Workers Movement, (MST), swarmed around bonfires alongside the highway. They marched, drank cane liquor, shouted out lines from militant songs and popular music, and otherwise provoked the military police contingent that had been mobilized by the Bahian governor to block such undesirable elements from marring the festivities.

The people the state government of Bahia sought to bar from Brazil's quincentennial celebrations included the MST, indigenous rights leaders, participants in the Black Movement, anyone associated with the Workers Party, and, it seemed to us, poor people in general. Stuck in the traffic, and since his documents were not in order, Juan jumped out and began cutting through vacant lots so as to bypass checkpoints. We promised to pick him up on the other side. For hours we sat in traffic in our "popular" Volkswagen Gol alongside church groups from Brasilia in their Hyundai vans, excursion buses full of boisterous workers anxious to join the party and hit the beach, petit bourgeois families from the prosperous central state of Minas Gerais in their Volkswagen station wagons, left-leaning college students from São Paulo in a variety of automobiles, and late model Ford pickup trucks full of mustachioed ranchers from the Eunápolis area.

Soon the military police's infamous "Shock" Battalion, sent from Salvador for the festivities, approached and questioned us. Satisfying them with our documents and expressions of patriotic fervor, association with the U.S. and nuclear families, and apparent good intentions, we were, along with the ranch owners, one of the few parties chosen to line up behind the barriers that separated us from the 80 kilometers of traffic-free blacktop that led to the spot on the Bahian coast where the Portuguese expedition had touched down in April, 1500.

While stopped as the fourth or fifth car in the line inching toward the barriers, word came through that nobody would pass that night, the eve of the quincentennial. It seemed that indigenous and leftist political groups had clashed violently with police on the other highway leading to Porto Seguro. The governor had decided that too many "subversive elements," as the officer in charge put it, had already been allowed into the nation's celebration of its discovery. As the members of the MST danced on the side of the road, seemingly oblivious to our desire to witness the celebrations and satisfied that their very presence unnerved the police, a great roar went up from the crowd in response to the rumor that Porto Seguro was now closed to visitors. "But how can we not be permitted to travel to Porto Seguro?!?" wailed a mother from the church group, "We've driven thirty-five hours to get here! We want to celebrate the discovery of Brazil, to see the land of Cabral [the Portuguese explorer]!"

"Into your cars, engines off, headlights off, interior lights on!" ordered the military police commander, a colonel from Salvador. As he stood alongside my door, I asked with patient formality, "Sir, would you give me one moment, please?" as I heard his radio crackling with reports as to the movements of the MST and rumors that they were preparing to march and overwhelm his checkpoint.

"Just a moment," he replied as he finished looking at the documents from the car and driver in front of us. "That black guy [negão] isn't going anywhere tonight. I know he's drunk, pull him out of the car!" he ordered a lieutenant, as he turned to my passport. I wanted to protest that I'd been watching the driver for hours and he hadn't been drinking. But I also wanted desperately, cowardly, and in direct response to a series of violent encounters with Bahia's police over the previous two years, to leave behind the traffic jam, the police, and the MST protesters.

I began to plead our case. "Sir, it's like this: My wife, baby son, and I have traveled from Salvador for the quincentennial. I am an academic in Brazil at the invitation of the federal government. Here is my card from Itamaraty, which explains my work.[51] We humbly request that we be permitted to proceed."

"Where do you live?"

"In Salvador, sir. In the neighborhood of Barbalho," my wife answered. I added, for good measure, "Just behind the 7th Military Police Battalion Headquarters." Following our claim to residence in a "traditional" neighborhood that fit nicely into Bahian spatial distinctions between "people" and *marginais*, and my calculated claim to proximity to and familiarity with the battalion headquarters, he returned my documents and said simply, "You may go. Enjoy your time in Porto Seguro." As we drove away I saw the colonel striding imperiously toward the car and supposedly drunk driver who had been in front of us seconds before.

Juan leapt from the bushes and flagged us down about a kilometer past the barricades. We sped quickly through the night, the only car on the highway. No one else seemed to have crossed the police lines. We tried to imagine the fate of the man in front of us. Juan commented, "The other day I saw the Shock [special police unit] catch a *negão*. They beat him so badly, calling him "*negão sujo*" [dirty black man] and they were almost all black. It's like Caetano [Veloso] says. We can denounce it afterward, but if we speak up at the moment they're giving out the beatings then our ribs will feel their boots too, neh?"[52] Accustomed to, but not comfortable with, such violence, we nonetheless yammered on and felt badly for the families stuck in hot vans who, despite their travel from the farthest reaches of Brazil, would not have an opportunity to join in their nation's festivities. Just before we reached the next checkpoint a number of the high-powered pickups owned by landowners passed us, apparently having been let through by the same colonel who had concluded that they, like the bourgeois family associated with the United States, represented no threat to national security.

To make a long story slightly shorter, after multiple checkpoints, continued rumors about the MST's overrunning of barricades, thorough searches, and numerous mosquito bites as we pled our cases to various commanders in different crossroads filled with stranded Brazilians of every stripe, we arrived at dawn in Porto Seguro. The city was not quite empty. But not surprisingly, given the difficulties involved in traveling across this historical territory by land, it lacked the huge crowds anticipated by the state and merchants. Storekeepers complained of poor business. Reports filtered in that the "Indians" up the coastal highway—we had arrived on the highway from the interior—continued to confront the police.

When we returned to Salvador we would learn that the police had literally walked upon the protesting indigenous residents of the Porto Seguro area and their guests from throughout Brazil. And they had beaten severely a number of protesters from the Black Movement and Workers Party. During the festivities, unable to leave due to police blockades, we made our way downtown at night to the site of a large amphitheater that had been set up so that invited guests, including the Bahian governor, the president of Portugal, and Brazil's President Fernando Henrique Cardoso, could view a re-enactment of the Portuguese "discovery" complete with mockups of Cabral's flotilla and actors dressed in appropriate costumes. Yet the majority of visitors and residents milling about could not enter the amphitheater and therefore missed the re-enactment of the European arrival in their land. They did not hold the passes that would allow them inside the reenactment of Brazilian history. So they massed around the retaining walls and fences, hoping to catch a glimpse of something or someone. Also lacking tickets, we soon found ourselves standing in the crowd near one of the entrances as provincial politicians and their wives filed by, dressed in fine dark suits and baroque dresses.

The crowd became angry, blocking the way of burly men who, accustomed to getting their way, pushed us aside. Soon people began to rain down abuse on the small groups of invited guests. As the dignitaries passed through, the crowd chanted "F-F-F-F-Filho da Puta!" or "S-S-S-S-Son of a bitch!" and individuals began to spit and throw objects at the regional bosses. The continual arrival of new groups became an occasion for their popular upbraiding since, due to their paranoia about the MST and the many political figures invited to the celebrations, the military police had apparently forgotten about the entrance used by minor officials. One spectator, a tall, blond man from southern Brazil, began to tweak the ears of the arriving gentry. He would reach out from the crowd and yank mightily on the lobes of the powerful men who accompanied their wives down the gauntlet populated by assorted rabble, disappearing into the crowd after each jerk. Some attendees would turn and seek to find the source of the tugs at their ears—a form of punishment typically directed by parents in Bahia at naughty children who must be pulled home for further correction—and find nothing but a sea of grinning, yet hostile, faces.

Eventually, police patrols caught on to what was happening and charged the crowd, beating and arresting a number, including the ear-puller and a group of men who sought to lift my wallet as we watched the action. A squad of military police from Salvador advised the rest of us to go home "or else."

The uproar over the privatization of the quincentennial commemorations was so intense that Porto Seguro's mayor decided that they would be repeated the next night, with the doors opened to all who desired to attend. After picking up tickets from city hall earlier in the afternoon, citizens filled the outdoor amphitheater for the second nighttime rendition. Yet most stayed away, preferring to dance, drink, or try to earn some money from the tourists. And as one young man told me, "There're no more fireworks, it's not worth standing in line." And sure enough, the fireworks had run out during the first show. Or, perhaps, they had just begun. We would know only upon our return to Salvador, to its Historical Center, and to the people not simply excluded from Brazilian history, but absolutely central to it.

Sincerely,

John Collins

CHAPTER 3

Prostitution's Bureaucracy

Making Up People in the "City of Women"

A pproximately one month before her death, which was registered officially as heart failure, Dona Katia Alves de Souza turned to me as she dispensed R$5 and R$10 pieces of crack cocaine to a room full of waiting customers, some of whom had been her clients for different illicit drugs for more than twenty years. She whispered, in a throaty mix of the *sertão* and the Maciel,

> John, I never wanted to sell drugs to other women's children. I never wanted to be the cause of others' deaths. My boys are all gone: Moreno, Nilsinho and Josué are dead, killed by others' greed and envy, Pateta is locked up, and I have nothing. The lady killed Moreno and the crooked policeman in Cosme de Farias took my Nilsinho.[1] But I never wanted to kill other women's children.

As I listened to our taped conversations for the first time from the lush confines of a North American university town in summer, I recalled Dona Katia's home built onto the rotting planks of the eighteenth-century "big house" with a collapsed roof and fire-damaged beams shrouded in damp cardboard. These produced a bouncy floor that would not cave in as long as one stepped on or near the beams. Today I still hear the flicking of lighters and the sucking of mouths on the aluminum tops of the plastic mineral water cups used as crack pipes in Salvador. And I remember Dona Katia interrupting the messages she wanted me to carry away for my book so as to conclude deals and to scold misbehaving users who might drown out our taping. Most of all, I remember my friend sitting in a brilliant orange and yellow dress on a three-legged stool propped against a protruding iron balcony that hung feebly to the building's Baroque façade. I think often about the struggles and the power of this Pelourinho mother.

I still admire Dona Katia's authority over Salvador's armed robbers, its priests, its heritage bureaucrats and social workers, its Pelourinho prostitutes, its pickpockets, and the lawyers whose pockets she lined in frequent attempts to remain free. I marvel at Dona Katia's control over the city hall employees who bought and used her products in her bedroom on their lunch breaks, her influence that extended through her former husband "Da Esporra" to the docks of Rio de Janeiro, and her battle to gain wealth and respectability after emigrating from the drought-stricken countryside before she turned thirteen to work as a domestic servant in what she always called "a rich white woman's house."

All this leads me to ponder Dona Katia's place in accounts of Bahia in general and the post–World War II Maciel/Pelourinho neighborhood in particular, representations that have taken on vital importance in defining racial identities and citizenship categories today: Dona Katia's participation in activities coded as illegal and configured as marginal by a variety of commentators somehow came to place her at the center of Bahian history and society at the end of the twentieth century. This process of drawing in the human beings typically called "marginals" but often recognized as central to social life, which is the subject of this third chapter, has been critical to the constitution of a particular type of state-sanctioned history, and phalanx of historical figures, emanating from the Pelourinho over the last three decades.

Dona Katia stands out within a group of influential Afro-Bahian women born in the sertão, that dry interior of Brazil's Northeast recognized since at least the mid-nineteenth century as the home of threatening mixed-raced backlanders, who came to the capital of the state of Bahia to work as domestic servants for wealthy families and who, for a variety of reasons, left those positions to "make a life" (*fazer vida*) as street vendors, restaurant owners, prostitutes, market women, and mothers in the Maciel red light district. Pelourinho women of Dona Katia's age recall her generosity and her skill in ministering to wounds, in scaring up change for medicines, or in facing down crooked policemen and abusive partners. In part as a result, in the late 1990s Dona Katia could walk into Salvador's men's prison to see her son at will, even carrying cocaine and, if caught, simply have it taken away by guards who would fetch her a juice and return the contraband upon her exit. Prisoners would line up against the grates, mumbling "Bença mãe" (Bless me mother) while offering her their limp palms and first sips of valuable soft drinks bought on visiting day. To know Dona Katia was insurance for me against hassles on Salvador's streets as I would find myself at the market or outside the bank and hard young men would lean out bus windows to shout, "what's up *gringo*, gringo of the strong blood [*gringo sangue bom*]; you're the old lady's son's friend, *sangue baaaaaom!!*"

In Salvador today it is common to represent Dona Katia and her peers as strong mothers and powerful lawbreakers, or as figures in the Pelourinho community whom dominant approaches in Bahian popular culture and social science indicate should be respected and analyzed at length, although not always as mothers. What, then, is the role of the "divergent" working-class and Afro-Brazilian mother in the making of a sanitized temple and a folkloric historical center? How does a state institution's focus on Pelourinho women in the 1970s and 1980s produce knowledge about Afro-Bahians that gives rise to something called "national patrimony"? And how does this specifically Brazilian and racialized engagement between an expanding social science and its working-class "subjects" inflect something called "Bahian," and, by extension, Brazilian, history?

Accounting for a Pillory and Its Population

In 1967, in an attempt to satisfy UNESCO criteria for world-heritage-site designation, the Bahian state established the "Bahian Foundation for Cultural and Artistic Patrimony and the Library Foundation" (FPACBa), the precursor to IPAC which, along with the state-level CONDER, would largely direct the Pelourinho restoration from 1992 to the present.[2] The Foundation, run for most of the 1970s by Vivaldo da Costa Lima, a respected anthropologist at the Federal University of Bahia (UFBA) well known for his studies of Afro-Brazilian religion, drew its personnel from a new corps of social scientists educated in universities that were undergoing expansion during the military government that lasted from 1964 to 1985. By the late 1970s these professionals, often more influenced by North American social science than the previous generation, began to replace the "men of letters" and medical doctors attached to coroners' offices preeminent at previous moments in Bahian intellectual life.[3] IPAC, then, constitutes a Bahian site for understanding the lopsided negotiations of knowledge and everyday life coconstructed by social scientists and "minority" communities across the Americas during the post–World War II era of United States–championed developmentalism. These ranged from Old San Juan, Puerto Rico's La Perla neighborhood, and the "streetcorner society" of Afro-North American neighborhoods more generally, to Brazilian programs directed at contacting, studying, and "pacifying" Amazonian groups.[4]

Although directed by its bylaws at the rescue of a disappearing architectural patrimony and the care of state archives, the FPACBa instead initiated

its heritage activities with a research program directed at Pelourinho prostitutes. IPAC regulation of, and focus on, prostitution made the practice an object of Bahian sociological, as opposed to police or hygienist, analysis for the
first time. And this entanglement of historical patrimony with sexual mores in
Salvador altered them both.[5]

A publication from 1997, *The Socioeconomic Study of the Pelourinho* (Levantamento Socioeconômico do Pelourinho), illustrates the extent to which IPAC
and its institutional predecessors focused on women's morality and everyday
life rather than the cathedrals and monuments more typically included in
global definitions of patrimony in the 1970s. The 1997 version of the *Study* is
a reprint—put out at a moment of mounting criticism of IPAC's removal of Pelourinho residents and designed ostensibly to commemorate IPAC's thirtieth
anniversary—of the 1969 publication of IPAC fieldwork conducted between
1967 and 1968.

In 1997, IPAC director Adriana Castro thus presented the glossy volume as
a "foundational landmark":

Directed by Professor Vivaldo da Costa Lima, the research [1967–68 study]
has taken on proportions that transcend its original impact. It is both a
foundational event and a valuable sociological study girded by extremely secure methodological foundations. It has established itself as the beginning
of a new way for approaching patrimony. *Previously, "patrimony" meant almost exclusively the privileging of material goods in the form of household fur-
nishings or real estate. The populations of the areas registered as historic sites
were relegated to a lower level or else completely forgotten.*[6]

This reprint of a study published in 1967, whose text includes as many pages
treating prostitution, morality, and policing as it does pages addressing monuments, is thus more than a sociological record or a chart of IPAC "progress." It
is a history of institutional beginnings that responds to criticisms of the expulsion of Pelourinho residents during the 1990s. The document establishes an origin, in the form of sociological data reconfigured as an historical "event," that
Director Castro authenticates by emphasizing "secure methodological foundations." The document also argues, on the basis of the fieldwork conducted between 1967 and 1968, that the population of Bahia's heritage zone is no longer
"forgotten" or "relegated to a lower level." This claim, enunciated in a language
of moral uplift and state-directed care, is critical to IPAC's conceptualization
of Bahian patrimony.

In 1997 Director Castro drew on the report to argue that, in its "new way
for approaching patrimony," IPAC included people when most institutions
simply catalogued historic sites and buildings. This is curious, given that her

predecessor, the anthropologist Vivaldo da Costa Lima, told me in August 2001 that he resigned from IPAC in 1993 in protest over the removal of residents during the restoration. Furthermore, in 2000 an expert panel composed of personnel from IPAC, UFBA's Architecture School, Salvador's municipal planning authority (SEPLAM), the Bahian state development organ (CONDER), and from IPHAN noted, "In spite of the generalized recuperation of real estate, the 1991–2000 program has not paid any attention to policies related to housing. This has resulted in a historical center directed exclusively at . . . tourist services and leisure."[7]

Rather than suggesting that Adriana Castro was bending the truth to defend her institution, I take the director at her word, reading her claims with, rather than against, the grain.[8] This means that IPAC attention to, or care of, the historical center's people must be understood in a slightly different way. After all, Director Castro's direct superior, Bahian Secretary of Culture and Tourism Paulo Gaudenzi, wrote in his preface to the reissue in 1997 that IPAC's efforts to protect Bahia's patrimony must be "measured [not] in time, but in political will, work, in seriousness, and in the coherence of the greatest values that accrue to this nation-state through what it holds most human and valuable—its people, its art, its culture and its traditions."[9]

Moral Calculus: Producing the Pelourinho as a City of Women

IPAC's approaches to the Pelourinho's buildings and population have oscillated across the institution's almost fifty-year history in relation to shifting movements in Brazilian political economic policy, democratic governance, and even whether or not an anthropologist or architect sits in the director's chair. The institution's practices should not be bundled into a neat account of a growing, neoliberal multicultural-type replacement of people by their practices; indeed, after 2008, IPAC would make great progress in opening itself up to public scrutiny and engaging the community in an effort to democratize Bahian patrimony. Nonetheless, IPAC policy across time does seem to track, at least in some diffuse manner, the dissemination of particular development models as well as trends in Brazilian national and global political economy more generally. Thus across the second half of the 1990s, IPAC's planners did find themselves working within a Bahian state, and in relation to a federal government, interested rather intensely in the marketing of culture. And this means that the institution's policies and practices in relation to Pelourinho residents offer a specifically Bahian story of the development of a city, a region, and its social science in the face of shifts in politics and developmental models.

Director Castro's self-legitimizing suggestion that IPAC is exceptional because it humanized patrimony through a focus on people is not simply a defense against critics of the post-1992 restoration or a manifestation of UNESCO's new intangible patrimony programs and a burgeoning, worldwide treatment of identities as branded, fungible goods: It is a response crafted in a language of concern about Brazil's mixed-race populations and purportedly degenerate modes of urban planning dating back to Portugal. This response draws on global instruments like UNESCO cultural heritage directives as well as a specifically Bahian gathering and interpretation of data about a population painted to varying degrees as problematic, diseased, and immoral. Thus the *Survey* might be read most productively as a means of understanding a longer, shifting discourse on people, national landscapes, and propriety. Men of letters like Manuel Bandeira put forth something similar as early as the 1920s. But by the 1970s these analyses had come to be enunciated in the language of social science in ways quite different, and yet at times rather reminiscent of, mid-twentieth-century idioms.

The extent to which the confusion of people and buildings in the 1990s explored in subsequent chapters arose as part of phenomena that need to be explored carefully in relation to Brazilian engagements with the world, rather than assimilated quickly into global patterns in the commodification of culture, soon becomes clear. After an introduction explaining that a desire for IDB funding spurred IPAC's early work, chapter 2 of the *Survey* offers a history of the Pillory that gave rise to the designation "Pelourinho." Here the report trumpets the Pelourinho's Portuguese-inspired beauty and lists monuments "contiguous to obvious houses of prostitution, to ruins that shelter a varied and suffering population."[10] From this moment on, a concern with prostitution, households, and social and moral ruination dominates IPAC's autobiography. This institution, directed by its original bylaws to the care of archives and the safeguarding of cultural manifestations, seems to have been directed in practice to the evaluation of Afro-Bahian morality.

Of the thirty-four pages of prose about the neighborhood, the methods, results, and tabulations that make up the 1969 study, twelve are dedicated entirely to explicit discussions of morality, commercial sex, and Pelourinho families. In other words, if taken seriously, Director Castro's mixture of emphasis on the marketing of heritage and IPAC attention to a population points to something quite specific about Bahian heritage-making of the last three decades of the twentieth century. Cultural heritage takes form in Bahia of the second half of the twentieth century as a concern with culture and tourism, which are dependent on the state's social scientific identification and manipulation of specific, very Brazilian conceptions of hygiene and morality among Afro-Brazilians. In support of this point, the *Survey* includes not just data and a discussion of their significance and production, but a number of documents reprinted from newspapers and Catholic Church sources. Among these is a denunciation in 1967 of the Pelourinho's ruin. In their response to the Church's outrage at the neighborhood's physical and moral decay, IPAC authors argue that the redemption of the Pelourinho and its population requires a sociological, as opposed to spiritual or monument-based, plan of action. The *Survey* thus explains that while prostitution is not its object of analysis, it is the area's major problem. It then points out that despite a significant ecclesiastical presence, the Church offered no social programs or plan for restoring the neighborhood even as it owned a majority of the buildings housing the Pelourinho's brothels. In this way the report anchors IPAC in a modern social science established in opposition to clerical authority and made understandable in terms of long-standing Brazilian concerns with tensions between landscapes and national progress, or the lack thereof.

After attacking Rome's influence, IPAC takes aim at more secular targets and moves to the police, arguing that their efforts against prostitution were ineffectual. Chapter 2 concludes by citing the noted Bahian geographer Milton Santos' call in 1959 for a holistic approach to the problems of prostitution and restoration. Such recourse to the state's most important intellectuals functions in tandem with the *Study*'s rhetoric, manipulations of data, and insertion of graphic objects from other sources in order to validate the heritage institution's place in absorbing, or at least to laying claim to, the Catholic Church's pastoral authority as well as the public safety authorities' powers to police the ostensibly unruly populace of a neighborhood renowned for its architecture, infamous for commercial sex, and increasingly celebrated as a source of Afro-Brazilian culture. This narrative depicts IPAC as the only institution prepared to treat the Pelourinho's problems, and it does so by usurping the right to care for and police the historical center's inhabitants so as to safeguard its monuments. And over the course of this broad engagement with what IPAC spokespeople would describe to me some two decades later as the "moralization of the ground" (*a moralização do solo*), residents' moral aptitudes became an object of sociological analysis. This focus transforms those people and their habits into the core content of the texts through which IPAC would come to define the Pelourinho as a historical center, as well as justify its place in the Bahian state structure.

Like the *Survey*'s text, questionnaires and postsurvey analysis published in both the 1969 and 1997 editions concentrate on prostitutes and their activities. They focus on women who owned or occupied Pelourinho real estate, especially in relation to their marital and educational statuses, occupations, and rural birthplaces. All data are mustered as evidence about moral status in twenty-three tables grouped under the following headings:

1. Income, Rent, and Sex (feminine)
2. Type of Real Estate, Conditions of the Occupation of the Domicile
3. Value of Rent, Type of Building
4. Occupation, Age Group, Sex (masculine)
5. Why One Wants to Move, Neighborhood to Which One Would Like to Move
6. Number of Rooms Occupied, Number of People in the Rooms, and Sex
7. Occupation, Age Group, Sex (feminine)
8. Age Group, Educational Level of Minors and Dependents
9. Material Conditions of the Building
10. Income Levels and Age by Sex
11. Income Levels, Birthplace and Sex
12. Employment, Birthplace and Sex (masculine)
13. Employment, Birthplace and Sex (feminine)
14. Employment, Whether or not they can Acquire Financing (mortgages), Sex
15. Number of Rooms Occupied, Number of People in the Rooms
16. Occupation, Whether or not they will accept Financing from the Municipality, Sex
17. Potable Water and Sanitation
18. Income, Rent and Sex (masculine)
19. Type of Building and How Obtained
20. Family Income and Number of Dependents
21. Number of Rooms and Floors
22. Type of Building, Repairs Necessary to Restoring the Building, Owner or Renter
23. Kitchens, Baths and Toilets

The arrangement of figures in a table, beginning with women's income and the rents paid for living spaces and ending with a table quantifying people's bathing and cooking facilities, reveals much about IPAC's logic: This "moral science" points to concerns with the intimate details of health, reproduction, and the occupancy of valuable central real estate during Brazil's 1960s and 1970s "economic miracle," a period characterized by rapid and disorienting urbanization.[11] But the *Survey* does much more: In an attempt to discern its assumptions and regularities, and thus IPAC's logics, one might group the report's twenty-three tables into four larger categories, namely "income and economic activities"; "sanitary concerns"; "care of and potential for removal from real estate"; and "birthplace." Bunched this way, the details of IPAC research underscore even more sharply the institution's preoccupation with family structure, morality, and its relationship to property regimes and propriety, or "proper" behavior and ways of making use of Brazil's patrimony, Salvador's city center. Three different tables—Income, Rent and Sex; Employment, Birthplace and Sex; and Occupation, Age Group and Sex—are repeated and divided, to be presented on separate pages according to gender. Yet they do not necessarily appear as pairs, standing alongside one another on successive pages: While the entire analysis begins with an exposition of women's income and the rents paid for their living quarters, the correlate table detailing men's incomes and rents does not appear until item eighteen! Given that newspapers and entry logs from Salvador's downtown police stations are filled with concerns over the exploitation of women and minors from the interior by pimps and avaricious exprostitutes running Pelourinho boarding houses during this time period, this table seems aimed at identifying single women of dubious virtue. It presents these women not simply as problematic, but as victims of an unsavory environment requiring state intervention.

The *Survey*'s text also emphasizes disparities between "excessive" rents in the Pelourinho and "normal" rents in outlying working-class neighborhoods. Such recourse to the market highlights the supposed impropriety of unruly women's occupation of Salvador's downtown, and related arguments would be used in the mid-1990s to justify residents' removal to their "proper" places in Salvador's urban geography. But IPAC concerns with prostitution and unruly women did not end with the *Survey*'s analytic attention to prostitutes, their families, and the suggestion that they would be better off economically if they took their places in the peripheral neighborhoods and shantytowns popping up during this period of high rural-urban migration. In a follow-up questionnaire administered to the fieldworkers who conducted the *Survey*, the authors attempted to hone their research tool by asking for researchers' opinions as to the study's efficacy and design. The fourth of these six questions posed to fieldworkers reads, "How did the prostitutes behave in the face of these questions and how was this related to the formulation of the questions?" IPAC singles out no other group in the follow-up in which open-ended questions are on the order of "What did you think of the research," "In general, what was the reaction of those interviewed," and "Cite some of the curious incidents that occurred." The IPAC questionnaire, although "about" the population of the Pelourinho and its relationship to the buildings to be designated as world heritage, is directed at and concerned with female prostitutes and their families.

Both IPAC's 1969 Study and its 1997 republication reveal how the institution came to focus on people, rather than buildings or monuments, nearly thirty years before the widespread dissemination of UNESCO categories like "masterpieces of oral and intangible patrimony."[12] Thus even as across the 1990s IPAC waged a war against residents as its personnel struggled to limit indemnifications and evict the families it identified through ethnography and the administration of questionnaires, Director Castro does not appear to be incorrect in arguing that IPAC developed a new approach to patrimony.

The way IPAC approached Pelourinho residents at the end of the twentieth century was nowhere near as benign or accommodating as Director Castro would have the public believe. Yet the research instruments and reports employed in the 1960s, like their subsequent re-elaboration as the raw material of histories of the Pelourinho together with the Bahian state's ostensible vigilance in protecting threatened cultural heritage, support Director Castro's contention that IPAC long placed people at the forefront of Bahian patrimony. How this focus on people rather than monuments took form, and how it changed over the three decades bracketed by the *Study* and explored across this book, is an important aspect not simply of the definition of Bahian cultural heritage, but also of the racial politics that would sweep Brazil at the turn of the millennium.

The Military Years: IPAC as Protector and Patron

The repression so central to Brazil's military dictatorship between 1964 and 1985 was geographically variable. While the military pursued important figures in Salvador's universities and forced Bahian recording stars like Caetano Veloso and Gilberto Gil—who would become Minister of Culture under President Lula—into exile, authorities left a contingent of intellectuals relatively free to pursue their activities. Salvador's planning magazine, *Revista de planejamento municipal*, became a forum for partially obscured discussions of Marxist theory. According to the sociologist and former IPAC head of research Carlos "Gey" Espinheira, censors simply ignored these debates. It is unclear whether such regional differences in levels of repression stemmed from the vagaries of interviewees' memories, intellectuals' almost incomprehensibly privileged status in Bahia, their ties to Antonio Carlos Magalhães—who was raised by the Federal University of Bahia's rector and chosen by the military as Salvador's mayor from 1967 to 1970 and governor from 1971 to 1975 as well as from 1979 to 1983—or a decline in regional importance that left Salvador something of a backwater in relation to São Paulo or Rio de Janeiro. But the relative freedom of action of intellectuals working for IPAC had an effect on the linkage of the Pelourinho's populace and wider society: Ethnographic research, accepted as a tool in national development under the authoritarian regime, provided a mantle under which social scientists established a special relationship with residents of Salvador's red light district. In turn, these people, who had often labored in the domestic spaces of the bourgeois home, came to know in a related yet slightly different way their city's bourgeoisie and the state institutions that directed an authoritarian care at their everyday activities.

In the 1970s IPAC aligned itself with Maciel residents as their protector, frequently intervening in disputes with police and even posting bonds for those detained. As Director Castro suggested in 1997, social scientists in the 1970s had indeed begun to carve out a new way of treating the Brazilian people. Their investigations would demonstrate that both buildings and people suffered from a lack of attention and thus provide evidence as to the importance of supplanting police action with social programs. And during the darkest days of the dictatorship, IPAC began to hire Maciel/Pelourinho residents as office assistants, archivists, art restorers, and cleaning crews. This was novel in the early 1970s, a time when the majority of Bahian public employees were "white" and middle class. According to a number of IPAC managers with whom I spoke during the latest round of reforms, the bonds between middle-class personnel and residents led to a whispering campaign among public servants, and IPAC became known among civil servants as "prostitution's bureaucracy" and the "Institute of the Children of the Prostitutes" (*O Instituto dos Filhos da Puta*).[13]

In an interview in 1968 with Flávio Costa, the head of Salvador's newly established tourist authority, IPAC's director was clear in his focus on the integrated care of monuments and residents. Vivaldo da Costa Lima also recognized the effects of these actions on social science and state archives, which he juxtaposed to the people who "live in the Pelourinho":

> *We now boast a considerable archive of basic information about the Pelourinho's human element. That is, the people who live in the Pelourinho. . . . It is for them* that we restore things, reform houses and monuments. The man who lives there. The quotidian being, an actor in the landscape. The resident. The permanent and stable dweller. This is who must be considered first. Even in the midst of a project with clear touristic ends . . . the Foundation must direct its reforms at the existential condition of the residents of the area . . . to promote its residents: to valorize and humanize the thousands of people who live there in utterly precarious conditions. So for whom are we reforming the neighborhood? For those who will come to visit? Or also, and above all, for those who are there? *It would be an enormous lie on the part of urbanizers if the Foundation [IPAC], for example, were to emphasize the eviction of residents.*[14]

Costa Lima's concern with the permanence of residents in the face of the Pelourinho's restoration contrasts with an appeal on July 7, 1967 to police/military authorities, published in the crime pages of Salvador's major newspaper:

An unbelievable, inconceivable, unnamable absurdity . . . committed due to the repaving of Joao de Deus Street . . . and the detour of minibuses . . . through Gregório de Mattos street, the . . . most sordid of lows of this city's red light district . . . passengers, especially the housewives and young women (*especialmente senhoras e senhoritas*), oftentimes returning from work or even from the cinema, are obliged to witness shameful and immoral scenes. . . . Last Monday I witnessed a scene that caused great indignation in all of us, especially two married woman and a young woman (*duas senhoras e uma moçinha*), passengers in a van . . . along Gregório de Mattos street. A woman of the night, fighting with some marginal . . . took off . . . her clothes in the middle of the street even as she let loose with a barrage of curses! . . . In the name of decent families in four large neighborhoods, please find a solution any way you can and change the bus route, colonel![15]

The married women and the young *moça*—a word for "girl" that is also strongly associated with virginity—coming home from work or sanctioned leisure could not face the Maciel. Their exposure to so-called indecent women warranted a full-page newspaper article, appeals to military authorities, and an editorial in northeastern Brazil's oldest and most influential daily. *A Tarde* published another editorial calling for a rerouting of buses on September 14, 1967, pieces of which IPAC again reprinted in the study's 1969 and 1997 publications. Although the municipality eventually resolved the problem by returning buses to their original routes, the unexpected contact between different classes of Bahian women demonstrates the moral divisions within the city. It also left clear the prejudice and suspicion of Maciel residents that IPAC argued it would combat in the name of preserving the city's heritage and caring for an Afro-Bahian population configured in the process as both basic and threatening to society's fundaments. The first move in the restoration effort was to map the population and in the process codify the domestic norms of women understood as outside normal social systems. Ironically, as the *Survey* makes clear, a substantial percentage of those women surveyed in what is now the historical center had once worked as servants in one of the most private areas of Bahian life, the bourgeois home. How these former domestic servants, who had become seamstresses, prostitutes, street vendors, washwomen, nursemaids for their neighbor's children, and mothers in a teeming red light district, engaged, and became engaged by, Bahia's new cultural heritage bureaucracy presents an important means of exploring the public face of the nationalist fantasy of interracial romance. And this, in turn, suggests new ways of understanding shifts in Bahian racial politics that over the next decades would come to turn ever more tightly around ideas of rooted, African purity.

"Bohemia" and Social Science

Due in no small part to the ways civil society actors mobilized against military rule, the 1970s are a key moment in the rise of Brazil's Unified Black Movement and today's challenges to the myth of racial democracy. These were also critical years in the professionalization of a Bahian social science from whose ranks, some two decades later, IPAC Director Adriana Castro would claim to privilege human beings in and as Bahian heritage. Again, I suspect that her assertion, while emerging in the neoliberal 1990s, is more than a self-serving means of veiling or justifying the commodification of Afro-Bahian lifeways and the expulsion of the inhabitants of the Pelourinho.

Military and civilian technocrats who served the dictatorship in the 1970s, like their opponents on the Left, came to draw increasingly on social scientists' concerns with supposedly marginal people and techniques for documenting everyday life. In this environment, Bahian sociology and ethnography grew increasingly influential as methods for managing formative contradictions like "civilization and barbarism," or the concerns with degeneracy and a non-white citizenry that pop up in various guises and with varying effects across the Brazilian history that planners claim the Pelourinho "restoration" both preserves and brings to life.

Vivaldo da Costa Lima, one of Bahia's most influential twentieth-century social scientists, served as a broker between public intellectuals and international visitors, university professors, Candomblé practitioners, and Antonio Carlos Magalhães' coalition within the Bahian state while also directing IPAC in the greater part of the 1970s, and again during the earliest period of the 1992-to-present Pelourinho reforms. Although Costa Lima published relatively little before his death in 2010, preferring to formulate his thoughts in brilliant seminars or in meetings with his disciples in Pelourinho nightspots, this erudite teacher played a key role in training students, institutionalizing UFBA social science, and advancing the study of Afro-Bahian culture in Brazil and abroad. In fact, Professor Vivaldo, as he was usually referred to by Bahian social scientists, might be understood as straddling the border between elite, northeastern men of letters schooled in "essays and small facts drawn from national life" and the professional anthropologists, sociologists, and political scientists who would make the Bahian university system a vibrant center of investigation by the 1980s.[16]

Costa Lima's career, and his views of Bahian culture, took form in dialogue with his engagement with Afro-Brazilian religiosity. Trained as a dentist and heir to a distilled spirits empire, Professor Vivaldo was part of a long line of intellectuals fascinated by and active in trance and possession-based Candomblé.

Although its rites were outlawed officially until 1976, and actively suppressed through the 1940s by the same Bahian civil-police vice squad charged with regulating prostitution and gambling, Candomblé has been enormously influential in Bahian popular and elite religiosity, and self-definitions. It was also central to the populist political project of Professor Vivaldo's former school chum, Governor Antonio Carlos Magalhães, that extended from the 1950s to the first decade of the twenty-first century.[17] But while Magalhães is often accused of appropriating Afro-Bahian religion in a transformation of sacred rites into a commodifiable public culture, Costa Lima is recognized as an academic expert and active participant in Candomblé.

Professor Vivaldo's master's thesis is a classic in the study of Afro-Brazilian religion.[18] The analysis benefits from its author's status as advisor to one of Bahia's most illustrious Candomblé houses of worship (*terreiros*). It draws also on data from questionnaires administered at 113 terreiros associated with the Federal University of Bahia's Center for Afro-Oriental Studies (CEAO), an institution that Costa Lima helped establish as an intellectual and political force.[19] Here it seems important to note that Professor Vivaldo's work is acclaimed for its importance in social scientific debates over the preeminence of Jejé, or Nagô-based, African religion and ethnicity in Bahia. Costa Lima argued that the Jejé-Nagô version of Candomblé serves as an "orthodox ideal" for a majority of Bahian terreiros, thus indicating a widely-disseminated valorization of "the African origins of the older Candomblés" in Bahia.[20]

The director of IPAC, in an academic study written ten years after the "foundational" socioeconomic study of the Pelourinho and during a moment of increasing black politicization across Brazil, stresses African roots and the ongoing reinvention as well as preservation of African origins, rather than some mixed-race view of national progress. Such valorization suggests that even as broad sectors of the Bahian and federal states focused on narratives about brownness and hybridity in the 1970s and 1980s, the government's position was not monolithic. It would appear that Costa Lima rejected aspects of, even as he participated institutionally in, attempts to valorize an instrumentalized Afro-Bahian culture on the part of governments linked to the Magalhães political coalition during the military years. Yet my discussion here of Costa Lima's involvement in Candomblé and directorship of IPAC should not be read as the beginning of an argument about a neat, top-down colonization of the formerly reviled Pelourinho, and thus some culture manager's "invention" of Afro-Brazilian concerns with history and African origins.

Recently, anthropologists have emphasized the extent to which academics who study Candomblé may have overlooked the historical importance of global networks of African and Afro-Brazilian intellectuals.[21] These Black Atlantic travelers and ritual specialists played a major role in the nineteenth-century construction of Bahia as a region and Brazil as a nation. Such recognition of black intellectuals' agency sharpens existing arguments about academics' role in the canonization of certain Afro-Brazilian ritual forms and the marginalization of others, demonstrating that modern Candomblé is part of an often fractious dialogue, and never a simple or clear-cut imposition by elites who would manipulate a citizenry.[22] It also bears a conceptual and methodological affinity to my argument that the Pelourinho is more than a Disneyified simulacrum imposed by Bahian elites. Rather, it is a coconstruction worked out between bourgeois intellectuals who often participated in Candomblé and working-class, Afro-Bahian intellectuals located throughout Salvador. Among Bahia's most important intellectuals are Candomblé's priests and priestesses.

Candomblé and its initiates have been influential in the development of Brazilian nationalism and Bahian social science since at least the nineteenth century.[23] Nonetheless, and even as anthropologists and historians have begun to produce detailed studies of the making of Brazilian culture of the early and mid-twentieth century, and thus of Candomblé's move into a Bahian public sphere and tourist industry, the specific historical connections or modes of transmission that tie Candomblé's often secret ritual grammars, origin stories, and high priests and priestesses from Salvador's outlying neighborhoods to IPAC, as well as to the Pelourinho-based social movements like Olodum that by the 1980s had become so much a part of the historical center's landscape, remain understudied.[24] But it is clear that Costa Lima, both during and after his tenures as IPAC director, was part of a group of Bahian cultural experts who worked diligently with Candomblé leaders to establish Afro-Bahian traditions as canonically Brazilian. In doing so he sought proudly to reveal Afro-Brazilian religion in all of its beauty.[25] At times this effort seems to have supported a national level "racial democracy," and at other moments, especially within Salvador, it involved the celebration of African purity even as the country as a whole was supposedly characterized at this juncture by an emphasis on brownness.[26]

One result of attempts to valorize African heritage on the part of middle-class and wealthy intellectuals associated with Candomblé during the military regime and the subsequent redemocratization process was an increasingly resonant sense of the Pelourinho, and thus Bahia as a whole, as a bit of Africa in Brazil. This positioning of Bahia as Brazil's blackest and most traditional region, even if not intended by those who sought to valorize African roots, nonetheless supported a national-level narrative of racial mixture in which politicians and culture managers portrayed Bahia as making up one of the three legs of Brazil's Portuguese, African, and Native Brazilian triad. As my reader has experienced since being introduced to Manuel Bandeira's first impressions of the Pelourinho, this is not a new role. But Costa Lima's apparent attachment to and insistent valorization of an African root of the nation, rather than to and of a miscegenated national culture, complicates a neat narrative that would equate mid-1970s national-level emphases on hybridity to the actions of IPAC in the Pelourinho.[27]

Again, Costa Lima served as an *ogã* to one of Bahia's most eminent houses of Candomblé.[28] The ogã often sits on a special stool alongside the head priests or priestesses during rituals and special events.[29] He is typically something of an upper-class patron of a temple, and thus in certain ways a survival of earlier periods of police repression. These allies, often drawn in the past from academia or politics because their presence might inhibit or generate warnings about police raids while providing access to powerful members of society, are not required to pass through the ritual induction process expected of full participants (*filhos do santo*). In my experience, an ogã is often several skin-tones lighter than the people surrounding him. However, this observation about color points to a certain disparity between my U.S.-influenced racial commonsense and that at play in Bahia, especially prior to the late 1980s.

From my naturalized North American perspective, unless they are "passing" and obscuring an invisible origin, people who appear white are indeed not black. Nonetheless, in a Bahian racial ideology in which even those whose lighter phenotypes might permit them to avoid blackness typically trace their Brazilian selves at least in part to a real or imagined black origin, the genealogical or historically and genetically substantiable relationship between surface appearances and actual origins is much less clear. Within this breach, a variety of people who a U.S. citizen might describe as appearing European may in Brazil claim African ancestry. This enables them to affirm selectively their relationship to blackness without being classified permanently as black. The possibility of such a move is important in a city like Salvador, which is usually considered to be about 80 percent black and where black people still make up a disproportionate percentage of the poor, the unemployed, and those murdered by police.

Costa Lima, who was decidedly elite and who I used to visit in his home in a gated community in one of Salvador's most expensive neighborhoods, was indeed classified by at least some noted outsiders, including Simone de Beauvoir whom he once squired about Salvador, as "swarthy."[30] He was, as at least one of his most eminent students told me, a *branco da Bahia*, or "Bahian white."[31] This means he appeared white in Brazil's blackest state, but carried with him a selectively acknowledged African ancestry that set him off as exceptional within the larger Brazilian nation. This branco da Bahia category highlights the space between phenotypical qualities and ancestry, a problematic that comes to the fore in a public and increasingly objectified manner in Brazil's racial shifts after the 1990s. And the reifications of origins and African culture that are so much a part of IPAC, police, and NGO activity in the Pelourinho are, as accentuated by the sorts of social scientific techniques, personal relationships, and approaches to culture I am beginning to focus on ethnographically in introducing the social scientists who built IPAC, a key part of this process. This is why Costa Lima's attachment to African roots and Candomblé, rather than mixed-race futures, is a critical part of charting the relationship between IPAC and residents within Bahia's race relations.

Ilê Axé Opô Afonjá, the Candomblé temple or "house" to which Costa Lima belonged, is well known as one of the sites where a valorization of African authenticity and a rejection of syncretism, especially between Catholic saints and African deities, emerged by the 1980s. Costa Lima's valorization of African roots may very well have been forged in dialogue with the members of Ilê Axé Opô Afonjá, or even contributed to its development. One might thus uncover Afro-Bahian sources for the state-directed machinations that produced the Pelourinho as Brazil's heart and cradle and, as I explore subsequently, played an important role in transforming how African origins and Brazil's public culture were configured by the end of the twentieth century. Yet dialogues between the recognized intellectuals in charge of the Pelourinho and Candomblé's organic intellectuals require more careful consideration in order to be brought into an argument about the ways that what went on within terreiros may have played a role in the interclass dialogues that have shaped Bahian patrimony. This is not something I have performed yet. Additionally, and to complicate matters, by the early 1990s a significant number of Pelourinho residents vehemently rejected Candomblé and its imagery. This may be due to residents' tendency to associate Candomblé with Antonio Carlos Magalhães' coalition and their state's attempt to commodify their lifeways. Or it may have to do with the influence of neo-Pentecostal churches, which have over the last two decades attacked Candomblé in increasingly aggressive, and even violent, manners. Nonetheless, and in spite of neighborhood leaders' and local social movements' recourse to Afro-Bahian religious imagery in their political programs, there is little convincing evidence that Candomblé played an important role in the lives of the majority of Pelourinho residents, even in the 1970s and 1980s. In fact, by the 1990s, many of these people argued to me that Candomblé represented a state-sponsored and elite mechanism for making them "folkloric," or enactors of a version of Afro-Brazilianness that corresponded more closely to the desires of people like Vivaldo da Costa Lima than to their own conceptions of what it is to be black in Brazil.

Whatever Costa Lima's ultimate relationship to something called "racial democracy" or to the sources of what is now a profound emphasis on authentic African roots practiced in Salvador's preeminent houses of Candomblé, the physically decaying and notorious Maciel/Pelourinho "to which he was attached by an umbilical cord" offered him a chance to ground his love of Bahian culture, to attempt to produce a monument to Afro-Bahianness as he envisioned it, and to work to mold that character as he saw fit.[32] And, in addition to the influence of Candomblé—something that remains to be described adequately on the basis of future research—the documentation available in IPAC's archives today suggests yet another means by which Costa Lima and his associates came to coproduce public culture and Bahian history with the people of the Pelourinho. This path involves sexuality.

Candomblé, while serving as a ritual grammar and source of power in myriad Bahian social realms, has long been linked complexly to sexuality. From elite fears about licentious slaves, to Ruth Landes' near banishment from the corpus of professional social scientists in the late 1940s due to her rumored relationship with the Bahian folklorist Edson Carneiro and her broaching of the subject of Candomblé priestesses' sexuality, and on to more contemporary disputes about priests' association with homosexuality and the historical development of gender roles in this Afro-Bahian religion, Candomblé's ties to sexuality are something of a Brazilian public secret.[33] In Paul Christopher Johnson's recent analysis of the transformation of Candomblé into national culture, or the patrimony of the nation, secrecy becomes an incitement to discourse that preserves an imagined Africa as the nation's and its religions' root. Johnson is explicit about this argument's debt to Michel Foucault's analysis of the creation of modern subjectivity in relation to public talk about private sexuality in Europe.[34] This is an important point in relation to the Pelourinho, where I have begun to suggest that a group of powerful social scientists linked to Candomblé came to configure cultural heritage as part of a dialogue about morality and Brazilian origins. Even more than it drew on religion, this exchange took form in relation to sexual practices and gendered norms that point at a very different set of publicly circulating myths about the roots of Luso-Brazilian civilization.

As Professor Jeferson Bacelar, former head of the CEAO, Costa Lima's student at UFBA, and IPAC's director of research in the late 1970s, told me, "We admired Vivaldo so much. We thought he was the only person capable of driving the Pelourinho project, that Vivaldo was interested in the situation of the poor. I mean it was all a romantic vision woven around one figure . . . Vivaldo was the owner of the Pelourinho." Like his schoolmate, "Governor" Antonio Carlos Magalhães, Costa Lima was a bohemian and a carouser and a wonderful talker who rarely shied away from a boisterous philosophical discussion, a fight, or a night of drinking in the city's houses of ill-repute.[35] Less famous members of the research team may also have been schooled in the same lifestyle. As Bacelar told me,

> [when I became an IPAC researcher] I already had lots of experience with prostitution. I'd already made lots of [male and female] friendships through prostitution. . . . My generation spent lots of time in brothels. . . . I used to go to . . . a beautiful cabaret where we practically lived. Once in a while we'd go to the beach, go swimming with the girls. I mean, this was another reality. I mean, I've lived in that world, because that was the world of, well, sex. And for making friends too.

This homosocial space of the red light district was vital to political life, especially for populist politicians. In 2008, former governor João Durval and Salvador's former mayor Mário Kertesz, who in the mid-1980s initiated a restoration of the Pelourinho that remained underfunded due to opposition from Antonio Carlos Magalhães, who occupied the governorship at the time and with whom Kertesz had broken politically, engaged in a glowing, nostalgic discussion of the red light district's importance to their masculinity, their lives, and thus to Bahian politics. Entitled "It's the Prostitution Zone, It's the Red Light District: That's Where People Constructed Themselves and their Sociabilities," this edition of a left-leaning political magazine celebrates memories of barroom brawls and masculine kinship, gay chamber maids, anal sex with specific prostitutes, the location of the "best" brothels, and generous madames who sponsored Candomblé-related feasts for the neighborhood.[36] Ordep Serra, chair of UFBA's Department of Anthropology from 1997 to 1999, my esteemed teacher, and another former director of IPAC during the administration of Governor João Durval (1983–87), has also written about this environment, albeit in a somewhat more analytic manner:

> There was . . . considerable separation between girls and boys. . . . We had lots of girlfriends, up to a point, and "love" was perhaps the only context in which youths of opposite sexes entered into any relationship. . . . There was little friendship outside of flirting and dating, and dating was fairly timid. . . . I lived through a time in which we had our virgin and upstanding girlfriend and another "flip-flop," as we used to say. . . . This means that the young boy had his girlfriend and was at the same time a steady customer of a prostitute.[37]

These statements underscore the extent to which masculinity was performed in visits to brothels, and thus the Pelourinho. Given the influence of Costa Lima, Bacelar, and Serra in producing the historical center and Bahian

Figure 3.1. Sketch of Pelourinho women and "bohemians" or malandros by the local artist Reginaldo Bonfim, a former student of noted modernist painter Di Cavalcanti.

culture as objects of admiration throughout Brazil and the world, and Kertesz and Durval to late-twentieth-century Bahian politics, their relationships to the red light district point to the role of sexuality in heritage. This is not, however, to boil down researchers' ties to the Pelourinho as revolving around sexuality, to tie sexuality within Candomblé directly to sexuality in the red light district, or to suggest that Bahia's best-known anthropologists all support a myth of racial democracy predicated on intimacy between powerful men and non-white women. In fact, as far as I know, none of these anthropologists has espoused a nationalist version of brownness. Yet sexuality does seem to have played a role in the social scientific approach to the people and cultural manifestations developed by IPAC personnel in the Pelourinho. As Bacelar emphasizes and IPAC publications point out, the downtown red light district was off-limits to respectable women and children. There, men of a particular class position could appear with working-class women as sexual partners, friends, and social scientific subjects at a moment when Bahia's intellectual and political establishment was celebrating Candomblé as a matriarchy as well as Bahia's quintessential religion and cultural expression.

Jaime Quatro, today a carpenter for IPAC, describes the Maciel of the 1970s in the following manner: "My father is a Sá, a cousin of Angelo Calmon. He left his family to live with my mom who 'made life' (*fazia vida*) in the Maciel. That's why I'm a *sarará*; my mother's black and my father's white."[38] This space of encounters is also where Umbuzada, a sanitation supervisor mentioned in chapter 1, moved after he left his first family in order to live with Dona Pió. And it is the place to which Dona Pió fled after deciding that walking for five days along the beach to escape her father in a village on the north coast of Bahia should not serve as a path into a career cleaning the bathrooms and kitchens of Salvador's bourgeoisie. And finally, it is the neighborhood in which Dona Pió's contemporary, Dona Katia, escaped the terrors of the sertão and the rich white woman's house into which she had been placed as a servant.

The Maciel/Pelourinho is and was a zone of mixture, but a mixture that is both celebrated as a source of social solidarity and employed as a symbol of an Afro-Bahianness against which modernity and non-Black Bahian identities have been secured since the 1940s. Such hybridity looks little like the seamless account of some "thing" called racial democracy so often located at the heart of Brazil and analyzed by social scientists today, especially in North America. Rather, it is a space for constructing inclusionary and exclusionary impetuses that lie at the core of the production of national history and community. In this sense, mixture works as a figure akin to what J. Lorand Matory describes as "'African purity,' [which] in the end, is less a consensual norm of belief and cooperative action than a shared symbolic meta-logic available for use in cooperative or competitive projects."[39] And it appears, as I detail in subsequent chapters, that this metalogic is becoming more generalized in Salvador today, in the context of the Pelourinho restoration.

Like the myth of racial democracy, generally understood as a culturalist response to European disqualification of a purportedly racially degenerate Brazil, Bahian social scientists' relativist explanation of Pelourinho residents' insalubriousness during the 1970s sought to replace explanations of and solutions to the neighborhood's degeneracy couched in a language of Christian religion with an objective, developmentalist social science. Led by Costa Lima, the progressive researchers responsible for the knowledge that would help secure UNESCO approval of Salvador as a world heritage center wove accounts of Pelourinho residents' extraordinary resilience and battles for survival.[40] However, even as they sought to argue that Pelourinho residents did in fact have their own culture and social systems that "made sense," IPAC researchers often employed metaphors that recalled Church denigrations of people's lifeways. One example involves Professor Vivaldo's comments in 1969 about the foundational study he conducted in 1967: "Nor did we direct our research toward the sanitary and public health aspects of the local population, something that would undoubtedly reveal the pathetic situation of its disgraced humanity."[41] Sexuality was the object on which IPAC focused in working to resolve, and thus in constructing, this fallenness. Yet sexuality, like race, was and is never pure, or a thing in itself. Rather, and as an incitement to discourse, sexuality functioned as a path for passage from interior spaces like brothels, colonial mansions, and colonial-mansions-turned-brothels, to the public life of the nation and the "beauty" of Bahia.

IPAC Ethnographers and their "Sexy Subjects"

After Professor Vivaldo moved to the IPAC director's office in 1969 he appointed as research director his student, Carlos "Gey" Espinheira. Assisting was Jeferson Bacelar, who would take over when Espinheira resigned in the wake of an unflattering film on Pelourinho poverty produced by his brother, Tuna. As director, Bacelar worked also with researchers like Enrique Moreira and Carlos Caroso. The latter would help educate a generation of anthropologists, including the author of this chapter, and then, later in his career, take on the presidency of Brazil's national anthropological association (ABA) and the directorship of Salvador's Museum of Archaeology and Ethnology (MAE). These IPAC ethnographers who would become so influential sought, alongside their associates in the 1970s and early 1980s, to identify the special aspects of the Maciel and its people. In doing so they produced masses of reports such as "The Nursemaids of the Maciel" (1977) by João Jorge Amado, son of noted novelist Jorge Amado; "Leisure and Poverty" (1980); "Marriage as Understood and Lived by a Female Resident of the Maciel" (1980); "The Artists of Hunger" (1979); "Diagnosis of the Health of a Marginal Community" (1974); and "A Study of Morbidity in the Maciel" (1976).[42] Their interventions in the Maciel would, as read through their ethnographic production, follow North American anthropology in both opposing and reinforcing ideas about the "culture of poverty" with a new relativizing emphasis on community and resistance in the face of economic discrimination.

In 1984 Espinheira published *Divergência e prostituição: Uma análise sociológica da comunidade prostitucional do Maciel* (Divergence and Prostitution: A Sociological Analysis of the Maciel Community of Prostitution). It reworks the author's master's thesis supervised by Professor Vivaldo in 1972. Espinheira based his writings on life histories conducted between 1970 and 1973 with a randomly selected group of one third of the prostitutes included in the 1967–68 study, which gave rise to IPAC's foundational *Survey*. In spite of a naturalization of a hydraulic model of male sexuality, *Divergence and Prostitution* remains one of the most historically grounded and nuanced ethnographic representations of the Maciel produced to date.[43] Written near the apogee of rural-to-urban migration, it argues for an understanding of prostitution based not on physical difference, mental incapacity, or moral degradation, but on the inequitable socioeconomic conditions characteristic of Brazil's "economic miracle" supervised by the dictatorship.

Espinheira presents prostitution as a rational choice for working-class women, whom he argues could earn more in the Maciel than they might in the jobs open to them, especially the domestic service that Dona Katia fled. He describes prostitution as an "escape hatch" or "emergency valve" that makes sense for women who find themselves at the margins of society. Espinheira argues further that prostitution preserves the bourgeois family by satisfying men's desires for sex outside of marriage. He thus links prostitution and bourgeois morality, albeit in a different manner than I do in this book. In Espinheira's view, prostitution enables the continuation of "official" kinship relations by providing a natural realm for sex outside of the family. *Divergence and Prostitution*, as relativistic ethnographies tend to do by definition, thus makes prostitution understandable in light of Bahian socioeconomic, moral, and kin structures. And in putting forth this linkage, it provides a social scientific justification of the presence of poor Afro-Bahian migrants at the symbolic heart of Brazil.

Espinheira, the son of a prominent lawyer, explains to a Bahian "society" he addresses directly in his text that the feared, syphilitic, black, licentious, crumbling, and exotic historical center makes sense, and therefore should not be condemned, in light of Bahian social structure since "prostitution cannot be seen as a phenomenon that interferes with social process, but as a part of this social process that maintains it."[44] Like IPAC's foundational study in 1967, Espinheira counters explanations offered by the Church, police, and the hygienists. In this move to integrate, explain, and thus in a sense recuperate as logical and moral an Afro-Brazilian population, Espinheira presented those people as different in their lifeways, but nonetheless a part of Bahian society.

Espinheira's intervention recalls Janice Perlman's roughly contemporaneous attempt to show the extent to which residents of squatter settlements were an integrated and necessary part of Rio de Janeiro's economy, as well as Fernando Henrique Cardoso and Ernesto Faletto's related argument on a world-systems level.[45] Finally, and more in line with this chapter's argument, Espinheira's research is enduringly significant in terms of Bahian representations of the Pelourinho. It influences contemporary understandings in that it is precisely the sort of IPAC text enshrined in the institution's library and trundled out today for the benefit of schoolchildren, reporters, and foreign social scientists who arrive seeking to understand the neighborhood's transformation and roles in Brazilian life. Like Director Adriana Castro's redeployment of the foundational *Survey* in her story in 1997 of IPAC's rise, Espinheira's document is significant due not only to what it says, but also to what it performs today.

Jeferson Bacelar continued Professor Vivaldo's students' attempts to understand and resignify the Maciel in his *A Família da Prostituta* (The Family of the Prostitute), published in 1982. In this description of the lives of sex workers he encountered while at IPAC, Bacelar argues that Pelourinho families were not characterized by a lack of structure and affection. Instead, kinship in the Maciel/Pelourinho worked differently from the unmarked structures coded as normal elsewhere in Salvador. And this particular system of alliance gave rise to a variety of functional family relationships. Here Bacelar, along with his peers in IPAC, approached residents as a specific group bound by a culture of poverty whose values contrasted with those of the mainstream. Yet as expressed in his speech in 1976 at the "Seminar on Education in the Maciel," Bacelar did so to argue that they did not warrant censure:

> These people think, eat, drink, sit, love, and have families just like we do. But they live, too, although in a different way, as a result of differences in occupation, the subhuman conditions of their housing stock, police repression, hunger, and the ecological and economic segregation that characterizes the Maciel in our society. . . . This is the real portrait of the Maciel, a region of "poor people" whose minimal levels of subsistence and survival are the fruit of a system whose structural logic is inhuman.

Earlier in this keynote address he had pointed out,

> It is the obligation of the educator to identify opportunities for pedagogical interventions by educational institutions, especially as diagnosed by social scientists. . . . This is the "educational position" of the Foundation [IPAC] in the Maciel. Once we diagnosed the area, the Foundation elaborated an educational plan adjusted to the socioeconomic and cultural characteristics of the neighborhood. . . . This research allowed us to apply the concept of community to the Maciel. . . . The Maciel is a community due to its status as a human grouping with specific social, economic and cultural characteristics, tied together geographically. More specifically, it is a prostitutional zone configured around eight streets.[46]

This attempt to integrate, or explain, Maciel people and practices into and to a wider Bahian society illustrates how IPAC scientists, as part of a relativistic effort at inclusion, repeatedly configured the Maciel as a space characterized by a group of prostitutes with specific cultural characteristics. In a process akin to the research conducted in 1967 that led to the *Survey*, prostitutes' families thus took over the social scientific representations by and of Bahia's heritage institution: At the same time IPAC became known as the bureaucracy loaded with prostitutes, the community it served was, in the words of its most eminent scientist, "a prostitutional zone configured around eight streets." The institution's response in the 1970s, as opposed to its policies in the 1990s, was to educate.

Sexuality, Authoritarian Development, and Popular Culture

From 1970 to 1975 Professor Vivaldo and his students established a handicraft atelier, a daycare center, a cooking school, and ceded space to residents for neighborhood musical performances. In the words of the son of a former director of the handicraft school, they "sought to produce an autochthonous version of Pelourinho art. Just as each Indian group in the Amazon has its own crafts, well, Vivaldo wanted . . . residents to have their own way of making pottery, of painting landscapes, of making things that one can find only here!" Stories of the initiatives make up an important part of IPAC official history today but, curiously, they are little remembered by long-term Pelourinho residents.

Technico-folkloric educational efforts piggybacked on the Brazilian Literacy Movement (MOBRAL), a program established under the dictatorship through the incorporation of pedagogical techniques developed by progressive educators in the heady period of political and cultural ferment just prior to the suspension of democratic process. Designed to provide basic education to working-class Brazilians, MOBRAL began to function in Bahia in 1970 as a part of the military's push to produce a version of national culture that would establish the dictatorship as a "continuity, and not a rupture, thus making concrete its association with an ideology of national origins" related to the racialized incorporation of Brazil's Northeast.[47] This region has long been the nation's poorest and its residents face great prejudice in southern cities like São Paulo. Programs like MOBRAL made financing available to IPAC, money that Costa Lima and his team employed to fund ethnography and educational efforts that would begin to make concrete his transformation of the Maciel into the Pelourinho, and its population into folkloric subjects of the nation-state.

Bahia's first MOBRAL unit, designed to "give an integrated education," appeared between 1967 and 1968 in the Pelourinho, on the same Gregório de Mattos Street involved in the polemic over bus routes.[48] Newspapers touted its presentation of the history of carnival and other pre-Lenten public festivals. Soon, and following the growing federal emphasis after 1974 on establishing institutions designed to produce national culture, MOBRAL became "MOBRAL Cultural" even as its curriculum came to include sanitary education. According to Dona Erpidia, owner of a brothel on João de Deus Street from the early 1970s until the early 1990s, MOBRAL classes taught her to write her name. She could then sign her identity card. But she learned little else. When I asked about carnival or culture, she responded, in reference to the activities of those who occupied the spaces within her Catholic Church–owned apartment that she rented out to short-stay customers, "Carnival, carnival! I had carnival every night. . . . I heard some serious samba every night. What is IPAC gonna teach *me* about carnival?!? They gonna dance some saint dances for me, huh? *Oxente!!*"[49] Her statement is significant not only in terms of a rejection of carnival that associates MOBRAL with the iconic cultural festival, but also in her linkage of IPAC's educational efforts to "saint dances," or the possession-based rituals and trances at the core of the practice of Candomblé. This implied criticism of Candomblé as "high" Bahian culture in the 1970s, even as enunciated in an interview conducted in 2000, gestures at residents' perception that the final decades of the twentieth century had given rise in the Pelourinho to seemingly interrelated and parallel growth in Candomblé as a publicly available Bahian religion; a social science-based effort to recuperate the Maciel/Pelourinho and its populace as cultural heritage; and a snowballing engagement between IPAC and neighborhood residents around culture and moral education.

Dona Erpidia's peers with whom I spoke also remembered little, or chose to speak little, about MOBRAL efforts that they understood as "just another IPAC program" (*mais um programa da Fundação*). What Dona Erpidia recalled best from the 1970s, a memory seemingly reinforced by the institution's censuses of the 1990s, which were designed to prepare the removal and indemnification of residents, are social scientific questionnaires of the type employed in the 1969 *Survey*. But she was not really interested in the surveys' content. As she once told me as I began to quiz her about her education, her employment after arrival in Salvador as a domestic servant, and her understandings of family structure and kinship: "Goddamnit, John! Stop asking me those stupid questions—this is the same shit that IPAC has asked me a thousand times. You sound just like those pricks from IPAC!" As I write this chapter I heed her advice, as I did throughout the rest of the time I spent researching the relations between Pelourinho residents and their state: Rather than mimic IPAC's agendas in an attempt to produce data that would be "better," and hence challenge the institution's conclusions directly and on their own terms, I seek to understand the methods for, and effects of, generating such information. Or, put another way, I work to understand how IPAC's identification of areas of social life that required state intervention spurred additional talk about related topics. And such talk typically involved attempts to define the hidden bases of sociability in the Maciel so as to explain, and recuperate, them.

People recall much about the 1970s, including police raids, fights, sexual trysts, and the movements, research agendas, and peccadilloes of IPAC employees. But MOBRAL and handicraft classes are not important in the histories told by anyone besides current and former IPAC employees. There are hundreds of artisans working in jewelry, stone, leather, and a plumbing resin called "Durepoxi," but none admit to having been trained by IPAC. Dona Erpidia's fifty-four-year-old son, Neném, and his schoolmate Jubiací, both born and raised in the Maciel, recall classes in handicrafts in their elementary school curricula. But neither really remembers what they learned, who taught them, and how long they studied. This is true for a majority of their subjects, not just handicrafts. The classes may well have been arts and crafts lessons as part of a standard curriculum, and thus may have had little to do with the professionalizing programs that IPAC officials report were instituted in the 1970s. Dona Miuda, employed in IPAC's library across the 1990s, claims to have taught some of these crafts classes and to have helped in establishing the Foundation's *Casa do Artesão* (Crafter's House). But she too can remember nothing of the curriculum or her students. Dona Miuda's overall disengagement from the texts she catalogues today and resolute clockwatching suggest to me that she may have expressed about the same level of interest in her position in the handicrafts courses of the 1970s! Yet my intuition is untested, and may very well be incorrect.

The paucity of memory around the handicrafts projects called "Professionalizing Schools" (*Escolas Profissionalizantes*), as well as IPAC's mid-1970s "Center for Attention to Minors" (*Centro de Atenção ao Menor*), and the "Maciel Recreational and Cultural Center" (*Centro Cultural Recreativo do Maciel*), suggests the programs were more ad hoc initiatives than totalizing institutions. Like many state projects, they may have been "phantasms" or public relations ploys designed to give the appearance of attention to popular needs while facilitating the management of unruly populations. Thus it is unclear whether residents' memories reflect IPAC programs accurately. But it *is* significant that the tools people remember best are not classes designed to make them productive artisans. They are the questionnaires administered to examine family arrangements and domestic space.[50] And the data produced make up a significant percentage of the material stored in IPAC archives today.

IPAC archives, like the interactions between residents and researchers, became a site for producing the histories that the Pelourinho would begin to instantiate and authorize in the 1990s. As Michel-Rolph Trouillot has argued influentially, the production of history might usefully be broken into four stages: the moment of "fact creation (the making of *sources*) . . . fact assembly (the making of *archives*) . . . fact retrieval (the making of *narratives*) and . . . retrospective significance (the making of *history* in the final instance)."[51] In Salvador, IPAC's shelves are packed with training manuals and educational plans, some of which appear in this chapter. The programs described, alongside the even more influential studies and questionnaires, seem to have encouraged a specific disposition toward history in the Pelourinho: The historical facts produced about the Pelourinho, and redeployed in narratives in manners exemplified by IPAC's 1997 institutional history, are not accounts of what most people involved consider to be important events. Rather, they are the crystallized records of specific habits, dispositions, desires, and tastes teased out of the everyday lives of Pelourinho residents by social scientists at various points in time, or what Trouillot describes as the moment of "fact creation" by means of a "making of sources" to be assembled by IPAC archivists.

Written into government-commissioned ethnographies, or historical interpretations of accretions of facts that are in turn stored alongside an array of questionnaires, unfinished projects, blueprints, letters, and internal memoranda, these human dispositions become a part of IPAC's store of knowledge about the Pelourinho and its people. Thus the interactions between the Pelourinho's working-class populace and state gentrification officials who rose from the ranks of, and took form as intellectuals among, Bahia's bohemians produce the raw material of history. This "evidence" includes the mass of documents contained in IPAC's archives and consulted by reporters, students, and visiting academics today.

As Dona Erpidia's reactions to me suggest, the process of information collection, or what might be termed governance through research, does more than produce content, or facts for consumption and re-elaboration. It helps spur among Pelourinho residents a mode of relating to their state government that may have had something to do with Dona Katia's encouragement of my own collection of her life history as she lay dying, still selling cocaine from her bedroom.

The Looping Effect: Pelourinho Representations

In June 2000 Jeferson Bacelar told me,

> The population of the Maciel became expert in social scientific research. It's the same as people involved in Candomblé today, who are all experts in research. . . . IPAC did so many quantitative studies. Every year we had to check out the population. They [residents] already knew, they were so used to researchers that when you asked . . . the questionnaire was like "name, sex, age" and if you passed on the "sex" they'd say, "Hey, you're gonna ask my sex, aren't you?" They already knew all the questions by heart. They'd say "You didn't ask me this and that!" Do you know what I mean? This happened so much that I stopped doing that sort of research.

In support of Bacelar's claims, in March 1999 I interviewed a man I will call Bulindo, a somewhat successful forty-eight-year-old drug wholesaler on the 28, the area presented by IPAC social scientists in the 1990s as full of "deviants." Yet Bulindo worked also as a security guard for a corporation that protected IPAC buildings and he arrived in the Maciel in the late 1970s, a period from which he claims to recall IPAC scientists scurrying about, measuring the population. Across his adult life, then, Bulindo maintained a close relationship to IPAC as a contract employee, as a potential producer of Bahian expressive culture, and as the occupant of a problematic building famed for drug selling that IPAC sought repeatedly to quantify, know, and pacify through research. He is also a heterosexual man who arrived in the Pelourinho on his own and who is therefore not a part of a family group headed by a woman like Dona Katia. I provide this information, and discuss his statements, because Bulindo employs a language of research and sexual morality that helps illustrate the extent to which research has impacted the stories of Pelourinho identity told by residents.[52]

During one of our meetings, Bulindo received a visitor who brought him a threatening letter from a prison inmate with whom he was involved in a dispute. "This one's for the archive, for the dossier," he told me in a menacing tone as he slipped the paper into a plastic binder of the type carried by IPAC social scientists and construction foremen. "I want this in case something happens to that boy." He then stated, in response to a question about the differences between the Pelourinho and peripheral working-class neighborhoods,

> Here there are no taboos. Here, a guy wants to be gay, he comes out when he's twelve and starts living with an old guy, some fifty-year-old fart. In the neighborhood it's at age eighteen, twenty, and the kid still has to study, graduate, get a job so that he can build his own space, his place for winning his independence. Here a person, when he is born, is born into a powerful disgrace. Back in the days when the Maciel was the Maciel you had thieves' wives screwing policemen, the same thieves hooking up with their prostitute neighbors, damned stool pigeons taking it from behind from drug dealers, pickpockets fooling around with shoplifters. And a bunch of sweet-talking "bohemians" on the weekends. It was some . . . life, that Maciel.

Bulindo's shift from the present to the old life of the Maciel marks the neighborhood as both a spatial and temporal concept. Today the Maciel, as opposed to the Pelourinho, is a fading but still powerful image of decay, marginalization, freedom, and sexual licentiousness. The avowedly heterosexual Bulindo recalls this time/space through the possibilities the neighborhood offers to a gay and apparently fictional teenager. Earlier in our interview, Bulindo had recounted his arrival as a street child too wild for his home neighborhood, the working-class suburb of São Caetano. He claimed to prefer hanging out downtown, smoking marijuana and picking people's pockets, over joining the boys in his neighborhood in catching crabs and snatching mangoes from neighbors' trees. But in his description of what the Maciel was "really" like before its transformation into the Pelourinho, he employs a non-normative sexuality to narrate a boyhood voyage downtown and toward a wider world of new identities.

This Maciel stands as a place for coming out, for a young man's struggle to express his inner self, as Bulindo did in making a name and a substantial amount of money after moving downtown. Rather than emerging from a domestic sphere fully formed and prepared for life in the city center, Bulindo and his doppelgänger emplot themselves in a journey in which one's own space is possible only outside the home and the arduous work of childhood education and domestic responsibility. According to Bulindo, true personhood is available in the swirling Maciel red light district of ruined colonial-mansions-turned-brothels where it seems that a "powerful disgrace" permits one to be whomever one wants.

Bulindo's story of a coming out in the Maciel, which makes the city center stand as a fallen public sphere to which subjects arrive from the domestic spaces of homes in far-off neighborhoods, turns on a narration of interior dispositions and domestic habits. His story of an unnamed protagonist's becoming a publicly imagined or recognized gay man involves a coupling with another older, and hence by association wealthier and perhaps dominant, man. In this account the Maciel takes form via a taxonomy of ostensibly hidden sexual acts and neighborhood types, mainly lawbreakers. These locate people in a continuum of power extending from thieves' wives to the police, and on to a police informant who Bulindo indicates deserves penetration. Here relations in a public sphere responsible in great part for defining cultural citizenship are imagined in terms of obscured, private, sexual, and affective ties that distinguish people according to their competencies, moral statuses, and practices in the Maciel. The claim that it is thieves' wives who are having sex with policemen, and not the policemen who are having sex with thieves' wives, suggests the power of Maciel women to choose their own partners and to use sexual relations instrumentally, perhaps to aid their husbands or perhaps as a sign of their independence from those spouses.

Even as he contrasts the small-town morals of Salvador's neighborhoods with the Pelourinho's licentiousness, thus dichotomizing the two types of neighborhood, Bulindo emphasizes that the Pelourinho's sociability emanates from domestic and affective relationships permitted in a space whose very publicness is constructed in tension with the private. This move rests on domestic relations that Bulindo reveals to the visiting foreign anthropologist in a manner that suggests his familiarity with the sorts of classifications and accretions of evidence so much a part of IPAC ethnographies of his neighborhood.

As should be clear, and in spite of dominant representations about its populace's immorality, the Pelourinho is more than a venue for sexual relations and social scientists' cataloguing of relations between powerful men and less powerful women whom I struggle to empower through anthropological narrative. Rather, according to Bulindo, the Maciel/Pelourinho permits youths from Salvador's periphery to find themselves in a world of distinct human types established through their sexuality. Bulindo thus offers a history of morality and social structures that corresponds in important ways to IPAC researchers' discussions of disgrace and a Pelourinho exceptionalism. Meanwhile, Espinheira argued that prostitution in the Maciel of the 1960s and 1970s works alongside, and makes sense in light of, the dominant structures of bourgeois kinship in the Bahia of the 1970s. And the Maciel appears as a special place for Bulindo because it allows for escape from the strictures of the neighborhood. And Bulindo tells his story in a manner that recalls IPAC ethnographers' categories of analysis.

In employing archives and dossiers, and a language of collection, in amassing information about his rivals, Bulindo produces a history that is close to what I present as the IPAC production of histories around its archives. To make my point clearer, let us recall that in writing about North America, Lauren Berlant and Michael Warner argue that the nation's "intimate public sphere" is produced around "a historical relation to futurity . . . restricted to generational narrative and reproduction" through the normalization of heterosexuality, rather than through alternative versions of community "imagined through scenes of intimacy, coupling, and kinship."[53] From this perspective, a public sphere arises in opposition to stories of homosexual intimacy and coming out. The analogy to the Pelourinho, a space that stands as both counterpoint and essential component of the Brazilian imaginary, is thus pertinent. Yet the account of Pelourinho community put together by Bulindo, a thrice-married, forty-five-year-old man now living with the nineteen-year-old daughter of his long-term friend, revolves around homosexual intimacy. Bulindo recollects his own journey to the Pelourinho around a gay teenager destined to encounter his own space by living downtown with his older lover. Even as Bulindo suggests that such aspirations are impossible in the rest of Salvador, he places them at the center of the Pelourinho's history. And the Pelourinho's history is that which the state government of Bahia employed to narrate *all* Brazilian history. Most important, the very terms by which this history is recountable have been coconstructed by Pelourinho residents and IPAC social scientists during the struggle from 1967 to the present to transform the Maciel into a UNESCO World Heritage site.

To point out that emphases granted to non-normative sexuality in Brazil and the United States diverge is not to argue that Brazilians are somehow more tropically open than the puritanical Yankees. Instead, it is to rework for the case of Bahia the "historical relation to futurity" that Berlant and Warner claim occurs in the United States through a normalization of heterosexual reproduction that leaves no space for alternative sexualities. Hence futurity in the United States may be constructed around the reproduction of properly heterosexual relationships, while in the Pelourinho history and heritage are produced by a cataloguing and a taxonomizing of homosexual and heterosexual relationships rescued from the "margins" by IPAC ethnographers involved in the Pelourinho's "reconstruction." This recuperation is the most critical aspect of the last three decades' ethnographic production of national history in Bahia. But it is not simply categories and grammars for producing history that emerge from the interactions between a moralizing IPAC and the Pelourinho's population in the 1970s and 1980s.

Bulindo's discussion of Pelourinho types and their sexual relations includes, almost as an aside, the "bohemians." The term, used infrequently in Salvador today except by older journalists who specialize in writing cultural pieces for the city's dailies, was employed regularly through the 1980s by both the wealthy and the poor to refer to Bahian men famed for their drinking, dancing, singing, and sexual activity in the Pelourinho. To be a bohemian was to exercise one's privilege in a space for politicking, commercial dealings, and the establishment of fictive kinship between men of the same class and men and women of different classes. And such "being" bohemian arose in relation to the modes of being Afro-Bahian that IPAC and residents alike surveyed, practiced, and represented.

Recognition in Death: Dona Katia, the Bohemian, and Memorialization

When Dona Katia died in July 1999, her remains lay in the morgue outside the Hospital Ana Nery until her former landlady Stella Manhattan and I broke into her room, found her clothing, and took a bus to the neighborhood of Pau Miudo to dress the body. When we arrived nobody could tell us if Katia had really died and, if so, where the body lay. The two of us, a bedraggled white gringo and a pot-bellied cross-dressing father of two without his wig and makeup but clad in a sequined T-shirt that set off his silicone breasts, drew stares as we were not the normal fare of this public hospital. Finally, an elderly gentleman wearing the white clothes and polished two-tone shoes of a 1970s dandy approached and asked, "Is that the woman from the Pelourinho? Are you two looking for the old lady from the Pelourinho who died last night of heart failure?" "Yes, thank God," we replied almost in unison as he took us down a corridor while promising to discover her whereabouts.

The man, part of that group of cash-rich public servants so important to Salvador's postwar growth and intellectual production, told us, "I *knew* that woman. She was famous in the Pelourinho, wasn't she? *Everyone knew her.* She used to be quite beautiful, but was in really bad shape when they brought her in! Did you see her swollen legs? Come down here with me and I'll show you where she is." The elderly "bohemian" took us to the morgue where he flung open the doors to reveal Katia's ashen body amid a smell that disturbs as I write.

There, next to the Hospital Ana Nery's garbage dumpsters and parking lot, we stared numbly at Dona Katia as the bohemian babbled on, "Yeah, I'll tell you, man, in my day I'd spend every weekend in the red light district (*brega*). That's a part of my life I don't really think about now, but I remember with pleasure. I wouldn't be who I am today if it weren't for the Maciel." Like an Angel of History measuring the movement of a life lived well against Dona Katia's already rigid body, the bohemian prattled on, narrating himself and his exploits in the Maciel/Pelourinho of the 1960s and 1970s. Without really listening, but nonetheless feeling his words rolling across Dona Katia's corpse and penetrating me, I experienced an enormous emptiness as my jailed friend's mother lay on a slab, seemingly inert like a writing pad or a thick book the bohemian consulted so as to load his memories with people and events while charting his progress across life. As I wondered what would come next, Stella, ever practical and accustomed to this role due to the frequent deaths of his peers, moved to dress the body so the ambulance could carry it to a burial paid for by a city assemblywoman.

Dona Katia had been quite famous, first as a prostitute, thief, and lover to powerful men outside the neighborhood and then as "Katia Agafan," one of the Maciel's most famous drug dealers. She made and lost fortunes selling marijuana and the injectibles popular in the years before cocaine. Among them was the depressant Agafan, which gave Dona Katia one of her nicknames, and whose use and damage to her circulatory system may have caused her massively swollen legs in the 1990s. She had come to own two refrigerators and two cars and had been made *comadre* to a French priest from the opulent Igreja de São Francisco, all while supporting a legion of lovers and husbands.[54] Dona

Katia had even managed to buy a house in Salvador's outlying working-class neighborhood of Mata Escura. She supported her brother in her home city of Feira de Santana and paid for her mother's stay in a nursing home in Salvador.

While Dona Katia's peers sometimes criticized her excessive desire and "hunger" for men who lived off her work, she chose those men and controlled her household finances, something stigmatized by the IPAC statistics and their mode of presentation. At the height of her power and fame, Dona Katia found herself a long way from the country-bumpkin teenager who had fled the white woman's house on the vaguely European side of town after, as she remembers it, throwing a pot of boiling water on her employer when she complained that Katia had eaten too much while preparing the family's meal.

Dona Katia seems quite heroic. She is an exceptional woman who fought the whirlwind of rural-urban migration, familial disaggregation, and domestic service that IPAC science offers as an explanation for the marginalization, and the resilience, of the working class in Salvador's post-1964 emergence from the "Bahian enigma," or the long decline that began with the transfer in 1763 of the national capital to Rio de Janeiro.[55] But that is a problem.

A Message in the Explanation

Given the history of the uses of the field of knowledge produced about the Pelourinho and its residents, Dona Katia's life cannot simply be rescued by a North American anthropologist who argues for some distinctive and experiential affinity to the people of the Pelourinho. This "people" or "population" is a discursive construct substantially indebted to IPAC ethnographic research that serves to code a host of actors, usually male social scientists, politicians, and cultural managers from outside the community, as authentic connoisseurs and purveyors of Bahianness. Like the bohemian who could tell his autobiography across Dona Katia's corpse, or Don Quixote's narrator who discovered the long-lost, soiled text, they know Bahia because they know the Pelourinho's residents and their everyday lives. And in Bahia, the greater the interlocutor's knowledge of the Pelourinho's population, the greater that person's authority and sense of personhood: Perpetual "Governor" Antonio Carlos Magalhães, Professor Vivaldo da Costa Lima, Professor Jeferson Bacelar, Professor Gey Espinheira, the "bohemian" hospital employee, and Professor John Collins are but a miniscule and variegated sampling of those who have lived in or passed through Bahia and been blessed as being "of the land" (*da terra*) through their association with the Pelourinho and its Afro-descendent people.

Idealized representations of motherhood and working-class struggle constitute a sentimental idiom through which IPAC ethnographers present Pelou-

Figure 3.2. Dona Katia and the foreign social scientist while her son was imprisoned, 1998.

rinho landscapes and residents as the ground of a national history coded as the erudite product of professional historians, anthropologists, and sociologists. For example, my reader may recall that Dona Katia wanted a version of her story to be told. She wanted people to know, by means of the account that her son's friend and a North American anthropologist would produce, that she did not mean to kill others' children. And she hoped to enunciate that she was not a bad mother, despite the fact that she rejected both the paid and unpaid domestic roles expected of her. Dona Katia's attempts to tell her story through the relatively powerful anthropologist who, like those IPAC social scientists in charge of documenting the lifeways of Pelourinho women, now presents a part of her life history to a public, reveal important details about mechanisms for the crafting of Bahian history in the late twentieth century.

On the one hand, by emphasizing the ways that Pelourinho residents, and especially women, stand as a misunderstood minority whose lifeways are in fact understandable and sensible in light of dominant morals, IPAC's social scientists of the 1970s produced a body of knowledge that filled the archives from which the history of the Pelourinho's restoration, and Bahia's role in the nation, would come to be written in the moment in the 1990s when I interviewed Dona Katia. This history helped establish the boundaries between "moral" families and residents of the red light district, and thus the standpoint from which Katia spoke. By focusing on the ways that Pelourinho residents, and especially women, took form as a special group whose lifeways were supposedly understandable and sensible in light of dominant morals, IPAC's social scientists produced a body of knowledge that continues to help codify the boundaries between "moral" bourgeois and elite families and residents of the red light district.

This situation, then, even as it supports a Brazilian ideology of purportedly salutary and exceptional national mixture, or racial democracy, also sets up a series of exclusions that help establish different social groups through oppositions. Both the Pelourinho and racial democracy are, in ways both similar and dissimilar, impossible spaces in which a series of contradictions are mediated and covered, at least contingently, by structures of feeling tied to the interactions between the Pelourinho's mainly female and Afro-Bahian population and middle-class men. And this is a relationship that produces, or parades as, national history.

Mothers, Authenticities, and Voices

This chapter began with Dona Katia lamenting her status as a mother whose children had been taken away and whose selling of crack cocaine seems to her to have spirited away the children of other women. Yet Dona Katia told me on numerous occasions that she never wanted children who would be burdens and prevent her from living as she desired. Often, in the same moments, I would see her brighten at the sight of the arrival of her youngest son. Or she would remember how nicely she fixed up her house with new refrigerators, soft drinks, beer, and a fresh coat of paint before Detective Barbosinha put her in jail and separated her from her children who found themselves struggling to survive on their own. I suppose that Dona Katia, like any person, experienced a range of emotions, and I will not try to pin her down in death in my pursuit of a cogent conclusion. Instead I try to recuperate something from IPAC's and my attempts to write a history of the Pelourinho around Dona Katia and her peers.

In standing around Dona Katia's corpse at the Hospital Ana Nery, the bohemian hospital employee measured his life in relation to the Pelourinho body heavily battered throughout its lifetime. He remembered Katia when she was beautiful, but in 1998 Dona Katia was a ground for the bohemian's voice and for this chapter's narrative. In telling a history of the Pelourinho through an ethnographic account intended to shed light on the structures of governance, political action, and the production of the past in Brazil in the 1990s, I struggle to avoid reproducing the bohemian's use of Dona Katia's body. Yet I recognize how much my account is also animated by my friend, her corpse, and her corpus of stories. This is a horrible recognition that reveals how much bodies, archived documents, and the act of translating everyday life into an ethnographic report gird the authority of those most empowered by the Pelourinho to set themselves up as arbiters of what has happened, and what should be done. But it is also something that I have discussed frankly not only with my erudite peers, but with one of my closest friends in Bahia, Dona Katia's son. He agrees with me that this account of his mother's life should be published. And he is able to list many reasons for making this information public in new ways, including a number I cannot reproduce here in good faith, or even know in their entirety.

Here it seems worth recognizing that I opened this chapter with an elegy to Dona Katia laced with first-person exclamations like "I think of" and "I remember," all spurred by my memories of, and attempts to recall, or perhaps re-member, Dona Katia. This did more than interrogate my own subjectivity, showcase an ethnographic sensibility, or provide an unfathomable primal scene for anthropological musings on the nature of fieldwork. It has shown instead how participant observation and autobiography conceived of by IPAC in relation to Maciel/Pelourinho women like Dona Katia is key to producing the evidentiary base that secures the truths that permit Brazil to be narrated into existence today. The same materials from which future historians might tell the story of Bahia's evolution, or degeneration, are those coproduced by people like Dona Katia and her son and Jeferson Bacelar and John Collins. Thus I might rescue one of the voices listed in the previous sentence and permit the product of my self-making in dialogue with the Pelourinho's population to masquerade as "social history" or "intellectual history," depending on which one I extract through my intensive research and analytical efforts. But I think it more just, and enlightening, to show how John Collins and Dona Katia Alves— only one of whom must appear in these pages under a pseudonym—require one another even as they are separated in the social cleavages whose negotiation by privileged bohemians and Pelourinho residents establishes the most basic myths of Brazilianness.

Rather than seeking only to describe what happened in the late 1960s, I have therefore studied the exchanges that structured the ways that the people of the Pelourinho became a Bahian and a Brazilian people. These exchanges generated a range of documents that I read in order to make my claims about the 1970s. Yet the account produced from these documents is not really a story of what happened. It is more a study of how the remarkable accretion and ethnographic invention of sources about the Pelourinho's population comes to trace an outline not only of these people, but also of the state apparatus and the intellectuals charged with authorizing knowledge about an Afro-Bahian working class in the 1970s.

Given the fact that the paperwork I examined in order to tell a story of Dona Katia and IPAC social science is safeguarded by IPAC for the use of experts and students from Bahia and around the world, Professor Vivaldo da Costa Lima and his team's research efforts have paid off. The archive that contains their data is now a place for successive reinterpretations, and hence reconstructions—of the sort Michel-Rolph Trouillot describes in the third and fourth stages of the "production of history"—of a Brazilian people anchored in the Pelourinho. But this is not to argue that there is no place for representing Dona Katia. After reading this chapter it may appear that Dona Katia plays little role except as the inert material of history. This is not, however, exactly the situation.

National Brands: The "People's" Fetishization of Social Science

By July 2000 Dona Katia's son—whom I will call Pateta—had been released from the almost three-year prison sentence that began when he accepted as his own 256 grams of his mother's marijuana. Once, on a Saturday afternoon, we sat on the 28th of September Street in the bar run by Dona Célia, the old friend of the famous bohemian Jeová de Carvalho who is said to be the father of one member of S.O.S. Children of the Historical Center. Carvalho was also a well known writer and a good friend of Professor Vivaldo. We sat under one of the blue plaques that read "Praça Jeová de Carvalho" and which he had distributed to his favorite establishments. As we talked, we remembered the times Célia "killed" Pateta's childhood hunger with her okra, peanut, and dendé palm oil stew (caruru) during his mother's absences. The street was eerily quiet. It had been cleared of the hundreds of drug users attracted to the area by dealing and encouraged to stay on by IPAC so that residents would accept the indemnifications offered in exchange for their homes. Military police stood on each corner, guarding the colonial buildings sealed up by IPAC crews. Workers and planners circulated in hard hats, carrying ladders and instruments for measuring doorways, windows, and façades. Pateta wore a special shirt that he had painted with the help of cellmates and that he claimed would empower him in his new, postprison struggles in a Pelourinho now devoid of the people with whom he had grown up.

As we left the bar, an animated gentleman, about fifty years old, entered, embraced, and kissed seventy-six-year-old Dona Célia, ordering us to stay put and drink the beer he bought for all present. We did, for many hours, as he strummed his guitar and sang about love, desire, the "mangrove," or red light district, and Bahia. Atailton is a university professor, initiated by Dona Célia into "life" as he put it, in an echo of Dona Katia and her colleagues' descriptions of beginning a life of prostitution. He was happy he could visit the bar. He felt safe now that the crackheads, or "sacis," no longer dominated the 28th of September Street. As Pateta, whom I will identify as Alberto Silva Mendes, and I walked home afterward, I took another look at the department store brand names, lightning bolts, helicopter, and tank drawn on the back of his prison T-shirt. Across the front of his belly I read "Alberto Silva Mendes, *Cientista Social*," or "Alberto Silva Mendes, Social Scientist."[56]

As we walked, and talked, Pateta told me that the figures on this shirt that he painted with his cellmates during the last weeks of his incarceration represent his hopes for a new life and mark powerful objects that impacted his time in prison and might protect him from the experience of incarceration in the future. Across the back of the shirt are a host of military and commercial images. The canvas mixes iconography promiscuously, leaping from images of war to favorite automobile and clothing brands and the Brazilian flag. On his left sleeve Pateta emblazoned the word "Plancton," a brand of surfwear. Here Brazil, the T-shirt, and social science seem to stand as a social skin akin to Malaquias' placards or Dandinha's bikini. But the multiple trademarks Pateta arrays are something of a collage. They do not add up to a history that he is prepared to tell, or even threaten to strip away so as to reveal something frightening or mysterious. "I dunno," he exclaimed, "I don't care what these things mean. I just put them there. But look under my name, look what it says." The figure on the T-shirt that "tells" is, according to Pateta, the title "cientista social" or "social scientist."

Pateta's unauthorized graphic archive may some day spur a more complete interpretation, or take form as a narrative of incarceration and struggle told in the language of commodities, the nation, and social science in opposition to what its wearer refers to insistently as "the system." If that were to take place, social science might be read as a mediating term or locus of control for the mass of warring images splashed across the shirt. When I mentioned this conclusion to Pateta, he looked at me blankly. Then he said, slowly, "Listen, if I were a social scientist, I'd know what this all means. But in jail, it's better not to know."

In the chapters that follow I will explore further the overlaps between Pelourinho women's morality and Brazilian patrimony as forms of property, commodities desired by outsiders and locals alike, and aspects of a heritage-based system of governmentality enacted through social science. And I will do so in light of what it means to know, or not know. This will suggest that Pateta's shirt is emblematic of residents' appropriations of IPAC's language and techniques over the course of the restoration of the Pelourinho. It will also put forth the argument that the transformation of everyday life into a valuable property, together with residents' interactions with social scientists and their craft, has altered definitions of Bahian patrimony in ways that also cause shifts in salient ideas about racial identities, or the relationship between signs that lie on one's body and the invisible properties of the human that lie underneath. But, most basically, it will begin to make clearer some of the specific ways that history-making in the Pelourinho involves occupying the space that brings together, and oversees, the transformations of knowledge that produce the heritage zone. As Pateta struggled to make clear to me on so many occasions without spelling it out, such history is not about knowing what has happened. It is about doing something in the present.

CHAPTER 4

A Metaphysics for Our Time

Pelourinho Properties, Bahian Social Bodies,
and the Shifting Meanings of Rams and Fetuses

Pateta and I used to talk about life, death, and his time in prison as
we contemplated the Bay of All Saints from the hill behind the Bahian Academy of Medicine, Brazil's first medical school. Once, in
May 2000, our conversation was interrupted as Seu José and Gavião,
two respected residents of this steep Pelourinho subsection called the
"Rocinha," began to argue about a pathway that passed from a patch
of bananas into Seu José's garden and along a ridge that gave Gavião
access to his home. Joseval, an artisan who lived behind Seu José,
with whom he had clashed over another piece of the Rocinha, sat
with us. As the shouts grew and José brandished a machete, Joseval
exclaimed,

> "Owner?!?" . . . Bullshit!! This Pelourinho has so many owners!
> Everyone here is an owner. You looked at a piece of territory? You
> own it. You move in, set up shop, and that's it, you own it. But no-
> body owns shit here. It all belongs to no one! Everyone's an owner!
> It all belongs to IPAC and the Navy.[1] Our Pelourinho has so many
> owners!

Soon after Joseval's clarification of a gap between claims to ownership based on occupation—something common in rural regions and
urban peripheries and based on legal codes that allow for the award-
ing of title to those "improving" and holding onto territory for at least
five years—and the abstract or seemingly "natural" rights exercised

Figure 4.1. The view over the Bay of All Saints from near the Rocinha.

by a federal government symbolized by IPAC and the Brazilian Navy, Gavião and José returned to their weeding and sank into a muted, mutual cursing. Just then an IPAC team moved into the Rocinha's lower section in response to the collapse of a wall below the neighborhood's only flat area, the Avenida Esperança (Alley of Hope). The sixteen attached houses sheltering just over ninety people in the Avenida Esperança, a *cortiço* or group of homes built around a shared pathway of the sort common in nineteenth century Brazilian cities, had been destroyed by a gunman/overseer (*capanga*) hired by Seu Angelo. Angelo, the son of Italian immigrants and the self-described owner of the entire Rocinha, feared residents displaced elsewhere in the historical center might invade the houses and demand indemnification.[2]

At various moments Angelo has presented legal documents that he claims prove that his father purchased the Rocinha. But given the complexities of Bahian land dealings, the papers are not necessarily bona fide. Ownership has rested instead on the occupation and manipulation of a judiciary that favors the powerful.[3] As a result, although residents have contested Angelo for decades, they have found it difficult to advance their case. Yet due to his fears of violence from inhabitants of the land he claims, Angelo cannot collect rent. People's construction of homes, cultivation of gardens, and establishment of informal bars on land Angelo claims but is unable to control completely have

Figure 4.2. Avenida Esperança after being sealed by IPAC.

granted them certain rights under Brazilian usufruct law. These claims have been strengthened by the proximity of the Federal University's Medical School, a venerable institution that faces onto the Pelourinho's Terreiro de Jesus Square but whose rear section towers over the Rocinha. This uncertain meeting of differently registered properties confounds eminent domain laws that permit IPAC to transform private, but not federal, lands into part of Bahia's cultural heritage. IPAC was therefore unable to confiscate this territory, force residents to accept indemnification, and grant restored buildings to political allies as it has done elsewhere in the Pelourinho.

Despite the importance of law in land contests, the bundling of territory and human practices as historical properties in the Pelourinho is not really a story of court disputes, physical extension, hired *capangas*, and the interpretation of legal documents, which are the staples of most such accounts in a nation where 1 percent of the population controls nearly 50 percent of landed property. Instead, the disputes over the properties that leak most forcefully into residents' perceptions of their changing landscapes, and thus their techniques for making claims to the historical center and related political and psychic imaginaries, have turned since the early 1990s on their perspicacity in answering questionnaires.

Ethnography as Suspended State

As we watched Seu José and Gavião, I recalled also the meeting I should have been attending at one of Salvador's most exclusive establishments, the Hotel da Bahia. Sponsored by the Inter-American Development Bank (IDB) and SIRCHAL, a mixed private/French government corporation, the reunion of heritage professionals promised to reveal the details of infighting and recent technical initiatives since Salvador's municipal planning commission, SEPLAM, sought to employ the event to wrest control of the Pelourinho from IPAC.[4] But the strife, the companionship, the sun, and the view across the Bay of All Saints convinced me to stay in the Rocinha. I decided to skip the meeting of experts who fretted about the Bahians' inability to qualify for the Monumenta Program, a line of credit designed by the IDB to strengthen heritage institutions and encourage Brazilian institutions to train professionals to care for the nation's patrimony. I thus consoled myself with the thought that I would learn more with the occupiers of one of the last pockets of the pregentrification Pelourinho, or people who declared themselves "maroons" (quilombolas) fighting against "slavocratic" machinations, than I would at a meeting I considered a dispute between bureaucrats.

Soon former Pelourinho residents Morrão, Edinaldo, and Branco arrived from the neighborhood of São Gonçalo do Retiro with a born-again Christian reggae band sponsored by a former Pelourinho numbers-runner-turned-community-radio-empresario, cocaine distributor, and ward boss linked at the time to Antonio Carlos Magalhães.[5] We began singing, dancing, and reminiscing while gossiping about IPAC employees' peccadilloes. When I stumbled home I remembered little about Pelourinho ownership. I knew only that I should attend that day's SIRCHAL meeting. Yet my head was full of residents' insights into planning policies. These pointed to how much people enjoyed confounding IPAC by creating fanciful stories, citing impossibly low household incomes, and overstating their time of residence before driving off researchers by launching the urine- and feces-filled bags (balões) that compensated for colonial buildings' lack of working plumbing.[6]

In laughing about cozying up to and fooling the state they struggled to analyze so as to claim buildings or indemnifications, residents tacitly recognized IPAC's right to oversee the Pelourinho. But they emphasized that something had changed in an institution they had once considered a font of patronage concerned with their health, cultural production, family structure, disputes with police, and spatial practices: By 1991 IPAC had refocused on counting the populace while arguing publicly that it was deeply involved in people's health and well-being. Yet residents received little support. Instead, and rather than following the customs of the 1970s and socializing with researchers with whom they hoped to enter into patron/client relations, people waited to be transformed into social scientific data. Or, if they wanted to cultivate IPAC patrons, they spied on neighbors and denounced those who sought indemnification but no longer lived in the neighborhood.

Residents awaited their state because if they failed to be counted they would be unable to claim indemnification or press for the right to remain, a dispensation IPAC sometimes granted to those with political connections or capable of demonstrating that they produced sanctioned cultural expressions important to the Pelourinho's animation. To attach oneself to a building thus involved not simply joining neighbors in using a shared courtyard or spigot, but participating in the construction of the social category IPAC questionnaires framed as "residents." Some who remembered IPAC's first offices on the Pelourinho Square argued that the situation recalled efforts to document inhabitants in the late 1960s. But they pointed out that at a turn-of-the-millennium characterized by a marked strengthening of democratic institutions and social movements, Afro-Bahian political victories, and the dismantling of direct state participation in industry and basic services such as power and light, they expected IPAC to cheat them rather than invite them to join in community development. Thus the Pelourinho's inhabitants stayed home, making sure census takers got their numbers right, as IPAC experts plotted a future predicated on ostensibly collective pasts.[7]

A Meeting of Experts, or the Shifting Meanings of Rams and Fetuses

A day after listening to residents' analyses of IPAC's counting and culling, I found myself talking with Director Maria Adriana Couto de Castro during the SIRCHAL meeting. She asked if I had heard her keynote speech. When I responded that I was sorry I had not, she exclaimed, "You really missed something. You needed to have seen the pictures in order to really understand what we have done in the Pelourinho." I answered only, "I heard about them."

Vociferous critiques of Bahian heritage planning marred SIRCHAL's meetings in May and June 2000. French delegates who elicited appreciative gasps

Figure 4.3. Left to right: Paulo Gaudenzi, Minister of Culture and Tourism, "Governor" Antonio Carlos Magalhães, and Adriana Castro, IPAC director, survey the Pelourinho reforms, March 1999.

during presentations about European restorations declared the Pelourinho a "Disneyworld."[8] Echoing opposition politicians, they argued that the reforms were an ethnocide. Meanwhile, Colombian and Chilean planners received applause for their care of historical centers' populations. Organizers praised the Ecuadorians for their attention to housing and capture of funds in financial markets. Most participants, following IDB publications by a Washington-based consultant who organized the event, lambasted Bahian officials for subordinating patrimony to commercial considerations, for expelling the population scrutinized by the 1970s-era IPAC, and for failing to follow established architectural protocols.[9]

Municipal planners gloated at IPAC's comeuppance as technicians from CONDER, IPAC's fellow state-level planning bureaucracy, leapt to their colleagues' aid, explaining, "You do not understand the conditions under which we operate. Ours is more of a political process than one determined by planning . . . needs." French urbanists informed me that they had not heard of Antonio Carlos Magalhães. Yet CONDER engineers confirmed Magalhães as the force that overwhelmed rational criteria. This tension between rationality and political power added something to the descriptions of the reforms put forth in IPAC Director Castro's plenary speech:

> It would [not] be correct to claim that our fellow citizens . . . are miserable beings who we are duty-bound to assist. When one adopts a housing policy or transforms a neighborhood, there is no nation in the world that does not

require paying tenants. If there existed an ideal solution, it would have been applied without sacrifice a long time ago and all nations would have adopted it. . . . It is necessary to know in a brutal, very cruel form, what is the price that you sirs would like to pay for the conservation of your cultural nuclei?[10]

Castro's defense conformed to a then-ascendant neoliberal emphasis on responsibility, "paying tenants," and thus a formalization of property intended to generate revenues and convert the poor into stakeholders in the nation. Here IPAC's director, in addition to supporting the transformations in property regimes put forth under *favela*-"upgrading" and land-titling programs directed at Brazilian cities since the early 1990s, espoused a narrative well developed in IPAC public relations. In it, residents appear as symbols of physical and moral degeneration. It thus makes sense that Castro's paper had opened with a story of colonial florescence before moving to the Northeast's degeneration in a national period culminating in the "near-disappearance" of Portuguese inheritances. At this moment of collapse, she brought in archetypes made real in the dialogues between her IPAC predecessors and the state-directed archive of fieldwork materials available for re-elaboration in histories of the Pelourinho and the Brazil supposedly born there.

Among the recollected personas Castro trundled out were the Pelourinho mother and child. Animated by slides, Castro highlighted her institution's divergence from the IPAC of the 1970s by describing the "physical and social ruin of the Pelourinho":

[These are] conditions under which the population lived, children alongside animals and a total lack of hygiene during the epoch. I'd like to especially comment on *that last photograph, in which you see a ram, well, that's precisely the sign put out by one of the residents that she is selling drugs, that she has product for sale.* This takes place on a street, João de Deus street, quite close to where the IPAC headquarters functions today. In the 1970s IPAC began to pay more attention to the human aspect of cultural heritage.[11]

The source of Castro's data was IPAC sociologist Jorge Maurício's "Survival in the Maciel," a 1980 monograph of the type that I argued in the previous chapter is held in IPAC's archive as a standing reserve for elaborating Pelourinho-based histories. In it Maurício celebrates a ram as a symbol of the wistful sentimentalism, and thus the humanity, of a resident hoping to soften life under Brazil's economic "miracle" of the 1970s. Like Manuel Bandeira in 1927, Maurício emphasized that the population made a life where none seemed possible and that people should be commended for such creative sociality. The text describes the lives of four residents of the Maciel. Illustrated by Francisco

Santos, a former Pelourinho resident, a student in IPAC crafts programs from 1975 to 1979, and a member of the IPAC restoration teams in the early 1980s, the booklet was printed in 1980 by IPAC's public affairs office. It presents residents who, as the author warns in the introduction, should not be taken as "typical" figures but who nonetheless stand as archetypes. These are Dona Maria de Lourdes, a middle-aged woman who sells roast meat to passersby on the Praça da Sé, Salvador's main square; Elias, the discreetly homosexual barber; Dona Maria Luiza, the "caregiver" (*criadeira*) who takes care of Maciel women's children when they are imprisoned or incapacitated; and Elisa, a migrant from the countryside. Elisa claims to earn a living by selling beer and soft drinks to patrons in nearby brothels and by taking photographs with tourists attracted by a ram named Kojak, a goat, roosters, and a monkey that she keeps in her house on João de Deus Street.

All four people described by Maurício appear incipiently folkloric. Elisa claims explicitly that she is aware of her folkloric, and hence special, status. Such recognition of the power of the social scientific and tourist gaze, and how it might be reworked in engagements with the state, would be fully generalized across the Pelourinho's population only in the 1990s. Yet here I bring up this status simply to demonstrate its relationship to IPAC's surveys and representations of the populace in the 1970s and 1980s, something exacerbated in the 1990s when IPAC began to monetize habits and living spaces through indemnification. And at this later moment of neoliberal dispossession of the Pelourinho's inhabitants Elisa's ram is no longer presented by IPAC as folkloric. Rather, it is a "secret" or masked sign of Elisa's illegal activities, and thus her unsuitability to the historical center. But Castro goes even farther in reinterpreting IPAC's ethnographic archive so as to paint a new, evolving picture of the Pelourinho she seeks to sanitize so as to market Afro-Brazilian culture. She speeds from the ram as a sign of illicit activity to a "dramatic image, of an abortion":

> [The abortion was] observed by the community and when the police arrived, the woman had fled. This . . . is being presented here for the first time . . . but since ours is a relatively closed environment just for specialists, you need to know what sort of conditions of life the population of the Pelourinho faced.[12]

While I did not attend, instead watching Seu José and Gavião argue in the Rocinha, the director's assistant later passed me a color photocopy of a corpse atop rough boards, below a streaked wall. Although the image's quality is poor, the fetus seems to have been in late stages of gestation, suggesting the scene is a stillbirth. I have not encountered residents who remember the incident, although stories of abortion and abandonment in the prerestoration Maciel are common.

Castro's veracity is not critical. Rather, her defense illustrates a shift in deployments of data about residents. She transforms proletarian lifeways from justifications for the rejuvenation of national culture into technocratic reasons for exclusion. This takes place at a juncture in the 1990s when an amalgam of land titles and moral fitness, and not simply the occupation of buildings, became the basis for assessing residents' suitability for permanence or inclusion in IPAC's spatial representations of national history. But in a city in which few beyond Catholic religious orders held actual title to Pelourinho buildings, law and real estate documents seemed almost incidental. Instead, the ongoing, usually social science–based negotiation of Afro-Brazilian habits established a key means of claiming land, and thus permanence, in a neighborhood being enshrined as Brazil's point of origin and locus of rebirth.

If residents' lifeways once provided a rationale for a state-directed crafting of a paradigmatically Bahian everyday, during Director Castro's tenure from 1994 to 2002 the population appeared mainly as a problem requiring disposal. While IPAC took form by arguing against those who would impugn the Pelourinho's population, even as its own attempts at relativism continued to pathologize people presented as in need of government help, by the 1990s its language of care had gained a viciousness. To keep a ram as a sign that drugs are available is, according to Castro, not only illegal but also an affront to public health. To undergo an abortion and then to flee is to be not simply an unfit mother, but also a murderer under Brazilian law and Bahian public opinion.[13] The new tone IPAC adopted was eerily reminiscent of the Church and journalistic denunciations against which then-director Costa Lima had positioned the new heritage institution at the end of the 1960s.[14]

As suggested by Gueto residents' decision to call their neighborhood association "S.O.S. Children of the Historical Center," childhood is a key idiom for arguing for permanence and state attention in the Pelourinho. Bahians often talk about its pure potentiality and are enormously accommodating of children. Thus, when Castro aligns a fetus and a ram and then showcases this symbol for the foreign anthropologist who missed her presentation, she mobilizes evidence about simultaneously problematic and richly folkloric lifeways. Even as she claims to protect cultural heritage, her move authorizes an exclusion of locals from decency, citizenship, and the historical center. This takes place as part of an emphasis on human rights and social responsibility. And yet, due to the contested and dialogical production of its contents over the course of conflicts over homes and permanence in the neighborhood, the establishment of an archive that justifies the exclusions of the 1990s means that the evidentiary base that authenticates IPAC accounts has been coproduced with the population it both silences and represents.

The commodification of Pelourinho culture, while tied to UNESCO heritage guidelines and IDB initiatives, turns on conceptions of property and subjectivity established across the last three decades of the twentieth century within the unequal give and take between IPAC and its human subjects. This version of patrimony includes specific approaches to emotions and habits coded as collective possessions. These gain patrimonialized status not simply through technical evaluations, but as sentimental objects in a historical landscape put together around evidence produced through IPAC's attempts to extend a strange form of care to people and buildings. IPAC research in the 1990s is thus part of a longer history of state-citizen contests around living spaces and claims to personhood that become objectified in the very data whose fabrication serves to justify, and push forward, the Pelourinho reforms. The at-times carefully preserved, and at other moments highly disorganized, results of IPAC research provide content for subsequent histories like the one deployed by Director Castro in defending her institution. Yet history is never about the past alone. Residents' exclusion, accomplished alongside their memorialization in social scientific data and receipt of copious, albeit short-lived and ultimately cynical, state attention has resulted in shifts in their understandings of personhood and shared pasts that hinge on their ways of facing the state's knowledge production today. Understanding these alterations, and the politics they enable, requires a focus on how residents established themselves in the 28th of September. It turns also on the techniques through which IPAC came to account for and remove them just a few years later.

Moving and Building

In 1827, a moment of economic crisis and revolts that led to the transshipment of many Bahian slaves to Rio de Janeiro's expanding coffee groves, a tax debt forced the Portuguese trader Alvelos Espinola to sell number 18 Saldanha da Gama Street to the Santa Casa da Misericórdia, the Americas' oldest philanthropic organization.[15] Located just off colonial Salvador's main square, the Praça da Sé, this Gueto, disputed at the end of the twentieth century by its residents and IPAC, lay neatly within nineteenth-century Salvador's nucleus. Given its proximity to the 28th of September, a hub of male sociability and Bahian public life across the twentieth century, it remained a central part of Salvador as the colonial downtown became a red light district. By the 1940s, the Santa Casa rented sections of the building to women who sublet them to other working-class people.[16] Records of these transactions, together with oral

Figure 4.4. A home built into the crumbling Gueto at number 18 Saldanha da Gama Street.

histories that extend to the 1960s and indicate that number 18 Saldanha da Gama Street was indeed run by women who took in boarders, suggest that, like surrounding buildings, it housed poor and usually unmarried women involved in a range of economic activities similar to those detailed in IPAC's 1967 survey. This is supported by the shifting uses of the infamous "Guaciara," a house of prostitution across the street that served Salvador's bohemians in the 1960s and early 1970s before being broken up in the 1980s into a warren of plywood rooms rented to individuals and families. Perhaps fittingly, yet in a restoration that galls former occupants, the Guaciara now houses part of the IPAC administrative appparatus.

In the 1980s a fire displaced the majority of renters in the Gueto, or number 18 Saldanha da Gama Street. It lay empty, save for transients, until the movement of people between 1992 and 1993, during the initial phases of today's reform. At this time, Miguel, a lifelong Maciel resident, entered the shell and erected shacks out of scavenged lumber. He did not object when Seu Bude, a waiter, moved into an unclaimed section with his wife and two children. Miguel then built a three-room home in the building's southwest corner and sold one room to Dinha, a homemaker, and her husband Dodô, a repairman and percussionist from the Maciel with three teenaged children. A childhood friend of Miguel's, Pipino, later occupied the storerooms near the entranceway framed by ancient beams that had survived earlier fires. Pipino sold three of his four rooms to a fervent Rastafarian preacher, who had found religion while imprisoned, and his wife, Gude. The two survived as musicians and from donations by their working-class families who live near Salvador's Abaeté Lake, a tourist destination outfitted with a new visitor center and an increased police presence during the time of the Pelourinho restoration. Eurydice, a former prostitute, and her adolescent son and daughter, bought another room. They earned a pittance by serving as *aviões*, or "airplanes," the lowest level drug dealers who mediate between customers and drug-dealing spots (*bocas*).

When Pipino divided his holdings, Miguel followed suit, selling the northwest wall to Malaquias. Malaquias built a two-story home and sold the bottom to Caboré, his business partner (*parceiro*) from adolescence who is still recognized throughout Salvador for his purposeful bearing and cone-shaped packaging of marijuana. After Caboré's arrival, Jurema, one of the Maciel's most powerful women, invaded a section adjoining Seu João's home. Pipino and Miguel permitted Jurema to build multi-storied living quarters without payment since her almost-three-hundred well-muscled pounds had, at one time or another, helped her knock down many of the Maciel's men. She lived with her husband, Mão Grande, her son, and her two daughters while caring for Gordo, Reginaldo, and Gaiola, nephews infamous for their violent daring. Like Jurema, Augusto, another respected member of the community, entered without paying by constructing a three-story dwelling in the northeast corner, a precarious space neglected by Miguel and accessible only by ladders.

Augusto invited his former schoolmate Pepeta, the author of the song "Eighteenth Battalion of Love" discussed in this book's first chapter, to live with him. They ceded a room to Diego, a friend of Malaquias' from prison who, as recounted in chapter 2, passed me the copy of Caminha's letter that catalyzed

Figure 4.5. A friend climbs one of the series of ladders that leads to Augusto's home in the Gueto.

Figure 4.6. Residents of the Gueto repair the building's front door after its removal by IPAC and police.

chapter 3's history of Brazilian heritage. Valter, Malaquias' boyhood friend, then moved into another of Pipino's rooms after legal troubles forced another friend, to whom Pipino had ceded this space first, to abandon Salvador.

By 1994, unable to hold on against people dislodged elsewhere, Miguel, the Gueto's original 1990s invader, began to subdivide further. He sold one room to Tatau, recently arrived from the rural town of Jequié, who invited his teen-aged girlfriend to live with him. Pipino sold another to Lucymery, her partner Ronaldo, and her daughter Cisinha. Caboré, who had purchased the bottom of

Figure 4.7. The door to Caboré's home, painted with slogans invoking Jesus Christ and designed to ward off harm, requests moral comportment from visitors.

Malaquias' house, sold a portion to his sister, Regina, and her husband, who operated a cigarette stand in the tourist neighborhood of Porto da Barra. Shortly afterward, when Caboré separated from his wife, Jaciara, she bought a large room across the courtyard for about US$300. Caboré's new partner, Morena, moved in. Next, Miguel reinforced Jaciara's roof and built rooms atop it, in front of Malaquias' second-floor home. Jô, a former prostitute from the state of Sergipe and a mother of two, bought the larger of the two. When the roof collapsed on the space Eurydice had bought from Pipino, she moved upstairs, alongside Jô. Malaquias, anticipating additional indemnifications, walled off another room. When IPAC arrived he reported that his mother and sister lived there. Both women, who resided in the peripheral neighborhood of Fazenda Coutos, received indemnifications that they divided with Malaquias.

In 1998 the Gueto housed nearly forty permanent residents, including eight women, fourteen men, and about thirteen children. Most had received indem-

Figure 4.8. A Gueto resident works to repair the front door to his building.

nifications so as to leave the Maciel, the first Pelourinho sector to be restored. Only Pepeta, Jô, and her children, Tatau and his girlfriend, Valter, and Caboré's new wife, Morena, had not lived in the Maciel. And only Pepeta, Valter, and Morena had not paid for their spaces in the Gueto. The money that Miguel and Pipino earned from 1992 to 1994, and that materialized the two men's positions as the building's "owners," thus came almost entirely from indemnifications paid to their former neighbors in the Maciel. Thus the calculation between 1992 and 1993 of indemnifications in the first subdistricts depopulated by IPAC enabled a speculative, and increasingly necessary, occupation of the 28 in the mid-1990s by former Maciel residents.[17]

The restoration of the Pelourinho's central Maciel in the early 1990s, together with the anticipation of future reforms by both IPAC and residents, meant that a building subject to collapse and frequent police raids, and known as a violent space for the purchase of marijuana, had become recognized by the state as a living space. Everyday sociality and face-to-face negotiations with the state gave the edifice a special identity as, in spite of police raids and perceptions of violence in the streets outside, Gueto inhabitants worked to convince IPAC of their propriety while bragging also that the long entranceway that opened into their courtyard provided protection. As Augusto put it, anyone "who does anything bad here has to pay the price right here, inside, before getting out."[18] Such claims about the Gueto's specialness grew as IPAC continued to measure homes and register occupants for an oft-postponed indemnification process. Residents interpreted this ongoing surveillance of their social life as the state's admission that the Gueto had become, in practice, their own.

Counting and Paying

After 1992, IPAC social scientists and their undergraduate assistants conducted overlapping surveys to specify buildings' occupants and uses. They started in the former Maciel rather than in the 28th of September, a region emptied only after 1999. Since people moved frequently and listed friends and relatives so as to inflate indemnifications, IPAC repeated its efforts regularly. But databases would go missing, criteria and units of analysis would shift, and administrators would determine that research needed to be repeated. The result was a movement into and out of homes by IPAC units uninterested in the nuanced ethnography of the 1970s. The teams, relying on questionnaires, included many junior members who failed to develop friendships or business and fictive kin relationships with residents.

In the wake of the indemnifications paid in the Maciel in 1992 and 1993, the city center became the scene of the conspicuous consumption of food, electronics, drugs, and alcohol. People would cash checks, go on drinking binges, or disappear overnight to new houses in distant neighborhoods. Most speculated as to how much neighbors received, the places to which they moved, and the results of these peregrinations. Many did not want anyone to know where they lived and would return to the center to meet and socialize, never revealing their addresses. Some even gave incorrect information—corrected only en route—to the moving crews IPAC provided to transport people and their possessions. Others reported being robbed on their way out or in new homes. Disputes with new neighbors unaccustomed to vocabularies and behaviors common in the red light district, together with the lack of services on the periphery, gave rise to talk about the "barbarism" of inhabitants of the neighborhoods (*bairros*) they contrasted with downtown. These stories exacerbated divisions between the center—the Maciel, or "the mangrove"—and the periphery. In a mirroring of IPAC's attacks on research subjects as immoral or barbarous, former residents stressed that people on the periphery were bumpkins, ignorant of the forms of solidarity employed by astute inhabitants of the former mangrove.[19] Yet many in distant *bairros* copied the vocabularies, dress, economic activities, reggae bars and musical tastes, and trips downtown of displaced Pelourinho residents, constructing them as figuras, mediators, and leaders in a working-class vernacular public sphere tied closely to the evaluation of private morality in Pelourinho homes.

As far as I have been able to make out from the numbers kept secret by both IPAC and residents, the indemnifications granted between 1992 and 1994 averaged ten to fifteen minimum salaries, or between US$1,000 and US$2,000 per household. These varied according to one's ability to manipulate IPAC's definition of family groups and one's skill in negotiating with Tatá, Dona Karla, Luciano Diniz, and later Lúcia Sepulveda, the heads of field research, social services, public relations, and legal services, respectively. Officially, IPAC employed a secret formula to calculate indemnifications. According to Dona Karla, head of social services, payments were based on square meters occupied, family size, length of residence, and whether the space was used as a domicile, place of business, or both. Yet much business fell outside IPAC definitions. Also, IPAC stretched criteria: As one official explained, "the real formula . . . is really very simple: No prostitutes, no thieves, no transvestites, and no drug dealers," even as many people who argued to me that they filled those categories received indemnifications, and often more than once.

In April 1998 the head social worker, speaking about Dona Katia, the woman whose life history motivates the previous chapter, told me, "She has already received three indemnifications, or rather, three with this one she is going to receive now. She has no rights to anything more, but due to her health problems we have allowed her to receive [an indemnification] one more time." When Katia died before cashing her check, I spoke to an IPAC employee about her imprisoned son's need for a lawyer, suggesting that he might receive his mother's payment. The official replied that this was impossible. But when I took a cue from residents and argued that patrimony is passed down within a family, and that an indemnification is an inheritance left by a mother in a manner that raises a moral obligation for the state, he included Pateta in the Gueto's 1999 indemnifications.

Such unclear dealings animated rumors as residents watched IPAC employees' spending in bars and on houses, cars, and clothing. When a resident attracted notice, neighbors argued that he or she had managed to put relatives on indemnification lists. During the two years before Brazil's anti-inflationary

Figure 4.9. Residents, personal archives under their arms, confront an IPAC team surveying the Gueto.

conversion in 1994 to a new currency, the *real*, people explained delays as the result of IPAC "working" money so as to benefit from spiraling inflation. They reported signing agreements containing sums marked in pencil, with IPAC employees then typing in another, higher figure, and pocketing the difference. I have no direct knowledge of such corruption, although a number of officials were transferred in 1999 amid rumors of scandal.

More significant than corruption is the argument that indemnification was manipulated and that key to such maneuvers was not law or protocol, or even land records, but rather evidence about everyday lives. In their complaints, residents argued that monies received were tainted, led to death and suffering, and could not be employed productively, instead running through one's fingers like water. These moralizing claims about cash were not necessarily borne out in practice, as family members would consolidate indemnifications and acquire a house. But many, especially the elderly, spent quickly the indemnifications they considered to be polluted by their associations with the state, and then found themselves on the streets. The indemnifications and collections of evidence then came to be described in terms of death, social advancement, and one's inner strength—phenomenal unities associated in various ways with one's status as a producer of a culture conceptualized as arising from within Afro-Brazilian subjects.

Living Human Treasures, Pelourinho-Style

During the rainy season in 1999, as water pooled in the marble entranceway and chunks of the eighteenth-century façade thundered to the ground, Gueto residents huddled around a set of documents. IPAC's Dona Karla had left behind her syntheses of the questionnaires administered so as to establish the size of indemnifications. In the ledgers were the names of over forty heads of household, but only nine families remained. People cursed their misfortune for not having gotten more friends listed, for their inability to create "phantasms" to facilitate gain. Just then, a teenager called up, "Malaquias, visitors. It's the lady from IPAC." Malaquias hid the papers and met the employee.

"My boss says that she left some documents with you."

"Oh, yeah? Documents?" answered Malaquias.

"Yes, those copies of your indemnification agreement, well, there were some of Dona Karla's papers mixed in."

"Gosh, I had no idea," answered Malaquias, "You know, like I told you when you interviewed me all those times, I'm illiterate. It's too bad, because my sister just left here and took them to my mother's house for safekeeping. You know [from your research] how poor our living conditions are. I didn't want them to get wet. Are they important?"

The intern responded affirmatively.

"Well, then you tell Dona Karla that I'm going to visit my mother tonight and I can get them. But if she can't wait and needs them now, I can dart out by cab. The fare is only about R$10. You can bring the money by if Karla really needs her documents."

When the intern left, residents dissolved into laughter and Malaquias exclaimed, "They say they're the patrimony, well, I'm patrimony. I'm the one who's folkloric. They wanna put me in their questionnaires and put me up there, 'Big Black guy from the Pelourinho,' well those milktoasts are gonna pay me what I deserve! I do my own research. I have my own dossier, I know what they're trying to do," even as one of his neighbors added, "and don't forget to include in that dossier, 'left-handed, toothless and a stutterer!'"[20]

Malaquias' creative deformation of disability and moralizing claims about his racialized self that reflect IPAC's language and emphasis on reconstruction illustrate how residents came to wrap themselves within patrimonializing techniques so as to slip into a productive landscape in which state-directed burnishings of human beings became more than a disciplinary mechanism or a technology for commodifying culture. Thus I am not presenting the trickster I call Malaquias—my good friend and interlocutor in writing this book and dealing with IPAC—as a romantic, resistant figure even as I enjoyed his creative confounding of state authorities. Rather, and even as he seeks to ransom Karla's records, Malaquias demonstrates "a metaphysics for our time," or a stealthy concern with skills, identities, and interiorized conceptions of personhood reminiscent of the "Masters of Intangible Heritage" and "Living Human Treasures" that UNESCO and Brazil's IPHAN had begun to institute by the end of the 1990s. Nonetheless, Malaquias' imagination and attachment of self to heritage techniques did not filter down from a Brazilian federal or UNESCO intangible heritage program at the dawn of a new millennium. It emerged in dialogue with IPAC techniques developed in Bahian dialogues with international initiatives since the late 1960s.

By 1999, most residents had come to see themselves as a part of an archived past serving state interests and produced through the distillation of data collected about them. As such, they believed, and still believe, that they may make demands on the basis of identity and that they deserve access to the windfall understood to result from reforms and from their state's particular manner of arraying history in this process. The subjectivities that ground compensation involve a rooted Afro-Bahianness, pronouncements about being from "antiquity" (*da antiguidade*), and the suggestion that ruined buildings would have crashed to the ground were it not for their inhabitants' conservation efforts.

Many "from antiquity" claim that they are both patrimony, and, like Dona Katia's son whose T-shirt proclaims his status, social scientists. As social scientists, they not only speak to and demand things from IPAC, but also mine landscapes for meaning and profit by means of personal properties objectified in IPAC surveys. In chapter 5 I will examine this burgeoning "hermeneutics of depth" that is associated with both landscape and IPAC social science in order to tie it to IPAC reconstruction, the objects that make up Bahian patrimony, and racial ideologies.[21] But here, and even more basically, I suggest that Malaquias' demands based on his representation in surveys partake of a Lockean-inspired version of intellectual labor and property even as they point also to a sympathy between the different objects of cultural heritage, and thus to a certain confusion between subjects and objects that empowers rather than disempowers.

By making tangible his personhood and culture through appropriated dossiers and lists, Malaquias believes that he gains rights to the Pelourinho as a national space and as a source of value mobilized by institutions that market culture. If Brazilian patrimony involves the entification of habits as possessions, and Afro-Brazilians as possessors of distinctly Bahian qualities, Malaquias' assertion about his entitlement to his commodified persona seems to follow a similar possessive logic. Additionally, he understands the labors expended in being represented by IPAC as constitutive of rights. This idea, that one should be paid for the work of appearing in a questionnaire, an ethnography, or a tourist video-tape, is common in the post-1992 Pelourinho. Yet while Malaquias argues that he is human patrimony—a type of property—he emphasizes in his confound-ing of the IPAC intern that he cannot store documents in the Gueto because the building is not a suitable environment. His assertion about leaks and the pro-tection of documents, and thus hygiene and proper living quarters, illustrates how dossiers and research sanction evidence about his valuable folkloric and black status to IPAC officials, neighbors, and the North American participant observer. Preservation and representation, then, stand as ambiguous sources of value tied together by the correct care for people, buildings, and the documents that connote and gird such efforts.

To argue that Malaquias owes his self-conceptualizations to IPAC, or that he sees himself as black thanks to attempts to remove him from the Pelourinho, would be to overemphasize, as is the case in much recent work on cultural commodification, the extent to which taxonomies generate identities and com-modification gives rise to extremely rational attempts to profit from objectifica-tion.[22] Yet experience with questionnaires that supports IPAC's reconstruction of people and buildings has indeed impacted Malaquias' ways of conceiving personhood: As he told the intern, he does his own research. Even today he strolls the restored Pelourinho with a notebook or folder of documents under his arm. This habit recalls the habits of the IPAC researchers who visited the Gueto and the bohemian men of letters and university professor practitioners of "armpit literature" who carried copies of Claude Lévi-Strauss' structural-ist tomes when they visited Pelourinho bars and castles during the 1960s and 1970s.

In claiming an identity and power around dossiers, something also a part of the politics of "Governor" Antonio Carlos Magalhães, whose manipulation of secret information earned him vast power and forced his resignation from the senate, Malaquias highlights a particular disposition to the gathering and storing of knowledge. Such knowledge, as mediated by documents as material signs deployed within debates over historical properties that ranged from colo-nial buildings to residents' identities, and thus Malaquias' interpellation within files and archives constitutive of Bahian histories like IPAC accounts of rams and unfit mothers, played an important role in the ways he and his neighbors came together as a political force in the changing Pelourinho.

Indemnification in the Gueto: S.O.S. Children of the Historical Center

As IPAC began to indemnify Gueto residents in 1999, a group made up of Jô's son Pierre, Malaquias, Jorginho and Gude, Pepeta, Caboré and Morena, Augusto, and Juciara's mother, Dona Neinha, who had moved into her daughter's quarters after her arrest, decided to fight for the Gueto. They had observed the difficulties faced by neighbors since the first indemnifications. And, they argued, they were a special type of person who by dint of their historical and patrimonial statuses deserved a place in the restored Pelourinho. As a result, they decided to work to take over the Gueto. The project gained strength alongside Augusto's and Malaquias' reggae band, the Bem Aventurados, or "The Blessed," after the group's vocalist, Gula, who claims to be the son of a prostitute and the bohemian writer Jeová de Carvalho who frequented Dona Célia's bar on the 28, revived his friendship with Edinho, his high school classmate who now served as chief of staff of the Workers Party city councilman Zilton

Figure 4.10. Carrying a banner that reads "The Right to a Place to Live," members of S.O.S. Children of the Historical Center march through the historical center's streets on Ash Wednesday—the day after carnival—when Pelourinho residents typically hold an additional day of carnival celebrations. Photograph by Shanti Avirgnan. Used by permission.

Rocha. Contact with Rocha led to the Bem Aventurados' coalescence as the social movement "S.O.S. Children of the Historical Center" and participation in events with Paulo Anunciação, a sanitation workers' union and Unified Black Movement leader, city councilman, and fellow Rastafarian. Construed by opposition politicians as authentic representatives of the community's desires, S.O.S. emphasized ever more vociferously that almost all of its members were either ex-street children or the children of prostitutes. Yet the group included five or six people who had registered as Gueto residents in order to receive indemnifications, but did not live in the building, and a number of participants who rejected the claim that they were associated with street children or prostitution. But in spite of such divergences within the group, S.O.S. moved through the 28th of September attempting to convert residents to their cause.

Ravaged by crack, the 28 was not fertile ground for community organizing. People not involved in the drug trade waited for indemnifications that would allow them to flee. Those selling illegal substances sought to avoid attention. Crack users who hoped to shake loose a meal, a shirt, or an indemnification attached themselves to the movement as S.O.S. organized protests and remained in the Gueto. Despite their efforts, most of the real estate around the building soon emptied, since people could not resist exchanging homes for cash. IPAC-supplied moving trucks trundled through, carrying possessions to neighborhoods and into the interior of Bahia and adjoining states.

Jurema, the well-known Gueto resident, took advantage of S.O.S.'s frustrations of IPAC by delaying her departure until three of her teenagers completed their eighteenth birthdays. As adults, and aided by the fact that Jurema had become a *comadre* to an IPAC bureaucrat who baptized her child, each became a "head of household" entitled to indemnification. Jurema received almost US$10,000 and departed for her husband's home city of Simões Dias in the state of Sergipe. They purchased three houses and lived, without working, for one year until Jurema's nephews, bored with life in the interior, began to commit serious crimes. With money running out, Jurema's son, frightened by an arrest as an adult before leaving Salvador, found work in a slaughterhouse. But Jurema's husband, Mão Grande, began to deal cocaine in Simões Dias and was arrested and forced to pay a bribe, thus losing their remaining savings.

In June 2000, Jurema and her family prepared to return to Salvador and invade another building. She told me, "IPAC was so good to me, I want to see them again. I miss them so much." Such "goodness" has much to do with money. But it cannot be reduced to a rational calculation: Many, especially those less guileful than Jurema, seemed moved by IPAC's attention. Like AIDS patients who receive state and NGO care after documenting infection, residents who once lacked birth certificates, social security numbers, working papers,

Figure 4.11. Opposition politicians and Gueto residents negotiate with military police sent to dislodge the building's inhabitants.

and identification cards found themselves ushered through bureaucracies by IPAC. Authorities contacted barbers and discovered clean clothing for those who would have pictures taken so as to gain the identity documents that impoverished, illiterate, or illegitimately born Bahians often lack. Social workers taught people to sign their names and open bank accounts. Most of all, IPAC employees spent time with and talked to Bahians who had not considered themselves full citizens because they had received scant attention from state emissaries other than police and jailors. As S.O.S. member Gula loved to joke, "The police are my psychiatrists and the Nina is my undertaker!" "Nina," a reference to the founder of Bahian physical anthropology and Bahian criminal forensics, Raimundo Nina Rodrigues, is slang for the city morgue. Gula thus emphasized that his contact with the state, and its production of subjects, had been limited to its most violent institutions.

IPAC care was more formal than substantive. People gained documents but little else, and they soon denounced these as Trojan horses (*engodos*). Initially, many joined drug treatment facilities, NGOs "recuperating" street children, and churches. Some worked in tourism and many entered schools. Yet this enthusiasm usually lasted only two or three weeks as documents counted for little in a tight job market and, lacking secure homes, those who did not have anywhere to store their papers saw them stolen, burnt, or damaged by water. Many became homeless, worse off than before.

A significant number found that they had exchanged their right to the historical center for a perplexing, formal attention meted out by a state that coveted their homes and habits. Thus the extent to which people warmed to IPAC's handholding operation and participated in its questionnaires in an attempt to guarantee indemnifications suggests how the restoration, a populace's patrimonialization, and the Bahian cultural heritage industry relied on a state-directed governmentality that not only supported designs on buildings but transformed lives, often detrimentally, in the name of social hygiene and reconstruction. This also produced the evidence that lent veracity to the very narratives that produced what residents argued was their status as Brazilian patrimony. What took place, then, was not some progressive individualization, or subjectification of individuals outside of history. Rather, an IPAC-catalyzed motivation of new subjects and objects with the potential to act in concert, or sympathy, came into being around the redeployment of evidence via techniques made visible in a catalogue not simply of people and buildings, but of data about them. Nonetheless, this new, almost sacral condition as the absent producers, as well as content, of the preserved representations that filled the memories around which the Pelourinho project congealed did not enable residents to avoid expulsion. In fact, their beatification as problematic yet celebrated forbears to the nation supported by their inventoried practices made their removal necessary.

The End of the Gueto

While Jurema and her family were in Simões Dias, S.O.S. Children of the Historical Center and PT politicians filed a legal motion for possession of the Gueto. Under Brazil's usufruct laws, a group demonstrating occupancy and "improving" a property for a period of five years may gain title. In April 1999 IPAC responded by sending the military police Choque Battalion to vacate the Gueto.[23] Residents used Caboré's cellular phone to call the city council. Within minutes Zilton, Paulo Anunciação, and additional opposition party politicians, including Green Party Councilman Juca Ferreira, who would become Brazil's minister of culture under President Lula, entered the Gueto. The police backed down and Anunciação mediated a meeting with IPAC in which S.O.S. demanded a restored building. In response, IPAC pressured those remaining to accept their offers, raising the amounts and stating that any who did not acquiesce would be evicted. A majority accepted and Tatau was arrested for selling marijuana, leading his girlfriend to abandon their room. IPAC workers began to destroy the homes of those who accepted indemnifications, ostensibly to prevent others from occupying abandoned spaces.

Figure 4.12. Gueto *residents celebrate the initial withdrawal of military police sent to dislodge them from their homes.*

The destruction resulted in the occupation of the empty rooms by crack abusers or robbers who used them to divide up spoils. Jurema's nephews came to use the Gueto's trashed corridors as hideouts during forays from Simões Dias. People defecated throughout the building, and the roofs and supports removed by IPAC caused walls to collapse. Had Tatau not been imprisoned, he may have died as several thousand pounds of brick crashed into his empty room one night.

The Children of the Historical Center decided that they could no longer hold out and, by June 1999, they reached agreements with IPAC. Members received an average of US$2,000 each. Caboré bought a room in a nearby building much like the Gueto, Valter moved down the 28th of September to a building Pipino had just invaded—and from which he would receive another indemnification in 2001—while Augusto transferred his belongings to his wife's house in the suburb of Lauro de Freitas. Malaquias and Pepeta moved five blocks to the west, to the Rocinha.

In the interactions with IPAC, S.O.S. had learned to speak wisely to cultural bureaucrats, police, and elected officials about members' moral states and rights to historical properties. They had conceived of themselves in ways that, much more than slotting them into preexisting categories of identity, facilitated their attempts to benefit from interactions with managers of historical properties. Perhaps this was a reincarnation of the opaque *politicagem,* or politricks, about which Malaquias had complained bitterly when he marched, like a human sandwich, onto the Pelourinho Square in 1998. And as displaced residents fanned out across the still-unrestored sections of the city center and into new neighborhoods, they would carry with them this knowledge of self, bureaucracy, and the data necessary to make narratives convincing. While consumed by dreams of material success, and fascinated by the ways that everyday life had become valuable, residents' experience in affairs of state meant that the negotiation of history and quotidian habits had become both linked to and an integral part of a broader ethos. This approach to life and truth turned on a certain confusion of subjects and objects that, in a nod to its catalyzation in the reforms of the 1990s, recalled the sorts of confusions over patrimonial categories and tangibility and intangibility discussed in chapter 2 above.

Tombamento: Structures of Properly Historical Being

Malaquias' and the Bem Aventurados' deformations of IPAC structures of feeling and knowing—whether by hiding field notes, answering questions falsely, or seizing the discourse of health and cultural rights—suggest the extent to which living in the Pelourinho as one of the few inhabitants allowed to remain, or as one of the majority who departed the neighborhood that produces folkloric afterlives manipulated by the Bahian state, generates a certain consciousness about representation, transformation, and belonging. For example, residents emphasize the extent to which they believe that IPAC knowledge-gathering activities carried away some aspect of their human essences. And they usually peppered conversations about such appropriations of lifeways with discussions of death.

Amid the reforms and the rebuilding of moral selves and colonial edifices, Pelourinho residents talked constantly about death. They would start rumors that a friend, or neighbor, or famous neighborhood figura had died. Friends spent hours explaining to me that IPAC money was polluted and caused neighbors to die. Many others, as detailed in the next chapter, claimed their neighborhood was riddled with the skeletons of slaves sealed up under squares and in thick colonial walls. In a telling use of language, Dona Guilhermina, a former Maciel criadeira, or caretaker of neighbors' children, linked these concerns to patrimonialization when she told me, "Esse povo doido pra pegar a indenização. Eles é que vai tombar morto antes de serem tombados!" This phrase, spoken in a working-class Bahian register, means "Those people, crazy to receive [take hold of] their indemnifications. They're the ones that are going to drop dead before they're turned into patrimony!"

Dona Guilhermina's wordplay relies on the verb tombar. "Tombar" means to fall or knock down, to die, or to become frozen or preserved in time. It is used to describe patrimonialization, or registry in a ledger of historical objects like IPAC's, IPHAN's, or UNESCO's archives. The word is confusing, or ambivalent: In a suggestive summary of destructive urbanism, to "tombar" a building is both to preserve it and to demolish it. Linguists are divided over the word's etymology, with some claiming a Lusitanian origin in Lisbon's Torre [Tower] do Tombo, the Portuguese national archive. Others argue that the Latin word *tumulum* (storehouse, archive) is the root of tombar.[24] In either case, the word as employed in Brazil today means to preserve something in an archive or to fall down, dead or wounded. Employed in this manner, the verb recalls the word "cadaver" (*cadáver*), derived from the Latin *cadere*, which, like tombar, means to fall down or be unable to stand on one's own. Thus the words for "patrimonializing" and "dying" demonstrate substantial etymological and practical overlap. And the care of the everyday needs of the Pelourinho's population as configured in the 1990s by IPAC is an attention designed to celebrate, prolong, and commemorate the elision of people in order to facilitate their celebration through representation. In fact, residents claim that Brazil's "cradle" is not about life for life's sake, but life in dialogue with death. They argue that the Pelourinho preserves life in the service of death because the state demonstrates its own efficacy by wrapping its people in the formal signs of care while preparing their physical removal and memorialization in registries hidden in the bowels of its headquarters. And yet, this lethal form of care makes people grounded, material, and substantive like a cathedral or a stone plaza. In residents' views, this is not simply an objectification of Afro-Brazilians as some sort of decoration for a UNESCO historical center. It represents instead their conversion into a specific form of material sign of historical rootedness and popular experience from which they might begin to make the sorts of demands afforded only to those most sacred members of society. Such demands are part and parcel of the specific ways Pelourinho residents have been inserted, and have placed themselves within, the flow of a history dependent for its truth claims on evidence about their everyday lives configured in turn as properties of the nation.

IPAC and the Archives of Everyday Life

In the 1990s, as IPAC attempted to quantify Pelourinho residents, the codification of habits permitted the state institution to produce accounts of its own efficacy and Bahian identities even as the net result of this exercise was the expulsion of the Pelourinho's population: As the state government insisted in newspaper articles, press releases, its own publications, interviews with foreign researchers, and reports to the federal government, UNESCO, and the

IDB that it cared for the people of the Pelourinho, it waged systematic war against them. Those who actively challenged the state received beatings and even bullets from police. Those who trusted in the veracity of IPAC's professions of concern with citizens' well-being found themselves in a special sort of bureaucratic limbo. This liminal state involved assurances that IPAC was taking care of health, buildings, and financial matters even as the institution did little more than produce data about residents' hygiene and family structures; the physical integrity, size, and layout of their homes; and the purportedly inspiring economic strategies through which they made do.

The archive coproduced around IPAC surveillance of habits of Pelourinho residents—a people configured simultaneously by the information-gathering process and by the existence of the archive as Brazil's most representative population and Bahia's most pressing problem—is in itself a type of governance that turns the state's records of people's habits into collective possessions of the nation. IPAC's spaces for housing its descriptions of residents' lifeways are monuments to its own, and to the state's in general, apparent efficacy and care of an exceptionally Bahian people. They are also testaments to the enfolding history of a neighborhood designed to make explicit its own historicity.

In the 1990s, prior to its move to the restored 28th of September, IPAC separated its archives into two parts. In the basement of its headquarters on Gregório de Mattos Street, the institution set up an efficient archive that included original field notes and rough tabulations of data from all major sociological studies of the neighborhood carried out by IPAC personnel, personal data on residents indemnified from 1992 to the present, legal documents pertaining to disputes over the ownership of neighborhood buildings, and information, including the original signed agreements between the state and residents, regarding the indemnification process. This area was strictly off limits to all but a few authorized employees. My knowledge of it comes from select members of the group that oversees it, knowledge I will not detail so as not to compromise their positions.

At the same time, in the shadows of the golden Church of São Francisco, one of Brazil's most prized Baroque jewels, sat the "Biblioteca de IPAC," or the IPAC library. The IPAC library remains open to the public and includes one of the state's best collections of published materials pertaining to Bahian culture, historical reconstruction, and architecture. Today located on the 28 in IPAC's refurbished headquarters, it houses the mass of reports written by IPAC technicians since 1967 and working papers produced for the benefit of visiting researchers and dignitaries. At the core of the collection sit thousands of newspaper clippings, carefully pasted into binders, that document Pelourinho and Bahian history since the late 1950s.

The newspaper collection reads like a who's who of Pelourinho residents. Archivists have divided the array of scrapbooks by year and then broken each year into multiple topics or themes. The person in charge of newspaper articles since 1986 has followed her predecessors and organized them thematically according to her understanding of their importance to the institution at any given moment. She told me that her ad hoc cataloguing may arise from her discussions with colleagues, from suggestions from superiors, or from her personal feelings about the public's interests and IPAC activities. Categories for organizing this enormous scrapbook thus move into and out of existence across time, becoming bloated with materials and then, toward the last years of their usefulness, slimming down in relation to formal and informal discussions.

One example of the invention, the waxing, and the waning of archival categories is "Minors, Prostitution and Police Occurrences," a folder present since 1971. In the late 1970s and 1980s the hundreds of pages of "Minors, Prostitution and Police Occurrences" were filled with stories of street children, rapes, Dickensian characters who exploit youths, and drug offenses. By the first years of the new millennium, however, as the Pelourinho became increasingly gentrified, "Minors, Prostitution and Police Occurrences" developed into a compendium of stories about NGOs, state-directed philanthropies for children, schools' restorations, and new posts for truant officers from the Juizado de Menores. Alongside this, new folders, such as "Olodum"—a file dedicated exclusively to the Afrocentric NGO and carnival band—and "Popular Festivals" come into existence only to be filled with clippings that no longer accrue to binders like "Minors, Prostitution, and Police Occurrences."

The categorizations in IPAC's archives provide an indirect yet perceptive picture of changes in the Pelourinho. Their shapes, silences, and regularities permit a reading of what is most important to the making of history: As "Minors, Prostitution and Police Occurrences" shrinks and "Popular Festivals" swells, the effect is akin to an ordering of Pelourinho time. "Popular Festivals," which existed in the late 1960s and was then abandoned by IPAC as Salvador's population paid less and less attention to pre-Lenten celebrations, becomes a type of a community calendar that presents important events in the neighborhood's, and the region's, ritual cycles during the reinvention of tradition today. Over the last decade more events have been added and attended by greater and greater numbers of people, and this renovation of tradition appears in the city's dailies, which then make their way into IPAC's folders. As a result, IPAC moves from a history of the Pelourinho told around descriptions of everyday life, minors, prostitution, and arrests-as-events, to celebrations of Bahian religion and culture in which "popular festivals" stand as the city's most diacritical events. Like the neoliberal policies Director Castro trumpeted and, arguably, misrepresented to SIRCHAL, these gain unity in relation to a patina of earlier immoral activities rectified and preserved by the archive.

The shifts and continuities in IPAC's archives testify to the ways that IPAC organization of information produces events, personages, and feelings of temporality and social solidarity. In-depth examination of their construction and manipulation by a variety of users would surely reveal much more about silencings and animations of Pelourinho pasts. But I am most concerned with the practices that give rise to IPAC's two archives and the role of the production of these ledgers in the political processes going on in the neighborhood over the last decades. Principle among these are the different types of social scientific field research performed on the Pelourinho's population during the institution's lifetime. This research establishes a system of "cultured governmentality" by allowing IPAC researchers to insinuate themselves into people's most intimate spaces as they materialize a mass of information ostensibly designed to allow society to know itself. And in contributing to IPAC's archives by allowing researchers to attempt to chart their inner selves and everyday movements, certain Pelourinho residents have themselves come to value archives in a manner quite reminiscent of the state's attempt to replace living people with their ambivalent representation.

A salient result of patrimonialization has been that residents, already familiar with IPAC, have begun to declare themselves—like Malaquias whom I discuss above and Pateta whom I describe in concluding chapter 3—both patrimony and social scientists. They are, in their view, both a collective object of the nation and the group of technicians who produce that object. It is common in the Pelourinho today to hear "I'm researching you" as a warning that a person is keeping another under close watch. I have never heard this from any Bahians except for Pelourinho residents. People also point out that facts and histories can be produced through "research." They laugh at IPAC attempts to do so, but they also learn. They weave their own stories of the Pelourinho's past in rhetorics and through methods very close to IPAC's. Residents joke that they are historians, slurring the first syllable so that the word also means storytellers. These new skills have been useful for staking a claim to the restored neighborhood, and the transformation of historians into storytellers is emblematic of one of the main points in this essay. The residents generally do not actively argue head on and challenge the very bases of state policies. Rather, they appropriate methods and narrative forms, deforming them slightly in the process.

Of the approximately 1,300 families resident in the Pelourinho in 1992, only about 150 have managed to remain through the end of 2002, frequently by using IPAC's techniques against the institution. People keep field notes, maintain dossiers, and write questionnaires so as to present arguments about themselves and their neighbors when facing the heritage bureaucracy. Good ethnographers, they often claim ignorance, pretending they know little about an issue, so as to draw out others' commentaries and gain new perspectives on debates with politicians or IPAC. But most of all, it seems, they have come to associate their own everyday with state power by means of archives and research programs. Together, these repositories and the actions that fill them produce Bahian heritage as a collection of special objects by attesting to these entities' special qualities. Yet heritage objects in the Pelourinho are not simply cathedrals and monuments. Rather, in the eyes of residents and in the logics of the state, they include the collection of Afro-Bahians at the center of the state-directed attempt to consecrate the Pelourinho as the source of Brazil.

Properly Historical Populations and a Metaphysics for Our Time

Property is not simply a market relationship. Or, put somewhat better, like markets, property relations help order society around different forms of price and value. In fact, property has long been linked in a variety of ways to propriety.[25] And modernity's most expressive genre conventions and representational techniques—or the ways that signs assign communicative value at a specific juncture—have often taken form in direct relation to circulations of money and goods.[26]

Pelourinho residents have approached IPAC indemnification as a compensation for people's removal as well as evidence of a malfeasance that is nonetheless presented by their state as a sign of care or beneficence. The IPAC questions and research techniques that motivate such circulations by defining the amounts paid to residents revolve around concepts of responsibility and, especially, moral accountability. And this accounting conducted since the end of the 1960s by IPAC fills archives with a content that residents describe as a form of social death that nonetheless sets them up as much more than sacrificial victims. They are instead part and parcel, like cathedrals, monuments, and folkloric dances, of a historical center to which they become attached by means of IPAC's iterative knowledge-gathering activities. This highlights the extent to which, as a moral discourse, national history is an idiom tightly imbricated in the construction of property. And such properties are not simply physical, intellectual, or "immaterial" entities. Rather, they are concatenations of all three that emanate from practices related to the production of knowledge, and the commodification of such knowledge, about the Bahian red light district. Such social ontologies leach out from knowledge-producing activities as a type of substance or thing that binds people to landscapes even as those people argue that such substantive connections are, due to their relationship to IPAC's alienation of their human properties, threatening and basically immoral.

I turn now to some results of these objectifications to look, in chapter 5, at the ways a configuration of people as patrimony, and thus of humanity as a species of property, impact the ways people discern themselves and analyze the Pelourinho's historical landscape. Then, in chapter 6, I return conceptually to this property/propriety hybrid to specify how proper historicity functions as an agentive quality or source of empowerment that brings the flesh of Pelourinho residents back into history.

CHAPTER 5

Treasure Tales and National Bodies

Mystery and Metaphor in Bahian Life

On March 29, 1999, the government of the State of Bahia unveiled the results of its reform of Salvador's Praça da Sé, the seat of ecclesiastical power during colonial times and the largest public square in the Pelourinho Historical Center today. The new layout highlighted an archaeological site at the recently exposed foundations of the Igreja da Sé Primacial do Brasil, the Portuguese Americas' first cathedral that, according to the State Government of Bahia, the voyager Gabriel Soares de Souza declared in 1584 to be "the most sumptuous temple in all of the Americas."[1] But what most fascinated visitors to the recently uncovered vestiges of the shrine, torn down in 1933 by urbanists eager to reproduce the Parisian-inspired reforms of Rio de Janeiro and please English shareholders in Salvador's streetcar company, were a number of exposed human skeletons strewn atop and alongside one another.

A quarter century before the unexpected reappearance of the human remains, residents outraged by the razing in 1975 of Salvador's ornate public library to clear room for a modernist city hall annex had come to call the side of the Praça da Sé "the Sucupira." This was an ironic reference to a pharaonic cemetery funded from public coffers by Sr. Odorico Paraguaçu, the corrupt mayor of the fictional Bahian village of Sucupira and the protagonist of *O Bem Amado*, a well known, prime-time, serialized television drama that aired in 1973.[2] And in the days before the reinauguration in 1999, as workers hurried to uncover, catalogue, and remove the skeletons to the nearby

Figure 5.1. Members of an excavation supervised by Dr. Carlos Etchevarne uncover human remains, February 1999.

Museu de Arqueologia e Etnologia (Museum of Archaeology and Ethnology) located within the Bahian Faculty of Medicine building that towers over the Rocinha, the public began to comment on the work and remains uncovered at the Sucupira. As municipal and state bureaucracies planted competing articles in the local press in attempts to gain control of the project, passersby and neighborhood regulars climbed the nearby Edifício Themis in search of an overarching view of the activity they believed would reveal the mysteries of their familiar city center. Pelourinho residents, who frequently told stories of human skeletons and valuable treasure lying under the floors and in the walls of their homes, saw their claims validated as accounts of gold, tiles, ornate rings, and jewels found by workers and smuggled out under the eyes of heritage authorities and foremen circulated freely.

On the night of the plaza's reinauguration, following speeches by Governor César Borges and Mayor Antônio Imbassahy, the public flocked to examine

Figure 5.2. View of the Sucupira from the Edifício Themis.

the graves and the exposed bones. A crowd of well-wishers, some dressed in folkloric costumes, mobbed the two men's political godfather, Antonio Carlos Magalhães. During his speech, Mayor Imbassahy had presented the first public history of Bahian origins mediated by the Praça da Sé's archaeological site. He claimed, "the team of archaeologists . . . has . . . already found coins, jewelry, necklaces and tools, fragments of indigenous Tupi ceramics, and Portuguese pottery shards. They have even registered indigenous ceramics, dated to the period between 1339 and 1389, thus proving that the Tupinambá inhabited this area." For the mayor, the excavation and its artifacts rooted Bahian, and by extension, Brazilian, history in the intermingling of Portuguese and Native Brazilian ceramics at a site dated as settled before the Portuguese conquest.

Despite Imbassahy's attempt to define what had emerged from his city's soil, at the actual site of the former cathedral's foundations, just beyond the frenzied greetings and currying of political favor, visitors found a slightly drunk worker surrounded by skeletons. The man offered yet another "official" explanation of the tear in a ground that, frequented in recent memory by prostitutes, hot dog vendors, pickpockets, tourists, and sellers of Chinese toys smuggled from Paraguay, had been resacralized through the uncovering of the hidden ruins of Brazil's first cathedral and the unveiling of a forgotten cemetery. The worker, clad in hard hat and overalls, called himself a "field architect" even though the archaeologist in charge of the site later told me that no such job description existed among his employees.

The tone and rhetoric of the self-proclaimed field architect's explanations—reproduced at length below—echoed the cadences and concerns in the speeches politicians had proffered just minutes earlier. But his message was highly critical. Surrounded by skeletons, he suggested that Brazil's transition to "free" labor was a sham, that the Pelourinho's colonial architecture was the materialization of the sins of an avaricious white elite interested in killing slaves whose bones now lay in full view, and that he, like the slaves before him, had secretly but righteously appropriated all manner of valuable objects during his workdays. Yet the worker also praised Magalhães' political alliance and defended an economic system that favors a privileged few while excluding or underpaying the vast majority of Bahians.[3]

Two tourist police officers arrived quickly to shoo onlookers beyond the site's protective cords and cut short the field architect's tenure within colonial Lusitania's once-buried ruins. As soon as he spied them, the first priest of what I will call the "Oracle of the Sucupira" took advantage of the confusion and slipped off into the crowd.[4] The police immediately "corrected" the worker/historian, claiming that only a fool would imagine that slaves could be buried in such an important place and that the bones were those of nobles laid to rest alongside the cathedral, hence close to God. This reinterpretation continued throughout 1999 and 2000 at the hands of politicians, military police, and university students hired by Salvador's tourist agency to disseminate an official story of harmonious racial mixture and monumental national patrimony overseen by the government of Bahia.

Among the speeches that preceded, and that seem to have influenced the field architect's vocabulary and bearing, was a flowery discourse—complete with the studied grammatical miscues and transpositions of consonants that Antonio Carlos Magalhães recommended to his associate so as to render their talks "popular" and thus blur the boundaries between the erudite and the vernacular—offered by Governor César Borges. The governor's message revolved around spirituality, or a soulful self, tied to a landscape, presented as an "economy of signs" put together by his government and all who call themselves Bahians. As the governor declared, "the primary duty of every citizen is that of preserving his or her land." Therefore, he continued,

> During this celebration of the 450 years of our city, the very best present we might give to Salvador is to make sure that things and identities become more and more untouchable. The point is to permit them to last centuries by means of an economy of signs that we should cultivate as sacred. There is nothing that particularizes more our city than its good populace. For those who have been here since the cradle as well as those who might stop by here for a time, whether short or long, whether to put down or not to put down roots, to care for Salvador is to incorporate into your personal world a piece of this spirituality, singular in its essence but plural in its manifestations—of affectivity, hospitality, sincerity and solidarity.

The speech mixed midcentury Brazilian corporatist interest in collective representations and sacred objects with liberal ideas about property, citizens' labor, and free and responsible members of a community. According to the man who governed Bahia at the time, landscapes help produce selves; responsible selves work to preserve communal landscapes and possessions by extracting them from everyday contexts; and such skilled and useful selves are characterized by four manifestations of a unifying spirituality, namely, "affectivity, hospitality, sincerity and solidarity."

At the root of the four "virtues" lies spirituality—at least in the version of the world advocated publicly by Borges—or a soulful inner private self, tied to a public landscape presented as carefully constructed by all who call themselves citizens. Borges employed heritage to mold citizens, to champion responsible selves in a neoliberal order under which patrimony plays a growing role in Salvador's political economy, and thus to "teach Bahians how to be Bahians," as

IPAC's spokesman once claimed to me when describing the importance of the Pelourinho reforms.

Yet souls are largely invisible, or secret. The apperception of a soul, like the attempt to delineate a person's race, involves a relationship between the visible and invisible in which certain material, perceivable sign vehicles or observable dispositions supposedly point at interior qualities that are otherwise unavailable for direct contemplation.[5] These potentials, which are typically presented in modern racial thought as metaphysical entities that indicate something definitive about the nature of their bearers, may range from intelligence to slothfulness, moral probity to outright licentiousness, or descent and connection to other people on the basis of biology or experience. A race-based identification, like the attempt to specify whether the skeletons encountered under the Praça da Sé were colonial elites or African slaves, thus relies on the perceptual and interpretive repertoire available to a community. And given the extent to which cultural heritage discourse presents the nation's patrimony as something authentic, pre-given, and enduring that must be uncovered and preserved, the interpretive or semiotic techniques encouraged by heritage's growing influence in Bahia might work also in a variety of related domains to "harden" understandings of groups' and people's ostensibly defining features. This is one reason Borges' sentimental appeal to affectivity, hospitality, sincerity, and solidarity—or four specific ways of suturing together a Bahian people—is so indicative of what has taken place in the Pelourinho.

Jens Andermann, in his discussion of the influence of natural history museums on shifting ideas of race and nation in late-nineteenth-century Brazil and Argentina, refers to something akin to Borges' "affectivity, hospitality, sincerity and solidarity" as a "national being" produced as officials translated evolutionary histories into museum displays. Such spatializations of national development produced in museums an "'invisible' that mediated between the real and its representations," or "a form of truth located neither on the level of the museum object nor on that of the context to which it referred, but, rather, in that which made it possible to represent, in the relation between things and signs."[6] A century later, the density of dialogue in the Pelourinho around vestiges of Bahian ancestors made visible and arrayed within Salvador's four hundred and fiftieth anniversary commemorations suggests the rather similar, and special, role of the Praça da Sé in a historical center that the Secretary of Culture and Tourism dubbed "this brown and generous mother, whose ample lap shelters all of our ancestral secrets."[7]

Like Dona Katia and her body for the bohemian hospital employee—and, in spite of his academic gymnastics, perhaps also for the author of this book—the morally ambiguous Pelourinho mother functions as a field for the production of knowledges essential to Brazilian identities. Whether in promotional literature for carnival, the fiction of Jorge Amado, reports by IPAC researchers, or in representations of overlapping female bodies and colonial buildings both disgorging and being entered by stylized, masculine figures in the paintings of the red light district by well-known Bahian artists like Carybé, Pelourinho women enable a masculine discernment of invisible attributes supposedly lurking below the surface of social life and within otherwise inert material objects.[8] In the logic of the state, the tokens of Bahianness, or supposedly eternal national truths both held and shielded from clear view by the Afro-Brazilian woman, might be explained and brought to the surface by the types of social scientific research around which IPAC, modern Bahian anthropology, and the Pelourinho gained form after 1967.[9] But they might also be defined by Pelourinho residents and field architects who take pride in acting as "social scientists" by amassing dossiers, questionnaires, and reports on neighborhood phenomena. They might also be preserved and made untouchable as mysteries, as Governor Borges suggests in his speech, or be left somewhere in-between as part of a citzenry's and state's coproduction of belonging in a region where, as politicians reminded the crowds repeatedly, "Brazil was born."

Despite official attempts at "correcting" interpretations, Bahians, like their elected leaders, comment even today on the ways that human remains arrived on the plaza, the identities of those remains, the propriety of the display of skeletons on a public square, and the government's moral authority in offering a version of the histories of the dead these bones have come to represent.[10] The plaza is thus a place where people support, question, and mock others' interpretations, often screaming out their views to contest versions they leave in silence elsewhere in the Pelourinho. How then, in this setting, do manipulations of surface signs over the course of the reconstruction of the Praça da Sé come to influence a wider, turn-of-the-millennium politics in which race and slavery came to the fore within an incipient, Brazilian multiculturalism? How might people from across Salvador, in the midst of drinking a beer, filling a prescription, or picking up a new copy of their own birth certificate at a downtown notarial office, walk through and process an archaeological site that the state government of Bahia worked to code as supporting racial democracy? And, perhaps most centrally to this book's concerns, how do Pelourinho residents, so accustomed to having their domestic spaces opened up and analyzed by IPAC research, make sense of the state-directed revelation of what supposedly lies within the landscapes to which the patrimonialization process has joined them so tightly?

Different actors' methods for approaching the mysteries said to lie underground and within the Pelourinho's walls reveal how evidence, narratives, and historical value are produced in exchanges between citizens and institutions. The ways people move to resolve historical problems, and thus their approaches to making visible what is said to lie at the source of their society, elucidate mechanisms through which versions of the past become believable and real in a historical center designed to encourage its visitors to dig down deep and encounter, or make present, the essence of Bahia. But it remains to be seen whether or not that core functions exactly like the core imagined by IPAC and the politicians who inaugurated the Praça da Sé. In fact, it is not even entirely clear that residents accept the assertion that if one works in the proper manner, then one will encounter the objects and sentiments that the state argues it stewards as enduring, Bahian wellsprings of personhood, property, and future-oriented community.

Mysteries of Bahianness

The well-known public historian Cid Teixeira, touted in Salvador's press as "the father of Bahian history" in a curious tension with the brown mothers of mysterious Bahian culture, was much sought-after in the days following the inauguration of the Praça da Sé. He commented on the popular insistence that the Pelourinho was pockmarked with gold and riddled with tunnels: "The only way to research subterranean structures is digging up the earth. Almost all of them are aqueducts and sewage systems. The rest is simply the fruit of the imagination."[11] But Professor Teixeira's empiricist approach to "real" objects he counterposed to popular imaginings would not, as excitement built around what one IPAC official described to me as a "wonderful touristic opportunity, a mini-Pompeii right in our own backyard," do much to alter what appeared to be the Bahian state's rather consistent approaches to evidence and interpretation of the subsoil.

Mayor Imbassahy opened the commemorations by stressing, like Governor Borges as well as Professor Teixeira, the importance to Bahian identity of the preservation of heritage. But he then moved quickly to spirituality and mystery to proclaim,

> In this city everyone belongs to Oxum. This city of the Casa Branca *terreiro* from which the nationwide diffusion of Afro-Brazilian religious manifestations originated. In our impressive syncretism, the only of its type anywhere in the world, where the saints and symbols of Catholicism . . . fuse with the African deities and drums of Candomblé. *Ladies and gentlemen, to understand these mysteries is to live Salvador, to love this land, just as we are doing right now in inaugurating this new plaza.* Might we be capable of making

a new mark in its landscape? . . . This locale has extraordinary historical power. We have given it a careful landscaping and a new bronze monument to Tomé de Souza, Bahia's first governor. We have restored the bust of . . . Brazil's first bishop . . . and [we have] put in a special lighting system and an iron plaque . . . so that the populace and our visitors can see the foundations, which emerge from the age of monism.[12]

Mayor Imbassahy's assertion that new infrastructure would illuminate the cathedral's foundations, which serve as a door to an early modern period of "monism," suggests that his government's attempts to set off the opening in the ground might permit visitors to experience a sixteenth-century moment that predates the rest of the Pelourinho, a neighborhood often described in promotional materials as Latin America's largest Baroque architectural complex. This move is significant on at least two levels. First, by counterposing the Baroque to monism, or a premodern philosophical tradition characterized by an approach to an undifferentiated reality based on a shared substance and a single supreme god, Imbassahy calls attention to the Baroque's status as a symptom, or even a diagnostic, of the Enlightenment and its legacies.

Generally understood as arising in Europe in the early seventeenth century, the Baroque emphasis on artifice, interiority, and the passions reflects the "dissociationism" so constitutive of a modernity based on distinctions between selves and the world, spectators and participants, minds and bodies, and thus knowing subjects and the senses on which they rely.[13] The artistic and philosophical movement thus accompanied, and commented on metaphorically, a historically specific separation of an interiorized, knowing subject from something that would come to be coded as "reality." This took place around the time of René Descartes' valorization of reason as related to, but somehow different from, emotion and sense perception.

A Luso-American Baroque, and here we arrive at the second major implication of the word choices of Mayor Imbassahy's speechwriter, marks historically the Brazilian colonies', and Bahia's, seventeenth-century preeminence in the production of tropical commodities, especially cane sugar. Mid-twentieth-century Brazilian nationalists overwhelmingly associated this period with a creative cultural and racial mixture arising from plantations presented as spaces of intimacy, rather than violence. The speeches proffered on the Praça da Sé in 1999 emphasized repeatedly such tropical hybridity at the core of the modern nation, as well as the transcultural qualities of a Baroque that developed in Portugal's American colony, whose size and wealth threatened to overwhelm the metropole. They did so as part of a celebration of a Bahian citizenry understood as a collection of individual subjects animated by attachment to a special land. From the perspective enunciated on the Praça da Sé, these sovereign individuals might be molded by a state invested in protecting a symbolic landscape that knowing subjects might engage with, interpret, and thus come to know in ways that would influence them even as they were no longer tied to that backdrop by a premodern, monadic episteme.

While the ruptures so important to Imbassahy's attempt to set off Bahia's colonial Baroque as special, and distinct, took place across the Americas and Europe in historically and geographically uneven engagements, they are generally associated with the enshrinement of reason and representation—two bugaboos of a contemporary anthropology still reeling from late-twentieth-century critiques of culture and currently heavily influenced by strands of critical realist thought indebted to the object-oriented meditations of Bruno Latour—as essential to the production, testing, and circulation of claims about a world that lay outside, or anterior to, its interpreters.[14] Painted in overly broad strokes, this world open to apprehension on the part of knowing, bounded subjects, came to stand as the ultimate source of a reality that humans would need to struggle to discern.

Given the importance to modern thought of semiotic mediation, or the claim that people cannot know the world directly and thus depend on the senses and sign vehicles to achieve such enlightenment, it is not surprising that Imbassahy sought legitimacy through the *orixás*, or Candomblé deities. Within Candomblé, and across Bahia, the orixás mediate between humans and the highest of gods, Olorun. In still-dominant approaches to the religion, which are nonetheless increasingly rejected by Bahia's most esteemed practitioners who argue that their practices are authentically African, and thus seek to purify them of European influence, the orixás' mediations of African religiosity and Christianity include individual deities' association with Catholic saints.[15] This approach to the relationships between religious traditions guides the mayor's claims on the Praça da Sé, and he places Bahia's "impressive" syncretism—again, a word often contested by Candomblé practitioners and Black Movement activists because of the extent to which it functions in Bahia as a synonym for the miscegenation so often deployed to marginalize black Brazilians—at the root of the mysteries symbolized by the Casa Branca, or Bahia's oldest continuously functioning house of Candomblé.[16] In doing so, Imbassahy refers specifically to the *orixá* known as Oxum. He thus echoes a famous carnival song by the Bahian singer Gerónimo and plays on the fact that the feast of Salvador's patron saint, Nossa Senhora da Conceição, falls on December 8, the day devotees honor this cunning and mysterious female figure.[17]

Oxum vies with Iansã for the attention of the orixá known as Xangô, appearing in some accounts as Xangô's second wife. She is often sexually available and agentive, the vain goddess of the river who loves gold, jewelry, and other women's men. Here Oxum recalls the 1970s-era middle- and upper-class man's second girlfriend—generally a nonwhite working-class woman who may have exchanged sex for money, gifts, or her own enjoyment and resided in the historical center—described in chapter 3 by Ordep Serra, the anthropologist who once directed IPAC and has played such an important role in the declaration of Bahain *terreiros*, or Candomblé temples, as national patrimony. And, according to Salvador's mayor, everyone in Bahia belongs to Oxum. Imbassahy therefore bases his account of producing responsible citizens on a sensual Bahian culture tied to mysterious and not-quite-controllable women of the sort who are so foundational to making the Pelourinho a historical center.

In a move relatively common in nationalisms around the world, Imbassahy celebrates the enabling myth of modern Brazil as a wonderful enigma. Like the minister of culture and tourism's above-mentioned invocation of Pelourinho secrets harbored in the "laps of brown mothers," the mayor portrays cultural heritage as a mystery associated with such racial mixture. And the history and memories that the state claims to have rescued, even though purportedly arising from IPAC's "extremely secure" methods for revealing the intimate details of a population rendered folkloric, are explicitly about the production and cultivation of gendered Bahian mysteries that tie people to, and arise from, the landscape.[18] Rather than seeking clarity, Mayor Imbassahy appears to favor mystery as a correlate to a nationalist account of Portuguese, African, and Native Brazilian origins and their subsequent blurring within dominant twentieth-century racial politics.

Social scientific investigation and citizens' concern for their history, according to pronouncements by Bahian politicians on the Praça da Sé, produce knowledge of mysteries. Rather than paths into a clearer knowledge of social relations, these mysteries rise up as the cultural attributes or goods that stand behind Bahia's sacred signs. Mysteries, at least for politicians, and apparently for some Brazilians and visitors, are therefore valuable and foundational beyond the realm of language. In fact, they function as metonyms of, and even synonyms for, Bahian culture. From Imbassahy's perspective, to know and comprehend mysteries is to approach them, taste them, and experience their powers without working to resolve that which makes them inscrutable. Knowledge comes not from demystification, but through a contemplation of the beauty of the mystery, taken as an entity in itself. Such celebrations of well-known unknowns may appear contradictory to an outsider. Yet they make a certain sense in Bahia.

Discussions of Bahia's mysteries have long appeared in travelers' accounts, in the work of the novelist Jorge Amado and the urbanists charged with Salvador's development during the 1970s and 1980s, in tourist brochures and, notably, in foreign social scientific representations of the post–World War II period.[19] Bahians describing their land to outsiders will also often speak about its great mysteries. Those in the Pelourinho accustomed to contact with tourists will most likely break into their "gringo pidgin" at this moment, mixing Portuguese, Italian, and Spanish under a perceived English or German accent. Yet it is rare to hear a Bahian who is not a politician, social scientist, or tourism professional discuss such "mysteries" without recognizing his or her own participation in a dissimulatory discourse, or one designed to hide meanings and generate pragmatic effects as much as, if not more than, it transmits sincere perceptions.[20] Nonetheless, mystery pervaded the certainties put forth by the field architect during his interpretation of the hidden depths of the symbolic heart of Brazil.

Slavery Makes Its Way into History

Soon after the official inauguration of the "restored" Praça da Sé in 1999, the field architect—a man who both dissimulates and reveals the secrets of the past to his fellow citizens—climbed into the archaeological site and initiated the following dialogue. I pepper my transcription with italics to indicate rising speech, capitalized italics in cases of extreme excitement, ellipsis to indicate pauses, and dashes to indicate interruptions. The portion of the dialogue I taped went as follows:

> Field Architect: When the blacks [slaves] didn't want to work, when they couldn't take it any more, they chained them inside the . . . inside these tunnels and killed them right there.
>
> Woman:[21] *Ah.*
>
> Field Architect: So that today, they . . . we should find all of them dead, still inside those tunnels. Inside those tunnels.
>
> First Woman: *Ah, eh,* you've got to mark them off for excavation.
>
> Field Architect: *Ah, exactly!* They brought them to build this thing here, look. The stones . . .
>
> Second Woman: *And the bones! The bones are from what, whose bones are they, anyway?*
>
> Field Architect: We are digging up every last bone, we have every last one . . .
>
> Second Woman: *Are you gonna put them back here?*
>
> Field Architect: No, certain things are going to remain in the museum. The bones will go to a laboratory so that . . . so that we can figure out

how many millions of years old they are. We've got bones that are five hundred, a thousand years old. No? They'd [slaves] carry these stones here in order to create this architectural complex[22] that we see today, the churches, the beautiful buildings, the tiles, no? As a matter of fact, I have . . . I saved[23] a tile, a plate that today, should be worth . . . six or seven hundred *reais*, easily.[24]

First Woman: Eh, old stuff, neh???

Field Architect: I grabbed it, I saved it for me, because . . . I have a colleague, he saved . . .

Second Woman: *THE LORD'S CHILD.*[25]

Field Architect: I had to take it too.

First Woman: Eh, well, you're working, *arent' you?!?*

First Man: And these tunnels, are they going to remain exposed afterward?

Field Architect: No, this tunnel, if they recuperate it, and, and might be open for visitation or it might not, depending on the extent that it's damaged. If it is damaged.

John Collins: Where's the mouth of the tunnel?

Field Architect: The mouth of the tunnel is there, over there, look. [coughs loudly] That hole over here. That square hole. In the middle. The tunnel starts down here comes out in that staircase over there. Look. That staircase where that open area is, do you see that tent, that sign over there? Look.

First Woman: Yes, I see.

Field Architect: Going down the staircase. The tunnel goes from there all the way to the Calçada, underneath the whole city. And the, and the Lower City's tunnel, it begins here underneath the, the docks here, where the old Pães Mendonça supermarket was, where the old Pães Mendonça was. And it goes from here underground a long way until it hits a long hallway, exactly where the blacks walked, carrying everything on their backs in order to make their way up the hill—they came underground—in order to come out up here. And when they weren't carrying things, when they fled so they could explore the city, which at the time belonged to the barons of the epoch, no? The whites that produced it all, all the wealth, and then they killed the blacks and buried them here, right here in this place that you're standing.

Second Man: And it's true that there's a tunnel from Lapinha to here?

Field Architect: There's a tunnel from Lapinha to here. Exactly. It's one of them.

Second Man: *It comes from Lapinha all the way here??*

Field Architect: It comes from Lapinha all the way here. [1.5 seconds] All, all, all the way . . . Now this project is going to take more or less, to do everything that's needed, four more years in order to set up all of the necessary structure. And in order to accomplish this we have to elect another government that's ready to do all that, because if we go and put another group in power . . . [1 second]

Second Man: *Ave Maria*, that'll be the end of everything—

Field Architect: Yep, the end. They'll make us close up the tunnel and bury everyone.

John Collins: What do you do here at the site?

Field Architect: I'm a field architect.

John Collins: Mmmmm.

Field Architect: I'm an engineer, a field architect.

John Collins: I'm asking, I'm only asking because I'm an anthropologist from the U.S.—

Field Architect: Ah, you're an anthropologist!

John Collins: and I'm trying to write about the changes here in the neighborhood.

Field Architect: Wow, no, there's gonna be. There's a book. We have a book here in Bahiatursa[26] and we're going to have a copy too in here in the café.

John Collins: Sorry, you were saying, whose bones are these [showing him the microphone and tape recorder]?

Field Architect: The bones are those of black people, of slaves, of whites, and of . . . women. Children too who were killed because. Well, it's like this [clears throat]: At the time, as the story goes, the blacks had children. And in order that they not be born . . . they would go and kill the father, the mother, and the child. That's why we found over there [turning back on crowd and facing the skeletons] in that space over there. Look.

Second Man: Over there?

Field Architect: Yeah, yeah, do you see the *R* over there? The *R* and the *S*, there. Right there, there was a mummy all rolled up that's the father, the mother, and the child. We've already researched the area. It's a black man, a black woman, and their black child. [1 second] They were killed and chained together, the three of them, sleeping holding one another. [1.5 seconds]. And a black man with a golden jug, a gold bar with a golden cup in his hand, dead, chained together with another black man.

Third Man: Where's the golden cup?

Field Architect: Everything was taken away.

[Generalized laughter from onlookers, as if doubting that anything will return or mocking third man's naïve question.]

John Collins: Will they show the pieces in the museum?

Field Architect: They're going to show them—

[More incredulous laughter]

Third Man: Where's the gold . . . the golden cup [laughing skeptically].

Field Architect: No, this here doesn't belong to anyone. This here is ours, it's ours, it's ours—

Third Man: It's history, it is part of—

Field Architect: It's not just Brazil that's astonished by this discovery here, the whole world is astonished. This was a real shot in the arm for Bahia, because [2 seconds] there's unemployment around the world, war everywhere, but Bahia—

Fourth Man [Addicted to crack, born in the Maciel/Pelourinho and now living in a suburban slum]: Unemployment . . . Bahia's in first place, first place—

Field Architect: Yeah, Bahia, unemployment. That's not the point [Isso aí não interessa].

Fourth Man: *First Place.*

Field Architect: That's the way it is everywhere. That sort of thing happens everywhere. It's normal. Somebody has to get left out in the story, don't they [Alguém tem que sobrar na estória, não tem]?

Crowd: *Yeah.*

Fourth Man: *Yeah, someone has to die in order to give a job to the next guy.*

Field Architect: Hey, hey, hey, didn't black people get left out back in those days? And today what happens? Look, I'm white, but I would never . . . I'd never go against a race that contains the same, the same blood as mine. We're all human beings. But back in those times nobody wanted to hear this, back then the story was different. Now I personally think that a worker in today's world is worse off than the slaves of that period. Because at least in those days they killed slaves because they . . . resisted. And today you don't resist, one doesn't resist, and they're still killing us for small change. Today they're killing us in the street, like it's nothing [Estão matando a gente a migué, assim na rua].

Fifth Man: Like recently [1 second] they kill with *triolétricos*[27] and everything.

Field Architect: Yesterday the bus driver at the stadium. Yesterday the driver got all juiced at the game, got in his bus and hit two young men. One with a jersey from (the soccer team) "Bahia." And the two even [1 second] and worse, the two came close to dying holding one another. They were together, fighting, holding onto each other. Bahia and Vitória. "Your Vitória is worthless. I'm Bahia." The bus came, the guy got drunk, and killed the two of them. They died locked together. Two died together.

Fifth Man: It was a bus from the Monte Serrat Company.

Field Architect: Yeah, and it killed the two of them together. You can see the union of the two. One had his Vitória shirt on, and the other was Bahia. Shit, so there you see today's mentality. I think this is idiocy, ten thousand times worse than in the old days.

Fourth Man: But all that is the work of God.

[Incomprehensible as the field architect turns his back to show details of the bones to a newly arrived group of middle-class-looking women]

Field Architect: Did you write down my name? I'll look for you there. I'll fix things up with the congressman, I'll talk to him, we'll find a way to get it done. Quietly, quietly. Nobody knows! *Ciao, ciao.* [Turns to anthropologist who'd like to ask a question] Yes?

John Collins: And that cup, did you really find lots of gold?

Field Architect: No, well, let's just say, silver, gold.

First Woman: *Coins, porcelain.*

Field Architect: *Porcelain*, sterling silver, everything you can imagine.

John Collins: And that gold was right here, err, by the skeletons?

Field Architect: Yeah, that's it, in special places. In special safes that in those days were made of, of [1 second] wood with stones, in hiding places. They'd go and hide the gold. And that's why in our excavations we've come across various objects.

John Collins: But if the majority of those buried were slaves, how is it that they had so much gold, as slaves?

Field Architect: Don't people rob today? [.5 seconds] They used to steal.

And they saved things too.[28] The guy would work, work, work, and as a child of God he'd hide something. The slaves from that time, ehh, are you gonna come across a gold bar and not hold onto it? Who wouldn't pick it up? I'm working away, carrying a mountain of these stones, you see a piece of gold, aren't you going to save it? Of course you're gonna keep it! If the role of the white person, I'm talking about those days, no . . . the function of the, the white human being from that period was to kill black people, keep everything for himself, and put the others to work? Isn't that the way it was? So today . . .

[Various voices, incomprehensible]

Field Architect: No, all this was discovered because, when they started to rip up the pavement the bulldozers began to dig, to dig and when the machines uncovered the street a skeleton would appear out of nowhere. So they stopped all the work and we waited six months for this to be finished. To study, to put makeup on the site [*maquiar*], to map [*mapear*] everything. It slowed down our work, but . . . now everyone's proud of the fact that we waited, that we've got this work that's marvelous, it's really a very pretty job.

First Woman: Are you going to continue with the research in the area as a whole?

Field Architect: Everything! No, we're going to dig everything here. It's all going to be dug up!

While I was unable to talk with the field architect again, and none of the archaeologists and construction workers employed at the Sucupira could identify him, his metaphors and interpretations recall an earlier analysis of the Pelourinho's landscape by an eighty-two-year-old retired tailor, born on a plantation outside Salvador. After working in the city center for just over fifty years, Oswaldo's failing eyesight obliged him to take employment as a handyman in the Hotel Colon, a boarding house in the Maciel run by a Galician immigrant who was also one of Bahia's most notorious black market money changers. As Oswaldo aged, his employer stopped paying a salary and the ex-tailor began to work for room or board alone. Approximately two years before his death in 1995, following the Spaniard's command that he reach out "like a monkey" and take a banana, Oswaldo spat and called out, pointing at the square in front of him,

Yeah, boy, this life is really nutty. Ehhehehehehehehehehehehehehe . . . You know, boy, below that cross there's a bunch of dead people [*gente morta*] . . . Eh, the other day, when they dug it up; when they reformed the area[29]

and tore up the cobblestones,[30] the workers found a bunch of dead people. Skeletons, skulls; they were slaves stuck in the wide hole filled with dead people. Whole skeletons. When the workers [*lavradores*] got killed on the job, they'd just seal 'em up. Bury them right there. Yep, those sons of bitches would just pack them up any old way [*de banda*] in the walls, in the streets. That's why the walls are all so thick here. Look, look around you. All these buildings are filled with dead people.

The field architect and Oswaldo seem to make out little mystery surrounding the objects that lie below the ground on which they work. They understand the landscape as riddled with bodies of workers like themselves whose contributions led to entombment in the monuments from which elites derive financial gain. Yet Mayor Imbassahy has also seen the bodies. Imbassahy's bodies have similarly clear identities, although these have been substantiated by experts. Nonetheless, such clear factual support props up stories of mystery told by Bahia's political leadership. And Imbassahy, Oswaldo, and the field architect are not alone in their interest in surprising encounters with the dead: the North American novelist Josephine Humphreys, writing in a special travel supplement in the *New York Times*, claims in her article contradictorily entitled "Celebration":

> You may suddenly encounter a mysterious breeze that seems to rise out of nowhere. I suppose it comes from the sea, slipping into the Bay of All Saints just as the Portuguese did in 1549, then eddying at the base of the headland before climbing one of the many ladeiras, or steep hill-streets, toward the upper city and the colonial district known as the Pelourinho. . . . an enthusiastic young Carmelite showed me a famous statue by Francisco Xavier das Chagas, an 18th-century slave sculptor. The Chagas Cristo lies life-size and lifelike in a glass case. His wounds are meticulously carved, and the droplets of blood are rubies. . . . My Carmelite, who spoke no English, pointed me down the hall. "Catacombs," I thought he said. . . . And I was reminded, Salvador is a spirited city.[31]

Humphrey's account, like Imbassahy's, differs from Oswaldo's in that it revolves around the uncanny appearance of underground graves and an associated mystery and spirits thought to inhabit the Pelourinho's twisting alleys and manor houses. It seems a rather North American approach to haunting, whereby spirits and mediators appear in relation to places rather, as in Candomblé, to their own desires or people's actions in calling them down. In my experience, beliefs in ghosts and talk about the spirits of the dead are entirely absent among Pelourinho residents unless they happen to be guiding a tourist.[32]

My research suggests that stories of haunted houses are, in the historical center and across Bahia, restricted to intellectuals' accounts or novelistic depictions of the city.[33] But whether or not Pelourinho residents place any emphasis on ghosts and uncanny apparitions within their homes, mystery as a metaphor for pasts that gain power in their unknown qualities, which in turn aid in reworking the relationships between past and present in the exploitation of Afro-descendent bodies, helps sell Salvador to a cosmopolitan travel community. The *New York Times* article marked an opportunity for the expanding tourism trade, as indicated by the worried call from the president of the Bahian Association of Tourist Guides for further sanitization of the neighborhood[34] due to the fact that Humphreys introduced her long discussion of African-inspired Bahian cuisine by writing,

> Times are good now. . . . Yet wander astray in Salvador and you see the edges of serious poverty and desperation . . . no one will ever forget that the streets ran with blood. The name is a constant reminder. O Pelourinho. The whipping post. It was set in the public square for all to see.[35]

Humphreys, taken by Bahian authorities as a representative of the desires of affluent tourists interested in the Pelourinho as a cultural destination, then moves from the whipping post to the dining room. And this carries the text back to the author's governing trope, the *mysterious* breeze:

> breezes of Salvador carry with them . . . a smoky-citrus amalgam of what everyone's cooking at any given moment, in the *lancherias*[36] on every block, or the stands of the street vendors in the parks and squares. It was an exotic aroma to me, with a strong element of something heavy and tropical, totally unfamiliar. That something turned out to be red dendê oil, a staple of West African and Bahian cooking, often flavored with hot pepper.[37]

In Humphrey's account, poverty and a history of exploitation linked to African slavery appear as a discrete background for a tourist industry and identity politics based on redemptive beauty and a tasty exotic mixture made real in the same type of peppery *moqueca* stew that fascinated Manuel Bandeira in 1927. And experiences on the "whipping post" seem a gift to the future offered by suffering ancestors to be enshrined through mystery and "remembered" in the present through "celebration" by visitors and politicians.

Tourists and Bahian politicians appear to adore mystery. Mystery is valuable, it attracts dollars, and it allows Imbassahy to cover up poverty in outlying neighborhoods by tying people to his historical center. But mystery in the Pelourinho is also much more subtle, and works on many levels.

The Treasure in History

While I did not speak again with the field architect about his linkage of slavery and treasure on the Praça da Sé, I did discuss the density of residents' talk about buried treasure and skeletons with Luciano Diniz, IPAC's chief spokesman. Diniz confirmed that skeletons had been found in various places in the Pelourinho. Yet he scoffed at popular claims about treasure, undercutting such assertions to knowledge through a familiar Bahian expression used to counter malicious gossip and "folk" beliefs: He told me that stories of wealth lying under the Pelourinho's streets and in its walls were simply "an invention of the people" (uma invenção do povo), but added almost immediately,

> Well, there *was* one occasion when we found a horde of silver. It was during the renovation of the cathedral.[38] Up there, beside the organ, in a hidden compartment behind a plaster wall that was painted over, the workmen discovered a room full of enormous silver candlesticks. It seems that a priest or someone working in the church must have horded them and perhaps he died before he was able to retrieve them. But there have been no other discoveries of hidden precious metals here in the Pelourinho! That's ridiculous, it's just the people talking.

Diniz's approach to the past, and to the subterranean depths of the Pelourinho, is challenged not only by his own interest in and admission of exceptional discoveries of treasure, but also by Dona Niza and Seu Jorge, two long-term residents of the Pelourinho. Having lived together for just over twenty years, Dona Niza and Seu Jorge received an indemnification in 1998 from the State of Bahia in exchange for their house on the Pelourinho's Ladeira da Misericórdia. After moving with a number of former Maciel/Pelourinho neighbors to the working-class city of Simões Filho just outside of Salvador, neither remained in regular physical contact with the Pelourinho and its modifications. Unable to afford the bus fare to visit downtown regularly, they usually asked me for accounts of their former neighborhood's ongoing reforms even as new neighbors in Simões Filho often flocked to their front step to hear accounts of derring-do in the city center. During one of my visits, they became agitated as I told them of my trip to Rio de Janeiro to examine the archives of the national heritage organ, IPHAN, and my attempts to confirm residents' skeleton stories in light of those official archives.

Dona Niza and Seu Jorge's reactions help demonstrate that claims about the Pelourinho's subsoil by Oswaldo and the field architect come not as individual musings, but as part of widespread talk about bodies, treasure, and buildings in a neighborhood in which the presence of foreigners, multiple state institutions

Figure 5.3. Dona Niza, her daughter, and a neighbor at Niza's candy and cigarette stand in front of the Sucupira.

and NGOs, as well as a thriving trade in illicit substances and sex means that residents face the possibility of rapid but often officially unexplainable or publicly invisible enrichment. And they show how stories about homes occupied prior to 1992, seemingly spurred in part by IPAC indemnifications that demonstrated to residents a valorization of their domestic spaces, have come to conform in certain ways to the outlines of government accounts of mysterious, powerful, and yet ultimately unreachable communal objects and origins.

For example, in 1999 Dona Niza and Seu Jorge remarked, squabbling and cutting one another off, on the discovery in 1993 of skeletons in front of the

Church of São Francisco (Igreja de São Francisco). This was something that Oswaldo had employed to comment on, and perhaps explain, his slavelike status.

Jorge: On that day that they, that they took out all the gold, there were a ton of policemen on the square. Police, guys taking photographs—

Niza: Reporters, news teams—

Jorge: And they found skeletons, many skeletons there too. All this just because they wanted to put in a sewer system!

Niza: The news, it was the television, "televisioning" all that stuff—

Jorge: Now, the gold, nobody knows where it went. They say that it went to the museum—

Niza: They say it went to, to, to, to the university—

Jorge: No! The gold went to the *museum*, and the *university* took the bones, woman!

Niza: No, it all went to the university. It all went to the university so that from the university it could go to the museum—

Jorge: But nobody knows if it's really in the museum—

Niza: Now you've got me, I don't know—

Jorge: Whether all of it went, or just a bit . . .

Later that week, when I visited again, the two continued:

Jorge: I don't remember the year, but there was a little square showing flush against the wall and—

Niza: Where we cooked!

Jorge: Yes, where we cooked . . . A little frame, little like this [indicating with his hands a square approximately 18 inches by 18 inches]. So I decided that I had to dig there, because maybe I would find something of value. I had an intuition. So I waited because she was out in the street and when she got home I said, man—

Niza: It was, logically, the day that the, the prince—

Jorge: Yeah . . .

Niza: arrived to visit

Jorge: So she got home—

Niza: *Where was that prince from? You have to tell him where the prince was from. The prince arrived from where, pops?*

Jorge: *Oh, yeah, I don't remember any more.* So she told me not to touch anything there, that it might be bones, and that we'd find a cadaver and then the police would want an explanation for the corpse over there. So I got real scared and I didn't finish digging.

Niza: He didn't finish digging—

Jorge: Even by digging just a bit, I disturbed a lot of sand. Lots of sand came out. I saw some bricks, like the ones you see there under the table, kind of like a catacomb down below like this—

Niza: But tell it all, there was the Padilha too.[39]

Jorge: So I started to dig. Only sand came out. So the people up top were looking down through the floorboards at me. There even arose a discussion, a rumor that I was digging so that I could find gold or somesuch thing.

Niza: Treasure!

Jorge: Yeah, so afterward we had to leave that house, the number 7 run by Parafuso.[40] You see, it's really not a very good house.

Whether or not Niza and Jorge left Parafuso's house because it was not a good place to live, or because of Jorge's digging, or because they fought too much with their upstairs neighbors who later moved to an abandoned nightclub on the Ladeira da Misericórdia, where they would be visited by the health professionals discussed in chapter 6, or because they drank too much of the alcohol they were supposed to sell for the owner in lieu of rent, they never successfully put their hands on any treasure. However, they claim that the gold was eventually discovered by representatives of the Bahian state, whom they came to know well in the course of sociological investigations that allowed IPAC to define them, fuzzily, in negotiations over the value of their indemnification that helped the family associate that state bureaucracy with treasure.

Jorge: Afterward, I found out that after we left, they dug down and found a chest stuffed with gold coins. They found a gold crown. And a gold braid.

Niza: A golden braid and a chest full of gold!

Jorge: Everything in antique coins, gold coins, you see? It was a dog's skull and a person's skull too, wasn't it?

Niza: No, just the dog's skull—

Jorge: Ah, a dog's skull—

Niza: With a collar and a bunch of gold!

Jorge: In the chest—

Niza: And the dog had a gold crown!

Jorge: I'd have been rich if I had gotten a hold of that gold. I wouldn't have given it to anyone, no way! What goddamned state?!? It would have been mine, mine! Nobody was going to know. I'd melt it all with a torch. I'd sell it in little pieces. Today here, tomorrow there, afterward out that way. I'd never sell it all in one place. I'd just sell small pieces little by little. Melted gold!

Niza: Did you know that they found lots of gold in front of the São Francisco Church too? Near the cross.

John Collins: Um hum—

Niza: You knew about it?

John Collins: I know that officially they did not find gold, just bones and skeletons—

Niza: They found gold! I was there!

Jorge: And in the São Francisco [Church] they found gold too.

Niza: I was there that day. They took out a bag—this big [motioning with hands apart]—transparent. A white plastic bag, a big one, right. I was there with [my children] Guilherme, Tainara, Alberto, João, everyone was there. The kids were saying, "What is it mom, is that a gold mine?" Even today they can't figure out where all the gold went, understand?

Jorge: Antique gold chains, medals—

Niza: Thick braided cord, like my finger.

If IPAC spokesman Diniz just barely allows treasure to slip into his story of the Pelourinho restoration, Dona Niza and Seu Jorge make it central to their account of the changes to their neighborhood, the removal of families, and the value of the past: On the day the "prince," a foreign dignitary—who I believe was the President of Portugal—came to visit the Pelourinho, workers supposedly uncovered a dog's skull and a gold crown, a quite unhomely bit of the past that lay undiscovered, but intuited, within the family's by-then defamiliarized former abode.

The crumbling building whose interior details suggested to Seu Jorge that there might be treasure lying somewhere becomes synonymous with wealth when "restored" through patrimonialization. The past becomes valuable for Niza and Jorge in a process that begins with their indemnification in return for relinquishing the homes that, in theory, they own under squatters' rights laws and that are filled with valuables that seem to stand in for their understandings of the extent to which labor and value crystallized in those buildings remains hidden or tantalizingly out of reach. I will return to Dona Niza and Seu Jorge later in this chapter. For the moment I move, once again, to the Praça da

Figure 5.4. University student "explaining" the Praça da Sé skeletons, July 1999.

Sé to look at the memories woven around architectural and archaeological detail and newly discovered bones. And I do so in a way intended to clarify how stories of proper burial in the Pelourinho today become a part of much longer debates over people, bodies, and the power of institutions to structure Bahians' ethical worlds.

Revolts over Bones: 1999

The university students and the police who replaced the field architect as interpreters of the Praça da Sé archaeological site, which is the only place in the Pelourinho where government employees are called upon to explain landscape, history, or tourist sites, face Bahians who insist that they possess the correct information about the bones and the processes that brought them to the plaza and, later, to light. The state's sanctioned interpreters must therefore interact in a civil way with the bearers of alternative messages so as to offer an official history of bones that often relies on an emphasis on mystery grafted onto methodological certainties derived from social science. For example, I overheard a slightly inebriated, middle-aged man whom I knew as a Pelourinho resident who earned a living as a street vendor, complain,

> You don't know shit about the history of this plaza. You weren't even born when this all happened. You're from Bahiatursa [state tourist authority] and you're gonna give me explanations about the history of Bahia? That's for

you all [pointing to the anthropologist]. . . . There're so many cemeteries in Salvador and they need to show these damned bones here? What they did, what they did was go to a cemetery and get a bunch of bones, then they stuck them here for tourists to see. That's ridiculous—the public health authorities [SUCAM, the municipal hygiene authorities] come into my house to hunt mosquitoes and then the government goes and puts this garbage in the middle of the plaza!

The tourist policewoman on duty that day replied patiently, "Well, sir, if you'd like to see the objects and hear their explanation by the archaeologist in charge of the project, you may walk over to the Museum of Archaeology and Ethnology on the Terreiro de Jesus." As she turned back to me, she rolled her eyes and began to describe the litany of "crazy" claims made by people about the Praça da Sé bones: "They keep insisting that they're [the skeletons] from slaves. Why would these people think that slaves would be buried in such an important place, overlooking the harbor, next to the cathedral and alongside the Archbishop's residence? These people were priests. Fat, rich, priests covered in gold. They were rich—just look how many valuables the archaeologist found!"

The bones are in no way mysterious for the man who comments on their proper place. He has no doubt about where they should go and how they got to the plaza. The beautiful mystery emphasized by the mayor is not an issue for the man who worries about the pollution of his familiar space or for the policewoman who answers him. While the street vendor does not discuss their identities and does not reveal *how* he knows their story, he is sure about the political uses of the bones on the Praça da Sé: They are for pleasing tourists, not Bahians. And they arrived on the plaza as a result of the government's attempts to cater to such visitors.

Augusto, another long-term Pelourinho resident and one of the founders of S.O.S. Children of the Historical Center, understands mysteries and skeletons somewhat differently. While starring in a reggae music video filmed inside the Gueto at number 18 Saldanha da Gama Street, he commented in reaction to the director's discussion of the possible uses of camera angles for fixing and presenting the ongoing illicit "action" in this building as a context for the video,

Yeah, there are a thousand and one angles for filming in this *Gueto*. Man, there're a lot of things that never come to light in this place [turning to his bandmate]. Have you seen the skeletons? We have to get this cameraman to film the bones. Yeah. There they are, lying there. All of them from the rich. You can tell from the ways they're buried, one on top of the other. They got offed. The guys they were battling for power wiped the floor with those people. Poor suckers. Dutch. English. Wasn't that a church? There's a bunch of priests down there too. They'd chuck the cadavers out the window under cover of darkness. That's the way it is: You, John, you're here in Brazil, but if you're not in agreement with them, they wipe the floor with you [*passam o rodo*]. At night "Joe Blow" [*nego*] goes and chucks you in the hole and nobody knows anything about anything.[41]

As with the passerby who points out the state's lack of propriety in displaying the bones on the plaza, Augusto assigns definite identities to the individual skeletons even though he does not understand the remains as slaves or bodies recently placed on display for tourist consumption. And his words seem to be designed to intimidate the foreign visitor, or at least to make him aware of the situation faced by residents of the Gueto who suffered significant abuses at the hands of the local police battalion, the "18th Battalion of Love": Augusto does not revel in the mystery of fusions and cultural manifestations arising from Bahian history as does Mayor Imbassahy. Instead, he identifies the skeletons as priests and vanquished foes of the Portuguese, fitting them into his version of a history that corresponds to his perceptions of strife and the relative powerlessness of all in Bahia when faced with political might. The mystery involved in his formulation is that which confronts in its obviousness: In Augusto's view, people have gotten themselves killed throughout history for offending the powers that be. Most everyone may claim to know this to be true, yet the act of throwing an enemy into a hole under the cover of darkness remains shrouded in mystery even as it is frighteningly clear. This public secret is mysterious because it cannot be brought to light, even as all know it takes place.[42]

Augusto indicates that what happened to the murdered person is in fact nothing of a mystery—he implies that people do not "know" what happened to the murdered individual due to their own fear of similar fates, not because the action of killing people and throwing them in hidden graves is mysterious in Bahia. Rather, it appears somewhat common, much like the attitude of Roque, a worker digging up bones on the Praça da Sé in July 2000 who told me that the skeletons did not really garner his attention because dead bodies were nothing new to him, a daily feature on the periphery where people's "diversion" often includes visiting cadavers left by police and thieves.

Augusto's interpretations seem also to be a way of understanding the bureaucracy that, as he spoke to me, attempted to exercise a right of eminent domain over the Gueto, his home. He begins to make out this structure of power in light of mysteries. These are not mysteries that the state presents as mysterious but rather mysteries that leave public, state-sponsored mysteries bare, demonstrating that the history of the Gueto should not be articulated publicly due to its nefariousness. If heritage derives from official mysteries produced through the careful cultivation of objects and events by means of state attempts to patrimonialize and thus withdraw them from everyday use and exchange, then the Gueto's history is also one of both dissimulation and extraction of clearer interpretations from public exchanges. In pointing this out I am not, in a manner akin to those who would separate memory and history, arguing that mystery accrues to one side of the erudite/popular divide. Rather, I am looking at how state and citizen draw on one another in what is at base a coconstruction on the Praça da Sé of the conditions of possibility for ongoing reinterpretations of Bahian history.

Speaking and Acting through, for, about, and as Others

In speaking about the past as a figure of their contemporary landscape, Pelourinho residents produce interpretations of their state government around heritage and history even as that government works to produce a people around the same symbols. The two sides create images of one another in mutual exchanges over skeletons that connote human bodies and treasure that point in turn to homes converted into valuable architectural heritage. A Pelourinho population that was specifically targeted by IPAC educational projects from 1967 onward in an attempt to produce a representative Afro-Brazilian and properly historical folkloric group thus employs its experiences with, and that state's representations of the workings of, IPAC so as to analyze and depict that same bureaucracy within a broader narrative of exploitation. Thus state and citizen make use of similar evidence, devices, and characters in a manner that often results in their mutual confusion and distinct actors' manipulations of evidence and curiosity about treasure and the subsoil fail to rise to a neat, bounded approach to history that might come to be identified with one side of the state-citizenry nexus.

In an example of the dynamic between state and citizen, the field architect employs certain devices to turn himself into the putative representative of the Bahian state as he stands over the skeletons. He is clear in his message—he compares the present to slavery, making the objects of cultural heritage management into signs of the bodies of a population brought to Salvador in chains and killed by white elites—but his delivery and vocabulary comment on the ways that the population to which he refers becomes a part of the national patrimony. Like Antonio Carlos Magalhães, who entered his limousine as the field architect began his dialogue, the construction worker seeks to be a patron or a conduit to another more powerful figure as he says to those who solicit his aid, "Did you write down my name? I'll look for you there. I'll fix things up with the congressman, I'll talk to him, we'll find a way to get it done. Quietly, quietly. Nobody knows! *Ciao, ciao.*" Even as the worker enunciates a critique of the inequalities that surround him, he employs the rhetorical and political strategies of the people who maintain such structures. Given a small audience, he puffs out his chest and acts like ACM did minutes before, mixing populist social critique, patronage, and personal power with technical terms that sound like those I had overheard the head archaeologist employ while talking to his workers. But the field architect does not stop with a mimicry of archaeologists or Magalhães' mannerisms.

Compare, for example, the field architect's final descriptions of his work, the items found, and the goals of the excavation on the Praça da Sé reproduced above to the fragment below, extracted from Mayor Imbassahy's speech on March 29 on the Praça da Sé:

> The team of archaeologists, coordinated by the director of the Museum of Anthropology and Ethnology of the Federal University of Bahia, Professor Carlos Etchevarne, has been conducting an urban archaeology project. Here they have already found coins, jewelry, necklaces and tools, fragments of indigenous Tupi ceramics, and Portuguese pottery sherds. They have even registered indigenous ceramics, dated to the period between 1339 and 1389, thus proving that the Tupinambás inhabited this area. This work, we can all see, is going to continue. When we begin the second stage of the revitalization of this plaza we will build, next to the cathedral, in an area that once belonged to the Jesuit College, a memorial to the Holy See, a memorial to our city. This plaza is the result of many cold nights of labor by construction workers, the fruits of the efforts of Governor Borges and Senator Antonio Carlos Magalhães, whose hard work allows us to present this plaza to you tonight, in the name of Bahian and of Brazilian pride!!

The field architect tells the audience, before listing his finds and the objects he has taken home, that he is going to dig everything up to uncover every last bone and jewel to take to the museum so as to determine their age. Although he is not sure exactly how old they are, like the mayor he catalogues the items, dates them, and promises an edifice that will serve as a memorial to the city and, it seems, his "administration."

The field architect was not alone in his performance of and parasitism on ways of speaking that are designed to mimic and produce distinct social groups. Mayor Imbassahy and Governor Borges, trained as an engineer and a medical doctor, respectively, sound like art historians or cultural anthropologists who have just learned that traditions may be invented.[43] Their speeches confused many working-class listeners on the plaza and led Bahian social scientists to whom I showed transcriptions to marvel at the extent to which the politicians had appropriated "their" ways of talking about culture and history.

Again, Antonio Carlos Magalhães used to encourage "his" politicians to make intentional grammatical and morphological errors, replacing, for example, "problema" with "pobrema," so as to approximate working-class ways of speaking Bahian Portuguese. On the night of the Praça da Sé's inauguration, this produced strange collisions as the mayor and governor struggled with a language of social constructivism and patrimony interspersed with imitations of the language of the poorest members of society. The field architect's and the politicians' appropriations exemplify the entanglement of content, genres, grammars, and prosody in the making of memories in the Pelourinho. And they demonstrate the extent to which an IPAC attempt to interpret, or map, the "people," like the people's struggle to understand their state, ends up reifying both people and state in ways that make each more available to the other's political agendas.

Bahian History via Problematic Populations and Fortress Cities

I have not yet determined the author of Borges' speech, but municipal planning officials identified the author of Imbassahy's text as Francisco Senna, a historian of architecture who headed the Fundação Gregório de Mattos, Salvador's municipal cultural institution and archive. Professor Senna never, to my knowledge, commented directly and publicly in his own name on the bones discovered on the Praça da Sé. But his pronouncements are important to thinking about the interpretations of the past and Brazilian bodies on the Praça da Sé: Within six months of the Praça da Sé's inauguration, Senna, the author of Imbassahy's interpretation of the restoration and investigation of buried skeletons, would produce another public speech about political participation, Salvador's landscape, and working people.

In late October 1999 Professor Senna offered a lecture entitled "Evolução Física de Salvador" (The Physical Evolution of Salvador) at Salvador's old city hall, which stands near the Sucupira and alongside the field architect's recently discovered archaeological site. Sponsored by the Instituto da Memória Pedro Calmon, a municipal foundation dedicated to preserving Bahian social memory and named after one of the state's wealthiest and most illustrious families, Senna's speech celebrated Salvador's 450th anniversary and the recent reissue by his Fundação Gregório de Mattos of a glossy planning text that bore the same title as the talk. His appearance also helped him vie for inclusion in the Bahian Academy of Letters. And it supported the re-election bid of Mayor Imbassahy, who won another four-year term in October 2000. The talk thus had the feeling of a triumphant party as Bahia's cultural elite crowded the hall. Present were the former state secretary of education and culture; the undersecretary of culture and tourism; the rector of the Federal University; the managing editor, the owner, and the business manager of *A Tarde*, northeastern Brazil's most influential newspaper; and the head of the Bahian Geographical and Historical Institute.

In the midst of such rich Bahian tradition, the speaker performed admirably. Without the aid of notes, he offered an erudite and seamless lecture loaded with historical detail that chronicled Salvador's rise from a Portuguese fortress city to its current position as Brazil's "cradle of culture," a center of arts and learning characterized by a beautiful yet mysterious culture with roots in the mixture of Portuguese, Native Brazilian, and African peoples. The move from the figure of a city conceived as a "cidade fortaleza," or the fortified home of local elites and Portuguese colonizers who required defenses against their slaves and Native Brazilians, to the culturally dynamic and tropically sensual center of Brazilian heritage, stands in general accordance with hegemonic ideas about twentieth-century Brazilian racial democracy.

Within his account of cultural evolution, Senna added the problematic of Salvador's population: poor workers, who in Bahia are usually thought to exhibit fewer Portuguese and more African cultural traits, necessarily gained limited access to the city of Salvador as a result of the rural-to-urban migration so prevalent in Brazil's post–World War II history. Senna made this demographic shift, its accompanying urban problems, and their attention at the hands of municipal government the main theme of his talk as he returned across his account of different periods of the city's growth to the issue of impoverished citizens. Their supposed disruption of the social fabric became especially pressing during the 1960s and 1970s, a period Senna described as characterized by a crush of migrants from the countryside who flooded into previously well-ordered neighborhoods, overwhelming the economic networks and social services of the Bahian capital. Nonetheless, as Senna reached the 1990s, he offered hope for a reversal of this situation, crediting international and federal programs for limiting population growth and claiming that this demographic shift meant that municipal and state governments were finally catching up and providing education and infrastructure. Examples of this success included the reform of the Praça da Sé, the Ministry of Education's dial-in registration system for public school students, and the CONDER program "Viver Melhor" (Live Better), which involves the "moralization" and "legalization" of plots of land and autoconstructed homes on Salvador's periphery.

Senna's message was that people—people out of place, people who had too many children, rural people who did not know how to live in a cultured city, and people who did not understand proper hygiene and morality—rather than urban services or their management, have long constituted Salvador's most pressing problem. In the midst of his narrative of order and progress, which culminated with an increasingly well-managed urbanization under Mayor Imbassahy, Senna described the mid-nineteenth-century reform of a public space that seemed to offer empirical evidence, of a sort quite different from the "reading" of tunnels and bones conducted by the field architect, about the relationship between Salvador's most important public plazas and African slaves.

Senna recounted the making of Salvador's best-known plaza after the Praça da Sé, the "Campo do Forte de São Pedro." This large, open space was later renamed "Praça Dois de Julho" in order to commemorate the date of Salvador's freedom from Portuguese military occupation. Today it is commonly called "Campo Grande" (Large Field). According to Senna, Campo Grande's urbanization arose in an interesting manner as an English preacher, part of the group of European traders and bankers so important to Salvador's nineteenth-century economy, pushed for the reform of the parade ground at the center of the British neighborhood along the Corredor da Vitória Avenue. The expatriates who lived there, so important to changing perceptions among Bahian elites about the desirability of modern, seaside homes rather than Pelourinho mansions, had become tired of the mud and dust that hindered their leisure in the large unfinished square. In the mid-nineteenth century they demanded that the area be urbanized.

"Para ingles ver," or "for English eyes," is a common saying in Portuguese that describes dissimulatory surface appearances designed to satisfy foreigners who might pry into Brazilian affairs and uncover information to which they should not be privy.[44] The expression arose in the nineteenth century as slave traders succeeded in avoiding British squadrons authorized by Brazilian authorities to intercept and confiscate all such cargoes after 1845. It suggests that Brazilians are more aware of the reality of their social and cultural environments than foreigners are, and that, in a move akin to Michael Herzfeld's delineation of "cultural intimacy," they generate solidarity around types of rueful recognition that they do not necessarily wish to share with those from afar.[45]

The British residents, as presented in Senna's talk, made demands on the city's infrastructure that, although he did not make this comparison, would lead to improvements in Salvador's urban milieu and, thus, under Lamarckian logics, the Bahians' level of civilization. According to Senna, an unnamed English preacher somehow gained control of a group of Africans, destined for slavery, who had been liberated by the British navy due to the empire's attempt to stamp out the slave trade.[46] The Africans landed at Salvador, neither slave nor free. For Senna, this served as an example of the types of reforms that are possible when Bahians work in conjunction with foreign eyes in support of the fortress city's inevitable and hard-fought march toward development and modernity.

Some months later, when I visited Professor Senna and asked for details about the Africans who built Campo Grande, he did not recall supporting documents that might help me in my understanding of the incident and its relationship to Salvador's modernization and social struggles. The Africans' incorporation into work brigades, it appeared, had come to his knowledge either as a result of his stewardship of Salvador's municipal archive or as a part of the fascinating oral history of Bahia that the lettered classes discuss at great length at the IGHB over cold drinks, under slowly spinning fans, and below portraits of their ancestors who earned renown in politics or intellectual affairs.

"Taking Advantage of the Good Disposition of the Reverend Parker" (and of African Labor)

On March 1, 1852, Judge Francisco Gonçalves Martins, the president of the Province of Bahia, opened the Legislative Assembly by reporting on his administration's activities over the previous year.[47] He concentrated on taxation and the state treasury, improvements to infrastructure, mortality among newborns left for adoption on the city's wheel designed for this purpose, and the rescue by his police chief of close to three hundred of the five hundred Africans loaded on the slave ship *Relámpago* near Lagos. At the behest of the Bahian planter and smuggler Higino Pires Gomes, the human cargo had been dispatched by Domingos José Martins, a mulatto born in Bahia and resident in Africa.[48]

The British consul in Bahia, himself a slave trader until 1815, would soon investigate Pires Gomes as a habitual offender of the Aberdeen Act of 1846, or the decree that all ships caught on the high seas with human cargoes would fall under the jurisdiction of British Admiralty courts. Even as Pires Gomes remained successfully on Brazilian soil, dueling with the consul in Bahian courts following Brazil's agreement in 1850 that all smuggling of human cargoes would be treated as piracy, Provincial President Martins forged a more productive relationship with another Englishman resident in Bahia, the Reverend Edward [Eduardo] Parker. Parker, a leader of the English community centered around Campo Grande, had become concerned about the plaza's pools of standing water, which were understood to harbor mosquitoes during a period of recurrent outbreaks of yellow fever and cholera. He approached the governor, who granted him 120 of the Africans rescued from the *Relámpago* and confined in hospitals, military installations, and Salvador's jail. They were to work on the plaza, that "upon conclusion would be . . . the most beautiful and perfect place in the city, where military parades and reviews could be held as well as any manner of the diversions to which *civilized peoples give themselves over.*"[49] The president convinced the plaza's owners to accept an indemnification of two *contos de reis*, rather than the sixteen that they had originally demanded, and the work went on, eventually costing substantially less than budgeted due, according to the president, to the cooperation of neighboring landowners.

Although he complained that the Legislature had cut his budgets and forced him to suspend work, Martins lauded the use of the "rescued" Africans,

> not as a matter of significant economizing of worker expenses, but as a means of occupying slothful arms because the Africans found themselves deplorably housed in hospitals and warehouses where they consumed public funds without providing anything of public utility in return and were in fact having their human rights and dignity violated.[50]

Here Martins employed a language of rights, dignity, and public utility and their relationship to work. Martins' use of the Africans in a move that spared the state coffers, even as these purportedly free people "rescued" from slavers were kept in bondage, expresses the contradictions of this age of revolution. The Africans' supposed lack of competence and skills, as we will see below, provides excuses for their only partial incorporation into Brazilian society and their slavelike labor in their new home.

The president revealed that not all the Africans ended up on Campo Grande:

> Of the remaining Africans not sent to philanthropic institutions and who lay wasting away in the storehouses of the Naval Arsenal, from which they were taken in deplorable states of health to fill up valuable space in our hospitals, I ordered that an additional 100 be distributed among the diverse firms undertaking public works projects, contingent upon the firms' payment of a reasonable indemnification to the Public Coffers. In this way I have arranged to disengage the public authorities from an onerous burden of support in a way that permits the Africans to acquire correct work habits and suitable tradesmen's skills through specific forms of guidance so that they may someday be ready to execute similar projects with local firms that might employ them directly.
>
> Once the Africans are trained, have learned our tongue, and are free from the danger of becoming lost, the government might more conveniently employ them in works in the interior of the Province.
>
> Besides the nourishment, clothing, medication of, and expenses incurred in apprehending them, the Province will not incur any further costs related to the said Africans.[51]

Martins described the indenture as an apprenticeship that would permit Africans to learn Portuguese and acquire Bahian habits. His discussion of habits and their relation to work is intriguing as presented in the Portuguese for he declared, "adquirindo elles também debaixo de inspecção particular os hábitos do trabalho e as convenientes habilitações," which I translate as, "permits the Africans to acquire correct work habits and suitable tradesmen's skills through specific forms of guidance." The word *habilitações* refers specifically to the trades, or vocational education, while *hábitos do trabalho* are work habits. Martins thus makes clear that the Africans required skills as well as a more fundamental work ethic. This ability to labor became, quite literally, a Protestant, albeit Anglican, attribute since Martins reported that the Africans' habits were to be acquired under *inspecção particular*, or special supervision.

Since Martins mentions only the Reverend Parker as responsible for the Africans, it seems that the English chaplain oversaw the *emancipados*' (emancipated ones') work regimen.[52] Perhaps I am imputing too much, but as a reader familiar with the extent to which Brazilian elites faced European condemnation as trapped in a backward and mixed-race nation may recognize, the opportunity to have an English chaplain mold the values and habits of newly arrived Africans in mid-nineteenth-century Bahia may have seemed to some to be almost too good to be true. Or it may have been a just, and even poisonous, reward for the representative of a nation that had just done much to deprive Bahia's planters of their labor force by interdicting slave ships in Brazilian and international waters.

In spite of any tutoring they may have received, the Africans' situation was tenuous. Martins' concerns that they learn Portuguese and not get lost—"livres do perigo de serem extraviados" or "free of the danger of being misplaced," as if they were children, objects with no agency of their own, or property like slaves—underscore their liminal status. Neither slave nor free, they had arrived at a time when slavery as an institution still existed but the importation of slaves was illegal. As a result, they could not be legally treated as slaves by the authorities who captured them after a hasty disembarkation from the ship that Martins took the care to note "criminally imported them to Brazil." Nor did the authorities treat them as free people. They found themselves instead in a land of partial freedom, jailed and obliged to labor without payment as a means of picking up Brazilian values and busying "their unoccupied and lazy arms."[53]

Revolts over Bones: 1836

As Martins' description of the beneficial aspects of guidance reveals, he did not allot the Africans to the English reverend alone. He also distributed well over one hundred to other institutions, mainly public works projects run by the state and by Roman Catholic philanthropies. Among this second group were twenty-five sent to help maintain Quinta dos Lázaros, Salvador's first cemetery run by a religious order. Thus a portion of the African workers were to begin work on Salvador's second cemetery intended for Brazilian, as opposed to foreign, corpses. They would help the Franciscans create a walled resting place for segregating the dead from the living and thus discourage the then-common private burials in homes and houses of worship that produced the skeletons brought to light during the Pelourinho's twentieth-century reforms discussed above. Hence the semi-free Africans, with one foot still in slavery and another in some form of the modified wage labor that is still prevalent in Salvador and characteristic of the labor force that has restored the Pelourinho since the 1990s, were touted as a solution to concerns over the dead that had challenged the power of the Bahian political elite in an 1836 cemetery riot.[54] Although it would be ridiculous to assert some unbroken tradition of popular resistance around death and burial, it is significant that again in 1999 debates over the state's treatment of corpses allow for a harsh critique of Bahia's dominant classes, political organization, and the commodification of practices understood as best performed in private.

Corpses in Salvador during the first half of the nineteenth century were a flashpoint for public protest as urban planners declared cemeteries to be absolutely necessary as a matter of public health and a signal of Brazil's place in the civilized world. But Bahians, both slave and free, resisted shifting their burial practices to these new institutions. Government attempts to force families to forego laying their relatives to rest beneath churches and to curtail home funerals, which often involved African ways of honoring individuals sold into slavery and therefore struck fear into the hearts of planters well aware of recent events in Haiti, culminated in an uprising on October 25, 1836. An enraged public, led by Catholic lay brotherhoods and sisterhoods accustomed to burying their members within churches, marched throughout Salvador. Protesting against the *cemiteristas*, as the proprietors of the privately owned Campo Santo, Salvador's first and main cemetery, were called, the crowd destroyed the graveyard with the chaplain barely escaping with his life. Next, they returned to the center wielding sticks and iron bars while triumphantly exhibiting chunks of tombs, cloth torn from burial shrouds, and pieces of funerary carts.

Most historians' interpretations of the riot that became known as the *cemiterada* revolve around the outcry by, and influence over the populace of, Church authorities and leaders of lay sodalities who would lose the fees paid by the public for burial in churches.[55] Martins, who as chief of police during the 1836 cemiterada uprisings had warned the crowd to cease and desist, supports the second interpretation, as he claimed in 1852 that his offering of captured Africans for the construction of the Quinta dos Lázaros would include workers, not just for the construction of the cemetery, but for its posterior operation. These priests, who have much to lose [financially] due to the end of burials in churches, will recuperate their losses by having at their disposition a cemetery like this one being built at the [Quinta dos] Lázaros . . . so that they can bury the bodies that they currently dispose of within their church.[56]

Bahian historian João Reis argues that the cemiterada revolts of 1836, while related to the concerns of the clergy and lay brotherhoods who stood to lose burial fees, were also the result of public outrage that such an intimate and symbolically resonant aspect of humanity should come to be run by a for-profit firm that limited their preparations and care of the dead.[57] Catholic Bahians associated burial inside churches with salvation, and all classes, even those buried just outside the doors of the church like those skeletons uncovered on the Praça da Sé, engaged in elaborate funeral processions and burial rituals. Free working people of color and slaves made up the principal constituencies of lay brotherhoods that cared for members in retirement and death and were responsible for some of the most expressive rituals around death and burial. They thus joined in protest with members of the middle class whose elaborate preparations for death within churches and within their version of Roman Catholicism were also threatened by cemeteries.

Martins' order that twenty-five Africans help out at the Campo Santo is significant in light of the cemetery revolts of just over fifteen years earlier. In his address in 1852 Martins expressed anxiety and frustration at the slow pace of growth in Salvador's urban infrastructure, suggesting, as did the cemetery revolts, the importance and contested nature of public and private space, and the borders between the two, in ordering his society. By sending twenty-five virtual slaves, who may or may not have stayed on "for its posterior operation" under terms still to be worked out between the state, the Church, and, whether Martins recognizes it or not, the Africans, the provincial president may have sent a symbolic peace offering to the ecclesiastical authorities whose power and influence he had come to know as police chief during the cemiterada. This interpretation is supported by the fact that he explicitly recognized that the religious organizations "have much to lose due to the end of burials in churches."

The symbolism of extending help to the religious organizations that had opposed him as chief of police might also have extended to the granting of Africans to the English community's chaplain, the Reverend Parker. In turning over Africans captured by slavers, Martins may have increased the possibilities that British authorities would take notice of Brazilian compliance with new laws instituted due to British pressure. He would thus have proven at an international level, as well as a local level as demonstrated also by making the English colony's main square suitable for recreation appropriate to civilized peoples, that Brazil was ready to join the community of civilized nations.

Why Do You Want to Know about the Africans?

When I first visited him, Professor Senna, somewhat taken aback for reasons unknown to me, asked, "Why do you want to know about the Africans?" In a partial and delayed response, I point out here that the Africans exemplify the development of the sorts of barriers to full inclusion that would be employed following emancipation approximately forty years after Martins' address. Also, they provide evidence about conflicts over urban space; the roles of Afro-Bahians in debates over citizenship, work, and property; and different methods by which Bahian interpreters conjure up the presence, or at least memories, of African slaves and free people who played key roles in depositing the sorts of bodies uncovered in the Pelourinho.

As emancipados—not quite citizens and not quite slaves—the Africans recall the tutelage offered by IPAC to Pelourinho residents today, even as their experiences promise a vantage point from which to ground a more nuanced understanding of the relations that both separate and connect liberalism and neoliberalism, nineteenth-century imperial power and twenty-first-century global capitalism, and freedom and bondage. But in terms of the current book, they are part of a historical memory summoned by Professor Senna—the author of at least one of the speeches pronounced upon the Praça da Sé at the end of the twentieth century—so as to explain, and even celebrate, an unjust present composed around the grooming of Salvador's urban form and Afro-descendent population. Such problematic positioning constitutes yet another reason I am interested in the Africans.

Both the field architect and Professor Senna have taken me to the Africans who built Campo Grande. The two men's stories about slaves and Salvador's topography reveal the depth of a historical imaginary constructed around the built environment in molding citizens today. And this landscape, as interpreted by Pelourinho residents, leads toward the figure of the African slave. The management of the writing history around public space is critical to determining the distance between those slaves and Bahian workers today, as well as to Pelourinho residents' growing understandings that the use of the past is just one of the many idioms of control imposed upon them since their ancestors' arrival and ambiguous emancipation in Brazil.

Conquering the Bahian Enigma: The Physical Evolution of Salvador

Senna based his "job talk" for the Academy of Letters on the book *Evolução Física de Salvador: 1549 a 1800* (The Physical Evolution of Salvador: 1549 to 1800). Originally published in 1978 under the direction of the Bahian landscape painter Diógenes Rebouças and the architect Américo Simas Filho who, like the poet Godofredo Filho, was a director of the Bahian office of IPHAN. *The Physical Evolution of Salvador* also played a role in the development of Bahian heritage initiatives. These include IPAC's institution of the Pelourinho reforms that give rise to the speeches on the Praça da Sé in 1999.[58]

Simas Filho and Rebouças produced their beautifully illustrated text as Salvador's economy emerged at the end of the 1970s from a dependence on Brazil's largest oilfields, located in the Bay of All Saints, which had helped pull the city out of a period of industrial and cultural decline known as the "Bahian Enigma." As Bahian reserves became less critical to the nation's oil production, new fiscal incentives attracted firms that produced consumer and petrochemical goods, thus integrating the state into the national economy at a moment when Brazil suffered through the debt crises of the 1980s. Although Bahia was not as harshly impacted as southern states were, and in fact grew substantially on the basis of the military's efforts to diversify industry geographically, Brazil's struggles convinced Antonio Carlos Magalhães' administrations to augment Bahia's industrial base. They began to do so through the production of culture, especially in the form of heritage. This was possible due in part to the contacts that Magalhães had developed during his earlier administrations as mayor of Salvador and during his childhood, part of which he spent in the home of Edgard Santos, the Federal University of Bahia's first rector.[59]

In addition to running in the same circles as Santos, Rebouças and Simas Filho—perhaps the most important figure in Bahia's post–World War II architectural heritage and restoration movement—had both served on the Bahian Conselho Cultural, or Cultural Advisory Board. There they joined Antonio Carlos Magalhães' father, university professor and medical doctor Francisco Peixoto de Magalhães Neto. The Conselho Cultural coordinated cultural activities and patrimony as an advisory body to the Ministry of Education and Culture between 1965 and 1970, a period during which ACM served as mayor of Salvador. The Conselho Cultural's debates, reproduced and commented upon every month in the back of its journal, the *Revista da Cultura da Bahia*, thus helped determine the form IPAC took when it was founded in 1967.[60] The resuscitation and re-elaboration of these debates during the recession of the early 1980s written by a team of technocratic planners drawn from Antonio Carlos

Magalhães' peers, as opposed to the artists, philosophers, and anthropologists of Francisco Peixoto de Magalhães Neto's generation who had advised and dominated the Ministry of Education and Culture, would gird the Pelourinho plan of the 1990s that, to an extent unprecedented in Brazil, tied urban planning and political power to a packaging of the past.

After serving as governor from 1971 to 1975, Antonio Carlos Magalhães did not hold office from 1976 to 1978 and eventual friction with Roberto Santos, his successor, limited his access to IPAC and the regional development agency CONDER. Seemingly as a result of these divergences, Salvador's municipal government, which Magalhães controlled, bypassed the state-level bureaucracy to create the Centro de Estudos da Arquitetura Baiana (CEAB) as a technical body that might "study the physical occupation of the city of Salvador, from its origin to the present."[61] The CEAB, together with its ally, the municipal-level PLANDURB (Plan for Urban Development) group, turned out to be instrumental in training many of the people who would guide the Pelourinho's IPAC during the 1980s and 1990s.

The CEAB team envisioned the cultivation of differentiated spaces of meaning, or urban sites where citizens would interact with specific, controlled environments that might provide places for specific types of cultural and economic activities that would be tailored to the urban landscape. Planners' attempts to foment interactions between citizens and the landscape—as in, for example, a field architect who might lead a group of people in interpreting the refurbished Praça da Sé—thus gained favor alongside industrial plans. The value of urban space now lay also in the meanings it could produce that might result in civic or economic development, rather than in supporting industrial production along the lines of the incentives designed to spur investment in Bahia's Aratu Industrial Center (CIA) of the late 1960s and 1970s. This shift mirrored tendencies in international currents in urban studies, but it also resuscitated parts of an earlier plan, known as the EPUCS project, created by Mario Leal Ferreira, a sanitary engineer trained at Harvard through the Rockefeller Foundation's public health initiatives of the 1930s.[62]

EPUCS, although never implemented during its director's lifetime, provided a blueprint for urban reform marked by holistic attention to health, housing, leisure, sanitation, morality, traffic flow, and aesthetics. Ferreira's vision is important not just in the context of urban planning, but as a way of understanding how history, or knowledge of the past, would come to be so important in Magalhães' and his advisors' future projects. It would gird the Pelourinho's reform in the 1990s.

This planning relied on a strong historical determinism, with history understood as factors that could be shown scientifically to determine a forward trajectory. According to Ferreira, by plotting these influences planners might graph the future:

> The use of all of society's cooperative elements, representatives of all of the sectors of human knowledge . . . organized around the study of the evolutive process of the city's formation in a way that makes it possible to describe that city's trajectory, which is not a straight line, but instead a continuous curve that permits a certain facility in extrapolating the future as long as we know the points that marked evolution in the past.[63]

Ferreira, writing in the late 1930s and early 1940s, worked in public affairs during and after Getúlio Vargas' Estado Novo, a period marked by the rise of authoritarian and then left-leaning populist governments based on corporatist doctrines of organic society and technocratic state management. Not coincidentally, the Estado Novo represented a moment of relative toleration and encouragement of Afro-Brazilian cultural manifestations of the type performed and exhibited in the Pelourinho today.

In the 1970s and 1980s Magalhães and his allies would seek to revive Ferreira's work and augment government involvement in Afro-Brazilian culture. Ferreira's plans were attractive to politicians preaching national consolidation in the wake of the military coup in 1964. By knowing a society's past its leaders could, they claimed, repair or avoid errors and plot future action. Antonio Carlos Magalhães made this an important motto in his many political administrations that focused on "reconstructing Bahia," noting in a paraphrase of Ferreira on the plaque outside his new Administrative Center for the State Government of Bahia, "Here we construct the future without destroying the past." Knowing, documenting, and preserving the past constituted, then, an important political strategy. A knowable and properly historic Bahian past provided Magalhães' political machine with a scientific method for managing the future. But even more important than a theory of history's directionalities, was Magalhães' ability to manage history for political benefit, something that became clear when he returned to the governor's mansion in 1978 and again in 1991.

Senna's talk thus serves as a conceptual link between political practices that consciously draw on something called "history" or "memory" and Salvador's differentiated urban spaces called on by politicians to provide specific versions of such history as part of political economic plans that have come to draw not simply on Africans' labor, but also on the forms of commemoration and packaging of culture developed in the final decades of the twentieth century. Thus Senna's, and EPUCS planners', history of the city of Salvador does more than posit the people as a problem and celebrate the municipal regime's purported near-victory in the war between population and infrastructure. Its basis in and updating of the CEAB history of Salvador, conceived of as a foundational plotting of a past that might predict the future, helps reveal the alliances and details in the Bahian move toward planning methods that would inflect the "reconstruction" directed at the sentimental landscapes of today's Pelourinho.

Urbanism in Brazil, like elsewhere, has long been a source of population control and a harbinger and supposed-generator of civilization, or a lack thereof. However, as the discussions of memories arising from the Pelourinho indicate, urbanism at the beginning of the twenty-first century is not limited to the control of Salvador's physical space and unruly people. Instead, it has moved into the realm of historical discourse and social scientific research and become a method by which space and time are combined to produce subjectivities and structures of governance, and thus interpretive conventions, useful to the Bahian state.

If state authorities portrayed work on Campo Grande Square or in cemeteries as redemptive for emancipados in the mid-nineteenth century, then memories related to those African workers appear useful to authorities' attempts to cultivate citizens today. Such concern with history parallels not just attention to the sorts of people coded as "problematic" when displaced in urban renewal programs, but to Afro-Brazilian culture in general: Magalhães' regime discovered tradition at about the same time that Eric Hobsbawm and Terence Ranger wrote about its invention. But the care for memory, signs, and objects that Borges recommends for all Bahians in 1999 is not simply the production of a tradition around public symbols into which Bahians are written and "rooted in the remotest antiquity."[64] Pelourinho residents are decidedly, to use Mayor Imbassahy's words, "of Oxum." These people are celebrated for their sexualized mystery, but must be carefully controlled by the state in part because, like Oxum, and like the Bahian state, they tend to covet the Pelourinho's heritage objects and spend significant amounts of time imagining how they might get their hands on some gold.

Histories and Mysteries

The expression "for English eyes" has many uses. Looking back over transcripts and listening again to taped interviews with Seu Jorge and Dona Niza, I began to nurse the suspicion that I had been duped. I now believe that the pauses, the gestures, the implied and explicit requests that one spouse fill in the other's gaps, and the at-times too-neat intercalations of evidence and experience are not simply a husband and wife squabbling: Over the course of our interactions, Jorge and Niza made up memories that might draw me in, to their benefit. Yet they fabricated these memories as part of a historically situated corpus of practices about which they commented in ways that reveal *how* they create objects or relationships where none seem to have existed before.

My two friends, even as I know that they discussed hidden treasure regularly with neighbors, seem to have mobilized the talk of untold riches just beyond their reach for rather specific ends. One of these involved offering the foreign anthropologist what he wanted since, especially during the early stages of fieldwork, I searched for powerful narratives of memories and the actual past that might counter the versions of things put forth by state authorities. In response to my verificationist impulse, Jorge and Niza fed me a story much like Governor Borges' discussions of mysterious heritage objects.[65]

Niza and Jorge's creative ability to describe in painstaking detail objects they encountered only in their imaginations produced real effects on the world as they drew into their daily orbit a relatively empowered visitor able to buy soft drinks or beer, or lend cash to the family in difficult moments, and even serve as a seemingly sensitive ally among a lettered class that Seu Jorge used to curse as "interested only in coming down here and telling us what we are, and then sending that back to IPAC headquarters so they can kick us out." Their analysis of treasure and bones also permitted them to join a moral community, or public sphere, on the basis of their participation in a shared discourse about the hidden bases of Bahian life. Like the field architect, who spun remarkably detailed accounts of materials that supported his claims to appropriation but that he never actually displayed in any empirical sense, two people who seem to have nothing tangible to show for their labors as fodder for IPAC social science brought into being no-longer-imaginary objects in ways that altered, materially, their conditions of existence. Like Bahia's figuras, whose surfeit of energy and charisma somehow demand fulfillment and respect, and are thus made materially significant in Salvador and early Christian theology, Jorge and Niza's imaginative hermeneutics of depth, even if it never resulted in the couple's discovery of a literal treasure beneath their floor, generated real effects in the historical center's spaces of everyday life.

Niza and Jorge's narrative strategies for enticing the foreign anthropologist into their home put into the world a number of insightful critiques of the production of value, the commodification of bodies and everyday habits, and thus the confiscation of labor and property taking place in the Pelourinho at a moment when accumulation increasingly involves the labor of performing the self as part of a historical center. Niza and Jorge were willing to engage me in extensive life histories, as they had done for decades with IPAC researchers, and would continue to do when necessary or beneficial to them. As took place with the actions of Dandinha, whose oppositional striptease helped to establish him across Brazil as one of the Pelourinho's colorful and ambiguous figures whose larger-than-life Bahianness supports the Pelourinho's showcasing of bits of everyday life sacralized through state attention, Niza and Jorge's criticisms of their state may be, and have been, recorded on tape and in writing at multiple moments. Even as these representations may transmit some oppositional content, their passage into an archive of everyday life on which IPAC can draw to authenticate the Pelourinho may support, or even motivate, the very terms of the patrimonialization process that has led to their indemnification and expulsion. They add to the IPAC-supported discussions of rooted, Bahian origins going on in the Pelourinho at the end of the twentieth century. Yet such dense sites of agreement and contradiction tend at times to bunch or fold up, generating or revealing a certain knottiness and, as a result, additional spaces of curiosity and questioning.

Stories and data about a brave, resistant Pelourinho people often work in the Pelourinho in manners quite similar to accounts of uniquely Brazilian Baroque architecture produced by slave artisans who challenged Portuguese convention to produce an object of desire or space of aesthetic contemplation. Such invitations to contemplation and identification in a space of densely packed forms of attention that masquerade as care while leading to little more than bureaucratic dead ends are indispensable to the Pelourinho. They add to its allure as a curious place of foundations that officials like IPAC Director Castro, Mayor Imbassahy, and Governor Borges assured their constituents were, simultaneously, extremely "secure" symbols of a knowable past as well as fonts of nearly unfathomable mystery: Pockmarked with contradictory plays of shadow and light, the surfaces and depths of the Pelourinho landscape thus bedazzle in their ability to generate feelings of grounded substantiality that so often fall away into a pure immediacy of illusion that scholars of the Baroque nonetheless tie to the production of bounded subjects.[66] But, at least from within that space of feints, dodges, and the denial of originality, it would seem that artifice is redolent with possibility.

Problems of Presence

Faced with an intimidating employer who draws on memories of slavery to denigrate him in a historical center undergoing disorienting change that involves the commodification of everyday life, Oswaldo the tailor sees skeletons that no one else is able to find. His contemporary, Dona Niza, observes authorities and workmen carrying away translucent plastic bags weighted with gold. And IPAC officials contradict themselves vociferously in denying the discovery of such jewels. Meanwhile, Seu Jorge intuits the presence of treasure that he is ultimately afraid—prevented, in great part, by fear of his landlord and dread of agents of the state in the form of police—to dig up. The field architect explains publicly a web of tunnels that supposedly extend for miles and he appropriates objects and job descriptions whose existence local archaeologists deny. In spite of divergences in the details of these subjects' quests, each is sure that something lies down there, belowground. Even more important, all manage to bundle those intuitions in ways that permit suspicions, rumors, hunches, and worries to transmogrify in an anthropological account of the making of the Pelourinho and of symbols batted about by groups of Bahians standing around revelatory fissures on the Praça da Sé. In the wake of these transformations, the barely perceivable hunches residents put forth in quotidian banter became nuggets of evidence in accounts of shared origins.

The stories emerging on the Praça da Sé, whether they involve the cultural anthropologist who sought to analyze an urban transformation, the archaeologists who sought to define and understand the lifeways of the people and objects encountered under the plaza, or the visitors, workers, and neighborhood residents who sought to seize hold of pieces of their past and place them in their proper resting spots (whether a wallet or a graveyard), point insistently at something akin to what Matthew Engelke has described as a "problem of presence."[67] In the case of the Pelourinho, this involves demonstrating, or making visible, that which participants know to be true about the world even if such truths are made manifest only with great difficulty and through techniques that participants find troubling or fail to trust. Such attempts at unveiling are not quite the same as an intentional, goal-oriented attempt to follow a particular rationality. Rather, they reveal how people may both deny and seize on almost any logic that might help them accomplish their representational, and thus in the case of the Pelourinho, pragmatic, goals.

It is worth recalling here that, as part of the long engagement around the skeletons and treasure, the field architect tells the assembled public that he and his compatriots are going to *maquiar*, or "put makeup" on, the Sucupira so that its historical secrets might be revealed.[68] But then he repeats himself slightly differently to report, hastily, that what the workers and archaeologists are really going to do is to *mapear*, or "map," the historical site. This alteration hinges on a quick shift in phonemes. The field architect recovers from the confusion between the two verbs by stressing that the act of mapping, and making something legible by diagramming it, is the team's ultimate goal. I recall distinctly that, as he shifted from "maquiar" to "mapear," the field architect reddened and stuttered, just a bit, as if embarrassed by his slipup.

In correcting his "error," the field architect skated from an additive process involving a slathering of new substances upon the surface of the excavation to an apparently more properly scientific attempt to produce a diagram of what really lay within the archaeological site. Such self-correction, like Niza's strategies for reeling the anthropologist into her life and space, highlights the diligence and facility with which Pelourinho residents and workers occupy the contours of a scientific and political rationality, which they nonetheless distrust, as they go about, and represent, their everydays: Even as supposedly marginalized Bahians, it is not uncommon for Maciel/Pelourinho residents living within Brazil's preeminent site of blackness to have a foreigner drop by to listen to rumor-mongering about neighbors. Nor is it strange for that interloper to imagine that this activity might lead to insights into the nature of modern state power and the production of history. In such "contact zones," where enormous state and institutional attention is directed rather explicitly at so many spheres of social life, the dissimulations and mysteries employed by both state and citizen are quickly picked up and improved upon by the other side.[69] And that other side is never quite a discrete Other, something that Seu Jorge used to emphasize to me as he labored in his electronics workshop on the Ladeira da Misericórdia.

Although I know relatively little about electronics and electricity, and I do not share a passion for the gadgets and new technologies so much a part of constructions of masculinity in Bahia, I used to sit in Seu Jorge's workshop for hours, talking as he fixed televisions and computers that his children would salvage in Salvador's nearby Comércio neighborhood. Born to Bahian parents who migrated to São Paulo, Jorge had taken advantage of one of the high-quality vocational high school programs available in that city, generally understood as a beacon of commercial and technical modernity. Thus his knowledge of physics challenged my memories from high school in New York. I often struggled with his explanations as to how things worked, even as the conceptual overlaps between economies of signs and circuits of energy transfer intrigued me as we sat together, gossiping and swatting at flies, on hot summer afternoons. I typically left the foot of Jorge's workbench with the distinct impression that when he lectured me on pathways, transformers, and switches, while complaining about his own inability to make gold materialize under his floorboards, he was talking about more than AC and DC current. In fact, Seu Jorge often stressed that, at base and in the view of physicists, what he was really doing when repairing castoff machines was giving new life to mechanisms for transforming, or translating, energy and insights from one corner of the world into new vessels that would in another context perform work with that energy.[70]

A national community's collectively held cultural property is typically conceptualized today around a powerful, Lockean "possessive individualism" whereby felt attachment to the nation, like the classic liberal conception of the

Figure 5.5. Seu Jorge repairing electronics as his son looks on.

individual based on the relationships between people and property, is developed in relation to the "possession" of objects like patrimonies, literatures, histories, or cultures.[71] Of course, when observed by anthropologists, these are more properly considered collections of practices and sentiments. But from the perspectives afforded by possessive individualism, culture-as-thing must be held onto, rescued, and protected as a potentially discrete good that attaches only to particular communities. At least in part, this situation is one effect of so many anthropologists' insistence on cultural particularity, on "their" often reified and thus artificially bounded communities of research, and on pilgrimages aimed at revealing sites of fundamental alterity that might help relativize the so-called Western condition. Such a (mis)conceptualization of culture, and the political subjects seen as "holding" and protecting it, seemed very much in evidence during the inauguration in 1999 of the reconstructed Praça da Sé on the part of both citizens and representatives of the state. Yet from within the swirling claims to ownership that emerged around the Sucupira, Seu Jorge and Dona Niza stress their *inability* to hold onto the spaces and practices claimed by IPAC for the nation.

Seu Jorge always insisted to me that there was no mystery to the treasure he knew lay under his home, but was unable to access even as the IPAC scientists who visited and disturbed him almost daily denied the presence of any such prizes. If he had his way, he would bellow, he would have dug up and melted the crowns, crucifixes, and gold braid into ingots and bars, or generalizable media of exchange that would be useful for the purchase of the materials his family lacks even today. But due in part to his forced removal from the neighborhood via an exchange of irresistible and fleeting cash money for his home, Jorge ends up a spectator of a different sort. Instead of serving as a participant in the extraction of hidden value in a neglected and then carefully scrutinized historical center, he is reduced to sitting in his two-room house in an impoverished suburb where he becomes a spectator to the foreign academic's accounts of the emergence, and ultimate repositories, of the objects he always knew lay underneath his former neighborhood.

Over the course of the dialogues with me that support the current chapter, Niza and Jorge followed what was happening just feet from their former home as the gold they claim they would have transformed into money so as to improve their economic positions emerged from the ground and then "melted" into museums, university holdings, the hands of IPAC, and the few construction workers daring enough to pilfer the horde coveted by Pelourinho residents. Such movement away from the Praça da Sé is, admittedly, a strange and highly metaphorical form of melting. It takes place as a patrimonialization of objects, which residents have for decades insisted are real, gives shape to what was once only intuited or rumored. Yet as the objects take form as material entities, they slip through the fingers of those who declare themselves the rightful owners, and discoverers, of this bounty. The things emerging from the Sucupira are never quite tangible as physical entities amenable to possession or alienation as individual wealth or circulating currency on the part of buildings' occupants. Instead, a team of experts lifts the valuables out of the ground and sends them on to Bahia's Museum of Archaeology and Ethnology, an institution Jorge, Niza, Oswaldo, and most of the other Pelourinho residents drawn on in this chapter have never visited. The pieces of gold that they once configured as potentially available, although contingently out of reach due to problems like landlords' prohibition of digging into walls and floors, turn out to be definitively out of reach for people who would rather melt them down than contemplate their historical significance.

Anthropologists working in such apparently diverse areas as science and technology studies, heritage and commemoration, and the spatialization of affect have focused recently on sense-perceptions, imagination—and even absence itself—as material entities rather than as contexts or footings for the "really real" stuff of rational contemplation and fact-based interpretation.[72] In his essay "The Architecture of Theories," C. S. Peirce enunciated something similar to these insights, as well as to recent moves in global cultural heritage planning that seek to make the "intangible" tangible. For Peirce, the "one intelligible theory of the universe is that of objective idealism, *that matter is effete mind, inveterate habits becoming physical laws*."[73] This formulation may seem strange to readers unaccustomed to the Victorian thinker's fascination with the ways qualities, or still-unrealized potentials (or what he called "firsts"), may become instantiated as particular occurrences or illustrations ("seconds"), or even habitual explanations that array phenomena as lawlike generalities ("thirds," of which arbitrary meanings are one instantiation). Yet, at least in my experience, such wonder may morph into appreciative understanding as it becomes clear that the movement toward a hardened thirdness Peirce describes as "effete mind," or firsts and seconds evacuated of their vital openness and reliance on the sign vehicle's materiality for significance as they gain and transmit conventional, arbitrarily assigned meanings, reveals how much supposedly inert matter is in fact invested with what are often dubbed immaterial features. As Karl Marx insisted through a focus on praxis, manifestations of innovative, oh-so-social, and motivating "spirit" are not divorced from the material stuff of everyday life and capital accumulation. The situation at the Sucupira suggests that such manifestations of "immateriality" are byproducts of, as well as internal to objects and their constitution. In observing that "at any time, however, an element of pure chance survives," Peirce makes explicit this relationality of what we still call, for lack of better terms, matter and spirit.[74]

It appears that, in the Pelourinho, inchoate feelings may take on the status of objects, even as objects may degenerate, as Peirce put it, into qualities. From this perspective, matter contains pure chance—or a first that impacts the world only through its potential, which is thus in effect material—as a dimly preserved possibility, muted and incapable of taking on a definitive form while nonetheless wrapped up in a sign that signifies arbitrarily (a relative third). And this describes a rather special way of belonging to something or someone as a "property."

Mystery and Dissimulation

Originally, as I marched down the Ladeira da Misericórdia to visit Niza and Jorge, I imagined that the ethnographic material I was collecting would permit me, some day and after careful analysis, to replace IPAC's stories of residents' barbarousness with alternative representations that would destabilize the hardened portraits of cultural difference so valuable to ethnographers, as well as states, invested in the marginal and the ungoverned. My hoped-for portraits of dignified ways of being would thus foster social justice on the basis of the truths contained in, and extracted from, otherwise silenced voices. But the people with whom I spent hundreds of hours on the Misericórdia usually confounded such plans.

Once, after returning from a visit to the IPHAN archives held in a magnificent high modernist building in downtown Rio de Janeiro, I reported excitedly to Jorge and Niza that I had come across a densely catalogued collection of written records attesting to official concern with the earlier sets of stories of skeletons and treasure that arose around the time that the Sucupira replaced Salvador's colonial Baroque library building. Dona Niza looked at me and smiled softly. Seemingly nonplussed, she responded, "Yeah, yeah, there's something there under the cloth, something that we don't know or understand that's hidden underneath thick gravy. I'd just like to know if that gravy hides meat or if there's really hot pepper down there underneath it. Because if you were to look closely, I think you'd discover hot pepper."

Niza nods at, but fails to lift, the white cloth used to protect from flies the surfaces of stews and pots of beans left on stoves in the absence of refrigerators. And her metaphorical movement through the broth to its underlying objects recalls similar movements through the earth's surfaces and Bahia's histories undertaken by actors as diverse as the field architect, Governor Borges, and Oswaldo the tailor. She warns, however, that what some take to be meat is in fact pepper, a rather special substance. Many Bahians claim to nurture the plant by tossing urine onto its roots in order to make the fruit more pungent as their own wastes course to the *pharmakon*, enhancing its ambiguous status as both tonic and poison.[75] Therefore, in a stew like Niza's—if used moderately—this pepper does not so much stand on its own as translate flavors into fundamentally new registers that are reliant on their previous states, and yet somehow different from that anterior condition. In such small dosages, pepper permeates its milieu and sets up and even amplifies the pathways between the qualities that congeal to determine the objects around it. It shifts shapes, and tastes, suggesting a plasticity and an ultimate lack of boundaries. In larger amounts, or in particular syntheses with some foods and spices, it may also shut down an ability to taste discrete objects, causing burns or even digestive problems. Here movements inward may push back outward, like a blinding veil of tears or rumbling of the gut liable to produce moments of intense clarity, toward an exteriority that ties the human to the landscape in yet another lesson in the fluidity and potentially eruptive nature of subjectivity.

It is by now widely accepted in the social sciences that history and memory do not lie below the surface of things, awaiting rescue or irruption. But this does not mean that the metaphors of surface and depth that support models of the wholesale resuscitation of past events, or even preexisting but "hidden" oppositional narratives otherwise obscured by a dominant discourse, have disappeared. This is one reason I have concentrated on technique at a time when Pelourinho residents have come to be configured as a type of collective ancestor to, and property of, the nation. As such, they function not only as citizens, but also as a species of heritage or historical object set askance from the nation they make possible: In spite of a widespread deconstruction of its supposed objects, namely, discrete, enduring histories that remain uncontaminated by their transmission or unsullied by their dialogical coming-into-existence, a salvage model of culture and history continues to play a powerful role in anthropology's cousin, cultural heritage management. And as Brazilians increasingly accept an architecture of racial belonging that solidifies the borders between what used to pass for mutable and overlapping assemblages, a "hermeneutics of depth" predicated on looking down, into the ground, within selves, and across time, seems to find fertile ground in the identification of what makes groups corporate.[76] This interpretive stance may encourage configurations of identity as a possession. But such possessions may not look much like the possessive individualism on which dominant strands of cultural heritage management, and even racial thought, are usually imagined.

Dona Niza seems to agree. Or, at the very least, she puts forth a kitchen-based allegorization that addresses historical objects that, by being besides themselves and adding something to the stew as a whole, may take on rather agentive qualities without requiring a definitive form. For Niza, in whose house I was sitting at the moment of arrival of the public health team around which the next chapter unfolds, depths are important. Yet from the perspective afforded by her perch on the Ladeira da Misericórdia, when one looks closely at what's really "down there," one finds peppers, rather than chunks of beef. In passing on their properties, the peppers may make the broth more savory, or more painful, for all those who sample it. What that means, and what those peppers do, are among my principal concerns in chapter 6. They are also key to understanding the "nature" of race and subjectivity in the Pelourinho today.

CHAPTER 6

"But Madame, What If I Should Need to Defecate in Your Neighborhood?"

To determine . . . the boundary at which the past has to be forgotten if it is not to become the gravedigger of the present, one would have to know exactly how great the plastic power of man, a people, a culture is: I mean by plastic power the capacity to develop out of oneself in one's own way, to transform and incorporate into oneself what is past and foreign, to heal wounds, to replace what has been lost, to recreate broken moulds.

—Friedrich Nietzsche, "On the Uses and Disadvantages of History for Life"

Adilson used to tell me, as we closed out afternoons drinking beer and eating acarajé near the Sucupira, how glad he was that on a Sunday morning "during the rainy season; after carnival but before the Feast of St. John," he had decided to forego his regular game of soccer (o baba). Lounging in front of his mother's store in the working-class neighborhood of Valéria, he happened to bump into his cousin Luis. Luis had left home in the Mussurunga neighborhood to visit Janete, his maternal aunt and godmother. As Janete served her nephew and son a gluey plate of mocotó, or boiled cow's feet with hot pepper and manioc gruel, the two men caught up. Luis reported that he had found a rewarding job downtown, with a group of archaeologists who encouraged feedback from workers and taught them new skills. These involved sifting through soil while paying attention to stratigraphy and carefully delimited quadrants that needed to be excavated in ten-centimeter intervals. Luis reported that they would soon move to rescue the skeletons that had been dislodged when a construction team broke ground for a new snack bar just across from where we sat. And, according to Adilson's account of the cousins' exchange, Luis emphasized that the archaeologists were looking for additional, trustworthy workers.

At the time, Adilson had not yet been able to save the cash necessary to put up a one-bedroom brick house in the empty space that his father had reserved for his older children when the family arrived from the Bahian village of Cruz das Almas. To make matters worse, Adilson owed his mother money, and his girlfriend—the mother of their three-year-old daughter—had begun warning that if they did not move into their own home soon, she would leave their child with her mother and depart for the position as a domestic servant that her sister had promised to secure for her in São Paulo. My interlocutor was therefore delighted when Luis took him by the archaeological site on the Praça da Sé and, as Adilson declared, "I got hired on the spot!"

The Pelourinho put Adilson, who as the eldest child in his family had arrived in his state capital as an eighteen-year-old, into contact with types of people he had not known in Cruz das Almas. He considered Dandinha irresistible in her exaggeratedly feminine masculinity and, as he manned the archaeological site's sieve, he found himself beginning to make sense of some of the questions put forth by camera-toting tourists speaking in foreign tongues. The drums and bright uniforms of the neighborhood social movement and musical group Olodum, which Adilson had experienced only from afar during carnival and on television and radio before encountering work in the Pelourinho, thrilled him. He began inviting his girlfriend to accompany him back downtown on Tuesday evenings when Olodum would put on a practice concert and sing about black empowerment and the beauty of African civilization. As he put it to me, "That was when I really got to know Olodum, and I saw it was a group *of tradition*."[1]

In his use of the word "tradition," Adilson followed Pelourinho-based lexical conventions, whereby words like "culture" and "tradition" serve as valorizing descriptors.[2] Intrigued by his statement, which he made on a day I had requested permission to tape our conversations and which he enunciated in a manner that is as clunky in Portuguese as the English translation, I asked/told Adilson, "Speaking about 'tradition,' you are, at least in some way, also working with tradition right here, downtown, neh?"

To this, Adilson responded, smiling contentedly and seemingly sincerely, "Yup, it's because this job is so good that I don't want any other one besides this one right here, nope!"

Adilson stressed that, working with the archaeologists, he was treated better than his fellow construction workers who stacked bricks or mixed cement to restore nearby buildings. However, the most positive aspect of his job was not that it was less physically demanding, but that "We learn lots of good things. Take me for example; now, with the knowledge I have, it's much better than what I had before."

"What sort of knowledge do you have?" I pressed.

"My knowledge is," he paused, as if searching for the correct description, "precisely those materials I uncover. Now I know the human part of our bodies. That's what the knowledge is."

I never followed up with explicit questions about Adilson's assertions that the knowledge gained on the Praça da Sé, which he equated to the materials he uncovered, allowed him to know "the human part of our bodies." I failed to do so because, as happened so often in our conversations, I feared that he linked knowledge, objects, and the human because of how I pressed him to make arguments about topics and in speech genres that may not have been important or familiar to him. Such self-consciousness is basic to ethical and rewarding research. And yet, my assumptions about how construction workers might—or should—speak to me about the pasts they were busy claiming across our conversations and during their workdays encouraged an ethnographic timidity that probably exaggerated my own role in Adilson's descriptive vocabularies.

Despite my inability to slide smoothly into discussions so as to articulate questions that would "cut to the chase" without leading me to believe I had forced us into a register that belonged to one or the other, but not both of us, Adilson's phrasing offers a felicitous opening for considering the interplay of surface signs and assertions about Bahian pasts around the depths of the Praça da Sé and surrounding areas of the historical center. "To know the human part of our bodies," or to put a finger on the vitality, or soul, or ethics, or spark of life, and thus the diacritical mark that supposedly defines the line between subjects and objects, people and beasts, and the flesh of being and the crumbling remains of skeletons, stands at the origin of so much modern social theory.[3] It seems similarly important to Adilson's understanding of the knowledge in which, by operating the archaeologist's sieve, he had become embroiled.

Adilson spoke frequently about the racialized oppression he saw as basic to Bahian politics. Like many on the Praça da Sé, he believed that he had uncovered evidence that the bodies encountered belonged to slaves to whom he tied himself as an Afro-descendent worker. He explained that this affiliation across time with remains that needed to be interpreted so as to become human arose as he and his colleagues would look at bones and imagine the "nature" of the flesh-and-blood people who once completed the skeletons. He insisted that especially robust skeletons, as well as those scattered around outside the cathedral's foundations, belonged to slaves. The most important evidence that supported these identifications emerged from Adilson's ability to discern special objects while running the sieve, or "things that I identify to them [the archaeologists] because they don't know what they are." He continued, "Lots of times we find, you now what? We find the spurs of a fighting cock [for example]. And the archaeologist doesn't know what it is! But I do. They don't know what we know" because "those there professors, one of them from Minas Gerais, another from Rio, and one from Buenos Aires. Those of us who are Bahians here, we know lots of things. All Bahians know what a cockspur is!"

On Evidentiary Regimes

As Pelourinho residents, visitors from outlying neighborhoods, and representatives of the Bahian state stood at the symbolic center of colonial Brazil and peered into the ground in order to discuss the skeletons, Dr. Carlos Etchevarne, or the professor from Buenos Aires referred to by Adilson, curated an exposition of materials at the Museum of Archaeology and Ethnology.[4] The exhibit highlighted tools and osteological evidence. According to Etchevarne and the museum catalogue, the skeletons bore the marks of trauma and forms of arthritis that the archaeologist attributed to years of hard labor. The most clearly institutionally authorized analyst of the site thus concurred that the skeletons were those of slaves: Despite the Bahian state's initial efforts to correct the interpretations enunciated by working people, the argument that slave bodies had been interred around Brazil's first cathedral had not only gained currency, but had become official. A few Bahians entered the museum and looked closely at the displays. A much larger number continued to flock to the cathedral's exposed foundations. There they listened as Pelourinho residents and frequenters of the Praça da Sé exclaimed boldly that the human remains were evidence of slave attempts to regain humanity and provide proper burials for their friends and family. At times, workers would join these dialogues. But they usually remained silent in public, preferring to converse among themselves.

Hélio, one of Adilson's fellow workers, once sat with us and sought to correct his peer. He argued that while Adilson was spot-on in identifying the skeletons as slaves, his methods were less than exact: "Some say there are only slaves and Indians," Hélio pointed out. "Others say that it's not just slaves, but whites too. But there you have it, for us to be certain we'd have to do a DNA test. And, right now they're doing one. But DNA is not our speciality. Those who worked at the site don't know the results. The results of what and who it was and why they died."

Intrigued, I responded, "The archaeologist doesn't know yet? Has he already received the DNA?" to which Hélio answered, "No, he's still doing it. In fact, there's one that's gonna go out this week."

"How do you choose one for DNA?" I pressed him.

"For DNA, we take the one who's most perfect. The position in which he was buried. And when he's perfect we haven't put any chemicals on him. We work (normally, in the case of "imperfect" skeletons) with some gluey stuff, you see? We put this liquidy-thing on top of the bones and it has acetone and polyester inside of it. We always put it on to give form and to unite the bones, and when teeth are weak or fragmented or breaking. That's what we work with."

Hélio participates in a widespread, global fascination with genetic coding and shared substance, one that seems to be colonizing race and ethnicity-based identifications predicated, like Adilson's, on experience.[5] Here the most basically human, or universal, aspects of the skeletons uncovered are configured as a mutating master code whose high-tech manipulation by unseen experts at a level above and beyond the workers might unlock the mysteries that, while in some way already known by the people who participated in the excavation, must be authorized by a type of evidence with greater weight than the discovery of cockspurs by a man running his eyes and hands across the sieve.

As emphasized in the discussions of surfaces and depths and objects and their varied interpretations presented across chapter 5, visitors, state officials, and workers on the Praça da Sé share a number of diagnostic technologies. They do so as part of a scene where it is difficult to correlate specific approaches to interpretation to distinct social groups. In this context, IPAC and archaeologists appropriate methods and vocabularies used by workers. And workers and residents who recognize the social power of techniques like DNA also seek to step into the modes of analysis and technical languages of their state. All participants attend to a wildly productive incitement to look down, across, and behind as part of attempts to reveal an "underneath of things."[6] Such digging, whether conducted as a divining around visible signs put together by residents who claim an authority to explain their city center to crowds of Bahians from distant neighborhoods, or a technical operation predicated on encountering a representative, relatively intact, skeletal remains for laboratory analysis, is not a sign of constitutive difference. Rather, it illustrates how competing claims to knowledge of the past and the appropriation of objects as "property" of a specific person may draw diverse actors into particular types of relatedness.[7] The multiple contradictions that make up the "regularities" of this chatter highlight its ability to order and then, in an instant, re-array practices and viewpoints in an ongoing coproduction of truths about the foundations of Bahian, and human, life. Nonetheless, differentially situated Bahians who flocked to the

Sucupira to stare at the skeletons and, in the process, look deep into their city's landscapes, their histories, and their selves did develop a number of patterned responses to the tear in the urban fabric.

In mid-1999, as the Bahian state's interpretation of the identities of the bones began to shift from "nobles" to "slaves," visitors from distant neighborhoods would often identify the skeletons as slaves while nonetheless denying their own genealogical relations to them. Their attitude contrasted with that of a majority of Pelourinho inhabitants. More closely involved with IPAC, tourists from throughout the African diaspora, and neighborhood social movements like the Afrocentric Olodum, these residents of the city center would almost always claim formal or direct equivalence to, and descent from, the bodies entombed in buildings and plazas. As illustrated by Adilson's growing appreciation of the Pelourinho as a source of earnings, leisure, and knowledge, the construction workers employed in the alteration of the Pelourinho's landscape represented a group from Salvador's outskirts who entered into ongoing commerce and dialogue with the residents and institutions who tended to link themselves genealogically to the people whose identities they derived from the skeletons. Adilson's and Hélio's distinct, yet complementary, readings of the site suggest that this intercourse has altered their understandings of the historical center, and thus themselves.

In contrast to both Pelourinho residents and construction workers, arguments about slavery and history put together by working-class Bahians who would come downtown to visit the Praça da Sé from distant periurban areas typically involved statements like, "Well, I'm brown, but I can understand their position, we're being treated like slaves today." However, in May and June, a larger group of people from working-class suburbs began to claim, "Those people were slaves. I know because we black people know those sorts of things."

While I have been able to focus on Pelourinho-based construction workers as mediators between a highly politicized, downtown transnational space and life in Salvador's working-class neighborhoods, where concerns with defining origins seem to be less pronounced, I still do not understand exactly how, and why, dominant readings of the skeleton's identities by Bahians from Salvador's periphery shifted in mid-1999. But they did.[8] And to argue for a specialized knowledge of the past on the basis of a public declaration that one is a black descendent of slaves is to contradict salient claims in the literature on race in Brazil, if not quite the tenets of "actually existing" racial ideologies: According to most twentieth-century studies, Brazilians of a variety of social positions have sought, at a number of junctures since emancipation in 1889, to deny a racialized relationship to slavery and, thus, blackness as a historical marker of that status.[9] In fact, Edward Telles, one of the most insightful of North American sociologists of Brazilian race relations, states in the first paragraph of the introduction to his 2005 *Race in Another America*, "Unlike in the United States, race in Brazil refers mostly to skin color or physical appearance rather than ancestry."[10] Nonetheless, in 1999, in front of the remains of Brazil's first cathedral, working-class Bahians from throughout Salvador stood at their nation's symbolic origin and declared themselves descendents of slaves on the basis of diverse concatenations of race as an experiential, embodied, human, biological, and, above all, historical condition. Yet a generalized reckoning of descent from slaves is basic to arguments about race mixture.

Despite salient shifts in people's recognition of racism and a growing movement toward claiming blackness as well as indigenous ethnicity, a majority of Brazilians still claims a brown identity that may or may not rely on an active linkage to Africa or slavery.[11] They often put forth such a vision of hybrid, brown status around the primal scene of celebrations of mixture, or the dimly remembered yet at-times celebrated interaction between kitchen and master's bedroom so formative in Gilberto Freyre's fantasies of national unity. Even noted sociologist and former president of Brazil Fernando Henrique Cardoso infamously referred to this association by stating to reporters in the mid-1990s, "I have one foot in the kitchen." But the banalization of a violent relationship between female domestics and male slave owners has come under intense scrutiny precisely at the historical juncture in which cultural heritage has become something of a fever across Brazil, and around the world.

Although I stress the novelty of a genealogical account of racial belonging in the Pelourinho, there are a variety of spheres—most notably Afro-Brazilian religiosity, capoeira, carnival groups, maroon communities (*quilombos*), and even soap operas—in which discussions of slave roots have been salient for decades.[12] And Brazil's Unified Black Movement has worked diligently to foster a racial consciousness that might take appearance into account as an explicit mark of descent, and thus corporate identity. Furthermore, the transmission in Candomblé of *axé*, or force, is a basic link in the genealogical relationships between temples and religious practitioners and the fictive or consanguineal kin relations that tie together different generations of leaders. This axé is a word commonly used in Salvador to refer to the interior of persons, and students and practitioners of Candomblé such as Ordep Serra, Júlio Braga, and Vivaldo da Costa Lima have played important roles in constituting the Pelourinho as a heritage center. So it would be incorrect to ignore the influence of multiple factors on the claims made about the skeletons as remains of slaves.

I suggest, instead, that across Brazil a variety of realignments in producing truths about pasts and human subjectivities unavailable to direct experience have been catalyzed by legal, philanthropic, and religious debates, educational initiatives, and ritual grammars. These mediate relationships between political-economic processes and racial politics in ways that respond to, but never emanate directly from, citizens' clear analysis of the true shape of those social relations. Among them seems to be the creative appropriation in the Pelourinho of certain of the conventions of social science and cultural heritage. Residents of the historical center, interpellated by a social scientific evaluation that has material effects on the sizes of indemnifications, on those subjects' ability to remain in the historical center, and on the type of work performed in transforming the red light district into a space of memory, have thus come to look deep inside themselves and at their habits as indexes of something else. And that something else is a historical condition, whether it involves DNA analysis or cultural memories such as the importance of roosters' spurs to conceptions of Afro-Bahian masculinity. But a recognition of historical continuity is not a given. Nor do such linkages of past and present unfold around the world in the same ways. Thus, as I have emphasized across this book, *how*, rather than with what particular data, one faces the past and makes claims on it is critical to changing perceptions of personhood and racial belonging.

Commuting, Smoking, and Eating: Engaging Figuras

Once, as we enjoyed yet another acarajé in the afternoon light on the Praça da Sé, a resident of the nearby Ladeira da Misericórdia approached our table. Her face scarred from a lifetime of disputes and her hands swollen from intravenous drug use, she commanded me to buy her a snack. My construction worker companions stiffened, as Bahians familiar with the city center often interpret such demands, common among street children, as an affront to their ability to circulate unimpeded in public space. Concerned about my performance of proper masculinity, which required that I demand "respect" (*respeito*), my tablemates followed closely as I reached meekly into my pocket and handed a five-real note to the woman, a close friend and a well-known Pelourinho figura named Topa. As I brandished the bill with an exaggerated flourish, I affected a strong "gringo" accent to proclaim formally, "Miss (*senhorita*), if, upon finishing your acarajé, you would be so kind as to give me a tour of this beautiful neighborhood's alleys and mysteries (*becos e mistérios*), then you may keep even the change from this large bill which demonstrates my enormous wealth." To this, Topa responded with a smack of her lips that played on her sexuality, "I don't eat acarajé, I like juicy abará. And I'm not even going to eat with this money. I'm gonna smoke rock (crack cocaine)!" She then ordered, and devoured, an acarajé from the stand in front of us.

Topa engaged us through her own well-known love of illegal substances, Pelourinho conventions for demanding favors from visitors—an idiom I reversed as part of a running joke in which we would follow all-too-faithfully the contours of well-known Pelourinho social practices so as to alter their meanings, playfully—and common Bahian wordplays around the "abará." The abará, a sibling to the acarajé, is a mass of ground black-eyed peas patted together and boiled in a banana leaf, rather than fried in palm oil like the acarajé. Next, and like the acarajé, it is filled with hot pepper, dried shrimp, fish paste, chopped onions and tomatoes, and okra and peanut stew (*caruru*). The word "abará" is used in Bahian slang to refer to female genitalia, and Topa and I, unbeknownst to my tablemates, often lent small sums or paid for meals if one or the other was hungry and without change at the moment. Witnessing the exchange, Hélio sucked in his breath and said, "That one, that one is dangerous. She's a real devil (*capeta*). She's a hot pepper (*pimenta*). I see her all the time on the Misericórdia. She's trouble (*é pobrema*).[13] But she's actually really good inside, or to have on your side."

Hélio was correct. Topa was an important ally in the Pelourinho and, in spite of her reputation for violence and the knife she secreted in her brassiere, she possessed a genuine sweetness and an aching vulnerability. Hélio, like Adilson and a number of their colleagues, had come to know the residents of the Misericórdia when, after becoming a client of Dona Niza's cigarette and coffee stand set up in the shadow of the Sucupira, he began to join the gossip in the doorway of her house located further down the sloping Misericórdia. This led to a familiarity with the approximately seventy-five people resident on the hillside, something that permitted Hélio to use the street as a shortcut between his workplace on the Sucupira and the bus terminal below. Yet the scene on the Misericórdia, Topa's home and a street he admitted he had been afraid to set foot on prior to his experiences with the archaeologists, shocked Hélio. Drug use, extreme violence, nudity, widespread profanity, transvestitism, the blatant display of weapons, and the division of spoils from robberies did not take place in the open in any neighborhood in which he had lived. Yet they were common on the Misericórdia.

As construction workers had done years before in relation to Dandinha when rebuilding the more central areas of the historical center, the men who excavated the Sucupira spoke with reverence and, at times, fear about Topa's remarkable powers, scarred body, and attractive personality. They knew little about the details of her youth in the working-class neighborhood of Fazenda Grande do Retiro, or what Topa's mother described to me later as the trials of a young woman who was too smart, too beautiful, too full of plans—and thus too "wild"—for a working-class neighborhood where she was expected to become a housewife or, if she ventured into paid employment, a domestic servant isolated behind the walls of a distant middle-class household. But the workers recognized Topa as a figura, or a devil, or a hot pepper, who possessed the remarkable powers and tolerance for abuse so often attributed to Maciel/Pelourinho residents and, as the Maciel became but a fading memory at the beginning of the twenty-first century, to those small pockets at the edges of the Pelourinho to which long-term residents moved in an attempt to extract more indemnification or remain in the cash-rich historical center.

This chapter, which builds on and complicates the ways that the incitements to discourse around the Sucupira encourage Bahians to recognize identities as more than "skin deep," is not really about Hélio, Adilson, or skeletons and their interpretation. Instead, I am intrigued by the idioms—romantic love, racial degeneracy, hygienic redemption, technocratic research, for example—through which the voyages into self-knowledge animated by the techniques central to the Pelourinho's restoration become enunciable. These provide paths into the types, and sources, of knowledge of selves developed by the residents of the Misericórdia, a group of people who function as quintessential Others against and with whom IPAC scientists have forged a simultaneously technocratic and affective bond that continues to inflect how patrimony, and thus the properties of a Bahian people, is conceptualized in Salvador. In other words, the remainder of this chapter focuses in on Topa and the transformations undergone by certain Pelourinho residents I refer to as properly historical subjects, or people who have developed remarkable approaches to their embeddedness in the narration of the past and the commodification of culture.

The Hill of Mercy

The Ladeira da Misericórdia, or Hill of Mercy, testifies to rent and spent flesh, to feet beaten by sharp granite designed to keep straining slaves and top-heavy mules from slipping, and thus to the ongoing laminations of renewal and decay that emanate from the urbanization schemes within which Pelourinho residents have become expert at objectifying themselves. The narrow street scratched into the merciful, merciless hillside, also called the "Ladeira da Misericórdia," twists, in the shape of a squared-off horseshoe, some five hundred yards down the cliff separating the Upper and Lower Cities, thus permitting its sinuous outline to connect the Praça da Sé to Salvador's waterfront, the most important point of arrival of African slaves to the Americas in the seventeenth and eighteenth centuries. The Misericórdia's occupants often told me that the street's scarred walls recall the backs of those who entered the New World through this passageway from Salvador's docks to its Pillory. Tucked behind the Hospital of the Santa Casa da Misericórdia (The Holy House of Mercy),

Figure 6.1. Ladeira da Misericórdia: "It is the hill without an origin/or in its very origins, it is without an end."

the oldest philanthropy in the Americas and the institution from which the hill and its street take their name, the Ladeira is mentioned frequently in eighteenth-century ecclesiastical and colonial authorities' concerns with public health. It was also denounced by virtuous citizens who opposed the dumping of animal carcasses and the performance of libidinous acts there at night. A center of luxurious houses of prostitution by the early twentieth century, the street also appears prominently in mid-twentieth-century Bahian landscape painting, newspaper reports, EPUCS planning documents, modernist proposals to animate Bahia's heritage, and oral histories of prostitution and bohemian nightlife.[14]

In 1948, the poet and long-term Bahian Regional IPHAN director Godofredo Filho published the poem "Ladeira da Misericórdia." This ode to a place made special in part through Godofredo Filho's artistry plays with origins, landscape, and the sexualized, interclass relations that gird Bahian heritage planning and representations of the Pelourinho today. The poem opens with,

It is the hill without an origin
or in its very origins, it is without an end
It is the hill that begins
where I'd like to end

This is the hill of Bahia
A cruel, lost hill
That in the greatest irony
Claims that it arises from mercy
It is the hill of Bahia[15]

Godofredo Filho seems to have recognized in his "Ladeira da Misericórdia" that there are no true ends or beginnings to regional and national identities, but only attempts to define their limits through different types of slippages or substitutions. After recalling drunken nights and lovers' quarrels, he names women and particular buildings he loved on the street behind the hospital, mixing his self with the stones, architecture, and body fluids so constitutive of the Misericórdia of the late 1940s and bohemian and ethnographic knowledge of Salvador's intimate spaces today:

You were the street of crèches
But today you are the hill of negressess,
Of syphilitic mulattas,
Of soldiers and drunks
The street of miserable whores . . .

Carnal love, blood,
Saliva and acidic kisses . . .

Over the following decades IPAC social science would translate Godofredo's masculine, regional poetry into expert knowledge and public memory. This would, in effect, realize Godofredo Filho's conclusion that,

I am the one who kisses your stones
I, who, in a transformative lament
Find myself thickening, becoming densely real, through your mystery;
Who lashes myself to those, your lips,
Mashed by bondage and cruelty
My love without name
My love that knows not its name
But translates it in the light of the pre-dawn
Because I want you embraced
In this tomorrow that tarries

In rescuing me from my torment . . .
the enigmatic depth of Christ
The flower of red flame
Touching on unreal whiteness . . .
Hill that is my life
The hill that is my love

The extent to which Godofredo Filho depends on his city's landscape and fallen lovers' "acidic kisses" underscores yet again how, for intellectuals of his generation, an important route into the self lay in sleeping with, fighting with, and loving the Misericórdia's "miserable whores" and ancient stones so as to become "densely real" through their mystery. Powerful men's identities, then, rested in no small part on an ability to know, and engage, the women of the red light district. Filho's poetic description of this process moves in time, but not through space, beginning at the crèches of the Santa Casa da Misericórdia, the hospital that once housed the public wheel at which mothers left the sort of unwanted children who now become "street children."[16] It ends with an unrealized, Christian redemption around battered, scarred, and yet apparently beloved women of ill repute on the "Hill that is my life / The hill that is my love." The verses thus participate in a trope common even in the late twentieth century, a time when the employees of the Santa Casa da Misericórdia, today one of Bahia's most important archives and an institution on whose board sit a number of descendents of the state's best-known planter families, used to invite me to peer out the window and watch the hillside's residents who Godofredo Filho had described as,

Crushed faces, asleep.
Atop traumatized stones
I step upon the exposed throats
of the voices I do not hear[17]

The archivists at the Santa Casa da Misericórdia tended to describe the people below us as a mix of "poor things" (coitados), dangerous marginals (marginais), and, like the woman who addressed the field architect at the unveiling of the Praça da Sé site located just a few meters from the Misericórdia, "children of God" (filhos de Deus). We would look down from the archive and see people I knew secreting stolen cameras, arms, or illicit substances atop walls that from the street promised hiding places but from our lofty position were open to easy inspection. I used to enjoy teasing people about their subterfuges and thus I would revel playfully—and perhaps too uncritically—in an unraveling of their secrets made possible by my archival perspective. On one occasion, the head

Figure 6.2. Storekeeper on the Misericórdia accompanied by his son.

archivist reported to me that she had heard shots and witnessed a slaughter as the police gunned down a man in one of the patios visible only from above.

I did not need the perspective afforded by the archive, as that was the day Quisinho and Cachorrão died, chased across the thick grass that backs up to the Misericórdia and assassinated by the Civil Police. The two had dared to burglarize an antiques dealer, rumored to be a cousin of a judge close to Antonio Carlos Magalhães. Bilisca, the son of Renata, a former Maciel resident who now works as a community health organizer for a Bahian NGO, denounced them so as not to die himself. Crazed by guilt and promised death by Quisinho and Cachorrão's other colleagues, Bilisca fled the Misericórdia that is now silent, entirely bereft of residents, and divided neatly by a large, locked gate. Municipal security guards open this barrier only to facilitate dignitaries' passage from the modern avenues of the Lower City to the city hall parking garage in the basement of the Sucupira. Often, when I telephone Bahia, an anthropologist friend says she encounters Bilisca lying in a stupor alongside Salvador's Barra lighthouse, not far from the antiques dealer he burglarized with two friends who are no more.

But here I get ahead of myself one more time and add details that do not fit in a chapter intended as an exploration of details that do not quite fit, but

Figure 6.3. Residents, circa 1994, of one of the houses on the Misericórdia that served as a brothel during Godofredo Filho's times on the Hill of Mercy. In 1994 it was a residence. Today it is empty, awaiting "reconstruction."

nonetheless converge in the elaboration of histories that make sense to some. It thus seems more than coincidental that in the final years of the twentieth century the Bahian trope of degeneration, so powerful during Brazil's First Republic when speaking of mixed-race backlanders, and animated once again around the residents of the Misericórdia in Godofredo Filho's poetry of the 1940s, found purchase on the hill without beginnings and ends. Few from the archive would believe me when I would tell them that I knew, liked, and trusted many of the people they spied upon through their window. Kind public servants would tell me, "No, no, John, those people are not to be trusted. They're thieves, the worst there are. They're dangerous. Bandits. Degenerates. People even say they have AIDS!"

Once, near the start of fieldwork, I sat on the bleachers in front of city hall and alongside the drop-off to the Ladeira da Misericórdia with the youngest nephew of Jurema, the most powerful woman resident in the 28's Gueto. Like those of many North American stadiums, the seats were open from underneath so that they exposed their occupants' legs to anyone approaching from behind. We were happy, exchanging news as he had just been released from juvenile detention and had never met my infant son who I cradled on my lap. In the midst of our conversation in front of Salvador's seat of municipal governance, one of the guards from city hall stole up on us. Quickly, he tried to stab the boy with a long fish knife (*peixeira*).

When I protested, screaming as the child ran for his life, the guard turned back and snarled, "Shameless, faceless one (*descarado*). Don't talk to me. I know what you are. Talking to those marginals, those animals (*marginais, animais*) on the Misericórdia. You think I don't see you down there. I know what you are!" as he threatened me with his knife. Yet such threats to foreigners are rare. And the attempt to extinguish violently the residents of the Misericórdia and the 28 is fairly new. It is part of a shifting set of IPAC and police practices established in dialogue with previous generations' interactions with Pelourinho residents and with contemporary philanthropic organizations' attempts to rescue those people from what are presented as their degraded conditions. As such, it exemplifies and reproduces the blurry boundaries between extirpation and care that are so essential to the heritage-based management of the life of an Afro-Bahian populace in the Pelourinho.

AIDS Education: "You Are the Owners of Your Bodies"

At the end of August 1997 I visited Dona Niza and Seu Jorge, the couple introduced in the previous chapter who intuited treasure in their Maciel home. Up until their removal from the historical center to the impoverished suburb of Simões Filho in 1998, Seu Jorge and Dona Niza had lived with their children at number 18 Ladeira da Misericórdia. In yet another example of people's attempts to remain in the city center following indemnification, Jorge and Niza had invaded this building after IPAC paid them to leave their former home in the Maciel in preparation for that region's restoration between 1992 and 1993. Jorge and Niza's number 18 Ladeira da Misericórdia was not the "18th Battalion of Love" memorialized by the Bem Aventurados, but a different building that a reader of Godofredo Filho's poetry may recognize as one of the houses of prostitution celebrated in his verse some fifty years earlier.

In spite of Filho's attempt to memorialize the hillside's brothels as the source of Bahia, on the day in 1997 that I visited Niza and Jorge, memories of bohemian extravagance were largely absent. Instead, residents were concerned with their own access to indemnifications and to the possibility of remaining in this

Figure 6.4. Misericórdia resident in front of the Coaty, 1995.

privileged territory. But even these anxieties vanished like the morning rains as a small procession of microbuses that residents described as belonging to the Ministry of Health spun their tires as they climbed the Ladeira's mossy stones. They strained to carry their cargoes of well-dressed medical personnel up to the building that at the time we called the Coaty nightclub. This "Coaty" was an eighteenth-century edifice reworked in the 1980s in a poured concrete modernist style, reminiscent of a dimpled Starship Enterprise, by the famous architect Lina Bo Bardi who had been invited to Salvador as part of then-Mayor Mario Kertesz's attempt to restore the Pelourinho.[18]

As the health professionals stepped from their vans, we filed into the Coaty and sat in front of its stage from which a large mango tree jutted through the central opening in Bo Bardi's well-designed roof. The visitors to this space reoccupied by displaced people, but which the modernist architect had concep-

Figure 6.5. A mother and her sons, residents in the Coaty, pose atop the building's stage and in front of its mango tree, November 1997.

tualized as a challenge to the "folklorization" of Afro-Bahian culture and the transformation of Salvador into a tourist city, handed out shiny red folders, pads, new pencils and pens, and AIDS education literature intended to encourage residents' participation in the street theater. This CETAD team, whose members deserve recognition as dedicated professionals in spite of the reversals their presentation would soon face in the hands of residents, had even listed two of the three adult women living in the Coaty as organizers of the event. Such respect, as well as the quality of their outreach and science, reflects CETAD's contributions to public health and to the residents of the city center. For this reason, the interactions that followed are so revealing: Rather than a problematic institution that ignores a citizenry's needs so as to displace a majority and enrich a few, as I suggest IPAC had become at the level of its directorate in the mid- to late-1990s, CETAD is a model institution in the field of harm reduction.[19]

Figure 6.6. Topa plays with the children next door, August 1994.

As they entered the Coaty's cool yet naturally lighted space, the educators handed all present a sheet entitled "Awareness: Preventive Information about STDS/AIDS, Drug Abuse, and Quality of Life," which described the meeting's themes.[20] Most residents did not know how to make the ink in their new pens begin flowing, indicating how little time they had spent in schoolrooms. Yet we soon began drawing, having been asked to define "health" and encouraged by facilitators to sketch our physical outlines as we listened to lectures about the need to take responsibility for our bodies. CETAD quickly built a rapport with their audience, many of whom drew enthusiastically. But those assembled, closely associated with injectable drugs and sex work, also whispered among one another and commented on how discomforting it was that the bourgeoisie should speak, and ask *them* to speak, in graphic terms about their bodies and inner being.

One of the women listed on the CETAD sheet as part of the "Organizing Team" drifted in and out of the central presentation area. Topa, whose actual nickname—which in Bahian slang means to be ready for something, to overcome, or to accept a challenge—I employ here because she is now deceased, was quite drunk and high on the powerful depressant Rohypnol. She stood listening, for a moment. Then, agitated, she pulled out a sheet of paper and scrawled furiously. Walking over to where I sat at the back of the audience, she dropped the paper into my lap. It read, "For those who know, 2 + 2 = 4."

Farther down the page she had written, alongside the number four, "I am José. No, I am nena, neno," as she allowed her pen to trail off in a long squiggle.[21] After that, Topa remained still, at least for a time.

Following a presentation by the head doctor from the Santo Antônio medical post, the nurse from the main Pelourinho medical post began a dialogue about hygiene. She asked that we act out household and "private" activities, such as bathing, cooking, and washing dishes. My notes, taken on CETAD paper, indicate that she emphasized repeatedly, "Each person is the owner of her body" and "You have value."[22]

Topa, one of the three women who lived with their common-law husbands in different areas of the Coaty, interrupted the nurse repeatedly. In response to a question about parasites, the nurse instructed residents on the inadvisability of tossing toilet paper and feces on the street. Topa mumbled and became belligerent as her neighbors laughed sheepishly, embarrassed and energized by her character traits, which they called "problematic." Although CETAD is a private NGO linked to the Federal University, the Ministry of Health, and a number of development organizations that ultimately lead back to USAID and associated private for-profit "social marketing" corporations, residents assured me that it was a state institution linked to IPAC. Therefore its experts needed to be respected. Residents so convinced me of this that I had to be corrected several times by Dr. Tarcísio, one of its directors, who explained that the NGO relied on corporations, international aid organizations, and private philanthropies for a majority of its operating expenses.

As the nurse finished her instructions about toilet paper and feces, Topa stood up and, suddenly giving off cues that suggested she was now coherent, raised her hand and announced that she had a question. The nurse stepped back and began to listen to the soft-spoken resident of the Coaty while I scribbled her words in my improvised field notebook provided by the people I thought represented the Ministry of Health. Topa asked, "Doctor, I just want to ask one question. I have just one doubt that needs to be cleared up about this issue of feces. Doctor, you say that we should not throw our shit-laden—sorry, I mean our soiled—toilet paper on the ground. This is an important issue for me. I just want to understand it a little better." The nurse who Topa called *doutora* (doctor) nodded eagerly and underscored the importance of the lesson, saying, "Yes, I'm glad you're asking. . . . We really need to talk about hygiene."

Topa continued, "So as I understand it. Well, let me ask it this way. If I am walking on a Saturday afternoon, out looking for useful items in the trash in your neighborhood, say Pituba or Caminho das Arvores, and I need to defecate, I should look for a bathroom.[23] There's no way I should crap—I mean defecate—in the street. Right?"

"Right!" answered the nurse, excited by her apparent progress.

"Well, OK, so let's say that I walk up to your house on a Sunday and knock on the door because I really need to defecate. Or rather, if I am in danger of soiling my pants [pause] No! What I really mean is, what I'm really going to do is to make poop. If I am going to make [pause] No! Not poop! If I am going to shit all over myself and the street, and instead I walk up to the door and knock, and you answer the door [pause] No, sorry, not you, but your maid, answers the door—"

"Eh, eh, eh, eh," sputtered the now worried nurse.

Topa continued, "And I say, 'Excuse me, I need to use your bathroom so that I don't shit all over the sidewalk and soil the street and endanger public health,' what do you think your maid is going to tell me? Is she going to let me in to use your bathroom that she's been scrubbing all morning? Or when she calls back and you answer 'Who is it?' Are you going to tell her to let me into your house to use your clean toilet, so I don't get shit and toilet paper on the sidewalk? What if I should need to defecate in *your* neighborhood, madame?"

The educator stood speechless, mouth agape, as she toyed with one of her gold bracelets.

Topa awaited an answer, her eyes glistening with tears, as her neighbors sat on the floor, drawing and playing with their stationery kits. Kleber, a theologian and sociologist who works with CETAD, responded, "Well, what would *you* do in that case, Topa?"

Topa hissed fiercely in response, "Don't butt in! *I'm* doing the asking!"[24]

Without options, the nurse, a kind professional I later came to know through my son's checkups at the Pelourinho health post, responded, "Ah ah ah ah ah, well, I would hope that anyone who answered the door in my house would let you in."

"But would *you* tell your maid to let me in?" asked Topa.

"This is truly a difficult question," responded the nurse, honestly, as the other health professionals buzzed about the back of the room and a long silence settled over a group of professionals and a group of people with AIDS. Friends hushed Topa as her husband pulled her from the room. She ran into her sleeping area, separated from the main room by a hanging sheet, and began crying, refusing to come out and join the lesson, which quickly became chaotic. Another woman raised her hand and announced, "I have a question!"

When called on, this woman, known as Dona Coroa (Old Lady), asked somewhat crankily, "I just want to know when the doctors are going to come see us. I've had enough with this education stuff. When are the doctors coming?" The members of the CETAD team announced abruptly that the meeting and street theater were over.

Figure 6.7. Topa engages the anthropologist and his lens, pensively.

Soon the health professionals returned to their vans, somewhat concerned about what the foreign ethnographer had witnessed and, it seemed, genuinely chagrined by a setback in their efforts to continue their work with a population at high risk of contamination with HIV. Promising to return the next week, they disappeared down the Hill of Mercy toward the fountain at the base of "the hill without an origin / or [that] in its very origins . . . is without an end."[25]

It would make little sense to distance myself from the medical team so as to appear as an unsullied "friend" of the residents of the Ladeira da Misericórdia. I was, and am, a friend to the few who still survive and who, in the wake of indemnification, now live throughout Salvador and the interior. And, like most members of CETAD, I am a professional social scientist who, from 1997 to 2000, was affiliated with UFBA's Institute of Collective Health.

Yet my presence that day, and my resistance to taping, pencils, notebooks, and structured interviews while working with the population of the Misericórdia—activities and tools I replaced with long hours of rumor-mongering and toil as I helped residents shore up their buildings, negotiate their indemnifications, or pack their belongings when IPAC sent its moving trucks—provided me with a special understanding of their relationship to me, to their hillside, to IPAC, and to my colleagues such as CETAD's health professionals.[26] This is not to argue that I exist or write from a position outside a transnational apparatus of NGOs, state bureaucrats, and social scientific knowledge in which the residents of the Ladeira are constructed, and construct themselves, as different types of political subjects. But it is to suggest the power of ethnography in helping me to perceive our interactions in novel ways. These make clearer just how proper Topa really was, even in her extreme impropriety.

Densities: A Marginal at the Epicenter

Topa's acting up in the midst of a public health drama designed to convince residents they "have value" at a moment when IPAC construed her habits as patrimony makes visible a number of concordances and contradictions. On one level, by reproducing the incident here I run the risk of presenting the anthropologist as occupying an "outside" that is more real than the circuits of knowledge activated by CETAD or IPAC. But if such a position were possible it would configure Topa and her neighbors as authentic exemplars of a popular consciousness into which I, and I alone, tap in order to produce myself as a subject that exists because he knows the "Other" so well, and so authentically. This is a claim I struggle to contest even as I remain convinced that years of living alongside residents of the Misericórdia and their neighbors has changed me in ways that I know only incompletely, but that permeate the account unfolding here. And, as should be apparent, I enjoyed, and continue to find inspiration in, Topa's creativity. But backtalk did not prevent her from losing her home or from serving as fodder for IPAC and accounts such as the one my reader digests here. This is a contradiction I cannot resolve at this moment.

Topa and I engaged one another in myriad ways, and we used to speak at length about friendship in the face of glaring inequality and markedly different experiences. My sense is that Topa understood well, as highlighted by her performance in the Coaty, the intersubjective space between the two of us and between institutions like CETAD and IPAC and the Pelourinho's population: In speaking to CETAD, she politicizes her living quarters and its surveillance through interruption. Her first move involves what seems a plea to be heard, to have her knowledge and opinion quite literally add up, or "count," within the manipulations of selves going on as medical personnel sought to convince her that she had "value."[27] She enunciates this appeal through a written message deposited in my lap while pursing her lips angrily at Kleber, the CETAD member speaking at the time. When we talked later, Topa admitted that she felt threatened and wanted to return to her room and get away from "those people." Her initial response, a private letter passed to the person who most obviously bridged the social gaps between those in the room, put forth a claim to personhood that shifted between proper name and nickname, and male and female, before literally trailing off the page.

Next, Topa broke the tension between the fluid yet fragile sense of self expressed in the secret communication and CETAD's rather intense work of reworking selves, an activity that seems to have motivated her look inward at a subject that refused to remain stable or contained. In asking her question to the nurse, Topa mimics magisterially, drawing the professionals out of their pedagogical roles and transforming them into actors within their own theater. This flipping of the naturalized position of actor and pedagogue is significant in itself. But Topa then sets another trap for her instructors by voicing "just one doubt that needs to be cleared up about this issue of feces" before moving through a glossary of slang terms for excrement. She does so while narrating her approach to the nurse's home. Here Topa, who once worked as a servant, raises the possibility of the wrong-type-of-woman's entrance into the bourgeois home, precisely the scene of the narrative of national purification/hybridity so important to modern Brazilianness. A maid who guards this space then checks whether to admit the woman from the Pelourinho. Yet Topa, a former prostitute and hence the doorkeeper's immoral doppelgänger, paralyzes the *patroa* ("patron" or employer; in this case, the nurse) by performing an imagined interaction on the threshold of house and street.[28] This solicitation of a toilet enables Topa to interpellate the hygienicist who arrived on the Misericórdia so as to educate, and perhaps render palatable to the public that would soon flock to the historical center, some of Salvador's most marginalized quasi-citizens.

Since from residents' perspectives, CETAD and IPAC are both state institutions, Topa's "gutsy insurrection" may be read as an analysis of state appropriations of her quotidian through surveillance of hygiene, sexuality, and domestic habits. Her inversions permit Topa to situate those objectifications within a longer history of IPAC cleansing. More than a Rabelasian overturning or even an anthropological fetishization of abjection, Topa's challenge recalls Begoña Aretxaga's description of political prisoners' "dirty protest." There, Irish Republican Army partisans' complaints forged around feces, urine, and menstrual blood reconstituted colonial representations of Irish filth "as a materialization of the buried 'shit' of British colonization, a de-metaphorization of the 'savage, dirty Irish.'"[29] Like prisoners' manipulations of excreta that made manifest their relations to the state, colonial history, and Ireland's place within Britain, Topa's upending of IPAC constructions helps make real, or palpable, the histories of Brazil that revolve around her own habits. Yet unlike the Irish prisoners, Topa never manipulates feces directly, even as her treatment of the emergence of human waste turns on a discursive calling up of impure substance and the people whose everyday habits inflect its shapes and textures. Nor, and especially significantly, does she come out and tell CETAD who and what she really is so as to correct them in any affirmative way. Rather, she treats the hillside residents' waste as an admittedly pungent, but undoubtedly fecund, sign of the lifeways under CETAD surveillance. This draws her public into interactions that she structures in ways that undercut the health team's presumptions, even as the outcomes of this communication remain somewhat undefined.

Roguishness as Habit

People like Topa—or the Mago, who appeared in the Preface, or Dona Niza, who warned me that I might be looking at peppers rather than meat—destabilize claims and identities by occupying multiple positions, mimicking ostensible social superiors' habits, and blurring categories touted as secure. This crafty disposition, usually referred to as *malandragem* (roguery or trick-sterdom), is a prized quality, albeit one often reserved for men, in hierarchical Brazil.[30] Roberto da Matta approaches this conceptual correlate to racial democracy's blurring and veiling of exclusionary racial categories as a source of power through which individuals caught in impossible situations may bend the structures that isolate them in order to demand the status of rights-bearing subjects. Across the present text I lean on malandragem in order to lay claim to quasi-insider status and to "speak between the lines" in obvious as well as sly ways that will be apparent to varying extents to different readers. One example is the pseudonym I use to refer to my friend who marched onto the Pelourinho Square like a human sandwich. In obscuring his identity I call him "Malaquias," a name well known within our peer group as that of a trickster. So this appellation is but a feint that might amuse, or peeve slightly, N_____ when he reads this text some day.

Macunaíma, "the hero without any character," is a quintessential rogue established as archetypically Brazilian in Mário de Andrade's prose. Yet his salience in Brazilian mythology underscores how a tendency to shift habits may become habitual, and thus problematic in new ways, even for those who perform it. Pelourinho residents, while they value malandragem, frequently characterize this disposition as an impediment to community organizing. Many argue that in failing to take a position and constantly undermining those loci occupied by his or her associates, the *malandro* renders real political action impossible. Nonetheless, people commonly explained that since they were not quite sure what they wanted or expected in their dealings with IPAC, they had to be malandros when engaging the heritage bureaucracy. After all, many had found themselves in the Pelourinho because it was where, as individuals without a firm claim to full personhood in Bahia, they could "make do" in a fold in a larger, exclusionary landscape. The crumbling Maciel/Pelourinho was the best place not simply for surviving—residents stressed that surviving is not living— but also for realizing their desires. So they strove, and continue to strive today, to avoid having to return to Salvador's periphery or the Bahian interior, a destiny encouraged by IPAC's paltry indemnifications. This struggle in the ruins of colonial Brazil made "malandragem" necessary. And the repositionings involved in its enactment seem to have inflected, if not quite structured, much of the neighborhood's social life. From one perspective, then, Topa's actions become significant in relation to a rather canonical way of being in and making sense of Brazilian national life. However, and much like a reading of Bahian race relations today as either an instantiation or a contestation of racial democracy, to reduce Topa's manipulations to a particular instance of a generalized tendency called "malandragem" is to miss the nuances and real significance of her performance. It also reduces a specific historical juncture, and a series of relations between Pelourinho residents and the state that seeks to configure them as authentic primitives, to a cultural condition rather than a contested series of "renewals" intended to transform residents into what they are not, but may end up being.

A Grand Tour in the Land of Data

When Topa places the nurse in the position of informant, she proffers a "grand tour question," or a query that allows the ethnographer to "know at least one setting in which the informant carries out routine activities." According to James Spradley, author of a rather standard North American fieldwork methods guide, such questions "are intended to encourage an informant to talk about a particular cultural scene" and to "elicit a large sample of utterances in the informant's native language."[31] Yet Topa answers her grand tour question by going into a bit too much detail about the nurse's home and domestic servant. And, like so many ethnographers, she frontloads her interrogative and details her own terms for feces rather than drawing out the nurse's emic perspective. Nonetheless, she has asked a large question about the nurse's home, her hired help, her hygienic practices, and, by implication, her focal vocabulary. She has asked the nurse to describe her typical weekend and her normal practices for dealing with public and private space, a source of anxiety in Bahia, especially as concerns doorsteps.[32] Most important for my understanding of the interaction, in posing questions that leave health professionals speechless, Topa avoids fashioning an alternative reality or educational program that might replace the bit of street theater designed to educate her. Instead, she produces a pause in those actors' standard ways of understanding the world. Into this gap, which I will argue is also a history that inserts Topa into a longer flow of history in rather special ways, steps Dona Coroa, who asks the question that really interests residents: "When are the doctors coming?" As Dona Coroa's pragmatic response indicates, those assembled do not really care about the meaning of the interactions in which they are enmeshed. They are interested in the practical effects of those engagements, even as any mobilization of evidence is, at least in some way, indebted to a process of making sense of a world. Thus my claim developed below, namely that Topa avoids interpretation in favor of a rather strange, in-between status akin to that of a datum in an archive or field note, involves a certain level of interpretation on her part. Yet, as I have emphasized throughout this account, not all sense-making works on the same plane.

At a most basic, rather blatantly "realist" level, Topa's forcing of the nurse to acknowledge that an impoverished yet conscientious Pelourinho woman may very well appear on a bourgeois doorstep looking for a bathroom makes clear how special such a well-tiled, modern space with running water is for inhabitants of the remains of eighteenth- and nineteenth-century buildings. Topa thus underscores to the CETAD team that residents do not leave toilet paper and feces on the ground because they know no better. Rather, there was nowhere to defecate, properly, close to home in the prerestoration Maciel/Pelourinho.

Not only does Topa point out implicitly that the Misericórdia lacked running water, but she raises to a level of consciousness the forms of care and lopsided concerns with working-class citizens' "propriety" so common in Salvador. By asking ethnographic questions of the nurse, Topa inverts the standard terms for interactions between researchers and Pelourinho residents. In chapter 3, I quote IPAC's head of field research Jeferson Bacelar, who argued that residents had become so habituated to questionnaires that they anticipated the questions presented by IPAC researchers in the 1970s. In Topa's case, she has altered and flipped the questions. The nurse's ultimately pained expression to me when we discussed Topa later, as she gave my young son his annual check-up in the Pelourinho health post, indicated that she had not been able to naturalize completely the interruption and that it had caused her to consider the nature of her presentation. Dr. Tarcísio, the head of the CETAD team and an extraordinarily dedicated professional, also shook his head ruefully to me as his team left the Misericórdia following Topa's acting up.

Instead of skating between and undermining hierarchical social relations, as Roberto Da Matta proposes that malandros tend to do, this female *malandra* calls up the techniques that naturalize those inequalities. She does so by objectifying them. She focuses in on and entifies performatively the social scientific interactions brought to bear in the ostensible alleviation of a social problem, and thus her own naturalization as a problematic person. In addition to her highlighting of the structural violence basic to her interactions with CETAD's lack of focus on physical infrastructure, Topa forces the nurse to produce data for the Coaty audience with which the hygienists had conducted careful epidemiological and ethnographic research. Within this interaction, the professionals and their practices become, if only for a moment, part of an elicited evidentiary base that makes visible the building blocks that pave the way for Topa's dispossession. This opens up the critical-perceptual landscapes that have over the last decades transformed Topa and her neighbors into bits of data and objects of CETAD pedagogy and helped ground her own claims to a unique form of self-possession. In undercutting structuring differences, Topa the iconoclastic rogue thus objectifies those differences in a manner that forces all present to inhabit them, differentially. But again, a celebration of roguishness is, by now, rather stale in Brazilian studies and national life.

Rethinking Agency

An ability to impact the world, or "agency," is in the United States frequently equated with individual intent. While efforts to conceive of a more distributed form of agency, which include attending to the ways objects and material forms make themselves present in interactions with humans, are today central to anthropological theorizations of politics, I would be remiss if I argued that the fluted concrete stage in the middle of the Coaty played a major role in what went on in the CETAD meeting in ways participants or the ethnographer found material. But in the space between "philanthropic" institutions and the Pelourinho's population, in relation to the multiple and often anticipatory self-objectifications described across the present chapter, and by means of blurrings of subjects and objects so much a part of the Pelourinho-based concern with "tombamento" discussed in chapter 4, residents' historically embedded proximity to and intense mimicry of signs and objects in the Pelourinho provides those subject to IPAC/CETAD care with resources for assembling themselves differently. This is especially true when those people are objectified as evidence about Bahia's "problems."[33] And the techniques deployed at such moments, a sort of "touching up" against the referents of accounts and performances, do not always make perfect sense. But they definitely "make do."

Topa's questioning during her imagined trip to the nurse's house is both an engagement that demands response and a form of witnessing that reiterates the very similar interaction that arose when the CETAD team members knocked on the Coaty door and, while not quite requesting a bathroom, implicitly asked residents why they did not use bathrooms so as to safeguard public health. Topa's questioning is therefore also a metacommentary, or talk about talk, that draws together the interaction's participants as a speech community because it reveals something of the shape of shared assumptions about what is correct, moral, and sensible.[34] Yet the fissures between Topa's experiences and the nurse's professional goals are rather difficult to bridge. The nurse demonstrated this chasm when, during my son's medical exam, she brought up Topa and that day on the Misericórdia. Initially, given the pained and kind expression on her face, I imagined that she had come to some understanding of her own implication in Topa's disorderliness. But this was not what had happened: "These people," the nurse explained sadly, "are quite difficult. They're really needy. One never knows what they put in their bodies and how those substances are going to make them react."

The health services provider to whom Topa and I both looked for care had put together an explanation for an unruly woman's insurrection, or refusal and recombination, of their dialectical relationship as pedagogue and nonhygienic subject. The nurse had re-established the hegemony of a habitual description of the Pelourinho's population as composed of drug abusing, dangerous, and needy people whose problems stood as objects of treatment for CETAD experts, rather than a specific form of fallenness in which the nurse and the social scientists surrounding her are implicated. From this perspective, the nurse was not needy. Nor was I needy. But Topa was, it seemed. What, then, of this apparent neediness? Might one distend further the concept of "making life" (fazendo vida), or the Pelourinho women's term for engaging in prostitution and thus making do following their escape from abusive male relatives; overbearing employers who in the privacy of the bourgeois home may beat, starve, and burn the young girls from the countryside consigned to domestic service; or the near absence of money and hope for a different life in the dust of the twentieth-century Bahian sertão?[35] Might the pain and struggle of a teenager who, like Dona Pió, walked along the beach for nearly a week so as to reach Salvador and escape her father, be translated into an idiom that goes beyond neediness even as it remains faithful to that pilgrim's suffering, dislocation, and hopes for a better future in a downtown, sexualized, and historical space incoherently sacralized by her voyage? Could it be that Topa somehow speaks through what might at first glance appear as little more than raw data that, seemingly inert, appears to make up a ground for the ostensibly real work of reconstituting a verifiable past? Might Topa situate herself in the experience of surveillance that lashes her very being to CETAD and then, nearly at the same time, force the members of the health team to come up with a different outcome, which she nonetheless inflects?

Topa, like the women who once surrounded her in Salvador's red light district, bridges different spaces of Bahian society in ways that place her at the core of Brazil's history as enacted in the Pelourinho. This mediation demands intimacy and makes it difficult to construe participants, and discourses, as separate entities.[36] Yet the nurse seemed unable to interpret Topa's interruption in any way beyond reinstating the moat between two intelligent and courageous Bahian women of different class positions. Topa seemed to realize this, in advance: Would the nurse tell her servant to invite the explosive trash picker into their kitchen, and would the domestic servant who had just finished polishing tiles accede to such a request? Of course not. And Topa knew this. As Erich Auerbach notes of a different sort of figura, far-removed in time and space from the Coaty, "in the figural interpretation the fact is subordinated to an interpretation which is fully secured to begin with: the event is enacted according to an ideal model . . . situated in the future and thus far only promised."[37] In a slight modification of Auerbach's insights produced in a mid-twentieth-century Europe scarred by National Socialism, Topa recognizes that as a disfigured, potentially diseased vector from and to the Maciel/Pelourinho, her future reception—and her interpretation in the hands of Others who nonetheless claim to know her domestic spaces so very well—was overdetermined, but not quite predetermined.

In his discussion of anthropological hermeneutics, Vincent Crapanzano notes in the landmark collection *Writing Culture*, "When Hermes took the post of messenger of the gods, he promised Zeus not to lie. He did not promise to tell the whole truth. Zeus understood. The ethnographer has not."[38] Hermes' "partial truths"—the subtitle of James Clifford's introduction to the volume— open to critique those ethnographers who would configure anthropological knowledge as objective by ignoring the extent to which representations are always situated and mediated, and thus partial. Clearly, Topa, as a symbol of Pelourinho degeneracy, and thus as matter out of place in the nurse's doorway, shifts in relation to the contexts in which she finds herself. And she does not open herself fully to the social scientific gaze. But she never ventures into an interpretation of the nurse or the maid's reactions. She does not put forth a positive claim about her ontological status. She simply asks the nurse what *she* would do in the hypothetical interaction described. Thus the central issue brought up by Topa the trickster and mediator does not seem to be the extent to which all representations must be "partial" knowledge. Instead, Topa works through a version of representation in which she, as what might be described as the agentive object and fleshly sign of an expert gaze, avoids standing back and commenting on the reality before her: Rather than focusing on the situatedness of the social scientific knowledge directed upon her lifeways, Topa formulates a demand that another perform an act of analysis for her. She obliges the nurse to proffer a commentary on her own fears and desires, as well as Topa's status as a garbage picker knocking on a middle-class door so that she might defecate in the proper manner.

Again, in suggesting that Topa first makes the nurse serve as a datum, and then demands that the health professional occupy a vaunted subject position made concrete precisely by Topa's forcing of the nurse to specify the meanings of their interactions, I do not claim that Topa fails to interpret in any manner. After all, to present oneself in an interaction with health professionals involves, like any communicative event, some level of description, and thus interpretation. This is just what the CETAD team requested, and began to propagate, with its pads and incantations that "you have value." Residents were asked to express, and thus interpret, their selves. Yet such "degenerate" or crippled, crawling, interpretation dependent on the configuration of the residents of the Coaty as fallen beings to be redeemed and understood or educated by health professionals may fail to rise to the level of a general claim, or a lawlike analysis of what has happened and how things are.[39] Topa makes this clear in her requests for clarification: Within her resituation of the nurse's charade, Topa configures herself more like an energetic datum demanding fulfillment than a scientist able to make broad assertions about the world.

Topa demands a future interpretation influenced by her display of specific signs related to her status as an apparently problematic, unhygienic, and thus tutelary subject. Her self-objectifying description of setting out to find discarded items in the trash, and self-conscious proto-interpretation that she probably would not be accepted in the nurse's hygienic space, is more an exhibition of her stigmata and "inappropriate" behavior than an explicit claim to be able to evaluate and explain the world in ways that open and close doors to people from the Misericórdia. Not quite a fully accepted interpreter, and still a frustrated mediator, Topa thus comes to look more like a number that does not yet add up, or an ill-formed interpreter whose understandings of what has taken place must remain implicit and inchoate until they are made to add up by someone able to do the math, or account for her.[40] Yet Topa has established herself as this denigrated being, in opposition to CETAD's attempt to educate her. How, from within this density of self-presentation, she demands an act of interpretation speaks to her situation as an object of care whose practices are objectified by CETAD and heritage authorities in ways that her self-positioning begins to make clear.

Topa-as-datum is more a fallen Christian saint than a Greek messenger. As made evident by the New Testament account of St. Peter disowning Jesus, saints do not simply leave out aspects of the truth because they are messengers who re-present reality; they may also deny the truth, outright, because they are fallible humans mired in that reality, and thus open to fear, intimidation, and self-interest. And those lying saints, unlike angels or Hermes, are not spiritual beings. Unlike angels—or even the dead, who in Catholic doctrine are souls who have ascended to heaven—saints are hybrid, material entities who begin life as humans and come to be embodied in earthly shrine images and altars after they ascend to heaven. There, they never undergo apotheosis and instead take on the status of "persons" in heaven. Physical and metaphorical attachment to a sinful world and human personhood, together with the fact that many saints engaged in immoral acts before putting together the denials of the world that make them saints and reinforce perversely their attachment to that world, establishes them as mediators par excellence. And their mediation rests in no small part on their qualities and the physical manifestation of those attributes.

Historically, in a melding of image and object that points to the extent to which different semiotic practices may narrow the gaps between representations, what they re-present, and interpretations made of this process, various Latin American and Iberian communities have conflated saints with their images, and even the physical locations of their shrines.[41] And the historian Catarina Pizzigoni, drawing on indigenous households' wills and testaments, even identifies a "conception of saints as objects, material components of the property that is bequeathed to the heirs" in areas of seventeenth-century Mexico.[42] The saints' interventions, at least in the Iberian, African, and Latin American Catholic world of Bahia, are therefore not necessarily partial like those of angels or a Hermes unwilling or unable to bundle the whole of "the real." They are powerfully practical and material, and their power stems in part from their attachment to, as opposed to their provision of information about, the world. Such pragmatic interventions mediate the transcendent, ultimately meaning-making space of Christian heaven in relation to the reality of painful life on earth. And the saints who operate and take form within this dynamic space between a defiled, earthly materiality and the heavenly space of interpretive authority are resolutely thinglike, rather than ethereal.

I recall speaking to a fellow anthropologist at a meeting in Lisbon and expressing my wonder at early modern Iberian handling of saints' images by congregants who demanded that those mediators pass on messages to the Christian God in order to effect change on earth. I mentioned to her the practice of extracting the statue of a child typically cradled in the arms of images of St. Anthony, the Lusitanian patron of lost objects and thus, somewhat like St. Valentine in the United States, a "saintly finder" of lovers for those who encounter themselves alone.[43] The faithful kidnap the image of the child in order to motivate St. Anthony who, suddenly lonely and sympathetic to his interlocutor's own solitary status, might intervene and arrange a lover for his manipulator. My friend, raised in bustling, decidedly modern São Paulo, and an activist inspired by her reading of Marx to join the Workers Party, smiled knowingly and confirmed the utility of this operation, saying, "Oh, whenever I wanted a boyfriend I used to do that to my mom's saints!"

Saints stand as a special type of concrete metaphor that enlivens, and I hope clarifies, my account of the ways that Topa configures herself as an "affordance," or an object that demands, but is never guaranteed, a specific type of interpretation or use. As Timothy Ingold describes the concept, "affordances are not acquired . . . but are said to exist as invariant properties of the objects themselves, quite independently of their being put to use by a subject."[44] Unlike Hermes, the son of Zeus and one of the Pleiades who hides the truth by delivering only a contextually dependent and incomplete version of the object of discourse, saints' properties help determine how they may be called upon. The material signs of their struggles are part and parcel of who they are, rather than some earthly background called "reality" or "sin" or "the human condition" that they must overcome and make sense of so as to transcend that world and pass into heaven. On the contrary, as "persons in heaven" saints remain—perhaps a bit like St. Peter who guards the pearly gates—partially attached to the world and its travails. As a result, saints' invocations in Brazil, as made evident in processions during which the faithful pin money to their robes, drop stones at their tombs, light candles and sprinkle body fluids on their altars, leave ex-voto offerings that recall iconically the afflictions for which petitioners seek intervention, or wrench babies from their arms, involve powerfully pragmatic interactions.[45]

Saints' passage into heaven as persons, something accomplished by a Roman Catholic canonization process predicated on authorities' documentation of their good deeds and self-abnegation in the face of the world's fallenness, reinforces their imbrication in—or only partial escape from—that world. In my hands, it also highlights saints' kinship with humans who today face UNESCO and Bahian guidelines for listing and preserving the objects of national patrimonies. Due in part to the ways saints and saintly images come together at religious pilgrimage sites from which the UNESCO heritage zone is descended, they mark a productive confusion of the space between an object (a referent) and its sign vehicle while revealing one way a populace construed as objects, and as raw data for stories of bohemian self-mastery and national redemption, may speak for itself by making Others speak. In the Coaty-based interactions described above, these Others are the social scientists who, rather than imposing their arbitrary reading of things, must hew to a certain extent to Topa's earthly insistence on what Donna Haraway describes as the "fullness of life . . . so rich and so strong that its manifestations force their way into the listener's soul independently of any interpretation."[46] But contra Haraway's understanding of figuration, the signs of Topa's struggle do not seem to force their way into the nurse's soul at a communicative level entirely below or beyond the interpretive. Instead, Topa's "modest witnessing" of the ethnographic conventions that mark her help establish the conditions of possibility for these sign vehicles' reception and use. As Topa makes clear about herself in her dialogue with CETAD, saints in Bahia are not built up as but the inert, impressionable, objects of an arbitrary, construing discourse. Rather— and often around inappropriate vocabularies, accretions of objects, or worshippers' imitation of stigmata and suffering over the course of pilgrimages to shrines—saintly interventions, and thus their place in the universe, are made real through manipulation.

While it is currently fashionable for anthropologists to claim that, as with the culture concept itself, they have lost control of an ethnography seized by everyone from political scientists to development professionals and "informants," Topa does not transform herself into an ethnographer in her habitation of the CETAD drama. Unwilling to occupy fully the space of interpretation and define who and what she is, Topa remains a scarred resident of the Maciel/ Pelourinho who travels, as she did regularly across her life, to wealthier neighborhoods in search of the means to survive and to gain pleasure in doing so. Here her impoverished status and marginalization by the bourgeoisie are called forth by indexical marks indicative of her citizenship status. What is most interesting, however, is that in reiterating her journey to the middle-class neighborhood of Pituba within the CETAD script, Topa summons up and draws even closer to a history of interactions with middle-class social scientists and health professionals. And she enacts this proximity with a difference.

In her iconic status as a datum sanctified but not yet interpreted fully, or as an example of those the nurse would both educate and exclude from her house in interactions subsequently archived and then turned into histories authenticated by that "evidence," Topa revels in her exclusion by objectifying herself in a way that clarifies in turn the very mechanisms of that marginalizing care. Again, Topa does not respond to the nurse's denigration of her habits by defining her ontological state. Instead, *she* demands a response: "But would *you* tell your maid to let me in?" Topa insisted. Like Malaquias who ransoms the field notes that an IPAC researcher forgot in his home, Topa "plays dumb" in a way that leaves the ground of interpretation to the more powerful participant in the interaction. Seemingly conscious of the importance of interpretation, she foists the requirement that the world be made meaningful onto precisely those empowered health workers who claim an ability to interpret, and thus to objectify and instruct, residents of the Coaty. Topa's questions to the nurse thus force the CETAD team to oscillate between the status of "informants" to Topa as social scientist and interpreters who must accept the demand that they make sense of Topa the informant/datum.[47]

Across my time in the Pelourinho, residents insisted that they lacked the authority to tell their neighborhood's history even as they had witnessed the relations and events that make up history. Residents therefore maintained that they could provide information about what took place, but I would have to re-work that data and write "history." Topa reinstantiates this position in an agen-tive, allegorical mode when she takes on the position of someone or something who requires a response from CETAD. Her refusal of the health team's invasion of her privacy is not a walling off of herself, but a demand that those empow-ered to interpret and improve upon her reality speak the words that leave clear the contradictions—if not quite the hypocrisy—of their project. Topa might thus be seen as an actor who shakes the powerful from their script. This would be an accurate characterization of my friend. But it would also leave out how, and the importance of how, she achieves this feat.

In one of the most ethnographically sensitive anthropologies of race and Brazilian everyday life available in English, Robin Sheriff suggests that racial democracy is an illusory but enduring dream, or a story about how Brazil ought to be. As such, true "racial democracy" remains largely unrealized in the face of a valorization of hybridity that permits veiled, yet active and virulent, dis-crimination. But Sheriff also suggests how, at certain disjunctive or unguarded moments of crisis, a pressing, popular recognition of race-based discrimina-tion as well as belonging gurgles past Brazilians' polite "cultural censorship" to reveal how people really perceive the world.[48] As my discussion of malan-dragem and my recognition of the power of particularly Brazilian linguistic and social conventions should suggest, such an intercalation of truths and veil-ings is basic to social life in Bahia, as in most, if not all, of the world. Thus one might characterize Topa's arrogation of the right to full interpretation as yet another manifestation of salient Brazilian conflict-avoidance mechanisms related to popular deference, or illusory submission, to bourgeois authority. I have no doubt that such a dynamic related to "English eyes" operates in the

Pelourinho. Yet, in the Pelourinho, the call and response of social scientific research is a richly contested discursive space, and one to which people make ongoing claims in public spaces like the Praça da Sé. And residents, so intimate with their state and its cultural technicians, do so with a greater tenacity and via insights more attuned to the experience of Pelourinho history-making than do people from far-off neighborhoods.

Rather than just some generalized, national code like malandragem or the rules of politeness emphasized by Sheriff, Topa's performance is about a particular time and a particular space in which people gain power by standing like weak data that require manipulation by those authorized to perform such magic. But that data is not weak. It structures, to a certain extent, the interpretations it forces subjects to perform. Topa performs this positioning by revealing her life, and its accrual of toxic symbols she cannot control completely, so as to influence still-unformed representations and those qualified to put them forward because they seem to be subjects to her doubly objectified self. She refuses, and gains, recognition not by failing to speak but—like social scientists—by making Others speak and by speaking through Others.

Michel-Rolph Trouillot notes that "data never speak for themselves, [but] anthropologists cannot speak without data" and that "this awareness calls upon us to reinforce the validity of that base by taking more seriously the construction of our object of observation."[49] If one takes seriously the concept of affordance, or the extent to which the materiality of objects or sign vehicles undercuts the possibility of any purely contextual or arbitrary reading of their meanings, then the experience of spending a life being made to stand as an emissary from an imagined past, of being re-collected as a stand-in for collective origins by having one's habits parsed by social scientists for IPAC and UNESCO registers, presents a specific form of agentive potential. This arises in relation to the possibility of becoming a part of an archive of stories and collected information that has largely replaced the physical presence of Pelourinho residents with the material signs of their past lives. In their replacement of people, these documents become nodes of distributed agency since agency might be imagined as "mediated via images of ourselves" so that, "as social persons, we are present, not just in our singular bodies, but in everything in our surroundings which bears witness to our existence, our attributes."[50] The practice of forcing those who would interpret Topa as a mute datum to understand her instead as an information-saturated object that makes demands upon them is, if not the realization of Hegel's allegory of Lord and bondsman, then a serious wrinkle in how dialectics have been drawn into modern social science.

After Topa's death I spent time with her family in the working-class neighborhood of Fazenda Grande do Retiro. Her ability to mobilize social science is

Figure 6.8. Topa kisses Jôjô, the youngest son of Dona Niza and Seu Jorge.

not explained by the fact that her father was a teacher and her family is composed of some of the most important local intellectuals in her area of Fazenda Grande. But it is significant. It is significant because in fleeing what she always described to me as the boredom and stultifying claims to morality in Fazenda Grande, Topa entered into a collectivity specifically configured by IPAC as a Bahian community requiring education and hygiene. The resultant experience of surveillance, normalization, and the codification of morality is the most powerful influence on what I call "properly historical populations," or those in the Pelourinho who inhabit knowledge-producing operations so fully that they are able to extend their logics faithfully enough to end up speaking, originally and forcefully, as objects of another's gaze. In her daily experience of the social scientific drawing of Bahia's internal frontiers, Topa became a properly historical subject because she understood that, in the Pelourinho, $2 + 2 = 4$ not due to some fundamental identity of the two twos, but because "for those who know,

2 + 2 = 4." Since CETAD forces Topa into the position of one who stands as knowledge for those who know, she forces CETAD's experts (who know better) to speak in ways that respond to, and comment on, her experience as data.

When Topa reiterated IPAC and CETAD technique in the Coaty, she revealed performatively how those institutions entify people and events as both problems and monuments that produce Brazilian identity and history. But she did so not simply, as people like Judith Butler have explored, by taking advantage of some contingent misreading. Rather, she directed specific types of evidence, and evidentiary regimes, at the claims to interpretive authority of middle-class people who would teach her to valorize her self and cleanse her own domestic space. And she demanded that these be interpreted in relation to the terms she helped set up by serving as the object of that interpretation, as well as the material sign vehicle that made it possible. Topa thus makes clear the distinct bases of her own and the educators' participation in a project configured as pedagogical and restorative, in the process forcing the CETAD team to inhabit even more fully their *own* discursive space.

Topa required all present, as the Pelourinho nurse and I discussed in subsequent meetings, to recognize how erudite knowledge and popular practice become entwined in producing a particular version of Bahian origins around the Pelourinho. And she did so by demanding that all those involved interpret their own historical situations in a more patently historical manner that attended to the objects of inquiry and the people who represent those conditions. Topa, then, helps make apparent the sedimentation of IPAC representations that constitute the ground from which she must speak and from which her state configures her as a source of information about Bahian society. This ability to demonstrate history's constructedness in real time and alongside its production of materiality around human figures by demanding a future interpretation as a reconfigured, agentive, datum may appear to be a small contribution by one woman, especially when viewed in light of the weight of some undifferentiated, or even quite specifically defined, entity called "history." But if the interpreter of the present text recognizes how deeply Topa has pushed herself into the constitution of the archive of stories that will come to serve as a basis of claims about her community, then it becomes apparent that within a communicative event performed in the present, Topa has gone back in time in a way that will come to influence that which had not yet taken place when she stood up and demanded that the nurse make sense of her life. Standing metaphorically on the nurse's well-scrubbed doorstep, Topa forced the nurse to make impossible sense of the scene. And the nurse sputtered, and admitted to the difficulty of such a public interpretation. Only later, with the aid of hindsight and in the power of her consulting room, did she venture to "explain" what had happened as she charted my son's growth and applied her stethoscope to his chest so as to unlock the secrets of his beating heart.

The choking and clarifying reach of Topa "the pepper" makes for a rather remarkable account of the actions of a quite special woman. Yet the Maciel/Pelourinho was populated by many such perceptive and creative people. I knew Topa better than I knew many of her neighbors and I struggle to represent something of her life here without reducing her to a datum even as I celebrate her as a datum that demands interpretation. I describe her on the basis of what she performed—or made necessary—by deploying her supposedly mute, objectified status, which required interpretation as a special sort of fulfillment. But I can never really know Topa in a final, or assured, sense even as my text participates in yet another facet of her ventriloquization of, and by, social scientific researchers. Thus I am often puzzled by my own attempts to interpret her, whether as data or agent, or agentive, iconic data. Perhaps that is entirely proper: Phyllis Passariello argues that "an icon is a person whose being becomes an enduring symbol of cultural specialness, often with a tinge of religion-like awe."[51] And perhaps, in the face of this awe and wonder, it makes sense to zoom back out, into the crowds and resolutely public spaces of the Pelourinho, as part of an attempt to link "proper historicity" and the life of "properly historical subjects" to approaches to race and origins put forth by the crowds of Bahians who travel downtown in search of joy and diversion on Salvador's central cobblestone square named after a pillory.

CHAPTER 7

"Chatty Chatty Mouth, You Want to Know Your Culture"

At the turn of the millennium the Pelourinho and its frequenters appeared to be enveloped in, and consumed by, debates over music and language as assertions of national and transnational identities. With the *real* stabilized in relationship to the dollar, then-President Fernando Henrique Cardoso championed the competitiveness of soon-to-be-privatized industries and sought to "chart a new course" for Brazil.[1] As widespread enchantment with the Internet and its promises of global connectivity meshed with programming like the popular soap opera *A Indomada* (The Indomnitable One), set in an Anglo-Brazilian village called "Greenville" (pronounced Greeeen-vee-lee) and scripted by talented writers who punned incessantly across English and Portuguese, millions of Brazilians incorporated into their everyday vocabularies Anglicisms like the almost-very British "weeeeeeeelll . . ." and "Helpeeeeee! Helpeeee." English, then, seemed influential in a Brazil involved in a neoliberal experiment that included, as we have seen, concerted attempts to make everyday practices on the Pelourinho's squares and streets into an alienable "culture." During this period of political economic restructuring and uncertainty that preceded the election of Lula in 2002, and thus the growth over the next decade of federal initiatives directed at democratizing culture and redistributing some of Brazil's riches, language schools flourished, even in nonelite neighborhoods.

Middle-class Bahians who feared for their futures sought to learn basic English. Parents pushed their children to gain fluency so they might make a life abroad or participate in Bahia's growing tourist trade and Brazil's expanding informatics industry. Meanwhile, teenagers clamored to produce rock and reggae bands in English, and the streets in front of exclusive foreign language academies pulsed with the sounds of young people working on their transnational connections. One school, the Centro Cultural Anglo-Americano (Anglo-American Cultural Center, or CCAA), featured a television commercial that depicted the capture by a group of black, presumably African, "headhunters" of a blond-haired, blue-eyed Portuguese-speaking male clad in safari-wear. This prize, when presented to the "native" queen, a blonde white woman, let out a sigh of relief as she softened, seemingly attracted to the captive. Yet this moment of desire and race-based identification evaporated as the ruler asked in a London accent, "Ah, do you speak English?" and the captive responded with a negative "*não*" that degenerated into frenzied gurgling, neither English nor Portuguese, as the African queen's troops dragged him to a waiting cauldron.

The commercial by CCAA reworks *antropofagia*, or the early twentieth-century modernist focus on cannibalism as a productive metaphor for the development of a native, cosmopolitan, and specifically Brazilian identity. Antropofagia inspired Brazil's *tropicália*, or tropicalist, movement of the early 1970s that featured prominent contributions by the Bahian singer, and future Minister of Culture, Gilberto Gil.[2] This tropicália, which resuscitated aspects of the creative nationalism of the modernists, gave rise also to Nelson Pereira dos Santos' 1971 *Como era gostoso o meu francês* (How Tasty Was My Little Frenchman). The film, which underwrites CCAA's advertisement three decades later, recounts the travails of a seventeenth-century French explorer captured on the coast of Brazil, coddled, fed, loved, and eventually eaten by his native Brazilian wife and affines, with whom he could not communicate verbally. Nonetheless, CCAA's advertisement turns on their head several of the metaphors central to *Como era gostoso o meu francês*. In CCAA's advertisement, the televised specter of the Brazilian male's inability to speak the Queen's English renders him helpless, and, the viewer is led to believe, a meal on the Dark Continent. In a reworking of Brazilian "incomplete" liberalism, or a nineteenth-and-early-twentieth-century concern with civilizational degeneracy and seemingly anachronistic politics charted in relation to Europe and often associated with Brazil's involvement with slavery and "peripheral" position within capitalism, lack of English proficiency marks the prisoner as an imperfect, and thus recognizably Brazilian, colonist even before he begins his project.[3] This contrasts with early- and mid-twentieth-century anthropophagistic representations of *foreign* linguistic and cultural incompetence in a "whitening" Brazil where the Luso-tropicalist natives set the terms of, and are nourished by, such intercourse.[4] But according to CCAA, a Brazilian linguistic incompetence at the end of the twentieth century results in the denial of sexual relations and shared identities followed by the protagonist's consumption by a mass of black men. The advertisement seems symptomatic of broader, and perhaps less visible, re-alignments at a moment when the celebration of a mixed-race Brazil associated with the tropicalistas' and antropofagistas' emphasis on cultural hybridity may have come to exert less of a pull on a working-class Afro-Bahian public.

The white Bahian interested in traveling abroad—targeted by the expen-sive CCAA school, and perhaps threatened professionally by the apparent lack of progress during the Cardoso administration's political economic restructur-ings that raised fears about a national backsliding in which Brazil might even become a "Haiti"—does not necessarily represent the majority of Bahians in-terested in or defined through English or antropofagia today.[5] On Tuesday and Sunday nights, thousands of working-class youth from across metropolitan Sal-vador gather to dance and to sing in the Pelourinho touted in tourist brochures as "open to the world." The youths are the sorts of Bahians generally excluded from the possibility of travel or study in elite English schools due to their eco-nomic status and skin color. Nonetheless, these regular visitors to the Pelouri-nho demonstrate a marked interest in foreign languages and burst frequently into a perplexing, anglophonic song in which they "translate" or mimic Jamai-can lyrics in Bahian Portuguese. They do so by following the songs' prosodic structures while inventing or substituting new vocabularies on the basis of those rhythms.

An invention of lyrics on the basis of phrasing and rhythms is not necessarily a form of translation as commonly defined. Nonetheless, many of the revelers insist when questioned, or even among themselves, that they are "translating" English.[6] Some, if challenged, will burst into a version of "mock English" based entirely on the reproduction of the sounds of an exaggerated English that, to my ear, sounds uncannily like my native tongue even as I recognize none of the words.[7] I thus accept revelers' claims that they are translating from English to Portuguese. This is not a means of arguing for a new theory of translation, or of assuring myself that they are indeed "translating," but a way of listening to what the message says in this transformational practice and the commentaries that surround it in the Pelourinho.

The message enunciated in the public spaces of Tuesday and Sunday celebra-tions does not emanate from the specific linguistic objects translated. Instead, it skips across overlapping transformations of knowledge, objectifications of people's quotidian movements, and talk about race and origins in the UNESCO World Heritage site. Rather than stopping this dance cold so that I might spec-ify exactly what is going on in order to make some neat pronouncement about identities produced in relation to categories like "race," "space," and "place"—or even "race," "gender," and "class"—I struggle to join in the rhythm, if only for a flat-footed moment.[8] In doing so I never deign to peer across my interlocutors' shoulders and imagine I can see clearly how Pelourinho translators read some shared cultural script of their own.[9] Instead, packed against other revelers who work to pick my pockets and appropriate my tape recorder—and even the pens I might in an emergency use to textualize their actions—I stretch, anticipatorily, my interpretive faculties and strive to *balançar* (bounce, oscillate; or, in Bahia, dance). What is most energizing about such dancing is that, at certain moments, it carries me into a sweaty communion I cannot really objectify as some kernel of meaning even as my social skin scrapes up against other, similarly permeable membranes. But at other moments this communion, which might at first glance serve as some embodied antidote to metacultural categories like race, class and gender, rises up into precise or ironic mimicry, citation, and thus rather clear commentary on the action that surrounds it.[10]

Walter Benjamin observed that translation, so often misidentified as an instrumental attempt at equivalence between words and across languages, serves most basically to specify a broad relationship between different types, or levels, of language.[11] A translation thus "touches the original lightly and only at the infinitely small point of the sense, thereupon pursuing its own course according to the laws of fidelity in the freedom of linguistic flux."[12] Benjamin's formulation pushes toward a rather novel, or in a sense "higher," form of fidelity based not on conformity to an existing original, but on the evolving conventions of a language moving closer to truth by means of its very freedom. This is an interesting proposition, given the apparent autonomy from referential conventions of the Pelourinho-based translations. And yet it is also a productively dangerous concept: Creative linguistic practices might leave bare certain fictions of cultural heritage restoration, and thus the often arbitrary, self-interested, and contingent decisions put forth by an IPAC that claims attention to buildings' and people's supposedly enduring content, but in reality restores specific buildings in a hodgepodge of styles and techniques that attends to the requirements of a prospective tenant or the need to save funds. And, in a related vein, an attempt to follow the implications of a bouncing, often belittled transformational practice that incites attachment to an enjoyable, cosmopolitan imagery may produce a suspicion about the sutures that bind us, as subjects, to the stable identities and treasured objects we hold most dear. Thus I am interested in something related to the often unvoiced recognition that what passes for historical reconstruction may be mere invention, or what is often taken to be unstable or recently-invented "imitation." This interest involves the contention, developed across this book, that conceptions of genealogical linkage are growing in the Pelourinho in relation to technologies and concerns directed at shared heritage, commodified identities, and the grooming and exhibition of Afro-Brazilians and their habits as ancestral to the national body. Here it bears noting that flux and fidelity—commonly expressed in patrimonializing discourse in relation to debates about restorations and originals—are central to salient, post-Enlightenment conceptions of identity.

In dominant models of personhood in the United States, to be "true to oneself" is seen as expressing something inside, preexisting, that, if only it could be represented faithfully and transparently, would make manifest what all of us really are.[13] Yet such appeals to "sincerity," as John Jackson has argued in relation to race in the United States, are also virtuoso performances that array a density of signs in a constellation that permits the illusory but often effective or necessary—and thus "real"—presentation of identities as lying securely within such a subject.[14] Thus, in an affirmation of Benjamin's insight that "no translation would be possible if in its ultimate essence it strove for likeness to the original," the Pelourinho revelers seem to formulate a collective voice that manifests the "*intentio* of the original not as a reproduction but as harmony, as a supplement to the language in which it expresses itself, as its own kind of *intentio*."[15] Perhaps, then, the tense stretching of language performed in the bouncing, playful translations on the Pelourinho Square will add to, or help both the readers and author(s) of this book step into, Topa's adumbrations of CETAD's racializing, hygienic surveillance so as to understand better how the forms of agency and approaches to interpretation emerging in the Pelourinho speak to broader shifts in Brazil's racial politics.

The Prisonhouse of Reggae

Jamaican reggae of the 1970s and 1980s, as sung by Jacob Miller, Bob Marley and the Wailers, The Gladiators, Peter Tosh, the Starlights, Max Romeo, Culture, Jimmy Cliff, and Gregory Isaacs, has filled Salvador's airwaves, neighborhoods, and public spaces since the late 1980s.[16] In fact, Jimmy Cliff spent a good portion of the 1990s living in the Bahian city of Feira de Santana, and Olodum's singers used to enjoy imitating Cliff's distinctive version of heavily accented Portuguese so as to momentarily trick concertgoers into thinking that the Jamaican star had stopped by for an impromptu appearance.[17] Yet contemporary Jamaican dancehall is little-known in Salvador, except among a small number of musicians and cultural elites in close contact with Europe and the United States. Likewise, Rio de Janeiro's Brazilian "funk" and southern Brazilian rock are generally disliked by working-class residents of Salvador, a cosmopolitan yet insular city that has given rise to a majority of Brazilian musical fads over

Figure 7.1. Antonio Carlos Magalhães, Bob Marley, and César Borges, juxtaposed.

the last forty years. Alongside the Jamaican classics, then, Bahians tend to favor an evolving array of songs related to the local form of *pagode*, country music (*música sertaneja*), and Brazilian popular music crooners like Roberto Carlos.[18] Natives of Salvador, or *soteropolitanos*, commonly describe their beloved 1970s–1980s era reggae as "roots reggae," a genre they link to a Jamaica commonly confused with Africa. These reggae aficionados are more likely to self-identify as black than are Bahians in general, and pagode fans in particular.[19]

It is common to walk down a street today in Salvador and be bombarded by Bob Marley's invocation to "Get up, stand up, stand up for your rights" or Peter Tosh's argument to "Legalize it." People often struggle to make out these lyrics, and a few listeners take pride in seeking out their meanings in Jamaican English, whether through foreigners' translations, dictionary definitions, or both. The effort to delineate standard meanings tends to make those Bahians more aware of the differences in English as spoken in Europe, North America, Asia, and the Caribbean. This recognition of multiple types of English provokes a pride in Portuguese as spoken in working-class Salvador. But a majority of reggae fans who "translate" on and around the Pelourinho Square simply insert pleasing or funny Portuguese words into the songs and sing along to their favorite tunes.[20]

The Tuesday and Sunday night Pelourinho festivities arose as the profane continuations of lay sodalities' weekly masses and offerings, and of working-class Bahians' search for spaces for leisure on Sundays.[21] In the 1980s, the events began to take on greater economic importance and local renown due in part to state government–supported concerts by Olodum. On nights Olodum performs, visitors circulate through the neighborhood, dancing, singing, meeting friends, and sharing drinks.[22] Across the 1990s this black and working-class public would typically move between the Pelourinho's three reggae bars, the Bar do Reggae (Reggae Bar), the Negru's Bar (Blacks' Bar), and the Bar Cravo Rastafari (Rastafarian Clove Bar).

In November 1998, under pressure from many storekeepers in the "new" Pelourinho who feared the thousands of black teenagers who moved from establishment to establishment but spent little money, the state government forced all three bars to move to the newly constructed, walled plaza it dubbed the "Praça do Reggae" (Reggae Square). Those who could not afford the R$1 entry fee would gather out front, on the Pelourinho Square, to dance and sing in much the same way as their friends inside.[23] In 2012 Bahia's state government closed the Praça do Reggae, declaring that they would upgrade the facilities with a nearly two-million-dollar, movable stage intended to be ready for the 2014 World Cup. The plaza remains shuttered, lacking any sort of stage and filled with rubble, as I finish writing this book in 2014. But young people who come downtown in search of fun still circulate across the Pelourinho in the ways that the transfer of the "reggae bars" to the high-walled Praça do Reggae was intended to inhibit.

Albino Apolinário, the military policeman, host of the concert that gave rise to the "18th Battalion of Love" described in chapter 1, and the proprietor of both the Negru's Bar and Bar do Reggae from the mid-1990s until the Reggae Square's closing, claims that his receipts dropped 60 percent after his move in 1998 to that Praça do Reggae. He describes this as something forced upon him by "the new businesspeople" who are "uncomfortable with our clientele. The music, their ways of dressing, their behavior . . . they are absolutely terrified of those people." Apolinário, who as a police officer claims to have entered into harsh conflict with his "corporation" due to his affiliation with music associated with blackness, drug use, and marginality, thus decided that the only move open to him was to accept confinement in the new, highly restrictive Praça do Reggae.

Locals still refer with anger to the renovated Praça do Reggae as "The Reggae Prison" (A Prisão do Reggae), "Bob Marley's Jail" (Cadeia de Bob Marley), and a "Cage for Blacks" (Jaula para Negros) while commenting ironically that its occupants are "caged savages" (feras enjauladas). Nevertheless, many Tuesday and Sunday revelers from Salvador's neighborhoods admired the space's smooth lines and "modern construction," as more than one person emphasized to me.

The story of the making of the Praça do Reggae, or the bringing in from what Bahians usually call the "street" of an Afro-Brazilian cultural form members

Figure 7.2. "Smooth lines and modern construction."

of the bourgeoisie often associate with deviance and blackness, deserves to be told in the sort of detail directed to similar attempts to "domesticate" Candomblé and capoeira. I have followed this process closely, but I focus here on a story of expansion, rather than constriction, around the working-class Bahians from outlying neighborhoods who continue to flock to the Pelourinho to translate reggae lyrics, dance, and enjoy themselves. They are the sort of public around whose racialized aura and cultural manifestations IPAC designed the restored Pelourinho. Yet they also represent a category of person IPAC discourages from visiting the Pelourinho in spite of the state's reliance for legitimacy and foreign exchange on the expressive cultural forms invented by such people.

The working-class visitors highlight many of the heritage zone's contradictions, especially as they reinterpret Jamaican reggae songs and catch the attention of IPAC's social scientists who admire the creativity of what many have described to me as a "mixed Bahian people" who find a way to "overcome adversity and express their creative resistance." As one IPAC observer told me, by "translating" songs whose "lyrics they could never understand, these people embody what is beautiful about Bahia." Yet in recognizing such expressive qualities, which he recruits into a creative Brazilian exceptionalism tied in turn to an African-derived antropofagia, the heritage official misses out on what the revelers are saying in their playful reworking of lyrics.

Much as a focus on the most obvious, naturalized markers and effects of race may at times elide the range of issues at the core of racial politics, IPAC commentators who focus on the *fact* or category of hybridity, rather than its ragged

Figure 7.3. "Smooth lines and modern construction" one year later as signs supporting Magalhães' bid for senator, Governor Borges' re-election, and IPAC bureaucrats adorn the Praça do Reggae.

deployment, tend to lose sight of ambiguous yet critical comments offered in the Pelourinho translations. Thus it is worthwhile to take seriously the invocation to "listen to what the message says" contained in the "translation" of the song "Dip Dem Jah Jah" by the Jamaican Bahian Starlights. In transforming the song, the revelers string together Portuguese sentences and phrases that share a rhythm with the English they hear. In the process, they put forth a chorus that encourages us all, as I indicate above is my goal in this chapter, to "listen to what the message says." The Pelourinho-based "translation" proceeds as follows:

"DIP DEM JAH JAH" (*Bahian version in Portuguese*)

"Venha, caia na gandaia, tire essa cara e vem cantar assim!
Balanço no corpo, sorriso no rosto, o reggae é mais bonito assim!
Ouça o som dos Starlight ou Gregory Isaque, ouca o que a mensagem diz.
Ô, venha, venha, caia na gandaia, tire essa cara e vem cantar assim,
Balanço no corpo, sorriso no rosto, o reggae é mais bonito assim"

"DIP DEM JAH JAH" ENGLISH VERSION (*North American English translation, by John Collins, of Bahian version; italics are my own*)

"Come on now, jump into the fray, wipe that frown off and sing along!
A bounce in your body, a smile on your face, reggae's a lot prettier that way!

Listen to the sound of the Starlights or Gregory Isaacs, *listen to what the message says.*

Oh, come on, come on, jump into the fray, wipe that frown off and sing along.

A bounce in your body, a smile on your face, reggae's a lot prettier that way."

In listening to what the message says, I tack between the lexical features of Bahian translations as relatively arbitrary signs that create meaning on the basis of shared conventions, and an understanding of the Portuguese words as indexes or icons that gesture at or rub up against a variety of states and identities. So when Pelourinho crowds sing about marijuana, their vocabularies should at times be taken as discussions or references to marijuana itself. However, at other moments, that talk is more a poetic, playful, "stepping" into rhythms. This version of the reggae fans' activities is less referentially specific and my approach to it leans toward an engagement in diffuse yet palpable diasporic ties fashioned around a sensuous interface with sound. Nonetheless, and even as it moves toward a deeper engagement with poetics than is normal in cultural anthropology, my double-sided attempt to perceive the revelers' message may overprivilege a very North American emphasis on language's denotative capabilities, or a focus on words' meanings rather than linguistic form or pragmatics.[24] Yet my hybrid strategy is purposeful, designed to nudge up against an admittedly strange form of "translation" in the hope that the Bahian versions of Jamaican songs, and subsequent commentary on that commentary, will provide more grounded paths into the redefinitions of racial politics and subjectivities occurring on the Pelourinho Square, and across Bahia.

Here I interject with an aside that is more than an aside: As I discuss marijuana use I note also that social scientific examination of black citizens' association with illegal drugs is too often filled with either saccharine, patronizing attempts at empathy or else what Fred Moten has called "endless recitations of the ghastly and terrible."[25] To describe the use or sale of prohibited substances may thrill an audience of outsiders or anchor my text within the very pathologizations of Afro-Brazilians against which I mean to write. However, to fail to consider how the state configures marijuana use—a common practice, as is true elsewhere in the world and among Bahians of all races and classes—as a source of social isolation and discrimination is to ignore the contestations that are so much a part of the relationship between that state and soteropolitano youth. I thus tread a thin line here, as I have elsewhere: I describe illegal activities while emphasizing the extent to which that illegality, and thus also those practices' strategic deployment by subaltern subjects, speak to attempts to disenfranchise and control the less powerful in the name of law and social hygiene. Most of all, I struggle to depict how I arrive at these representations so that you, my reader, may evaluate their efficacy and empathy (as well as whether efficacy and empathy make sense at that juncture). Perhaps, then, I am seeking to protect myself by mimicking Topa and arrogating the space of involved or satisfying interpretation to our audiences. If that is true, it underscores the importance of understanding the position from which we all translate, and thus interpret, the shape of the evidence that authorizes our claims to similarities and differences.

"Você Vacilou, Não Vai Fumar da Massa" / "You Want to Know Your Culture"

In the Salvador I know and love it is difficult to find a working-class person between the ages of fifteen and forty who does not know the Bahian Portuguese refrain to "Dip Dem Jah Jah" (1976) by the Starlights, "Tenement Yard" (1974) by Jacob Miller, and "Chatty Mouth" (1976) by The Gladiators. The latter two have tended to be the most popular, especially "Chatty Mouth," a song that in its Jamaican English "original" warns the implied addressee that in spite of any desire to come to "know your culture," that person is a traitor to class consciousness if he or she denigrates "the meek" at the behest of a violent boss. And yet, when the Bahian youth on the Pelourinho Square sing, or translate, "Chatty Mouth!," they do so in the following manner:

"HEY MISTER CHATTY MOUTH!" (*Bahian prosodic "translation," in Portuguese*)

Você vacilou, não vai fumar da massa
Você vacilou, não vai fumar da massa
fumar da massa

Você vacilou
não vai fumar da massa
Você vacilou

"HEY MISTER CHATTY MOUTH!" (*North American English translation, by John Collins, of Bahian version*)

You screwed up and got us caught, you're not gonna smoke MY dope
You screwed up and got us caught, you're not gonna smoke my dope
Smoke my dope
You screwed up
You're not gonna smoke any dope
You screwed up

Meanwhile, the revelers belt out the song's chorus, "We shall overcome / One fine day," in a recognizable English. They place an emphasis on the final line, "One fine day," and repeat this, letting the words roll off the tongue, inserting syllable breaks where none exist in English, and reveling in the sounds of English with a Bahian accent. They also emphasize the word "Jah" in the Jamaican original's line "By the power of Jah-I." Soteropolitanos commonly use this term for God as shorthand for Rastafarianism, holiness, and blackness. It even serves as a descriptive greeting, employed jokingly by non-Rastarian Bahians to engage Rastafarians, along the lines of "Hey, what's up, Jah? (*E aí, Jah?*)" in the same way an imagined speaker of Hollywood's version of twentieth-century English might say, "Hey, what's up, cowboy?"

It may strike an English speaker as ironic, or tragic, that the Gladiators' denunciation of working-class traitors who side with their employers in exploiting the meek becomes a riff about smoking marijuana. Yet cannabis, prohibited by law and dominant morals in Salvador's working-class neighborhoods until its decriminalization under the Lula government, is associated in Bahia with Jamaica and has long been a mark of Pelourinho specificity. For example, Umbuzada, the seventy-five-year-old retired sanitation supervisor and grandfather whose move to the Pelourinho from the Liberdade neighborhood I mention in chapter 1 as part of my discussion of the habits of a group of friends who would play dominoes each afternoon in the Gueto, once claimed,

> I came down here for the first time because of this, [holding aloft a joint]. I never robbed. I always worked. There were guys in my neighborhood who I knew liked to smoke, but we couldn't. So I said "fuck it" I need my little psychology every day, so I just moved to the Maciel [Pelourinho]. Now I have my [original family]—they live in Boca do Rio—and another place to stay down here too.

Irrespective of the story's ultimate truth—and my research indicates that he moved to the Pelourinho for quite different reasons—Umbuzada's account reveals relative tolerance of drug use at a time when the rumor that someone smoked marijuana was sufficient to cause ostracization, and perhaps expulsion, from Salvador's working-class neighborhoods. Through the mid-1990s, residents of peripheral neighborhoods considered marijuana use to be the first sign that a person had embarked on a life of violent crime which made that person a marginal or *bicho solto* (wild animal), outside of "correct" society. Thus, whether or not Umbuzada really moved downtown to smoke in peace, or to rob, or to live with a certain woman, or for all three or none of these reasons, his account highlights the Maciel/Pelourinho's association with a politicized marijuana use that is symbolic of inclusion in the category of "marginal."

Some of the young people who travel to the Pelourinho challenge authorities by seeking to smoke in public so as to mark or dominate symbolically areas of the city through their use of an illicit substance.[26] They often brag of the multiple sites around town where they have cleaned a *dolinha* (nickel bag) of its seeds and stems and rolled and smoked without discovery. Since the Pelourinho is so symbolically important, visitors to the Praça do Reggae would, prior to its closing, take advantage of the crowds that pack the square so as to smoke in full view of overwhelmed police unable to wade through the mass of people to beat or arrest them.

Here it is useful to note that my translation above of the Bahian "você vacilou" as "you screwed up" is poor. The verb *vacilar* also means to break up the flow, to call attention to oneself by disturbing the even surfaces of normal life or official stories. To vacillate in the Praça do Reggae prior to its closing, or on the Pelourinho Square when smoking in full view of the police, may have meant passing close to the representatives of the law on the way out the door or failing to notice their approach. At times, this generated a beating, the confiscation of marijuana by those officers, or arrest. Today it gives rise to sentencing to a drug treatment program or, more common, to confiscation and a beating. Should a joint belonging to someone else, but smoked by a different reveler, be apprehended by the police, the penalty for both men and women meted out by its owner and peers may be another beating, a severe dressing down, or exclusion from future trips downtown. Of course, it is important to note that the majority of frequenters of the Praça do Reggae would never engage in such violence, or even marijuana use.

Nonetheless, and in the case of men, there are few more degrading situations for many of the people who travel downtown than police confiscation of marijuana. Thus, on the Praça do Reggae, "you screwed up, you ain't gonna smoke my dope" is not simply a playful filling in of the pleasing rhythms of a language one does not quite understand with talk about an illegal product associated with Rastafarianism. It is also a pointed commentary, by way of Bahian imaginings of Jamaica, as to the activities going on around the singer in Salvador's Pelourinho. These words substituted for the English lyrics in the Bahian chorus of "Chatty Mouth" show how boundaries and identities are drawn between the state and citizens; between proper citizens and those stigmatized as "marginals" and associated with (in some quarters) Jamaica and blackness; and between different spaces of the city. They do so by mirroring, in their poetic manner, the social relations within which the wordplay is performed.

Yet the process of producing new versions of Jamaican songs in Salvador has little to do with the semantic content of the original phrasing. Instead, listeners reinterpret the sounds of reggae lyrics and the rhythms produced by instruments in order to create a new vocabulary. Rather than a shared diasporic "code" dependent on a mysterious hybridity of the sort that Paul Gilroy associates with the power of song in the Black Atlantic, the language put together by Bahians indexes an imagined Jamaica as a sonic place.[27] For the middle classes, to claim to know English is to project a sense of cosmopolitanism related to Salvador, to prepare for the unexpected, or to engage in something they enjoy. For the Pelourinho translators, such projection, preparation, and enjoyment involves touching or pointing to blackness/Jamaica through communicative acts that in their pleasure challenge how a variety of people tell themselves they put together meaning.

Pelourinho revelers often elide the differences between, and the historical specificities of, Jamaica and Africa, arguing that they are the same place or that Jamaica is a nation on the African continent. The red, green, gold, and black of Rastafarianism are commonly known as the "colors of Africa," and people who live in both Africa and Jamaica are often described as "blue black" (*preto retinto*). Such claims suggest the extent to which Africa is reinvented in the Americas today and the ways that a new Africa is growing in Brazil as an important part of diasporic consciousness.[28] There is much to say about this Africa—including how it is different from or similar to the Africas invented through Afro-Bahian religion or martial art, or those Africas salient in earlier periods—but for purposes of understanding how the Pelourinho reforms call upon a particular sense of origins that I suspect are germane to conceptions of Afro-Bahianness, I am more interested in the techniques through which an imagined foundation is established and invoked.

Shaking Secrets Free

Pelourinho residents and visitors from outlying neighborhoods refer to crowds' playful replacement of English vocabulary with Portuguese words not only as "translation" but also as the act of *chacoalhar*. "To chacoalhar" is a regional version of the verb *chocalhar*, which means to shake, rattle, or, when used intransitively, to laugh uproariously or to divulge secrets. The noun *chacota* is both "an old-fashioned irreverent and loud popular song" and a "satirical or burlesque lyrical verse."[29] As the IPAC social scientists pointed out to me about the translations, chacoalhar exemplifies a Pelourinho-based approach to language, or a playfully poetic and quintessentially Bahian signifying practice predicated on satire and hybrid destabilization of dominant meanings.

Social scientists and literary critics often link linguistic and interpretive irreverence to subaltern groups, especially African Americans. What seems most important about such undercutting is not that it takes place, but what arises in the reworkings. If *vacilar* (to vacillate) is a disturbance of everyday life used in talk about the marijuana smoking censured in Salvador, to rattle (*cha-coalhar*) and to "divulge secrets" is to talk about the ways that youth from the city's periphery employ a practice understood as the "translation" of Jamaican English to discuss pilgrimages to the Pelourinho. But this rattling through the divulging of what the music really says does not just make public the brutal-ity of the police apparatus that ushers middle-class, white, and foreign pass-ersby through its barricades while forcing thousands of Afro-Brazilian youth to line up for up to an hour and be searched before entering their city center's Reggae Square. It does not simply conjure an Africa/Jamaica that people know they come from and that is gaining in importance in Bahian self-conceptions. Instead it fluctuates to shake up common understandings of commodities, identities, and what I will describe as "racial properties," pointing in the pro-cess to some of the ways the three are entwined in the Pelourinho.

A Bahian Counterpoint: Nestlé Quik and Nestlé Nescau

Commodities and ritual objects—especially dress, food and drink, and bodily adornment—play key roles in identity construction in the Pelourinho.[30] In fact, conversion of everyday experience and history into commodities may well be one of the signature operations of the heritage zone. But more traditional trop-ical commodities like sugar, tobacco, and cocoa seem to lie at the heart of the translation of the second-most popular Pelourinho reggae song transformed in Bahia in the late 1990s, Jacob Miller's "Tenement Yard." The Pelourinho ver-sion of this song about crowded living conditions, gossip, and working-class be-trayal works in the following way:

"TENEMENT YARD" *(Bahian version of chorus in Portuguese)*

"Beba whiskey mas não beba Nescau
Beba whiskey mas não beba Nescau
Dê a Doogie, Hollywood, mas não
    dê especial,[31]
Dê a Doogie, Hollywood, mas não
    dê especial,
Beba whiskey mas não beba Nescau,
Beba whiskey mas não beba Nescau,
O cigarro é dez centavos, a maconha
    é um real,
O cigarro é dez centavos, a maconha
    é um real

"TENEMENT YARD" (*North American English translation, by John Collins, of Bahian version*)

Drink Whiskey, but Don't Drink Nestlé Nescau
Drink Whiskey, but Don't Drink Nestlé Nescau
Give Doogie (Howser MD) a Hollywood (brand cigarette), but don't give
   him a special one (a joint)
Give Doogie a Hollywood, but don't give
   him a special one
Drink Whiskey, but Don't Drink Nestlé Nescau
Drink Whiskey, but Don't Drink Nestlé Nescau
A cigarette costs ten cents, but a joint costs a *real*
A cigarette costs ten cents, but a joint costs a *real*

In the Bahian translation, the crowd advocates drinking whiskey, as opposed to the sugary breakfast or children's drink Nescau, while singers compare the cost of a joint and a cigarette offered to a television character from the United States (Doogie Howser, MD). They rue the fact that a joint is ten times the price of a cigarette, telling me that the playful translations reflect their desire to "fazer à cabeça" or, translated literally, "to make one's head." Here a desire to become intoxicated, or to enter an altered state, supports representations of Bahia as a continual party and the Pelourinho as a space for festivities that occur all day and all night. In fact, the arm of IPAC that contracted paid musicians so as to "animate" the increasingly empty Pelourinho in the wake of residents' indemnification was called "Pelourinho Day and Night" (Pelourinho Dia e Noite).[32] But to point out that the Pelourinho is a ludic space, and that Bahians know how to have fun, is to emphasize the obvious, as well as the ideological, by accepting the state-sanctioned versions of Bahianness constructed around what Osmundo Araújo Pinho, one of the most perceptive ethnographers of the changing Pelourinho and Bahian race relations, describes as "supposedly universal and popular cultural diversity directed at hiding or symbolically resolving racial contradictions that are not addressed on a concrete, social plane."[33] Whether or not their fun covers up what is really going on, the youth on the Pelourinho Square enjoy themselves. Seemingly oblivious to whether IPAC authorities or ethnographers are looking over their shoulders in an attempt to make sense of the scene, they circulate fluidly, calling out to friends and greeting rivals and allies with continuously updated dance steps and language that Araújo Pinho argues permits them to claim urban space. A favorite wordplay during the first decade of the twenty-first century involved rhyming "Nescau" and Brazil's unit of currency, the *real*, (pronounced like the English utterance hay-ow) before sliding into a paean to whiskey. Yet whiskey—presumably Scotch—but more probably a Paraguayan imitation, or even a bootleg of that Paraguayan imitation of the sort produced in a clandestine factory in Salvador itself, is not really a beverage consumed in the Pelourinho. The inexpensive sugar-cane liquor called *cachaça*, sometimes flavored with cloves, is the revelers' drink of choice.

Whiskey is a mark of distinction in Salvador, and many working-class men who can afford it display bottles in their homes, often in the living room. These displays generally boast the cheapest brands of local whiskey, while bourgeois households show off the occasional non-Paraguayan, imported bottle. The choice of "whiskey"—a word used to induce those posing for pictures to smile, as in "cheese" in the United States—reflects the rhythms of the Jamaican music and also expresses a desire for altered states and for a specific image of leisure and material success. Despite its all-too-common local provenance, Bahian/Paraguayan/Scotch whiskey bears the marks of importation, and these attach to its consumers to underscore how much the Pelourinho translations reflect desires and identities. In this vein, another common iteration in the "translation" of Jacob Miller's song "Tenement Yard" makes even clearer how the crowds' participatory wordplay speaks to commodification and concerns with access to the world through commodities.

The second common Pelourinho version of "Tenement Yard" replaces "Beba whiskey mas não beba Nescau" (Drink whiskey, but don't drink Nestlé Nescau) with "Beba Quik, mas não beba Nescau," or "Drink [Nestlé] Quik, but don't drink Nestlé Nescau." If an opposition between whiskey and a sugary drink suggests the power of both the Pelourinho's intoxicating party and commodities associated with a cosmopolitan world, the tensions between the two Nestlé chocolate drinks Quik and Nescau recall Fernando Ortiz's "contrapuntal" approach to Cuban nation-state formation. By building up a density of metaphors around what begin as the "competing" entities of tobacco and sugar, Ortiz destabilizes both, demonstrating their surprising overlaps and eventual synthesis into the transcultural space—and people—of Cuba.[34] Whether one reads *Cuban Counterpoint* as a celebration of a hybridity frighteningly similar to the racist, sexist version distilled from the everyday life of the Brazilian plantation by Gilberto Freyre, or else as an opening salvo in challenging imperial histories, Ortiz's ability to tear apart and then weave together a density of metaphors around commodities offers a remarkable tool for analyzing capitalism's abstractions.[35] Yet in Bahia today the agentive commodities that rise to consciousness in delineating a national "people" in the Pelourinho are not tobacco and sugar produced in Bahia, and manipulated by the types of slave labor brigades and petit bourgeois immigrant families in Cuba whom Ortiz initially counterposes, but their finished products as packaged by companies like the Swiss multinational Nestlé.

Nestlé Quik, like the Quik pitched on North American television by a rascally rabbit, is in Brazil a frothy, brown chocolate drink available in both powdered and ready-to-consume form.[36] The powder may be mixed with milk or water, but is not very prestigious among frequenters of the Praça do Reggae. The drink is rather pedestrian, and well known in Bahia. Quik is newer on the scene, first appearing in the 1980s in its powdered form and available as a pre-mixed drink in the mid- to late 1990s. Offered too in strawberry/chocolate flavor, the more expensive Quik is packaged in a one-hundred-gram box while Nescau comes in a variety of large cans and bags. In speaking to people who profess a preference for Quik, I have been told that Quik is "cooler" because of its pink color, pre-mixed form, and strawberry flavor. Pelourinho regulars living in the neighborhoods of São Gonçalo do Retiro and Sussuarana have also argued to me that Nescau is something mixed with whiteness when put into milk, and thus problematic. As a result of these claims I sometimes suspect that at least some of the Pelourinho revelers were speaking of the milky white gruel called *mingau* made for infants by mothers out of canned milk since their argument is somewhat confusing—both Quik and Nescau can be mixed into milk as powder, and, depending on the amounts used, both leave the milk a nonwhite color. Such contradictions suggest that I may be paying too much attention to the meanings so commonly believed to attach to particular words, and thus reading poetic language in a too-literal sense, rather than concentrating on the playful, nondenotative nature of lyrics that entertain thousands of people. Indeed, the wordplays require analysis in a decidedly nonreferential vein. As Roman Jakobson observed, "the supremacy of poetic function over referential function does not obliterate the reference but makes it ambiguous. . . . In poetry the internal form of a name, that is, the semantic load of its constituents, regains its pertinence. The 'Cocktails' may resume their obliterated kinship with plumage."[37]

Perhaps I ruffle Jakobson's feathers in arguing that non-referential translation helps denaturalize the brand name "Nescau." Nonetheless, the translations bring to light a series of relations implied by Nescau, sibling to the instant coffee Nescafé.[38] Nancy Scheper-Hughes has scrutinized the canned milks and infant formulas so closely related to Nescau by Bahians in Salvador. Drawing on research in the neighboring state of Pernambuco, she concludes that poor mothers' replacement of breast milk with Nestlé products makes manifest social structures established around rural wage labor.[39] Scheper-Hughes' research is often controversial. But her conclusions about the symbolic power of Nestlé products among working-class northeasterners ring true in relation to my research among Pelourinho mothers and families living in three of Salvador's poorest neighborhoods, my discussions with Bahian medical anthropologists, and my experience caring for my son, born two months before I began fieldwork. According to Scheper-Hughes, the "pretty cans of milk, displayed on the table in the front room, symbolized her newborn son's birth certificate and her own proof that she, too, was 'claimed.'"[40] Condensed milk plays a similar role in working-class Salvador, suggesting the analytic brilliance of Ortiz's means of engaging commodities' metaphorical extensions into relational forms of personhood and community identity. Quik and Nescau point perversely to the extent to which commodification, in its elision of alternative values, associations, and forms of labor in favor of the pricing of goods through their circulation in markets, offers a technology for forgetting as well as the possibility of fresh forms of association.

The prosodics employed to interpret Jamaican lyrics bypass established lexical messages while opening up spaces and rhythms for commentary, and thus for contextualizations that may attach sounds to significance and significance to sounds. Translations are thus further evidence that the heritage zone, if approached as an ongoing set of practices rather than as a text, spectacle, or simulacrum to be lamented or mined for meaning, is not necessarily a place for the whitewashing of what may have really happened in national pasts: More than a site for the elision of authentic history, the Pelourinho gives rise to new types of histories, affiliations, and identities, both impoverished as well as full of promise. The Pelourinho as a space of consumption energizes new, influential practices and images even though consumption is more of a deferred desire than a reality among many working-class Pelourinho revelers. The Lula (2002–2010) and Rousseff (2011–present) years saw a sharp uptick in consumption, especially among the working class and northeasterners. But even today, a majority of the translators/singers arrives by bus with little more than their return fare and then lines up to be searched by police before being allowed to walk up the Pelourinho hill to the Reggae Square.

Until it was shuttered for renovation, visitors arriving from peripheral neighborhoods who were able to afford the admission price would often proceed to the Reggae Square. But because they could not afford the entrance fee, or because they appreciated the freedom to come and go offered by the street, a majority would listen and sing to the concerts outside the Reggae Square's walls. Wherever they located themselves within this performance interpreted by Pelourinho heritage officials as another example of what they told me was a quintessential Bahian "creativity" directed at reworking a hodgepodge of cultural forms, thousands of working-class youths came to amuse themselves by singing about versions of personhood intimately related to their relatively frustrated wish to consume a Swiss multinational's packaged derivatives of Bahia's tropical commodities. Their activities recall a relation basic to commodities and to aspects of racial identity as commonly understood in both Brazil and the United States. This involves the space between appearance and reality, or exterior manifestations and the true sources of value and identity.

Karl Marx grounded his theory of ideology in alienation and expressed the gap between appearance and reality most poetically and revealingly in his theorizations of exchange and use value.[41] But strange things happen with commodification in the Pelourinho: While the circulation in global markets of sugar and cocoa extracted from plantations near Salvador deprives workers of the full fruits of their labor, the rematerialization of such value forms as branded, foreign, items of consumption to be batted about in collective verbal performances seems to support Marilyn Strathern's observation that objects may be "created not in contradistinction to persons but out of persons."[42] Pelourinho revelers treat the verbal objects conjured up on Tuesdays and Sundays as sensuous nodes of enjoyment thrown up against one another in spiraling plays of metaphors. Invocations of joints, breakfast drinks, and North American television characters come, in their sonic weightiness and often ridiculous recontextualizations, to focus playful attention on abstraction and identification. The dexterity with which revelers protrude into Jamaican reggae and multinational marketing by wrapping themselves in and then relating transculturally the sounds of language enchants, drawing together the crowd and leading observers to comment on this rather special process.[43] Yet such "popular" or Afro-Brazilian cultural production of selves is also critical to the building up of the Pelourinho as an alluring space, and thus to the success of a historical reconstruction project predicated on packaging black Bahians' practices.

A simple story of the replacement of diverse ontologies and diffuse practices with post-Enlightenment or scientific ways of knowing, or use value by exchange value, would not only ignore the variegated genealogies of so-called Western knowledges but would tamp down the variety of Bahian responses to patrimonialization as well as the promiscuity of race and racial thought in contests over exclusion and inclusion. Translators' rhythms encourage Pelourinho revelers to shake and rattle in sympathy with thousands of their peers. And these are Bahians whom the state and shopkeepers seek to control through spatial as well as interpretive measures. Like the heritage officials who celebrate the crowds' "Afro-Brazilian" creativity, the young translators are quite sure that they are inventive, sensually Brazilian, and blessed (as Bahians) by their ability to take part in multiple projects and to draw from distinct traditions in the sort of transcultural hybridity celebrated—perhaps ambiguously, perhaps in different ways, but nonetheless celebrated—by thinkers like Gilberto Freyre and Fernando Ortiz. But they are also often sure that as Afro-Brazilians they are actively excluded on the basis of their race from national life as depicted in the Pelourinho. And their anthropophagistic renderings of Jamaican lyrics both reproduce the Pelourinho as a magical realm of mixture and, if one really listens to what the messages say, make visible or notable the commodification of everyday life and Afro-Brazilian qualities. But they also make visible the limits of, or at least the tense alignments and remnants of qualities and practices that escape naked objectification within, such commodification.

Singers, and young people from the periphery, often refer ironically to white Bahians and foreigners as "Parmalat," the brand name of one of Brazil's highest priced milks. And these revelers engage passersby and friends by modifying slightly their dance steps or their already playful lyrics so as to comment on, call out to, or provide an opening that permits a type of embodied invitation to join the party, and the group. On more than one occasion I watched someone pretend to fire a pair of pistols as a part of a song either punctuated by alternative beats or understood referentially as discussing "rude boys" in Jamaica passed across a sound system. Moving up and down, the dancers pulled in passersby and associates while gesturing with their hands as if firing guns. Pantomimed gunplay may seem a strange way of making friends, but it works on the Pelourinho Square. In a related case of verbal dexterity that opens up particular social spaces, I have observed people "break" their translation and, in the midst of singing about drinking Nescau, interject a comment about a passing foreigner "white as milk," and thus a "Parmalat." This interruption may be friendly or aggressive. In either case, such engagements add to the panoply of Brazilian color terms documented by social scientists while marking milky white complexions as worthy of comment and permitting youth from the periphery room for maneuver in downtown Salvador.

Before its bankruptcy and purchase by another conglomerate, Parmalat Brazil's website bragged, "the search for quality is deeply rooted in its [Parmalat's] own culture and tradition. . . . Quality becomes a reality only if it can be perceived by consumers."[44] "Quality" (qualidade), as a sign of inner essences potentially made apparent by exterior appearances or marks like brands, is precisely the word that was most commonly used in Bahia until the early 1980s in place of the term "race" (raça), which is much more common today. Ironically, or perhaps in a further demonstration of the extent to which racial essences, histories, and cultural heritages are painstakingly conjured rather than decidedly present or enduring, in May 2011 the ex-president of Parmalat's Italian holding company was imprisoned for fraud related to the company's bankruptcy.

To ask an elderly Bahian today to identify herself in terms of "race" is often to elicit puzzled silence. A question about "quality," however, will generally result in one or more of Brazil's multiple and much-studied "racial" categories. The plays, and interpretations made, of external signs and interior qualities are critical to understanding current contests over race and racial mixture in the Black Atlantic. They provide a way of understanding entwined local and transnational processes, as well as how human essences are produced in spaces like heritage zones. If race, which means so many things across time and space, can be understood as a concern with the ascription and differentiation of inner essences or qualities understood as basic to humans, whether morality, genetic materials, industriousness, or intelligence, on the basis of what pass as exterior signs—skin color, hair, speech, odor, sexual proclivities, and cleanliness to name just a few common categories—then changes in the particular ways that exterior signs are thought to index core human qualities are pertinent to understandings of race and personhood.[45]

Again, certain Tuesday night and Sunday visitors to the Pelourinho grab hold of the sensuous qualities of signs that circulate in advertisements, political messages, techniques for registering habits as world patrimony, and celebrations of Bahia and the Pelourinho and attach them to English sounds that they do not understand, at least as defined in dictionaries.[46] Such creative bricolage is, as the IPAC representatives made a point of telling me, "very Bahian." In fact, once over lunch, one sociologist told me, "It's like this salad, rice, beans and manioc powder (*farinha*). I bet you take a bit of each and put it in your mouth. Look what I do. I put hot pepper on top and mix it all up!" as he folded the manioc powder into the liquid from his beans. Yet that does not mean that all Bahians find such mixtures altogether appealing.

A Frightening Mixture

In September 1999 IPAC bureaucrats offered a ritual meal for São Cosme and São Damião (Saints Cosmas and Damian), the Roman Catholic saints/Bahian *orixás* who are associated in Candomblé with the Ibêji, the Yorubá deity who watches over twins. This meal, called a "caruru" after its principal course of okra and palm oil stew, involved distributing food and candy to the neighborhood's children. And as they handed out gifts, bureaucrats offered pronouncements about Bahianness by linking the regional identity to the mixture that the state, but not all practitioners of the religion, portrayed as intrinsic to Candomblé as a public culture (rather than a religious tradition). In fact, such a dish, if offered in one of the most canonical of Candomblé temples, would most certainly be directed at orixás considered African. But distributed in the Pelourinho, a neighborhood whose residents typically do not practice Candomblé and associate the religion with celebrations of a Bahian culture painted by the state as resting soundly on mixtures of African, Catholic, and Native Brazilian influences, this caruru meant something else.

On the day that I observed IPAC's distribution of caruru, Pelourinho mothers were aghast at the acceptance of food from the same heritage officials who had run community soup kitchens throughout the 1970s and 1980s and then sought to displace them, rather violently, in the 1990s. One screamed at her son, "Jesus Christ! You're taking the Devil's food!" Another yelled, "That mixture, that oil, that's the Devil's Food! Get in the house!" as she smacked her preadolescent son about the head and neck. Another told me, "Those things, those voodoo offerings (bozós), they make the children sick. All that oil and coconut milk!! I don't eat that stuff." This objection came from a woman I had often seen preparing and eating *moqueca*, or fish stewed in palm oil and coconut milk! This woman had often sought to entangle me in her disputes with IPAC. Frequently, as I walked into the Rocinha, she would shout out something along the lines of "Hey, John, the devils (*capetas*) beat you here this morning. They say they're gonna make this whole space folkloric, and you're not gonna have anywhere else to hang out with your friends!" The capetas, or devils, to whom she referred were IPAC technicians.

I have never seen people on Salvador's periphery reject a caruru, a nexus for establishing affinities and mutual obligations. The same is true of the countryside. Caruru is an important part of sociability in August and September, and as I discuss in chapter 3, Dona Katia's son Pateta and the bar owner Dona Célia spent happy moments in the late 1990s recalling his childhood participation in the carurus she offered when he was a hungry, lonely adolescent struggling to survive while his mother was imprisoned. I suspect that part of the reason residents considered the IPAC caruru problematic had to do with their recent experiences with IPAC. This frustration with an IPAC that celebrated a Bahian popular culture based on mixture meant that residents, who at the time were also in direct contact with the Black Movement activists' strident critiques of racial democracy, came to focus a series of engagements with discriminatory experiences and the Bahian state around the caruru. Additionally, people recognize that caruru is offered to the saints associated with African twins, and that the ingredients are paradigmatic signs of the Candomblé ceremonies that the Bahian state, in a move related to the appropriation of everyday practices in the Pelourinho, seeks to appropriate as part of politicians' attempts at popular legitimation. As a result, many Pelourinho residents associate Candomblé with marketing campaigns that celebrate a fantastical Bahia that they understand full well is an abstraction, if not an outright misrepresentation. Thus most Pelourinho residents I know, even as they continue to associate Candomblé with mysteries, and perhaps even fear and respect its ritual efficacy and powerful practitioners, approach its public symbols as resolutely fabricated and suspect in their association with a Bahian state invested in the appropriation of working-class, Afro-Bahian life.

Bourgeois Bahians unaffiliated with the state's cultural heritage efforts also flock to the Pelourinho Square on São Cosme and Damião's day. They pass out candy and when I asked one group of clearly wealthy women who self-identified as "white" what they were doing, they became excited, explaining that it is a "Bahian custom" to give out candy to children on the feast day of the twins, St. Cosmas and St. Damian. When I asked why, and what the offerings represented, the women became flustered, laughing at me: "It's a Bahian thing" they repeated, "These are things from Bahia, you know, it's about our mixture, that sort of thing," as they tried to get away from the pesky foreigner.[47] I interpret the women's response not as the dissimulation of religious practitioners guarding their secret knowledge, but rather the bewilderment of people doing something because it was Bahian even though they do not want, or quite know how, to explain its origins or meaning. What they were doing, at a most basic level, was distributing to a wider public symbolically marked—or sacred—foods favored by specific orixás. Independently of how they interpreted this action, or how they explained it to me, the participants were involved in a series of practical and symbolic exchanges typical of Candomblé. In such engagements, food serves as a vehicle for distributing axé, or the life force at the core of the religion.

At the end of a Candomblé ceremony, for example, a special ritual specialist (*Iyabassê*) who is versed in the tastes of each orixá passes out to each member of the remaining public a carefully assembled plate of symbolic delicacies to be consumed before leaving the temple. This distributes the axé to worshippers and spectators before they return home. In a related vein, the acarajé sold today by women dressed in the white lace associated with Candomblé first moved into public as women gave out the bean fritters without charge on special dates in order to "pay" their obligations to their orixás.[48] Within the Ketu tradition in Candomblé, food serves a similar function when placed on the heads of those seeking initiation or within specific bowls or containers (*assentos*) left on altars within Candomblé temples. This display converts the altar into a shrine through which the religious practitioner "seats" (calls down and receives) a particular orixá. And the "feeding of the saint" atop the head of the initiate, as well as someone suffering from affliction who seeks help from a priestess (*mãe de santo*), creates a reciprocal bond between the petitioner, the priestess, and the orixá. In all cases, practitioners offer quite specific foods, understood as those favored by the particular "saint" with whom a link is sought, in the attempt to reconstruct the person by entangling that orixá in webs of mutual obligation.[49] To an extent, then, it did not really matter that the women giving out candy and caruru failed to explain what their actions meant. They were engaged in efficacious activities that satisfied obligations and that are understood in Bahia to activate networks. Independent of participants' concerns with the meanings of the gifts, or even their ability to objectify and explain their intentions, they performed a form of religion, and public culture, that engaged the world and both linked and divided people through the exchange of carefully prepared materials.

None of the people I saw rejecting the IPAC caruru in the Rocinha were Protestants. But due in part to the emphasis in Candomblé on practitioners' public dispersal of often hidden forces, the "foods of the saint" (comida de santo) associated with this religion of spiritual possession are a common target of the ire of Pentecostal ministers who demonize competing religions. It is not uncommon to witness a Pentecostal expressing disgust at the vats of palm oil set up by acarajé sellers in a park or at a bus stop. Thus whether or not Rocinha residents really believed that caruru was a devil's food is almost beside the point—they adopted and adapted existing idioms for castigating the "people of the saint" (povo do santo) in order to express their own discomfort at being brought into IPAC patron-client relations through food associated with the Candomblé rituals that their state sought to colonize as its own. And this colonization of Afro-Bahian religiosity, many Pelourinho residents told me repeatedly even if they self-identified as Catholic or Protestant and thus kept their distance from "people of the saint," was a correlate to what they faced in relation to the state's attempt to appropriate their everyday habits as goods marketable to tourists.

As the variety of phenomena and relations associated with caruru demonstrate, qualities may circulate around signs like food—or Nescau, roots reggae, and cigarettes and whiskey—and be picked up for varied purposes. In such appropriations, the foods carry with them vestiges of their former associations. So an okra stew given out by IPAC indexes that institution's relationship to Candomblé, and thus the state's transformation of Afro-Bahian practices into folklore. But it also carries associations with the recent history of Pentecostal attacks on Candomblé. Residents then direct this vocabulary, perhaps liberated from Protestant pastors but still carrying the bundled signs of that experience, at issues like their relationship to IPAC technicians who seek to disappropriate them. In yet another materialization of Benjamin's insight that "translation passes through continua of transformation, not abstract ideas of identity and similarity," then, an opposition to mixture or the devil's food is not necessarily about religion or race. It may very well emanate from strife with IPAC technicians who knock down houses and pay paltry indemnifications while employed by a state that trumpets its attachment to Candomblé. Even a condemnation of caruru enunciated in a language of Christian sin and claims that palm oil and coconut milk are devil foods is not necessarily a rejection of Afro-Bahian religions (although it may very well be reappropriated for precisely that goal and, in the majority of cases in Salvador today, such denunciations are a direct assault on Candomblé and its practitioners).[50] It is also a relatively undetermined symbolic resource that may land in new places, and in new ways. This is especially true today, as practitioners of Candomblé and Pentecostal Protestantism increasingly enter into acrimonious conflict in spite of—or perhaps due to—the fundamental overlaps and crossfertilizations in the ritual practices of these two competing strands in Brazilian religiosity.[51]

The claim that words and things may mean something new when they are recontextualized is basic to any modern theory of signification. But how they come to signify, and thus how they construct claims to identities and belonging in ways that do not depend entirely on some preexisting context, is not always basic, or clear. Yet it seems critical to making out details of a mounting ontologization of race in Brazil today.

Talking about Translation: "Sin, Fornication, and Idiocy"

Some of the holiest, and most respected, people in the Pelourinho are members of a group of Pentecostal Protestant Rastafarians. These organic intellectuals embody roots and blackness and serve as mediators between the community and cosmopolitan capitals around the globe. By 2002 the leaders of the best-known and most cohesive group of Rastafarians in the Pelourinho had moved to the Rocinha after IPAC forced nearly everyone out of the 28. Then, when IPAC sealed off and emptied the Rocinha of residents in 2012, these people moved to neighborhoods across metropolitan Salvador. From there they await the promised return of their homes in the Rocinha and they travel by bus to meet up in the historical center. Included in this group of wanderers are members of S.O.S. Children of the Historical Center, or the Bem Aventurados with whom this book opens. And over the last decade, these important actors in the historical center have expressed outrage at how the mass of youth from far-off neighborhoods plays with the roots reggae lyrics they consider to be sacred.

Jorginho, a reggae musician convicted of a serious crime as a young man, a follower of Rastafarian teachings, and an advocate of the literal interpretation of the word in reggae or the Bible, commented to me on the prosodic translations: "This is a sin, a fornication, idiocy. It's the bottlemouth (a "Boquinha da Garrafa," a popular sexualized pagode dance and song). It's good only for deluded people who bump and grind without morality and without stopping to listen to the Lord." For Jorginho, who studies Malcolm X, Gandhi, and Mao through their writings and through North American films, this sin against the word is similar to problems with Candomblé, which, in another example of the extent to which Pentecostals across Brazil denounce, and even attack, the religion and its daily practice, he calls "a devil's religion worshipped by *negrólogos* and the godless state invested in cash money, brainwashing, and the negation of our African roots." Yet unlike many members of neo-Pentecostal churches like the Universal Church of the Reign of God (IURD), and in ways that recall the negotiations of freedom and moral censure so much a part of Jamaican religiosity, Jorginho advocates against attacking, or even criticizing publicly, practitioners of Candomblé.[52] He makes clear in all discussions of what he recognizes as another of Brazil's "black" religions that, given its historical ties to Africa, one should avoid providing ammunition for racists. Instead, Jorginho emphasizes, the correct targets for public critique—as opposed to his private musings and personal choices—are violent police officers, elites who foster economic inequality, and an IPAC heritage bureaucracy that "collects and kills" black culture.

The word *negrólogos* (negrologists) is a censorious neologism that I have heard in the Pelourinho and among some UFBA social scientists who criticize those who canonize African traditions so as to make popular practices subservient to the contemporary politics of Bahianness. The deployment of the term by Jorginho suggests his recognition of the social scientific objectifications of something called "Afro-Bahian culture." It also demonstrates the high stakes and the depth of feeling—or tacit agreements—about black culture and "African" roots and practices understood as properly authentic that unite Pelourinho residents and academics who assess the state's reliance for legitimacy on the appropriation of Afro-Bahian culture.

In my years of conversations with Jorginho, he has emphasized a stark division between his attachment to roots, truth, and fidelity to origins, and what he presents as an immoral promiscuity as regards sources and appropriations of valuable, symbolic resources on the part of the Bahian state and many "deluded" people from peripheral neighborhoods. His emphasis on roots and the literalness of the word—what he calls the elaboration of "the true truth behind the words" (*a verdadeira verdade*)—is not just a rejection of mixture but an attachment to origins, whether African or Jamaican songwriters' words, as essential to his identity and politics. Jorginho has pointed out to me on multiple occasions that one reason he opposes revelers' playful alteration of Jamaican lyrics is because this "dilutes" them and opens the door for a hybridization that strips sacred objects and ideas of their association with a truth he ties to their entwined sacral qualities and association with Africa. Opposition to the Praça do Reggae translations on the part of Jorginho and his fellow reggae musicians thus corresponds broadly to IPAC social scientists' association of such "free" translation with Brazilian racial ideologies, although they evaluate this ligature differently.

Jorginho opposes a translational practice painted by IPAC interpreters as quintessentially Brazilian in its antropofagia, and he is a member of a Rastafarian community portrayed throughout working-class Salvador as "roots" and close to Africa. Yet the members of this group are among the Pelourinho residents most likely to ride in airplanes, speak English, manipulate imported technology gleaned from contacts around the world, obtain dollars, and live in Europe, Asia, or North America. Five of Jorginho's close associates are now abroad—one in London, one in Spain's Basque region, one in Japan where he has appeared as an exotic figure in automobile advertisements, one in Munich, and another in the Bronx, New York, from where he frequently travels to offer dance classes at the City University of New York. Another has married a British woman and each summer performs on the English reggae festival circuit. These people who present themselves as most faithful to Bahian and African origins are precisely those most likely to participate more fully than their neighbors in a world of consumption, travel, and stereotypical modernity. They are also more likely than their peers to marry outside "their" race. But this does not mean that they are unfaithful to their roots. It means only that touching, transmitting, or even conjuring up those roots may be a bit more complex than they perceive or admit.

Shooting Up with the Lord

The revelers feared and celebrated by IPAC planners and criticized by self-consciously rooted Rastafarians have produced a type of commentary on consumption that, like the inventions of tradition so essential to Rastafarian authenticity in the Pelourinho, is itself a product of the heritage zone. Thus, at least from my perspective, it comes as little surprise that the Pelourinho-based Rastafarians have also forged identities and expressive forms that speak to the neighborhood's contradictions. They partake extensively of, and even depend for authenticity on, the modernity against which they define themselves. Given these tendencies, one way that Jorginho distinguishes himself as what he describes as a pure and originary African part of the Pelourinho's cultural landscape involves sound.

Jorginho favors, and accentuates, onomatopoeic verbs in everyday speech. He thus punctuates his talk with the sounds of bullets, with shouts, and with open, supplementing descriptors and substantives like "bābābā" (pronounced like the English "banbanban," and functionally, but not lexically, reminiscent of something like "la-dee-dah" in English), which Bahians employ at the end of sentences when they do not want to specify what has happened or wish to indicate that more than they are willing to describe has taken place. Much of Jorginho's language and performances during reggae shows rests on communications that draw attention to their sound as he gurgles, speaks in tongues, and shouts out streams of descriptions that often overwhelm listeners in their sonic complexity or volume but contain little referential content.[53]

In a related phenomenon, Vincent Crapanzano has suggested, even as he never mentions the sonic, that certain fundamentalist and Pentecostal Protestant representations in the United States might be treated as "iconic" due to their reliance on an almost figural power of images to drive out alternative meanings or contrapuntal readings.[54] Jorginho engages in something related to this crowding out of alternative readings. He engages his interlocutors through metaphors like the "bottlemouth" that take over the center of a conversation, imposing a diagrammatic stamp, or when he performs and drives himself into a frenzy, singing for long periods without putting forth recognizable Portuguese words. Sometimes Jorginho contents himself with guttural groans. Or, when lambasting the *sacis* (crack abusers) so common in his region of the 28 until just a few years ago, he will stand on stage and double over as if vomiting, or borrow a lighter from an audience member and pretend to smoke crack. In spite of, or perhaps due to, his engagement with politics, the world beyond Bahia, and Rastafarianism, Jorginho's performances and everyday speech rely to a marked extent on an embodied or mimetic calling up of sensations and physical movements.

Like Gula, his former neighbor in the Gueto who now lives in London and plays in a reggae band with a group of St. Lucians who find his version of religion quite strange, Jorginho frequently bares and smacks forcefully the veins in his arm while shouting out to an appreciative Pelourinho audience, "Prepare yourselves for Christ. Prepare yourself for an overdose of Jesus Christ! Roll up your sleeves and take him, take him straight in the vein! Tonight you're going to get an overdose of the Lord! Glory Hallelu-Jah!" The image is powerful, and when Jorginho performs it by smashing his palm into his forearm until his skin is red and his veins stand out, one can almost feel a needle penetrating flesh opened to a coursing, godlike power. Jorginho's narrative of religious conversion while imprisoned also relies on weighty metaphors and the coursing, eruptive power of fluid connection:

> Everyone but me in Quadrant III got these big boils, tumors, all over them. They'd start in the crotch and spread everywhere, to the armpits, to the backs of the legs and inside the thighs, and finally the face. They'd get infected and burst with great gobs of puss. I don't know if it was the food or

what. For some reason I never got any. I watched everybody moaning and screaming, "ay, ay ay," all night long. I couldn't take it any more so I started to clean some of my cellmates' bodies. You don't touch another man's body that way in prison unless you want to spend the rest of your time with the cops and transvestites locked up in the infirmary. I had to clean their groins. I'd lift up their penises and clean underneath. I was terrified. I thought I was going to be raped for my trouble, when it was over. But I had to do it. I had to go on. When the epidemic passed I was the hero. Before I went to prison I was big, strong, full of steroids. Look at me now [holding out a bony arm]. But now I'm stronger, with the Holy Spirit. You can hit me, kick me. I'll jump aside, but I won't hit back, by the grace of God.

Jorginho makes clear through his metaphors and the comment "You don't touch another man's body that way in prison" that touch, penetration, eruption, and movement are critical to his messages and his conversion.[55] If Jorge's passage into grace took place as a performance of good deeds made necessary by the affliction that surrounded him in prison, in his harangue to concertgoers a syringe pricks the addressee and burrows through flesh, directly into a vein. In this overdose—surely a "crowding" out of other concerns and meanings—faith made material as content turns conversion into a literal attachment to God's overpowering substance.[56] Yet Jorginho never mentions this syringe, a sensational form like a reggae song, or a Bible read and declaimed across Salvador's streetcorners as a means of attaining salvation or transcendence.

In spite of the needle's centrality to the act of conversion Jorginho presents so richly, the lack of direct reference to the central vehicle for the transmission of the substance of God seems to support Birgit Meyer's point that "media become so entangled in what they contribute to mediate that they are not visible as such" and this generates "a sense of the immediate presence of the divine."[57] Meyer's insight is potentially important for thinking about race and its naturalization. After all, ethno-racial identification is often presented in both the United States and Brazil as part of felt attachments to tradition, biology, and a collective being connected to both the correction or amelioration of injustice, and thus a potential for additional atrocities. But the power of this identification may very well blot out the particular ways that one begins to perceive that belonging.[58] Such disregard for the workings of rather standard post-Enlightenment separations of form and content—divisions both reinforced and undermined by the attachment to saints and saint images salient in Bahian Catholicism as well as people's engagement of higher powers through carurus and the propitiation of orixás who become literally present on Candomblé altars by means of their ritual "seating"—is nonetheless brought into partial view by the discordances between Rastafarian approaches to texts and the playfulness of the Praça do Reggae "translators."[59]

To a certain extent, the liberties taken with language by youth from across Salvador who look to the "incorrect" spaces of semiotic form in order to make sense of Jamaican songs they supposedly do not understand come to rattle, or shake up, understandings of the transfer of meaning and the establishment of connections. But a putatively incorrect and thus troubling emphasis on form, as opposed to the original messages supposedly contained securely in words—or from IPAC's perspective the true Bahian histories supposedly lying dormant and readymade within plazas and monuments—is not incorrect per se. Rather, it raises to consciousness the extent to which the exchanges of meaning circulating across the Pelourinho on a variety of interconnected but rather different planes depend on the specific nature of the sign vehicles that permit that meaning to be distinguished as meaning.

On the day we sat down to talk about approaches to Jamaican texts, Jorginho's bandmate Malaquias helped make clear how Pelourinho translators' ability to derive content from form, and thus obviate or forget that separation in a way that naturalizes that content as the essence of language and communication, may raise to consciousness certain normally occluded semiotic operations. Malaquias insisted on the importance of fidelity to the word and the basic immorality and involvement in a racist "racial democracy" of anyone who would ignore the sacred, authoritative status of the roots reggae lyrics that he described as arising from Jamaican holy men's direct links to God. But when I pressed him as to how such unimpeded access to meaning could be possible if he rejected the Praça do Reggae crowd's ability to make sensuous engagement with sound significant, Malaquias quickly admitted something strange: Bahians, he claimed, are unable to interact with texts directly. Due to their overwhelming illiteracy and their status as sinners, they cannot in fact come to know the literal meaning of the word of God. He emphasized that this is the case with all people, but it is especially pronounced given the impact of social inequality on Bahians' education. Thus, for Malaquias, even as it stands as an ideal, fidelity to the text is impossible in light of humans' fallen status and the nature of a world filled with sins like gluttony and usury.

Malaquias' argument instantiates a separation of form and content since he claims in part that an inability to read, or to deal with the word of God through the specific material medium in which it is presented, means that God's truths contained in those texts are unavailable to him and to his neighbors (at the time, Malaquias did not know how to read). It also does something else: Like Jorginho's failure to name the syringe that rose in my own imagination as a great, gleaming, blood-flecked instrument for the transmission of bodily fluids and charisma, Malaquias' story about the impossibility of a literal reading generated a focus on the very media he ignored in making his points. One of the fundaments of Pentecostalism more generally involves a faith, as Jorginho's concerns with an overdose of Jesus suggested, in the possibility of an unmediated access to God. Yet Malaquias yielded this terrain. And he did so in a special way, namely, by blaming people's lack of interpretive skills rather than some shortcoming in the communicative capabilities of the word of God or Jah-Rastafari. Clara Mafra offers one explanation of this phenomenon by noting that Brazilian Pentecostalism is "contaminated" by centuries of framing by Catholicism.[60] This argument about the semiotic conflations and alignments that might usefully be dubbed "bundling," and that necessarily leak out to form new hybrids due to the ongoing qualities of semiosis, is congruent with recent work on similarities in ritual grammars between Candomblé and the Pentecostal churches that attack it.[61] Most important for the present analysis, however, it highlights the issue of semiotic entailments, or the ways the contents of a bundle of signs and qualisigns, or what becomes material and significant only in a specific conjuncture or arena, may leak into those spaces and beings adjacent or subsequent to it.

Jorginho's shooting up with the Lord reveals more than the presence of a mediating syringe. In light of standard practices in the Pelourinho, this manifestation of spirit implies also a sharing of needles and contact with other people's blood, thus establishing a consanguineous relationship between God and his assembled children. And blood is a substance associated powerfully with race and descent in the United States and, increasingly, in Brazil. Again, an important component of many citizens', NGOs', and state institutions' projects in Bahia today involves the adoption, as well as the modification, of North American–style racial definitions.[62] In these models, via the "one drop rule," Afro-Brazilian identity may be thought of in terms of rules of descent, rather than negotiated in relation to physical appearance and a host of perceptions and habits that attach to and modify what passes as a biological or material givenness of the human body. Nonetheless, as evinced in the divergence between Adilson, who stressed experience, and Hélio, who relied on DNA to establish the identity of the skeletons on the Praça da Sé, a number of different, and even competing, racial ideologies are at play in Bahian conceptions of racial belonging. Hence this "something" that takes form as a real substance passed down across generations and held in common in defining attachment to a collective identity need not be blood. It may be culture. What is critical, however, is that in the new racial ideologies being put together in the Pelourinho it be some *thing*, or substantive entity, in uniting a people. Rather than a constellation of qualities, then, race is gaining certain more formally recognized properties. Yet this movement into a more definable, even essentialized, set of relations carries with it traces of former associations and seemingly outdated interpretations.

Across this book I have argued that concerns with civilizational aptitudes and the qualities of a national population make up a long-standing site of concern in Brazilian national life. This preoccupation is being reconfigured today in an environment in which an interest in biologized or essentialized models of racial belonging meshes complexly with an emphasis on environment and mutability. Malaquias' concerns with the fallenness of "man" in general, and especially with an undereducated Bahian citizenry, seem to tap into such worries about national deficiency. They also recall Topa's acceptance of this positioning and agentive resituation of hygienists' interventions in her redemption. Thus it would appear that, in addition to Clara Mafra's suggestion that semiotic dispositions in Brazilian Pentecostalism are contextualized by Catholicism, these dispositions are tempered in the Pelourinho by the lived experience of the secular sacred, collective representation, and commodity form known as "cultural heritage." And within cultural heritage, as with arguments about the literalness of language or the fixity and ultimate "truth" of social ontologies like race, content is so often (misre-)presented as coming into being as pure content, or a thing or property somehow disengaged from the everyday so that it may be possessed.

Race as Property, Personhood as Extension

Critical legal scholar Cheryl Harris has proposed that the very definition of property in the United States turns on white privilege. Thus whiteness "is valuable and is property."[63] Given the extent to which culture and personhood have been commodified in the Pelourinho by a Bahian state that employs bureaucracies like IPAC to appropriate ever more complexly the labor and "being" of its populace, race and subjectivity often take form as possessions. Here I define "possession" as the fruit of a relation between a subject and the world onto which that subject projects—and thus constructs—itself through a process of appropriation.[64] Within classical liberal political theory, the act of enclosing what is presented as formerly unoccupied, or unproductive, is thought to grant that actor certain properties. Property thus defines the individual, or the collectivity, by serving as a sign of and space for action and extension. This is what is usually dubbed an "agency" essential to defining an acting, and thus "true," subject.[65]

In this well-known story of human extension, or a labor theory of value crystallized by John Locke and transformed into the core of Marx's critique of classical economics, property is an effect of the human action that wrenches unmarked or "natural" ways of being and acting from their Edenic state.[66] A right to objects conceptualized as part and parcel of nature up until their extraction by human actors takes form as a moral drama about the reach and obligations of the sovereign, the labors of subjects, and the passivity of that nature as a field for human action.[67] But what of properties like those of pepper, which spread out, and penetrate, even in the absence of human volition? What of the Pelourinho discourse of tombamento in which the objectification of Pelourinho residents as properties seems to extend to them certain powers, akin to those usually associated with subjectivity? And what of the status of landed property in a Pelourinho in which incomplete or problematic forms of self-possession, understood as responsible behavior and the types of "self-valorization" encouraged by institutions like CETAD, serve as signs of individuals' fitness to stay on and claim the buildings restored by IPAC?

In the wake of IPAC's interventions in the central Maciel in 1992 and 1993, large numbers of residents moved to the 28 and the Misericórdia. When IPAC began to empty and restore those ruined buildings, their occupants sought new residences elsewhere, moving to the Rocinha or to surrounding areas in Santo Antônio, the Saúde, the Gravatá, the Taboão, and the Pilar. Sometimes this search for a domicile involved paying rent or buying spaces from people who had already occupied, with or without legal documents, existing buildings. Often, however, residents would leave early in the morning and survey prospective residences, searching for signs of occupancy. Yet given the dislocations faced by thousands, only a few houses remained empty. More often than not, people needed to employ persuasion, violence, or affective and kin ties to convince those already ensconced to permit them to settle into a corner, a basement, or a forgotten entranceway where they might build shacks with scavenged lumber.

The techniques employed to stake claims to home and territory meant that ownership, as is common in Brazil more generally, rested on possession rather than legal authority or documents.[68] This meant that the new occupiers could not pretend that they were moving into empty, unoccupied, or even "natural" spaces of the type that gird John Locke's seminal, if contradictory and exclusionary, theorizations of capitalist property relations based on a making productive of unused resources.[69] Unless those searching for domiciles came to inhabit the perspective of the wealthy Bahian families who had forgotten the ownership of Pelourinho buildings abandoned generations ago, there could be no fiction of unwanted, "empty" lands. Nor, in the sort of operation common in frontier societies in which economic activities and property ownership index racial, class-based, and "civilizational" differences between social groups competing for territory, could residents distinguish themselves easily from their relatives, friends, enemies, and former neighbors who had claimed decaying buildings.[70] Instead, people recognized that their property claims were resolutely social, and staked out in relation to citizens who, like themselves, struggled to stay on in the few corners of the historical center that had not been restored for the tourist trade or sealed in durable concrete in anticipation of that fate. Extending oneself and claiming landed property thus meant risky interactions with peers liable to burst out of a basement to confront and confound interlopers, at times violently, and engaging people in face-to-face interactions without the aid of settler ideologies that placed newcomers on a higher civilizational level than those whom they sought to supplant.

The efforts of IPAC and CETAD to define and valorize Pelourinho souls compounded the foreignness, at least in Pelourinho residents' eyes, of standard capitalist justifications of "rights" to putatively empty landed property. Intelligent people who carried on love affairs with, blackmailed, or cleaned the houses of wealthy Bahians or outsiders found themselves back home in the crumbling Pelourinho, listening to well-meaning social workers who sought to inculcate the knowledge that they had value. Yet most knew, beforehand, that they had value even if that value far exceeded their wages in kind and quantity. Nonetheless, in the face of an inability to make the world understand that they could make 2 + 2 = 4, residents often presented themselves as perpetrators of a clutching fallenness that permitted them to survive but excluded them from many of the benefits of full inclusion in Bahian society. In this light, Malaquias' concerns with human failure are not simply a function of religious indoctrination or a view of an abstract humanity facing God, but an ambivalent reaction to historical exclusion dependent on ongoing incorporation of the very terms of that exclusion, or what Ann Stoler synthesizes as a "ruination" characterized by a caustic "eating away of less visible elements of soil and soul."[71] Such a contradictory habitation of the already-degraded seems characteristic of the layerings and reinventions that are so much a part of turning one of the world's most important slave ports into a UNESCO-sanctioned celebration of humankind's basic creativity.

As enunciated and described in chapter 3 by Bulindo, Malaquias' cellmate while both were teenagers incarcerated in Salvador's infamous and now-shuttered Pedra Preta (Black Rock) Penitentiary, "Here a person, when he is born, is born into a powerful disgrace." However, the lilting exclamation "desgra-ça!" (disgra-ced one!) is not directly disparaging in the Pelourinho, or in Salvador. It may even serve as a sign of affection as old friends spy one another and call out. Like Topa, a "marginal at the epicenter of history," Bulindo, Malaquias, and their neighbors confront daily the overlaps of dispossession from land, the government-mandated care of the self, and thus the contradictions of what Paul Christopher Johnson describes as "the occupied body and spoken-through person" that link modern Atlantic notions of sovereignty, contract, and attempts to control the inner states of the occupants of colonized lands.[72] Clearly, then, many competing or even antithetical movements join together in order to constitute uneasily a modern conception of possession in Bahia today, as is true in different ways around the world. Thus the claim that something like race is a "property," which people hold like an object or resources as a part of some form of possessive individualism, may complicate much more than it clarifies.[73] And, yet, I have suggested that as part of the entifications of inner states and the possessive markings of culture so essential to the Pelourinho's transformation into a historical center for the marketing of Afro-Brazilianness, race has become something of a property. But I have employed this concept of "property" in a rather specific way, related to the ostensible fallenness of the Pelourinho's residents and the techniques they employ for making already-claimed spaces their own. Or, put another way, the properties that exist in the Pelourinho are a rather direct function of the techniques wielded in laying claim to them. Thus properties in the Pelourinho take a rather special form.

Contemporary anthropology is marked by strong, at this point almost reflexive, tendencies to bewail modernity's categorizations, or its taxonomic approach to a world that somehow becomes hardened when "being" is translated into "knowing." I share and applaud such a utopian attachment to relations, rather than reifications and objectifications. And yet a language of "attachment to" rather ironically underscores my reference to pure relationality by means of a distancing operation that construes inchoate tendencies and respectful recognition as properties that attach to certain enlightened subjects—like careful, seemingly theoretically sophisticated ethnographers—who nonetheless recognize the constructedness of such properties. Evidence as to the salience of this self-positioning in anthropology today includes Jean Jackson's careful explorations of the methodological and ethico-political conundrums that anthropologists face when subaltern groups appropriate, and reify, the culture concept in ways that "we" might find problematic.[74] Essential to such noblesse oblige are arguments that even as "we" know that culture is a mobile, relational set of symbols, those who seek to turn culture into a resource might need to objectify it in some sort of strategic, and thus understandable, essentialism. Such an ultimately patronizing move approximates Malaquias' condemnation of Pelourinho revelers' inability to recognize the "real," and essentialized, meanings of texts.

A formal affinity between an anthropological celebration of relationality and smugness about "natives'" essentializations and Malaquias' attempt to fix the meanings of the world as the word of God becomes even clearer in light of his explanation of why people cannot get to true meaning. From Malaquias' perspective, Bahian citizens who become disadvantaged due to structural violence somehow fail to "get it." They do not recognize the true truths that the Bem Aventurados, as a cosmopolitan, and yet apparently "rooted" or "grounded," intellectual group, is able to perceive. Here, the well-traveled, worldly, Rastafarian resident of the historical center, or someone who argues that he is organically attached to the historical patina of tradition, accounts for what then becomes a somewhat understandable lack of sophistication among a population he presents as misguided, albeit through no fault of its own. Yet Malaquias, like so many in my professional guild, is blind to his own blindness.

Any communicative event requires cues and contextual winks and nods so as to become understandable. It seems that such "becoming comprehensible" usually involves going through the sorts of questioning and authorization that gird claims to its truth or efficacy. This is a process that I have approached, drawing on Peirce, as a progressive movement into fully symbolic meaning, or the contextual delimitation of blurry iconic and imprecise indexical relations into messages with significance across time and space. Here the cutting down of potential, but still-unrealized, interpretations and usages—or what Malaquias seeks to effect by denying the truth or efficacy of Pelourinho revelers' apparent ability to produce linguistic value out of pure sound—into a lawlike, generalizing, and thus rather rational interpretation with comparative validity, generates a specific type of symbolic or interpretive system. E. Valentine Daniel has described this state of affairs, so common in the textualization of cultures, as "metacultural and not cultural" due to the fact that it does not take into account the slippages between the varied and yet nested communicative levels that produce truly multiplex knowledge of and action in the world.[75] Among these are sign vehicles whose importance to the communicative event seems to require their erasure.

Jorginho seems blissfully unaware of the mediating instrument that facilitates his overdose of Jesus. He forgets, or misses the importance of, the sharp syringe that takes on the status of sign vehicle when it punctures flesh to deliver an overdose of a "White light/White heat" that would undoubtedly make Lou Reed flush. Without that syringe, there would be no transmission of what Jorginho finds so essential, and powerful, that he simultaneously accentuates and ignores its mode of transmission as he slaps his arm so intently, and screams out the names of God so forcefully, that it almost appears that the syringe is there. But Jorginho never mentions the vehicle for his transformation into a Christian. Perhaps there is no need to. And it is precisely this "no need" that I am seeking to address, in dialogue with Bahians who range from IPAC, to the anonymous Pelourinho translators, and on the Bem Aventurados.

Veins and Identification

According to many observers, for so long racial identity in Brazil presented an ambiguity in which systematic discrimination coexisted with systems of color-based classification that became notable, and hence discernible, around visible, surface signs taken by analysts as but a system of classification that Charles Wagley called "social race."[76] From this perspective, much like the claims put forth by social constructivists in North America today, race, or color, was not about a shared, biological substance. The signs of one's racial identity were recognized instead as systems of classification, or situational social constructs that made contextual sense out of human biological diversity. And they did so in a very structuralist play of difference that referred to a universe of diacritical marks and circulating signs, rather than particular forms of embedded reference to something outside that socially constructed sphere of circulation. Hence, as a function of social location and the variable existence of categories of identity, the intermediate, or seemingly "brown," Brazilian could change race or have a biological child of a different race. Mid-twentieth-century social scientific models correspondingly portray Brazilian racial ideologies as predicated on the denial of an essence, and thus multiplex and situational in their contingent calling up of ideas about membership in a group. But what happens when race becomes increasingly essentialized, as is taking place in Brazil today? Or, put better, how is race configured as a shared substance, transmitted by specific instruments and actions, in a world in which such categorization may violate salient ethical principles, or at least public codes of politeness?

My honest answer to the final question above must be, "I am not yet sure." But I have begun to examine such configurations in relation to the historical center and to cultural heritage as a set of techniques that locates an identity, deep in time, that must be cared for by the cultivation of signs in the present. Therefore the different ways that Pelourinho revelers make sense of lyrics formerly known as Jamaican (my apologies to Prince), and then the ways social scientific and Rastafarian observers make sense of those efforts at significance, bring to light some of the semiotic operations that permit the linkage of what are, in the end, inchoate and often unlike qualities. So while I recognize the ultimate lack of transcendent logic in North America's "one drop rule," I frequently carry on as if the identities it makes real are real, and make sense. And, indeed, they *do* make sense. Yet most people with whom I have spoken have argued that the claim that one can translate the "true" meaning of an English word on the basis of its sound, or by listening to the vibrations that form it, makes no sense. This may be true. But, then again, it often made little sense to elders on the maternal side of his family when, across our time in Bahia, someone argued that my light-complexioned son, whose mother is a recognizably Afro-Brazilian woman, is in some way black or Afro-Brazilian. But it typically made great sense to his young cousins, or Bahians attuned to recent alterations in Brazilian racial calculations.

Such anecdotal evidence of a significant shift in forms of racial identification is much more than evidence. It is a pathway into the importance of considering not the identities of those subject to the performances and manipulations of signification, but the details of those vectors. In making this claim I am not telling us all, once again, to attend to categories or even categorization. Instead, and like Topa, I am stopping, midway along the path to smooth interpretation, and asking us all to think through the mechanisms that generate the results of such interpretation. By halting, if only temporarily, I am trying to suggest that to think through—rather than about—those braidings and bundlings would involve an openness to creative possibility in which creation and possibility become visible as engagements with the actions of others, rather than the efforts of a diligent self. And that would be more than a celebration of some beautiful dialogue. It would instead show how tightly we are all lashed to that which we deny. In the process, the nature and value of that knot might be recognized as an unequal but nonetheless shared engagement with what we might be, rather than a search for who we really are.

A Forgotten Sign

In writing of becoming, and suggesting the power of halting at the nodes that provoke, I think again of Malaquias-the-sandwichman and his parade onto the Pelourinho Square narrated in chapter 1. In moving out into public without being noticed, Malaquias seemed to have generated little, or no, effect on the world. He was, at the time, what C. S. Peirce dubs a "rheme," or a future-oriented sign of still-unrealized possibility, but little concrete significance. Our group of friends in Salvador still laughs, and teases Malaquias, about his frustration on that hot summer day. But as I work to wind up this chapter in our lives in some way that would make it comprehensible to a public who might then compare our experiences to those elsewhere and in other times so as to make broader claims about the world, I wonder about what has become of the potential that was deferred that day. Perhaps I am simply tired, or incapable, or again being lazy and asking my readers to do the hard work of interpretation for me. Or perhaps I am being productively pragmatic and admitting simply that I still do not know. But in revealing this blindness, I must admit something else.

After the 18th Battalion of Love, or the Gueto, or number 18 Saldanha da Gama street, became resolutely uninhabitable due to falling beams, collapsing façades, the presence of sacis who defecated throughout the building, violent police patrols, and IPAC indemnifications, Malaquias and I sat and talked, one last time, before he signed his indemnification agreement and turned over to IPAC the keys to the small padlock that secured his doorway. Glancing about the˙room as he stuffed some last items into a bag, I saw a somewhat familiar crumpled cardboard sign lying in the corner. I walked over, picked it up, and began to read the red, green, gold, and black letters that opened with the words,

> *Denucia* [sic]
> Do You Know what IS
> happening here?
> IPAC (Instituto Patrimônio Artistico e cultural)
> takes our houses, I Passed
> my entire childhood here.
> Now my house, Is this Justice?
> Where are our rights?

Malaquias looked at me, surprised and I think a bit put off that I would be interested in that item that he had somehow saved for over a year but had consigned to the dustbin of histories accumulating in the corner of his soon-to-be-abandoned home. I blush, now, as I admit to scrounging through my friend's trash and seizing an item of great significance to me, but which he had apparently cast off. And I admit also that I dropped the sign back into the trash. But then, as we were moving to lock up, I asked Malaquias why he was leaving the sign behind. "I don't want it," he answered, "Take it if you want it."

Last night I went to my office in the Department of Anthropology where I had stored that sign. Memory tells me that I, like Malaquias, careless and yet seemingly unaccountably attached to the text, had dropped the placard in a corner, atop a pile of books and papers that soon engulfed it like a sandwich. But my search turned up nothing. That secure fragment, so weighty in its smudged inscriptions that we imagined would carry our concerns out onto the Pelourinho Square, was gone. And yet it seems to have produced something in the world, namely, an attempt at connection that some might describe as ephemeral, but that I find essential.

Conclusion

Saints, Not Angels

On January 22, 1927, eight days after first detailing Bahia's charms to Mário de Andrade, Manuel Bandeira followed up with two postcards. One bears a photograph of Salvador's dockside customs house, today a bustling, tourist-oriented handicrafts market known as the Mercado Modelo. On the back of the card, Bandeira instructed Andrade to "Look at this stupendous warehouse. It's the customs house. A colonial building. The windows are made of white marble."[1] This description and the injunction to look accord rather well with Bandeira's fascination with colonial buildings as well as with his initial letter to Andrade, dated January 14. There, as recounted in this book's introduction, Bandeira linked poorly maintained but imposing Pelourinho mansions to Portugal's colonial venture while describing these buildings' occupation by Afro-Brazilian women whose presence he noted on the basis of the shadows thrown by their home altars. This engagement with the visible, the invisible, and the almost visible, like his concern with witnessing, experience, and the knowing subject's relationship to colonial Brazil, is also an important part of the second card Bandeira mailed to Andrade on January 22. That "other" communication provides a slightly different perspective on Salvador's Comércio district and the epistemic connections whose analysis make up the core of this book.

The face of what I will describe as the second postcard—I have been unable to uncover the order of their assembly on January 22, so it may have been the first—reproduces the view afforded even today by dangling one's head over the railings of the Plano Inclinado (Inclined Plane), the funicular that links Salvador's Upper and Lower Cities, and thus the Pelourinho Historical Center to the Comércio neighborhood below (see figure 1.7). The enframed scene slopes sharply downward, away from the camera, pushing the viewer's gaze toward the point at which the funicular's steel tracks disappear into a tangle of colonial and Beaux-Arts buildings in the Lower City's dockside commercial area. Suspended near the midpoint of their trajectory sit two counterweighted cable cars tied into the chain, veiled by its emplacement within a concrete trench, which still pulls these vehicles up and down the slope. In the distance stretches Salvador's Lower City, encircled by the Bay of All Saints. On the back, Bandeira wrote, "This is not a modernist portrait, it is old Bahia, so close to us."[2]

Bandeira materializes the past and secures his own position through a perspective on the cityscape, and the technologies or infrastructures that connect it, that his penned description suggests permit him to look back in time. But the path of the funicular at the center of the rectangular offering that connects past and present leads into a jumble of buildings. Like its unmoored origins in the camera's optics, the railway's final coordinates thus remain indistinct in spite of the precision with which Bandeira links the perspective it affords on "old Bahia." This breathtakingly, yet misleadingly, clear passageway between the camera lens and the rails' vanishing point is precisely the space traversed by this book: Despite the poet's explicit denial of the face of the postcard as a portrait of something—and thus a representation—in favor of a claim to an unmediated "old Bahia, so close to us," the card is indeed a "modernist portrait" all the way down.

What better metaphor could there be for that moment, for Bandeira's voyage of discovery into Brazil's most traditional region, and for the cultural heritage-based sleights of hand that have become more and more pervasive in the nearly nine decades since Bandeira's journey? In helping the viewer to understand and delineate as an object of contemplation and manipulation the urban life whose distillation this book has posed as a fundament of Bahian history, Bandeira's postcard brings antiquity into view as a function of equipment that facilitates a passage between the two early-twentieth-century neighborhoods it arrays as spatio-temporally distinct.[3] The card thus illustrates as well as enacts a thread, and a disjuncture. As a photograph, it ties the mind's eye of the unmarked viewer atop the Plano Inclinado to the rails' vanishing point in what, over the course of Bandeira's clipped description, the card's circulation, and ensuing decades' cultural heritage management, becomes something akin to the nation's Baroque origins. And as a circulating object addressed to Brazil's best-known modernist thinker, the card carves out a representational space by means of its passage across Brazil's postal system, through the hands of people like Andrade, and into the archives and anthologies from which I have been privileged to extract it, for just a moment, as a xeroxed copy.[4]

In presenting the postcard as evidence of the presence of national beginnings he enjoins Andrade to study, Bandeira foregrounds an ideological formation called "old Bahia" as a relic that supposedly rises unmediated from the past. The infrastructure that, depending on one's perspective, either produces or permits access to that past thus sits on the face of the postcard—which might also be understood as part of the assemblage that makes Bahian heritage thinkable—as an unmarked or relatively unnoticed detail. Yet this funicular disappears from the caption that announces what the communicative vehicle performs as the physical form of this circulating sign molds a specific interpretation that draws attention away from what sits in the middle of the photograph, in plain sight.

Richard Price has described attending a meeting with Martinican cultural heritage authorities who announced that citizens no longer make use of a type of fishing canoe plainly visible on the beach beyond the conference room's windows. In the face of such elisions, Price describes the reification of popular practices as cultural heritage as a "postcarding of the past."[5] His reliance on the metaphor of the postcard, or an attractive if relatively flimsy piece of tourist memorabilia, highlights the flattenings of history that so often follow from attempts to commemorate human and institutional interactions in the monumentalized, or what some argue are truncated or stereotyped, forms of remembering evident in historical centers. And, based on my experience, there is little doubt that the mechanisms of collective memory nurtured there are remarkably exclusionary, and oftentimes flimsily authenticated. Similarly, a postcard is not the same as a thick, historical monograph, an interview with a community elder who may be able to authenticate what has happened, or even a coffee table book that allows the viewer to peer at or learn something of the authorized history of Pelourinho monuments' baroque folds. But as I have argued, and work by scholars like Price has demonstrated in detail for the Atlantic world, constriction and attempts to strip away existing social relations may also make the process of representing more complicated, thus generating new forms of experience and new semiotic attunements.[6]

"Degenerate" or resituated sign vehicles that signify improperly, and that thus fail to live up to the interpretive norms of, for example, the guild of professional historians on whose authority an ostensible thinness may take form as a quality of the postcard, may provoke or even require unexpected readings. Unlike a sealed letter, and like Topa who sends herself off to the nurse's home in search of an interpretation she both demands and inflects, a postcard is a patently vernacular, often-denigrated, and "open" sign I associate with both the monumentality of Chartres, Machu Picchu, and the Tower of London as well as the bad taste of Florida's Panhandle, Bahian depictions of palm-fringed beaches and sexually available "brown" women clad in bikinis, and Las Vegas casinos plastered with garish billboards. Swathed in an image that permits its sender to claim to have "been there," the card is not an appropriate space for deep, academic reflection about significance. But it is a photograph whose competing flimsiness and artifactuality, together with its fragmentary and public status in the face of the rather reserved conventions of proper letter-writing, helps configure it as iconic of the old Bahia conjured by Bandeira and his writings. So while I emphasize that Bandeira's postcard is a representation rather than a relic from and of old Bahia, its very dissimulation and physical status as an unsealed and unmoored thing in the world suggests that postcards, like cultural heritage management, are much more than impoverished or baroquely exaggerated representations of what has really taken place. My assertion draws on a realization that, as tokens, postcards must be supplemented by supporting evidence like the seemingly more complete accounts provided in letters, photo albums, or summaries of the voyage put together by travelers upon their return home. Only then might they appear to represent "correctly" and tell the sort of story that grounds so-called real history and real events.

Nonetheless, like stories of buried treasure and the race-based identification of ancestors lying under plazas and within buildings' walls, gutsy claims to health authorities' pedagogical authority, or an ability to make out and up the meanings of English on the basis of reggae songs' prosody, the postcard's circulating, ongoing affirmations of human creativity and perspicacity—and even, we should recognize, poor taste—push the boundaries of history and sensibility. One might even argue that the postcard of a modern funicular serves Bandeira as a potent metaphor for thinking through the operations necessary to set off old Bahia as a thing in itself. Such "analogic returns" highlight the extent to which representations have lives, and afterlives, of their own.[7] Thus, and in working to wrap up and recapitulate aspects of my argument by looking at postcards and the erection of cultural heritage programs, or two objects that those invested in "real" histories might understand as putting out similarly flimsy but influential claims to knowledge and its production, I am not turning my back on what has happened. Rather, I am seeking to amplify that empiricism, and thus attend to history not simply as what has happened or what is said to have taken place, but as what is happening, and even what will happen.

Once, sitting on the floor with Dona Niza, I asked her what I should call my book-in-progress. She immediately replied, in proper Pelourinho fashion designed to elicit sympathy and perhaps even funds from the powerful, "Call it the *Poor, Suffering People of the Pelourinho and the Injustices done to them by* IPAC *and Tony Rotten!*"[8] Her teenage daughter looked up, laughing, and, warning me not to mind her mother's exaggerations, announced, "Call it *The African People of the Pelourinho!*"[9]

The space between a "poor suffering people" designed to elicit compassion and support and an "African people" celebrated so insistently in so many ways in Bahia today is one that, like the gap between a modernist portrait and a relic of "old Bahia," may at times become confused in the contemporary world. Yet in engaging both suffering and Afro-Brazilian struggles for equality I have tried to avoid equating the two or fetishizing, as some essential truth, the points of view of those who suffer over those who rule.[10] But I have done so without abandoning the truths of history or suggesting that a consideration of one member of either dyad described here is possible without addressing their entanglement. Instead, I have examined relationships, noting how concerns with suffering, moral fitness, care, and Afro-Brazilianness may both come together and diverge as Pelourinho residents struggle to forge alliances, dominate (one) an Other, and attach themselves to power as it flashes by or is transformed while ricocheting across their selves. Similarly, I have not sought to celebrate Bahia's African character in a way that recalls the modernist reification of primitive alterity, or the sense of foundational difference that Manuel Bandeira seems to have so loved as he scanned Bahia for Brazilian traditions that might stand up to France's Arc de Triomphe.

Instead, I have begun to work out some of the ways that, in a highly unequal fashion, the residents of the Pelourinho and the IPAC social scientists charged with knowing those people have coauthored a version of Bahian history that is, again and as the tourist literature affirms, open to the world today. This Pelourinho and its "people," then, are critical to the construction of modern Brazil. They were critical in Manuel Bandeira's time because they stood metonymically for urban orders and a quasi-citizenry that supposedly needed to be recuperated so the nation might move beyond cosmopolitan prognostications of racialized degeneracy. Ironically, during the midcentury period in which Brazil's intellectuals struggled to tell a story of mixed-race exceptionalism, the Pelourinho was left to crumble, inhabited mainly by the people who Bandeira did not quite see when he visited Bahia in 1927. And today, as they did in different ways at earlier moments, the Pelourinho and its population support the sorts of spatializations and racializations of people and their habits that enable the nation's apparent coherence. Nonetheless, the approaches to tradition and reified versions of cultural belonging apparent in the Pelourinho have been appropriated also by many of the communities that challenge that nation-form today. In southern Brazil, descendents of Polish and German settlers now enunciate a diacritical identity opposed to the mixed-race nation and, especially, northeastern and "backward" regions like Bahia.[11] In the Amazon, the Kayapó have taken possession of a video project, begun alongside North American anthropologists, that promises to increase their ability to enunciate their desires, and even their autonomy, in the face of state power and a global marketplace.[12] And throughout the city of Salvador, reggae bars and carnival and neighborhood groups have sprung up that enunciate a black consciousness of the type that prompted Dona Niza's daughter to celebrate the African in naming the ethnographic venture of which she is a part. Such movements suggest a growing search for independence, sovereignty, or community autonomy around ethno-racial lines. Yet I have stressed that the Pelourinho's population is not looking for autonomy.

For the most part, residents did not work, and are not working, to separate from the nation-state or carve out a special space like the indigenous groups whose engagements of and by the national state may have influenced Professor Vivaldo da Costa Lima's directions for IPAC in the 1970s. They would rather be included in the benefits that their elected representatives argue will emanate from a restored historical center. Although inhabitants of culture-based development and monumentalized history in Salvador's Pelourinho take part in many of the practices employed by indigenous communities throughout the world so as to demand rights and justice in the face of the commodification of culture, their struggles to analyze their state and lay claim to particular forms of selfhood pertain mostly to an attempt to remain a part of the polity as it exists, rather than to force major modifications in law or practice. It would thus be incorrect to configure the Pelourinho as a community, in the sense of many Latin American indigenous groups, that might be analyzed primarily in terms of its challenges to the state's sovereignty or right to govern.

Nonetheless, like many of their counterparts in the Andes or Amazonia, residents of the Pelourinho rely on creative claims to a self-consciously traditional position, anterior to the nation-state, on the basis of their special skills, knowledge, race, and rooted condition as *da antiguidade*. This has involved appropriating and working through social scientific and heritage technologies such as censuses, field notes, archives, questionnaires, and ideas about culture as a resource or discrete entity. As a result, residents have come at times to understand themselves as a possession, or an object, that both belongs to and helps construct the nation. Such understandings have multiple effects. Among these is an awareness not only of the work that goes into building nations, and peoples, but also of their critical role in the contradictory engagements between state and nation.

Those who chart the rise of black consciousness in Brazil look often to the Estado Novo as an important site for the manipulations of popular culture, and a concerted effort to produce a national people on the part of an authoritarian state invested in statistics and documentation, which articulated complexly with Afro-Brazilian political organizing.[13] Social scientists also concentrate on Brazil's *abertura* (opening) in the 1980s, and thus the creativity and energy of civil society actors whose fight against discrimination tied into the battles for civil rights so essential to the return from military rule.[14] And historical and ethnographic analysis of the trajectories of Bahian civil society organizations like Olodum, Ilê Aiyê, Malê Debalê, and Muzenza has illustrated how lessons learned and associations formed during redemocratization continue to inflect racial politics today.[15] Yet this book has approached Brazil's racial politics from a different, more recent, moment characterized by neoliberal "reforms" associated with novel as well as shopworn state structures and property regimes, the rise or exacerbation of cultural commodification, and approaches to identity. As such, the turn of the millennium and the series of engagements it presents in Salvador serve as something of a bridge that links a twentieth-century, corporatist, and "racial democratic" Brazil to a nation of multicultural initiatives, affirmative action policies, and redistributive federal programs intended to alleviate as well as undermine the nation's glaring inequalities.[16]

The late 1990s and first years of the new millennium were important to today's politics, and not solely in relation to the actions of vaunted, nationally recognized organizations like Olodum, the MNU, or Salvador's most beautiful and famous Candomblé temples. As a result, and in a move similar to Keisha-Khan Perry, who argues for the importance of moving away from the best-known and most frequently recognized of organizations toward smaller, neighborhood associations often missed or discounted by the social scientists who flock to Bahia as a paradigmatic site for studies in the Black Atlantic, I have looked away from the Pelourinho's most expressive social movements.[17] As a function of this approach, as well as my long-term familiarity with the Pelourinho, I became a part of a nascent, and not-quite, social movement called "S.O.S. Children of the Historical Center." Drawing in turn on this position, I have focused on the engagements between state and citizen that help make clear how institutions and individual actors see one another, understand themselves, and tap into grammars or technologies that may permit them to alter the world. And this orientation has led me to the conclusion that weaving a "better" ethnography of race and history in Brazil today is not an issue of scale or of catching that which has been missed because it is small, subjugated, and thus flies under the radar. Rather, I have suggested that *how* we as anthropologists look is often the most glaring issue.

In one of the few recent ethnographies to take seriously the influence on Brazilian racial ideologies of historical processes and people's insertions into those flows, John Burdick lays out a discomfort with what he characterizes as social scientists' "metaphor statements" filled with bland talk of "vehicles" and verbs like "shapes" and "expresses." For Burdick, these open signifiers render analysis loose and, in a sense, uneventful. In response, he suggests that anthropologists search for meaning, and he offers the ostensible groundedness of "place," "body," and "history" as key, experiential—I might even say "authoritative"—sites for this crusade for relevance. Burdick, who has long woven nuanced approaches to race and religion in Brazil, is no doubt correct, in a way. By this, I mean that recourse to such putatively grounded categories, or to phenomenal unities on whose "materiality" and relevance we as professional social scientists can somehow agree without questioning in detail why we agree, reflects the conventions of an engaged ethnography as typically performed today.[18] In fact, given that *Revolt of the Saints* is at base about the mutating-but-historically entwined technologies that tie Bandeira to "old Bahia" and contemporary Bahians to their sidewalks and plazas' hidden contents, and thus also to the identities of slave bodies lying beneath their feet and second-order ideas about racial affiliation and descent, my own approach to the production of knowledge through ethnography is allied rather tightly with Burdick's project of gaining "some sense of priority in the processes . . . that make one good to think the other with."[19] But my ethnography moves in slightly different, and yet significant, directions in relation to the imbrication of phenomenal unities called bodies, race, and history in a place called the Pelourinho.

As demonstrated by Bahians' appropriation of IPAC's and IPHAN's investigative equipment—and especially the discourse of tombamento—the Pelourinho is marked by a powerful lack of clarity in relation to the borders that separate a body subject to a eugenicist burnishing, data about that body and its trajectories, and a statue or colonial building covered with scaffolding so as to have its rotten beams replaced and mortar repointed.[20] And, today, around the world, pieces of human bodies are not simply reproduced in laboratories, but have been colonized as the very tools, or technologies, that perform the work of Big Pharma: Rather than prediscursive things on which we may lean, securely, bodies are semiotically produced materialities and a consideration of their meaningfulness must attend to that semiosis. This assertion is not an attempt to claim bodies as products of language. Rather, it is part of the work of expanding ethnographers' engagements with the world by recognizing the instability, and thus the primacy, of an expanded conception of materiality.

If Topa revels in and wields like a rapier a proleptic or imaginary history performed on the nurse's doorstep and authorized by her ongoing manipulation of technocratic interactions between residents of the Misericórdia and CETAD, where does history really lie and is an imaginary history projected into the future actually a history? Is history the meaning or felt identification attached to events and dead people in some fully symbolic, synthesizing account of what has happened? And if that history can be ordered, and prioritized—or if it prioritizes and orders—has it thus described better those people and events? Or is history that moment of interaction between Pelourinho residents and the IPAC teams who survey them in order to put together the documents that will ground future accounts of what has happened? My ethnography suggests that it is all of the above and therefore most fully understood as the series of oftentimes nested connections and truth claims that depend on and authorize subjects' specific locations in, and ability to step into and manipulate, an interconnected world so often sundered by the elision, or denigration, of the technologies that join it as an unstable constellation.

In a related question, then, is race but a system of color classifications that give life to social exclusions, or is it, like official representations of a society's patrimony, a historicized substance that passes by means of specific types of connection between and across generations? In light of my analysis in this book, race is both a classificatory system and the substance and knowledge made to fill or connect and validate the both, as well as one or the other. And this claim highlights how, by seizing on a fragment from Burdick's attempt to array body, place, and history so as to obtain some ranked purchase on what really counts in the analysis of Christian gospel and race in Brazil, I am not simply suggesting that we substitute one triumvirate with three novel terms that would secure what pass for real meanings. In fact, if I were searching for such conventionally grounded figures in relation to the Pelourinho and this conclusion, I might even seize on postcards, funiculars, and handicrafts markets as figures that do substantially more analytical work than do bodies, histories, and places. After all, the Latin root of funicular, *funiculus*, is a rope, cord, or bundle of fibers.

As Hans-Jorg Rheinberger has argued recently for laboratory notes, the transfer of experimental protocols onto paper effects a "redimensionalization" that facilitates a deeper exploration of data, or the sorts of abductive reorderings associated with new knowledge.[21] In fact, to a certain extent I have argued that it is not only the process whereby Pelourinho residents' lives are transformed into ethnographic field notes and then redimensionalized in IPAC archives that is so important to understanding changes in personhood and historical consciousness, but also the very experience of feeling oneself being transferred into a data that, in the hands of certain people like IPAC managers, is then reinflated in a conferral of substance to new social types or categories of citizen. These perches and their associated labels may range from *morador* (resident) to "marginal" and on to "Living Human Treasures."

So while it may be true that "vehicles" and verbs that go no farther than nodding at vague concepts may stand as relatively flat metaphors whose lack of precision encourages fluffy thinking, so too is it true that body, place, and history are bundles of signifiers in movement. As signs of and participants in something more than unmediated experiences or pathways into "true" origins and "real" facts, histories refer to the world in a wide variety of ways with differing significance. Or, as Joanne Rappaport puts it, "History is not a matter of 'truth,' but of the choice of a particular expository style that is itself determined historically."[22] Hence the suggestion that a loose language about sign vehicles fails to specify the true nature of politics is both enlightening and itself a generalization that leads to a certain conceptual fluffiness: Ethnographers, like early-twentieth-century Brazilian folklorists, heritage professionals around the world, and even religious and social visionaries like Jorginho and Malaquias, might benefit instead from a move away from a focus on the "true truth of things" (*a verdadeira verdade*) and come to appreciate the technologies and standpoints, and thus the epistemic labor, required to make such connections. This assertion is not a simple reiteration of the realization, put forth so eloquently by people such as Michel-Rolph Trouillot and Hayden White, that historical truth is a function of narrative or archival convention. Nor is it yet another plea for a social constructivist approach. Rather, it is one reason I have opened this final section of this account with a story of a postcard, and what it reveals and what it hides.

My orthogonal approach enacted ethnographically in *Revolt of the Saints* has been spurred by the recognition that meaning-as-content as usually imagined by North Americans, and even social scientists around the world, is but one type of significance. Or, put better, meaning and history are at least in part dependent on the shape and materiality of the vehicle that transmits them, rather than some ability of a sign to signal transparently and "honestly" the true nature of its object or referent. Thus whether or not, and how, a fountain, a slave, and a self-described master speak is dependent not simply on the contents of their speech or on that speaker's categorical status as "physical object," "human property," or "legally empowered citizen of many liberal democratic republics," but also on the burbling of water, the rhythms of a work song, and the physical enactment of privilege as manifested in tokens like broken teeth and poorly healed fractures or qualities like corpulence, bathing habits, or dress. And abstract, general ideas and lawlike propositions about the world such as the three categorical statuses arrayed in quotation marks in the previous sentence must necessarily be enacted in specific, materially mediated interchanges like the sending of postcards, the exercise of a particular person's vocal chords, or the appropriation of snippets of stereotyped, social scientific interview methods and exchanges like that performed by Topa. As sonic, physical, and/or emotional objects and signs, these interactive nodes carry with them qualities that necessarily reverberate in ways that are a function of their material form, rather than solely their content. And yet meaning as we typically know it is about a significance that so often moves away from tokens in the world in favor of a dematerialized, and thus abstract, claim about their value.[23] One result, I would venture to argue, is a social science that speaks either to theoretical canons and traditions or to some "real life" supposedly available to the intrepid and diligent ethnographer. But the interface and the interfaces that make up life, those moments of realignment that so often pass unnoticed and uncommented on by researchers determined to get to the bottom of things or to make an intervention into existing ways of representing the world, still structure so very thinly the ways we as social scientists claim to touch reality and intervene in erudite debate.

I am suggesting that an emphasis on proliferation and hybridization in today's Pelourinho is not a celebration of excess or yet another deconstructive fetishization of the emergence of meaning in ways unintended by its enunciators or predicted by rhetorical structures. It is rather a suggestion that, due to an unwillingness or conceptual inability to link smells, winks, never-expressed compliments and criticisms, and frustrated goals to supposedly staid and "existing" interpretation-based entities like histories, places, persons, and political systems, anthropologists have been unable to track the real transformations of the actual sites and amalgams that mean something to people. And over the course of my fieldwork I found that history, understood as the projection of meaning onto supposedly objectively available events and processes, meant almost nothing to most Pelourinho residents. Similarly, affective ties to place were typically approached as part of a public discourse "for English eyes" that meant little to people who would much rather live in seaside apartments than crumbling ruins located on extremely dangerous streets. Meanwhile, full "personhood" (in Bahia, the attainment of the status of *gente*, or people, rather than "marginal") was something that Pelourinho residents often argued escaped them due to the fierce prejudice they faced across Bahian society. And, as generations of anthropologists have noted, something so viscerally important to me as "race" often failed to resonate in twentieth-century Brazil to the extent it did in the United States. To note this situation is not to argue that such categories are unimportant. But it is to suggest the importance, and difficulty, of reducing how I have engaged the Pelourinho to an analytic claim about what that means. I am thus tempted simply to appropriate Stephen Kern's point about the varied acceptance of Mendelian genetics' challenges to Charles Darwin's pangenesis, and announce that my research allows me to make out a "new approach to hereditary transmission . . . [that is] part of a broad cultural shift in thinking about the causes of human experience generally."[24] In other words, my ethnography may have made visible some of the techniques through which people link threads that permit them to make out the past, and even weave causal explanations. Exchanging postcards, transforming experience into field notes, and, as Tim Ingold points out, signing one's name and drawing kinship diagrams, are practices that build up threads of explanation and causality.[25] Yet explanation, or one type of interpretation, is typically understood in modernity as the result of the mental activities of human subjects who move away from objects, into abstraction, in performing feats of analytic dexterity. As a result, and across this book, I have leaned loosely on Peirce's semiotics, and Pelourinho residents' approaches to the production of history, so as to find a way back toward objects and their sensuousness without simply assigning an agency to those objects themselves.

Perhaps then, in the wake of the redimensionalizations put forth by a postcard that permitted me to make out the importance of a representation of a funicular on which Bandeira refused to comment, and on which I have ridden hundreds of times, Malaquias and I might both locate and look even more closely at the placards he wore out onto the Praça da Sé on a day the assembled public failed even to note his protest. And in light of the redimensionalizations effected by heritage protocols, it might also be worth emphasizing that as things become even more specifiable, and subject to ramped up and apparently improved techniques for investigation in and of the world, those things and techniques change in relation to one another. This is a real change and not a function of blurred vision. The resulting alterations in barely perceivable phenomena that take form as evidence at so many different scales and from so many different perspectives make our conclusions more complex, rather than simpler.[26] I take this to be, rather than some poorly specified "navel-gazing" or postmodern gobbledygook, a hallmark of a social science that does things like alert us all to our blind spots and ask us, as I recount in this book's preface the Mago and Fat Carlos suggested I should do, to coproduce with our interlocutors the means of turning those disabilities into sources of insight. And given the importance today to the Bahian economy of Afro-Brazilian culture, or practices long maligned and even persecuted by Bahian authorities who nonetheless appropriated them in building a regional identity, such moves need not be relegated to some "culturalist" or "symbolic" sphere divorced from political

356 CONCLUSION

economy. Routes into tradition, then, are painstakingly crafted pathways that play an important role in international organizations' lending policies and evaluations of democratic inclusiveness today. Somewhat like the railways of the industrial revolution, or an inclined plane that amplifies human force in pushing objects uphill, cultural heritage has contributed to profound alterations in urban form and salient senses of time, place, and human extension in the world.[27]

Even more than altering the physical composition of cityscapes, heritage shifts how and what things factor into landscapes as material objects. As Lynn Meskell defines it, "materiality [rather than solely a physical relationship] represents a presence of power in realizing the world, crafting things from nothing, subjects from nonsubjects."[28] If people's feelings and intimate practices can be bundled as patrimony, then people may stand alongside "immaterial" entities or qualities like affect, desire, or absence as a species of vibrant, human patrimony and a type of infrastructure akin to the archive and its contents. As I suggested in the introduction, being historical means looking through the archive in new ways. And looking through the archive in the Pelourinho requires that the subject seeking to do so understand that she is not simply an interpreter, and thus an effect or the author of meanings of history that are somehow distilled from the evidence contained there, but a part of the archive and its materials.

Engagements with minor techniques and elaborate, suturing technologies wielded by bureaucrats who seek to open to view the homes and lives of Pelourinho residents, and who produced the raw material of IPAC-authenticated histories, were basic to the research that leads me here, in this conclusion, to work to put forth a theory of the ethnographic production of history that strives to make out significance in the collection of objects—whether texts, people as monuments, or field notes about habits (objectified practices)—rather than their synthesis. How difficult, but how potentially rich as well as fun, funny, and uncomfortable this can be was brought home to me when, as I worked to finish this book, I bumped into Dandinha, the cross-dressing former marine and community leader. We were walking along the Baixa do Sapateiro, a street filled with clothing and household articles for working-class Bahians when, happy to see my wife and me again, Dandinha reached out with a deep squeal and, amidst hugs, informed us gravely that he had suffered a series of heart attacks while we were away. Yet he had survived, he noted with pride. In fact, as he put it while showing off the scars across his chest, "I'm still here!" It's because "St. Peter told me it wasn't my time, that I had to go back because I still have a lot of ass to give up down here. Nope, no way I'm going away any time soon." His voice rising into a shriek that caused the vendors and shoppers around us to glance up, Dandinha then repeated loudly, "St. Peter said to me, 'Go back! It's not your time yet. You still have to give up a lot of ass down there!'"[29]

In spite of the recurring risk of titillating readers with stories from the highly sexualized version of Brazil that is still so much in vogue today, Dandinha's slightly scandalous announcement of his permanence on earth seems a proper ending to a book about proper historicity and the details of ways that productions of history speak to changes in political identities. Proper historicity is a concept I have approached laterally at multiple points throughout *Revolt of the Saints* as a component of Pelourinho residents' ways of facing their state, their pasts, and their desires by engaging and transforming existing conceptualizations of property and propriety. In the Pelourinho, this is often a highly sexualized interaction, one nearly always about morality, family structures, and domesticity, and thus properties of selves and communities packaged by means of UNESCO-authorized conventions apparently aimed at demonstrating humankind's common origins and multiplex futures. What seems most interesting about Dandinha's claims, then, is that the "giving up of his ass" grants history and Dandinha's life a directionality. He must return to earth, quite literally turned away from an ultimate Christian redemption in heaven. It is as if the redemption, and the meaning of his life, eludes him as St. Peter shuts the gates and condemns him to his scarred body. But Dandinha celebrates this move as permitting him to locate himself firmly in his promised land, the life of the Pelourinho where his sexual appetites have not yet been sated.

Unlike the ephemeral, backward-facing angel who in Walter Benjamin's hands glides away from the detritus of a history temporalized as detritus by the angel's departure, and for which that backward-facing movement seeks or promises to make those ruins meaningful, Dandinha plummets triumphantly to earth on the basis of the sorts of stigmatized activities associated with the Pelourinho as a red light district, and later a folkloric space.[30] He returns— ass-backward, one might even argue—to the detritus of "old Bahia" in a life-giving manner sanctioned by St. Peter, perhaps because the saint recognizes the importance of what Dandinha does, and enjoys, in that life. And Dandinha recounts this journey in a doubling or reiterative style: In his description of his fall, he first summarizes what St. Peter says and then returns to quote the gatekeeper, supposedly verbatim. Like historical reconstructions in the Pelourinho, which are a species of return whose pragmatic importance and ultimately ridiculous impossibility Pelourinho residents recognize and Topa mimics with a difference in her return (in the future, and in her imaginative recounting) to the nurse's doorstep, Dandinha's account of a dialogue with heaven's gatekeeper enchants in its re-presentation of origins as more than symbolic sources that make our lives meaningful.

Across this book I have argued that halting interventions into the finality or potentiality of interpretation provide a contested space for the development of novel technologies of the self, and thus of the flows of history producing those selves. St. Peter seems to recognize the importance of such novel sites. His words permit Dandinha to approach (and depart) the pearly gates not as a sinner, but as someone who must return to earth to engage in worldly, sometimes-stigmatized practices. These are implicitly accepted, and perhaps even sacralized, by the saint's affirmation of a sinner as a participant in a life so well lived that it beckons in its pleasurable sensuousness. The return, then, to a space that some might find sullied, or immoral, grants Dandinha a glimpse of transcendence or the self-realization of absolute identity—something ordinarily approached within a Hegelian philosophical tradition as an endpoint, as a "spirit" lying in the future—that he rejects for the embodied pleasures of sinful life.[31] Yet in Dandinha's return those tarnished origins become something besides past experience, the marks of social exclusion, or an object that must be recognized and overcome in the movement toward synthesis.[32]

While true saints are persons in heaven, Dandinha is a person located between heaven and earth and potentially able to access both, depending on his volition, his skills, and St. Peter's evaluation. After all, he makes this apparent in a bit of autobiography recounted to a social scientist, reformulated in an ethnography written in English, and now consumed by you, my esteemed reader. In facing death only to return to life, he carries us all—in a manner akin to Topa's transportation of the nurse, CETAD workers, and her audience of neighbors "back" to the nurse's doorstep—into an imagined but never-realized encounter that grounds an interaction in the present subjunctively, or in an "if I should" or "if I should (ever) need to defecate in your neighborhood." It is as if this possible history has in fact taken place, and thus established in an earthly sense the conditions of possibility out of which Topa and Dandinha both reconfigure their interactions in the present with the CETAD nurse or St. Peter.

We thus return narratively, as a group, to the primal scene of racial democracy. This novel but familiar origin that has arisen in my text recalls the Pelourinho Historical Center in its exposition of sexuality, domestic arrangements, smells, desires, and consumption—after all, in Bahia "to eat" (comer) is "to have sex" or even "to fuck"—of foods, people, and lives within a brutalizing and yet hopeful narrative that once promised to make Brazil and Brazilians equal, and "democratic." But today the inequalities and veiling of violence so much a part of that account have been made much more visible, in no small part due to the actions of militants in the Black Movement like Senator Luiz Alberto, the former city council member Paulo Anunciação, and the citizens like Malaquias, Gula, and Caboré with whom they interact. Yet if I have tried to pass on any message in this book, from my strange perch as an outsider located deeply within these interactions, it is that the size—and not simply the shape—of our blindness is so rarely apparent.

When Dandinha saw me that day on the Baixa do Sapateiro, he lifted his shirt nearly immediately after our initial greeting. This gesture announced a story of near-death, and return, in which his status as a respected man with breasts, who some might refer to as folkloric and tombado (patrimonialized and ruined), was not so much a living death or suspended state as a return to life. There, on a working-class shopping street known as the "Valley of the Shoemakers," built upon a cemented-over creek called the Rio das Tripas (River of Guts) in recognition of the tanneries that once ringed it, Dandinha invited me to peer across his stigmata, but not directly into his self. And the mark of a surgical violence that saved his life invites me to consider Dandinha's presentation of what I could not see, but have come to draw on as real in formulating my interpretations.

The ability to see what is not immediately present, or at least to speak about and organize into chains of cause and effect that which one has not experienced directly, is critical to how I have approached race. In concentrating on the processes that authenticate genealogical linkages so important to dominant theories of race in the United States and, increasingly, in Brazil, I have suggested that cultural heritage is one of many technologies that encourages people to associate themselves with the past, and thus to talk about that which they have not experienced. Thus I have suggested also that people close to the Pelourinho's patrimonialization seem to be associated with a more noticeable configuration of race as a historical property than are many people who live in Salvador's peripheral neighborhoods and who are not associated with the city's famed blocos afros or political organizations linked to the Black Movement. Meanwhile, I have argued also that in the Pelourinho there exist a number of social conventions, ranging from rules of politeness to the moral sense that one cannot ever really know another person, that discourage people from speculating about the relationship between visible signs and the sorts of civilizational qualities to which visible marks are linked in, for example, North American racial ideologies. And in this conclusion I have described an interaction with Dandinha in which he formulates a connection to the world, and a fortuitous escape from death, that seems to suggest the importance of what I have discussed across this book as the rather iconoclastic historical practices of Pelourinho residents.

Given a specifically Brazilian or at least Pelourinho-based approach to historical objects and their manipulation and significance, it would seem that even though racial ideologies are changing in Brazil, one should not expect

Brazilian racial politics to simply converge with those in the United States. And, indeed, I do not believe that understandings of race in Brazil and the United States will converge. But this is beside the point I wish to make: I have emphasized that, in the Pelourinho, there exist multiple, and even at-times antithetical, approaches to history, race, and belonging. Thus the dispositions toward the past discussed should not be ontologized as distinct ways of being in history that loop back to define some constitutive difference on the part of Pelourinho residents. Such a move would relegate them to precisely the sort of closed, corporate, and "folkloric" community into which IPAC sought to dragoon them in the 1970s and 1980s. I have therefore followed as Pelourinho residents reject interpretation, defer interpretation, project the interpretive faculty onto professional social scientists, and engage in all manner of objectifying and self-objectifying activities. So while regimes of representation shift alongside the state-directed objectification of everyday life as heritage, I have not followed IPAC's lead and placed Pelourinho residents on some "primitive" plane whereby their approach to interpretation serves as a mark of constitutive, existential difference.

On the contrary, as made evident in Topa's gutsy insurrection in the context of CETAD pedagogy or Malaquias' definition of a racialized self as part of a dispute with IPAC over the possession of field notes, the ways that Pelourinho residents approach history, selves, and interpretation are always coproductions. Just as Bahia's political class alters how it speaks when addressing the working class, so too does the working class alter how it speaks when engaging state institutions. And residents of the Pelourinho are among the world's populations that most intensely engage, and find themselves interpellated by, state institutions. Like prisoners or the hospitalized, Pelourinho residents are subject to concentrated regimes of discipline and normalization. Thus, the ways they approach archives are not some manifestations of a medieval Catholicism or African religiosity that has somehow survived in one of Brazil's poorer and blacker religions: on the contrary, in the Pelourinho we see a confluence of Catholic approaches to saints and their mediating roles, an increasingly strident engagement with images and claims to purity on the part of Pentecostal Christians, and an attempt by the state government of Bahia to commodify a citizenry's everyday habits. This is a dynamic situation, and one that is as historically specific as it is productive of seemingly novel semiotic attunements.

My argument in this book is thus at base methodological. Building on Peirce's theorization of the sign as a triad in which an object or referent, a sign vehicle or representamen, and an interpretant or claim about significance are copresent within semiotic mediations, I have focused on the materiality of the sign vehicle as an important determinate of what history is, and does, for all people (and not simply Pelourinho residents). My endpoint that arises from doing so is really rather simple. Rather than suggesting that social groups can be arrayed in terms of how they relate to history or to the materiality of the sign vehicle, I have sought to illustrate how, when a concentration on the work performed by that sign vehicle (or the mediating technology) drops away, the human beings with whom I am in contact tend to ontologize themselves, their surroundings, and their Others. Blindness, then, is absolutely essential. But recovering from blindness is not necessarily about seeing again or realizing that one's vision is but partial. Rather, it is about understanding how much we can see, and feel, in light of all of our blind spots.

Acronyms Used

Acronym	Portuguese	English Translation
CAB	Centro Administrativo da Bahia	Bahian Administrative Center
CCAA	Centro Cultural Anglo-Americano	Anglo-American Cultural Center
CEAB	Centro de Estudos da Arquitetura Baiana	Center for Bahian Architectural Studies
CETAD	Centro de Estudos e Terapia de Abuso de Drogas	Center for Therapy and Studies of Drug Abuse
CIA	Centro Industrial de Aratu	Aratu Industrial Center
CIAM	Congrès internationaux d'architecture moderne	International Congresses of Modern Architecture
CNBB	Conferência Nacional dos Bispos do Brasil	Brazilian National Bishops' Conference
CODESAL	Comissão de Defesa Civil do Salvador	Commission for the Civil Defense of Salvador
CONDER	Companhia do Desenvolvimento Urbano do Estado da Bahia	Bahian State Urban Development Company
EPUCS	Escritório do Plano de Urbanismo da Cidade do Salvador	Office of the Urbanizing Plan of the City of Salvador

Acronym	Portuguese	English Translation
FGM	Fundação Gregório de Mattos	Gregório de Mattos Foundation
FPACBa	Fundacao do Patrimônio Artístico e Cultural da Bahia	Bahian Foundation for Cultural and Artistic Patrimony and the Library Foundation (precursor to IPAC)
IPHAN	Instituto do Patrimônio Histórico e Artístico Nacional	National Institute of Historical and Artistic Patrimony (formerly SPHAN)
IPAC	Instituto do Patrimônio Artístico e Cultural da Bahia	Bahian Institute of Architectural and Cultural Patrimony
IURO	Igreja Universal do Reino de Deus	Universal Church of the Reign of God
MOBRAL	Movimento Brasileiro de Alfabetização	Brazilian Literacy Movement
MNU	Movimento Negro Unificado	Unified Black Movement
MST	Movimento Sem Terra	Landless People's Movement
PERSH	Programa Especial de Recuperação dos Sítios Históricos	Special Program for the Recuperation of Historical Sites
PFL	Partido do Frente Liberal	Party of the Liberal Front (now called Democratas)
PT	Partido dos Trabalhadores	Workers Party
PLANDURB	Plano de Desenvolvimento Urbano da Cidade do Salvador	Urban Development Plan for the City of Salvador
SIRCHAL	Séminaire Internationale sur la Réhabilitation des Centres Historiques des Villes de l'Amerique Latine	International Seminar on the Rehabilitation of the Historical Centers of Latin American Cities
SPHAN	Secretaria do Patrimônio Histórico Artístico Nacional	Secretariat of National Artistic and Historical Patrimony
SEPLAM	Secretaria do Planejamento Municipal	Municipal Planning Secretariat

Notes

Introduction

1. The Commission for the Civil Defense of Salvador (Comissão de Defesa Civil do Salvador, or CODESAL) is the municipal institution in charge of preventing and reacting to landslides, which are extremely common in this hilly, tropical city once covered by a deep-rooted Atlantic rain forest now largely replaced by auto-constructed housing. See http://www.defesacivil.salvador.ba.gov.br/, the CODESAL website, for updates on emergency responses and initiatives (last accessed August 15, 2014).

2. Monteiro Lobato 2008. The term *folclórico* (folkloric) is both a compliment and an insult in the Pelourinho, where it is used to describe or upbraid someone who performs his or her Bahian or Afro-Bahian identity too self-consciously. I employ the word in this book in a number of ways, at times ironically, but usually in reference to the nationalist celebration of a pantheon of popular customs and habits presented as typically Brazilian and authentically of the people. These traits, imagined to ground the nation in an essential *volksgeist*, were an important focus of cultural policy in the period after World War II, a period marked in Brazil by spiraling interest in creative approaches to national culture that ended with the U.S.-supported military coup of March 30, 1964 that ushered in a dictatorship that lasted until the election of president Tancredo Neves in January 1985. Ortiz 1984, 1992 outlines the transformation of earlier discussions of Brazilian national culture within military attempts to reconfigure the national-popular in the service of their centralizing and violently authoritarian national development efforts. Andrade 1966, in a text of great importance given his influence on cultural policy across the nation, discusses the role of folklore studies in the 1930s and 1940s under the populist dictator Getúlio Vargas. See also the collection of letters between Andrade and the dean of Brazilian folklore studies, Luís da Câmara Cascudo 2010.

3. In an example of the braiding of past, present, and future so essential to the "heritage zone," historical centers are also commonly referred to as "cultural heritage" or simply "heritage" centers. I employ all three terms interchangeably in this book despite recognizing the ways that "patrimony"—a term that I also employ in-

terchangeably with "heritage"—emphasizes property and its transmission among corporate groups across time (Chelcea 2003).

4. The lyrics suggest that the strange forms of folklorization, or concurrent celebration and denigration of Afro-Brazilian culture by the Bahian state in spaces like the Pelourinho, produce a paranoid structure of feeling. The term *a paranoia* (to be paranoid) is a synonym in Brazil, and especially in São Paulo, where crack abusers are referred to as '*noias*, for the state of being high on cocaine (Heckenberger 2012).

5. Harvey 2004, 2008 suggests that such "creative destruction" is basic to urbanization schemes that reflect the contradictions of a capitalist system in which attempts to resolve issues of overaccumulation generate spatial and temporal, and thus urban-renewal and credit-based, "fixes" that both destabilize and propel forward what he dubs the "new imperialism."

6. James 2012.

7. The "care" proffered in relation to experiments in segregation justified as humanitarian responses to war, famine, and natural disaster has become central to ethnographies of contemporary philanthropy and attempts to determine "the political" in light of attention to an ostensibly basic humanity and its associated rights (Agier and Bouchet-Saulnier 2004; Redfield 2013; Schuller 2012). Ticktin 2012 examines how such depoliticized appeals to moral responsibility naturalize political orders, and Biehl 2005 suggests that they may open spaces of contestation in a neoliberal Brazil marked by the medicalization of social issues. While IPAC seeks to justify its actions in the Pelourinho in relation to similar appeals to humanitarianism, residents and a wider Bahian public appear to support and update Viotti da Costa's observation that nineteenth-century Brazilians "could not but be aware that . . . liberal theory did not have anything to do with the reality . . . around them" and deployed liberalism as an imported bauble (2000, 75–76). Given the salience of this claim about a Brazilian, peripheral, ability to "see through" ideological formations that confuse elsewhere, I follow Pelourinho residents' lead and resist drawing a boundary between ethics and politics. Instead I treat all engagements between IPAC and local people as potentially political, and thus as political.

8. Kelly 1998 presents a devastating critique of the power differentials reproduced by social scientists' fascination with and misrepresentations of African American urban life in the United States.

9. Rubim and Barbalho 2007 offer a historical introduction to this attempted democratization of cultural policy under the Workers Party (PT). Marilena Chaui, a theorist within the PT and one of the most innovative critics of Brazilian cultural policy, analyzes these measures' continuing subservience to capital (2006) from a position within the Party. At the center of the new policies developed under the PT lies a concern with so-called intangible or immaterial cultural property, or the sorts of folkloric, everyday practices associated with orality and working-class and minority communities. This curiously named resource was first introduced into Brazilian legislation with Decree 3.551 of August 2000 as "knowledges," "forms of expression," "celebrations," and "places," and in 2006 Brazil ratified UNESCO's 2003 Convention for the Safeguarding of Immaterial Patrimony. Attention to this more labile category of heritage, which supplemented the existing "natural" and "cultural" heritage designations (Collins 2011b; Silverman and Ruggles 2007; Smith

and Akagawa 2009), exemplifies a growing concern in Brazil with multicultural inclusion, and thus with a more clearly anthropological, processual, and historicized approach that focuses not simply on monuments or individuals but also on landscapes and "living traditions" (Cavalcanti and Fonseca 2008).

10. This approach is indebted to Stoler's (1997; see also 1995) insights into the extent to which modern accounts of race and racisms both make up and rest on malleable and extremely convincing types of truth claims. Such "racial histories and their regimes of truth" are typically dependent on a redemptive story of overcoming racial and racist flaws that are so often associated with historical mistakes or ancestors, as well as those citizens in the present who lack enlightenment, but that "we" as enlightened moderns might overcome through some rational excavation of origins and relationships of cause and effect. Stoler emphasizes the importance of looking instead at the very explanations for, and uses of, racial discourse—including triumphant narratives of overcoming—put forth in the often social scientifically authorized production of knowledge and class-based claims to rationality so much a part of public sphere debates about racisms. And she suggests that standard ways of seeking to overcome racialized exclusion may play a role in configuring "interpretive space" between the "'seen' and the 'unseen'" (1997, 187), or a semiotic relationship and a definition of race that rests in the gap between that which is visible and those human qualities or baskets of attributes that somehow become attached to visible marks of difference. Across this book I am interested in how distinct manipulations of memory and pastness (as well as futurity) may encourage institutional and popular historicizations of the links between the visible and invisible. Bendix 2009 is one of the few commentators on the patrimonialization process who has begun to link perception and semiotic arrangements to particular political economic forms.

11. As Hale contends in relation to the politics of indigeneity in Guatemala, "the rise of official multiculturalism, paradoxically enough, has made racial hierarchy more resilient" (2006, 210). Rahier 2013 makes a similar point about the continuation under neoliberalism of long-standing sources of discrimination against Afro-Ecuadoreans. The record in Brazil under the PT is more mixed (Ansell 2013). While some commentators suggest Latin America is somehow post-neoliberal, I read the Brazilian state's multicultural and redistributive work as a complex entailment of neoliberalism whereby the politics of identity and the state's alleged attention to cultural difference are basic components of attempts at the political economic disempowerment of precisely those communities targeted by multiculturalist discourse. My claim emanates in part from the observation that neoliberalism is characterized not simply by some bald retreat of the state in favor of the market, but also by complex realignments in its structures and means of funding citizens' initiatives put in place around attempts to monetize novel areas of social life (Collins 2008b). Thus spiraling investments in culture put together with an eye toward market returns are, rather than the education of consent or the consolidation of the national-popular around patriotic fervor, an important facet of shifting approaches to capitalism that I continue to refer to as "neoliberal" and that continue to be tied to multicultural initiatives in Brazil. This is not to discount the social gains and political reforms wrought since Lula's election, but it is to take seriously Cardoso's

(1998) analysis of the contradictions of Left politics in a Brazil facing a world evermore blanketed by market logics as well as leftist governments' ongoing, if troubled, engagements with neoliberal policy (Navia 2009).

12. I understand the Northeast's "Regionalists"—a group that includes Godofredo Filho and Bahian novelists like Jorge Amado—as geographically specific participants in the Brazilian modernist movement. For some of the most influential pronouncements and analyses of this regionalism by Brazil's best-known midcentury intellectual and a leader of the movement, see especially Freyre 1942, 1952.

13. Tavares 1961, 131. On the creation of IPHAN (Instituto do Patrimonio Historico e Artistico Nacional), or the National Artistic and Historical Patrimony Institute—originally SPHAN—in relation to modernist initiatives, see especially chapter 3 below as well as Arantes 2007, Bomeny 1995, Castro 1991, Gonçalves 2003, and Williams 2001.

14. By the 1920s the Pelourinho and Bahia had been consecrated as historical sources of blackness for the nation. This would become even more the case with the initial publication in 1933 of Gilberto Freyre's *The Masters and the Slaves* (1986), which drew on Bahian sources and discussions of planter families resident in Salvador for the author's influential claims about the colonial household as a site of the formative, sexual encounters between Portuguese planters and nonwhite women that would give rise to a modern Brazil that avoided the black/white polarities of the United States. Freyre's arguments found support in *O negro na Bahia* (The Negro in Bahia), published in 1946 by his Bahian interlocutor, Luiz Vianna Filho. Santos Silva 2000 provides a historical overview of the ongoing construction of Bahia as a source of African traditions during the 1930s and 1940s. Yet this early-to mid-twentieth-century linkage of Salvador's downtown and a Bahian people to Africa and blackness—terms I do not take as covalent, but whose careful consideration would require research directed specifically at that task (Matory 2005; Dawson 2014)—was not without precedent: Bahia's "African" character had already been discussed at length in a variety of contexts, including Luís dos Santos Vilhena's letters to Portugal from the final years of the eighteenth century (Amaral and Carneiro 1969), the nascent anthropology of Raymundo Nina Rodrigues and his disciples, and in foreign travelers' descriptions of the city of Salvador (Corrêa 1998). Among Rodrigues' most interesting—if contradictory and traumatic due to the extent to which the mixed-race Rodrigues struggled brilliantly to explain a "backwardness" attributed to black Brazilians—are *Os Africanos no Brasil* (The Africas in Brazil); *As Raças humanas e a responsabilidade penal no Brasil* (Human Races and Penal Responsibility in Brazil); *O animismo fetichista dos negros baianos* (The Fetishistic Animism of Black Bahians); and *As coletividades anormais* (Abnormal Collectivities). These last three texts were edited and published posthumously during the 1930s, the period of nation-building during which issues of race character were re-elaborated into a regenerative example of Brazilian exceptionalism. Schwarcz 1999 offers the most nuanced reading of this process available in either English or Portuguese.

15. This letter of January 14, 1927, has been published in Andrade, Bandeira, and Morães 2000, 332. All translations from Portuguese across this book, unless otherwise noted, are my own. All names of people other than state officials or public

figures have been altered to protect identities. Furthermore, as a means of fending off the possible use of this text to persecute or regulate members of the Pelourinho community, I hereby declare that, for reasons of privacy in but a few cases, I have slightly altered certain minor events and persons in order to render them fictitious to the hostile reader. Nonetheless, this strategy should not be understood as impacting significantly the truth-values or accuracy of my ethnography and the events it narrates. In fact, my approach to statements that some might claim as evidence in attempts to malign the people who appear in these pages, but which I here declare to be untrustworthy for such purposes, may very well increase their fidelity to what I understand to have taken place in a variety of instances. Should the declarations in this note confuse the reader, I suggest that he or she look immediately at the sections of the preface and chapter 6 that discuss what is known in Brazil as *malandragem*.

16. Caldwell 2007; Goldstein 2003; Guimarães 2001, 2007; Telles 2004; Twine 1998. Perry 2013 focuses on black women's lives, social exclusion, and the importance of local political associations in Gamboa, a neighborhood that, while not officially part of Salvador's Historical Center, lies near, and is linked historically to, the Maciel/Pelourinho.

17. Da Matta 1997, 60. Racial democracy, or ideas that have been dubbed "racial democratic" (Guimarães 2002) only in retrospect, has been treated as a myth (Bastide and Fernandes 1955); as an ideology related to slavery (Fernandes 1965); a form of political participation when described as an "ethnic democracy" (Freyre 1963); a mark of a Brazilian creativity or exceptionalism (Freyre 1986; Fry 1995); a subordination of race to class (Harris 1956; Wagley 1952); and an unfulfilled desire, or dream, and thus as an expression of a "lack" or "silence" (Bailey 2009; Hanchard 1994; Sheriff 2001) around race in Brazil.

18. Guimarães 2002 offers a nuanced genealogy of "racial democracy" in relation to Gilberto Freyre and his contemporaries. Burke and Pallares-Burke 2008 offer a detailed contextualization in English of Freyre's oeuvre.

19. In an example of the confusion of houses and women I will explore in chapter 3, Freyre uses the gerund form of the verb *trepar*, which means to climb, to wind around, or to engage in sexual relations.

20. Manuel Bandeira edited and published in the Rio de Janeiro newspaper *A Manhã* on September 10, 1944, Freyre's 1926 poem. Bandeira then included it in his *Antologia de Poetas Brasileiros Bissextos*, published in 1946.

21. In referring to Freyre's thesis in *The Masters and the Slaves* as a "whitening," I am relying on a historical shorthand that obscures the many shifts in the discourses glossed as "racial democracy" or a bundle of claims historicized by scholars such as Lesser 1999, Schwarcz 1999, and Skidmore 1974.

22. Skidmore 1974.

23. Agier 1995, 251.

24. On histories of the nation-state as moral narratives of becoming, see especially White 1980.

25. I employ Wallerstein's term "peoplehood" (1991) to underscore the important role of the Bahian state in actively producing a Bahian populace, or people, as part of shifting class relations that attend to shifts in global political economy.

26. The term "new world in the tropics" comes from Freyre 1969 and his argument that Brazil gained its strength, and novelty, from the "tropical" race mixture that emerged from the plantation and its particularly promiscuous mixtures of races, tastes, smells, and cultures.

27. See the debate between Bourdieu and Wacquant 1999, French 2000, 2003, and Hanchard 2003 over contemporary imperial formations, academic research, its funding by U.S. foundations, and race relations in Brazil.

28. Santos, Kent, and Gaspar Neto 2014, 38. For an impassioned defense of Brazil's specificity in race relations by a respected foreign anthropologist who has long added to debates in Brazil, and a Brazilian "creative" racial exceptionalism by a Bahian intellectual who has long served as one of the state's most insightful cultural critics and intellectual historians, see Fry 2005 and Risério 2007, respectively. Fry, Maggie, Chor Maio, Monteiro, and Ventura Santos 2007 offer an edited collection in which a number of prominent social scientists express their opposition to or doubts about the paths taken in recent attempts to alter racial politics in Brazil, including the quota system established in public universities beginning at the end of the 1990s. For rather different perspectives on recent changes from religious, social movement, and racial quota arenas, see especially Burdick 2013, Caldwell 2007, and Cicalo 2012, respectively.

29. Nogueira 1985, 78–79. See also Nogueira 1954.

30. Sansone 2003; Harris' statements about reference appear in 1970, 2.

31. Keane 2003, 2007 develops the term "semiotic ideology" in relation to recent work on "linguistic ideologies," or the presuppositions that govern how communicative utterances signify. The concept is helpful for unraveling the ways that different types of signs combine in producing what Latour 1993 refers to as "hybrids," as well as the ways that the nested relations between sign vehicles, their interpretants, and their objects or referents (Peirce 1955a) demonstrate rather different engagements with the materiality of the world represented, as well as the signifying process itself. This approach is consistent with Daniel's (1996) discussion of "dispositions to the past," or the ways that actors and interpreters face the past as an often-embodied, materialized semiotic braiding through which the specific forms taken by signs, or objectifications and representations of some object in relation to an interpretation, implicate in turn the pragmatic effects of such recollections. On this, see also the introduction and chapter 7 of Collins 2003. Such labile conceptualization of the distinct as well as complementary ways that different types of communicative vehicles—or "signs" or "symbols" in common anthropological parlance—engage one another, interpreters, and the world they represent makes Peirce's semiotic helpful in getting at the levels of cultural engagement produced by "natives" as well as the ethnographers who would seek to represent them. Appadurai 1981 addresses history and heritage to develop some of the same issues with respect to an invention and reliance on history in the present, albeit without the language and resultant sharpness of Peircean semiotics.

32. Agha 2007. My approach to the processes through which additional semiotic attachments come to specify meanings in new ways relies rather heavily on a recognition of the play of what Peirce called "qualisigns," or signs and material qualities

whose interpretations are still largely undetermined but nonetheless potentially impacted by the materiality of the sign vehicle. Manning 2008, 2012 and Munn 1986 offer especially rich ethnographic accounts of the workings of qualisigns while Parmentier 2014 offers a more conceptual outline of the influence on communication of such nonarbitrary signs Peirce referred to as "degenerate."

33. Alvarez 1989; Burdick 1998; Caldeira 2006; Cunha 1998; Rubin 2004.

34. Hacking 1999.

35. Hartigan 1999.

36. As Agha 2011 puts it, "A figure of personhood once abstracted from performance as a generic symbol may be subjected to various forms of decontextualized depiction" (173).

37. Daniel (1984, 1–58) offers what remains the clearest, most beautiful, and concise entrée into Peirce's theory, and use, of signs in a manner that expands significantly the Saussurean 1998 emphasis on arbitrary meaning.

38. Stoler 2002, 2009.

39. Stoler 2009, 33; see Feldman 2008 on filing systems.

40. Hull 2012, 13

41. Stoler 2009, 32.

42. This approach to what Stoler calls an "ethnography of the archives" (2002) is indebted to the anthropologists and historians who look closely at manipulations of documents (Feldman 2008; Hull 2012; Riles 2001; Weld 2014) and the impact of their material status on what has not yet transpired (Strassler 2008).

43. Burns 2010 focuses on the ways colonial notaries' ventriloquizations, and alteration of the voices, of their clients in colonial Peru generated a mass of concerns and discourse around archival practice. Strassler 2010 joins contemporary Indonesians' concerns about documentary evidence to photography to illustrate the importance of a "culture of documentation" to attempts to achieve modernity. Kjoster 2014 explores related concerns with archives around identification cards in northeastern Brazil today, and Cody 2009 suggests that lower-caste women's work in petitioning Indian government officials constituted a similar space of worries about full inclusion in the nation and the manipulation of the material and symbolic properties of documentary and self-referential media.

44. The delineation of the Pelourinho as a historical center alongside the painstaking manipulation of residents' lives recalls Foucault's attention to "biopolitics," or a form of power based on the regulation of a population through the delineation of biological processes, and thus to Agamben's interest in the "spaces of exception" and separations of biological and social life around which he argues that sovereignty and law are produced in modern states (1998, 1999). But my experiences in the Pelourinho leave me troubled by Agamben's sharply delineated, and relatively simplistic, bracketings of people in space and time: While the salience of modern concerns with sacred scapegoats and the shoring up of the norm through the exclusion of those who are rendered exceptional means that his approaches influence my arguments about the Pelourinho as chronotope and camp, they do not offer solid purchase on the ethnographic experiences that gird this book.

45. Araújo Pinho 2001; Butler 1998a; Gomes and Fernandes 1995; Nobre 2002;

Perry 2013; Rodrigues 1995; Rojas 1999; Sansone 1995; Saule Júnior and Menezes 2005; Williams 2013.

46. Lévy 1986; also Sansone 2001.

47. On Bahia's global interconnectedness from the seventeenth to the nineteenth centuries, see especially Verger 1976. The scholarly and popular literature on the Pelourinho is enormous. Three twentieth-century discussions of the neighborhood whose authors played important roles in the development of Bahian approaches to urban space and regional culture are Santos 1959, Simas Filho 1998, and Azevedo 1969. Santos was an influential geographer whose arguments that the decadent, mid-twentieth-century Pelourinho should be read as an effect of Bahian spatial relations that responded to the region's shifting historical role in the world economy would come to influence the arguments, which I examine in chapter 3, that IPAC deployed in working to gain control over the Pelourinho at the expense of representatives of the Catholic Church and the Bahian police forces. Simas Filho was the former director of the Bahian office of IPHAN and a member of the group of influential midcentury Bahian planners put together by Mário Leal Ferreira, whose ideas would be reappropriated by Antonio Carlos Magalhães from the 1970s through the present, as discussed in chapter 5. Azevedo was a critical figure in the development of Bahian anthropology, the former university teacher of many IPAC bureaucrats, and a collaborator with the international group of social scientists, especially Charles Wagley and Marvin Harris, who traveled to Bahia as part of the post–World War II UNESCO-sponsored investigation of Brazilian race relations (Chor Maio 1999). Azevedo's son, the architect Paulo Ormindo de Azevedo, served as the director of IPAC in the 1980s, and his daughter, Maria Brandão, directed Salvador's municipal planning organ (SEPLAM) in the early 1990s. In a further example of the close links among the people influential in Bahian urbanism and cultural policies of at least the last sixty years, see Filho (2007, 100) for a description of Thales and Paulo Azevedo's visit to Godofredo Filho's home for lunch in 1963.

48. Schwartz 1985 reports that Brazil's share of the world's sugar production declined from about one third to less than 10 percent in 1787. Although Bahian cane producers took advantage of the Haitian Revolution and expanded production at the very end of the eighteenth century and first decades of the nineteenth, Bahia's eighteenth-century preeminence in tropical commodities would never again be equaled as the Caribbean, and especially Cuba, came to lead the worldwide production of sugar.

49. The designation "white men" is, like all identity categories, relational: as Azevedo 1975 and Wagley 1952 have pointed out, to be "white" in Bahia—Brazil's "blackest" state—is not necessarily to be considered "white" elsewhere, as indicated by the term brancos da Bahia (Bahian whites). Yet I gloss the upper-class bohemians who once frequented the Pelourinho as white because this is how Pelourinho residents describe them. Their social position makes them white, even if many would not necessarily be considered white in São Paulo or New York. For a fascinating glimpse at the relationality of claims to whiteness from a Bahian/North American comparative perspective, see Landes 1994 for an account of her discussions of segregation in the United States with the Bahian intellectual Edson Carneiro. And for the discussion

of how interclass and interracial sexual relations supported elite men's claims to engagement with the "people" in Venezuela, which has influenced my understanding of *mestiçagem* in the Pelourinho, see Skurski 1994.

50. The 1980s are frequently referred to as a time of "re-africanization" (Risério 1980) of Bahia. Throughout Brazil, an awakening from twenty years of military rule generated an enormous upsurge in race-based identification as part of a generalized identity politics, frequently conducted around NGOs. On race relations and the key roles of the Black Movement in this period, see especially Alberto 2011, Covin 2006, and the overview in Hanchard 1999. On the roles of Olodum and other Pelourinho-based *blocos afros* in this period, see Dantas 1994, Perrone 1992, Rodrigues 1995, 1996, and Williamson 2011. Guimarães 1987 analyzes the effects on Bahian class relations of regional development efforts under the military dictatorship, an important dynamic in Bahia's racial transformations today due to the expansion of the petrochemical industry in the 1970s and 1980s. This helped form an Afro-descendent industrial working class in Salvador at a moment of intense migration from rural Bahia.

51. My estimates speak to what I define as the "Pelourinho," or the downtown region extending from the Ladeira da Praca to the Convento do Carmo. This geographical unit does not conform exactly to either the "Centro Histórico de Salvador" (Historical Center of Salvador) delineated by IPHAN in 1984; to the "Área de Proteção Rigorosa" (Area of Rigorous Protection) established by municipal law 3,298 of 1983; or the "Centro Antigo de Salvador" (Old City of Salvador), a term increasingly employed today to refer to the downtown region—including the docks in the Lower City—surrounding the Centro Antigo de Salvador and contemplated for cultural tourism-based development (Superintêndencia de Estudos Económicos e Sociais da Bahia 2013). It is instead a geographical and temporal unit that conforms to the ways residents of the colonial center carve up the various neighborhoods in downtown Salvador. And my estimate of the number of people who remain is a synthesis of experiential perceptions and a careful, house-by-house, mapping of the region in 1995, 1999, and again in 2009. Yet these numbers fluctuate widely in relation to the historical moment and the definition of the historical center's borders. See also Nobre 2002 and Zancheti and Gabriel 2010, an IDB document whose statistics conform rather closely to my own.

52. Brown 2003; Handler 1985, 1991; MacPherson 1964. On some of the varying ways cultural property structures a variety of political engagements, see especially Collins 2011b, Coombe 2011, Di Giovine 2009, Ferry 2005, Franquesa 2013, Reddy 2006, and Silverman and Ruggles 2007.

53. Abu El-Haj 2001; Lomnitz 2001; Verdery 1999.

54. MacCannell 1999.

55. Kirschenblatt-Gimblett 2004; Urban 2001.

56. Garber 1991, 10.

57. Brumann's work on Kyoto, Japan (2013, 2014) is a salient example of the argument that heritage need not be seen as some simulacrum or imposition, but works instead as a practice that makes sense alongside, and is integrated into, the lifeways of a particular community. A slightly different argument, in which heritage management is productive in the sense of inspiring further articulations and programs

in relation to its strictures and forms of subjectification and objectification, girds this book, Collins 2014, and Kirschenblatt-Gimblett 2006.

58. Adorno 2002, 15.

59. Heidegger 1993a, 1993b.

60. Handler 1985, 208.

61. Bunten 2008; Comaroff and Comaroff 2009; DeHart 2010; Vanthuyne 2009.

62. Foucault 1991.

63. Foucault 1990, 137. See also Alencar 1999 and Biehl 2009 in relation to the Pelourinho.

64. Sommer 1991, 6.

65. The "mansions and the shanties" and the "big house and the slave quarters" are the titles of Freyre 1963, 1986.

66. Rose 2007, 40.

67. Petryna 2002; Rapp, Heath, and Taussig 2003; Redfield 2013; Rose 2007.

68. Fassin 2009, 49.

69. Santos, Kent, and Gaspar Neto 2014, 53.

70. Weffort and Souza 1998 discuss this reversal of temporalities in their coffee-table volume produced by the Ministry of Culture. See also the remarks by Minister of Culture Francisco Weffort at the meeting of the World Bank in New Orleans in 1998, posted at www.iadb.org (last accessed November 21, 2004). Gonçalves 2003 outlines a longer Brazilian history of fears about the "loss" of patrimony.

71. On the construction of Brasilia, see especially Holston 1989, and for an official statement of the Cardoso administration's federal cultural policy support of the historical reconstruction of urban spaces, see Weffort and Souza 1998. Bernardes Ribeiro 2005 describes Brasilia's recent patrimonialization around a novel approach that preserves its architectural relationships, or scale, but not necessarily buildings.

72. Da Costa 2010a, 2010b; Dent 2009; Mattos and Abreu 2011; Perry 2004.

73. Dayan 1995, 36.

74. Bastide 1978, 2001; Della Cava 1970; Slater 1986.

75. Rancière 2010.

76. McGranahan 2010 refers to something similar, but differently configured in Tibet and its diaspora, as "historical arrest."

Chapter 1

1. Perhaps unsurprisingly, the Instituto Antonio Carlos Magalhães, or the private foundation begun after "Governor" Magalhães' death, turns "ACM" into "Ação, Cidadania, e Memória," or "Action, Citizenship, and Memory." It is headquartered at number 2 Rua Saldanha da Gama Street—just down from Malaquias' former home located at number 18 on the same street. See http://www.institutoacm.com.br/ (last accessed July 2014).

2. Salvador's current cathedral is the former church of the Jesuit Order, expelled from the Portuguese Americas during the Pombaline reforms designed to consolidate Portuguese imperial control during the latter half of the eighteenth century. The transfer of Salvador's cathedral was necessary because, in a process described in greater length in chapter 5, authorities tore down the city's and Brazil's first

cathedral, the Igreja da Sé, in 1933 as part of a modernizing reform movement. Baianas do acarajé are women who, dressed in white lace clothing reminiscent of ritual garb associated with Candomblé, sell blackeyed-pea fritters on street corners across Salvador.

3. See Herron 2003 for a related process involving government bankers' evaluations of peasants' loan applications, and self-presentation, in rural Colombia.

4. The literature on, as well as popular attention to, Brazil's "street children" is enormous and often contentious. As he recounts in *Tristes Tropiques*, none other than the ethnologist Claude Lévi-Strauss found himself detained by authorities in Salvador in 1936 when, after being approached by a group of "urchins" upon arrival on the city's docks, he took a photograph of them. This led the Estado Novo's police officers to claim that a photograph of black children in rags would besmirch Brazil's reputation. Lévi-Strauss thus found himself marched to the same Delegacia de Jogos e Costumes (Customs and Gaming, or "Vice" Squad) that regulated prostitution and entertainment in the mid-twentieth-century Pelourinho. One year later, the Bahian novelist Jorge Amado would fictionalize in his novel *Capitães da Areia* (Captains of the Sand) the lives of children who circulated across downtown Salvador begging, rummaging through garbage, performing small tasks for change, and at times involving themselves in petty crime. During the 1970s, a time of military dictatorship, authorities came to configure street children as a major problem in rapidly urbanizing cities. Hector Babenco's film *Pixote* (1981) depicts the growing brutality of the state response during this period, a reaction that would culminate, and begin to be reined in, with the murder by military policemen of eight street children asleep on the steps or Rio's Candelária Cathedral in 1993. For a consideration of the ongoing effects across social strata of this violence meted out by society and the state against homeless and wayward children, see Jose Padilha's 2002 film *Ônibus 174* (Bus 174), which draws on a hostage crisis perpetrated by one of the survivors of the Candelária massacre in order to unwrap layers of neglect and explore knowledge claims about street children and social inequality in urban Brazil.

5. Bahia, like all Brazilian states, has two main police forces: the Military Police, or Polícia Militar (PM), who are charged with "ostentatious" (*ostensivo*) or visible, repressive policing, and the feared Civil Police (Polícia Civil) who, like detectives in the United States, work in street clothes and investigate crimes and amass evidence to which the PM responds initially. The PM also relies on a number of specialized units, including Special Companies (*Companhias Especiais*) and the Shock (*Choque*) Battalion. Both are specialized units feared due to their status as types of SWAT units, and what my interlocutors describe as skilled death squads (Collins 2014).

6. Malinowski 1984, 4. This defaced perch from which I begin recounting my fieldwork endeavor and relationship to Pelourinho politics leans on Adorno's (1981) concept of negative dialectics, or a tension between necessity and contingency that suggests that history is not a spirited unfolding, as Hegel would have it, but an incomplete and bewildering play whose recognition requires not only negation, but also the attempt to read negation and objectification productively.

7. My approach to love's entailments, and obligations, is indebted to Barthes 2010, among others.

8. Today's pagode is a highly sexualized form of samba performed throughout Brazil, but dominated by Bahian musicians, that is influenced by an earlier, more traditional, and similarly named "pagode." This older form arose in working-class Rio de Janeiro as musicians sought to recuperate aspects of the samba sound, and dancing, that had come to be neglected in a city in which samba was increasingly confined to carnival, or the subgenre known as *samba de enredo*. For a discussion of the rise of the Rio-based pagode that influenced Bahian musicians, who in turn put together from the 1990s onward the sort of sound, and sexualized spectacle, offered by É o Tchan and decried by intellectuals, see Galinsky 1996 and Moehn 2012.

9. The name "timbalada" describes Brown's mass of drummers organized around players of the *timbau*, a large drum used in samba and somewhat reminiscent of the conga drums used in hispanophone Caribbean music.

10. At the end of the twentieth century, approximately 500,000 Brazilian students were enrolled at 148 campuses spread across 47 different public universities. From 2000 to 2012, however, the PT-led government established 18 new federal universities and the number of public campuses across Brazil grew to 321. Abreu 2010 provides a concise discussion of this expansion, and democratization, of higher education in a nation in which a majority of coveted spaces in the elite federal university system have been occupied historically by privileged students from private high schools. See Teles dos Santos 2013 for a Ford Foundation–sponsored overview of Brazil's growing, and innovative, class and ethnoracial affirmative action systems in public universities.

11. Da Matta 1991b, in an inversion of arguments emanating from Europe or the United States, argues that the domestic sphere functions in Brazil as the proper place of friendship, politics, and moral intercourse between citizens. Lauderdale Graham 1992 modifies this formulation by focusing on domestic servants, and thus the class and gender-specific nature of Da Matta's claims. See also Goldstein 2005.

12. Rama 1996, as part of his well-known consideration of urban form and literacy in Latin American nationhood, analyzes the role of Atlantic port cities' fading colonial downtown precincts in the gendered interactions between upper-class men and nonwhite women critical to the development of a particularly Latin American intimate public sphere, a process retold in the first person in Gabriel García Márquez's novella *Memories of My Melancholy Whores* (2006).

13. Throughout this book I will switch between the terms "Maciel," "Maciel/Pelourinho," "Pelourinho," and "Historical Center" in relation to the intent and context from which I make reference to the areas of downtown Salvador currently undergoing patrimonialization. I lean on the word "Maciel" to emphasize a previous moment, when the region was primarily a red light district. I employ "Historical Center" or "Pelourinho" to refer to a defined territory contemplated for, or undergoing, a transformation into an anachronistic space for leisure and patriotic identification around cultural heritage. Use of "Maciel/Pelourinho" represents a midpoint in time in this process, or the neighborhood's contradictory status as both an exalted historical center and a maligned space associated with illicit or denigrated forms of sexuality.

14. Dona Valmira said, "Aqui eu me criei, aquie eu dei cria, aqui eu o." See Jean Wyllys 1997.

15. Dona Valmira and her neighbor Dona Célia once described to me with great pride the elaborate means of, and architecture for, preserving the honor of women who worked in certain of the Pelourinho's better-run bawdy establishments. Principal among these were a number of cabarets in which a visible, male orchestra performed while women danced behind a screen so that only their profiles could be seen by audiences.

16. Bahian intellectuals typically agree with Dona Valmira's assessment of pagode's immorality, or tastelessness; Bahian sociologist and communications theorist Milton Moura claims, "Pagode lyrics and choreography often associate being black and Bahian with sexual innuendo and sensual dancing" and these "repertoires . . . set the standard by which young people . . . display their sensuality in public" (2002, 170).

17. The range and nature of transactional and commodified sexual relations in Bahia is quite broad. Kottak 2000 details the activities of women known as *raparigas*, or those single women, often in peripheral neighborhoods or the countryside, who trade sexual favors for goods on an informal basis with a limited array of sexual partners. Williams 2013 provides a sensitive and yet troubling portrait of the more fully monetized affective and sexual relations between foreigners and Bahians in the Pelourinho, something that Mitchell 2011 explores in relation to homosexual male sex tourists and the Bahians with whom they interact.

18. The designation "Mala" is more than a shortening of the name "Malaquias" since the Portuguese *mala*, or "suitcase," is a slang term used across Salvador to refer to someone who, as in the expression "drag" in English, needs to be carted around in a way that weighs on his or her companions and interactions.

19. "Eu posso ser gago, canhoto, banguelo, analfabeto e preto, mas eu levo qualquer um na gaiva." This conversation is based on my field notes written after Malaquias' return to the Gueto. Transcriptions, here and throughout this book, are thus often subject to the vagaries of my memory. I nonetheless believe they are accurate portrayals of the language used and sentiments expressed at the moment. I include the Portuguese snippets as I remember/have them written down so as to express better the nuances of the speech reported here. My depictions of Malaquias' stuttering are therefore substantially flawed, but I include them here as a means of emphasizing his own self-image as a *guerreiro*, or warrior, who uses to his advantage aspects of his person that others may portray as shortcomings. In fact, this strategy was something that Malaquias has made explicit to me throughout our friendship and encouraged me vociferously to make a part of my own everyday practices.

20. Rede Globo, founded by media magnate Roberto Marinho and directed today by his son, is Brazil's largest television conglomerate and, according to Globo itself, the world's fourth-most-watched network. Globo is regularly recognized as capable of making and destroying presidents, and is the single most powerful political force in Brazil. See http://redeglobo.globo.com/ (last accessed December 2013).

21. What he said in Portuguese was, "Você é teleguiado pelo diabo, rapaz! Todo mundo de olho duro no rabo da loira remexendo frente a Casa de Jorge Amado.

Pessoal me viu. Bati com Mundinho e o descarado me chamou de sanduiche humano. 'Que porra tá fazendo aqui, sanduiche humano?' Vá se catar, rapaz. A próxima vez é Augusto quem vai. E Gula, fala pra esse Edinho de Zilton pra se ajeitar, tô de saco cheio da politicagem dele."

22. The word "Babylon" is the Rastafarian designation for anything evil and sinful, in this case the sexualized dancing of Carla Perez and, it seems, by extension, the crowd on the Pelourinho Square that ignores Malaquias.

23. The word I translate as "politricks" is *politicagem*. Jean Jackson 2002 has discussed the use of the Spanish term *politicaje* in analogous situations by leaders of Colombia's indigenous movement. I cannot comment with any authority here on the diffusion of "politricks" as a description of patron-client politics, the rise and influence of NGOs, or double-dealings in Latin America, although a variety of travelers, politicians, members of NGOs and even song lyrics and statements by the Jamaican musician Peter Tosh might be pointed to as sources for international crossfertilizations between Colombia, the Caribbean, and Brazil and between black liberation and indigenous rights movements. In 2001, in an example of such exchanges, Malaquias, Pepeta, and I met the head of Cimarrón, one of the Colombian Black Movement's most important groups, at an event attended also by Bahian historian João Reis and North American anthropologist Sheila Walker. Malaquias' use of the term politicagem, as well as the juxtaposition of community leaders, Pelourinho residents, and North American and Brazilian intellectuals, gestures at a global ecumene constituted in relation to the culture concept that is increasingly influential in political economy.

24. The word *axé*, which derives from Afro-Brazilian religion and refers to a spirit or force, has come to describe a Bahian musical genre, extremely popular during carnival, that mixes heavy metal guitars with Spanish-speaking Caribbean rhythms and percussion.

25. Despite claims by the messenger/street child Avisa-lá, Brazil's most important television network, Rede Globo, was not filming the ersatz philanthropic event. Rather, a private film crew was busily capturing the action for the benefit of the organizers.

26. Katia Borges, "Ação Duvidosa," *A Tarde*, January 14, 1998. For media coverage lauding the event before the discovery of the organizers' deception, see "Estrelas fazem festa no Pelô em favor dos jovens carentes," *A Tarde*, January 7, 1998.

27. Here I transpose Judith Butler's (2004) concern with dispossession and affect as fonts for a reconceptualization of subjectivity, and ethical belonging, for imperial citizens into a broader concern with dispossession as a way of making do on the part of less-clearly empowered subjects such as the inhabitants of Salvador's Pelourinho.

28. Among the most active of these groups in or near the city center were Projeto Axé, Grupo Orla, the Pelourinho Clube das Mães, the Escola Criativa Olodum, the Sociedade Beneficiente Conceição Macedo, and Ibêji, together with state and municipal programs like "Cidade Mãe."

29. Herzfeld 1993.

30. The discourse of "marginality," or those excluded from proper social relations and thus known in Bahia as *bichos soltos* (wild or "escaped" animals) and open to

extermination, is remarkably powerful across Brazil, and especially Salvador. On this sense of marginality, see especially Wacquant 2008 and Huggins and Mesquita 2000.

31. Ethnographies of this part of the Pelourinho, and its inhabitants, include Kulick 1998, Motta and Cerqueira 1997, and Oliveira 1994. In his sensitive ethnography conducted on and around the Rua São Francisco, Kulick argues that the English translation "transvestite" misrepresents the extent to which Bahian travestis, given their investment in attracting male desire, perform an identity that turns on sexual desire rather than the argument that they are somehow men trapped in women's bodies, and thus miscategorized. This assertion, which blurs the lines between sexuality and gender, highlights the Bahian emphasis on practices, rather than a recourse to or expression of some already-existing, essentialized, internal self, as definitive of identity.

32. Blood, a substance apparently shared by all people and, at least in the United States, connotative of descent and corporate groups, is a powerful material in Bahia. There it plays a critical role in Candomblé offerings, and thus the efficacy of magic and religion, as well as everyday cuisine. For an analysis of how ideas about "good blood" (sangue bom) factored into debates about race in the Rio of the early 1990s, see Sheriff 2001. For an analysis of blood, descent, and ideas about tradition in Bahia in the late 1990s and first decade of the new millennium, see the chapters that follow.

33. Alencar 1999; Biehl 2009.

34. Dandinha and a number of his neighbors claim that Magalhães was bisexual and was involved in secret affairs with his bodyguards, all understood by these residents as hypermasculine, violent, current or former, military policemen. This speculation about the sexuality of the leader of Bahia emphasizes the extent to which issues related to gender and sexual moralities are central to debates in the Pelourinho around national history and politics. It also suggests how secrecy, and its supposed exposure, plays a role in making the Pelourinho meaningful.

35. Sifuentes-Jáuregeui 2002, 129.

36. Although I find the literature on transvestitism, particularly the work of Sifuentes-Jáuregeui 2002, helpful in thinking through Dandinha's performative laying bare of the illegitimacy of claims to naturalness of the original, as well as claims about authenticity in cultural heritage more generally, I follow Kulick (1998) in using the term "travesti" to differentiate the community of crossdressing, biological males in the Pelourinho from "transvestites" around the world. According to Kulick in Travesti, biological males in the Pelourinho who dress as women, alter their bodies with silicone, and desire men but do not however wish to become women or make claims about attuning outward appearances and ostensibly "true" interior or hidden identities, construct themselves as a third gender.

37. Keane 2005.

38. The Bahian artist Daniel Lisboa's Projeto Figuraça, an attempt to produce a "catalogue" of well-known Bahian figuras, is an example of the widespread currency of the concept in Salvador today. See http://gracc-ucsal.blogspot.com (last accessed June 2014).

39. Telles 1992.

40. Collins 2011a; Kottak 2000; Mafra 2011. Plotkin 2011 provides an important historical correlate, and potential corrective, to claims about Brazilian popular resistance to psychologizing techniques by emphasizing the extent to which mid-twentieth-century social scientists viewed psychoanalysis as a part of a "toolbox" that might serve "a large primitive population whose unconscious was supposedly located more on the surface than that of urban civilized European people" (2011, 129).

41. Auerbach 1984.

42. Officially designated the "Parque Histórico do Pelourinho" by Mayor Mário Kertesz's decree number 7,849 of September 4, 1987. See Santos 1959 for a discussion of notions of urban centrality and physical reform in postwar Salvador. Bomfim 1994, Carvalho Neto 1991, and Simas Filho 1977 provide analyses of the historical center's changing boundaries since the 1960s.

43. The newspaper *A Tarde* reported on December 20, 1932, that the police chief Tancredo Teixeira had supervised the transfer of prostitutes to the area from surrounding blocks and that he had gone so far as to negotiate with the owners of their previous residences so that the women could break their leases!

44. While R$97 million was, in 1993, approximately US$100 million, today it is worth about US$30 million.

45. Caldeira and Holston 2005.

46. Navaro-Yashin 2012, 6–8.

47. Agnew's (1986) study of the concomitant rise of Elizabethan markets and theater, and thus of means of representing the world and its values, underscores the importance of clarifying the epistemological and political economic structures that gird major shifts in modes of interpretation, or what Rancière 2010 refers to as "dissensus."

48. Performing one's identity for another, or "being ourselves for you" (Stanley 1998) as a part of a government or sovereign group's political economic programs, is an important part of "immaterial" or cultural labor today (Collins 2003; Comaroff and Comaroff 2009). Elyachar 2005 ties together the performance of self and the commodification of everyday life in her study of informal labor markets in Cairo in an ethnography that I interpret as an argument about the transformation and colonization of social relations as "social capital," or a type of infrastructure that goes far beyond bridges, railways, or even bureaucratic institutions.

49. For Benjamin, the sandwichman is the "final incarnation of the flâneur" marked by an "empathy with exchange value" (1999, 448).

50. At the time about US$950.

51. See Stoler (2002, 2009) for discussion of an oppositional reading "with the grain," or an interpretive maneuver that follows social logics so as to understand not only their contradictions, but the unexpected conjunctures and effects they incite or produce in the world.

52. Scott 1992.

53. *S.O.S. Filhos do Centro Histórico.* As is the case with the "Maciel," the "Maciel/ Pelourinho," and the "Historical Center," I approach in relational terms the designations for the group of Gueto residents who joined Malaquias in analyzing their

state: When I emphasize the group's proximity to history I employ the designation "Children of the Historical Center." When stressing the residents' near-coalescence as a social movement, I refer to their collectivity as "S.O.S. Children of the Historical Center," or simply "S.O.S."

54. Ahmed 2014, 134.

55. Feld 2012; Geertz 1973.

56. Following C. S. Peirce 1955a, I differentiate between "symbol" and "sign," with a symbol being a particular and more "complete" sign, and a sign a more general denomination that includes a number of "degenerate" vehicles whose meaning is less determined than that of symbols.

57. Here I suggest that dominoes, approached as an economy of signs whose manipulations propel the game forward, depends for its sensuousness on movement from the relatively inchoate, barely recognized feelings about pieces that Peirce would call "firstness," to moments of rupture or physical, indexical dislocation that Peirce dubs "secondness," and on to the more fully cognized "counting" of pieces that conforms rather closely to the habitual or objectified claims about the world that Peirce referred to as "thirdness" and that Ferdinand de Saussure generalized as the "arbitrariness" of the sign.

58. I extend the term *coronelismo*, or a mid-nineteenth to early-twentieth-century, historically specific, rural system of paternalistic control in which landowners carved out rural fiefdoms populated by their clients, or *agregados*, in their articulations with an emergent, liberal national state. Analyzed canonically by Leal 1977, coronelismo is no longer the most significant axis in most studies of hierarchical, intimate structures in Brazil's rural Northeast even as patron-client relations (Ansell 2013) and other, dispersed forms of obligation (Villela 2004) and violent reciprocity (Marques 2002) continue to organize politics in Salvador and across the region (Power 2000). Nonetheless, given his paternalistic, studied, and anachronistic engagement with political clients across Salvador and his role as a kingmaker in the articulations between political parties and Bahian politicians with the national state, Brazilians frequently dubbed Magalhães a "coronel."

59. Vianna 1994.

60. "Festa no Dia do Turismo," *Correio da Bahia*, September 25, 1997.

61. Romo 2010.

62. This wording is common around the world in UNESCO heritage projects. Yet "Governor" Magalhães appropriated it as his slogan in the 1990s. See, for example, the homage to his legacy on the website of Antonio Carlos Magalhães Neto, his grandson: http://www.acmneto.com.br (last accessed July 11, 2011).

63. Expedito Filho, "'Não vou desistir': Entrevista com Antônio Carlos Magalhães," *Veja*, June 3 1998.

64. As Hobsbawm 1983 observes, states tend to lean most heavily on invented traditions at moments of regime change and the transition between authoritarian and democratic governments.

65. Buarque de Holanda 1999, 96.

66. Williams 2001 offers a fascinating discussion in English of the importance of tradition to twentieth-century Brazilian modernism, something also touched upon by Holston 1989. Examples of the strong tendency to set off future-oriented projects

through recourse to folkloric pasts are rife in leading architectural journals such as *Módulo*, an influential publication begun in 1955 in Rio de Janeiro and suspended by the military after the coup in 1964. The table of contents of the initial issue, which boasts both the architect who designed Brasilia, Oscar Niemeyer, and the head of Brazil's national patrimony institution, Rodrigo M. F. de Andrade, on its board of directors, reveals a decisive intercalation of articles on modernist projects such as Brasilia and treatments of indigenous Amazonians' doll-making, rural Catholic chapels, and peasant's houses built on stilts so as to endure the shifting water levels of the Amazon River.

67. Sheriff 2001.

68. Hanks 2010, 163.

69. For the history of a similar dynamic evident in the nationalist incorporation of early-twentieth-century popular music, see Vianna 1994. For the case of capoeira, see especially Assunção 2002. However, the argument that elites seek simply to enclose and co-opt popular vitality tends to obscure the extent to which contested cultural forms are the coproductions, rather than properties, of specific social groups. Hertzman 2013 makes this point quite well in relation to the rise of samba as a quintessential marker of Brazilianness.

70. Through the first years of the 1990s it was not unheard of for Bahian police to punish, or torture, dreadlocked "lawbreakers" and "marginals" by cutting off their long hair with a knife or rusty pair of scissors.

71. My analysis of the ways the Reggae Square audience's productive misinterpretations spur new understandings of Pelourinho realities is indebted to Butler's (1997) concept of "excitable speech," or the ways in which mistakes in quoting established scripts may have unintended consequences that are a function of their recontextualization. Yet it should be clear from this chapter's emphasis on figuration and fulfillment, and thus on the materiality of the sign vehicle as well as the extent to which human action in the world may give rise to durable social ontologies, that I do not accompany Butler in understanding this process as but a function of the contingencies of reception.

72. Heidegger 1962, 1977. In leaning on Heidegger's approach to equipment in order to understand the national history in Brazil, and foreshadowing the confusion of people and things and interpretations and data that I will explore in subsequent chapters, I am indebted to E. Valentine Daniel's observations about violence and the "availability" of different histories in the context of Tamil-Sinhala conflicts in Sri Lanka.

Chapter 2

1. Caminha 1947, 41.

2. As Milan Kundera 1999 points out in introducing Cervantes' masterwork, "The principle character in his novel is a very original madman who believes himself to be a very conventional hero. . . . The fundamental fact of the protagonist's whole existence is his will to be what he is not."

3. The Spanish-speaking Moors, descendents of those who had conquered Spain and a community whose members continued to speak Arabic, were expelled officially from the Iberian Peninsula in 1609 and again in 1613.

4. Cervantes 1981, 66–67.

5. González Echevarria 2012 offers a fascinating reading of affect, landscape, and *Don Quixote*'s polyphonic emergence in relation to competing genres in early modern Iberia. I draw my approach to chronotopes from Bakhtin 1981.

6. Borges 1965, 43.

7. Cervantes' narrator recounts the discovery of the texts in the following manner: "As I am fond of reading even scraps of paper in the streets, my natural bent led me to take up one of the notebooks the boy had for sale. I saw it was in characters which I recognized as Arabic, but, despite that, was unable to read. I looked about to see if there was any Spanish-speaking Morisco at hand for me, and I had not great difficulty in finding such an interpreter" (1981, 66).

8. For a detailed discussion of the importance of the Pelourinho, or Maciel, to the development of Bahian social science written by an IPAC field researcher active during the period described in the next chapter, see Moreira 2007.

9. Complete Brazilian independence from the Portuguese royal family came only in November 1889, with the overthrow of Dom Pedro II and his daughter Princess Isabel by a Comtean positivism-inspired military. Albuquerque 1999 provides a history of public commemorations of Bahia's 1820s-era independence from the Portuguese, if not from their royal family.

10. *Bahia. 22 de abril de 1500*

De uma parte, a proa lusitana. De outra parte, a praia dos tupis. A noite estrelada passa em silêncio, mas cheia de presságios. Na manhã seguinte, a surpresa. Dois povos se medem, frente a frente. Trocam olhares, gestos, sinais. E vem a dança do encontro. A primeira manhã de um novo mundo. De um mundo chamado Brasil. Sim. O Brasil nasceu na Bahia. E logo chegaram os negros—com os seus risos, ritos e ritmos. Assim o coração se completou. E é por isso mesmo que a Bahia começa, desde já, a bater os seus tambores. A celebrar os 500 anos de vida do Brasil. E a convocar os brasileiros para colocar este país no centro de todas nossas atenções.

11. I add quasi-citizens as a means of recognizing the strong critiques enunciated by MNU theorists of the yet-incomplete acceptance, due to racial, sexual, gender, and class discrimination, of a wide variety of Brazilians in the national polity.

12. In writing of the MNU in Salvador I understand affiliated NGOs and neighborhood percussion and educational groups like Salvador's Ilé Aiyé, Malé Debalé, Olodum, Niger Okan, as members of the organized, or Unified, Black Movement.

13. Anderson 2006; Lomnitz 2001.

14. Léry 1990, 141–42.

15. For de Certeau, "It is the task of ethnology to articulate these rules of writing and to organize this space of the other into a picture of orality" (1988, 209).

16. Mitchell 1991, 5–10.

17. Lomnitz (2001, 130) has approached similar spaces of interaction in Mexico as structures, or "contact zones," that enframe, in the productive senses put forth by thinkers such as Erving Goffman and Michel Foucault, the "internal idioms of distinction that give shape to national culture" in relation to transnational networks of identity production. Through the metaphor of the "perch" I seek to expand these observations by emphasizing the possibility of a longer history of embodied agency on the part of participants in the Pelourinho-as-contact zone: Not only a series of

brackets constructed by privileged actors, the Pelourinho Historical Center is a space that most of the people who appear across this book struggled painfully to reach, and then inhabit.

18. As well as in the confluence of mutating imperial gazes and Bahian regional contributions to a national anthropology.

19. Coronil 1997. The descriptive term "civilization and barbarism" was popularized by Domingo Faustino Sarmiento in *Facundo: Civilization and Barbarism*, an account of gaucho life in Argentina, first published in 1845. Notable subsequent fictional treatments of the issue outside Brazil include Romulo Gallegos' *Doña Bárbara* in Venezuela, published in 1929, and José Eustacio Rivera's *La Vorágine* (The Vortex), which first appeared in Colombia in 1924.

20. Stocking 1982 describes the rejection of Lamarckianism in a twentieth-century Anglophone anthropology that would replace "race" with "culture" as an explanation for geohistorical difference even as Stepan 1991 explores its spreading influence across Latin America, especially in the decades on both sides of Modern Art Week in São Paulo. Yet Schwarcz 1999 and Blake 2010 focus more directly on specifically Brazilian debates that reveal the extent to which scientists in cities like Salvador, Recife, and Rio de Janeiro struggled creatively with competing, and often contradictory, approaches to the interactions of "nature" and "culture" in relation to Brazilian racial politics. Here it is worth noting recent European and North American anthropological approaches that focus on the extent to which a conceptual walling off of the genome and ideas about heredity from social processes misses the true power of genealogical thinking in understanding personhood, politics, and history today (Abu El-Haj 2012; Collins 2011a; Franklin 2007; Palmié 2008; Pálsson 2007).

21. Da Cunha 1944, 54.

22. CIAM, the Congrès Internationaux d'Architecture Moderne, was a modernist planning movement led by Le Corbusier in which the "city is conceived of as a city of salvation" (Holston 1989, 41).

23. Serviço de Proteção do Patrimônio Histórico e Artístico Nacional (SPHAN), which is today known as IPHAN.

24. Note Macunaíma's anxiety about transparent language, a concern similar to that presented in Caminha's letter of discovery in the selection quoted at the beginning of this chapter.

25. The description of Native Brazilians in Caminha's letter can be read in English in Caminha 1947, 5. Macunaíma's description of São Paulo's red light district appears in Andrade 1984, 72–73. In delineating the nationalities of women in São Paulo, and declaring that they all go by the designation "Frenchwoman" (*francesa*), Andrade's Macunaíma invokes a common early-twentieth-century slang term for prostitutes in Brazil.

26. Caulfield 1997; Guy 1991; Rago 1987, 1991; Soares 1992.

27. Schwarz 1992; Viotti da Costa 2000.

28. Andrade 1984, 77.

29. Lacerda 1938, 103.

30. Flynn 1979, 94.

31. Vargas 1938, 6:88.

32. Vargas 1938, 5:163.

33. Lacerda 1938, 58.

34. Hacking 1991, 194. Modern statistical analysis thus helps establish the limits of what may be thought, or how the world may be perceived, and it does so by abstracting everyday phenomena from their enunciative contexts so as to establish patterns of regularity and deviance. According to Francisco Martins of São Paulo's Geographical and Historical Institute, statistics "was, until the advent of Getúlio, the imprecise and unfaithful mirror of our deficiencies, weaknesses, destined to reproduce that which we always were, and not what we should be, as it is now" (1941, 69). Martins is instructive since he makes explicit the attempt during the Estado Novo to transform the science of statistics into a method of statecrafting that might conjure up "what we should be" since "statistics is much more than a matter of representation; it is a tool of political intervention" (Asad 2002, 82).

35. Letter from Minister Gustavo Capanema to President Getúlio Vargas, June 15, 1937, Gustavo Capanema Archive of the FGV/CPDOC, Rio de Janeiro, quoted in Cavalcanti 1999, 180.

36. On moral education in and around Vargas' Estado Novo, see especially Dávila 2003.

37. Andrade 1993, 40.

38. Andrade also proposed that each *livro de tombo*, or patrimonial registry, be complemented by a separate museum dedicated to one of the four categories of national possessions.

39. Andrade 1993, 41.

40. Andrade 1993, 45.

41. Andrade 1993, 45.

42. Bennett 1995.

43. Andrade made a special effort to, as he put it in a letter to Manuel Bandeira dated June 26, 1925, "Brazilianize my language" (1966, 140). One of the reasons that the novel *Macunaíma* is such a delight for a Portuguese speaker is that Andrade creates neologisms that make eminent sense in twentieth-century Portuguese, uses a wide variety of local words that he collected in his ethnographic journeys throughout the countryside, and sends up the pretentious language of nineteenth-century Brazilian science, law, and letters by means of puns, complex allusions, and irony.

44. Dent 2009 offers a more contemporary view of this cowboy region, as well as debates about folklore and intellectual property, in his recent study of Brazilian country (caipira) music in rural São Paulo.

45. Serra 2000b provides an overview of his own and fellow Bahian intellectuals' roles in challenging precedent so as to patrimonialize specifically Afro-Brazilian institutions such as Salvador's Candomblé temples. See also Sansi 2007.

46. "IDB President Calls for Heritage Preservation to Spur Economic and Social Development," Press Release, World Bank Headquarters, Washington, March 29, 2000.

47. These descriptions of intangible heritage and "Living Human Treasures" may be found at http://www.UNESCO.org (last accessed January 2010).

48. Other instruments include Resolution 1 of August 3, 2006, which complements Decree 3.551; Decree 5.040 of April 6, 2004, which created IPHAN's De-

partment of Intangible Patrimony; and FUNAI *Portaria* 693 of July 19, 2000, which created the Indigenous Cultural Heritage Registry. Brazil also ratified the 2003 Convention for the Safeguard of Intangible Cultural Heritage in 2006 and implemented it legally via Legal Decree 22 of February 1, 2006, and Presidential Decree 5.753 of April 12, 2006.

49. I thank Richard Price 2006 for the term "pastification."

50. See Collins 2009 and 2011c for more in-depth histories of Brazilian cultural heritage institution-building and engagements with the innovative initiatives coming out of IPHAN and other heritage institutions across Brazil. These extend the chronology, and details, presented here into the first decades of the twenty-first century, or a period during which the Workers Party has sought to democratize culture.

51. The Ministério das Relações Exteriores (Ministry of Foreign Affairs).

52. Here, Juan referred to the description of police beatings of "blacks and almost blacks" on the Pelourinho Square by the Bahian singers Caetano Veloso and Gilberto Gil in their song "Haiti" from the album *Tropicalia 2* (New York: Polygram), 1993.

Chapter 3

1. Cosme de Farias is a working-class neighborhood in Salvador that has received significant numbers of former Maciel residents during the period of evacuation of residents from the historical center.

2. First set up in September 1967 as part of the Ministry of Culture and Education, the Foundation was then "regulated," or established as an enduring part of the Bahian state, by Decree 20.530 of January 3, 1968.

3. Corrêa 1998; Ortiz 1984. The shifting tendency for Brazilian intellectuals to study abroad in Portugal during the colonial period and the nineteenth century, France in the early and mid-twentieth century, and the United States after the 1960s reflects changing alignments in imperial power.

4. Garfield 2001; Lewis 1966; Ramos 1998.

5. Prostitution is not illegal in Brazil and police attention throughout the twentieth century is usually associated not with the commodification of sex, but with its occurrence in public, with the activities of its promoters, or with violations of its contractual obligations. Additionally, the exchange of sex for material compensation in Salvador does not necessarily work through a strict North American definition of prostitute and customer. Kottak 2000 and Landes 1994 offer ethnographic portraits of the blurred boundaries that are so much a part of such "prostitution," or uncertainly remunerated sexual favors, in Salvador and its surrounding areas.

6. IPAC 1997, italics my own.

7. "Análise do caso Salvador, frente ao três eixos temáticos" Final Report (Relatório Final) from IV Meeting of SIRCHAL (Programa para a Revitalizacao dos Centros Historicos das Cidades da America Latina e do Caribe), Salvador, Bahia, May 29–June 2, 2000.

8. Stoler 2009.

9. IPAC 1997, Preface.

10. IPAC 1997, 1.

11. Bentham in Hacking 1986.

12. For updated lists of UNESCO-recognized manifestations of intangible patrimony, see http://www.UNESCO.org (last accessed December 2013).

13. Even as I have translated "filhos da puta" literally, as "children of the prostitute" here, a more accurate translation attuned to the way the phrase is typically used in Bahia would be "sons of the bitches."

14. Flávio Costa, "O Pelourinho pôsto em questão," *A Tarde*, January 14 and 15, 1968; emphasis my own.

15. Republished in IPAC's *Study*, this came from "Polícia Dia e Noite," *Jornal da Tarde*, July 7, 1967.

16. Ortiz 1984, 108.

17. The police unit in charge of repressing the practice of Candomblé was the *Delegacia de Jogos e Costumes*, or the same Customs and Gaming (Vice) Squad that set its sights on regulating the mid-twentieth-century Pelourinho's customs and mores.

18. Until the late 1990s there were relatively few doctoral-degree granting institutions in Salvador, and UFBA professors of Costa Lima's generation, unless they had studied abroad, typically held masters degrees.

19. The CEAO was begun by academics close to Professor Vivaldo and the French ethnographer Pierre Verger as a way of a fomenting a south-south dialogue envisioned to revolve mainly around Candomblé. Today CEAO is an important think tank for Bahia's black rights movements and UFBA faculty.

20. Costa Lima 1977, 4–8.

21. Bastide 1978; Carneiro da Cunha 1985; Matory 2005; Parés 2013; Verger 1976.

22. Stephania Capone 2010 captures this historical "fractiousness" rather well. Dantas 1987, 1988 and Serra 1995 tend to overestimate the power of Bahia's social scientists in inflecting twentieth-century Candomblé.

23. Matory 2005.

24. Capone 2010, Gonçalves da Silva 2000, Matory 2005, Sansi 2007, Stirling 2012, Teles dos Santos 2005, and Van de Port 2011 all help clarify the role of Candomblé in making contemporary Bahian public culture. While these authors begin to detail connections that suggest Candomblé's influence on the corps of social scientists who directed the Pelourinho reforms, no one but Gonçalves da Silva (2000) examines in detail the ethnographic exchanges going on as the Bahian social scientific community engaged the Pelourinho as a living laboratory of Brazilian origins and what it configured as folkloric practices. Johnson's (2002) focus on Candomblé in Rio de Janeiro adds to these studies in important ways by suggesting that as Candomblé has become the most Brazilian of Brazil's religions, and thus a part of public culture, it has turned in on itself to produce forms of secret knowledge whose mystical status grant the religion even more power and authority across the nation.

25. Risério 1995.

26. Guimarães 2002; Skidmore 1974.

27. This is supported by former IPAC director and UFBA cultural anthropologist Ordep Serra's key role in the landmarking of the Casa Branca terreiro in 1982.

28. Costa Lima attained the positions of Elemaxó and Obá Odofin of the Candomblé terreiro Ilé Axé Opô Afonjá, perhaps the most illustrious in Brazil.

29. Many types of ogã, or assistants to the Candomblé, may work behind the scenes in ritual duties. It seems that Costa Lima engaged in such activities.

30. Beauvoir 1965.

31. Azevedo 1955 and Wagley 1952 discuss the use of the term.

32. Bacelar 2007, 17.

33. Taussig 1999.

34. Johnson 2002.

35. "Bohemian" (boêmio) is the Bahian term for cash-rich middle-class men who enjoyed carousing in the Pelourinho in the period between 1940 and 1980. Today the term coroa, or crown, meaning "old guy," is more common in Salvador as well as Rio de Janeiro. On this, see Goldstein 2005. Nonetheless, coroa and boêmio are not synonyms, as to be a bohemian in the post–World War II fashion is today impossible. For an insider's view of Costa Lima's group of bohemians who frequented the Pelourinho in the 1960s and 1970s, see Carvalho 1980.

36. "E a zona, é o brega: Era lá que o pessoal se resolvia," Revista Metrópole 8 (January 25, 2008). See http://www.revistametropole.com (last accessed September 2014).

37. Serra 2000a, 69–70.

38. The Calmons, as well as the Sás, rank among Bahia's oldest and most important families. Angelo Calmon de Sá was president of Bahia's Banco Econômico—the oldest private bank in Brazil—until its failure amid a serious financial scandal in 1998 (Dantas Neto 2006; Henry 2003). Thus Jaime Quatro's claim unites the most powerful and the poorest of Bahians in a sexualized and racialized interaction in the Pelourinho that gives rise to intermediate racial types, such as the sarará, or mixed-race person with blond hair, blue eyes, and features recognized as black.

39. Matory 2005, 144.

40. Here, IPAC, as a well-funded governmental organization concerned with "marginal" groups during the military dictatorship, stands alongside FUNAI, the federal organ in charge of "discovering" and "civilizing" groups of Native Brazilians, especially in the Amazon region. FUNAI's use of patronage, trade goods, and technical educational programs is mirrored in certain important ways by IPAC's policies (Ramos 1998).

41. IPAC 1997, 39.

42. These reports, and thousands of others, are held today in the IPAC library.

43. Jorge Amado's novel Suor, set in the building at 18 Rua Alfredo Britto, and his Tenda dos Milagres are two of the richest fictional accounts of the neighborhood.

44. Espinheira 1984, 34.

45. Cardoso and Faletto 1977; Perlman 1976. I describe this work as contemporaneous with Espinheira's study of Pelourinho prostitutes because Divergência e prostituição, finished in 1975 and only published in 1984, was a reworking of Espinheira's master's thesis (1972).

46. "Documento de Abertura," Primeiro Seminario Sobre Educacao no Maciel, IPAC Library, Documento EDU 232, Salvador, 1976.

47. Henfrey 1981; Ortiz 1984, 85.

48. "Mobral cultural ampliará a educacao," Diario de noticias, January 15, 1974.

For a discussion of MOBRAL in English prepared by the military government's Ministry of Education and Culture and seemingly intended for U.S. government and funding entities, see Commission for International Affairs 1972. Kirkendall 2010 provides an overview of the MOBRAL program as part of a larger argument about radical pedagogy in Brazil.

49. *Oxente* is a phatic interjection in northeastern Brazil used similarly to "damn" in U.S. contexts. By "saint dances" Dona Erpidia refers to Candomblé ceremonies, thus indicating that the class-based criticisms of the Afro-Brazilian religious rites celebrated by and associated with IPAC intellectuals that I discuss in chapter 7 as related to Pentecostal Protestant groups today are also employed by a seventy-two-year-old woman who left the Pelourinho, never to return, in 1992.

50. Residents' memories of the administration of social scientific questionnaires during the military period are most probably influenced by these instruments' salience in the 1990s, and thus their reinforcement at a later date.

51. Trouillot 1995, 26.

52. Cataloguing or producing taxonomies of lawbreakers, sexual acts and preferences, and various types of deviancy is an important pastime among Pelourinho residents when they reminisce about the prerestoration neighborhood. Yet they do so apparently without casting aspersion on people's habits, in a manner that generally appears more like a bemused pride in the exceptionality of their neighborhood as "mangrove," or red light district.

53. Berlant and Warner 1998, 554.

54. To be a comadre, or a *compadre* (in the masculine case), involves entering into a fictive kin relationship on the basis of baptizing, or enjoining a friend or relative to baptize, a child.

55. Dias Tavares 1966, 2001.

56. This is not Pateta's real name, but despite his desire to be named in this text I have decided, in one more example of ethnographic authority, not to reveal his name or leave his face clear to my reader. Perhaps this is unfair. I am not sure. Surely, it is off-putting to me as a friend and an ethnographer. I look forward to Pateta's, and my readers', responses.

Chapter 4

1. "A Marinha," a common designation for the federal government that refers to the federal government's, and by association the nation's, unoccupied or "empty" property.

2. The *cortiço* occupies a privileged place in the Brazilian national imaginary as a symbol of urban degeneracy and struggle that predates the post–World War II growth of Brazil's other major symbol of spatial alterity, the *favela*. Azevedo's *O Cortiço* (The Slum), first published in 1890, is a canonical Brazilian account of life in an urban setting akin to the Rocinha's courtyard. Chalhoub 1996 and Meade 1997 provide a social historical counterpart to, and a focus on the impact of *belle époque* urban reforms on, Azevedo's novelistic *carioca* world. On peripheral settlements and working-class housing in Salvador, see especially Gordilho 2000.

3. Holston 1991 offers a detailed historical and ethnographic analysis of competing land claims and manipulations of legal documentation to that land in a peripheral area of São Paulo. According to Salvador's major newspaper, some 60 percent of land claims in the greater metropolitan area are either blatantly fraudulent or contested by multiple parties and thus tinged by a suspicion of fraud. See "600 mil imóveis estão irregulares," A Tarde, May 19, 2003.

4. SEPLAM stands for Secretaria do Planejamento Municipal, or Municipal Planning Secretariat (of the city of Salvador) and SIRCHAL for Séminaire Internationale sur la Réhabilitation des Centres Historiques des Villes de l'Amerique Latine, or the International Seminar on the Rehabilitation of Latin American Historical Centers.

5. In early 2004, this trafficker was arrested by the Civil Police, who dismantled his empire and, perhaps unwittingly, helped initiate a new phase in Salvador's drug trade in which the axis between the imprisoned dealer's network headquartered in the neighborhood of São Gonçalo do Retiro and the Pelourinho came to be replaced by multiple, competing, organizations and places for bringing to Salvador, and then marketing, cocaine. Bahians often speculate that the trafficker, once protected by important figures in government and the police, suffered this fate due to the waning power of the elderly Antonio Carlos Magalhães. Although I have no way of confirming this information, many in Salvador argue that a new, competing faction of the Civil Police, empowered by the novel coalitions seeking to control Bahian politics in the face of Magalhães' demise, began the process that helped change radically the drug trade. To make the issue more complex, over the last ten years a number of initiatives in southern and central Brazil seem to have inhibited organized, open sales of drugs in urban areas. Thus criminal factions from other parts of Brazil, such as São Paulo's feared Primeiro Comando da Capital, or "First Command of the Capital" (PCC), have expanded to northeastern cities in search of safety and new markets. Collins 2014 presents an account of this dynamic and its relationship to the Pelourinho, and Biondi 2010 has produced a fascinating, semi-insider ethnography of the PCC, its motile structures, and its operations inside São Paulo's prisons.

6. Length of residence in the neighborhood was one variable that IPAC plugged into its formulas for computing indemnifications.

7. Residents' perceptions of changes in IPAC policies' logics are telling both in terms of actual shifts and as illustrations of the workings of memory, since the ascription of an earlier, beneficent, status by a number of long-term inhabitants overlooks a series of struggles over buildings on the Pelourinho Square soon after the establishment of IPAC, at the time known as the FCABA. In fact, the recuperation of a building on the Pelourinho Square, which would serve as IPAC's first headquarters, dislocated a number of residents and these earlier "reforms" were accomplished, as in later decades, through a forced indemnification of residents. Additional dislocations of residents took place in the mid-1970s and then, albeit on a smaller scale, between 1986 and 1988 as Mayor Mário Kertesz, who had become a fierce opponent of his former ally Antonio Carlos Magalhães, sought to counter state-level influence on cultural and urban policy by establishing the municipal-level Fundação Gregório de Mattos and the Programa Especial de Recuperação dos Sítios Históricos (Special Program for the Recuperation of Historical Sites), or PERSH.

8. The French delegate who most vociferously expressed this opinion was an official from the city of Nantes. As Frazier points out (1990, 198–99), the citizens of Nantes, a birthplace of liberalism and center of participation in France's slave trade with and to the Caribbean, have systematically ignored the extent to which their own self-representations have arisen as part of a wider circuit that includes areas like northeastern Brazil and the Caribbean. In comparing the Pelourinho and Disney World and contrasting them to Europe, the official helped elide the extent to which, even as he spoke in a meeting organized by SIRCHAL, Nantes and Salvador are part of an interrelated circuit of technologies in the form of financings, experts, and materiel.

9. IPAC tended to ignore historical considerations and restore the interiors of buildings in a manner arrived at by architects as a function of perceived future use, a harmony of the building's shell and potential interior décor, or, as the reforms wore on, in the manner that would cost the state the least amount of money. For IDB-sanctioned critiques of the Pelourinho project, see Rojas 1999.

10. The speech may be viewed in Portuguese, French, or Spanish at http://www2 .archi.fr/SIRCHAL (last accessed October 15, 2014).

11. Castro 2000b, 3; italics my own.

12. Castro 2000b, 3.

13. Abortion is illegal under Brazil's penal code, except when there is no other means of saving a woman's life or when a pregnancy results from a rape, but it is widely practiced in Salvador and the rest of the country. The decision to undergo an abortion usually results in harsh social censure, but the newspaper *Folha de São Paulo* has estimated that 10 percent of the world's illegally induced abortions occur in Brazil. Those who can afford them make use of a variety of illegal clinics, including at least one in the Pelourinho, while a majority of women who seek to end unwanted pregnancies make use of a wide variety of home remedies and pharmaceuticals. The ulcer drug Cytotec, produced by Searle, is currently a popular method for terminating pregnancies among working-class Bahian women.

14. IPAC 1997, 12.

15. Archives of the Santa Casa de Misericórdia da Bahia (ASM), Documento Cofre, Saldanha da Gama 18, Documents 1–5.

16. ASM, "Conta Corrente de Inquilinos," Books 32–36.

17. The prices paid for spaces in the Gueto varied wildly in accordance with the buyer's friendship with Pipino and Miguel, the size of the space, the buyer's ability to promise future payment and then defer that payment indefinitely, and the rate of inflation at the moment of purchase. In dollar terms, those who bought their spaces before the Plano Real fiscal and exchange rate reforms in 1994 paid substantially less than those who arrived later. It thus makes little sense to discuss prices in dollars, or even in Brazilian *cruzeiros* or the post-1994 *real*. Most residents paid between one and five monthly minimum salaries as established by the government. The minimum salary varied between about US$40 and US$120 during the period in question. A simple house in one of Salvador's working-class neighborhoods typically cost between five and twenty minimum salaries during the same time period.

18. "Tem que pagar o pau aqui dentro, rapaz!"

19. Words typically used include "tabaréu," "os besta," "ignorantes," and "muito rude."

20. Here Malaquias' neighbor reworks one of Malaquias' favorite self-deprecating sayings. See chapter 1 for another example of how he employs it.

21. Dreyfus and Rabinow 1983.

22. Among the studies that posit an overly direct, strategic linkage between the commodification of identity and resistance and reappropriation, or an interpretation of subjects' ostensible entrepreneurism that I refer to here as too "rational"—even when it may involve misinterpretation or engagements with occult economies— are Collins 2003; Comaroff and Comaroff 2009; DeHart 2010; and Santillán 2011.

23. In calling the police unit loosed on the Gueto's inhabitants the "Choque," I am following residents' language even as I misrepresent slightly that unit—it was not indeed the Choque that invaded the Gueto but rather a slightly less elite police unit known as the *Companhia Especial* (Special Company).

24. My linkage of everyday life in Bahia today to the history of Lisbon's Torre do Tombo archives rests on d'Azevedo and Baião 1905.

25. Collins 2011b; Verdery 2003.

26. Agnew 1986; Coronil 1997.

Chapter 5

1. This claim appears on the commemorative postcard handed out by representatives of the state during the commemorations in March 1999. Yet Gabriel Soares' 1587—rather than 1584—*Tratado Descriptivo do Brazil em 1587* describes the cathedral only as "having three naves, of a true grandeur, high and well-aired, with five chapels very well done and nicely ornamented" (136–37). Perhaps additional writings from 1584 exist, but I have not yet discovered them. I do note, however, that Soares describes the nearby Jesuit complex, which would become Salvador's Cathedral following the destruction of the Cathedral da Se in 1933, as composed of "a sumptuous college . . . and a well-shaped and pleasing church."

2. Brazilian *telenovelas*, originally related to the North American soap opera in terms of episodic sequence and sponsorship, were important to debates about redemocratization in the early 1980s, and racial consciousness at the end of the decade. *O Bem Amado* is historic not just in its suggestion of quotidian modes of political resistance on the part of a populace facing a military suspension of democratic process, but also because it was Brazil's first color telenovela and the first of its genre to be exported. Written by the well-known dramaturge Dias Gomes, *O Bem Amado* helped spur the development of a national culture industry around telenovelas and has attracted attention in debates about the role of "the popular" in Brazilian intellectual and political life (Ortiz 1984).

3. As Scheele argues succinctly, "graveyards . . . and conflicts associated with them [illustrate] . . . not only how people deal with death and violence, but also how they construe social order, political legitimacy, and historical continuity (2006, 859). This is a point emphasized also by Verdery 1999 in relation to the "ends" of socialism in Eastern Europe.

4. I was therefore unable to interview the field architect again. I did conduct

more than thirty hours of taped interviews with other construction workers without ever finding the field architect. Construction workers are an important group for understanding the relations between Pelourinho residents and working-class Bahians from other neighborhoods since, demographically, they very much resemble Maciel/Pelourinho residents. These workers quickly become integrated into Pelourinho mores and ways of living, thus suggesting one way that racial ideologies, approaches to state power, music and fashion, and modes of understanding personhood may be disseminated between the Pelourinho and the rest of Bahia.

5. Stoler 1997.

6. Andermann 2007, 25.

7. IPAC 1997.

8. Caybé, or Héctor Julio Páride Bernabó, was a well-known artist and adopted "son of Bahia" born in Buenos Aires who played an important role in the postwar florescence in Bahian culture protagonized by people like Vivaldo da Costa Lima, Godofredo Filho, Jeová de Carvalho, Jorge Amado, the French ethnographer, photographer, and Candomblé practitioner Pierre Verger, the journalist Odorico Tavares, Antonio Carlos Magalhães, and the musician Dorival Caymmi. Caymmi contributed to a recognizably Bahian culture even after his move to Rio de Janeiro and is perhaps best-known to an Anglophone public as the author of *O Que É Que a Baiana Tem?* (What Is It about Bahian Women?), a song that cemented Carmen Miranda's fame in the United States. Romo 2010 and Ickes 2013 offer detailed histories in English of this period in Bahian cultural life.

9. Ickes (2013, 120–24) provides nuanced historical analyses of early- and mid-twentieth-century attention to Afro-Bahian women's roles in social reproduction and the domestic sphere in relation to the elaboration of public ideologies of Bahianness. According to Ickes, the linkage of "public" Afro-Brazilian women and Bahianness was so well known that the U.S. Consul in Bahia referred to the circuit of visits to women like "Black Eva," whose cooking so enchanted Manuel Bandeira, as the *rotina baiana*, or "Bahian routine."

10. The state and local authorities are not alone in their attention to the Praça da Sé skeletons. The archives of IPHAN that relate to the restoration and inclusion on UNESCO's list of historic cities of Salvador's Pelourinho dedicate enormous attention and space to the discovery of a number of skeletons in 1987 alongside the Church of São Francisco, in the adjacent Praça da Anchieta. See Pastos de Inventário I, I-D and I-B, in the IPHAN archive, Rio de Janeiro.

11. *A Tarde*, June 24, 1999.

12. Literally, "permitindo que a populacão, e os visitantes, possam ver as fundações do tempo de monism." The italics are my own.

13. Egginton 2005.

14. Latour's well-known book, and assertion, *We Have Never Been Modern* (1993) is not so much a plea to reverse the terms of the historical sketch of the detachment of subjects and objects and the rise of systems of representation that perform that work, as repeated in Imbassahy's speech and my gloss of the rise of the Baroque, as it is an argument about the fact that such accounts are in themselves representations that miss the heterogeneity of human engagements with sensuous, material

worlds. This insight is an important part of my interest in the boundaries, and overlaps, between heritage objects and human beings in the Pelourinho today. But, unlike Latour, I do not toss out the baby with the bathwater in order to abandon a close engagement with the details of how representations unfold in *variegated* engagements with materiality and experience, and thus around series of often qualitatively different interactions between signs, objects, and their interpreters of the sort made clear in the semiotic of C. S. Peirce.

15. On such attempts in Bahia's most respected terreiros to purge Candomblé of associations with Christianity, see especially Matory 2005 and Sansi 2007. Burdick 1998 offers a discussion of Brazilian Catholics' "inculturated" mass that seeks a certain rapprochement with Candomblé practitioners who emphasize their African heritages. Here it is noteworthy, and perhaps surprising given Matory's emphasis on transnational connection, that none involved in this debate consider Christianity's, and especially Iberian and Brazilian Catholicism's, variegated historical roots in the manners suggested by historians like Thornton 1998.

16. The Casa Branca is one of the places of worship registered by IPHAN and Bahian authorities as a piece of the nation's patrimony during the florescence in "popular" patrimonialization over the course of Brazil's return to civilian rule in the late 1970s and 1980s. See Serra 2000b.

17. Salvador's patron saint, Nossa Senhora da Conceição, is usually syncretized as or associated in Candomblé—depending on one's view of "syncretism"—with Yemenjá, the queen of the waters, rather than Oxum. Thus December 8 might be thought of as Yemenjá's, and not Oxum's, day. Nonetheless, Yemenjá is celebrated in Bahia on February 2, with the festival of Rio Vermelho, the day in the Christian calendar associated with the Virgin of Candeias, who is usually associated instead with Oxum. Oxum and Yemenjá, two female figures associated with the waters (Oxum with fresh and Yemenjá with salt water), have thus become somewhat joined in Bahia's festive calendar. And Salvador's saint's festival is popularly associated today with Oxum. I thank Ordep Serra for pointing out Gerónimo's lyrics and for help in understanding their state's competing calendars, temporalities, and archetypes in terms of Candomblé.

18. IPAC 1997, Preface.

19. The French Ethnologist Roger Bastide, so influential in studies of Afro-Brazilian religion and race relations, produced in 1945 a book entitled *Imagens do nordeste místico em branco e preto* (Images of the Mystic Northeast in Black and White). Bastide was a close associate of Jorge Amado and some of his earliest published work in Brazil examined landscape painting and the ties between human beings and transcendent divinity. Here mystery played an important role, as exemplified by the 1938 article "Pintura e mistica" (Painting and Mystique). Bastide's contemporary and fellow ethnographer of Candomblé, Ruth Landes, also leans on mystery in her published analyses (1994). Jorge Amado was part of a circle of intellectuals that included Bastide, and he was well acquainted with Lande's closest collaborator in Bahia, the reporter and "folklorist" Edson Carneiro. Ickes 2013 offers the most complete historical portrait in English of this period in Bahian life.

20. Lewis (1992) offers a related argument directed at capoeira in Bahia.

21. A middle-aged and apparently working-class Afro-Brazilian woman, dressed

in the conservative and often second-hand North American clothing common to evangelical Protestants in Bahia. I frequently saw her in the Pelourinho between 1999 and 2000 and usually assumed she was a former resident. However, as I did not interview her or stop her in the crowd on March 29 I know little about her and her group of friends who engaged the field architect on the night of the inauguration.

22. *Conjuntos arquitetónicos*, or literally, a collection of arquitectonic pieces.

23. Note that he talks about "guardando," meaning "putting away, holding onto for posterity." This word choice suggests the extent to which the field architect is privatizing the patrimony that the politicians were talking about as an ideal "common" good in their speeches proffered on the Praça da Sé.

24. US$300–US$350 at mid-1999 exchange rates.

25. Meaning that the field architect is another *filho de Deus*, or child of God, and that we're all *filhos de Deus* with the moral authority to take the treasure since it is an object that God left behind. I thank Ana Silva Collins for making this meaning clearer to me.

26. Bahiatursa is the Bahian state tourist authority.

27. The Bahian sound trucks piled high with speakers and topped by live bands used to "pull" dancing carnaval crowds through the city center.

28. Again, "guardar," whose ambiguous meaning means "save," as in to put away for posterity, as well as to "pick up and put in one's pocket."

29. The state government and IPAC conducted a much smaller reformation of the area around the Pelourinho Square in the 1970s. This earlier reform seems to be that to which Oswaldo refers, since the cross had not yet been refurbished at the time of the incident in the Hotel Colon doorway. "Outro dia," which I have translated as "the other day," implies a much longer temporal horizon in Bahian Portuguese than it does in English.

30. *Cabeça de nego* or, literally, "black people's heads."

31. Humphreys 2001. Josephine Humphreys is also the author of *Nowhere Else on Earth* (New York: Viking, 2001), a historical novel set in a Lumbee Indian settlement in Civil War North Carolina that revolves around the memories of the narrator's prohibited love.

32. Spirits of the dead, or *eguns*, constitute a difficult problem in the study of Candomblé since they are not generally spoken of or, according to public representations, recognized and worshipped in a majority of temples. While important to Candomblé's sister religion, Umbanda (Capone 2010), as far as I know eguns are cultivated only in a single temple in Bahia today, located on the Island of Itaparica (Braga 1992). Yet Parés 2013 reports that, historically, their presence or absence in terreiros constituted important ways of distinguishing different temples and their congregations. As Braga makes clear, such spirits are tied in Candomblé to ideas about ancestry, something that would seem important to the genealogies of the skeletons' identities being put together around the Sucupira. However, and even as the head archaeologist once whispered to me that he had been approached by members of the Candomblé community troubled by the revelation of human bodies, and then quickly changed the topic and refused to return to his earlier statements, the roles and power of eguns in Candomblé do not constitute something that I have been able to link in a convincing manner to the public debates on the Praça da Sé.

33. In this context, Gilberto Freyre's study of haunting in Recife, *Assombrações do Recife velho* (Hauntings in Old Recife), raises issues concerning well-known interpreters' fidelity to popular practices alongside their imposition of distinct, class-specific interpretations onto those practices.

34. "Salvador no limite entre a pobreza e o desespero," *Gazeta Mercantil*, April 9, 2000, Bahia Supplement.

35. Humphreys 2001.

36. This is Humphrey's incorrect version of the Bahian Portuguese word for a luncheonette.

37. Humphreys 2001.

38. This is the "new" Cathedral, the church built by the Jesuits who were expelled from Brazil during Portugal's mid-eighteenth-century Pombaline reforms. The Jesuit Church, located on the corner of the Praça da Sé and the Terreiro de Jesus Square, replaced the Cathedral of the Sé as Salvador's official cathedral following the former's demolition in 1933.

39. Dona Niza's nickname for a neighbor with whom she fought, and continues to fight, almost continually. Here she is suggesting that this neighbor used Jorge's digging as an excuse to cause problems for the family. It is significant that this designation, "Padilha," is the name for a Candomblé entity, related to the Christian devil, present in certain of the religion's variants, or traditions. Padilha is the sister of the also malicious and more commonly known *exu*, or relatively malignant figure, called the Pomba Gira. According to legend, the Padilha was both a very jealous and a very rich woman, due to her marriage to a king. She was also raped by her own brother at age fourteen and promised to avenge this violation by killing him with seven thrusts of a dagger. After abandoning her royal husband and moving to a *brega*, or working-class red light district like the Pelourinho, Padilha came across her estranged brother one afternoon. Inviting him for a drink, she stabbed him to death and drank his blood but was herself murdered by another prostitute as she stood above her brother's body. Padilha then descended into hell, where she became a female version or associate of the malignant god of the crossroads and underworld, Exú, and the patroness of prostitutes and red light zones. To complicate her story, she later murdered her own sister, Pomba Gira, who also descended to hell. According to Wafer (1991, 13), Padilha and Pomba Gira are both sworn enemies today and frequently confused, serving as devil figures. Dona Niza is a Candomblé practitioner and she seems to understand herself as a Pomba Gira to her neighbor's Padilha.

40. A well-known percussion teacher, now deceased, responsible for teaching drumming to many of the children who would go up to play in the Banda Olodum, or the musical component of the Olodum social movement.

41. The word *nego*—derived from *negro*, or black—is often both a term of endearment and a way of indicating an anonymous person in everyday Bahian speech. In this second connotation, the term is somewhat akin, but more specific in its racialization and proletarian associations, to "Joe Blow" in North American slang. Augusto's usage is in accord with this latter convention. Yet in Augusto's speech, as is common in Bahia, "nego" is not just virtuous, but indicative of a person capable of deceit and malfeasance. While the "nego" may at times be used to indicate someone

who suffers class and racial discrimination, and is thus a way of indexing virtue in the face of adversity, its racialized status allows for the smuggling in of pejorative associations.

42. Taussig 1999.

43. Hobsbawm 1983.

44. Fry 1982.

45. The "recognition of those aspects of cultural identity that are considered a source of external embarrassment but that nevertheless provide insiders with their assurance of common sociality" (Herzfeld 1997, 3).

46. At the time, as a result of the Brazilians' decision to enforce its 1845 Aberdeen Accords with Britain, the slave trade, but not slavery itself, had been declared illegal and had begun to be prosecuted actively, if ambivalently, by Bahian authorities.

47. Francisco Goncalves Martins uttered this phrase that serves as the title of the present subsection of this chapter in his address in 1852 to the Assembly. See Martins 1852, 20.

48. Verger 1999; Wetherell 1860.

49. Martins 1852, 20, italics my own.

50. Martins 1852, 20.

51. Martins 1852, 26.

52. Emancipados are Africans transported to Brazil by slave traders but declared, if not in practice made, "free" on the basis of British pressure in the mid-nineteenth century. See Conrad 1973.

53. Martins 1852, 20.

54. Reis 2003.

55. Amaral 1918; Casimiro 1996; Cortes de Oliveira 1988.

56. Martins 1852, 27.

57. Reis 2003.

58. Rebouças, Simas Filho, and Godofredo Filho were long-term colleagues and intellectual collaborators.

59. Risério 1995, 2013.

60. Simas Filho 1969a, 1969b, 1971a, 1971b.

61. CEAB 1998.

62. For examples of the rise of urban planning initiatives that sought to develop an urbanism that encourages differentiated spaces of urban "meaning" and that influenced Bahian planners, see, for example, Lynch 1960, 1976.

63. Sampaio 1999, 277.

64. Hobsbawm and Ranger 1983, 14.

65. Scott 1991 offers a sophisticated and influential challenge to such verificationism. Together with Trouillot's work on the "silencing of the past" (1995), this challenge to a naïvely empiricist history has been influential in my conceptualization of, and writing about, histories in Bahia.

66. According to Zamora, "Seventeenth-century Baroque portraiture depicts the birth of the modern self" (2006, 179).

67. Engelke 2007 observes that a Zimbabwean Apostolic Christian congregation's emphasis on interior faith, rather than material signs of that faith, leads to a series or practical and ideological issues related to the resolute rejection of thinglike

signs in their "live and direct" approach to religiosity. Although I am more interested here in the transfer of relatively intangible qualities into material form, I understand Pelourinho residents' attempts to make manifest a series of objects that seem to embody their aspirations and frustrations in the context of the reforms as bringing up a different sort of problem of presence, namely, their inability to produce tangible, accepted evidence of the "costs" of their dispossession and the alienation of their everyday habits as the cultural property of all Brazilians.

68. The field architect's implicit hesitancy to reveal histories, something potentially overcome when conditions for telling are correct, bears a certain resemblance to "arrested histories," or what McGranahan 2010 identifies among Tibetans as culturally specific inhibitions to telling certain types of history at certain historical junctures.

69. I appropriate this term from Lomnitz, for whom "internally homogeneous" contact zones in Mexico are "integrated into a broader 'region' of national identity production that includes a zone of state institutions that define rights and obligations for citizens and produce images and narratives of nationality" (2001, 130).

70. Anthropologists, following Silverstein 2003, have begun to use the term "transduction" for such energetic transfers whose force, and thus significance, depend on the material form of the transmission. In biology, the term "transduction" refers to the transfer of DNA between two different organisms by a mediating virus. In physics, transduction involves a transfer of a particular kind of energy, or motion, into another in a process in which the transformation is dependent on the very nature, or material form, of the vehicles involved in the exchange. Helmreich 2007 has sought to extend Silverstein's engagements into soundscapes and their punctive effects on the body.

71. Ferry 2005; Handler 1991; Coombe 1998.

72. I acknowledge and apologize to van de Port 2011 and his work on Candomblé for my resignification of his psychoanalytically inflected use of the "really real" in relation to Bahian culture. Meanwhile, Helmreich 2011 has examined the qualities of water, as well as the theories and cultural affordances that would account for the effects of such qualities, as real actants in the world. In a related vein, Navaro-Yashin sees ghostly presence as "what is retained in material objects and the physical environment in the aftermath of the disappearance of the human linked or associated with that thing or space" (2012, 17). Stoler's (2013) recent engagement with "ruination" constitutes yet another facet of these approaches, one which seeks to get at the lingering effects, and thus the historicity, of objects and their normally unrecognized surplus of potentials, which are, nonetheless, material. In a different orientation that nonetheless speaks to the materiality of what could be, and traces of what were, Meskell 2002 traces the "negative heritage" left over and mobilized as a resource for remembering in the wake of the destruction of New York's World Trade Center.

73. Peirce 1955b, 322; italics my own.

74. Peirce 1955b, 323.

75. Derrida 1983.

76. Dreyfus and Rabinow 1983.

Chapter 6

1. What Adilson said in Portuguese was "Eu conhecia assim, através da televisão, quando tocava as músicas no rádio, aí eu curtia. Aí depois eu conheci o Olodum mesmo, eu vi que é um grupo de tradição."

2. This resignification, or extension, of words like "tradition" and "culture" has increased in recent years. The son of one friend, a resident of the Rocinha, recently said to me, "I've got to go home now, and write up my *cultura* (homework)."

3. It is, for example, an essential move in Agamben's (1998, 1999, 2003) attempts to extend the reach of Foucault's version of biopolitics (1990, 1991) as well as Arendt's (1973) pathbreaking recognition of the contradictions of claims about "human" rights in the wake of the displacements of the Holocaust.

4. Etchevarne is perhaps also the excavation's "architect," or the figure performed mimetically by the field architect.

5. Henry Louis Gates' "Finding Your Roots" project is a salient example of the extent to which DNA has come to crowd out other forms of evidence in putting together genealogies and felt identities. See http://www.pbs.org (last accessed September 12, 2014).

6. Ferme 2001.

7. Foucault 1972. On property regimes, relatedness, and the genealogical imagination, see especially Strathern 2005, 2006.

8. French 2007, draws on her ethnography of *quilombola* (maroon) communities not far from Salvador and Gonçalves' (2005) suggestion that heritage's ability to convince, or claim truth, depends on "resonance, materiality, and subjectivity" to argue that the enunciation of black identities in relation to patrimonializing initiatives depends on the extent to which heritage protocols and legal regimes gain a historically contingent "resonance" in the contexts in which they emerge. This is an important insight in relation to what took place on the Praça da Sé because it addresses similar concerns with land rights, genealogies, and cultural heritage among rural Northeasterners that seem to generate an increased identification as "Afro-Brazilian" or black. Yet such broad brushstrokes aimed at specifying mechanisms of social change do not really attend to the extent to which subjects and objects tend to become confused, and inflect or produce their own contexts, in relation to legal and bureaucratic instruments associated with intangible heritage initiatives. French's approach also rests on the assumption that the simple presence of legal measures aimed at, for example, heritage, establishes a horizon of possibility that inflects "resonances." Indeed, such a horizon may do so. Yet the outlines of such legal horizons are, in the IPAC-overseen Pelourinho, rather muted and appear to do little to alter the conditions of possibility for social action in the face of the state institution's management of everyday life as patrimony.

9. Guimarães 2001; Mattos 1998; Reichmann 1999; Teles dos Santos 2005.

10. Teles dos Santos 2005, 1.

11. Bailey 2009; Bailey and Telles 2006; Bolaños 2010; Karam 2007; Nobles 2000; Warren 2001.

12. Bastide 1978; Dantas 2009; Downey 2005; Rodrigues 1996; Santos 1985.

13. I understand full well that the correct term for "problem" in Portuguese is

problema, not *pobrema*. Yet in my transcriptions and remembrances of conversations I strive to put down words that describe, or represent as faithfully as possible, the way all participants in exchanges actually spoke.

14. Rebouças and Filho 1985 provide a beautifully illustrated depiction of the Ladeira da Misericórdia. Rebouças' watercolors are accompanied by Godofredo Filho's historical descriptions and an introductory comment by the anthropologist Thales de Azevedo, a member of the Bahian Conselho de Cultura, which, as described in the previous chapter, helped set up IPAC by bringing together intellectuals involved in protecting Bahian culture and *sanitaristas* like Antonio Carlos Magalhães' father, Franciso.

15. Filho 1987.

16. On the role of the Santa Casa da Misericórdia's hospital in taking care of orphans and in housing and treating those considered threats to the Bahian social body in the eighteenth and nineteenth centuries, see Fraga Filho 1996 and Venâncio 1999.

17. Filho 1987, 287.

18. The Coaty Nightclub functioned for a time during the municipality's reform of the Misericórdia in the 1980s. It fell into disuse in the 1990s, eventually being abandoned and then invaded by former residents of the nearby Maciel after the reforms in 1992. Around 2004 it began to function as an African-themed bar and nightclub. Yet the Ladeira's continued isolation behind the imposing Santa Casa da Misericórdia, its association with crime and prostitution, and pressing security concerns occasioned by the hillside's poor lighting and Salvador's economic inequalities meant that patrons refused to descend to the establishment. Today this fascinating hybrid of colonial architecture and modernist innovation sits shuttered, off-limits to all but a few privileged city hall insiders. For details on the short-lived attempt by São Paulo–based architect Lina Bo Bardi to integrate in 1987 the Ladeira da Misericórdia into a more vibrant and inclusive version of Salvador's Historical Center, see Zeuler 2013.

19. Biehl 2009 offers a sensitive analysis of the institutionalization of NGO-based care in relation to AIDS in the Pelourinho, and Salvador more generally. The account is noteworthy for its attention to the affective relations so important to this process, as well as in relation to interactions between social scientists and residents of the Misericórdia in the present chapter because it includes a luminous photograph of Topa, identified under a pseudonym I have discarded here in favor of this deceased friend's nickname.

20. "Sensibilização: Informações Preventivas Sobre DSTs/AIDS, Abuso de Drogas e Qualidade de Vida."

21. Topa and I first met in 1992.

22. "Cada pessoa é dono do seu proprio corpo" and "você tem seu valor."

23. These are two wealthy neighborhoods on the modern northeastern side of the city of Salvador.

24. "Não se meta! *Eu* estou perguntando!"

25. Filho 1987, 287.

26. My reader may note that I have included extensive photographs of Miseri-

córdia residents. In most cases these are the results of long-term and close friendships with people who understood and explicitly desired to support my research. In certain other cases they result from an agreement I had with many residents of the historical center whereby I would photograph them and turn over sets of prints in return for their permission to use their images, for the most part anonymously, in a future ethnography of the making of the Pelourinho Historical Center.

27. See Rancière 2001 on "counting" and the policing of the sensorium.

28. Da Matta 1991a.

29. Aretxaga 1995, 135.

30. The statement by the Mago—reprinted in the preface—that "there are many children of Jesus in this world who take many positions, but the best position to take is none at all" is the best description of malandragem I have encountered.

31. Spradley 1979, 85.

32. The doorstep, as a space between house and street, is extraordinarily important to definitions of correct morality in Salvador. For example, it is still common for teenagers in Salvador to brag about their steady boyfriends (or girlfriends, to a lesser extent) in a language of "we conducted our relationship on the doorstep" ("Foi um namoro na porta de casa"). Azevedo 1986 discusses gendered propriety and dating around doorsteps in mid-twentieth-century Salvador.

33. See Kulick 1996 on the extent to which Pelourinho travestis produce an agentive "scandal" by pushing up closely, but with a difference, to established social codes.

34. Keane 2003, 32. See also Bauman 2004, 129–32.

35. I specify the "dusty" sertão as a temporal entity because under the federal redistributive programs put in place by Workers Parties administrations since 2002 life in the sertão has gotten substantially better, even as relatively more privileged, middle-class urban dwellers are more liable to argue that they have lost ground. For perspectives on this dynamic, see especially Ansell 2013.

36. Hill 1995; Parmentier and Mertz 1985.

37. Auerbach 1984, 59.

38. Crapanzano 1986, 53.

39. A Percean "third" or fully symbolic, generalizing claim that stands in opposition to icons (firsts) and indexes (seconds), which Peirce characterized as "degenerate" signs.

40. Rancière 2001.

41. Bastide 1978; Christian 1989; Gruzinski 2001; Sansi 2013. In an example of the confusion of saints and saints' images so much a part of early modern Iberian and, I suggest, Bahian popular Catholicism and Pelourinho residents' readings of the Pelourinho project, Brown points out that in the Mediterranean Christianity of late antiquity a new relationship between life and death set off Christianity from Islam and Judaism as tombs of saints became places where the saints were venerated, and literally "present" (1981, 12). For recent engagements with the materiality and denials of the materiality of the image more generally and in regions beyond Brazil, see especially Meyer 2011, 2012; Mitchell 2002; and Strassler 2010. Carpentier's melding of iconoclastic readings of commodity fetishism and Haitian vodou in his novel Kingdom of this World (2006) is the richest exploration of the dynamic I have

only begun to explore in describing Topa's self-objectifying, and thus contradictorily resistant, demand for completion by precisely those actors who oppress her. The place of vodou in Carpentier's attention to images that come "alive" suggests also the importance of a deep consideration of Candomblé practitioners' influence on Bahian engagements with images. This is a relationship at the heart of Sansi's (2007) and Stirling's (2012) studies of the making public of Candomblé as Bahian culture, but it is beyond the scope of *Revolt of the Saints*.

42. Pizzigoni 2013, 137.

43. Vainfas 2003, 104. Mott 1997 has explored St. Anthony's role as a "divine slave hunter" for *capitães-do-mato*, or the armed men who sought to recapture escaped slaves.

44. Ingold (1988, 13) draws the concept of affordance from Gibson 1979. See especially Daniel 1996, Manning 2012, Keane 2003, and Kockelman 2013 on the challenges such a recognition of the sign's materiality presents to more standard anthropological notions of agency and arbitrariness.

45. For a clear description of the evaluatory and truth-producing operations that make a saint, see the U.S. Catholic bishops' document at http://www.usccb.org (last accessed July 15, 2014). Yet as emphasized by a variety of commentators, Latin American "lay" Catholic traditions often rely on less carefully codified steps to sainthood even as such saints established in popular practice are often recognized by the Vatican at a later date.

46. Haraway 1997, 10.

47. Taussig 1993 examines mimesis in relation to a distinguishing alterity.

48. Sheriff 2001.

49. Trouillot 2003, 128.

50. Gell 1998, 103.

51. Passariello 2005, 75.

Chapter 7

1. Cardoso 1998, 2001.

2. In an example of the playfulness so much a part of antropofagia and tropicália, Gil's longtime collaborator, Caetano Veloso, reportedly responded "sexy" when asked in the 1990s what he thought of Antonio Carlos Magalhães.

3. Schwarz 1992; Viotti da Costa 2000.

4. Echoes of this long-standing Brazilian emphasis on "ingestion" of the foreign punctuated the speeches of Mayor Imbassahy and Governor Borges on the Praça da Sé in 1999.

5. In 1993 Caetano Veloso launched the song "Haiti" on the album *Tropicalia II*. In this song Veloso proclaims "O Haiti é aqui," or "Haiti Is Right Here." Since Veloso's verses are explicitly about racial discrimination and police violence on the Pelourinho Square, it is difficult to interpret "Haiti" as a direct commentary on bourgeois experience of neoliberal restructuring or the difficulties of hyperinflation in the 1990s. Nonetheless, the lyrics and choice of title do demonstrate the presence of a widespread fear about the rupturing of certain teleologies that had girded the Brazilian nation across much of the twentieth century.

6. There is precedent in Salvador for such "intuition" of linguistic content through

prosody since Bahians typically play with and alter the lyrics of famous carnival songs while dancing down "the Avenue" in this pre-Lenten rite. Many Bahians are also well versed in public, active participation in the singing of songs in a language that participants cannot make meaningful in a conventional sense. Salient examples include the conducting of Roman Catholic mass in Latin until the mid-1960s and Candomblé ceremonies, which include liturgical elements performed in Yorubá, a language most Bahians do not understand.

7. The "mock Spanish" (Hill 1993, 1998) from which I derive this term is a somewhat different phenomenon, whereby appropriation and deformation of aspects of Spanish by dominant Anglos in an indirect denigration of Spanish speakers supports a potentially deniable racism in the United States.

8. As Downey 2005 notes, "flat" feet held close to the ground are, in the more "traditional" forms of Bahian capoeira *angola* a mark of being *plantado* (planted) and sure-footed, thus a form of protection and strength from which to deal with the unexpected. I appreciate both the ethnographic perspicacity of this observation, and the fact that in Bahia to be "flatfooted" is to be well prepared to move nimbly and forcefully in the face of adversity.

9. Geertz 1973.

10. Here I think especially of the ability of capoeira to reach out to break up delimitations between participants and audience as practitioners use gesture, song, and percussive rhythms to comment on and react to the events surrounding the circle of mobile, clapping humans within which this dance/martial art is "played." Downey 2005; Lewis 1992.

11. Benjamin 1978, 325.

12. Benjamin 1968a, 80.

13. The contradictions of such an expression, and interpellation, of self are a critical component of modernist anthropology. Among the most insightful of recent ethnographies of selves, truths, and the politics of representing that self is Nelson's (2009) work on the tensions surrounding Guatemalan indigenous activist Rigoberta Menchu's autobiographies and political positioning.

14. Jackson 2005, 225–30. I add "ultimately real" in the sentence above because this is, as I interpret it, Jackson's ultimate point about the variegated ways in which Afro-North American subjects claim a race that is, if not natural or "social-constructed," definitively real. In a rather different, but nonetheless pertinent observation about the assumptions that gird salient approaches to modern subjectivity, Hirschkind (2004, 14) observes in his study of cassette sermons and Islamic counterpublics that "the very act of listening came to be seen as a danger to the autonomy of the enlightened liberal subject."

15. Benjamin 1968a, 79.

16. Pagode is also sometimes called "Axé," although axé music is more properly a genre, especially popular through the early 1990s, that mixes heavy metal guitars with Spanish-speaking Caribbean rhythms and percussion. In addition to Jamaican reggae singers, African musicians like Koko Dembele, Lucky Dube, and Alpha Blondy, are also wildly popular in the Pelourinho and Salvador's neighborhoods.

17. Olodum's signature drumming, invented in the mid- to late 1980s in the Pelourinho, is known as "samba reggae."

18. North American readers unfamiliar with Roberto Carlos might try to imagine a more politicized Neil Diamond who suffered through a military dictatorship.

19. Araújo Pinho 1997, 1998–99.

20. The creative deformation of well-known lyrics is, as attested to by the career of "Weird Al" Yankovic in the United States, common around the world. It is especially notable in Salvador, Brazil's capital of "street-based" carnival where musicians produce and perform new songs each year from atop sound trucks that circulate slowly through the crowds that pack the city's pre-Lenten celebrations. This proximity of performer and audience gives rise to a remarkable intimacy, and familiarity, that crowds seize upon to sing back to performers. Such responses range from a repetition of lyrics that leads vocalists to hold their microphones out to crowds, to listeners' seizure and alteration of lyrics that they sing back to overpowered performers.

21. Butler 1998b analyzes the postemancipation history of one of the Pelourinho's Afro-Bahian lay sodalities, as does Braga 1987. Costa Lima 1995 describes the rise of the Tuesday night "Benção" or "Bença" in the Pelourinho and Serra 2000c examines Bahian festivities more generally. For pointed insights in Salvador's youth culture and music scene of the 1990s, see Guerreiro 2000.

22. Browning 1995 describes this late-1980s moment in gatherings on the Pelourinho Square.

23. This sum has ranged from about US$0.80 to US$0.50 since 2000.

24. Graham 2002; Silverstein 1976, 1979.

25. Moten 2003, 3.

26. Araújo Pinho 2001.

27. Gilroy 1995.

28. Focusing his ethnography of West African culture brokers resident in Salvador, Dawson 2014 dissects some of the ways new generations of the sorts of transnational actors on whom Matory 2005 focuses for an earlier period have come to play important roles in the imagination of Africa in Bahia today. Reis' (1995) study of early-nineteenth-century slave rebellions, and especially as regards the role of Muslim religious conversion in those actions, offers an earlier engagement with the making of Africa in the Americas.

29. *Dicionário Aurélio—Seculo XXI.* I understand the problems inherent in posing such a genetic relationship in the context of the present argument, but I have not yet found any scholarly mentions of the word.

30. Araújo Pinho 1997; Dunn 1994; Mitchell 2011; Sansone 1994, 1995, 1996; Williams 2013.

31. This refrain also appears as "Jogue street mas nao jogue mortal" (Play it like in the street, but not like some mortal combat). This seems an invocation to become involved in Salvador's related rock-and-roll and hip-hop scenes, but to do so carefully and consciously.

32. Today, in an example of the contradictory attempts at redefining and incorporating existing and often neoliberal institutions into the new, more democratic and redistributive state structures established by the Workers Party, Pelourinho Day and Night has been taken over by the Ministry of Culture's new subsection, the Centro de Culturas Populares e Identitárias (Center for Popular and Identitarian Cultures).

33. Araújo Pinho 1998–99, 258.

34. Ortiz 1995.

35. Coronil 1995 understands Ortiz as a profound critic of occidentalist categories, while Allen 2011 suggests that Ortiz's fascinating theory of transculturation, or a fugue-like nonevolutionary process of contrapuntal interfaces, rests on a negation of Africans' culture followed by a naturalization in the Americas of their difference.

36. The iconic commercial can be viewed at http://www.youtube.com/watch?v=p26oRXYBFxw (last accessed April 5, 2014).

37. Jakobson 1999, 61.

38. Coffee and cocoa are major crops in Bahia. Although Brazil has now been surpassed by the Ivory Coast in cocoa exports due to the "witches' broom" mold that attacks trees in the Americas, until the early 1980s Bahia was the world's most important exporter of cocoa. The prime cocoa growing region is precisely the Recôncavo and the region to its south, areas to which a majority of the Pelourinho translators have close ties due to the intensity of rural-urban migration across the second half of the twentieth century.

39. Scheper-Hughes 1993, 326.

40. Scheper-Hughes 1993, 324.

41. Marx 1973, 1977.

42. Strathern 1988, 171. It is worth noting that Strathern's work, and sources of data in Melanesia, reflect a rather particular approach to capitalism and its analysis. On personhood, consumption, and material objects deployed as powerful signs within a Melanesian optic more attuned to the issues of commodification and consumption at the core of the present chapter, see especially Foster 2003.

43. Coombe 1998. As Strathern puts it, "nameless inventors . . . when they are not known they can reflect back a diffuse or generalized aura of capacity, enhancing people's sense that they are all heirs to a collective creativity" (2005, 95).

44. www.parmalat.net/www/mission/e_mission.htm. Site last accessed February 19, 2004. The Italian multinational Parmalat has since undergone a bankruptcy and reorganization and this page is no longer available.

45. The way I have described this relation here is intended to gesture at a formal resemblance between such racial signification and human beings' "hidden" qualities and the ways that marks, or signatures, on money or brand logos that circulate in market relations supposedly index deeply rooted qualities intrinsic to the market. Given these overlaps between racializing and capitalist logics, I direct this chapter not at proving the marks to be false, but at understanding how associations between signs in the market and signs of racial identities may draw on similar logics in becoming as necessary and believable as they are in the world today.

46. These are the relatively undetermined, but nonetheless sensuous, iconic signs that Peirce dubbed "qualisigns." Since such qualisigns, or iconic "firsts" in Peirce's lexicon, are contained in the "bundles of cables" in which semiosis occurs, even the more sedimented and more completely interpretive transferrals of significance of the type common in fully symbolic communication carry with them a history of these open, sensuous markings (Daniel 1984, 39–40). This is an important observation for considering how concerns with the sounds of language might "leap" conceptually and practically into an arena more properly described as

concerned with identity, and vice versa. Hull 2012, Keane 2003, 2007, and Manning 2004, 2012 offer especially fine-grained approaches to the promiscuity of such bundlings.

47. "São coisas da Bahia. São coisas da Bahia, viu? Aquela coisa de mistura, da terra."

48. Costa Lima 1997.

49. My variegated use of "saint" and "orixá" here, and elsewhere, is intended to emphasize how much the terms are used interchangeably in Bahia while, as mentioned several times so far, the leaders of Salvador's oldest and most prestigious temples typically reject a conflation of "Catholic" saints and "African" gods. On the multiple types of potential Africanness of Christian saints, see Thornton 1998.

50. Collins 2004.

51. Gonçalves da Silva 2006, 2007.

52. Austin-Broos 1997 offers a detailed ethnography of relationships between Jamaican Rastafarianism, more "mainstream" Protestant churches, and salient ideas about salvation, sin, and moral stricture.

53. Collins 2004.

54. Crapanzano 2000.

55. De Witte 2009 argues that different forms of "membership" in a Ghanian Christian congregation are established in relation to particular modalities of "touch," Abreu 2009 examines breath and air to hone in on the material dynamics through which a community as a communicative entity unfolds, and Strassler 2010 focuses on photography's framings and transpositions of subjects and techniques in the making of Indonesian national life.

56. Such immediacy is characteristic of Pentecostalism, a set of practices and religious communities that take their name from the Holy Spirit's descent to earth as tongues of fire.

57. Meyer 2011, 25. Meyer is also responsible for coining the term "sensational form," or iterative structures that offer access to religious transcendence.

58. This point underscores the insights of Jackson's (2005) discussion of "bling," or shiny stones and jewelry, in relation to the performance of black identity in the United States. "Bling" is not simply a shiny adornment, but a sound. This conjuncture suggests the possibility of rapid transductions between vision, hearing, and material items that, as Jackson explores, establish a relatively grounded form of subjectivity.

59. In spite of my assertion here that form/content distinctions make little sense in relation to Candomblé's ritual spaces, and Candomblé more generally (Sansi 2009), Johnson 2002 argues that along with the "protestantization" of Candomblé as a Brazilian public or national culture, an emphasis on secrecy for secrecy's sake has led to a differentiation between representations and the mysteries or entities thought to lie behind them.

60. Mafra 2011.

61. Keane 2003, 2007 as well as Manning 2008 focus especially on the ways that the circulation of Peircean "qualisigns" in one arena inflect interpretation in another. On bundling, see Keane 2003, 2007 and Daniel 1984.

62. But see Bairros 1996, 2008 for a Brazilian federal minister's, and Bahian

leader in the Black Movement's, ongoing recognition that while there is much to be learned from civil rights struggles in the United States, Brazilian racial ideologies work in manners that cannot, and should not, be equated with those in other American republics.

63. Harris 1993, 1721.

64. Handler 1985, 1991 extends E. B. Macpherson's theory of "possessive individualism" to cultural property, thus inflecting an enormous literature on cultural and intellectual property, human rights, and development discourse. Brown 2003 seeks to mitigate individual appropriation through public sphere remediation, while Ferry 2005 documents a fascinating case whereby the alienation of heritage objects by members of a Mexican mineral cooperative actually makes them much more resolutely public, or shared, objects than does their sequestering as patrimony.

65. But Gell 1998 as well as Strathern 2005, 2006 resituate within, or disaggregate across, a variety of objects and actors an agency that modern social theory typically concentrates within the subject.

66. Locke 1980.

67. This point builds on Keane's (2007) emphasis on the extent to which Christian moral codes and Marx's theory of fetishism both reject the agency of material objects and locate meaning, and virtue, in the associations of spirit, reason, and thus humanity with a denial or overcoming of ostensibly inert matter. For a discussion of the function of Pelourinho-based morality and archival storage in relation to the production of value around cultural labor and cultural properties, see Collins 2012.

68. Holston 1991; Saúle Junior and Cardoso 2005. But see Holston 2008, in which he suggests that in São Paulo today residents' engagements with land have shifted to a deep desire to be within the law. This perspective is not supported by my research in Salvador and may be a function of the communities studied, or a wider, regional difference in approaches to law and property within Brazil.

69. Seed 1992 offers a historical perspective on the multiple and often contradictory conceptualizations of property at play among different European powers competing for possession of newly discovered American territories immediately prior to Locke's labor-based theorization of ownership.

70. Chang 2010; Kosek 2006.

71. Stoler 2013, 1.

72. Johnson 2011, 395.

73. This is an issue too in the relatively rational, instrumental approach to identity and its commodifications at the core of Comaroff and Comaroff 2009.

74. Jackson 1995a, 1995b, 2009; Warren and Jackson 2002.

75. Daniel 1984, 33.

76. Wagley 1968.

Conclusion

1. Andrade, Bandeira and Morães 2000, 334, postcard dated January 22, 1927. The stone Bandeira highlights is a particular type of white, Portuguese marble.

2. Andrade, Bandeira and Morães 2000, 333, postcard dated January 22, 1927.

3. Here it is worth noting also that the funicular as machine helps set off the

city's vitality and, since at least the time of Descartes, the machine has functioned as an important conceptual model for the living organism.

4. On the postcard's circulation as a factor in its meaning, and thus on the importance of an indeterminacy or denial of a metaphysics of presence that adds to rather than detracts from its significance, see Derrida 1987.

5. Price 2006.

6. For a fine example of the creative resignifications engendered by whitewashings of the past and violent denials of identities, see, for example, Price 2007 on the Saramaka Maroons of Suriname and their exile in Guyane. Additionally, the creolization process, whereby practices and habits stripped of their social structures by the violence of the slave trade continued to mean something and orient Africans who combined culture traits in new ways in the Americas, gave rise to the "birth of Afro-American culture," as Mintz and Price 1992 put it.

7. Strassler (2010, 211) argues that "the photograph's miniaturized scale, mobility, and fragility . . . work to establish an intimate relationship to the historical past."

8. "Evil Tony" is my translation for the appellation "Tonho Malvadez" (literally "Bad Tony") used frequently to describe Antonio Carlos Magalhães. What Dona Aidil said was, "*O povo pobre e sofredor do Pelourinho e as injusticias feitos pelo IPAC e Tonho Malvadez!*"

9. "*O povo africano do Pelourinho.*"

10. This is not to claim, for even a second, that I favor those who rule.

11. Oliven 1996 provides an ethnography of the inventions of tradition so much a part of an earlier stage in the ongoing development of a specifically southern-Brazilian, "white" identity and political movement.

12. Turner 1992. See Boyer 2006 for an overview of Turner's work with video in conjunction with the Kayapo.

13. Bacelar 1996; Cunha 2002; Nascimento 1989.

14. Hasenbalg 1997; Williamson 2011.

15. Alberto 2011; Pinho 2009; Teles dos Santos 2005.

16. Ansell 2013 offers the most ethnographically sensitive, English-language analysis of this most recent period and the overlaps of redistributive food programs, multicultural initiatives by PT activists, and local-level politics in the northeastern state of Piauí.

17. Perry 2013.

18. See, for example, my emphasis on the naturalized interplay of history, landscape, and peoplehood in the Pelourinho (Collins 2003).

19. Burdick 2013, 181.

20. Or, as Mbembe 2003 argues, it may be true that "bodily integrity has been replaced by pieces, fragments, folds, even immense wounds that are difficult to close." Whether or not it is, Gell's (1998) version of distributed agency as well as recent work on figuration and technoscience (Haraway 1997) extend the emphasis on the plasticity of the human that is so much a part of anthropological investigations since the Victorian period. For discussions of contemporary scientific procedures as scaffolding that is inseparable from their results, see especially the overview of indeterminism and quantum mechanics in Kern 2004. Bynum 1990 offers a rather

different discussion of the distribution of the human and the body. She does so in relation to ideas of continuity, form, and inheritance by delving into the ways that early Christian debates over, for example, the human subjects to whom body parts consumed by cannibals would accrue on Judgment Day when heaven and earth and the dead (spirits) and the living (bodies) would be united.

21. Rheinberger 2010.

22. Rappaport 1998, 13.

23. My claims about historical meaning here are influenced by Adorno's (1995, 2002) view of redemption as a "negative dialectics" that would preserve the experience of the object as well as Keane's (2007) observations about the extent to which, within Christian modernity, abstraction supposedly provides a space for freedom and transcendence, while materiality is configured as an entangled space of silent objects that require explanation by thinking subjects.

24. Kern 2004, 48.

25. Ingold 2007.

26. Franklin 2013, Hartigan 2013, Hirschkind 2004, Jackson 2005, Kern 2004, and Stoler 2013 all offer, in relation to differing research sites and theoretical apertures, analyses that demonstrate the extent to which "ideas of relatedness . . . must be composed out of distinct idioms, such as love, care, genes, blood, naming, or place in order to function in a social context that requires constant adjustment" (Franklin 2013, 246).

27. On the importance of language and railways—to grab hold of what might at first glance seem an odd pair—to connection and separation in time and space, and thus to subjectivity, see Agha 2011 and Schivelbusch 2014.

28. Meskell 2005, 51.

29. *"São Pedro disse que não era a minha hora. Que eu tive que voltar. Porque eu ainda tinha que dar muito cú em baixo. Eu não vou embora não, John. São Pedro me disse, 'desca, não é sua hora não. Você ainda tem que dar muito cú la em baixo.'"*

30. Benjamin 1968b.

31. Hegel 1977.

32. Here I refer to the preface to Hegel's *Phenomenology* (1977), in which he suggests that the realization of identity requires the subject to recognize the self in the Other and to expend the labor necessary to confront, and live with, death. But in Dandinha's case St. Peter relieves him of this requirement and sends him back to life. See also Mbembe 2003 and Taussig 1999.

References

Archival Sources

Archives of the Santa Casa da Misericórdia da Bahia, Salvador, Bahia (ASM)
Public Archives of the State of Bahia, Salvador, Bahia (APEB)
IPAC Library, Salvador, Bahia

Books and Articles

Abreu, Maria Aparecida Azevedo. 2010. "Educação: Um novo patamar institucional." *Revista Novos Estudos (Cebrap)* 87:131–43.

Abreu, Maria José de. 2009. "Breath, Technology, and the Making of Community: *Cancão Nova* in Brazil." In *Aesthetic Formations: Media, Religion, and the Senses*, edited by Birgitte Meyer, 161–82. New York: Palgrave Macmillan.

———. 2013. "Technological Indeterminacy: Medium, Threat, Temporality." *Anthropological Theory* 13 (3): 267–84.

Abu El-Haj, Nadia. 2001. *Facts on the Ground: Archaeological Practice and Territorial Self-Fashioning in Israeli Society.* Chicago: University of Chicago Press.

———. 2012. *The Genealogical Science: The Search for Jewish Origins and the Politics of Epistemology.* Chicago: University of Chicago Press.

Adorno, Theodor. 1995. *Negative Dialectics.* Translated by E. B. Ashton. New York: Continuum.

———. 2002. *Minima Moralia: Reflections from a Damaged Life.* Translated by E. F. N. Jephcott. New York: Verso.

Agamben, Giorgio. 1998. *Homo Sacer: Sovereign Power and Bare Life.* Translated by D. Hellner-Roazen. Stanford: Stanford University Press.

———. 1999. *Remnants of Auschwitz: The Witness and the Archive.* New York: Zone Books.

———. 2003. *The Open: Man and Animal.* Translated by Kevin Attell. Chicago: University of Chicago Press.

Agha, Asif. 2007. "Recombinant Selves in Mass Mediated Spacetime." *Language & Communication* 27 (2007): 320–35.

———. 2011. "Large and Small Scale Forms of Personhood." *Language & Communication* 31:171–80.

Agier, Michel. 1995. "Racism, Culture and Black Identity in Bahia." *Bulletin of Latin American Research* 14 (3): 245–64.

Agier, Michel, and Françoise Bouchet-Saulnier. 2004. "Humanitarian Spaces: Spaces of Exception." In *The Shadow of Just Wars: Violence, Politics and Humanitarian Action*, edited by Fabrice Weissman, 297–313. Ithaca, N.Y.: Cornell University Press.

Agnew, Jean-Christophe. 1986. *Worlds Apart: The Market and the Theater in Anglo-American Thought, 1550–1750*. New York: Cambridge University Press.

Ahmed, Sara. 2014. *Willful Subjects*. Durham: Duke University Press.

Alberto, Paulina. 2011. *Terms of Inclusion: Black Intellectuals in Twentieth-Century Brazil*. Chapel Hill: University of North Carolina Press.

Albuquerque, Wlamyra R. de. 1999. *Algazarra nas ruas: Comemorações da independência na Bahia (1889–1923)*. São Paulo: Editora da UNICAMP.

Alencar, Rosilene. 1999. "Pelos meandros da subjectivação." Master's thesis, Institute of Collective Health, Federal University of Bahia.

Allen, Jafari. 2011. *¡Venceremos?: The Erotics of Black Self-making in Cuba*. Durham: Duke University Press.

Alvarez, Sonia. 1989. "Politicizing Gender and Engendering Democracy." In *Democratizing Brazil: Problems of Transition and Consolidation*, edited by Alfred Stepan, 205–51. Oxford: Oxford University Press.

Amado, Jorge. 1945. *Todos os Santos: Guia das ruas e dos mistérios da Cidade do Salvador*. São Paulo: Editora Martins.

———. 1995. *The War of the Saints*. Translated by Gregory Rabassa. New York: Bantam Books.

———. 2003. *Tent of Miracles*. Translated by Barbara Shelby Merello. Madison: University of Wisconsin Press.

———. 2011. *Suor*. São Paulo: Companhia das Letras.

———. 2013. *Captains of the Sands*. Translated by Gregory Rabassa. New York: Penguin.

Amaral, Braz do. 1918. "A cemiterada." *Revista do Instituto Geográfico e Histórico da Bahia* 24:43.

Amaral, Braz de, and Edson Carneiro. 1969. *A Bahia no século XVIII*. Salvador: Editora Itapuã.

Andermann, Jens. 2007. *The Optic of the State: Visuality and Power in Argentina and Brazil*. Pittsburgh: University of Pittsburgh Press.

Anderson, Benedict. 2006. *Imagined Communities: Reflections on the Origin and Spread of Nationalism*. New York: Verso.

Andrade, Mário de. 1966. *Cartas a Manuel Bandeira*. Rio de Janeiro: Edições de Ouro.

———. 1984. *Macunaíma*. Translated by E. A. Goodland. New York: Random House.

———. 1993. "Anteprojeto do patrimônio." In *Modernistas na repartição*, edited by Lauro Cavalcanti, 39–56. Rio de Janeiro: Editora UFRJ.

Andrade, Mário de, Manuel Bandeira, and Marcos A. de Morães. 2000. *Correspondência: Mário de Andrade & Manuel Bandeira*. São Paulo: EDUSP.

Ansell, Aaron. 2013. *Zero Hunger: Political Culture and Antipoverty Policy in Northeast Brazil.* Chapel Hill: University of North Carolina Press.

Appadurai, Arjun. 1981. "The Past as Scarce Resource." *Man* 16:201–19.

Arantes, Antônio Augusto. 1997. "Patrimônio cultural e nação." In *Trabalho, cultura e cidadania: Um balanço da história social brasileira*, edited by A. M. Carneiro Araújo, 275–90. São Paulo: Scritta.

———. 2007. "Diversity, Heritage and Cultural Politics." *Theory, Culture & Society* 24 (7/8): 290–96.

Araújo Pinho, Osmundo de. 1997. "'The Songs of Freedom': Notas etnográficas sobre cultura negra global e práticas contraculturais locais." In *Ritmos em trânsito: Sócio-antropologia da música baiana*, edited by L. Sansone and J. Teles dos Santos, 181–200. Salvador: Dynamis.

———. 1998–1999. "Espaço, poder e relações raciais: O caso do Centro Histórico de Salvador." *Afro-Ásia* 21–22:257–74.

———. 1999. "'Só se vê na Bahia': A imagem típica e a imagem crítica do Pelourinho afro baiano." In *Brasil: Um pais de negros?*, edited by Jefferson Bacelar and Carlos Caroso, 87–11. Salvador: CEAO.

———. 2001. "'Fogo na Babilonia': Reggae, Black Counterculture, and Globalization in Brazil." In *Brazilian Popular Music and Globalization*, edited by C. Perrone and C. Dunn, 192–206. Gainesville: University of Florida Press.

Araújo Pinho, José Wanderley. 1969. "Proteção dos monumentos públicos e objetos históricos." *Revista da Cultura da Bahia* (July/December 1969): 53–59.

Arendt, Hanna. 1973. *The Origins of Totalitarianism.* New York: Harcourt, Brace, Jovanovich.

Aretxaga, Begona. 1995. "Dirty Protest: Symbolic Overdetermination and Gender in Northern Ireland Ethnic Violence." *Ethos* 23 (2): 123–48.

Asad, Talal. 2002. "Ethnographic Representation, Statistics, and Modern Power." In *From the Margins: Historical Anthropology and Its Futures*, edited by Brian Axel, 66–94. Durham: Duke University Press.

Assunção, Matthias Röhrig. 2002. *Capoeira: The History of an Afro-Brazilian Martial Art.* New York: Routledge.

Auerbach, Erich. 1984. *Scenes from the Drama of European Literature.* Foreword by Paolo Valesio. Minneapolis: University of Minnesota Press.

———. 2003. *Mimesis: The Representation of Reality in Western Literature.* Translated by Willard Trask. Princeton: Princeton University Press.

Austin, John L. 1962. *How to Do Things with Words.* New York: Oxford University Press.

Austin-Broos. 1997. *Jamaica Genesis: Religion and the Politics of Moral Orders.* Chicago: University of Chicago Press.

Azevedo, Aluísio. 2000. *The Slum.* Translated by David Rosenthal. New York: Oxford University Press.

Azevedo, Paulo Ormindo de. 1984. "O caso Pelourinho." In *Produzindo o passado: Estratégias de construção do patrimônio cultural*, edited by Antônio Augusto Arantes, 219–55. São Paulo: Editora Brasiliense.

Azevedo, Thales de. 1955. *As elites de cor: Um estudo de ascensão social.* São Paulo: Companhia Editora Nacional.

———. 1969. *Povoamento da Cidade de Salvador*. Salvador: Editora Itapuã.

———. 1975. *Democracia racial: Ideologia e realidade*. Petrópolis: Editora Vozes.

———. 1984. *As ciências sociais na Bahia*. Salvador: Fundação Cultural.

———. 1986. *As regras do namoro à antiga*. São Paulo: Editora Ática.

Bacelar, Jeferson. 1982. *A família da prostituta*. São Paulo: Editora Ática.

———. 1996. "A Frente Negra Brasileira na Bahia." *Afro-Ásia* 17:73–85.

———. 2007. "Uma pedagogía do viver." In *Vivaldo da Costa Lima: Intérprete do Afro-Brasil*, edited by Jeferson Bacelar and Cláudio Pereira, 11–26. Salvador: EDUFBA.

Bailey, Stanley. 2009. *Legacies of Race: Identities, Attitudes, and Politics in Brazil*. Stanford: Stanford University Press.

Bailey, Stanley, and Edward E. Telles. 2006. "Multiracial vs. Collective Black Categories: Census Classification Debates in Brazil." *Ethnicities* 6 (1): 74–101.

Bairros, Luiza. 1996. "Orfeu e poder: Uma perspectiva Afro-Americana sobre a política racial no Brasil." *Afro-Ásia* 17:173–86.

———. 2008. "A Community of Destiny: New Configurations of Racial Politics in Brazil." *Souls* 10 (1): 50–53.

Bakhtin, Mikhail. 1981. *The Dialogic Imagination: Four Essays*. Translated by Caryl Emerson and Michael Holquist, 84–258. Austin: University of Texas Press.

Bandeira, Manuel. 1946. *Antologia de poetas brasileiros bissextos contemporâneos*. Rio de Janeiro: Z. Valverde.

Barickman, Bert. 1998. *A Bahian Counterpoint: Sugar, Tobacco, Cassava, and Slavery in the Recôncavo, 1780–1860*. Stanford: Stanford University Press.

Barthes, Roland. 2010. *A Lover's Discourse: Fragments*. Translated by Wayne Koestenbaum. New York: Hill and Wang.

Bastide, Roger. 1938. "Pintura e mística." *Revista do Arquivo Municipal* 5:47–61.

———. 1945. *Imagens do nordeste místico em branco e preto*. Rio de Janeiro: Empresa Gráfica O Cruzeiro.

———. 1965. "The Development of Race Relations in Brazil." In *Industrialisation and Race Relations*, edited by Guy Hunter, 9–29. New York: Oxford University Press.

———. 1978. *The African Religions of Brazil: Toward a Sociology of the Interpenetration of Civilizations*. Baltimore: Johns Hopkins University Press.

———. 2001. *O Candomblé da Bahia: Rito nagô*. Translated by M. I. Pereira de Queiroz. São Paulo: Companhia das Letras.

Bastide, Roger, and Florestan Fernandes. 1955. *Relações raciais entre negros e brancos em São Paulo*. São Paulo: UNESCO.

———. 1959. *Brancos e negros em São Paulo: Um ensaio sociológico sobre aspectos da formação, manifestações atuais e efeitos do preconceito de cor na sociedade paulistana*. São Paulo: Editora Nacional.

Bauman, Richard. 2004. *A World of Others' Words: Cross-Cultural Perspectives on Intertextuality*. Malden, Mass.: Blackwell Publishing.

Beauvoir, Simone de. 1965. *Force of Circumstance*. Translated by Richard Howard. New York: G. P. Putnam's Sons.

Bendix, Regina. 2009. "Heritage Between Economy and Politics: An Assessment from the Perspective of Anthropology." In *Intangible Heritage*, edited by Laura-jane Smith and Natsuko Akagawa, 253–69. New York: Routledge.

Benjamin, Walter. 1968a. "The Task of the Translator." In *Illuminations: Essays and Reflections*, edited by Hannah Arendt, 69–82. New York: Schocken Books.

———. 1968b. "Theses on the Philosophy of History." In *Illuminations: Essays and Reflections*, edited by Hannah Arendt, 253–64. New York: Schocken Books.

———. 1978. "On Language as Such and the Language of Man." In *Reflections: Essays, Aphorisms, Autobiographical Writings*, edited by Peter Demetz, 314–32. New York: Schocken Books.

———. 1999. *The Arcades Project*. Translated by Howard Eiland and Kevin McLaughlin. Cambridge, Mass.: Harvard University Press.

Bennett, Tony. 1995. *The Birth of the Museum: History, Theory, Politics*. New York: Routledge.

Berlant, Lauren, and Michael Warner. 1998. "Sex in Public." *Critical Inquiry* 24 (2): 547–66.

Bernardes Ribeiro, Sandra. 2005. *Brasilia: Memoria, cidadania e gestäo do patri-mônio cultural*. São Paulo: Annablume Editora, 2005.

Biehl, João Guilherme. 2009. *Will to Live: AIDS Therapies and the Politics of Sur-vival*. Berkeley: University of California Press.

———. 2005. *Vita: Life in a Zone of Abandonment*. Berkeley: University of Califor-nia Press.

Biondi, Karina. 2010. *Junto e misturado: Uma etnografía do PCC*. São Paulo: Editora Terceiro Nome.

Blake, Stanley. 2010. *The Vigorous Core of our Nationality: Race and Regional Iden-tity in Northeastern Brazil*. Pittsburgh: University of Pittsburgh Press.

Bolaños, Omaira. 2010. "Reconstructing Indigenous Ethnicities: The Arapium and Jaraqui Peoples of the Lower Amazon, Brazil." *Latin American Research Review* 45 (3): 63–86.

Bomeny, Helena Bousquet. 1995. "O patrimônio de Mário de Andrade." In *A invenção do Patrimônio: Continuidade e ruptura na constituição de uma política oficial de preservação no Brasil*, edited by Márcia Chuva and Helena Bousquet Bomeny, 11–25. Rio de Janeiro: Minc/IPHAN.

Bomfim, Juarez Duarte. 1994. "Políticas públicas para o Centro Histórico de Sal-vador: O caso do Parque Histórico do Pelourinho, investigação de originalidade numa ação do governo local." Master's thesis, School of Administration, Fed-eral University of Bahia.

Borges, Jorge Luis. 1965. "Partial Enchantments of the *Quixote*." In *Other Inquisi-tions: 1937–1952*, translated by Ruth Simms, 43–46. Austin: University of Texas Press.

Bourdieu, Pierre and Loïc Wacquant. 1999. "On the Cunning of Imperialist Rea-son." *Theory, Culture & Society* 16 (1): 41–58.

Boyer, Dominic. 2006. "Turner's Anthropology of Media and Its Legacies." *Cri-tique of Anthropology* 26 (1): 47–60.

Braga, Júlio. 1987. *Sociedade Protetora dos Desvalidos: Uma irmandade de cor*. Salva-dor: Ianamá.

———. 1992. *Ancestralidade Afro-Brasileira: O culto de babá egum.* Salvador: CEAO/ Edicoes Ianamá.

Brown, Michael. 2003. *Who Owns Native Culture?* Cambridge, Mass.: Harvard University Press.

Brown, Peter. 1981. *The Cult of the Saints: Its Rise and Function in Late Christianity.* Chicago: University of Chicago Press.

Browning, Barbara. 1995. *Samba: Resistance in Motion.* Bloomington: Indiana University Press.

Brumann, Christoph. 2013. *Tradition, Democracy and the Townscape of Kyoto: Claiming a Right to the Past.* New York: Routledge.

———. 2014. "Heritage Agnosticism: A Third Path for the Study of Cultural Heritage." *Social Anthropology* 22 (2): 173–88.

Buarque de Holanda, Sérgio. 1999. *Raizes do Brasil.* São Paulo: Companhia das Letras.

Bunten, Alexis. 2008. "Sharing Culture or Selling Out? Developing the Commodified Persona in the Heritage Industry." *American Ethnologist* 35 (3): 380–95.

Burdick, John. 1998. *Blessed Anastácia: Women, Race and Popular Christianity in Brazil.* New York: Routledge.

———. 2002. "Pentecostalismo e identidade negra no Brasil: Mistura impossível?" In *Raça como retorica: A construção da diferença*, edited by Yvonne Maggie and Claudia Barcellos Rezende, 185–212. Rio de Janeiro: Civilização Brasileira.

———. 2013. *The Color of Sound: Race, Religion, and Music in Brazil.* New York: New York University Press.

Burke, Peter, and Maria Lúcia G. Pallares-Burke. 2008. *Gilberto Freyre: Social Theory in the Tropics.* Oxford: Peter Lang.

Burns, Kathryn. 2010. *Into the Archive: Writing and Power in Colonial Peru.* Durham: Duke University Press.

Butler, Judith. 1997. *Excitable Speech: A Politics of the Performative.* New York: Routledge.

———. 2004. *Precarious Life: The Power of Mourning and Violence.* New York: Verso.

Butler, Kim. 1998a. "Afterword: *Ginga Baiana*; The Politics of Race, Class, Culture, and Power in Salvador, Bahia." In *Afro-Brazilian Culture and Politics: Bahia, 1790s to 1990s*, edited by Hendrik Kraay, 158–76. Armonk, N.Y.: M. E. Sharpe.

———. 1998b. *Freedoms Given, Freedoms Won: Afro-Brazilians in Post-Abolition Salvador and São Paulo.* New Brunswick: Rutgers University Press.

Bynum, Caroline Walker. 1990. "Material Continuity, Personal Survival, and the Resurrection of the Body: A Scholastic Discussion in Its Medieval and Modern Contexts." *History of Religions* 30 (1): 51–85.

Caldeira, Teresa. 2006. "'I Came to Sabotage Your Reasoning': Violence and Resignifications of Justice in Brazil." In *Law and Disorder in the Postcolony*, edited by Jean and John Comaroff, 102–49. Chicago: University of Chicago Press.

———. 2008. "From Modernism to Neoliberalism in Sao Paulo: Reconfiguring the City and Its Citizens." In *Other Cities, Other Worlds: Urban Imaginaries in a*

Globalizing Age, edited by Andreas Huyssen, 51–78. Durham: Duke University Press.

Caldeira, Teresa, and James Holston. 2005. "State and Urban Space in Brazil: From Modernist Planning to Democratic Interventions." In *Global Assemblages: Technology, Politics and Ethics as Anthropological Problems*, edited by Aihwa Ong and Stephen Collier, 354–72. Malden, Mass.: Blackwell.

Caldwell, Kia. 2007. *Negras in Brazil: Re-envisioning Black Women, Citizenship and the Politics of Identity*. New Brunswick: Rutgers University Press.

Caminha, Pero Vaz de. 1947. "The Discovery of Brazil: Letter of Pero Vaz de Caminha, Written in Porto-Seguro of Vera Cruz on the First Day of May in the Year 1500." In *Portuguese Voyages, 1498–1663*, edited by Charles David Ley, 41–59. New York: E. P. Dutton.

Capone, Stefania. 2010. *Searching for Africa in Brazil: Power and Tradition in Candomblé*. Durham: Duke University Press.

Cardoso, Fernando Henrique. 1998. *O Presidente segundo o sociólogo: Entrevista de Fernando Henrique Cardoso a Roberto Pompeu Toledo*. São Paulo: Companhia das Letras.

———. 2001. *Charting a New Course: The Politics of Globalization and Social Transformation*. Edited by Maurício Font. New York: Rowman and Littlefield.

Cardoso, Fernando Henrique, and Enzo Faletto. 1977. *Dependency and Development in Latin America*. Translated by Marjory Mattingly Urguidi. Berkeley: University of California Press.

Carneiro da Cunha, Manuela. 1985. *Negros estrangeiros*. São Paulo: Brasiliense.

———. 2009. *Cultura com aspas*. São Paulo: Editora Cosac Naify.

Caroso Soares, Carlos Alberto. 1979. "Expedientes de Vida: Um Ensaio de Antropologia Urbana." Master's thesis, Federal University of Bahia.

Carpentier, Alejo. 2006. *Kingdom of this World*. Translated by Harriet de Onis. New York: Farrar, Strauss and Giroux.

Carvalho, Jeová de. 1980. *A cidade que não dorme*. Salvador: Jeová de Carvalho.

Carvalho Neto, Isaias de. 1991. "Centralidade Urbana: Espaço & Lugar." Master's thesis, University of São Paulo, Faculdade de Arquitetura e Urbanismo.

Casimiro, Ana Palmira Bittencourt Santos. 1996. *Mentalidade e estética na Bahia colonial*, Salvador: Empresa Gráfica da Bahia.

Castro, Adriana Almeida Couto de. 2000a. *Centro Histórico de Salvador, Bahia*. Belo Horizonte: Horizonte Geográfico.

———. 2000b. "Palestra." IV Encontro SIRCHAL: Salvador, Bahia, Brazil. Xeroxed Copy, May 19.

Castro, Nadya Araújo. 1998. "Trabalho e desigualdades raciais: Hipoteses desafiantes e realidades por interpretar." In *Trabalhos e desigualdades raciais: Negros e brancos no mercado de trabalho de Salvador*, edited by Nadya Araújo Castro and Vanda Barreto, 15–21. São Paulo: Annablume Editora.

Castro, Sonia Rabello de. 1991. *O Estado na preservação de bens culturais*. Rio de Janeiro: Livraria e Editora Renovar Ltda.

Caulfield, Sueann. 1997. "The Birth of the Mangue: Race, Nation, and the Politics of Prostitution in Rio de Janeiro, 1850–1942." In *Sex and Sexuality in Latin*

America, edited by Daniel Balderston and Donna Guy, 86–100. New York: New York University Press.

Cavalcanti, Lauro. 1999. "Modernistas, arquitetura e patrimônio." In *Repensando O Estado Novo*, edited by Dulce Pandolfi, 178–96. Rio de Janeiro: Editora FGV.

Cavalcanti, Maria Laura Viveiros de Castro, and Maria Cecilia Londres Fonseca. 2008. *Patrimônio imaterial no Brasil: Legislação e políticas estaduais.* Brasilia: UNESCO/Educarte.

Cervantes Saavedra, Miguel de. 1981. *Don Quixote.* Translated by John Ormsby, Joseph Jones, and Kenneth Douglas. New York: W. W. Norton.

Chalhoub, Sidney. 1996. *Cidade febril: Cortiços e epidemias na Corte imperial.* São Paulo: Companhia das Letras.

Chang, David. 2010. *The Color of the Land: Race, Nation, and Politics of Land-ownership in Oklahoma, 1832–1929.* Chapel Hill: University of North Carolina Press.

Chaui, Marilena. 1989. *Cultura e democracia.* São Paulo: Cortez.

———. 2006. *Cidadania cultural: O direto à cultura.* São Paulo: Editora Fundação Perseu Abramo.

Chelcea, Liviu. 2003. "Ancestors, Domestic Groups and the Socialist State: Housing Nationalization and Restitution in Romania." *Comparative Studies in Society and History* 45 (4): 714–40.

Chor Maio, Marcos. 1999. "O projeto UNESCO e a agenda das ciências sociais no Brasil dos anos 40 e 50." *Revista Brasileira de Ciências Sociais* 14 (41): 141–58.

Chor Maio, Marcos, and Ricardo Ventura Santos. 2005. "Politica de cotas raciais, os 'olhos da sociedade' e os usos da antropologia: O caso do vestibular da Universidade de Brasília (UNB)." *Horizontes Antropológicos* 11 (23): 181–214.

Christian, William. 1989. *Local Religion in Sixteenth-Century Spain.* Princeton: Princeton University Press.

Cicalo, André. 2012. *Urban Encounters: Affirmative Action and Black Identities in Brazil.* New York: Palgrave MacMillan.

Cody, Francis. 2009. "Inscribing Subjects to Citizenship: Petitions, Literacy Activism, and the Performativity of Signature in Rural Tamil India." *Cultural Anthropology* 24 (3): 347–80.

Cohn, Gabriel. 1984. "A concepção oficial da política cultural nos anos 70." In *Estado e cultura no Brasil*, edited by Sérgio Miceli, 85–96. São Paulo: Difel.

Collins, John. 2003. "The Revolt of the Saints: Popular Memory, Urban Renewal and National Heritage in the Twilight of Brazilian 'Racial Democracy.'" PhD dissertation, University of Michigan.

———. 2004. "'X Marks the Future of Brazil': Racial Politics, Bedeviling Mixtures and Protestant Ethics in a Brazilian Cultural Heritage Center." In *Off Stage/ On Display: Intimacies and Ethnographies in the Age of Public Culture*, edited by Andrew Shryock, 191–224. Stanford: Stanford University Press.

———. 2007a. "The Sounds of Tradition: Arbitrariness and Agency in a Brazilian Cultural Heritage Center." *Ethnos* 72 (3): 383–407.

———. 2007b. "Recent Approaches in English to Brazilian Racial Ideologies: Ambiguity, Research Methods, and Semiotic Ideologies." *Comparative Studies in Society and History* 49 (4): 997–1009.

———. 2008a. "'But What if I Should Need to Defecate in Your Neighborhood, Madame?': Empire, Redemption and the 'Tradition of the Oppressed' in a Brazilian Historical Center." *Cultural Anthropology* 23 (2): 279–328.

———. 2008b. "Patrimony, Public Health, and National Culture: The Commodification and Redemption of Origins in Neoliberal Brazil." *Critique of Anthropology* 28 (2): 237–55.

———. 2009. "Historical and Cultural Patrimony in Brazil: Recent Works in Portuguese." *Latin American Research Review* 44 (1): 291–301.

———. 2011a. "Melted Gold and National Bodies: The Hermeneutics of Depth and the Value of History in Brazilian Racial Politics." *American Ethnologist* 38 (4): 683–700.

———. 2011b. "Culture, Content, and the Enclosure of Human Being: UNESCO's 'Intangible' Heritage in the New Millennium." *Radical History Review* 109:121–35.

———. 2011c. "Nation-State Consolidation and Cultural Patrimony." In *The Brazilian State: Paths and Prospects of Dirigisme and Liberalization*, edited by Mauricio Font and Laura Randall, 219–46. Lanham, Md.: Lexington Books.

———. 2012. "Reconstructing the 'Cradle of Brazil': The Detachability of Morality and the Nature of Cultural Labor in Salvador, Bahia's Pelourinho World Heritage Site." *International Journal of Cultural Property* 19:423–52.

———. 2014. "Policing's Productive Folds: Secretism and Authenticity in Brazilian Cultural Heritage." *The Journal of Latin American and Caribbean Anthropology* 19 (3): 473–501.

Comaroff, Jean, and John Comaroff. 2009. *Ethnicity, Inc.* Chicago: University of Chicago Press.

Commission for International Affairs. 1972. *Education in Brazil, 1971.* Brasilia: Ministry of Education and Culture.

Conrad, Robert. 1973. "Neither Slave nor Free: The Emancipados of Brazil, 1818–1868." *Hispanic American Historical Review* 53 (2): 50–70.

Coombe, Rosemary. 1998. *The Cultural Life of Intellectual Properties: Authorship, Appropriation, and the Law.* Durham: Duke University Press.

———. 2011. "'Possessing Culture': Political Economies of Community Subjects and their Properties." In *Ownership and Appropriation*, edited by Veronica Strang and Mark Busse, 105–30. New York: Berg.

Coronil, Fernando. 1995. "Introduction to the Duke University Press Edition." In *Cuban Counterpoint: Tobacco and Sugar*, ix–lvi. Durham: Duke University Press.

———. 1997. *The Magical State: Nature, Money and Modernity in Venezuela.* Chicago: University of Chicago Press.

Corrêa, Mariza. 1998. *As ilusões da liberdade: A escola Nina Rodrigues e a antropologia no Brasil.* Brangança Paulista: EDUSF.

Cortes de Oliveira, Maria Inés. 1998. *O Liberto: O seu mundo e os outros.* Salvador: Corrupio.

Costa Lima, Vivaldo da. 1977. "A família-de-santo nos candomblés jeje-nagô." Master's thesis, Federal University of Bahia, Division of Social Sciences.

———. 1995. "Festa e religião no Centro Histórico." *Afro-Ásia* 16:70–79.

———. 1997. "Etnocenologia: Etnoculinária do acarajé." Paper presented at the III Colóquio Internacional de Etnocenologia, Federal University of Bahia, September.

Covin, Daniel. 2006. *The Unified Black Movement in Brazil, 1978–2002*. Jefferson, N.C.: McFarland.

Crapanzano, Vincent. 1986. "Hermes' Dilemma: The Making of Subversion in Ethnographic Description." In *Writing Culture: The Poetics and Politics of Ethnography*, edited by James Clifford and George Marcus, 51–76. Berkeley: University of California Press.

———. 2000. *Serving the Word: Literalism in America from the Pulpit to the Bench*. New York: New Press.

Cunha, Olívia Maria Gomes da. 1993. "Fazendo a 'coisa certa': Reggae, rastas e pentecostais em Salvador." *Revista Brasileira de Ciencias Sociais* 8 (23): 120–37.

———. 1998. "Black Movements and the 'Politics of Identity' in Brazil." In *Cultures of Politics/Politics of Cultures: Re-Visioning Latin American Social Movements*, edited by Sonia Alvarez, Evelina Dagnino, and Arturo Escobar, 1–32. Boulder, Colo.: Westview Press.

———. 2002. *Intenção e gesto: Pessoa, cor e a produção cotidiana da (in)diferença no Rio de Janeiro, 1927–1942*. Rio de Janeiro: Arquivo Nacional.

D'Azevedo, Pedro A., and Antonio Baião. 1905. *O archivo da Torre do Tombo: Sua história, corpos que o compõem, e organisação*. Lisbon: Imprensa Commercial.

Da Costa, Alexandre Emboabo. 2010a. "Anti-Racism in Movement: Afro-Brazilian Afoxe and Contemporary Black Brazilian Struggles for Equality." *Journal of Historical Sociology* 23 (3): 372–97.

———. 2010b. "Afro-Brazilian Ancestralidade: Critical Perspectives on Knowledge and Development." *Third World Quarterly* 31 (4): 655–74.

Da Cunha, Euclides. 1944. *Rebellion in the Backlands*. Translated by Samuel Putnam. Chicago: University of Chicago Press.

Da Matta, Roberto. 1991a. *Carnivals, Rogues, and Heroes: An Interpretation of the Brazilian Dilemma*. Translated by John Drury. Notre Dame: University of Notre Dame Press.

———. 1991b. *A casa & e rua: Espaço, cidadania, mulher, e morte no Brasil*. Rio de Janeiro: Editora Guanabara.

———. 1997. *Relativizando: Uma introdução à antropologia social*. Rio de Janeiro: Editora Rocco.

Daniel, E. Valentine. 1984. *Fluid Signs: Being a Person the Tamil Way*. Berkeley: University of California Press.

———. 1996. *Charred Lullabies: Chapters in an Anthropography of Violence*. Princeton: Princeton University Press.

Dantas, Beatriz Góis. 1985. *Vovó nagô e papai branco: Usos e abusos da África no Brasil*. São Paulo: Brasiliense.

———. 1987. "Pureza e poder no mundo dos candomblés." In *Candomblé: Desvendando identidades*, edited by Carlos Eugênio Marcondes de Moura, 121–28. São Paulo: EMW Editora.

Dantas, Marcelo. 1994. *Olodum: De bloco afro a holding cultural*. Salvador, Bahia: Grupo Cultural Olodum/Fundação Casa de Jorge Amado.

Dantas Neto, Paulo Fábio. 2006. *Tradição, autocracia e carísma: A política de Antonio Carlos Magalhães na modernização da Bahia (1954–1974)*. Belo Horizonte: Editora UFMG.

Dávila, Jerry. 2003. *Diploma of Whiteness: Race and Social Policy in Brazil, 1917–1945*. Durham: Duke University Press.

Dawson, Allan. 2014. *In Light of Africa: Globalizing Blackness in Northeastern Brazil*. Toronto: University of Toronto Press.

Dayan, Joan. 1995. *Haiti, History, and the Gods*. Berkeley: University of California Press.

De Certeau, Michel. 1988. *The Writing of History*. New York: Columbia University Press.

De Witte, Marleen. 2009. "Modes of Binding, Moments of Bonding: Mediating Divine Touch in Ghanian Pentecosalism and Traditionalism." In *Aesthetic Formations: Media, Religion, and the Senses*, edited by Birgitte Meyer, 183–206. New York: Palgrave Macmillan.

DeHart, Monica 2010. *Ethnic Entrepreneurs: Identity and Development Politics in Latin America*. Stanford: Stanford University Press.

Della Cava, Ralph. 1970. *Miracle at Joaseiro*. New York: Columbia University Press.

Dent, Alexander. 2009. *River of Tears: Country Music, Memory, and Modernity in Brazil*. Durham: Duke University Press.

Derrida, Jacques. 1983. *Dissemination*. Translated by Barbara Johnson. Chicago: University of Chicago Press.

———. 1987. *The Post Card: From Socrates to Freud and Beyond*. Translated by Alan Bass. Chicago: University of Chicago Press.

Di Giovine, Michael. 2009. *The Heritage-Scape: UNESCO, World Heritage and Tourism*. New York: Lexington Books.

Dias Tavares, Luís Henrique. 1966. *O problema da involução industrial na Bahia*. Salvador: UFBA.

———. 2001. *História da Bahia*. Salvador: EDUFBA.

Downey, Gregory. 2005. *Learning Capoeira: Lessons in Cunning from an Afro-Brazilian Art*. New York: Oxford University Press.

Dreyfus, Hubert, and Paul Rabinow. 1983. *Michel Foucault: Beyond Structuralism and Hermeneutics*. Chicago: University of Chicago Press.

Dunn, Christopher. 1994. "Between Markets and Patrons: The Field of Afro-Bahian Carnival Music." *Lucero* 5:47–56.

Egginton, William. 2005. "Baroque Anxieties and Strategies of Survival of Baroque Holes and Baroque Folds." In *Hispanic Baroques: Reading Cultures in Context*, edited by Nicholas Spadaccini and Luis Martin-Estudillo, 55–71. Nashville: Vanderbilt University Press.

Elyachar, Julia. 2005. *Markets of Dispossession: NGOs, Economic Development, and the State in Cairo*. Durham: Duke University Press.

Engelke, Matthew. 2007. *A Problem of Presence: Beyond Scripture in an African Church*. Berkeley: University of California Press.

Espinheira, Gey. 1984. *Divergência e prostituição*. Salvador: Tempo Brasileiro.

Falcão, Joaquim Arruda. 1984. "Política cultural e democracia: A preservação do patrimônio histórico e artístico nacional." In *Estado e cultura no Brasil*, edited by Sérgio Miceli, 21–39. São Paulo: DIFEL.

Fassin, Didier. 2009. "Another Politics of Life Is Possible." *Theory, Culture & Society* 26 (5): 44–60.

Feld, Steven. 2012. *Sound and Sentiment: Birds, Weeping, Poetics, and Song in Kaluli Expression*. 3rd ed. Durham: Duke University Press.

Feldman, Ilana. 2008. *Governing Gaza: Bureaucracy, Authority, and the Work of Rule, 1917–1967*. Durham: Duke University Press.

Ferme, Mariane. 2001. *The Underneath of Things: Violence, History, and the Everyday in Sierra Leone*. Berkeley: University of California Press.

Fernandes, Florestan. 1965. *A integração do negro na sociedade de classes*. São Paulo: Companhia Editora Nacional.

———. 1977. *O folclore em questão*. São Paulo: Editora Hucitec.

Ferry, Elizabeth. 2005. *Not Ours Alone: Patrimony, Value, and Collectivity in Contemporary Mexico*. New York: Columbia University Press.

Filho, Godofredo. 1969. "Rodrigo Mello Franco de Andrade." *Revista da Cultura da Bahia* X (January/June): 11–14.

———. 1987. *Irmã poesia: Seleção de poemas, 1923–1986*. Salvador: Secretaria da Educacação e Cultura da Bahia, Academia de Letras da Bahia.

———. 2007. *Diário de Godofredo Filho*. Edited by Fernando da Rocha Peres and Vera Rollemberg. Salvador: EDUFBA.

Flynn, Peter. 1979. *Brazil: A Political Analysis*. Boulder, Colo.: Westview Press.

Fonseca, Maria Cecilia Londres. 1997. *O Patrimônio em processo: Trajetória da politica federal de preservação no Brasil*. Rio de Janeiro: UFRJ/Minc/IPHAN.

Foster, Robert. 2003. *Materializing the Nation: Commodities, Consumption and the Media in Papua New Guinea*. Bloomington: University of Indiana Press.

Foucault, Michel. 1991. "Governmentality." In *The Foucault Effect: Studies in Governmentality*, edited by Graham Burchell, Colin Gordon, and Peter Miller, 87–104. Chicago: University of Chicago Press.

———. 1990. *The History of Sexuality*, Volume I. New York: Vintage Books.

———. 1972. *The Archaeology of Knowledge and the Discourse on Language*. Translated by A. M. Sheridan Smith. New York: Pantheon Books.

Fraga Filho, Walter. 1996. *Mendigos, moleques, e vadios na Bahia do século XIX*. São Paulo: Editora Hucitec.

Franklin, Sarah. 2007. *Dolly Mixtures: The Remaking of Genealogy*. Durham: Duke University Press.

———. 2013. "Analogic Return: The Reproductive Life of Conceptuality." *Theory, Culture & Society* 31 (2/3): 243–61.

Franquesa, Jaume. 2013. "On Keeping and Selling: The Political Economy of Heritage Making in Contemporary Spain." *Current Anthropology* 54 (3): 346–69.

Frazier, E. Franklin. 1990. *The Caribbean: Genesis of a Fragmented Nationalism*. New York: Oxford University Press.

French, Jan Hoffman. 2007. "Performing Slave Descent: Cultural Heritage and the Right to Land in Brazil." In *Cultural Heritage and Human Rights*, edited by Helaine Silverman and D. Fairchild Ruggles, 106–32. New York: Springer.

———. 2009. *Legalizing Identities: Becoming Black or Indian in Brazil's Northeast.* Chapel Hill: University of North Carolina Press.

French, John. 2000. "The Missteps of Anti-Imperialist Reason: Bourdieu, Wacquant and Hanchard's Orpheus and Power." *Theory, Culture & Society* 17 (1): 107–28.

———. 2003. "Translation, Diasporic Dialogue, and the Errors of Pierre Bourdieu and Loïc Wacquant." *Nepantla* 4 (1): 375–89.

Freyre, Gilberto. 1942. "A condição de provinciano." *Cultura Política* 2 (15): 13–16.

———. 1944. *Na Bahia em 1943.* Rio de Janeiro: Livraria José Olympio.

———. 1952. "Manifesto regionalista de 1926." *Boletim do Instituto Joaquim Nabuco de Pesquisas Sociais. Recife* 1 (1): 21–43.

———. 1963. *The Mansions and the Shanties: The Making of Modern Brazil.* Translated by H. de Onís. New York: Knopf.

———. 1968. *Região e tradição.* Rio de Janeiro: Reccord.

———. 1969. *New World in the Tropics: The Culture of Modern Brazil.* New York: Knopf.

———. 1970. *Assombrações do Recife velho: Algumas notas históricas e outras tantas folclóricas em tôrno do sobrenatural do passado recifense.* Rio de Janeiro: J. Olympio.

———. 1986. *The Masters and the Slaves: A Study in the Development of Brazilian Civilization.* Translated by S. Putnam. Berkeley: University of California Press.

Fry, Peter. 1982. *Para Inglês ver: Identidade e política na cultura brasileira.* Rio de Janeiro: Zahar.

———. 1995. "Why Is Brazil Different?" *Times Literary Supplement* 8, December 6–7.

———. 2005. *A persistência da raça: Ensaios antropológicos sobre o Brasil e a África austral.* Rio de Janeiro: Civilização Brasileira.

Fry, Peter, Yvonne Maggie, Marcos Chor Maiio, Simone Monteiro, and Ricardo Ventura Santos, eds. 2007. *Divisões perigosas: Políticas raciais no Brasil contemporâneo.* Rio de Janeiro: Civlização Brasileira.

Galinsky, Philip. 1996. "Co-optation, Cultural Resistance, and Afro-Brazilian Identity: A History of the 'Pagode' Samba Movement in Rio de Janeiro." *Latin American Music Review* 17 (2): 120–49.

Gallegos, Rómulo. 2012. *Doña Barbara: A Novel.* Translated by Robert Malloy. Chicago: University of Chicago Press.

Garber, Marjorie. 1991. *Vested Interests: Transvestitism and Cultural Anxiety.* New York: Routledge.

García Canclini, Néstor. 2001. *Consumers and Citizens.* Minneapolis: University of Minnesota Press.

García Márquez, Gabriel. 2005. *Memories of my Melancholy Whores.* New York: Knopf.

Garfield, Seth. 2001. *Indigenous Struggle at the Heart of Brazil: State Policy, Frontier Expansion, and the Xavante Indians, 1937–1988.* Durham: Duke University Press.

Gaudenzi, Paulo. 1999. *Operário do Turismo: Retalhos de idéias e pensamentos.* Salvador: Omar G. Editora.

Geertz, Clifford. 1973. "Deep Play: Notes on the Balinese Cockfight." In *The Interpretation of Cultures: Selected Essays,* 412–54. New York: Basic Books.

Gell, Arthur. 1998. *Art and Agency: An Anthropological Theory.* New York: Oxford University Press.

Gibson, James. 1979. *The Ecological Approach to Visual Perception.* Boston: Houghton Mifflin.

Gil, Gilberto, and Caetano Veloso. 1994. *Tropicalia 2.* New York: Elecktra.

Gilroy, Paul. 1995. *The Black Atlantic: Modernity and Double-Consciousness.* Cambridge, Mass.: Harvard University Press.

Goffman, Erving. 1971. *Relations in Public: Microstudies of the Public Order.* New York: Basic Books.

Goldstein, Donna. 2003. *Race, Class, Violence and Sexuality in a Rio Shantytown.* Berkeley: University of California Press.

Gomes, Angela de Castro. 1996. *História e historiadores.* Rio de Janeiro: FGV.

Gomes, Marco, Aurélio A. de Filgueiras, and Ana Fernandes. 1995. "Pelourinho: Turismo, identidade e consumo cultural." In *Pelo Pelô: História, cultura e cidade,* edited by Marco Aurélio A. de Filgueiras Gomes, 47–58. Salvador: EDUFBA.

Gonçalves, José Reginaldo Santos. 2003. *A Retórica da perda: Os discursos do patrimônio cultural no Brasil.* Rio de Janeiro: Ed. da UFRJ/ Ministério da Cultura-IPHAN.

———. 2005. "Ressonância, materialidade e subjetividade: As culturas como patrimônios." *Horizontes Antropológicos* 11 (23): 15–36.

Gonçalves da Silva, Vagner. 2000. *O antropólogo e sua magia: Trabalho de campo e texto etnográfico nas pesquisas antropológicas sobre as religiões afro-brasileiras.* São Paulo: EDUSP.

———. 2006. "Transes em trânsito: Continuidades e rupturas entre neopentecostalismo e religiões afro-brasileiras." In *As religiões no Brasil: Continuidades e rupturas,* edited by Faustino Teixeira and Renata Menezes, 207–28. Petrópolis: Vozes.

———. 2007. "Entre a Gira de Fé e Jesus de Nazaré: Relações sócio-estruturais entre neopentecostalismo e religiões afro-brasileiras." In *Intolerância religiosa,* edited by Vagner Gonçalves da Silva, 191–260. São Paulo: EDUSP.

González Echevarría, Roberto. 2012. *Love and the Law in Cervantes.* New Haven: Yale University Press.

Gordilho Souza, Angela. 2000. *Limites do habitar: Segregação e exclusão na configuração urbana contemporânea de Salvador e perspectivas no final do século XX.* Salvador: EDUFBA.

Graham, Laura. 2002. "How Should an Indian Speak? Amazonian Indians and the Symbolic Politics of Language in the Global Public Sphere." In *Indigenous Movements, Self-Representation, and the State in Latin America,* edited by Kay Warren and Jean Jackson, 181–228. Austin: University of Texas Press.

Graham, Sandra Lauderdale. 1988. *House and Street: The Domestic World of Servants and Masters in Nineteenth-Century Rio de Janeiro.* Austin: University of Texas Press.

Gruzinski, Serge. 2001. *Images at War: Mexico from Columbus to Blade Runner (1492–2019)*. Translated by Heather MacLean. Durham: Duke University Press.

Guerreiro, Goli. 2000. *A trama dos tambores: A música afro-pop de Salvador*. São Paulo: Editora 34.

Guimarães, Antônio Sérgio. 1987. "Estrutura e formação das classes sociais na Bahia." *Cadernos* CRH 2:1–31.

———. 2001. "The Misadventures of Nonracialism in Brazil." In *Beyond Racism: Race and Inequality in Brazil, South Africa, and the United States*, edited by Charles Hamilton, Lynne Huntley, Neville Alexander, Antonio Sérgio Guimarães, and Wilmot James, 157–86. Boulder, Colo.: Lynn Rienner Publishers.

———. 2002. *Classes, raças e democracia*. São Paulo: Editora 34.

———. 2007. "Depois da democracia racial." *Tempo Social* 18 (2): 269–87.

Guy, Donna. 1991. *Sex and Danger in Buenos Aires*. Lincoln: University of Nebraska Press.

Hacking, Ian. 1986. "Self-Improvement." In *The Foucault Reader*, edited by David Hoy, 235–40. Oxford: Blackwell.

———. 1991. "How Should We Do the History of Statistics?" In *The Foucault Effect: Studies in Governmentality*, edited by Graham Burchell, Colin Gordon, and Peter Miller, 181–95. Chicago: University of Chicago Press.

———. 1999. *The Social Construction of What?* Cambridge, Mass.: Harvard University Press.

Hale, Charles. 2002. "Does Multiculturalism Menace? Governance, Cultural Rights and the Politics of Identity in Guatemala." *Journal of Latin American Studies* 34 (3): 485–524.

———. 2006. Mas que un Indio *(More Than an Indian): Racial Ambivalence and the Paradox of Neoliberal Multiculturalism in Guatemala*. Santa Fe: SAR Press.

Hanchard, Michael. 1994. *Orpheus and Power: The Movimento Negro of Rio de Janeiro and São Paulo, Brazil, 1945–1988*. Princeton: Princeton University Press.

———. 1999. "Introduction." In *Racial Politics in Contemporary Brazil*, edited by Michael Hanchard, 1–26. Durham: Duke University Press.

———. 2003. "Acts of Misrecognition: Transnational Black Politics, Anti-Imperialism and the Ethnocentrisms of Pierre Bourdieu and Loïc Wacquant." *Theory, Culture & Society* 20 (4): 5–29.

Handler, Richard. 1985. "On Having a Culture: Nationalism and the Preservation of Quebec's Patrimoine." In *Objects and Others: Essays in Museums and Material Culture*, edited by George Stocking, 192–217. Madison: University of Wisconsin Press.

———. 1991. "Who Owns the Past? History, Cultural Property, and the Logic of Possessive Individualism." In *The Politics of Culture*, edited by Brett Williams, 63–74. Washington, D.C.: Smithsonian Institution Press.

Handler, Richard, and Eric Gable. 1997. *The New History in an Old Museum*. Durham: Duke University Press.

Hanks, William. 2010. *Converting Words: Maya in the Age of the Cross*. Berkeley: University of California Press.

Haraway, Donna. 1997. *Modest_Witness@Second_Millennium.FemaleMan©_Meets_OncoMouse*.™ New York: Routledge.

Harris, Cheryl. 1993. "Whiteness as Property." *Harvard Law Review* 106 (8): 1707–91.

Harris, Marvin. 1956. *Town and Country in Brazil*. New York: Columbia University Press.

———. 1964. *Patterns of Race in the Americas*. New York: Walker.

———. 1970. "Referential Ambiguity and the Calculus of Brazilian Racial Identity." *Southwestern Journal of Anthropology* 26 (1): 1–14.

Harris, Marvin, and Conrad Kottak. 1963. "The Structural Significance of Brazilian Racial Categories." *Sociologia* 25:203–9.

Hartigan, John. 1999. *Racial Situations: Class Predicaments of Whiteness in Detroit*. Princeton: Princeton University Press.

———. 2013. "Knowing Race." In *Anthropology of Race: Genes, Biology and Culture*, edited by John Hartigan, 3–20. Santa Fe: School for Advanced Research.

Harvey, David. 2004. "The 'New' Imperialism: Accumulation by Dispossession." *Socialist Register* 40:63–87.

———. 2008. "The Right to the City." *New Left Review* 53:23–40.

Hasenbalg, Carlos. 1979. *Discriminação e desigualdades raciais no Brasil*. Rio de Janeiro: Graal.

Heckenberger, Michael. 2012. "Marginal Bodies, Altered States, and Subhumans: (Dis)Articulations between Physical and Virtual Realities in Centro, São Paulo." In *Human No More: Digital Subjectivities, Unhuman Subjects, and the End of Anthropology*, edited by Neil Whitehead and Michael Wesch, 199–216. Boulder: University Press of Colorado.

Hegel, George W. F. 1977. *Phenomenology of Spirit*. Translated by A. V. Miller. New York: Oxford University Press.

Heidegger, Martin. 1962. *Being and Time*. Translated by John Macquarrie and Edward Robinson. New York: Harper & Row.

———. 1977. *The Question Concerning Technology and Other Essays*. Translated by William Lovitt. New York: Garland Publishing.

———. 1993a. "The Question Concerning Technology." In *Basic Writings*, edited by David Farrell Krell, 307–42. New York: HarperCollins.

———. 1993b. "Building, Dwelling, Thinking." In *Basic Writings*, edited by David Farrell Krell, 343–65. New York: HarperCollins.

Helmreich, Stephan. 2007. "An Anthropologist Underwater: Immersive Soundscapes, Submarine Cyborgs, and Transductive Ethnography." *American Ethnologist* 34 (4): 621–41.

———. 2011. "Nature/Culture/Seawater." *American Anthropologist* 113 (1): 132–44.

Henfrey, Colin. 1981. "The Hungry Imagination: Social Formation, Popular Culture and Ideology in Bahia." In *The Logic of Poverty: The Case of the Brazilian Northeast*, edited by Simon Mitchell, 58–108. London: Routledge & Kegan Paul.

Henry, James. 2003. *The Blood Bankers: Tales from the Global Underground Economy*. New York: Four Walls Eight Windows.

Herron, James. 2003. "Animating the State: Discourses of Authority and Intimacy in the Colombian Agrarian Bank." PhD dissertation, University of Michigan.

Hertzman, Marc. 2013. *Making Samba: A New History of Race and Music in Brazil*. Durham: Duke University Press.

Herzfeld, Michael. 1993. *The Social Production of Indifference: Exploring the Symbolic Roots of Western Bureaucracy.* Chicago: University of Chicago Press.

———. 1997. *Cultural Intimacy: Social Poetics in the Nation-State.* New York: Routledge.

Hill, Jane. 1993. "Hasta la Vista, Baby: Anglo Spanish in the American Southwest." *Critique of Anthropology* 13 (2): 145–76.

———. 1995. "The Voices of Don Gabriel." In *The Dialogic Emergence of Culture,* edited by Dennis Tedlock and Bruce Mannheim, 97–147. Urbana: University of Illinois Press.

———. 1998. "Language, Race, and White Public Space." *American Anthropologist* 100 (3): 680–89.

Hirschkind, Charles. 2004. *The Ethical Soundscape: Cassette Sermons and Islamic Counterpublics.* New York: Columbia University Press.

Hobsbawm, Eric. 1983. "Introduction: The Invention of Tradition." In *The Invention of Tradition,* edited by Eric Hobsbawm and Terence Ranger, 1–14. Cambridge: Cambridge University Press.

Holston, James. 1989. *The Modernist City.* Chicago: University of Chicago Press.

———. 1991. "The Misrule of Law: Land and Usurpation in Brazil." *Comparative Studies in Society and History* 33 (4): 695–725.

———. 2008. *Insurgent Citizenship: Disjunctions of Democracy and Modernity in Brazil.* Princeton: Princeton University Press.

Huggins, Martha, and Myriam Mesquita. 2000. "Civic Invisibility, Marginality and Moral Exclusion: The Murder of Street Youth in Brazil." In *Children on the Streets of the Americas: Globalization, Homelessness and Education in the United States, Brazil, and Cuba,* edited by Roslyn Arlin Mickelson and Marian Wright Edelman, 257–68. New York: Routledge.

Hull, Matthew. 2012. *Government of Paper: The Materiality of Bureaucracy in Urban Pakistan.* Berkeley: University of California Press.

Humphreys, Josephine. 2001. "Celebration: Salvador da Bahia." *New York Times Sunday Magazine.* March 1.

Ickes, Scott. 2013. *African-Brazilian Culture and Regional Identity in Bahia, Brazil.* Gainesville: University of Florida Press.

Ingold, Tim. 1988. "Introduction." In *What Is an Animal?* edited by Tim Ingold, 1–16. New York: Routledge.

———. 2007. *Lines: A Brief History.* New York: Routledge.

Instituto do Patrimônio Cultural e Artístico da Bahia (IPAC). 1994. *Centro Histórico de Salvador: Programa de Recuperação/Salvador's Historic District, Recovery Program.* Salvador: Editora Corrupio.

———. 1997. *Pelourinho: Levantamento Sócio-Econômico,* 2nd ed. Salvador: Secretaria da Cultura e Turismo.

———. 1998. *Catedral Basílica do São Salvador da Bahia.* Salvador: Solisluna Design e Editora Ltda.

Jackson, Jean. 1995a. "Culture, Genuine and Spurious: The Politics of Indianness in the Vaupés, Colombia." *American Ethnologist* 22 (1): 3–27.

———. 1995b. "Preserving Indian Culture: Shaman Schools and Ethno-Education in the Vaupés, Colombia." *Cultural Anthropology* 10 (3): 302–29.

———. 2002. "Contested Discourses of Authority in Colombian National Indigenous Politics: The 1996 Summer Takeovers." In *Indigenous Movements, Self-Representation and the State in Latin America*, edited by Kay Warren and Jean Jackson, 81–122. Austin: University of Texas Press.

———. 2009. "Traditional, Transnational and Cosmopolitan: The Colombian Yanacona Look to the Past and to the Future." *American Ethnologist* 36 (3): 521–44.

Jackson, John. 2005. *Real Black: Adventures in Racial Sincerity*. Durham: Duke University Press.

Jakobson, Roman. 1999. "Linguistics and Poetics." In *The Discourse Reader*, edited by Adam Jaworski and Nikolas Coupland, 54–62. New York: Routledge.

James, Jason. 2012. *Preservation and National Belonging in Eastern Germany: Heritage Fetishism and Redeeming Germanness*. New York: Palgrave Macmillan.

Johnson, Paul Christopher. 2002. *Secrets, Gossip, and Gods: The Transformation of Brazilian Candomblé*. New York: Oxford University Press.

———. 2011. "An Atlantic Genealogy of 'Spirit Possession.'" *Comparative Studies in Society and History* 53 (2): 393–425.

Karam, John Tofik. 2007. *Another Arabesque: Syrian-Lebanese Ethnicity in Neoliberal Brazil*. Philadelphia: Temple University Press.

Keane, Webb. 2003. "Semiotics and the Social Analysis of Material Things." *Language and Communication* 23 (3–4): 409–25.

———. 2005. "Signs Are Not the Garb of Meaning: On the Social Analysis of Material Things." In *Materiality*, edited by Daniel Miller, 182–205. Durham: Duke University Press.

———. 2007. *Christian Moderns: Freedom and Fetish in the Mission Encounter*. Berkeley: University of California Press.

Kelly, Robin. 1998. "Check the Technique: Black Urban Culture and the Predicament of Social Science." In *In Near Ruins: Cultural Theory at the End of the Century*, edited by Nicholas Dirks, 39–66. Minneapolis: University of Minnesota Press.

Kern, Stephen. 2004. *A Cultural History of Causality: Science, Murder Novels, and Systems of Thought*. Princeton: Princeton University Press.

Kirkendall, Andrew. 2010. *Paulo Freire and the Cold War Politics of Literacy*. Chapel Hill: University of North Carolina Press.

Kirshenblatt-Gimblett, Barbara. 2004. "Intangible Heritage as Metacultural Production." *Museum International* 56 (1–2): 52–65.

———. 2006. "Exhibitionary Complexes." In *Museum Frictions: Public Cultures/Global Transformations*, edited by Ivan Karp, Anne Kratz Cori, Lynn Svaja, and Tomás Ybarra-Frausto, 35–45. Durham: Duke University Press.

Kjoster, Martijn. 2014. "Fear and Intimacy: Citizenship in a Recife Slum, Brazil." *Ethnos* 79 (2): 215–37.

Kockelman 2005. "The Semiotic Stance." *Semiotica* 157:233–304.

———. 2013. *Agent, Person, Subject, Self: A Theory of Ontology, Interaction, and Infrastructure*. New York: Oxford University Press.

Kosek, Jake. 2006. *Understories: The Political Life of Forests in Northern New Mexico*. Durham: Duke University Press.

Kottak, Conrad. 1966. "Race Relations in a Bahian Fishing Village." *Luso-Brazilian Review* 4:35–52.

———. 2000. *Assault on Paradise: Social Change in a Brazilian Village*. 3rd ed. New York: McGraw-Hill.

Kulick, Don. 1996. "Commotion: Public Scandal as Resistance among Brazilian Transgendered Prostitutes." *Anthropology Today* 12 (6): 3–7.

———. 1998. *Travesti: Sex, Gender, and Culture among Brazilian Transgendered Prostitutes*. Chicago: University of Chicago Press.

Kundera, Milan. 1999. "Introduction." In *Don Quixote de la Mancha*. Translated by Charles Jarvis. New York: Oxford University Press.

Lacerda, João. 1938. *O Estado Novo: Democracia e corporatismo, a posição do Brasil*. Rio de Janeiro: Editora Nacional.

Landes, Ruth. 1994. *City of Women*. Albuquerque: University of New Mexico Press.

Latour, Bruno. 1993. *We Have Never Been Modern*. Translated by Catherine Porter. Cambridge, Mass.: Harvard University Press.

Lauderdale Graham, Sandra. 1992. *House and Street: The Domestic World of Servants and Masters in Nineteenth-Century Rio de Janeiro*. Austin: University of Texas Press.

Leal, Victor Nunes. 1977. *Coronelismo: The Municipality and Representative Government in Brazil*. Cambridge: Cambridge University Press.

Leibing, Annette, and Sibylle Benninghoff-Lühl. 2001. *Devorando o tempo: Brasil, o país sem memória*. São Paulo: Editora Mandarim.

Léry, Jean de. 1990. *History of a Voyage to the Land of Brazil, Otherwise Called America*. Translated by Janet Whatley. Berkeley: University of California Press.

Lesser, Jeffrey. 1999. *Negotiating National Identity: Immigrants, Minorities, and the Struggle for Ethnicity in Brazil*. Durham: Duke University Press.

Lévi-Strauss, Claude. 1992. *Tristes Tropiques*. Translated by John and Doreen Weightman. New York: Penguin.

Lévy, André. 1986. *Nouvelles lettres édifiantes et curieuses d'Extrême-Occident, par des voyageurs lettrés chinois à la Belle Epoque*. Paris: Seghers.

Lewis, J. Lowell. 1992. *Ring of Liberation: Deceptive Discourse in Brazilian Capoeira*. Chicago: University of Chicago Press.

Lewis, Oscar. 1966. *La Vida: A Puerto Rican Family in the Culture of Poverty: San Juan and New York*. New York: Random House.

Locke, John. 1980. *Second Treatise of Government*. Edited by C. B. Macpherson. Indianapolis: Hackett Publishing.

Lomnitz, Claudio. 2001. *Deep Mexico, Silent Mexico: An Anthropology of Nationalism*. Minneapolis: University of Minnesota Press.

Lynch, Kevin. 1960. *The Image of the City*. Cambridge, Mass.: MIT Press.

———. 1976. *Managing the Sense of a Region*. Cambridge, Mass.: MIT Press.

MacCannell, Dean. 1999. *The Tourist: A New Theory of the Leisure Class*. Berkeley: University of California Press.

Machado, Paulo A. L. 1987. *Ação civil pública: Tombamento*. São Paulo: Editora Revista dos Tribunais.

MacPherson, C. B. 1964. *The Political Theory of Possessive Individualism: Hobbes to Locke*. New York: Oxford University Press.

Mafra, Clara Cristina Jost. 2011. "Saintliness and Sincerity in the Formation of the Christian Person." *Ethnos* 76 (4): 448–68.

Malinowski, Bronislaw. 1984. *Argonauts of the Western Pacific: An Account of Native Enterprise and Adventure in the Archipelagoes of Melanesian New Guinea*. Long Grove, Ill.: Waveland Press.

Manning, Paul. 2004. "Owning and Belonging: A Semiotic Investigation of the Affective Categories of Bourgeois Society." *Comparative Studies in Society and History* 46 (2004): 300–325.

———. 2008. "Materiality and Cosmology: Old Georgian Churches as Sacred, Sublime, and Secular Objects." *Ethnos* 73 (3): 327–60.

———. 2012. *Semiotics of Drink and Drinking*. New York: Bloomsbury Academic Press.

Marques, Ana Claudia. 2002. *Intrigas e questões: Vingança de família e tramas sociais no sertão de Pernambuco*. Rio de Janeiro: Relume Dumará.

Martins, Francisco Goncalves. 1852. *Falla que recitou o Presidente da Provincia da Bahia, o Desembargador Conselheiro Francisco Goncalves Martins, n'abertura da Assembleia Legislativa da mesma provincia, no 10 de março de 1852*. Salvador: Typographia Const. De Vicente Ribeiro Moreira.

Martins dos Santos, Francisco. 1941. *O fato moral e o fato social da década getuliana*. Rio de Janeiro: Z. Valverde.

Marx, Karl. 1973. *Grundrisse: Foundations of the Critique of Political Economy*. New York: Penguin Books.

———. 1977. *Capital*, Volume I: *A Critique of Political Economy*. New York: Vintage Books.

Matory, J. Lorand. 2005. *Black Atlantic Religion: Tradition, Transnationalism, and Matriarchy in the Afro-Brazilian Candomblé*. Princeton: Princeton University Press.

Mattos, Hebe. 1998. *Das cores do silêncio*. Rio de Janeiro: Arquivo Nacional.

Mattos, Hebe, and Marta Abreu. 2011. "'Remanescentes das Comunidades dos Quilombos': Memória do cativeiro, patrimônio cultural e direito á reparação." *Revista Iberoamericana* 42:147–60.

Mbembe, Achille. 2003. "Necropolitics." *Public Culture* 15 (1): 11–40.

McCallum, Cecilia. 2005. "Racialized Bodies, Naturalized Classes: Moving Through the City of Salvador da Bahia." *American Ethnologist* 32 (1): 100–117.

McGranahan, Carole. 2010. *Arrested Histories: Tibet, the CIA, and Memories of a Forgotten War*. Durham: Duke University Press.

Meade, Teresa. 1997. *"Civilizing" Rio: Reform and Resistance in a Brazilian City, 1889–1930*. College Park: Pennsylvania State University Press.

Meskell, Lynn. 2002. "Negative Heritage and Past Mastering in Archaeology." *Anthropological Quarterly* 75 (3): 557–74.

———. 2005. "Objects in the Mirror Appear Closer Than They Are." In *Materiality*, edited by Daniel Miller, 51–71. Durham: Duke University Press.

Meyer, Birgitte. 2011. "Mediation and Immediacy: Sensational Forms, Semiotic Ideologies, and the Question of the Medium." *Social Anthropology* 19:123–39.

———. 2012. "Material Religion: How Things Matter." In *Things: Religion and the Question of Materiality*, edited by Dick Houtman and Birgitte Meyer, 1–23. New York: Fordham University Press.

Miceli, Sérgio. 1984. "O processo de 'construção institucional' na área cultural federal (anos 70)." In *Estado e cultura no Brasil*, edited by Sérgio Miceli, 53–84. São Paulo: Difel.

Ministério da Cultura. 1995. *A invenção do patrimônio: Continuidade e ruptura na constituição de uma política oficial de preservação no Brasil*. Brasilia: IPHAN.

Mintz, Sidney, and Richard Price. 1992. *The Birth of African-American Culture: An Anthropological Perspective*. Boston: Beacon.

Miranda, Alberto. 1995. *Memorial de um repórter de polícia*. Salvador: Alberto Miranda.

Mitchell, Gregory. 2011. "Turboconsumers™ in Paradise: Tourism, Civil Rights, and Brazil's Gay Sex Industry." *American Ethnologist* 38 (4): 666–82.

Mitchell, Timothy. 1991. *Colonizing Egypt*. Berkeley: University of California Press.

Mitchell, W. J. T. 2002. *What Do Pictures Want? The Lives and Loves of Images*. Chicago: University of Chicago Press.

Moehn, Frederick. 2012. *Contemporary Carioca: Technologies of Mixing in a Brazilian Music Scene*. Durham: Duke University Press.

Monteiro Lobato, José Bento. 2008. *Saci Pererê, resultado de um inquérito*. Rio de Janeiro: Editora Globo.

Morães, Marcos Antônio, editor. 2000. *Correspondência: Mário de Andrade & Manuel Bandeira*. São Paulo: EDUSP.

———, ed. 2010. *Câmara Cascudo e Mário de Andrade: Cartas, 1924–1944*. São Paulo: Editora Global.

Moreira, Vicente Deocleciano. 1982. "Jovens ladrões: O caso do Maciel/Pelourinho." Master's thesis, Federal University of Bahia, Division of Social Sciences.

———. 2007. "Vivaldo e o Maciel." In *Vivaldo da Costa Lima: Intérprete do Afro-Brasil*, edited by Jeferson Bacelar and Claudio Pereira, 45–58. Salvador: EDUFBA.

Moten, Fred. 2003. *In the Break: The Aesthetics of the Black Radical Tradition*. Minneapolis: University of Minnesota Press.

Mott, Luiz. 1997. "Santo Antônio, o divino capitão-do-mato." In *Liberdade por um fio: História dos quilombos no Brasil*, edited by João Reis and Flávio dos Santos Gomes, 110–38. São Paulo: Companhia das Letras.

Mott, Luiz, and Marcelo Ferreira Cerqueira. 1997. *Os Travestis da Bahia & A AIDS: Prostituição, silicone e drogas*. Salvador: Grupo Gay da Bahia.

Moura, Milton Araújo. 2002. "World of Fantasy, Fantasy of the World: Geographic Space and Representation of Identity in the Carnival of Salvador, Bahia." In *Brazilian Popular Music and Globalization*, edited by Charles Perrone and Christopher Dune, 161–76. New York: Routledge.

Munn, Nancy. 1986. *The Fame of Gawa: A Symbolic Study of Value Transformation in a Massim Society*. Durham: Duke University Press.

Nascimento, Abdias. 1989. *Brazil: Mixture or Massacre? Essays in the Genocide of a Black People*. Translated by E. L. Nascimento. Dover, Mass.: Majority Press.

Navaro-Yashin, Yael. 2012. *The Make-Believe Space: Affective Geography in a Postwar Polity*. Durham: Duke University Press.

Navia, Patricio. 2009. "The Chilean Left: Socialist and Neoliberal." In *Beyond Neoliberalism in Latin America? Societies and Politics at the Crossroads*, edited by Philip Oxhorn, John Burdick, and Kenneth Roberts, 17–42. New York: Palgrave MacMillan.

Nelson, Diane. 2009. *Reckoning: The Ends of War in Guatemala.* Durham: Duke University Press.

Nietzsche, Friedrich. 1994. "On the Uses and Disadvantages of History for Life." In *Untimely Meditations,* translated by R. J. Hollingdale. New York: Cambridge University Press.

Nobles, Melissa. 2000. *Shades of Citizenship: Race and the Census in Modern Politics.* Stanford: Stanford University Press.

Nobre, Eduardo A. C. 2002. "Urban Regeneration Experiences in Brazil: Historical Preservation, Tourism Development and Gentrification in Salvador da Bahia." *Urban Design International* 7:109–24.

Nogueira, Oracy. 1954. "Preconceito racial de marca e preconceito racial de origem—Sugestão de um quadro de referência para a interpretação do material sobre relações raciais no Brasil." *Anais do XXXI Congresso Internacional de Americanistas.* Vol. 1. São Paulo.

———. 1985. *Tanto preto quanto branco: Estudos de relações raciais.* São Paulo: T.A. Queiroz.

Nujiten, Monique. 2013. "The Perversity of the 'Citizenship Game': Slum-Upgrading in the Urban Periphery of Recife, Brazil." *Critique of Anthropology* 33:8–25.

OCEPLAN. 1976. EPUCS—*uma experiência de planejamento urbano.* Salvador: PLANDURB.

Oliveira, Neuza Maria. 1994. *Damas de pau: O jogo aberto dos travestis no espelho da mulher.* Salvador: Centro Editorial e Didático da UFBA.

Oliven, Ruben. 1996. *Tradition Matters: Modern Gaúcho Identity in Brazil.* New York: Columbia University Press.

Ortiz, Fernando. 1995. *Cuban Counterpoint: Tobacco and Sugar.* Durham: Duke University Press.

Ortiz, Renato. 1984. *Cultura brasileira and identidade nacional.* São Paulo: Editora Brasiliense.

———. 1992. *Românticos e folcloristas: Cultura popular.* São Paulo: Editora Olho D'Agua.

Palmié, Stephan. 2008. "Genomics, Divination, 'Racecraft.'" *American Ethnologist* 34:203–20.

Pálsson, Gisli. 2007. *Anthropology and the New Genetics.* New York: Cambridge University Press.

Parés, Luis Nicolau. 2013. *The Formation of Candomblé: Vodun History and Ritual in Brazil.* Translated by Richard Vernon. Chapel Hill: University of North Carolina Press.

Parmentier, Richard. 1985. "Signs' Place in Medias Res: Peirce's Concept of Semiotic Mediation." In *Semiotic Mediation: Sociocultural and Psychological Perspectives.* Edited by Elizabeth Mertz and Richard Parmentier, 23–48. Orlando: Academic Press.

———. 2014. "Semiotic Degeneracy of Social Life: Prolegomenon to a Human Science of Semiosis." *Semiotica* 202:1–20.

Passariello, Phyllis. 2005. "Desperately Seeking Something: Che Guevara as Secular Saint." In *The Making of Saints: Contesting Sacred Ground*, edited by James Hopgood, 75–89. Tuscaloosa: University of Alabama Press.

Peirce, Charles S. 1955a. "Logic as Semiotic: The Theory of Signs." In *Philosophical Writings*, edited by J. Buchler, 98–119. New York: Dover Press.

———. 1955b. "The Law of Mind." In *Philosophical Writings*, edited by J. Buchler, 339–53. New York: Dover Press.

Perlman, Janice. 1976. *The Myth of Marginality: Urban Poverty and Politics in Rio de Janeiro*. Berkeley: University of California Press.

Perrone, Charles. 1992. "Axé, Ijexá, Olodum: The Rise of Afro and African Currents in Brazilian Popular Music." *Afro-Hispanic Review* XI (1–3): 42–50.

Perry, Keisha-Khan. 2004. "The Roots of Black Resistance: Race, Gender and the Struggle for Urban Land Rights in Salvador, Bahiba, Brazil." *Social Identities* 10 (6): 811–31.

———. 2013. *Black Women Against the Land Grab: The Fight for Racial Justice in Brazil*. Minneapolis: University of Minnesota Press.

Petryna, Adriana. 2002. *Life Exposed: Biological Citizens after Chernobyl*. Princeton: Princeton University Press.

Pinho, Patricia de Santana. 2009. *Mama Africa: Reinventing Blackness in Bahia*. Translator of original edition, Elena Langdon. Durham: Duke University Press.

Pizzigoni, Elizabeth. 2013. "Where Did All the Angels Go? An Interpretation of the Nahua Supernatural World." In *Angels, Demons and the New World*, edited by Fernando Cervantes and Andrew Redden, 126–45. New York: Cambridge University Press.

Plotkin, Mario Ben. 2011. "Psychoanalysis, Race Relations, and National Identity: The Reception of Psychoanalysis in Brazil, 1910 to 1940." In *Unconscious Dominions: Psychoanalysis, Colonial Trauma, and Global Sovereignties*, edited by Warwick Anderson, Deborah Jenson, and Richard Keller, 113–40. Durham: Duke University Press.

Power, Timothy. 2000. *The Political Right in Postauthoritarian Brazil: Elites, Institutions and Democratization*. College Park: Pennsylvania State University Press.

Price, Richard. 2006. *The Convict and the Colonel: A Story of Colonialism and Resistance in the Caribbean*. Durham: Duke University Press.

———. 2007. *Travels with Tooy: History, Memory, and the African American Imagination*. Chicago: University of Chicago Press.

Rago, Margareth. 1987. *Do cabare ao lar: A utopia da cidade disciplinar, Brasil; 1890–1930*. Rio de Janeiro: Paz e Terra.

———. 1991. *Os Prazeres da noite: Prostituição e códigos da sexualidade feminina em São Paulo (1890–1930)*. Rio de Janeiro: Paz e Terra.

Rahier, Jean Muteba. 2013. *Blackness in the Andes: Ethnographic Vignettes of Cultural Politics in the Time of Multiculturalism*. New York: Palgrave Macmillan.

Rama, Angel. 1996. *The Lettered City*. Translated by John Charles Chasteen. Durham: Duke University Press.

Ramos, Alcida. 1998. *Indigenism: Ethnic Politics in Brazil*. Madison: University of Wisconsin Press.

Rancière, Jacques. 2001. "Ten Thesis on Politics." *Theory & Event* 5 (3).

————. 2010. *Dissensus: On Politics and Aesthetics*. Edited and translated by Steven Corcoran. New York: Continuum.

Rapp, Rayna, Deborah Heath, and Karen Sue Taussig. 2003. "Flexible Eugenics: Technologies of the Self in the Age of Genetics." In *Genetic Nature/Culture: Anthropology and Science Beyond the Two Culture Divide*, edited by Alan Goodman, Deborah Heath, and Susan Lindee, 58–76. Berkeley: University of California Press.

————. 2004. "Genetic Citizenship." In *A Companion to the Anthropology of Politics*, edited by David Nugent and Joan Vincent, 152–67. Malden, Mass.: Blackwell.

Rappaport, Joanne. 1998. *The Politics of Memory: Native Historical Interpretation in the Colombian Andes*. Durham: Duke University Press.

Rebouças, Diógenes, and Godofredo Filho. 1985. *Salvador da Bahia de Todos os Santos no século XIX: Pintura Documental*. Salvador: Odebrecht, S.A.

Reddy, Sida. 2006. "Making Heritage Legible: Who Owns Traditional Medical Knowledge?" *International Journal of Cultural Property* 13:161–88.

Redfield, Peter. 2013. *Life in Crisis: The Ethical Journey of Doctors Without Borders*. Berkeley: University of California Press.

Reichmann, Rebecca. 1999. *Race in Contemporary Brazil: From Indifference to Inequality*. College Park: Penn State University Press.

Reis, João. 1995. *Slave Rebellion in Brazil: The Muslim Uprising of 1835 in Bahia*. Translated by Arthur Brakel. Baltimore: Johns Hopkins University Press.

————. 2003. *Death Is a Festival: Funeral Rites and Rebellion in Nineteenth-Century Brazil*. Translated by H. Sabrina Gledhill. Chapel Hill: University of North Carolina Press.

Rheinberger, Hans-Jörg. 2010. *An Epistemology of the Concrete: Twentieth-Century Histories of Life*. Durham: Duke University Press.

Richter, Gerhard. 2010. "Between Translation and Invention: The Photograph in Deconstruction." In *Copy, Archive, Signature: A Conversation on Photography*, edited by Gerhard Richter, translated by Jeff Fort, ix–xxxviii. Stanford: Stanford University Press.

Riles, Annelise. 2001. *The Network Inside Out*. Ann Arbor: University of Michigan Press.

Risério, Antonio. 1995. *Avant-garde na Bahia*. Salvador: Instituto Lina bo e p.m. bardi.

————. 2007. *A utopia brasileira e os movimentos negros*. São Paulo: Editora 34.

Rivera, José Eustacio. 2003. *The Vortex*. Translated by Earle K. James. Bogota: Panamericana Editora.

Rodrigues, João Jorge Santos. 1995. "O Olodum e o Pelourinho." In *Pelo Pelô: História, cultura e cidade*, edited by Marco Aurélio A. de Filgueiras Bomes, 81–92. Salvador: EDUFBA.

————. 1996. *Olodum: Estrada da paixão*. Salvador: Grupo Cultural Olodum/Casa de Jorge Amado.

Rodrigues, Raymundo Nina. 1935. *O animismo fetichista dos negros*. Rio de Janeiro: Livraria Civilização Brasileira.

————. 1938. *As raças humanas e a responsabilidade penal no Brasil*. São Paulo: Companhia Editora Nacional.

————. 1939. *As coletividades anormais.* Rio de Janeiro: Livraria Civilização Brasileira.

————. 1988. *Os africanos no Brasil.* Brasilia: Universidade de Brasilia.

Rojas, Eduardo. 1998. *Heritage Conservation in Latin America and the Caribbean: Recent Bank Experience.* Washington, D.C.: Inter-American Development Bank.

————. 1999. *Old Cities, New Assets: Preserving Latin America's Urban Heritage.* Washington, D.C.: Inter-American Development Bank.

Romo, Anadelia. 2010. *Brazil's Living Museum: Race, Reform, and Tradition in Bahia.* Chapel Hill: University of North Carolina Press.

Rose, Nikolas. 2007. *The Politics of Life Itself: Biomedicine, Power, and Subjectivity in the Twenty-first Century.* Princeton: Princeton University Press.

Rubin, Jeffrey. 2004. "Meanings and Mobilizations: A Cultural Politics Approach to Social Movements and States." *Latin American Research Review* 39 (3): 106–42.

Rubim, Antonio Albino Canelas, and Alexandre Barbalho. 2007. *Políticas culturais no Brasil.* Salvador: EDUFBA.

Sampaio, Antônio Heliodoro Lima. 1999. *Formas urbanas: Cidade real & cidade ideal, contribuição ao estudo urbanístico de Salvador.* Salvador: Quarteto Editora.

Sansi, Roger. 2007. *Fetishes and Monuments: Afro-Brazilian Art and Culture in the Twentieth Century.* New York: Berghahn.

————. 2009. "'Fazer o santo': Dom, iniciação e historicidade nas religiões afro-brasileiras." *Análise Social* 44 (1): 139–60.

————. 2013. "Encountering Images in Candomble." *Visual Anthropology* 26 (1): 18–33.

Sansone, Livio. 1994. "Pai preto, filho negro. Trabalho, cor e diferença geracio-nal." *Estudos Afro-Asiáticos* 25:73–98.

————. 1995. "O Pelourinho dos jovens negro-mestiços de classe baixa da grande Salvador." In *Pelo Pelô: história, cultura e cidade*, edited by Marco Aurélio A. de Filgueiras Bomes, 59–70. Salvador: EDUFBA.

————. 1996. "Nem somente preto our negro: O sistema de classificação racial no Brasil que Muda." *Afro-Ásia* 18:165–89.

————. 2000. "Os objetos da identidade negra: Consumo, mercantilização, global-ização e a criação de culturas negras no Brasil." *Mana: Estudos de Antropologia Social* 6 (1): 87–119.

————. 2001. "The Localization of Global Funk in Bahia and in Rio." In *Brazilian Popular Music and Globalization*, edited by C. Perrone and C. Dunn, 136–60. Gainesville: University of Florida Press.

————. 2003. *Blackness without Ethnicity: Constructing Race in Brazil.* New York: Palgrave Macmillan.

Santillán, Ricardo López. 2011. "Yucatecan Maya Professionals in Mérida and their Participation in the Cultural and Professional Fields." In *Selling Ethnicity: Urban Cultural Politics in the Americas*, edited by Olaf Kaltmeier, 205–20. Burlington, Vt.: Ashgate.

Santos, Joel Rufino dos. 1985. *O Movimento Negro e a crise brasileira.* São Paulo: Corrupio.

Santos, Juana Elbein dos. 1986. *Os Nàgô e a morte: Pàde, Asèsè e o culto Egun na Bahia.* 4th ed. Petropolis: Editora Vozes.

Santos, Milton. 1959. *O Centro da cidade do Salvador: Estudo de geografia urbana*. Salvador: Livraria Progresso.

Santos, Ricardo Ventura, Michael Kent, and Verlan Valle Gaspar Neto. 2014. "From Degeneration to Meeting Point: Historical Views on Race, Mixture, and the Biological Views on Diversity of the Brazilian Population." In *Mestizo Genomics, Race Mixture, Nation, and Science in Latin America*, edited by Peter Wade, Carlos López Beltrán, Eduardo Restrepo, and Ricardo Ventura Santos, 33–54. Durham: Duke University Press.

Santos Silva, Paulo. 2000. *Âncoras de tradição: Luta política, intelectuais e construção do discurso histórico na Bahia, 1930–1949*. Salvador: EDUFBA.

Sarmiento, Domingo. 2003. *Facundo: Civilization and Barbarism*. Translated by Kathleen Ross. Berkeley: University of California Press.

Saule Júnior, Nelson, and Patrícia de Menezes Cardoso. 2005. *Direito à moradia no Brasil*. São Paulo: Instituto Polis.

Saussure, Ferdinand de. 1998. *Course in General Linguistics*. Chicago: Open Court Publishing.

Scheele, Judith. 2006. "Algerian Graveyard Stories." *Journal of the Royal Anthropological Institute* 23 (4): 859–79.

Scheper-Hughes, Nancy. 1993. *Death Without Weeping: The Violence of Everyday Life in Brazil*. Berkeley: University of California Press.

Schivelbusch, Wolfgang. 2014. *The Great Railway Journey: The Industrialization of Time and Space in the Nineteenth Century*. Berkeley: University of California Press.

Schuller, Marc. 2012. *Killing with Kindness: Haiti, International Aid, and NGOs*. New Brunswick: Rutgers University Press.

Schwarcz, Lilia. 1999. *The Spectacle of the Races: Scientists, Institutions, and the Race Question in Brazil, 1870–1930*. Translated by Lilia Guyer. New York: Hill and Wang.

Schwartz, Stuart. 1985. *Sugar Plantations in the Formation of Brazilian Society, Bahia, 1550–1835*. Cambridge: Cambridge University Press.

Schwarz, Roberto. 1992. *Misplaced Ideas: Essays on Brazilian Culture*. Translated by John Gledson. New York: Verso.

Scott, David. 1991. "That Event, This Memory: Notes on the Anthropology of African Diasporas in the New World." *Diaspora* 1 (3): 261–84.

Scott, James. 1992. *Domination and the Arts of Resistance: Hidden Transcripts*. New Haven: Yale University Press.

Secretaria da Segurança Pública do Estado da Bahia. 1978. *Breve história do Instituto de Identificação Pedro Melo*. Salvador: Governo do Estado da Bahia.

Seed, Patricia. 1992. "Taking Possession and Reading Texts: Establishing the Authority of Overseas Empires." *William and Mary Quarterly* 49:183–209.

Serageldin, Ismail. 1998. *Culture and Development at the World Bank*. Washington, D.C.: World Bank.

Serra, Ordep. 1995. *Águas do rei*. Rio de Janeiro: Editora Vozes/Koinonia.

———. 2000a. "O sagrado na obra de Jorge Amado: a cidade de todos os santos." In *Ciclo de palestras: A Bahia de Jorge Amado*, edited by Myriam Fraga, 63–84. Salvador: Casa de Palavras.

———. 2000b. "O patrimônio negro, o povo-de-santo e a política de preservação." In *Faraimará: O caçador traz alegria*, edited by Cléo Martins & Raul Lody, 127–36. Rio de Janeiro: Editora Pallas.

———. 2000c. *Rumores da festa: O sagrado e o profano na Bahia*. Salvador: EDUFBA.

Sheriff, Robin. 2001. *Dreaming Equality: Color, Race, and Racism in Urban Brazil*. New Brunswick: Rutgers University Press.

Shryock, Andrew. 2004. "Other Culture/Self-Aware: First Thoughts on Cultural Intimacy and Mass Mediation." In *Off Stage/On Display: Intimacy and Ethnography in the Age of Public Culture*, edited by Andrew Shryock, 3–30. Stanford: Stanford University Press.

Sifuentes-Jáuregui, Ben. 2002. *Transvestitism, Masculinity and Latin American Literature: Genders Share Flesh*. New York: Palgrave.

Silva, Paula C. da. 1995. *Negros à luz dos fornos: Representações do trabalho e da cor entre metalúrgicos baianos*. Salvador: Dynamis Editorial.

Silva, Paulo Santos. 2000. *Âncoras de tradição: Luta política, intelectuais e construção do discurso histórico na Bahia (1930–1949)*. Salvador: EDUFBA.

Silverman, Helaine, and D. Fairchild Ruggles. 2007. "Cultural Heritage and Human Rights." In *Cultural Heritage and Human Rights*, edited by Helaine Silverman and D. Fairchild Ruggles, 3–22. New York: Springer.

Silverstein, Michael. 1976. "Shifters, Linguistic Categories, and Cultural Description." In *Meaning in Anthropology*, edited by Keith Basso, 11–55. Albuquerque: University of New Mexico Press.

———. 1979. "Language Structure and Linguistic Ideology." In *The Elements: A Parasession on Linguistic Units and Levels*, edited by Paul Clyne, William Hanks, and Carol Hofbauer, 193–247. Chicago: Chicago Linguistics Society.

———. 2003. "Translation, Transduction, Transformation: Skating Glossando on Thin Semiotic Ice." In *Cultures: Perspectives on Translation and Anthropology*, edited by Paula Rubel and Abraham Rosman, 75–105. Oxford: Berg.

Simas Filho, Américo. 1969a. "Legislação de proteção aos bens culturais." *Revista de Cultura da Bahia* (July/December): 39–71.

———. 1969b. "Considerações em tôrno de uma metodologia adequada para o estudo de centros históricos." *Revista de Cultura da Bahia* (July/December): 21–45.

———. 1971a. "Sistema de proteção aos bens culturais." *Revista de Cultura da Bahia* (July/December): 39–71.

———. 1971b. "Ensino e pesquisa na defesa dos bens culturais." *Revista de Cultura da Bahia* (July/December): 17–29.

———. 1977. "Problemática e critérios para delimitação das áreas de proteção histórica." Xerox of speech at the Seminário sobre o Centro da Cidade do Salvador, Public Library, Salvador, Bahia, January 28.

———. 1998. *Evolução física de Salvador, 1549 a 1800*. Salvador: UFBA/Prefeitura Municipal de Salvador.

Skidmore, Thomas. 1974. *Black into White: Race and Nationality in Brazilian Thought*. New York: Oxford University Press.

———. 1992. "Bi-Racial U.S.A. vs. Multi-Racial Brazil: Is the Contrast still Valid?" *Journal of Latin American Studies* 25 (2): 373–86.

Skurski, Julie. 1994. "The Ambiguities of Authenticity in Latin America: Doña Barbara and the Construction of National Identity." *Poetics Today*: 605–42.

Slater, Candace. 1986. *Trail of Miracles: Stories from a Pilgrimage in Northeast Brazil*. Berkeley: University of California Press.

Smith, Laurajane and Natsuko Akagawa. 2009. "Introduction." *Intangible Heritage*, edited by Laurajane Smith and Natsuko Akagawa, 1–10. New York: Routledge.

Soares, Luiz Carlos. 1992. *Rameiras, ilhoas, polacas: A prostituição no Rio de Janeiro do século XIX*. São Paulo: Editora Ática.

Sommer, Doris. 1991. *Foundational Fictions: The National Romances of Latin America*. Berkeley: University of California Press.

Sousa, Gabriel Soares de. 1938. *Tratado descriptivo do Brazil em 1587*. São Paulo: Companhia Nacional.

Souza, Márcio. 2000. *Fascínio e repulsa: Estado, cultura e sociedade no Brasil*. Rio de Janeiro: Edições Fundo Nacional de Cultura.

Spradley, James. 1979. *The Ethnographic Interview*. New York: Holt, Rinehart and Winston.

Stanley, Nick. 1998. *Being Ourselves for You: The Global Display of Cultures*. London: Middlesex University Press.

Stepan, Nancy. 1991. *"The Hour of Eugenics": Race, Gender and Nation in Latin America*. Ithaca, N.Y.: Cornell University Press.

Stirling, Cheryl. 2012. *African Roots, Brazilian Rites: Cultural and National Identity in Brazil*. New York: Palgrave MacMillan.

Stocking, George. 1982. *Race, Culture, and Evolution: Essays in the History of Anthropology*. Chicago: University of Chicago Press.

Stoler, Ann. 1995. *Race and the Education of Desire: Foucault's* History of Sexuality *and the Colonial Order of Things*. Durham: Duke University Press.

———. 1997. "Histories of Racisms and their Regimes of Truth." *Political Power and Social Theory* 11:183–255.

———. 2002. "Developing Historical Negatives: Race and the (Modernist) Visions of a Colonial State. In *From the Margins: Historical Anthropology and Its Futures*, edited by Brian Axel, 156–88. Durham: Duke University Press.

———. 2009. *Along the Archival Grain: Epistemic Anxieties and Colonial Common Sense*. Princeton: Princeton University Press.

———. 2013. "'The Rot Remains': From Ruins to Ruination." In *Imperial Debris: On Ruins and Ruination*, edited by Ann Laura Stoler, 2–38. Durham: Duke University Press.

Strassler, Karen. 2008. "Material Resources of the Historical Imagination: Documents and the Future of the Past in Post-Suharto Indonesia." In *Timely Assets: The Politics of Resources and their Temporalities*, edited by Elizabeth Ferry and Mandana Limbert, 215–42. Santa Fe: School for Advanced Research Press.

———. 2010. *Refracted Visions: Popular Photography and National Modernity*. Durham: Duke University Press.

Strathern, Marilyn. 1988. *The Gender of the Gift: Problems with Women and Problems with Society in Melanesia*. Berkeley: University of California Press.

———. 2005. *Kinship, Law, and the Unexpected: Relatives are Always a Surprise.* New York: Cambridge University Press.

———. 2006. "Divided Origins and the Arithmetic of Ownership." In *Accelerating Possession: Global Futures of Property and Personhood*, edited by Bill Maurer and Gabrielle Schwab, 136–73. New York: Columbia University Press.

Superintêndencia de Estudos Económicos e Sociais da Bahia. 2013. *Centro antigo de Salvador: Território de referência.* Salvador: Superintêndencia de Estudos Económicos e Sociais da Bahia.

Taussig, Michael. 1993. *Mimesis and Alterity: A Particular History of the Senses.* New York: Routledge.

———. 1999. *Defacement: Public Secrecy and the Labor of the Negative.* Stanford: Stanford University Press.

———. 2004. *My Cocaine Museum.* Chicago: University of Chicago Press.

Tavares, Odorico, ed. 1951. *Pelourinho: 27 desenhos de Carybé.* Salvador: Livraria Turista.

———, ed. 1961. *Bahia: Imagens da terra e do povo.* Rio de Janeiro: Editora Civilização Brasileira.

Teles dos Santos, Jocélio. 2005. *A cultura no poder e o poder da cultura: Disputa simbólica da herança cultural negra no Brasil.* Salvador: EDUFBA.

———. 2013. "Introdução." In *O impacto das cotas nas universidades brasileiras (2004–2012)*, edited by Jocélio Teles dos Santos. Salvador: CEAO.

Telles, Edward. 1992. "Residential Segregation by Skin Color in Brazil." *American Sociological Review* 57 (2): 186–97.

———. 2004. *Race in Another America: The Significance of Skin Color in Brazil.* Princeton: Princeton University Press.

Thornton, John. 1998. *The Kongolese Saint Anthony: Dona Beatriz Kimpa Vita and the Antonian Movement, 1684–1706.* New York: Cambridge University Press.

Ticktin, Miriam. 2012. *Casualties of Care: Immigration and the Politics of Humanitarianism in France.* Berkeley: University of California Press.

Trouillot, Michel-Rolph. 1995. *Silencing the Past: Power and the Production of History.* Boston: Beacon Press.

———. 2003. *Global Transformations: Anthropology and the Modern World.* New York: Palgrave Macmillan.

Turner, Terence. 1992. "Defiant Images: The Kayapo Appropriation of Video." *Anthropology Today* 8:5–15.

Twine, France Winddance. 1998. *Racism in a Racial Democracy: The Maintenance of White Supremacy in Brazil.* New Brunswick: Rutgers University Press.

Urban, Greg. 2001. *Metaculture: How Culture Moves Through the World.* Minneapolis: University of Minnesota Press.

Vainfas, Ronaldo. 2003. "St. Anthony in the Portuguese Americas: Saint of the Restoration." In *Colonial Saints: Discovering the Holy in the Americas*, edited by Allan Greer and Jodi Bilinkoff, 99–112. New York: Routledge.

Van de Port, Mattijs. 2011. *Ecstatic Encounters: Bahian Candomblé and the Quest for the Really Real.* Amsterdam: Amsterdam University Press.

Vanthuyne, Karine. 2009. "Becoming Maya? The Politics and Pragmatics of

'Being Indigenous' in Postgenocide Guatemala." *PoLAR: Political and Legal Anthropology Review* 32 (2): 195–217.

Vargas, Getúlio. 1938. *A nova política do Brasil.* Rio de Janeiro: J. Olympio, 11 volumes.

Venâncio, Renato Pinto. 1999. *Famílias abandonadas: Assistência à criança.* Campinas: Papirus.

Verdery, Katherine. 1999. *The Political Lives of Dead Bodies.* New York: Columbia University Press.

———. 2003. *The Vanishing Hectare: Property and Value in Postsocialist Transylvania.* Ithaca, N.Y.: Cornell University Press.

Verger, Pierre. 1976. *Trade Relations Between the Bight of Benin and Bahia from the 17th to the 19th Century.* Translated by Evelyn Crawford. Ibadan, Nigeria: Ibadan University Press.

———. 1989. *Centro Histórico de Salvador: 1946 a 1952.* São Paulo: Editora Corrupio.

———. 1999. *Notícias da Bahia, 1850.* Salvador: Editora Corrupio.

Vianna, Hildegardes. 1994. *Antigamente era assim.* Salvador: Fundação Cultural do Estado da Bahia.

Vianna Filho, Luiz. 1988. *O negro na Bahia.* Rio de Janeiro: Nova Fronteira.

Vilaça, Marcos Vinícios. 1984. *Por uma política nacional de cultura.* Brasilia: Fundação Nacional Pro-Memória.

Vilhena, Luis Rodolfo. 1997. *Projeto e missão: O movimento folclórico brasileiro, 1947–1964.* Rio de Janeiro: Funarte.

Villela, Jorge Mattar. 2004. *O povo em armas: Violência e política no sertão de Pernambuco.* Rio de Janeiro: Relume Dumará.

Viotti da Costa, Emília. 2000. *The Brazilian Empire: Myths and Histories.* Chapel Hill: University of North Carolina Press.

Wacquant, Loic. 2008. "The Militarization of Urban Marginality: Lessons from the Brazilian Metropolis." *International Political Sociology* 2 (1): 56–74.

Wafer, James. 1991. *The Taste of Blood: Spirit Possession in Brazilian Candomblé.* Philadelphia: University of Pennsylvania Press.

Wagley, Charles. 1952. "Introduction." In *Race and Class in Rural Brazil*, edited by Charles Wagley, 7–46. Paris: UNESCO.

———. 1968. "The Concept of Social Race in the Americas." In *The Latin American Tradition: Essays on the Unity and the Diversity of Latin American Culture*, edited by Charles Wagley, 155–74. New York: Columbia University Press.

———. 1971. *An Introduction to Brazil.* New York: Columbia University Press.

Wallerstein, Immanuel. 1991. "The Construction of Peoplehood: Racism, Nationalism, and Ethnicity." In *Race, Nation, Class: Ambiguous Identities*, edited by Etienne Balibar and Immanuel Wallerstein, 71–85. New York: Verso.

Warren, Jonathan. 2001. *Racial Revolutions: Antiracism and Indian Resurgence in Brazil.* Durham: Duke University Press.

Warren, Kay, and Jean Jackson. 2002. "Introduction: Studying Indigenous Activism in Latin America." In *Indigenous Movements, Self-Representation, and the State in Latin America*, edited by K. Warren and J. Jackson, 1–46. Austin: University of Texas Press.

Weffort, Francisco. 2000. *A cultura e as revoluções da modernização*. Rio de Janeiro: Edições Fundo Nacional de Cultura.

Weffort, Francisco, and Márcio Souza. 1998. *Um olhar sobre a cultura brasileira*. Brasilia: Minc.

Weld, Kristin. 2014. *Paper Cadavers: The Archives of Dictatorship in Guatemala*. Durham: Duke University Press.

Wetherell, James. 1860. *Stray Notes from Bahia, Being an Extract from Letters during Residence of Fifteen Years*. Liverpool: Webb & Hunt.

White, Hayden. 1980. "The Value of Narrativity in the Representation of Reality." *Critical Inquiry* 7 (1): 5–27.

Williams, Daryle. 2001. *Culture Wars in Brazil: The First Vargas Regime, 1930–1945*. Durham: Duke University Press.

Williams, Erica. 2013. *Sex Tourism in Bahia*. Chicago: University of Illinois Press.

Williamson, Kenneth. 2011. "Night Becomes Day: Carnival, Contested Spaces, and the Black Movement in Bahia." *Journal of Latin American and Caribbean Anthropology* 17 (2): 257–78.

Wyllys, Jean. 1997. "Boca do lixo: Moradores da Rua 28 de Setembro lamentam decadência da área." *Correio da Bahia*, June 10, 1997.

Yúdice, George. 2004. *The Expediency of Culture: Uses of Culture in the Global Era*. Durham: Duke University Press.

Zamora, Lois Parkinson. 2006. *The Inordinate Eye: New World Baroque and Latin American Fiction*. Chicago: University of Chicago Press.

Zancheti, Sílvio Mendes, and Jordelan Gabriel. 2010. "The Sustainability of Urban Heritage Preservation: The Case of Salvador de Bahia." Washington: Inter-American Development Bank.

Zeuler, R. M. de A. Lima. 2013. *Lina Bo Bardi*. New Haven: Yale University Press.

Index

Page numbers in italics refer to illustrations and captions.

Brazil, Brazilians: *abertura* and, 351; air force of, 135; Bahia as heart of, 50; Baroque and, 25, 258, 346; capitals of, 3, 8, 23, 25; colonial landscape of, 104; constitutions of, 121, 129, 132; cordiality of, 91; *coronelismo* and, 86; democracy and, 36, 42; economy of, 76, 198–99, 253, 305, 307, 323; ethos of, 35; exceptionalism of, 109, 135, 312, 349, 368; identity of, 25; industrialization and, 118; land ownership and, 183–84; as landlord in Pelourinho, 181, 182, 183; map of, *26*; military rule and, 28, 86–87, 91; Ministry of Culture, 71, 129; Ministry of Education, 145; Ministry of Education and Culture, 253, 254; Ministry of Education and Health, 123, 125, 127, 285; Ministry of Sports, 60; modernism and, 8, 118, 124; motto of, 70; multicultural initiatives in, 351; myths of, 177, 225, 290; national anthropological association of, 162; national degeneracy of, 92; national life of, 291; Natives of, *106*; navy of, 181, 182; Africa and, 318; origins of, 22, 23, 25–32, 40, 102–3, 107, 114, 135, 139, 346; patrimony of, 179; peripheral capitalism and, 7; presidents of, 5, 8, 71; quincentennial celebration of, 103, 107, 137–40; race in, 4, 7, 9, 14, 15, 25, 306, 307, 309; recording industry of, 80; as republic, 107, 116, 280; Senate of, 87; slavery and, 306; UNICEF and, 60; usufruct law in, 183, 206
Brazilian Communist Party (PCB), 88
Brazilianisms, 127
Brazilian Literacy Movement (MOBRAL), 165–66
Brazilian National Bishops' Council (CNBB), 60
Brazilianness, 106, 123, 128, 177, 289
British community in Bahia, 246, 247–48
brothels, 27, 46, 88, 159, 165, 170,

188, *280*, 281. *See also* prostitution, prostitutes
Brown, Carlinhos ("Charlie"), 52
Brown Mother, Pelourinho as, 27
brownness, 128, 154, 155, 160
Buarque de Holanda, Sérgio, 91, 92
Buenos Aires, 169, 170
buildings: collapse of, 1–2, 182, 200, 343–44; condition of, 44, 71, 72; of Ladeira da Misericórdia, *276*, *282*; of Lower City, 75; in Pelourinho, 77
Bulindo, 169–71, 339
bureaucracy, bureaucrats, 65, 67, 128, 213; of IPAC, 4, 205, 326

caboclo, 106
Caboré, 81, 195, 196, 359; as resident of Gueto, 192, 194–95, *195*, 203, 207
Cabral, Pedro Álvares, 107
cachaça (sugar-cane liquor), 321
Cachoeira, 132
Cachorrão, 279
Calçada, 227
Caminha, Pero Vaz de, Letter of Discovery of, 102–3, 108, 112, 118, 120, 192
Campo da Pólvora gang, 88
Campo Grande, 246–47, 252, 256
Campos, Francisco, 121, 122
Campo Santo, 250
Candeal de Brotas, 52
Candomblé, 38–39, 69, 93, 94, 232, 272; ACM and, 88, 91; *axé* (force) and, 272, 328; Bahia and, 106, 327–28; deities (*orixás*) of, 222–25, 326; canonization of, 312; Imbassahy on, 222–23; Pelourinho and, 153–62; Pentecostals vs., 330, 331, 336; possession in, 38; ritual of, 328–29, 334; symbolic exchanges of, 328; temples (*terreiros*) of, 129, 225, 351
canonization, 38–39; sanctification of Afro-Bahians and, 23
Capanema, Gustavo, 123–25
capanga (gunman/overseer), 182, 183
capoeira, 30, 46, 88, 132, 272, 312

Cardoso, Fernando Henrique, 120–21, 130, 139, 163, 272, 305, 307
care, 6, 36, 45, 52, 55, 209, 284–86, 293–94; contradictions of, 63–68; essence of Brazil and, 4; objectification and, 297–99
Carneiro, Edson, 158
carnival, 30, 67–68, 94, 165–66, *203*, 350; in Bahia, *9*; bands of, 211; *blocos afros* and, 28, 272; dancing of, 69; in Maragojipe, 132; Olodum at, 267; in Pelourinho Square, *111, 113*; promotional literature for, 221; songs of, 22
Caroso, Carlos, 162
carteira assinada (labor documents), bourgeoisie and, 47
caruru (okra and palm oil stew), 178, 326–27, 334
Carvalho, Jeová de, 178, 203
Carybé, paintings by, 221
Casa do Artesão, 167
castles (houses of prostitution), 27. *See also* brothels; prostitution, prostitutes
Castro, Maria Adriana Couto de, 144–45, 150, 153, 163, *186*, 188, 189, 190, 211, 258; author and, 185; on social scientists, 151; speeches of, 186–87
cathedrals, 38; of Salvador, 46
Catholicism, 38, 39, 69, 91, 123, 147, 166, 298, 329; folk, 39; medieval, 361; Pentecostalism and, 336, 337; religious orders of, 8, 71, 189, 232, 250; saints of, 297–98; symbols of, 222
Célia, Dona, 178, 327
cemeteries, 250; *cemiterada* uprisings and, 250–51. *See also* death
Center for Afro-Oriental Studies (CEAO), 154, 158
Center for Bahian Architectural Studies (CEAB), 254, 256
Centro Cultural Anglo-Americano (CCAA), advertisement for, 306–7
Cervantes Saavedra, Miguel de, 131; *Don Quixote*, 104–7

CETAD (Center for Therapy and Studies of Drug Abuse) 353; AIDS education and, 283, 284–88; nurse of, 285–86, 289, 291–96, 299–303; on self-valorization, 338, 339
chacoalhar, chacota, 318–19
Chagas, Francisco Xavier das, 232
childhood, children, 189; feast of São Cosme and São Damião and, 326–27, 328; of Ladeira da Misericórdia, *284*; of prostitutes, 204; sexual abuse of, 84. *See also* street children
Children of the Historical Center. *See* S.O.S. Children of the Historical Center
Chile, 136, 186
Choque (Shock) units, of military police, 51–52
Christianity, Christians, *195*, 224; born-again, 184; eschatology of, 69; Evangelical, 85; gospel of, 353; heaven of, 297; Protestant, 329; redemption in, 358; sin in, 330; theology of, 257. *See also* Catholicism; Pentecostalism, Pentecostals
chronotope, 105
civilization and barbarism 113–15, 153, 197; Brasilia and 115; Pelourinho residents and, 263
class conflict, at quincentennial celebration, 139–40
Cliff, Jimmy, 309
Coaty Bar, *282, 283*, 284, 285, 296, 300
cocaine. *See* crack cocaine; drug use
cockfighting, 45, 82, 99, 169, 273
cocoa, 319, 324
coffee, 113; plantations of, 190
Collor de Mello, Fernando, 129–30
Colombia, 186
colonial buildings, 190–91, *191*, 218, 246, 264, 346; of Bahia, 117; collapse of, 28, 53, 141, 345; on dockside, 345; lack of plumbing in, 184; repair of, 1, *196*, 352
colonial planter class, 11, 220, 249, 278

colonies, colonizers: British, 289–90; Portuguese, 112, 113, 223

color, skin, race and, 14, 16

Comércio, Salvador's Lower City as, 74, 75, 260

commodification: of Afro-Bahian lifeways, 63, 153, 325; of bodies, 257; of culture, 32, 34, 130, 146, 154, 190, 200, 202, 275, 351; of identities, 309; as technology of forgetting, 323

Como era gostoso o meu francês (film), 306

Compadre Washington, É o Tchan and, 51, 56

CONDER (Bahian Regional Development Company), 47, 145, 254; reconstruction of Pelourinho by, 1, 28–29, 47; "Viver Melhor" program of, 245

Conjunto ACM, as housing project, 72

Contorno (Gamboa neighborhood), 72

conversion experience, 333–35

Coroa, Dona, 286, 292

coronelismo (patron-based strongman politics), 86

corporatism, 123, 219, 351

Corredor da Vitória Avenue, 246

Correio da Bahia, 55, 63, 66, 87

cortiço (nineteenth-century group of houses), 182, *183*

Costa Lima, Vivaldo da, 143, 144–45, 151, 153, 156, 158, 161, 165, 174, 178, 189, 350; Candomblé and, 156, 157, 272; Espinheira and, 162; racial democracy and, 157–58

Costa, Flávio, 151

crack cocaine, 98, 184; 28th of September Street and, 2–3, 75–76, 204; Dona Katia and, 141, 176; sale of, 168; smoking, 273; users of, 179

creativity, human, 348

creoles, 114, 117

criadeira (caregiver), 188; women as, 208

Cruz das Almas, 267

Cuba, 321, 322

cultural censorship, 300

cultural heritage or cultural patrimony (*patrimônio cultural*), 30–32, 94, 130, 357; Andrade on, 124–27; of Bahia, 115; Baroque architecture and, 71; bureaucracy of, 104, 122, 124, 128, 213, 256, 291; as commodity, 337; critics of initiatives of, 110; definition of, 129; historical ethnography of, 37; industry of, 206; as inert resource, 33; inventions of, 111; management of, 29, 71, 78, 113, 131, 242, 265; as movement, 103; objects of, 39, 201; people canonized as, 39; planning of, 32, 262; programs of, 348; race and, 225, 342; reconstruction of, 69, 105; -scape, 33, 49; sexuality and, 143, 146–48, 160; technocratic impulses around, 122; tourism and, 146; translation and, 323; UNESCO and, 146; zones of, 71, 78, 319, 326. *See also* patrimonialization; patrimony

culture: commodification of, 32, 115, 146, 200, 202, 275, 337, 351; democratization of, 78, 305; marketing of, 145; materialization of, 30; as medium of empowerment, 5; national pride and, 130; objectification of, 82; policy, 5, 14; popular, 120, 123, 165–68, 327; of poverty, 162, 164; production of, 253; rights, 208; textualization of, 341; UNESCO view of, 3

Culture (reggae band), 309

da antiguidade, 39, 49, 201, 350

da Cunha, Euclides, *Rebellion in the Backlands*, 114–15

Da Esporra, 142

Dandinha, 66–68, 70, 257, 267, 274, 357–59, 360

Darwin, Charles, 114, 356

da Silva, Luiz Inácio "Lula," 83, 87, 121, 132, 150, 206, 316, 323; election of, 5, 305

Guilhermina, Dona, 208
Gula, 58, 59, 64, 205, 333, 359; Bem
    Aventurados and, 96, 203

Haiti, 250, 307
handicrafts trade, 46, 54, 72, 167, 345,
    353
Hélio, 269–70, 274, 336
Hermes, 295, 297
heterosexuality, 35
"Hey Mister Chatty Mouth" (reggae
    song), 315–16, 317
Hill of Mercy. *See* Ladeira da
    Misericórdia
historical determinism, 254
historicity, 37, 40, 42, 60–61, 65, 210–
    12, 304; legacy and, 31; property
    and 56–61; waiting and,185. *See also*
    proper historicity
history, histories, 37, 126, 242, 264;
    authentic, 323; of Bahia, 244–47;
    constructedness of, 303; ethno-
    graphic production of, 357; histo-
    riography and, 126; as idiom, 20;
    meaning and, 25, 354; mysteries
    and, 256–63; production of, 19, 167,
    178, 260; public, 222; slavery in,
    226–33; subjects of, 38–39, 61; theo-
    ries of, 125; treasure in, 234–39
HIV, 41, 64, 65, 287. *See also* AIDS
homosexuality, 84, 158, 169, 171, 188
Hospital Ana Nery, 172, 176
Hospital of the Santa Casa da
    Misericórdia, 275–76
Hotel da Bahia, 184
hybridity, hybridization, 155, 156, 318,
    321, 331, 355; cultural, 307; racial
    democracy and, 161; racial politics
    and, 312–13; transcultural, 324–25;
    valorization of, 300

Iansã, 224
Ibêji, 326
ICOMOS (International Commission
    on Monuments and Historic Sites),
    71, 127

identity, identities, 78, 106; Afro-
    Brazilian, 45; Bahian, 38; categories
    of, 17; collective, 112; commodifica-
    tion of, 309; ethnoracial, 134; gen-
    der, 84; politics of, 233
Igreja da Sé Primacial do Brasil,
    archaeology at, 215–17, 216, 217
Igreja de São Francisco (São Francisco
    Church), 46, 110; priests of, 173;
    skeletons at, 236–37, 238
Ilê Aiyê, 351
Ilê Axé Opô Afonjá, 157
Imbassahy, Antônio, 224, 232, 233, 241,
    244; as mayor of Salvador, 218, 246,
    258; speech of, 222–23, 243, 244, 256
immorality, 40, 60, 119, 171, 288, 331
indemnification, 23, 56, 150, 178, 182,
    185, 195–96, 197, 199, 200, 206, 208,
    235, 238, 258; amount of, 77, 79, 198,
    207, 273, 291; confiscation by, 106;
    demands for higher, 64; for Dona
    Niza and Seu Jorge, 281; failure of,
    183; forms for, 344; IPAC criteria and
    calculation, 198; by IPAC, 41; mon-
    etization of habits and living spaces
    by, 188; for Pelourinho residents and,
    22, 29, 72, 203–6, 213, 234, 282–82,
    287, 288; spent on daily needs, 78;
    used to purchase homes, 74
independence celebrations of Bahia, 106
Indio, 65
Institute of Artistic and Cultural Patri-
    mony. *See* IPAC

intangible patrimony (also immate-
    rial heritage), 201, 208; recent man-
    ifestations of, 132; UNESCO and,
    130–31, 146, 149–50. *See also* Living
    Human Treasures
intellectuals: Bahian, 128; black, 155;
    Estado Novo and, 123, 124; global
    networks of, 154; under military
    rule, 150; mixed-race exceptionalism
    and, 349; nationalist projects and,
    93, 120–21; prostitutes and, 278; on
    race mixture, 12

Etnologia; MAE), 162, 216, 240, 243, 262, 269

music, 95, 127, 305, 307; Axé, 60; Brazilian recording industry and, 80; carnival songs, 24; country, 310; funk, 309; *pagode*, 51, 310; salsa, 136; samba de roda, 132; Timbalada, 52. *See also* reggae

Mussurunga neighborhood, 266

Muzenza, 351

mystery, mysteries: Brazil's origins and, 225–26; dissimulation and, 263–65; histories and, 256–63; mythology and, 290; stories of, 232; value of, 233

National Institute of Historical and Artistic Patrimony. *See* IPHAN; SPHAN

nationalism, 8, 29, 94, 99, 116, 225; biopolitics of, 34; Candomblé and, 155; creative, 306; culture managers and, 25; intellectuals and, 93; Latin American, 35; milieu and, 62; miscegenation and, 13; novels and, 34–35; recuperation of mixed-race citizenry and, 120; Salvador and, 7; sexual politics of, 121

nation and nation-state, 220, 291; character of, 118; commemorations of, 135–36; consolidation of, 122, 255; construction of, 350; culture of, 126–27, 158; formation of, 321; historicity of, 25; history of, 80, 127, 175; identity of, 123, 131, 305; ideology of, 108; kinship, 63; memory of, 92; myths of, 9, 36, 121, 153; origins of, 16; patrimony of, 122, 126–27, 143, 184, 186, 242, 298; pride of, 130; production of, 172; race and gender and, 104; rise of, 121–23; statistics of, 122; unity of, 272

Native Brazilians, 9, 110; in advertisements, 107–8, 109; carnival decorations and, *111*, *113*; cultural productions of, 125; police vs., 139;

valorization of, 127; women as, *111*, 112, 118

natural rights, 181–82

natural selection, 114

negrólogos (negrologists), 331

negros lindos (beautiful blacks), 93

Negru's Bar, 311

neighborhoods: of Historical Center, 73, 195, 197, 274, 301; working-class, 149, 174, 266, 274, 316

Neinha, Dona, 203

Neném, 167

neoliberalism, 6, 32–33, 129, 188, 219, 305, 351

Nescau, 319, 320, 321, 322, 323, 329

Nestlé Quik, 321, 322, 323

newspapers, in IPAC archives, 210–11

NGOs, 52, 59, 157, 204, 205, 211, 235, 279, 285; S.O.S. Children of the Historical Center as, 81, 85

nightclubs, 282

Niza, Dona, 234–38, 256–57, 261–65, 274, 281, 290, 302, 348–50

Nogueira, Oracy, 14–15

Nossa Senhora da Conceição, 224

nostalgia, 98

O Bem Amado, 215

objects, objectification, 214, 361; of Afro-Bahian culture, 331; of Afro-Brazilians, 209; of inchoate feelings, 263; materiality of, 301; of Pelourinho residents, 275, 338; of self, 293; of status, 304; of urban life, 346

ogã, in Candomblé, 156

Olodum, 57, 94, 211, 267, 271, 309, 310, 351

Olorun, 224

one drop rule, 336, 342

origin stories: factual support for, 102–3; found texts and, 25, 103, 104. *See also* Afro-Brazilians; archive; Bahia

orixás, 224–25, 326, 327, 328, 334

Ortiz, Fernando, 323, 325; *Cuban Counterpoint*, 321–22

Oswaldo, 231–32, 234, 236, 264
Oxum, 256; as orixá, 224–25

economy of, 163; IPHAN archives in, 234; music in, 309

Rocha, Zilton, 81, 203–4, 206

Rocinha neighborhood, 74, 181, *182, 183*, 207, 216, 327, 329; collapse of structures in, 182; Pelourinho residents remove to, 338; Rastafarians in, 330

Rockefeller Foundation, 254

Rodrigues, Raimundo Nina, 205

Roque, 241

Romeo, Max, 309

Ronaldo, 194

Rousseff, Dilma, 5, 121, 323

Rua do Tijolo (Street of Bricks), 71

Rua Gregorio de Mattos, 44

Rua João de Deus, 44

Rua Saldanha da Gama, 96

Rua São Francisco, *48*, 64, 66, 84

ruins, 74, 97, 98, 170, 343–44

Rumba Dance Nightclub, 55

saci pererê, as trickster figure, 2

sacis (crack cocaine users), 2–3, 179, 333, 344

Saint Anthony, 298

Saint John, feast of, 266

Saint Peter, 297, 298, 357–59

saints, 38–39, 69, 223, 224, 297

Saldanha da Gama Street, 47, 53, 96, 190–91, *191*, 192, 240, 343–44

Salvador: Barra lighthouse in, 279; as Brazil's first capital, 7, 8, 36, 107, 245; cable cars in, 55; Candomblé in, 129, 158; Cathedral of, 46; cemeteries in, 250; Comércio district of, 345–46; expansion of, 27; historical center of, 70; landscape of, 244; Lower City of, 74, 75; maps of, 7, *26*; mayors of, 5, 86, 87, 150, 159, 282; Museum of Archaeology and Ethnology of, 162; natives of, 310, 314, 316; neighborhoods of, 49, 70–74, 138, 260; patron saint of, 224; physical evolution of, 253–58; police of,

149; political movements in, 28; prisons in, 74; red light district of, 150; suburbs of, 207; tourism and, 151, 219, 283; Upper City of, 74; upper classes of, 8; urban spaces of, 112; waterfront of, 275, 345; working class of, 49, 309, 310

sandwichmen, 78–79, 343

Santa Casa da Misericórdia, 47–48, 190, 278

Santo Antônio, 298

Santo Antônio Além do Carmo, 71, 87, 89

Santos, Edgard, 253

Santos, Francisco, 187–88

Santos, Luiz Alberto dos, 5, 7, 94, 359

Santos, Roberto, 254

São Caetano neighborhood, 170

São Gonçalo do Retiro neighborhood, 72, 184, 322

São Miguel neighborhood, 72

São João do Pelô, festival of, 66

São Paulo, 59, 74, 116, 118, 123, 150, 165, 260, 267, 298; modernism and, 8, 113; planning in, 128; red light district of, 107, 133; state of, 127; women in, 119

Saúde, 338

Saussure, Ferdinand de, 18

sculpture, Redemption, 45

secrecy, 66, 87, 90, 155, 158, 188, 198, 202, 220, 225–26, 259, 303, 317, 319; archival perspective and, 278; public 158, 231. *See also* intimacy; mystery

semiotic ideology, 15, 262

Senna, Francisco, 244, 245, 246, 247, 252, 255; *Evolução Física de Salvador*, 253

SEPLAM (Salvador's municipal planning authority), 145, 184

Sepulveda, Lúcia, 198

Sergipe state, 195, 204

Serra, Ordep, 128, 159–60, 225, 272

sertão (backlands), 44, 48, 53, 115, 141, 132, 142, 161, 294

Seu Angelo, as owner of Rocinha, 182–83

Seu Bude, as resident of Gueto, 192

Seu João, as resident of Gueto, 192

Seu Jorge, 234, 236–38, *261*, 261–62, 263–64; children of, *302*; Dona Niza and, 256–57; removal of, 281; workshop of, 260

Seu José, as resident of Rocinha, 181, 182

Seu Leal, as IPAC manager residents, 78

sex trade, 235; drug use and, 284; homosexuality and, 84; indemnification and, 74; of Pelourinho, 27–28, 146, 147

sexuality: biopower and, 34; Brazilian nationalism and, 121; Candomblé and, 158–60; under Estado Novo, 123; patrimonialization and, 41; Pelourinho restoration and, 161–62; popular culture and, 165–68; surveillance of, 289

shantytowns, of Pelourinho, 28

sign vehicles, 361; materiality of, 362

signification: Bahian, 318; in heritage zone, 319; Peirce and, 18; postcards and, 348; qualisigns and, 336; race and, 17; recontextualization and, 330; of silence, 83

signifiers: body as, 354; history as, 354; place as, 354

signs, 180, 209; of Brazilian pasts, 19; density of, 309; economies of, 83; economy of, 219; food as, 329; future-oriented, 343; of Malaquias, 344; Malaquias as, 79–80; mimicry of, 293; national belongings and, 104; of racial identity, 342; sacred, 225; signification and, 18–19, 82; of status, 296; street children as, 63; as triad, 361; vehicles of, 263, 299, 301, 303, 341, 347, 354; visible, 270

silence: racism and, 93; signification of, 83

Silva Mendes, Alberto, Pateta as, 179

Simas Filho, Américo, 253

Simões Dias, 204, 207

Simões Filho, as working class suburb, 281, 234

SIRCHAL (International Seminar on the Rehabilitation of the Historical Centers of Latin American Cities), 184–85, 212

skeletons: discovered near Sucupira, 267; discovered on Praça da Sé, 244; at Igreja da Sé Primacial, 215–17, *216*, *217*, 220; at Igreja de São Francisco, 236–37; in Pelourinho, 37, 41, 234; at Praça da Sé, 239, 240, 336; of slaves, 226, 228, 231, 232, 268–69; stories of, 264

skin color, terms for, 325

slave trade, 246; British interdiction of, 247

slavery, 113, 249, 321; in Brazil, 306; Brazilian multiculturalism and, 221; in history, 226–33; present and, 242; race and, 272; racialized relationship to, 271

slaves, 252; artisans as, 258; in Rio de Janeiro's coffee groves, 190; Salvador's plazas and, 246; skeletons of, 208, 218, 220, 226, 228, 231, 232, 240, 268–69, 271, 272

Soares de Souza, Gabriel, as Portuguese voyager, 215

sobrados (mansions): in Pelourinho, 4; restoration of, 46–47

sociability, caruru and, 327

social constructivism, 17, 244, 354

social hygiene, 115, 206, 210, 314–15. *See also* civilization and barbarism; Lamarckianism

social justice: in Brazil, 76; Workers Party policies in relation to, 5

social memory, of Bahia, 244

social movements, 57, 185; Bem Aventurados and, 204; launching of, 59, 82–83; of Pelourinho, 40, 50; in Salvador, 22

Thoreau, Henry David, 115

Timbalada, 97. *See also* police

tobacco, 319, 320, 321, 329

Tombamento, 208–13, 293, 338, 352, 360

Topa, 291, 294, 295, 309, 315, 337, 339, 343, 347, 352, 355, 358, 359, 361; as author's friend, 273–74, 288–89, 304; at CETAD AIDS education session, 284–86, 288, 292; family background of, 301–2; as figura, 275; insurrection of, 41–42; photos of, 284, 287, 302; self-objectification of, 299; as symbol of Pelourinho degeneracy, 295; as trickster, 296

Tosh, Peter, 309, 310

tourism, tourist trade, 72, 94, 192, 233, 283, 306, 307, 339; Candomblé and, 155; cultural heritage and, 146; IPAC and, 151; jobs in, 205; in Porto da Barra, 195; in Porto Seguro, 135; promotion of, 108, 226, 347, 349

tourists, 53, 105, 188, 202, 232–33, 329; attracting, 131; as middle class, 93; police and, 240; at Praça da Sé, 240, 267; touts and, 81

tradition: cohesion of, 103; in *Don Quixote*, 105; invention of, 110, 211, 256, 332; manufacture of, 33; modernism and, 115; as valorizing descriptor, 267

translation, of Jamaican reggae lyrics, 312, 313–14, 318–20, 323, 331–32, 335. *See also* interiority; race, racism; semiotic ideology

transvestitism, transvestites, 32, 67, 172, 274; AIDS and, 63–64; Dandinha as, 66–68; denied indemnification, 198; on Rua São Francisco, 64, 66, 84. *See also* cultural heritage; race, racism; semiotic ideology

treasure, 257; in history, 234–39; under Igreja da Sé Primacial do Brasil, 216; Seu Jorge on, 261–62; stories of, 264

trickster, 2, 94, 120, 200, 290–91, 296

Tropicália, 306, 307

Tupinambás, 109, 110, 218, 243

TV Globo, 56, 59

28th of September Street (the 28), 2, 4, 46, 47, 48, 71, 72, 190, 196, 207; ACM and, 88; bars on, 178, 203; brothels of, 56; drug trade and, 169, 204; homes on, 53, 55; impromptu bars on, 51; IPAC and, 197; removals from, 330; residents of, 95; restoration of, 74, 210

Umbuzada, 59, 161, 316

UNESCO (United Nations Educational, Scientific and Cultural Organization), 60, 69, 201; cultural bureaucrats of, 67; heritage guidelines and registries of, 110, 190, 301; humankind and, 30, 339; intangible patrimony and, 33–34, 130–31, 146, 149–50; officials of, 62

UNESCO World Heritage Sites, 1, 28, 49, 71, 127, 143 172, 298–99; Pelourinho as, 6, 15, 17, 25, 161, 209, 307

UNICEF (United Nations International Children's Emergency Fund), 60

Unified Black Movement (MNU), 5, 109, 153, 204, 272, 351

United Nations Educational, Scientific and Cultural Organization. *See* UNESCO

United States: bicentennial of, 135, 136; biological citizenship in, 35–36; developmentalism and, 143; personhood in, 309; racial politics of, 6, 14

Universal Church of the Reign of God (IURD), 331

Upper City of Salvador, 55, 74, 275, 346

urbanization, 148, 246, 256

urban life, objectification of, 346

urban planning, planners, 250, 254, 256